Tristram and Coote's
Probate Practice

Third Supplement to the Thirtieth Edition

Tristram and Coote's Probate Practice

Third Supplement to the Thirtieth edition

R D'Costa
District Probate Registrar, Oxford
JI Winegarten
The Chief Master of the Supreme Court, Chancery Division
T Synak
HMRC Inheritance Tax

LexisNexis®

Members of the LexisNexis Group worldwide

United Kingdom	LexisNexis, a Division of Reed Elsevier (UK) Ltd, Halsbury House, 35 Chancery Lane, London WC2A 1EL, and London House, 20–22 East London Street, Edinburgh EH7 4BQ
Australia	LexisNexis Butterworths, Chatswood, New South Wales
Austria	LexisNexis Verlag ARD Orac GmbH & Co KG, Vienna
Benelux	LexisNexis Benelux, Amsterdam
Canada	LexisNexis Canada, Markham, Ontario
China	LexisNexis China, Beijing and Shanghai
France	LexisNexis SA, Paris
Germany	LexisNexis Deutschland GmbH, Munster
Hong Kong	LexisNexis Hong Kong, Hong Kong
India	LexisNexis India, New Delhi
Italy	Giuffrè Editore, Milan
Japan	LexisNexis Japan, Tokyo
Malaysia	Malayan Law Journal Sdn Bhd, Kuala Lumpur
New Zealand	LexisNexis NZ Ltd, Wellington
Poland	Wydawnictwo Prawnicze LexisNexis Sp, Warsaw
Singapore	LexisNexis Singapore, Singapore
South Africa	LexisNexis Butterworths, Durban
USA	LexisNexis, Dayton, Ohio

© Reed Elsevier (UK) Ltd 2010

Published by LexisNexis

This is a Butterworths title

All rights reserved. No part of this publication may be reproduced in any material form (including photocopying or storing it in any medium by electronic means and whether or not transiently or incidentally to some other use of this publication) without the written permission of the copyright owner except in accordance with the provisions of the Copyright, Designs and Patents Act 1988 or under the terms of a licence issued by the Copyright Licensing Agency Ltd, Saffron House, 6–10 Kirby Street, London, England EC1N 8TS. Applications for the copyright owner's written permission to reproduce any part of this publication should be addressed to the publisher.

Warning: The doing of an unauthorised act in relation to a copyright work may result in both a civil claim for damages and criminal prosecution.

Crown copyright material is reproduced with the permission of the Controller of HMSO and the Queen's Printer for Scotland. Parliamentary copyright material is reproduced with the permission of the Controller of Her Majesty's Stationery Office on behalf of Parliament. Any European material in this work which has been reproduced from EUR-lex, the official European Communities legislation website, is European Communities copyright.

A CIP Catalogue record for this book is available from the British Library.

ISBN 13: 9781405750097

ISBN 978-1-4057-5009-7

Typeset by Letterpart Ltd, Reigate, Surrey

Printed and bound in Great Britain by Hobbs the Printers Ltd, Totton, Hampshire

Visit LexisNexis at www.lexisnexis.co.uk

Preface

Editor's Note: In addition to the Preface for the third edition (below) notes from the previous two Supplements are also included in order to illustrate the full content of this cumulative Supplement.

This cumulative Supplement further updates the main work. The Human Fertilisation and Embryology Act 2008 and consequential amendments to the Children Act 1989 extend parental responsibility for minors to include a mother and parent of a child to whom the Human Fertilisation and Embryology Act 2008 applies. The Non-Contentious Probate (Amendment) Rules 2009 reflect these changes which are explained here. This work includes also the Solicitors' (Non-Contentious Business) Remuneration Order 2009.

Recent decisions include *Re Ikin (decd), Court v Despallieres* [2009] EWHC 3340 (Ch) which confirms the conditions for preservation of a will upon the testator's subsequent marriage or formation of a civil partnership and *Re Servoz-Gavin, Ayling v Summers* [2009] EWHC 3168 (Ch) which further confirms the definition of a mariner or seaman at sea under s 11 of the Wills Act 1827.

The Supplement refers to recommendations on the practice of settling straightforward oaths to reduce the pressure on core services in some probate registries. Reference is also made to proposals of the Law Commission consultation paper *Intestacy and Family Provision Claims on Death*.

Currently the President of the Family Division has established a working group chaired by Lord Justice Munby to consider a substantive revision of the Non-Contentious Probate Rules 1987 and probate practice. The committee is expected to report to the President of the Family Division at the end of 2010. The editors anticipate that there will be significant changes to practice and procedure when the new rules come into force.

In respect of the Inheritance Tax aspects, the main change relates to the address for payment of Inheritance Tax and the revised methodologies that may be utilised for payment. There are also details of the change in the way the level of the interest rate appropriate on outstanding Inheritance Tax is centrally calculated together with the revised rates applicable.

In the section relating to contentious probate attention is drawn to a recent amendment to the Practice Direction to CPR Pt 57 which makes it clear that an application to remove or substitute an executor (but not an administrator) may be made before a grant of probate.

The Second Supplement was published in January 2009.

Preface

The Council for Licensed Conveyancers became an approved body for the purpose of granting licensed conveyancers an exemption from s 23(1) of the Solicitors Act 1974 and it was given power to make rules in relation to the probate practice of licensed conveyancers (Probate Services (Approved Bodies) Order 2008).

The increase of spouse's and civil partner's statutory legacy takes effect on 9 February 2009 in respect of deaths occurring on and after that date (Family Provision (Intestate Succession) Order 2008).

Part 2 of the Human Fertilisation and Embryology Act 2008 confirms definitions of 'mother', 'father' and 'parent' of a person born as result of assisted reproduction and it effects amendments to s 2 of the Children Act 1989 to rights of parental responsibility.

The effect of a codicil confirming an earlier revoked will is referred to following the ruling in *Hoare Trustees v Jacques* [2008] EWHC 2022 (Ch).

With regard to the changes in respect of the Inheritance Tax aspects, the major change relates to the introduction of the new Form of account IHT400 and accompanying schedules that replaces the previous Form IHT200 and schedules. The previous Form IHT200 will not be accepted by HMRC Inheritance Tax after 9 June 2009. There are also some amendments to the procedures involved in submitting the form.

The other substantive Inheritance Tax change relates to the new legislation contained in s 10 of and Sch 4 to the Finance Act 2008 regarding the pooling of the nil-rate thresholds for spouses and civil partners.

The First Supplement was published in December 2007.

So far as the changes to the Inheritance Tax aspects are concerned, the major points of the Supplement relate to the more detailed clarification of the amendments introduced by the Finance Act 2006. In particular, the changes relate to the definition of the beneficial estate chargeable on death with particular regard to settled property, together with the amendments in respect of lifetime transfers, some of which are now immediately chargeable when made. More detailed information is also provided regarding the appropriate forms and procedures to be used when applying for a second or subsequent grant.

Other matters highlighted include registered pension schemes, gifts with reservation and pre-owned assets. The procedure for the issue of clearance letters has also been amended and the revised procedure is now detailed within.

Although still subject to future parliamentary process, an indication of the potential amendments to the pooling of nil-rate thresholds by spouses or civil partners announced in the pre-Budget report on 9 October 2007 has also been included for guidance only.

RD'C

JIW

TS

February 2010

Publisher's Note

Paragraphs in this Supplement update and replace in their entirety those published in the Thirtieth edition main work and Second Supplement.

The Second Supplement may now be discarded.

Whilst every care has been taken to ensure the accuracy of this work, no responsibility for loss or damage occasioned to any person acting or refraining from action as a result of any statement in it can be accepted by the authors or publishers.

Note.—The Supreme Court Act 1981 is now known as the Senior Courts Act 1981 and all references should be read accordingly (substituted by the Constitutional Reform Act 2005 with effect from 1 October 2009).

Contents

Preface **v**
Table of statutes **xi**
Table of statutory instruments **xv**
Table of cases **xix**
Table of abbreviations **xxiv**

Part I   The Common Form Probate Practice

1   The probate jurisdiction of the Family Division **3**
2   General procedure in registry **5**
3   Wills and codicils **12**
4   Probates **19**
5   Letters of administration with the will annexed **29**
6   Letters of administration **36**
7   Minority or life interests and second administrators **59**
8   Inland Revenue accounts **62**
9   Trust corporations **105**
11 Limited grants **106**
12 Grant where deceased died domiciled out of England and Wales **127**
13 Grants 'de bonis non'—Cessate grants—Double probate **128**
14 Right of the court to select an administrator—'Commorientes' **132**
15 Renunciation and retraction **133**
16 Amendment and notation of grants **134**
17 Revocation and impounding of grants **136**
18 Resealing **139**
20 Deposit and registration of wills of living persons **140**
21 Searches and copies – Exemplifications – Duplicate grants **141**
25 Applications to District Judge, Registrar or High Court Judge (Non-Contentious Business) **144**

Part II   Contentious Business

26 Introduction **149**
28 Parties to claims **155**
32 Statements of case generally **158**
34 Defence and counterclaim **161**

Contents

39 Trial **196**
40 Costs **202**
41 Associated actions **214**

Appendices

I   Statutes **217**
II   Rules, Orders and Regulations **377**
III Fees (Non-Contentious Business) **465**
IV   Rates of Inheritance Tax and Capital Transfer Tax **475**
V   Costs (Non-Contentious Business) **481**
VI   Forms **487**
Index **515**

Table of Statutes

Paragraph references printed in **bold** type indicate where the Statute is set out in part or in full.

	PARA
Administration of Estates Act 1925	
s 11	**A1.223**
21	3.52
34(3)	4.273
Pt IV (ss 45–52)	6.18, 6.40
s 46	5.266, 6.18, 6.45, 6.384
(1)	5.194, 6.39
(i)	5.204, 6.37
47A	16.36
49	5.192
(1)	5.204
(aa)	5.266
55	41.02, **A1.127**
(1)(x)	6.45
Sch 1	4.273
Administration of Estates Act 1971	8.29
Administration of Justice Act 1985	
s 21(2)	1.32
50(3)	41.02
Adoption Act 1958	6.40
Adoption Act 1960	6.40
Adoption Act 1964	6.40
Adoption Act 1968	6.40
Adoption Act 1976	6.40
s 67	5.78
74	5.78
Adoption and Children Act 2002	
s 52	**A1.518**
67	5.73
144(1)	6.246
Sch 3	**A1.547**
Armed Forces Act 1981	8.109
Births and Deaths Registration Act 1953	
s 10ZA	**A1.148A**
10B	**A1.149A**

	PARA
Births and Deaths Registration Act 1953—*contd*	
s 10C	**A1.149B**
Children Act 1989	1.42
Pt I (ss 1–7)	11.159
s 2	11.124
(1)	7.25
(1A)	**11.161A**
(2A)	**11.161A**
(4Z)	**11.161A**
(7)	**11.152**
4	11.161A
(1)(a)	11.159A
4A	7.29
4ZA	**11.161A**, 11.161C, **A1.450A**
Pt II (ss 8–16A)	11.159
s 8	11.163
12	11.161C
(2)	11.163
14A	7.29
25(2)	7.29
33	7.29
105	**A1.463**
Sch 14	
para 4	11.159
6	11.159
Civil Partnership Act 2004	
s 213	**A1.567**
County Courts Act 1984	
s 18	26.12
32	26.12
33	26.12, **A1.394**
Courts and Legal Services Act 1990	1.32A
s 53	2.03, **A1.480A**
55	2.03
119	2.03A
Sch 17	
para 4	A1.487
13	A1.487

Table of Statutes

	PARA
Customs and Inland Revenue Act 1881	
s 30	16.53

Domicile and Matrimonial Proceedings Act 1973
s 1 .... 8.51
4 .... **A1.240**

Enduring Powers of Attorney
Act 1985 .... 3.455, 11.237, 11.254

Family Law Reform Act 1969
Pt II (ss 14–19) 6.18, 6.40
s 14 .... 6.40, 6.45
15 .... 6.40
17 .... 6.40

Family Law Reform Act 1987
s 1 .... 11.159A
(3) 11.161A
4(1) 11.159
18 .... 6.18, 6.37, 6.40, 6.85, 6.170
(2) **6.122**
(2A) **6.170A**
27(3) 6.172
28 .... 6.221A
33(4) 6.40

Family Provision Act 1966 .... 6.18
s 1 .... 6.39

Finance Act 1894
s 5(2) 8.75

Finance Act 1975
s 19 .... 8.06
20(2)–(4) 8.06
22 .... 8.10
(1) 8.09
(4) 8.75
23(1) 8.09
24(2) 8.06, 8.09
(3) 8.09
33 ff 8.75
35 .... 8.86
37 .... 8.13
46 .... 8.06
101 .... 8.118
Sch 4
  para 16 .... 8.23
  17 .... 8.135
Sch 5
  para 3(1) 8.11
  16(4) 8.11
Sch 6 .... 8.06
  para 1 .... 8.126
  10, 11 .... 8.126
  12, 13 .... 8.75, 8.126
  23(1) 8.126
Sch 7
  para 1 .... 8.10, 8.109
  3(1) 8.06
  5(1) 8.06
  6 .... 8.06

Finance Act 1975—*contd*
Sch 7—*contd*
  para 7(6) 8.111
Sch 8 .... 8.86
Sch 9 .... 8.10
Sch 10
  para 12(1) 8.10

Finance Act 1976
s 76 ff 8.75
84 .... 8.75
89–92 .... 8.06
96 .... 8.126
120 .... 8.09
Sch 10
  para 2 .... 8.77

Finance Act 1980
s 94(1) 8.02

Finance Act 1981
s 96 .... 8.86
104(3) 8.09
135 .... 8.10
Sch 14 .... 8.86

Finance Act 1982
s 93–95 .... 8.75
100 .... 8.10
Sch 16 .... 8.75

Finance Act 1985
s 83(2) 5.249
84(8) 5.249

Finance Act 1986
s 102 .... 8.02, 8.143, **A1.616**
(3) 8.11
102A(2) 8.02
102ZA 8.02, 8.143
Sch 20 .... 8.143

Finance Act 1976
s 58 .... 8.77
Sch 8
  para 5 .... 8.77

Finance Act 1989
s 178(1) 8.130

Finance Act 1996
s 154 .... 8.75
184(2) 8.77

Finance Act 1998
s 161 .... 8.75

Finance Act 2007
Sch 15 .... 8.143

Finance Act 2006
s 157 .... 8.09, 8.11
160 .... 8.11
Sch 22 .... 8.11

Finance Act 2007 .... 8.11
s 66 .... 8.143
Sch 20
  para 20 .... 8.63

Finance Act 2008
s 10 .... 8.13
Sch 4 .... 8.13

Table of Statutes

	PARA
Finance (No 2) Act 1992	
Sch 14	
para 1	8.77
Gender Recognition Act 2004	4.190, 6.221A
s 1	A1.584A
2	A1.584B
3	A1.584C
4	A1.584D
5	A1.584E
5A	A1.584F
6	A1.584G
7	A1.584H
8	A1.584I
9	A1.584J
10	A1.584K
11	A1.584L
12	6.18, A1.584M
13	A1.584N
14	A1.584O
15	A1.584P
16	A1.584Q
17	A1.584R
18	A1.584S
19	A1.584T
20	A1.584U
21	A1.584V
22	A1.584W
(4)(b)	4.105A
23	A1.584X
24	A1.584Y
25	A1.584Z
26	A1.584ZA
27	A1.584
Government Annuities Act 1929	
s 20, 21	1.82
56, 57	1.82
Human Fertilisation and Embryology Act 1990	6.221A
Human Fertilisation and Embryology Act 2008	1.42, 11.123, 11.124, 11.159
Pt 2 (ss 33–58)	6.40
s 33	A1.592A
34	A1.592B
35	A1.592C
36	A1.592D
37	11.159A, A1.592E
38	11.159A, A1.592F
39	11.159A, A1.592G
40	11.159A, A1.592H
41	A1.592I
42	A1.592J
43	6.171, 11.161C, A1.592K
44	11.161A, A1.592L
45	A1.592M
46	A1.592N
47	A1.592O

	PARA
Human Fertilisation and Embryology Act 2008—*contd*	
s 48	A1.592P
49	A1.592Q
50	A1.592R
51	A1.592S
52	A1.592T
53	A1.592U
54	A1.592V
55	A1.592W
56	A1.592X
57	A1.592Y
58	A1.592Z
Sch 6	6.40, A1.592AA
Inheritance (Provision for Family and Dependants) Act 1975	28.01
Inheritance Tax Act 1984	
s 1, 2	8.06
3(1), (2)	8.06
3A	8.06
4	8.10
(1)	8.09
5	A1.595
(1)	8.09
(2)	8.11
6	8.06, A1.596
(1)	8.09
7	8.13, A1.597
10–16	8.06
17	8.06
(a)	8.101
18	8.126
23, 24	8.126
25, 26	8.75, 8.126
27	8.75
30 ff	8.75
39A	8.128
46A, 46B	8.06
48	8.09, A1.598
(3), (3A)	8.11
49(1)	8.11
(1A)	8.11
49A, 49B	8.11
49D, 49E	8.11
64–69	8.63
71A	8.11
71C, 71D	8.11
86	8.11
89A(4)	8.11
102(4)	8.143
104	8.77
105(3)	8.77
115 ff	8.86
125	8.10
141	8.118
142(1), (2)	8.101
(5)	8.101
151(2)–(4)	8.11
151A–151C	8.11
152	8.11

Table of Statutes

	PARA
Inheritance Tax Act 1984—*contd*	
s 154	8.10
(1)	8.109
156	8.10
169	8.10
200	**A1.601**
216	8.01, **A1.606**
218A	8.101
230	8.135
234	8.23
239	8.142
245	8.101
245A	**A1.609**
256	**A1.610**
(1)	8.02
257	**A1.611**
267	8.11, 8.51
(1)	8.02
269	8.77
Sch 3	8.52
Sch 4	8.75
Sch 6	
para 2	8.75
Intestates' Estates Act 1952	6.18, 6.37
Sch 2	**A1.147**
Judicial Trustees Act 1896	
s 1	41.02
Law Reform (Succession) Act 1995	
s 1(1)	6.37
Legitimacy Act 1926	
s 9	6.40
Legitimacy Act 1959	6.40
Legitimacy Act 1976	
s 9	6.40
Lunacy Act 1890	11.246
Lunacy Act 1891	11.246
Lunacy Act 1908	11.246
Mental Capacity Act 1959	11.246
Mental Capacity Act 2005	3.455, 4.34, 4.81, 5.02, 5.258, 7.22, 7.23, 11.41, 11.42A, 11.237, 11.237F, 11.239, 11.240, 11.241, 11.242, 11.243, 11.244, 11.253, 11.254, 11.255, 11.270, 11.272, 11.274, 13.48, 13.49, 13.92, 13.93, 13.125, 15.43, 15.44, 15.45, 15.46, 17.16, 17.17, 25.12, 25.103
Pt 1 (ss 1–44)	11.237A

	PARA
Mental Capacity Act 2005—*contd*	
s 1	11.237B
2	11.237C
9	11.237A, 11.263A
11	**A1.583**
16	3.438, 11.237C, 11.246
(1)	3.455
(2)(a)	3.455
16A	**A1.586A**
17	11.246
18	11.246
(1)(i)	3.438, 3.455
(2)	3.439, 3.455
Pt 2 (ss 45–61)	11.237D
s 45	11.246
46	3.440
Sch 1	
para 16	11.237E
Sch 2	
para 3	3.455
Sch 4	
Pt 1, 2	**A1.591**
para 15	11.237E
Pt 8	**A1.591**
Mental Capacity Act 2007	17.13
Mental Health Act 1983	3.455, 15.43
Pt VII (ss 93–113)	3.438, 3.455, 11.237
National Assistance Act 1948	
s 21(1)(a)	25.103
Powers of Attorney Act 1971	
s 3	11.42A, 11.263D
Senior Courts Act 1981 (Supreme Court Act 1981)	
s 109	8.01
111	21.01
113(1)	8.33
114(2)	5.199, 6.122, 7.28, 11.244
116	5.02, 11.264, 13.53, 15.45, 25.102, 25.103
124	21.33
130	1.44
Solicitors Act 1974	
s 23(1)	1.32, 2.03
Stamp Act 1891	
Sch 1	5.249
Trustee Act 1925	
s 36	**A1.79**
Wills Act 1837	
s 9	3.70
20	34.70
33 ff	6.45
Wills Act 1963	3.408

Table of Statutory Instruments

	PARA
References in **bold** type indicate that the Statutory Instrument is set out in part or in full.	
Capital Transfer Tax (Delivery of Accounts) Regulations 1981, SI 1981/880	4.202, 8.02
Capital Transfer Tax (Delivery of Accounts) (No 3) Regulations 1983, SI 1983/1039	8.02
Charities (The Shrubbery) Order 2003, SI 2003/1688	8.02
Civil Procedure Rules 1998, SI 1998/3132	
Pt 30	
r 30.2(8)	39.01
Pt 44	
r 44.4(2), (3)	40.10
Pt 48	
r 48.4	40.10
Pt 49	27.20
Pt 57	
r 57.1	**A2.153**
57.2	**A2.154**
(3)	26.12
57.3	**A2.155**
57.4	**A2.156**
57.5	**A2.157**
57.6	**A2.158**
(1)	28.01
57.7	**A2.159**
(1), (2)	32.06
(5)	40.13
57.8	**A2.160**
57.9	**A2.161**
57.10	**A2.162**
57.11	**A2.163**
57.12	**A2.164**
57.13	**A2.165**
(2), (3)	41.02
57.14	**A2.166**
57.15	**A2.167**
57.16	**A2.168**

	PARA
Civil Procedure Rules 1998, SI 1998/3132—*contd*	
PD 57	
para 1.1	**A2.169**
1.2	**A2.169**
2.1	**A2.170**
2.2	**A2.170**
2.3	**A2.170**
2.4	**A2.170**
3.1	**A2.171**
3.2	**A2.171**
3.3	**A2.171**
4(1), (2)	**A2.172**
5.1, 5.2	**A2.173**
6.1(1)–(3)	**A2.174**
6.2	**A2.174**
7.1	**A2.175**
7.2	**A2.175**
7.3	**A2.175**
7.4	**A2.175**
8.1	**A2.176**
8.2	**A2.176**
8.3–8.5	**A2.176**
9	**A2.177**
10.1, 10.2	**A2.178**
11	**A2.179**
12	**A2.180**
13.1, 13.2	41.02, **A2.181**
14.1, 14.2	41.02, **A2.182**
15	**A2.183**
16	**A2.184**
17	**A2.185**
18.1–18.3	**A2.186**
Annex	**A2.187**
Court of Protection Rules 2001, SI 2001/824	3.441
Court of Protection Rules 2007, SI 2007/1734	
r 61	3.441
Court of Protection (Enduring Powers of Attorney) Rules 2001, SI 2001/825	11.258
Courts and Legal Services Act 1990 (Commencement No 11) Order 2004, SI 2004/2950	1.32

Table of Statutory Instruments

	PARA
Courts and Legal Services Act 1990 (Modification of Power to Make Rules about Licensed Conveyancers) Order 2008, SI 2008/537	1.32, 2.03
District Probate Registries Order 1982, SI 1982/379	2.59
art 1	A2.28
2	A2.29
3	A2.30
4	A2.31
5	A2.32
Schedule	A2.33
Double Taxation Relief (Estate Duty) (France) Order 1963, SI 1963/1319	8.111
Double Taxation Relief (Estate Duty) (Italy) Order 1968, SI 1968/304	8.111
Double Taxation Relief (Estate Duty) (Netherlands) Order 1950, SI 1950/1197	8.111
Double Taxation Reflief (Estate Duty) (South Africa) Order 1947, SR & O 1947/314	8.111
Double Taxation Relief (Estate Duty) (Sweden) Order 1961, SI 1961/578	8.111
Double Taxation Relief (Estate Duty) (Switzerland) Order 1957, SI 1957/426	8.111
Double Taxation Relief (Estate Duty) (USA) Order 1946, SR & O 1946/1351	8.111
Double Taxation Relief (Taxes on Estates of Deceased Persons and Inheritances and on Gifts) (Republic of Ireland) Order 1978, SI 1978/1107	8.111
Enduring Powers of Attorney (Prescribed Form) Regulations 1990, SI 1990/1376	11.41A, 11.258
Enduring Powers of Attorney (Prescribed Form) (Amendment) Regulations 2005, SI 2005/3116	11.41A
reg 3	11.42, 11.259
Enduring Powers of Attorney (Prescribed Form) (Amendment) Amendment Regulations 2007, SI 2007/548	11.41, 11.41A, 11.42, 11.259

	PARA
Enduring Powers of Attorney (Welsh Language Prescribed Form) (Amendment) Amendment Regulations 2007, SI 2007/549	11.41A, 11.42
Family Provision (Intestate Succession) Order 1972, SI 1972/916	6.39
Family Provision (Intestate Succession) Order 1977, SI 1977/415	6.39
Family Provision (Intestate Succession) Order 1981, SI 1981/255	6.39
Family Provision (Intestate Succession) Order 1987, SI 1987/799	6.39
Family Provision (Intestate Succession) Order 1993, SI 1993/2906	6.39
art 1	A2.116
2	A2.117
Family Provision (Intestate Succession) Order 2009, SI 2009/135	
art 1	A2.135U
2	A2.135V
Human Fertilisation and Embryology Act 2008 (Commencement No 1 and Transitional Provisions) Order 2009, SI 2009/479	
art 6(1)(d)	6.170A
Inheritance Tax (Delivery of Accounts) (Expected Estates) Regulations 2002, SI 2002/1733	4.202, 8.02
Inheritance Tax (Delivery of Accounts) (Expected Estates) Regulations 2004, SI 2004/2543	4.202, 8.02
Inheritance Tax (Delivery of Accounts) Regulations 1981, SI 1981/880	
reg 1	A2.20
2	A2.21
3	A2.22
4	A2.23
5	A2.24
6	A2.25
7	A2.26
8	A2.28
Inheritance Tax (Delivery of Accounts) Regulations 1987, SI 1987/1127	8.02
Inheritance Tax (Delivery of Accounts) Regulations 1989, SI 1989/1078	8.02
Inheritance Tax (Delivery of Accounts) Regulations 1990, SI 1990/1110	8.02
Inheritance Tax (Delivery of Accounts) Regulations 1991, SI 1991/1248	8.02

Table of Statutory Instruments

	PARA
Inheritance Tax (Delivery of Accounts) Regulations 1995, SI 1995/1461	8.02
Inheritance Tax (Delivery of Accounts) Regulations 1996, SI 1996/1470	8.02
Inheritance Tax (Delivery of Accounts) Regulations 1998, SI 1998/1431	8.02
Inheritance Tax (Delivery of Accounts) Regulations 2000, SI 2000/967	8.02
Inheritance Tax (Delivery of Accounts) (Expected Estates) Regulations 2004, SI 2004/2543	
reg 1	**A2.118**
2	**A2.119**
3	**A2.120**
4	**A2.121**
5	**A2.122**
6	**A2.123**
7	**A2.124**
8	**A2.125**
9	**A2.126**
10	**A2.127**
11	**A2.128**
Intestate Succession (Interest and Capitalisation) Order 1977, SI 1977/1491	6.37, 6.45, 16.36
art 1	**A2.07A**
2	**A2.07B**
3	**A2.07C**
Schedule	**A2.07D**
Intestate Succession (Interest and Capitalisation) Order 1977 (Amendment) Order 1983, SI 1983/1374	6.37, 6.45, 16.36
Intestate Succession (Interest and Capitalisation) (Amendment) Order 2008, SI 2008/3162	16.36
Lasting Powers of Attorney, Enduring Powers of Attorney and Public Guardian Regulations 2007, SI 2007/1253	11.259
art 1	A2.135A
2	A2.135B
3	11.42, **A2.135C**
4	A2.135D
6	A2.135E
7	A2.135F
8	A2.135G
9	A2.135H
10	**A2.135I**
11	**A2.135J**
23	**A2.135K**
24	**A2.135L**
25	**A2.135M**
26	**A2.135N**
27	**A2.135O**
28	**A2.135P**
29	**A2.135Q**

	PARA
Lasting Powers of Attorney, Enduring Powers of Attorney and Public Guardian Regulations 2007, SI 2007/1253—*contd*	
art 30	**A2.135R**
31	**A2.135S**
32	**A2.135T**
Sch 1	
Pt 1	11.42A, 11.263A
Pt 2	11.42A, 11.263A
Mental Capacity Act 2005 (Transitional and Consequential Provisions) Order 2007, SI 2007/1898	11.237F
Non-Contentious Probate Fees Order 2004, SI 2004/3120	1.45
art 1	A3.01
2	A3.02
3	A3.03
4	A3.04
5	A3.05
6	A3.06
7	A3.07
8	A3.08
Sch 1	A3.09
Fee 1	11.358
7	21.04, 21.34
8(a)–(c)	21.04
Sch 1a	4.261, A3.10
Sch 2	A3.11
Non-Contentious Probate Rules 1987, SI 1987/2024	1.43
r 1	A2.40
2	A2.41
3	A2.42
4	A2.43
5	A2.44
6	A2.45
7	A2.46
8	A2.47
9	A2.48
10	**A2.49**
11	**A2.50**
12	**A2.51**
13	**A2.52**
14	**A2.53**
15	**A2.54**
16	**A2.55**
17	**A2.56**
18	**A2.57**
19	**A2.58**
20	**A2.59**
(c)	5.200
(d)	5.198, 5.202
21	**A2.60**
22	7.35, 11.273, **A2.61**
(1)	11.272
23	1.42, **A2.62**
24	**A2.63**

Table of Statutory Instruments

	PARA
Non-Contentious Probate Rules 1987, SI 1987/2024—contd	
r 25	A2.64
(2)	7.28, 7.29
(3)(a)	7.25
26	A2.65
27	A2.66
28	A2.67
29	A2.68
30	A2.69
31	11.31, 25.103, A2.70
(1)	11.42A, 11.65
32	A2.71
(1)	7.29
(2), (3)	7.25
33	A2.72
34	A2.73
(1)	15.43
35	11.41A, 11.237F, 11.238, 17.15, 17.65, 25.103, A2.74
(1)	11.239, 11.241
(2)	11.244
(a)	11.246, 11.252
(b)	7.22
(c)	7.22, 11.265, 15.46
(3)	7.22, 11.244, 11.248, 11.266
(4)	7.23, 11.268, 11.274
(5)	11.149, 11.257
36	A2.75
37	A2.76
38	A2.77
39	A2.78
40	A2.79
41	A2.80
42	A2.81
43	A2.82
44	A2.83
45	A2.84
46	A2.85
47	A2.86
48	A2.87
49	A2.88
50	A2.89
51	A2.90
52	25.102, A2.91
53	A2.92
54	A2.93
55	A2.94
56	A2.95
57	A2.96
58	A2.97
59	A2.98
60	A2.99
61	A2.100
(1)	11.274
62	A2.101
62A	A2.102
63	A2.103

	PARA
Non-Contentious Probate Rules 1987, SI 1987/2024—contd	
r 64	A2.104
65	A2.105
66	A2.106
67	A2.107
68	A2.108
69	A2.109
Sch 1	A2.110
Sch 2	A2.111
Parental Responsibility Agreement Regulations 1991, SI 1991/1478	
reg 1	A2.112
2	A2.113
3	A2.114
Schedule	A2.115
Probate Services (Approved Bodies) Order 2008, SI 2008/1865	1.32
Probate Services (Approved Bodies) Order 2009, SI 2009/1588	1.32A
Public Trustee (Custodian Trustee) Rules 1975, SI 1975/1189	25.103
Solicitors' (Non-Contentious Business) Remuneration Order 1994, SI 1994/2616	4.272, 4.276
art 1	A5.01
2	A5.02
3	A5.03
4	A5.04
5	A5.05
6	A5.06
7	A5.07
8	A5.08
9	A5.09
10	A5.10
11	A5.11
12	A5.12
13	A5.13
14	A5.14
15	A5.15
Solicitors' (Non-Contentious Business) Remuneration Order 2009, SI 2009/1931	4.272
art 1	A5.16
2	4.273, A5.17
3	4.274, A5.18
4	4.276, A5.19
5	A5.20
Stamp Duty (Exempt Instruments) Regulations 1987, SI 1987/516	
Schedule	5.249
Taxes and Duties (Interest Rate) (Amendment) Regulations 2009, SI 2009/2032	8.130

Supplementary Table of Cases

	PARA
Abbott v Richardson [2006] EWHC 1291 (Ch), [2006] WTLR 1567, [2006] All ER (D) 54 (May)	3.133, 34.31
Abdul Hamid Bey's Goods, Re (1898) 67 LJP 59, 78 LT 202	11.65
Adams, Re [1990] Ch 601, [1990] 2 All ER 97, [1990] 2 WLR 924, [1990] 2 FLR 519, [1990] Fam Law 403, 134 Sol Jo 518	34.70
Anderson's Estate, Re, Anderson v Downes [1916] P 49, 85 LJP 21, 60 Sol Jo 254, 114 LT 519, 32 TLR 248	3.376
Atkinson v Morris [1897] P 40, 66 LJP 17, 45 WR 293, 41 Sol Jo 110, 75 LT 440, 13 TLR 83, CA	34.70
Atter v Atkinson (1869) LR 1 P & D 665, 33 JP 440, 20 LT 404	34.50
Austen's Goods, Re (1853) 2 Rob Eccl 611, 17 Jur 284, 21 LTOS 65	3.376
Baker, Re, Baker v Baker [1929] 1 Ch 668, 98 LJ Ch 174, 141 LT 29	3.188
Barker-Benfield, Re, Hansen v Barker-Benfield [2006] EWHC 1119 (Ch), 150 Sol Jo LB 708, [2006] WTLR 1141, [2006] All ER (D) 253 (May)	34.31
Barnes Goods, Re, Hodson v Barnes (1926) 96 LJP 26, 136 LT 380, 43 TLR 71	3.376
Barry v Butlin (1838) 2 Moo PCC 480	34.50
Battan Singh v Amirchand [1948] AC 161, [1948] 1 All ER 152, [1948] LJR 827, PC	34.31
Bibb v Thomas (1775) 2 Wm Bl 1043	34.70
Blewitt's Goods, Re (1880) 5 PD 116, 44 JP 768, 49 LJP 31, 28 WR 520, 42 LT 329	3.70
Booth, Re, Booth v Booth [1926] P 118, 95 LJP 64, 134 LT 229, 42 TLR 454	34.70
Boughey v Moreton (1758) 3 Hag Ecc 191, 2 Lee 532	34.70
Bowen-Buscarlet's Will Trusts, Re, Nathan v Bowen-Buscarlet [1972] Ch 463, [1971] 3 All ER 636, [1971] 3 WLR 742, 115 Sol Jo 872	5.204
Broadway v Fernandes [2007] EWHC 684 (Ch), [2007] All ER (D) 485 (Mar)	34.70
Brown v Executors of the Estate of Her Majesty Queen Elizabeth the Queen Mother [2007] EWHC 1607 (Fam), [2007] All ER (D) 66 (Jul); revsd [2008] EWCA Civ 56, [2008] 1 WLR 2327, (2008) Times, 19 February, [2008] All ER (D) 118 (Feb)	4.249
Brunt v Brunt (1873) LR 3 P & D 37, 37 JP 312, 21 WR 392, 28 LT 368	34.70
Buckenham v Dickinson [2000] WTLR 1083	34.50
Burrell's Goods, Re (1858) 1 Sw & Tr 64, 6 WR 461, 31 LTOS 41	11.279
C (children) (parent: purported marriage between two women: artificial insemination by donor), Re [2006] EWCA Civ 551, [2006] All ER (D) 216 (May), sub nom J v C [2007] Fam 1, [2006] 3 WLR 876, sub nom J v C (void marriage: status of children) [2006] 2 FLR 1098, [2006] Fam Law 742, (2006) Times, 1 June	6.221A

Supplementary Table of Cases

PARA

Cattermole v Prisk [2006] 1 FLR 693, [2006] Fam Law 98 .... 34.50
Chana v Chana [2001] WTLR 205 .... 34.70
Chanter's Goods, Re (1844) 1 Rob Eccl 273, 3 Notes of Cases 438 .... 11.358
Clancy v Clancy [2003] EWHC 1885 (Ch), [2003] 37 LS Gaz R 32, [2003] WTLR 1097, [2003] All ER (D) 536 (Jul) 34.31, 3.133
Clarke v Brothwood [2006] EWHC 2939 (Ch), [2006] All ER (D) 207 (Nov) 3.264
Clarke v Scripps (1852) 2 Rob Eccl 563, 16 Jur 783, 20 LTOS 83 .... 34.70
Cleare and Forster v Cleare (1869) LR 1 P & D 655, 38 LJP & M 81, 17 WR 687, 20 LT 497 .... 34.50
Cleaver, Re, Cleaver v Insley [1981] 2 All ER 1018, [1981] 1 WLR 939, 125 Sol Jo 445 .... 3.222
Combes' Case (1604) Noy 101, Moore KB 759 .... 34.31
Cook's Estate, Re, Murison v Cook [1960] 1 All ER 689, [1960] 1 WLR 353, 104 Sol Jo 311 .... 3.70
Court v Despallieres, Ikin (dec'd), Re [2009] EWHC 3340 (Ch), 154 Sol Jo (no 1) 30, [2009] All ER (D) 167 (Dec) 3.45
Cousins v Tubb (1891) 65 LT 716 ..... 40.14
Crispin v Doglioni (1860) 29 LJP 130, 2 Sw & Tr 17, 9 WR 19, 3 LT 179 .... 28.01
Cutcliffe's Estate, Re, Le Duc v Veness [1959] P 6, [1958] 3 All ER 642, [1958] 3 WLR 707, 102 Sol Jo 915, CA 40.13, 40.14

Dalton v Latham [2003] EWHC 796 (Ch), 147 Sol Jo LB 537, [2003] All ER (D) 305 (Apr) 5.187
Davies v Gregory (1873) LR 3 P & D 28, 37 JP 279, 42 LJP & M 33, 21 WR 462, 28 LT 239, [1861–73] All ER Rep Ext 1008 .... 40.14
Davis v Chanter (1848) 2 Ph 545, 15 Sim 300, 17 LJ Ch 297, 10 LTOS 477 .... 11.358
Dawson's Goods, Re, Maclean and Maclean v Dawson (1859) 1 Sw & Tr 425, 43 LTOS 53 .... 11.358
Dickson, Re [1984] LS Gaz R 3012, CA 34.70

PARA

Douglas's Will Trusts, Re, Lloyds Bank Ltd v Nelson [1959] 2 All ER 620, [1959] 1 WLR 744, 103 Sol Jo 657; affd [1959] 3 All ER 785, [1959] 1 WLR 1212, 104 Sol Jo 126, CA 5.204
Dufour v Pereira (1769) 1 Dick 419, 2 Hargrave Juridical Arguments 304 .... 3.222

Eccles' Goods, Re (1889) 15 PD 1, 54 JP 55, 59 LJP 5, 61 LT 652 ..... 11.279
Evans v Tyler (1849) 2 Rob Eccl 128, 14 Jur 47, 13 Jur 413, 13 LTOS 264, 14 LTOS 450, 7 Notes of Cases 296 .... 4.34, 11.241, 14.13
Eyre v Eyre [1903] P 131, 72 LJP 45, 51 WR 701, 88 LT 567, 19 TLR 380 .... 34.70

Fanshawe's Estate, Re (1983) Times, 17 November, CA 40.13
Franks v Sinclair [2006] EWHC 3365 (Ch), [2007] WTLR 439, [2006] All ER (D) 340 (Dec) 3.133, 34.50, 40.10
Fuller v Strum [2001] EWCA Civ 1879, [2002] 2 All ER 87, [2002] 1 WLR 1097, [2002] 1 FCR 608, (2002) Times, 22 January, [2001] All ER (D) 92 (Dec) 34.50

Galbraith's Goods, Re [1951] P 422, [1951] 2 All ER 470n, 95 Sol Jo 548, [1951] 2 TLR 412 .... 17.20
Giles v Warren (1872) LR 2 P & D 401, 36 JP 663, 41 LJP & M 59, 20 WR 827, 26 LT 780 .... 34.70
Gill v Gill [1909] P 157, 78 LJP 60, 53 Sol Jo 359, 100 LT 861, 25 TLR 400 .... 34.70
Good (dec'd), Re, Carapeto v Good [2002] EWHC 640 (Ch), (2002) Times, 22 May, [2002] WTLR 801, [2002] All ER (D) 141 (Apr) 34.50
Goodchild, Re, Goodchild v Goodchild [1997] 3 All ER 63, [1997] 1 WLR 1216, [1997] 3 FCR 601, [1997] 2 FLR 644, [1997] NLJR 758, CA 3.222
Goodman v Goodman [2006] EWHC 1757 (Ch), [2006] All ER (D) 193 (Jul) 3.264
Green, Re, Lindner v Green [1951] Ch 148, [1950] 2 All ER 913, 94 Sol Jo 742, 66 (pt 2) TLR 819 .... 3.222

Supplementary Table of Cases

	PARA
Green's Estate, Re, Ward v Bond (1962) 106 Sol Jo 1034	34.70
Guardhouse v Blackburn (1866) LR 1 P & D 109, 35 LJP & M 116, 12 Jur NS 278, 14 WR 463, [1861–73] All ER Rep 680, 14 LT 69	3.133
Gullan's Goods, Re (1858) 27 LJP & M 15, 4 Jur NS 196, 1 Sw & Tr 23, 5 WR 307, 30 LTOS 326	34.70
Hall-Dare, Re, Le Marchant v Lee Warner [1916] 1 Ch 272, 85 LJ Ch 365, 114 LT 559	40.14
Harding (dec'd), Re, Gibbs v Harding [2007] EWHC 3 (Ch), [2008] Ch 235, [2007] 1 All ER 747, [2008] 2 WLR 361, 9 ITELR 563, [2007] All ER (D) 28 (Jan)	5.88A
Harris v Berrall (1858) 1 Sw & Tr 153, 7 WR 19	34.70
Hart v Dabbs [2001] WTLR 527	34.50
Harwood v Baker (1840) 3 Moo PCC 282	34.31
Hastilow v Stobie (1865) LR 1 P & D 64, 35 LJP & M 18, 11 Jur NS 1039, 14 WR 211, 13 LT 473	3.133
Hastings' Goods, Re (1877) 4 PD 73, 42 JP 185, 47 LJP 30, 39 LT 45	11.279
Hegarty v King (1880) 5 LR Ir 249; affd (1880) 7 LR Ir 18, CA	34.50
Hey's Estate, Re, Walker v Gaskill [1914] P 192, 83 LJP 152, 59 Sol Jo 45, 111 LT 941, 30 TLR 637	3.222
Hoare Trustees v Jaques [2008] EWHC 2022 (Ch), [2008] All ER (D) 68 (Feb)	3.188
Hoff v Atherton [2004] EWCA Civ 1554, [2005] WTLR 99, [2004] All ER (D) 314 (Nov)	3.133, 34.31
Holland's Estate, Re [1936] 3 All ER 13, 105 LJP 113, 80 Sol Jo 838, 155 LT 417, 53 TLR 3	6.21
J v C (void marriage: status of children) [2006] 2 FLR 1098. See C (children) (parent: purported marriage between two women: artificial insemination by donor), Re	
J v C [2007] Fam 1. See C (children) (parent: purported marriage between two women: artificial insemination by donor), Re	
Jarrom v Sellars [2007] EWHC 1366 (Ch), [2007] WTLR 1219, [2007] All ER (D) 202 (Apr)	40.13

	PARA
Jenner v Ffinch (1879) 5 PD 106, 49 LJP 25, 28 WR 520, 42 LT 327	40.14
Jones's Estate, Re, Thomas v Jones. See Thomas v Jones	
Kipping and Barlow v Ash (1845) 1 Rob Eccl 270, 9 Jur 542, 4 Notes of Cases 177	28.01
Lamothe v Lamothe [2006] EWHC 1387 (Ch), [2006] WTLR 1431, [2006] All ER (D) 153 (Jun)	34.70
Lay's Goods, Re (1840) 2 Curt 375	3.376
Lemage v Goodban (1865) LR 1 P & D 57, 35 LJP & M 28, 12 Jur NS 32, 13 LT 508	40.14
Leonard v Leonard [1902] P 243, 71 LJP 117, 46 Sol Jo 666, 87 LT 145, 18 TLR 747	34.70
Lindsay v Lindsay (1872) LR 2 P & D 459, 36 JP 808, 27 LT 322	28.04
Liver, Re, Scott v Woods (1956) 106 L Jo 75	34.50
Long-Sutton's Estate, Re [1912] P 97, 81 LJP 28, 56 Sol Jo 293, 106 LT 643	4.151
Mack v Lockwood [2009] EWHC 1524 (Ch)	5.187
McKee, Re, Public Trustee v McKee [1931] 2 Ch 145, 100 LJ Ch 325, 75 Sol Jo 442, 145 LT 605, 47 TLR 424, CA	5.204
Mackenzie's Estate, Re [1909] P 305, 79 LJP 4, 26 TLR 39	34.70
M'Murdo's Goods, Re (1868) LR 1 P & D 540, 32 JP 72, 37 LJP & M 14, 3 Mar LC 37, 16 WR 283, 17 LT 393	3.376
Maltby v DJ Freeman & Co [1978] 2 All ER 913, [1978] 1 WLR 431, 122 Sol Jo 212	4.274
Marsh v Tyrrell and Harding (1828) 2 Hag Ecc 84; on appeal (1832) 3 Hag Ecc 471	34.31
Mills v Millward (1889) 15 PD 20, 59 LJP 23, 61 LT 651	34.70
Minns v Foster [2002] All ER (D) 225 (Dec)	3.133
Mitchell and Mitchell v Gard and Kingwell (1863) 28 JP 104, 33 LJPM & A 7, 10 Jur NS 51, 3 Sw & Tr 275, 12 WR 255, 9 LT 491	40.13, 40.14
Newland's Goods, Re [1952] P 71, [1952] 1 All ER 841, [1952] 1 Lloyd's Rep 280, 96 Sol Jo 230, [1952] 1 TLR 896	3.376

Supplementary Table of Cases

	PARA
Newton's Goods, Re (1843) 3 Curt 428, 7 Jur 219	17.17
O'Brien v Seagrave [2007] EWHC 1247 (Ch), [2007] 3 All ER 633, [2007] 1 WLR 2002, (2007) Times, 2 May, [2007] All ER (D) 56 (Apr)	28.01, 32.06
O'Keefe, Re, Poingdestre v Sherman [1940] Ch 124, [1940] 1 All ER 216, 109 LJ Ch 86, 84 Sol Jo 44, 162 LT 62, 56 TLR 204	3.408
Oldham, Re, Hadwen v Myles [1925] Ch 75, 95 LJ Ch 148, [1924] All ER Rep 288, 69 Sol Jo 193, 132 LT 658	3.222
Orton v Smith (1873) LR 3 P & D 23, 37 JP 503, 42 LJP & M 50, 28 LT 712	40.13
Palliser v Ord (1724) Bunb 166	11.65
Parker v Felgate (1883) 8 PD 171, 47 JP 808, 52 LJP 95, 32 WR 186	3.133, 34.31
Patten v Poulton (1858) 22 JP 180, 27 LJP & M 41, 4 Jur NS 341, 1 Sw & Tr 55, 6 WR 458, 31 LTOS 40	34.70
Patterson's Goods, Re (1898) 79 LT 123	3.376
Pearson, Re, Rowling v Crowther [1963] 3 All ER 763, [1963] 1 WLR 1358, 107 Sol Jo 872	3.188
Penny's Goods, Re (1846) 1 Rob Eccl 426, 4 Notes of Cases 659	11.279
Perotti v Watson [2001] EWCA Civ 116, [2001] All ER (D) 26 (Feb)	41.02
Phillips' Goods, Re (1824) 2 Add 335	17.17
Practice Direction (incapacity, evidence of) [1969] 1 All ER 494, [1969] WLR 301	11.256
Practice Direction [1981] 2 All ER 832, [1981] 1 WLR 1185	4.206
Practice Direction (probate: non-contentious probate: grant on behalf of minor) [1991] 4 All ER 562, [1991] 1 WLR 1069, [1991] 2 FLR 462, [1991] Fam Law 493	11.123, 11.159
Practice Direction (probate: grants of representation: computer records) [1999] 1 All ER 384, [1998] 1 WLR 1699	21.01
Practice Note [1962] 2 All ER 613, [1962] 1 WLR 738, 106 Sol Jo 456	11.256

	PARA
Practice Note [1975] CLY 266	16.53
Price v Craig [2006] EWHC 2561 (Ch), 9 ITELR 393, [2006] All ER (D) 249 (Oct)	3.264
R, Re [1951] P 10, [1950] 2 All ER 117, 94 Sol Jo 386, 66 (pt 2) TLR 26	34.50
Rapley's Estate, Re, Rapley v Rapley [1983] 3 All ER 248, [1983] 1 WLR 1069, [1984] FLR 173, 127 Sol Jo 394	3.376
Rogers (dec'd), Re [2006] EWHC 753 (Ch), [2006] 2 All ER 792, [2006] 1 WLR 1577, [2006] NLJR 644, (2006) Times, 3 May, [2006] All ER (D) 68 (Apr)	4.47, 4.48
Rose, Re (October 1940, unreported)	7.35
Rowe v Clarke [2006] EWHC 1292 (Ch), [2006] All ER (D) 124 (May)	40.14
Rowe v Clarke [2005] EWHC 3068 (Ch), 149 Sol Jo LB 1450, [2006] WTLR 347, [2005] All ER (D) 368 (Oct)	34.70
Sabatini, Re (1969) 114 Sol Jo 35	34.70
Saunders v Saunders (1848) 6 Notes of Cases 518	34.70
Scott, Re, Huggett v Reichman (1966) 110 Sol Jo 852	34.50
Segelman, Re [1996] Ch 171, [1995] 3 All ER 676, [1996] 2 WLR 173	3.264
Servoz-Gavin (dec'd), Re, Ayling v Summers [2009] EWHC 3168 (Ch), [2010] 1 All ER 410	3.376
Sharp v Adam [2006] EWCA Civ 449, 10 ITELR 419, [2006] WTLR 1059, [2006] All ER (D) 277 (Apr)	34.31
Shaw's Estate, Re [1905] P 92, 74 LJP 39, 92 LT 428	17.16
Shephard v Wheeler (2000) Times, 15 February, [2000] All ER (D) 19	25.102
Shuck v Loveridge [2005] EWHC 72 (Ch), [2005] All ER (D) 306 (Jan)	34.50
Simpson, Re, Schaniel v Simpson (1977) 121 Sol Jo 224, [1977] LS Gaz R 187, 127 NLJ 487	3.133, 34.50
Solicitor, a, Re [1975] QB 475, [1974] 3 All ER 853, [1975] 2 WLR 105, 118 Sol Jo 737	34.50

Supplementary Table of Cases

	PARA
Sowerby's Goods, Re (1891) 65 LT 764	17.16
Spiers v English [1907] P 122, 76 LJP 28, 96 LT 582	40.13
Sprigge v Sprigge (1868) LR 1 P & D 608, 33 JP 104, 38 LJP & M 4, 17 WR 80, 19 LT 462	34.70
Stone v Hoskins [1905] P 194, 74 LJP 110, 54 WR 64, 93 LT 441, 21 TLR 528, [1904–7] All ER Rep Ext 1406	3.222
Summerell v Clements (1862) 27 JP 41, 32 LJPM & A 33, 3 Sw & Tr 35, 11 WR 153, 8 LT 172	40.13
Sykes, Re, Drake v Sykes (1906) 22 TLR 741; affd (1907) 23 TLR 747, CA	34.70
Taylor's Estate, Re, National and Provincial and Union Bank of England v Taylor (1919) 64 Sol Jo 148	34.70
Thomas, Re, Davies v Davies [1949] P 336, [1949] 1 All ER 1048, [1949] LJR 1095, 93 Sol Jo 321, 65 TLR 313	26.12
Thomas v Jones [1928] P 162, [1928] All ER Rep 704, 72 Sol Jo 255, 139 LT 214, 44 TLR 467, sub nom Jones's Estate, Re, Thomas v Jones 97 LJP 81	34.31
Thomas and Agnes Carvel Foundation v Carvel [2007] EWHC 1314 (Ch), [2008] Ch 395, [2007] 4 All ER 81, [2008] 2 WLR 1234, 10 ITELR 455, [2007] All ER (D) 76 (Jun)	41.02
Treloar v Lean (1889) 14 PD 49, 58 LJP 39, 37 WR 560, 60 LT 512	34.70

	PARA
Twist v Tye [1902] P 92, 71 LJP 47, 46 Sol Jo 177, 86 LT 259, 18 TLR 211	40.13
Tyrrell v Painton [1894] P 151, 6 R 540, 42 WR 343, [1891–4] All ER Rep 1120, 70 LT 453, CA	34.50
Welch v Phillips (1836) 1 Moo PCC 299	34.70
Wilkes, In the Estate of, Wilkes v Wilkes [2006] WTLR 1097	34.50
Wilson's Estate, Re, Walker v Treasury Solicitor (1961) 105 Sol Jo 531	34.70
Wilson's Estate, Re, Wilson v Coleclough [1952] P 92, [1952] 1 All ER 852, [1952] 1 Lloyd's Rep 292, 96 Sol Jo 231, [1952] 1 TLR 911	3.376
Wintle v Nye [1959] 1 All ER 552, [1959] 1 WLR 284, 103 Sol Jo 220, HL	34.50
Wren v Wren [2006] EWHC 2243 (Ch), 9 ITELR 223, [2006] 3 FCR 18, [2006] All ER (D) 30 (Sep)	34.70
Wytcherley v Andrews (1871) LR 2 P & D 327, 35 JP 552, 40 LJP & M 57, 19 WR 1015, 25 LT 134	28.04
Young v Holloway [1895] P 87, 64 LJP 55, 11 R 596, 43 WR 429, 72 LT 118, 11 TLR 128, [1891–4] All ER Rep Ext 1478	28.04
Yule's Estate, Re (1965) 109 Sol Jo 317	34.70

Table of abbreviations

AC (preceded by date)	Law Reports, Appeal Cases, House of Lords and Privy Council
Add	Addams' Ecclesiastical Reports
A & E, Ad & El	Adolphus and Ellis, QB reports
Adam	Adam's Justiciary Reports
All ER (preceded by date)	All England Law Reports
All ER Rep (preceded by date)	All England Law Reports Reprint
App Cas	Law Reports, Appeal Cases
B & Ad	Barnewall and Adolphus
Beav	Beavan's Rolls Court
Bos & Pu	Bosanquet and Puller
Bro CC	Brown's Chancery Reports
CA	Court of Appeal
CB	Common Bench Reports
Ch	Law Reports, Chancery Division (1890 onwards)
Ch D	Law Reports, Chancery Division (1875–1890)
Cox	Cox's Chancery Reports
CPD	Law Reports, Common Pleas Division
CPR	Civil Procedure Rules
Curt	Curteis's Ecclesiastical Reports
Deane Ecc R	Deane's Ecclesiastical Reports
Dea & Sw	Dean and Swabey's Ecclesiastical Reports
De GM & G	De Gex, MacNaughten and Gordon's Reports
Dick	Dickens's Reports
Dir Ag	Directions to Agents
E & B	Ellis and Blackburn's Reports

Table of abbreviations

Eq Cas	Equity Cases
Fam	Family Division, Series of Law Reports
F & F	Foster and Finlayson's Reports
Gow	NP Gow's Nisi Prius Cases
Hag Cons	Haggard's Consistory Court Cases
Hag Ecc	Haggard's Ecclesiastical Reports
Hare	Hare's Chancery Reprots
HL	House of Lords
Ir Eq Rep	Irish Equity Reports
JP	Justice of the Peace Reports
JP Jo	Justice of the Peace and Local Government Review
Johns & H	Johnson and Hemming's Reports
Jur	Jurist Reports
KB (preceded by date)	Law Reports, King's Bench Division
Knapp	Knapp's Privy Council Cases
LGR	Local Government Reports
LJR	Law Journal Reports
LR Ir	Law Reports (Ireland)
LRP & D	Law Reports, Probate and Divorce
LT	Law Times Reports
LTJo	Law Times Newspaper
Lee	Lee's Ecclesiastical Reports
Lev	Levinz, KB
M & W	Meeson and Welsby's Reports
Moo	Moore's Privy Council Reports
NC	Notes of Cases
NC	Non-Contentious
NCPR	Non-Contentious Probate Rules 1987
NLJ	New Law Journal
P (preceded by date)	Law Reports, Probate, etc, Division
PC	Privy Council Cases
PCC	Prerogative Court of Chancery
PD	Law Reports, Probate Division
P & D	Law Reports, Probate and Matrimonial
P & M	Law Reports, Probate and Matrimonial
Phill	Phillimore's Ecclesiastical Reports
Phill Ch R	Phillip's Chancery Reports
Plowd	Plowden, KB

Table of abbreviations

Prec C	Precedents in Chancery
P Wms	Peere Williams' Chancery Reports
QB	Queen's Bench Reports
QBD	Law Reports, Queen's Bench Division
R	The Reports
RR	Revised Reports
Rob	Robertson's Ecclesiastical Reports
RSC	Rules of the Supreme Court
Russ Ch Rep	Russell's Chancery Reports
SCF	Supreme Court Fees
Sim	Simon's Chancery Reports
Sol Jo	Solicitor's Journal
Spinks	Spinks' Ecclesiastical and Admiralty Reports
S & T	Swabey and Tristram's Reports
Sw & Tr	Swabey and Tristram's Reports
Sugd Pow	Sugden on Powers
TLR	Times Law Reports
Vern	Vernon's Chancery Reports
Ves	Vesey's Chancery Reports
Ves Sen	Vesey's Chancery Reports
WLR	Weekly Law Reports
WN (preceded by date)	Law Reports, Weekly Notes
WR	Weekly Reporter
WW & D	Willmore, Woolaston and Davisson, KB or QB
Y & CCC	Young and Collier's Chancery Reports

Part I
THE COMMON FORM PROBATE PRACTICE OF THE FAMILY DIVISION OF THE HIGH COURT OF JUSTICE

Chapter 1
THE PROBATE JURISDICTION OF THE FAMILY DIVISION

COMMON FORM BUSINESS

1.32 Sections 53 and 55 of the Courts and Legal Services Act 1990 (see paras A1.480A and A1.482) came into force on 7 December 2004[1] and allows for new classes of probate practitioner to be appointed. Section 53 gives the Council for Licensed Conveyancers the powers necessary to enable it to become an approved body for the purpose of granting only to persons who are licensed conveyancers, in accordance with s 55 of that Act exemption from the provisions of s 23(1) of the Solicitors Act 1974. The Council became an approved body on 1 August 2008[2] and, further, was given power to make rules in relation to the probate practice of licenced conveyancers on 28 March 2008[3]. This extends the power that s 21(2) of the Administration of Justice 1985 gives the Council to make rules for the payment of compensation to people who suffer from fraud or dishonesty of licensed conveyancers in connection with their practice, or a failure to account for money they receive in connection with their practice. The Licensed Conveyancers' Probate Rules 2008 came into force on 30 November 2008. Accordingly the Council may now grant a probate licence to a person who qualifies under these rules. Such a person is a probate practitioner for the purposes of the Non-Contentious Probate Rules 1987 (as amended).

[1] Courts and Legal Services Act (Commencement No 11) Order 2004, SI 2004/2950.
[2] Probate Services (Approved Bodies) Order 2008, SI 2008/1865.
[3] Courts and Legal Services Act 1990 (Modification of Power to Make Rules about Licensed Conveyancers) Order 2008, SI 2008/537.

1.32A Similarly by virtue of the Probate Services (Approved Bodies) Order 2009, SI 2009/1588, the Association of Chartered Certified Accountants became an approved body on 1 August 2009 for the purpose of granting exemption under the 1990 Act.

Rules

1.42 The current rules are the Non-Contentious Probate Rules 1987, SI 1987/2024 (see 1.43 below), as amended by the Non-Contentious Probate

1.42 *The probate jurisdiction of the Family Division*

(Amendment) Rules 1991, 1998, 1999, 2003 and 2004. The Rules were further amended with effect from 1 October 2007 by the Mental Capacity Act (Transitional and Consequential Provisions) Order 2007, SI 2007/1898. The most recent are the Non-Contentious Probate (Amendment) Rules 2009, SI 2009/1893 (effective from 1 September 2009) which reflect amendments to the Children Act 1989 consequential upon the Human Fertilisation and Embryology Act 2008. These rules govern the practice in the case of death on or after 1 January 1926. Where the deceased died before 1 January 1926 the right to a grant is, subject to the provisions of any enactment, to be determined by the principles and rules under which the court would have acted at the date of the death (see r 23 of the 1987 Rules).

1.43 The Non-Contentious Probate Rules 1987, as further amended to date are reproduced in Appendix II to this Supplement.

Table of fees

1.44 By s 130 of the Senior Courts Act 1981[1], the power of prescribing fees to be taken in non-contentious probate business has been conferred on the Lord Chancellor with the concurrence of the Lord Chief Justice, the Master of the Rolls, the President of the Family Division and the Vice-Chancellor, or of any three of them, together with the concurrence of the Treasury.

[1] See para A1.356.

1.45 The current table of fees to be taken in non-contentious business is contained in the Non-Contentious Probate Fees Order 2004, SI 1999/688, as amended[1], which is reproduced in Appendix III, para A3.01 ff.

[1] Most recently with effect from 13 July 2009 by virtue of the Non-Contentious Probate Fees (Amendment) Order 2009, SI 2009/1497.

SMALL SUMS: PAYMENT WITHOUT GRANT

Government and savings bank annuities

1.82 Sums not exceeding £5,000 due in respect of 'National Debt' annuities[1] or savings bank annuities[2] may be paid without probate or other proof of title; and sums of any amount in respect of annuities of either class may be paid on production of a grant issued in the Isle of Man or the Channel Islands[3].

[1] Government Annuities Act 1929, s 21, as amended by Administration of Estates (Small Payments) Act 1965, s 1(1), the Administration of Estates (Small Payments) (Increase of Limit) Order 1975 (see para A2.03) to £1,500 in relation to deaths on or after 10 August 1975 and the Administration of Estates (Small Payments) (Increase of Limit) Order 1984 (see paras A2.34 ff) to £5,000 in relation to deaths on or after 11 May 1984. In the case of deaths prior to 10 August 1975, the limit is £500.
[2] Government Annuities Act 1929, s 57, as amended by Administration of Estates (Small Payments) Act 1965, s 1(1).
[3] Government Annuities Act 1929, ss 20, 56.

Chapter 2
GENERAL PROCEDURE IN REGISTRY

AT THE PRINCIPAL REGISTRY

By whom application made

2.03 The Council for Licensed Conveyancers and the Association of Certified Chartered Accountants are approved bodies for the purpose of granting to licensed conveyancers and certified chartered accountants respectively exemption from s 23(1) of the Solicitors Act 1974 (see paras 1.32, 1.32A). Exemption is granted by virtue of s 53 and in accordance with s 55 of the Courts and Legal Services Act 1990 (see para A1.482). The Courts and Legal Services Act 1990 (Modification of Power to make Rules about Licensed Conveyancers) Order 2008, SI 2008/537, which came into force on 28 March 2008, confirmed the power of the Council for Licensed Conveyancers to make rules in relation to the probate practices of licensed conveyancers in the same way as rules which apply to their practices of conveyancing. The Licensed Conveyancers' Probate Rules 2008 came into force on 30 November 2008 and, accordingly, the Council may grant a probate licence to members who qualify in accordance with these rules. The Probate Registry may require these members to produce proof of qualification on submitting probate papers. A copy of the licence is sufficient. Similarly the Probate Registry will initially require certified chartered accountants to produce a valid exemption certificate.

2.03A Probate practice has the same meaning as probate practice defined in s 119 of the Courts and Legal Services Act 1990:

'the drawing or preparation of any papers on which to found or oppose a grant of probate or a grant of letters of administration and the administration of the estate of a deceased person'.

2.06 In any case where it is desired, drafts of the oath or other documents to lead a grant of representation may be submitted to the probate department of the Registry for settling. The fee (payable on submission of the draft papers) for perusing and settling each document is £10[1]. The settled drafts must be lodged with the papers to lead the grant. The Probate Service is currently

2.06 *General procedure in registry*

considering revising the practice of settling oaths and other papers. This is an optional service for the benefit of practitioners in particular where a difficulty arises in a proposed application for representation. However, practitioners submit a significant number of straightforward oaths for executors or kin entitled on intestacy. This situation compromises the core functions at some registries. It is suggested that practitioners do not submit papers for settling as a matter of course but only those papers where there is a particular difficulty which is explained in covering correspondence.

1   NC Probate Fees Order 2004, Fee 11.

Lodging papers for grant

2.09 *See Chapter 8 of this Supplement for an update in respect of inheritance tax.*

2.14 It is now necessary for an HMRC account to be assessed in the Inheritance Tax office (HRMC Inheritance Tax) prior to issue of the grant. The solicitor should deal with this before sending the papers to the registry. The registry will not undertake the transmission of such accounts to the Capital Taxes Office. Similarly, whenever inheritance tax or capital transfer tax is payable on delivery of the account, the amount, as assessed either by the solicitor under the 'self assessment' procedure or by the Inheritanced Tax office, must be paid to the Finance Division, HMRC and a receipt endorsed on the account summary (Form IHT 241) before the probate papers are sent to the Principal Registry. The Inheritance Tax Helpline (0845 30 20 900) may be able to assist with general enquiries.

Postal, or document exchange, applications

2.15 Postal remittances for inheritance tax or capital transfer tax payable in England and Wales should be sent to:

HMRC Inheritance Tax
Ferrers House,
PO Box 38,
Castle Meadow Road
Nottingham
NG2 1BB
(DX 701201 Nottingham 4)

2.15A Inheritance tax may be paid by electronic transfer through Bank of England account number 234303303, sort code number 10-00-00 or bank giro credit using the same account number and sort code 10-53-92.

AT DISTRICT PROBATE REGISTRIES AND SUB-REGISTRIES

Situation of registries

2.59 District probate registries and sub-registries are situate at the following places[1]:

Registries	Sub-registries	Addresses, telephone numbers, fax number and document exchange number
Birmingham		The Priory Courts, 33 Bull Street, Birmingham B4 6DU Tel: 0121 681 3400 Fax: 0121 236 2465 DX 701990 Birmingham 7
	Stoke on Trent	Combined Court Centre, Bethesda Street, Hanley, Stoke on Trent ST1 3BP Tel: 01782 854065 Fax: 01782 274916 DX 703363 Hanley 3
Brighton		William Street, Brighton BN2 2LG Tel: 01273 573510 Fax: 01273 625845 DX 98073 Brighton 3
	Maidstone	The Law Courts, Barker Road, Maidstone ME16 8EQ Tel: 01622 202048/7 DX 130066 Maidstone 7
Bristol		Ground Floor, The Crescent Centre, Temple Back, Bristol BS1 6EP Tel 1: 0117 927 3915 Tel 2: 0117 926 4619 Fax: 0117 925 3549 DX 94400 Bristol 5
	Bodmin	The Law Courts, Launceston Road, Bodmin PL31 2AL Tel: 01208 261581 Fax: 01208 77542 DX 136847 Bodmin 2
	Exeter	First Floor, Exeter Crown and County Court, Sothernhay Gardens, Exeter EX1 1UH Tel: 01392 415 370 Fax: 01392 415 608 DX 98442Exeter 2
Probate Registry of Wales		3rd Floor, Cardiff Magistrates Court, Fitzalan House, Cardiff CF24 0RZ Tel: 029 2047 4373

2.59 *General procedure in registry*

Registries	Sub-registries	Addresses, telephone numbers, fax number and document exchange number
	Bangor/ Caernarfon (*with effect from April 2009*)	DX 743940 Cardiff 38 Caernarfon Criminal Justice Centre, Llanberis Road, Gwynedd LL55 2DF
	Carmarthen	14 King Street, Carmarthen SA31 1BL Tel: 01267 242560 Fax: 01267 229067 DX 51420 Carmarthen
Ipswich		Ground Floor, 8 Arcade Street, Ipswich IP1 1EJ Tel: 01473 284260 Fax: 01473 231951 DX 3279 Ipswich
	Norwich	Combined Court Building, The Law Courts, Bishopsgate, Norwich NR3 1UR Tel: 01603 728268 Fax: 01603 627469 DX 5202 Norwich
	Peterborough	1st Floor, Crown Buildings, Rivergate, Peterborough PE1 1EJ Tel: 01733 562802 Fax: 01733 313016 DX 12327 Peterborough 1
Leeds		3rd Floor, Coronet House, Queen Street, Leeds LS1 2BA Tel: 0113 386 3540 Fax: 0113 247 1893 DX 26451 Leeds Park Square
	Lincoln	360 High Street, Lincoln LN5 7PS Tel: 01522 523648 Fax: 01522 539903 DX 703233 Lincoln 6
	Sheffield	PO Box 832 The Law Courts, 50 West Bar, Sheffield S3 8YR Tel: 0114 281 2596 Fax: 0114 273 0848 DX 26054 Sheffield 2
Liverpool		Queen Elizabeth II Law Courts, Derby Square, Liverpool L2 1XA Tel: 0151 236 8264 Fax: 0151 227 4634

At district probate registries and sub-registries 2.59

Registries	Sub-registries	Addresses, telephone numbers, fax number and document exchange number
	Chester	DX 14246 Liverpool 1 2nd Floor, Civil Justice Centre, Trident House, Little John Street, Chester CH1 1RE Tel: 01244 345082 Fax: 01244 346243 DX 22162 Northgate
	Lancaster	Mitre House, Church Street, Lancaster LA1 1HE Tel: 01524 36625 Fax: 01524 35561 DX 63509 Lancaster
Manchester		Ground Floor, Manchester Civil Justice Centre, Bridge Street West, PO Box 4240, Manchester M60 1JW Tel: 0161 240 5702 Fax: 0161 839 7526 DX 724784 Manchester 44
	Nottingham	Butt Dyke House, Park Row, Nottingham NG1 6GR Tel: 0115 941 4288 Fax: 0115 950 3383 DX 10055 Nottingham
Newcastle upon Tyne		1 Waterloo Square, Newcastle upon Tyne NE1 4AL Tel: 0191 211 2170 Fax: 0191 211 2184 DX 61081 Newcastle upon Tyne 14
	Carlisle	Courts of Justice, Earl Street, Carlisle CA1 1DJ Tel: 01228 521751 DX 63034 Carlisle
	Middlesbrough	Teeside Combined Court Centre, Russell Street, Middlesbrough TS1 2AE Tel: 01642 340001 DX 60536 Middlesbrough
	York	Duncombe Place, York YO1 2EA Tel: 01904 671564 Fax: 01904 624210 DX 61543 York
Oxford		Combined Court Building, St Aldates, Oxford OX1 1LY Tel 1: 01865 793050 Tel 2: 01865 793055 Fax: 01865 793090 DX 96454 Oxford

2.59   *General procedure in registry*

Registries	Sub-registries	Addresses, telephone numbers, fax number and document exchange number
	Gloucester	2nd Floor, Combined Court Building, Kimbrose Way, Gloucester GL1 2DG Tel: 01452 834966 Fax: 01452 834970 DX 98663 Gloucester
	Leicester	90 Wellington Street, Leicester LE1 6HG Tel: 0116 285 3380 Fax: 0116 285 338 DX 17403 Leicester 3
Winchester		4th Floor, Cromwell House, Andover Road, Winchester SO23 7EW Tel 1: 01962 897024 Tel 2: 01962 897029 Fax: 01962 840796 DX 96900 Winchester 2

District probate registries and sub-registries are open every weekday, except Saturday, from 9.30 am until 4.00 pm.

[1]   The District Probate Registries Order 1982, SI 1982/379 as amended (see para A2.28 ff).

Administration pending determination of probate claim

2.65 A grant of administration pending determination of a probate claim (formerly administration pending suit) can be made only at the Principal Registry[1]. As to application for an order for such a grant, see paras 38.01 ff.

[1]   Direction, 1935; NCPR 7(1).

Application for grant at district registry

2.71 A solicitor or probate practitioner makes application for a grant at a district probate registry by lodging at, or sending by post or document exchange to, the registry, or a sub-registry attached to that registry (see para 2.59) the papers to lead the grant, namely, the will and codicils (if any), the oath, the HMRC account summary Form IHT 241 (unless such an account is not required, see Ch 8) or return of estate in Form IHT205/207 as appropriate (see Ch 8) and any affidavits etc, which the particular circumstances of the case may render necessary. A personal applicant may apply for a grant at the registry or sub-registry, or at a probate office (see paras 2.91 ff).

Payment of fees and tax

2.79 The former practice whereby district probate registries and sub-registries were generally prepared to forward, on behalf of solicitors, HMRC accounts with the remittance to the HMRC has been discontinued. The HMRC account summary (Form IHT421) must now be receipted before it is lodged with the oath at the registry or sub-registry. The account itself is retained by HMRC Inheritance Tax. Similarly, if no tax is payable, the account has to be controlled by HMRC Inheritance Tax before a grant may be issued, the account must be so controlled before Form IHT421 is lodged at the registry or sub-registry[1].

[1] Secretary's Circular 15 April 1999. See also Ch 8 for practice as to HMRC accounts.

Calendar

2.81 Depending upon the year of grant issue, the calendar containing a note of every grant passed in England and Wales in each year can be inspected at a district registry either in printed book form, microfiche records or the probateman computer.

Interested parties may now search the Probate calendars using computer terminals in most Probate Registries and sub-registries. Copies of any grant found may be ordered through the local registry.

PERSONAL APPLICATIONS

Inheritance tax or capital transfer tax

2.97 The personal applicant must complete and prepare any HMRC form necessary for the application, and he must deal directly with HMRC Inheritance Tax for the payment of inheritance tax or control of the account, if this is required before the registry issues the grant.

In cases where inheritance tax is payable the amount of this as provisionally assessed must be paid by the applicant before the grant can be issued. Form IHT421 is endorsed as to payment of the tax and it is filed with the application. As to inheritance tax and capital transfer tax, see Ch 8.

Chapter 3
WILLS AND CODICILS

REVOCATION OF WILLS

Revocation by subsequent formation of Civil Partnership

3.45 As can be seen from the above text, the changes made by the new statutory provisions allow for exceptions (see para 3.47 ff below) to the revocation of a will by the testator's subsequent marriage or formation of a civil partnership, in particular, the earlier references to heirship and the Statute of Distributions in s 18 of the 1837 Act when dealing with the exception relating to the exercise of a power of appointment are updated; in addition, clarification is given to the point that only the relevant disposition is preserved in such a case and not the whole will (sub-ss (2) of ss 18 and 18B). But perhaps the most important change is in relation to the exception permitted where a will is made in contemplation of marriage or in contemplation of the formation of a civil partnership. In respect of wills (including codicils) made on or after 1 January 1983, there is now a rebuttable presumption in favour of preservation of the whole will, where it appears from the will that it or part of it was intended to survive a particular marriage (s 18(3)) The same rebuttable presumption also applies where a testator subsequently formed a civil partnership on or after 5 December 2005 (s 18B(3)). The court has held that a general direction or mere statement in the will that it shall not be revoked by marriage or civil partnership is insufficient for the purposes of s 18(3) or 18B(3) to preserve it from revocation by a subsequent marriage/civil partnership (*Court v Despallieres, Re Ikin (decd)* [2009] EWHC 3340 (Ch), 154 Sol Jo (no 1) 30). The will should show that the testator intended to enter into a marriage or form a civil partnership with a particular person.

Exceptions

Will made in contemplation of marriage

3.50 As respects wills made on or after 1 January 1983, s 177 of the Law of Property Act 1925 is repealed and is replaced by s 18(3) and (4) of the Wills Act 1837, as substituted by s 18 of the Administration of Justice Act 1982.

The main effect of this change is to introduce a presumption in favour of the preservation of a will if it shows or appears to show an intention to survive a particular marriage (see para 3.45 above). For this purpose, and as an aid to construing the will, extrinsic evidence is admissible (see s 21 of the Administration of Justice Act 1982, para A1.375).

Will made in contemplation of formation of civil partnership

3.52 On the formation of a civil partnership the presumption in favour of preservation of a testator's will is given effect by s 18B(3) of the Wills Act 1837 as amended by Sch 4 to the Civil Partnership Act 2004. Although this Act came into force on 5 December 2005 a will that was made in contemplation of the formation of a civil partnership with a particular person before that date is preserved by that civil partnership (see para 3.45 above). The will is revoked if a civil partnership is formed with another person. Again as in the case of a marriage extrinsic evidence is admissible as an aid to interpreting or construing the will so as to survive the formation of a civil partnership (see s 21 of the Administration of Justice Act 1982).

EXECUTION OF WILLS—INTERNAL LAW OF ENGLAND AND WALES

Signature of testator

3.70 'Signed ... by the testator'. A will may be signed by the testator with his name, initials[1], or mark. The words 'Your loving mother' have been held to represent the name of the testatrix and to be a sufficient signature[2]. The signature however made must be original. A photocopied signature is not acceptable even if it is subsequently acknowledged in the presence of witnesses who then attested the photocopied paper. Section 9 of the Wills Act 1837 requires that the will be in writing and signed by the testator. A photocopy of a will with a photocopied signature is not a document which is signed by the testator. The (original) signature has to be made in the presence of two or more witnesses or acknowledged in the presence of those witnesses (*Lim v Thompson* [2009] EWHC 3341 (Ch)).

[1] *Re Blewitt's Goods* (1880) 5 PD 116.
[2] *Re Cook's Estate, Murison v Cook* [1960] 1 All ER 689, [1960] 1 WLR 353.

Will to be exhibited

Knowledge and approval

3.133 It is essential to the validity of a will that the testator should know and approve of its contents[1]. More recently this proposition was qualified when the court held that a will was validly executed even though the testatrix did not have testamentary capacity when she signed it. In *Clancy v Clancy* [2003] EWHC 1885 (Ch), [2003] 37 LS Gaz R 32 the court found for the validity of a will which had been properly drawn up in accordance with the instructions

3.133 *Wills and Codicils*

of the testatrix who had at least the capacity to understand that she was executing a will prepared in accordance with her instructions[2]. In *Hoff v Atherton* [2004] EWCA Civ 1554, [2004] All ER (D) 314 (Nov), the Court of Appeal drew a distinction between the ability to understand which is the test of capacity and actual understanding which is not. Unless suspicion attaches to the document, eg where it is signed by mark, or where the signature indicates extreme feebleness, the testator's execution is sufficient evidence of his knowledge and approval[3]. (See also para 34.16.)

See also updates in this Supplement to paras 34.31 and 34.50 for recent decisions touching on the tests for testamentary capacity and understanding of the testator viz. *Re Loxton dec'd Abbott v Richardson* [2006] WTLR 1567; *Franks v Sinclair* [2006] EWHC 3365 (Ch); *Cattermole v Prisk* [2006] 1 FLR 693.

[1] *Hastilow v Stobie* (1865) LR 1 P & D 64. See also *Re Simpson, Schaniel v Simpson* (1977) 121 Sol Jo 224; where, through age or infirmity, a testator's capacity is in doubt, the making of the will ought to be witnessed or approved by a medical practitioner.
[2] Applying *Parker v Felgate and Tilley* (1883) 8 PD 171. See also *Minns v Foster* [2002] All ER (D) 225 (Dec) where the testator suffered short-term memory loss but 'understood the business in which he was engaged' at the time he executed the will.
[3] *Guardhouse v Blackburn* (1866) LR 1 P & D 109.

Condition of will

3.156 If pin or clip marks etc were caused by documents of a non-testamentary nature being attached to the will or codicil, the production of such documents with a covering certificate to this effect by the practitioner, or other person having knowledge of the facts, may be required: in other cases an affidavit of plight and of search for any other testamentary document may be necessary (see Forms Nos 5 and 6).

Two wills: effect of codicil confirming earlier will

3.188 It is important to observe that where an earlier will is revived by a codicil, and that will contains a clear revocation clause, any intervening wills are revoked, the revocation clause in the earlier will being incorporated in, and republished by, the codicil[1]. Where a testatrix made a will and two codicils, and made a second will in the intervening period between the codicils, it was held the later will was effectively revoked by the second codicil which expressly referred to the earlier will. The solicitor who drafted the second codicil was unaware of the second will. It was implicit, if not express, that the testatrix intended that her earlier will and first codicil be revived in preference to the second will[2].

[1] *Re Pearson, Rowling v Crowther* [1963] 3 All ER 763, [1963] 1 WLR 1358 applying *Re Baker, Baker v Baker* [1929] 1 Ch 668.
[2] *Hoare Trustees v Jaques and ors* [2008] EWHC 2022 (Ch), [2008] All ER (D) 68 (Feb).

Joint and mutual wills

Revocation of joint and mutual wills

3.222 If after the death of one testator, the survivor revokes his will, the revocation is recognised in the probate registry as operative, but his personal representative may be directed[1] to hold the estate on trust to carry out the terms of the contract, or implied contract (if any), originally made[2]. It does not necessarily follow, because joint or mutual wills are made, that there was a contract: and this is a question to be decided in the Chancery Division[3], the probate registry being concerned only with the formal validity of the dispositions.

[1] By the Chancery Division.
[2] *Dufour v Pereira* (1769) 1 Dick 419; *Stone v Hoskins* [1905] P 194; *Re Oldham, Hadwen v Myles* [1925] Ch 75 (the probability of a contract is greater if the mutual gifts are for life only); *Re Green, Lindner v Green* [1951] Ch 148, [1950] 2 All ER 913 (the wills themselves may contain a clear indication of a contract); *Re Cleaver, Cleaver v Insley* [1981] 2 All ER 1018, [1981] 1 WLR 939 (the whole evidence must be looked at to determine whether there was a definite agreement between the testators: the mere fact that the wills were to the same effect, though a relevant circumstance, was not in itself sufficient).
[3] *Re Heys' Estate, Walker v Gaskill* [1914] P 192 at 200; *Re Goodchild* [1997] 3 All ER 63, [1997] 1 WLR 1216 (the court confirmed that for the doctrine of mutual wills to apply there had to be a contract at law between two testators that both wills would be irrevocable and remain unaltered. It was not sufficient that both testators merely had a mutual desire that the wills should remain unaltered).

Alterations in wills

Rectification and interpretation of wills (death on or after 1 January 1983)

3.264 The application must be supported by an affidavit, setting out the grounds of the application, together with such evidence as can be adduced as to the testator's intentions and whichever of the following matters are in issue:

(a) in what respects the testator's intentions were not understood; or
(b) the nature of any alleged clerical error[1].

[1] *Re Segeman* [1996] Ch 171, [1995] 3 All ER 676 (a solicitor's failure to amend a draft will was treated as a clerical error). *Clarke v Brothwood and others* [2006] EWHC 2939 (Ch) (a solicitor's failure to apply his mind to the effect of defective drafting in a will amounted to a clerical error); see also *Goodman v Goodman and others* [2006] EWHC 1757 (Ch) (draftsman misunderstanding testator's instructions) and *Price and others v Craig* [2006] EWHC 2561 (Ch) (testator's changed instructions inadvertently created a partial intestacy).

PRIVILEGED WILLS

Sailors' privileged wills

'At sea'

3.376 The words 'at sea' have been held to mean 'on maritime service', and apply to persons serving on board vessels permanently stationed in a harbour[1], or on service in a river[2]. A will made on shore, but in the course of a

3.376 Wills and Codicils

voyage, or by the employee of a ship owner between voyages, will be within the section[3]. The plain meaning of 'a mariner or seaman' means that the privilege is not restricted to usage only on British registered ships[4]. But it has been held that a pilot on a ship canal is not 'a mariner or seaman at sea' within the meaning of s 11 unless it is established that the document propounded was made either on board a ship or when proceeding to join, or return from, the ship[5]. A seaman on leave who had not received instructions to join a particular ship, and was not part of the complement of any particular ship, was not 'at sea' within the meaning of s 11 of the Wills Act 1837[6].

[1] *Re M'Murdo's Goods* (1868) LR 1 P & D 540.
[2] *Re Patterson's Goods* (1898) 79 LT 123; *Re Austen's Goods* (1853) 2 Rob Eccl 611.
[3] *Re Lay's Goods* (1840) 2 Curt 375; *Re Anderson's Estate, Anderson v Downes* [1916] P 49; *Re Newland's Goods* [1952] P 71, [1952] 1 All ER 841; *Re Wilson's Estate, Wilson v Coleclough* [1952] P 92, [1952] 1 All ER 852.
[4] *Re Servoz-Gavin (decd), Ayling v Summers* [2009] EWHC 3168 (Ch), [2010] 1 All ER 410 (Testator made wills when about to join ships registered in the Netherlands and in Panama. It was held that the later of the two wills was valid within the meaning of s 11 of the Wills Act 1837).
[5] *Re Barnes Goods, Hodson v Barnes* (1926) 136 LT 380.
[6] *Re Rapley's Estate, Rapley v Rapley* [1983] 3 All ER 248, [1983] 1 WLR 1069.

WILLS ACT 1963

Meaning of 'internal law'

3.408 This subsection provides for cases where internal systems of law such as those of the United Kingdom and Colonies or territories are in question. Where recourse is to be had to the law of the nationality of a testator who was, at the time of execution of the will, a citizen of the United Kingdom and Colonies or of a dependant or overseas territory, any one of a number of systems of law might otherwise be applicable (eg the law of England and Wales, of Scotland, or of a particular colonial or other territory). Similarly, the subsection applies in the case of a territory or state which applies different systems of law according to the religion, caste, tribe etc, of testators. If there is no rule in force throughout the territory or state indicating which system can properly be applied to the case in question, it will be necessary to ascertain with which system of law the testator was most closely connected at the relevant time (as defined above), and apply that system. The WA 1963 does not define the type of connection, and where this provision is relied upon in connection with the proof of a will, there should be affidavit evidence of the facts by reason of which it is contended that the testator's closest connection, at the time of execution of the will or at the time of death, as the case may require, was with a particular system of law as to the formal validity of wills (see also *Re O'Keefe, Poingdestre v Sherman* [1940] Ch 124, [1940] 1 All ER 216, and 'Practice' at paras 3.433 ff).

WILL MADE FOR MENTALLY DISORDERED PERSON

Power to make will for mentally disordered person

3.438 Chapter 7 (ss 93–113) of the Mental Health Act 1983 was repealed and replaced by the Mental Capacity Act 2005 (MCA 2005) on 1 October

2007. Section 16 of the Act gives the court—the reconstituted Court of Protection—power to make an order making decisions on a person's behalf if he lacks capacity within the meaning of the Act in relation to a matter or matters concerning his welfare or his property and affairs. The powers under s 16 extend to the execution of a will of the person (s 18(1)(i)) which he could have made if he did not lack mental capacity.

3.439 Section 18(2) of the Act provides that no will may be made at a time when a person who lacks mental capacity within the meaning of the Act has not attained 18 years of age.

3.440 Section 46 of the MCA 2005 makes provision for the powers of the Court of Protection to be exercised by:

a judge nominated for that purpose by—
- (a) the [Lord Chief Justice], or
- [(b) where nominated by the Lord Chief Justice to act on his behalf under this subsection—
    - (i) the President of the Court of Protection; or
    - (ii) a judicial office holder (as defined in section 109(4) of the Constitutional Reform Act 2005)].

(2) To be nominated, a judge must be—
- (a) the President of the Family Division,
- (b) the Vice-Chancellor,
- (c) a puisne judge of the High Court,
- (d) a circuit judge, or
- (e) a district judge.

Section 46(3) and (4) further provide for the appointments of President, Vice-President and Senior Judge of the Court from the list of nominated judges.

3.441 The Court of Protection Rules 2007 which replaced the previous (2001) Rules took effect on 1 October 2007. An application to the court for an order directing the making of a will or codicil for a person who lacks mental capacity is made under the general rules (r 61ff) for starting proceedings.

Mode of execution of will

3.442 *See para 3.455 (reproduced below) for the requirement for execution of a will by an authorised person for a testator who lacks mental capacity within the meaning of the MCA 2005.*

Effect of will

3.455 The Mental Capacity Act 2005 received Royal assent on 7 April 2005 and fully came into force on 1 October 2007. The Act followed extensive

3.455 Wills and Codicils

consultation flowing from the Law Commission Report (No 231) published in 1995 and the Government's policy statement 'Making Decisions' published in October 1999 which set out proposals to reform the law and clarify the decision-making process for people unable to make decisions for themselves. The Act replaced Part 7 of the Mental Health Act 1983 (ss 93–113) and the Enduring Powers of Attorney Act 1985. The Act further provided for the establishment of a new Court of Protection to replace the existing court.

By power given in s 16(1) and (2)(a) of the Act the court may by order make decisions concerning the personal welfare, property and affairs of a person who lacks capacity to make decisions for himself. Section 18 of the Act provides that these powers extend to making a will for such person (sub-s (1)(i)) but no will may be made under this section when the person has not attained 18 years (sub-s (2)).

Schedule 2 of the Act makes provision for the making and execution of a will on behalf of a person who lacks capacity. The will may make any provision (whether by disposing of property or exercising a power or otherwise) which could be made by a will executed by the person if he had capacity to make it.

The requirements relating to execution of the will are (Sch 2 para 3):

'the court makes an order or gives directions requiring or authorising a person ("the authorised person") to execute a will on behalf of the person lacking capacity (P).

Any will executed in pursuance of the order or direction—
   (a) must state that it is signed by P acting by the authorised person,
   (b) must be signed by the authorised person with the name of P and his own name, in the presence of two or more witnesses present at the same time,
   (c) must be attested and subscribed by those witnesses in the presence of the authorised person, and
   (d) must be sealed with the official seal of the court.'

In this regard the new procedure for making a will mirrors the procedure for making a will on behalf of a patient under the Mental Health Act 1983.

An extract of the Act may be found at para A1.560.

Chapter 4
PROBATES

Note.—This chapter deals with grants of probate in cases where the deceased died **domiciled in England and Wales**. For the practice in cases where the deceased died domiciled out of England and Wales, see Ch 12. For interpretation of wills (including codicils), see Ch 3.

EXECUTORS

Executor incapable

4.34 Mental incapacity or lack of capacity within the meaning of the Mental Capacity Act 2005 is a ground upon which an executor may be excluded from probate[1], but the usual practice where he is sole executor is to make a grant for his use and benefit (see para 11.237 ff).

[1] *Evans v Tyler* (1849) 2 Rob Eccl 128 at 131.

Partnership firm succeeded by limited liability partnership

4.47 The usual appointment of a partnership containing a succession clause (see para 4.43) has caused a difficulty where at the date of the testator's death a limited liability partnership succeeded the partnership. The district judges and registrars were of the view that the appointment failed in consequence of the limited liability partnership being a corporate body (with a legal personality) whose members were not partners. On a further scrutiny of the appointment clause it was held in *Re Rogers (decd)* [2006] EWHC 753 (Ch), [2006] 2 All ER 792, [2006] 1 WLR 1577 that the court should take a practical and common sense view in eliciting and giving effect to the intentions of the testatrix and that on a true construction probate should be granted to profit-sharing members of the limited liability partnership (they being the equivalent of partners in the previous partnership). Lightman J held that just as a partner in a partnership was a profit sharing partner the appointment could only apply to profit-sharing members unless a contrary intention is established in the will. In consequence of this the oath should confirm that the applicant executors are profit sharing or share-owning members of the limited liability partnership at the death of the deceased.

Other incorporated practices

4.48 Following *Re Rogers (decd)* (see para 4.47) similar considerations will apply to an incorporated practice such as a company recognised by the Law Society and it may be treated as a successor firm for the purpose of construing

4.48 *Probates*

the usual succession clause to a partnership firm. In this case (profit-sharing or share-owning) directors or members replace partners who may apply as executors.

4.49 *In cases of doubt about the wording of the form of appointment, the directions of the district judge or registrar should be taken before preparation of the papers.*

TRANSMISSION OF EXECUTORSHIP

Chain through grant for use and benefit of incapable executor

4.81 The chain of executorship is not broken by letters of administration (with will) of an estate granted for the use and benefit of an executor who has proved the will but has since become incapable or lacks capacity to manage his affairs and property within the meaning of the Mental Capacity Act 2005. Where such an executor dies without recovering his capacity, the grant, if it has been impounded under the former practice, may be handed out on a district judge's or registrar's order; see para 17.67 ff.

REQUIREMENTS ON PROVING A WILL

The executor's oath

Settling oaths

4.92 The Probate Service wishes to discourage the practice of submitting straightforward oaths for settling. Where there is a particular difficulty about the application which the practitioner should specify, he or she may submit the oath in draft for settling by the registry from which the grant is to issue. Examples of difficulty may be an ambiguous appointment of executor or imprecise attestation clause. The settled draft should be lodged with the sworn papers.

REQUIREMENTS ON PROVING A WILL

The executor's oath

Change of name

4.105A A title of an executor is not defeated if he or she has acquired, or is applying for, a gender recognition certificate under the Gender Recognition Act 2004. The oath should describe the executor in a changed name, if any. An affidavit of identity confirming the facts should be filed with the application. The grant will issue to the executor in the changed name without any reference to his or her description in the will. Owing to the sensitive nature of the information, the affidavit of identity will be sealed after inspection and not be open to public disclosure or inspection unless the executor gives permission[1]. Such permission, if given, should ideally be included in the affidavit of identity. This paragraph does not apply where a decree of divorce or nullity of the marriage (in existence at the date of the will) between the executor and the deceased was in force at the date of death of the deceased.

[1] Gender Recognition Act 2004, s 22(4)(b).

Date of death

4.151 If the *fact* of death is certain, but the exact date unknown, the oath should state that the deceased 'was last seen alive (*or* last known to be alive) on the   day of   , and that his dead body was found on the   day of   '[1].

[1] *Re Long-Sutton's Estate* [1912] P 97.

Relationship of the applicant

4.190 The following are examples of the circumstances in which the applicant's relationship to the deceased must be stated:

(a) where the appointment of the executor (or beneficiary) is by relationship and not by name (eg 'I appoint my son as sole executor'; or 'I leave all my estate to my wife (without naming her)');
(b) where there is some discrepancy or possible ambiguity in the appointment, and inclusion of the relationship assists in establishing the identity of the applicant;
(c) in cases where the applicant's title to a grant depends entirely on his relationship, ie where application for administration (with will) is made by a person entitled to the estate undisposed of by the will. Thus, in a case where a will appoints no executor and there is no gift of the residuary estate, the widow of the deceased must depose that she is 'the lawful widow of the deceased and the only person now entitled to the undisposed-of estate', or as the case may be.

But see para 4.105A above concerning the effect of the Gender Recognition Act 2004 on the title of an executor who has acquired, or is applying for, a gender recognition certificate.

Amount of estate in oath

4.202 Except in those cases where, pursuant to the Capital Transfer Tax (Delivery of Accounts) Regulations 1981, as amended and Inheritance Tax (Delivery of Accounts) (Excepted Estates) Regulations 2002 as amended[1] (see Ch 8), the need to deliver an account for the purposes of inheritance tax or capital transfer tax has been dispensed with, the oath must state the actual *gross* value of the estate to be covered by the grant, as indicated by the HMRC account. The account summary in the new Form IHT421 must be filed with

4.202 *Probates*

the papers to lead to the grant. This replaces the former requirement in applications made on or after 1 November 2004 where the deceased died after 5 April 2004 and Form D18 was stamped and authorised by the HMRC Inheritance Tax before being submitted with the application[2].

[1] The Inheritance Tax (Delivery of Accounts) (Excepted Estates) Regulations 2002 (as amended) is reproduced in Appendix II to this supplement.
[2] Inheritance Tax (Delivery of Accounts) (Excepted Estates) Regulations 2004 (as amended). (See Appendix II to this supplement.)

DEATH ON AND AFTER 6 APRIL 2004

4.204 *See Chapter 8 of this Supplement for the update and requirement for HMRC account forms.*

4.206 Every oath must contain a statement by the applicant as follows:

'To the best of my knowledge, information and belief the gross estate passing under the grant does not exceed/amounts to* £ and that the net estate does not exceed/amounts to* £ [and that this is not a case in which an HMRC Inheritance Tax Account is required to be delivered]*.'

The alternatives marked with an asterisk should be deleted as appropriate[1].

[1] *Practice Directions* [1981] 2 All ER 832, [1981] 1 WLR 1185. In relation to a death prior to 13 March 1975, a sworn HMRC Inheritance Tax affidavit is still required (see NCPR 42).

4.207 The relevant dates and gross limits are:

Death on or after	Gross limit
6 April 2009	£1,000,000/£325,000
1 April 2009	£1,000,000/£325,000
6 April 2008	£1,000,000/£312,000
6 April 2007	£1,000,000/£300,000
6 April 2006	£1,000,000/£285,000
6 April 2005	£1,000,000/£275,000
6 April 2004	£1,000,000/£263,000
6 April 2003	£240,000
6 April 2002	£220,000
6 April 2000	£210,000
6 April 1998	£200,000
6 April 1996	£180,000
6 April 1995	£145,000
1 April 1991	£125,000
1 April 1990	£115,000
1 April 1989	£100,000
1 April 1987	£70,000
1 April 1983	£40,000
1 April 1981	£25,000

Requirements on proving a will 4.229

and the relevant net limits and court fees payable are:

Exceeding	Not exceeding	Court fee
£——	£5,000	(no fee)
£5,000	(relevant gross limit stated above)	£50

4.212 An alteration made by HMRC Inheritance Tax in the amount of the estate shown in the HMRC account does not normally necessitate amendment of the figure sworn in the oath.

Estate for purposes of probate or administration

4.218 For the purposes of probate or administration, the local situation of property and the validity of debts and encumbrances for ascertaining the net value of an estate, are determined according to the general principles of English law, any rules or concessions which are peculiar to inheritance tax or capital transfer tax (eg under Double Taxation Conventions) being ignored. Thus, all property forming part of the estate must be included, notwithstanding that it may be exempt from inheritance tax or capital transfer tax.

Notice to Treasury Solicitor

4.227 In any case in which it appears that the Crown is or may be beneficially interested in the estate of a deceased person, notice of the intended application for a grant must be given by the applicant to the Treasury Solicitor. The district judge or registrar may direct that no grant shall issue within 28 days after such notice has been given[1]. The notice should be sent to: The Treasury Solicitor (BV), One Kemble Street, London WC2B 4TS *or* DX 123240 Kingsway (tel 020 7210 3116/7 or 3239).

[1]   NCPR 38.

Copies of wills

4.229 With effect from 1 January 2009, practitioners are responsible for preparing and submitting two copies each of the will and any codicils. The Probate Service has set out the following requirements for copies of wills and codicils:

(a) the copies must be made in good quality A4-size white paper from the original will and codicil after the oath has been sworn;
(b) the copies should be true and complete but it is not necessary to copy any covers or instructions for completion and signing of the will;
(c) the copies must be legible and clear and care should be taken to ensure that any faint typescript or writing or blue ink is clearly visible;
(d) the top and left-hand margins (at least 1 inch) should be left clear so that the grant can be attached; and

4.229 *Probates*

(e) if it is necessary to take the will apart in order to copy it, the practitioner should restore it to the same plight and condition that it was in before it was copied and further enclose a covering letter with the application confirming that this has been done and that nothing of a testamentary nature was attached or detached.

4.230 In certain special cases, however the practitioner must lodge an engrossment or a 'fiat copy' of the will (see further para 4.234 ff) and copies.

When copies of wills are necessary

4.231 Where alterations in a will have not been properly set up or the will has been altered after execution; in certain foreign cases, where the will is unsuitable for facsimile reproduction; and in special cases directed by the district judge or registrar, it is necessary to file a copy of the will[1]. Certain wills drawn on paper unsuitable for facsimile reproduction on account of size, and any codicil thereto, must be accompanied by an engrossment copy[2]. This copy is then photographed instead of the will (see also 'Fiat copies', para 4.234 ff). Care should be taken in the preparation of the engrossment as it will be examined in the registry and, if necessary, returned for correction.

[1] NCPR 11.
[2] This memorandum which is still relevant in part was issued by the Principal Registry, and published in the *Law Society's Gazette* for February 1956, and is as follows: 'All official copies of wills, whether for insertion in probates or for issue when bespoken afterwards, are now photographed, the system in use in the Principal Registry since 1931 having been extended to all other registries. It would be of assistance to the Probate Registry if solicitors would always bear in mind, when preparing wills, that it is desirable that they should be prepared in a form which lends itself easily to photographic reproduction. The ideal is for the will to be foolscap size, typed in black on white paper. Size of type is not in itself important, as a will in this form can be reproduced without reduction in size or loss of contrast.' A reminder to those preparing wills of the format preferred by the probate registries in order to facilitate facsimile copying appeared in (1974) 124 NLJ 1101. The usual size of paper used now is A4.

Will of member of the Royal Family

4.247 On the death of a member of the Royal Family it is usual for application to be made to the President of the Family Division for an order that the will be sealed up. Application for such an order is made by summons, which is served on the Treasury Solicitor. An official of HMRC Capital Taxes examines the will and HMRC account before the papers to lead the grant are lodged.

4.248 No copy of the will is annexed to the grant of probate: the grant bears a notation 'Probate granted without annexing a copy of the will by order of the President dated   '. The usual records of the grant are kept.

4.249 After the will has been sealed up it can be opened only by direction of the President[1].

[1] In *Brown v The Executors of the Estate of HM Queen Elizabeth the Queen Mother and others* [2007] EWHC 1607 (Fam), [2009] 1 WLR 2327 on a application for the unsealing of the wills of the late Queen Elizabeth the Queen Mother and Princess Margaret, Countess of Snowden the President struck out the claim as vexatious and an abuse of process, made solely for the purpose of seeking to establish an imaginary and baseless claim. On appeal the Court of Appeal concluded that the appellant was entitled to have a substantive hearing of his claim to inspect the wills and accordingly allowed his appeal ([2008] EWCA Civ 56).

Copies of grant for registration

4.250 The executor or administrator may obtain any number of sealed office copies of the grant for the purpose of expediting the registration of the grant, at a fee of £1 each, if he applies for them with the application for the grant. The copies will be sent to the solicitor with the original grant.

He may also obtain copies at any other time, either on personal attendance or by a postal application when the fee is £5[1] for the copy grant (including a copy of any will) and £1[2] for each additional copy. A grant with will annexed is treated as one copy[3].

[1] NC Probate Fees Order 2004, Fee 8(a).
[2] NC Probate Fees Order 2004, Fee 8(b).
[3] Secretariat Circular, 15 April 1999.

HMRC account

4.254 *See Chapter 8 of this Supplement for the most recent update of HMRC accounts.*

4.255 With effect from 31 March 2003 it has been possible to draw on funds in a deceased's bank and building society accounts to pay inheritance tax before the grant can be issued. Where the deceased had sufficient funds in the accounts the bank or building society transfer the amount of inheritance tax due directly to the HMRC. Details of this scheme may be obtained from the IR Capital Taxes (see paras 8.24, 8.133).

FEES

Fees on the grant

4.260 Similarly, in the district probate registries and sub-registries all fees are paid by cheque, or in cash (preferably by crossed cheque payable to 'HMCS' or 'HM Court Service'). For the time being it has not been possible to introduce payment by debit/credit card.

4.261 *Probates*

Remission of probate fees

4.261 The Non-Contentious Probate Fees Order 2004 as amended by the Non-Contentious Probate Fees (Amendment) Orders 2007 and 2008[1] sets out the criteria in Sch 1A for ascertaining whether a party is entitled to a remission or part remission of a fee prescribed by the Order. The Lord Chancellor may on the grounds of financial hardship or for other reasonable cause remit in whole or in part any fee prescribed by the Order. The amendment removes the element of discretion which the Order previously contained and Sch 1A contains a calculator for determining whether the applicant is entitled to a full remission or part remission. The application for remission of fees is made at the time when the fee is payable. All requests for reduction or remission of fees payable in the Principal Registry will be referred to the manager of the probate department; those made in the district probate registries should be referred to the probate manager.

[1] Non-Contentious Probate Fees Order 2004, SI 2004/3120 as amended by Non-Contentious Probate Fees (Amendment) Orders 2007, 2008 and 2009, SI 2007/2174, SI 2008/2854 and SI 2009/1497, included in Appendix III of this Supplement.

COSTS OF NON-CONTENTIOUS PROBATE PROCEEDINGS

Solicitors' charges

4.272 The Rules of the Supreme Court (Non-Contentious Probate Costs) 1956, which applied to all non-contentious or common form probate business for which instructions were accepted on or after 1 May 1956 were revoked as from 1 September 1994[1] and replaced by the Solicitors' (Non-Contentious Business) Remuneration Order 1994, SI 1994/2616, which came into force on 1 November 1994. This in turn was revoked and replaced by the Solicitors' (Non-Contentious Business) Remuneration Order 2009, SI 2009/1931[2] with effect from 11 August 2009 and applies to all non-contentious business for which bills are delivered on or after that date.

[1] Rules of the Supreme Court (Amendment) 1994, SI 1994/1975, r 24.
[2] See para A5.01.

4.273 Under these new rules there are no fixed items or scales of costs for extracting a grant, administering an estate, etc. A solicitor is entitled to charge and be paid[1] such sum as may be fair and reasonable (see para 4.274) to both solicitor and entitled person[2], having regard in particular to:

(a) the complexity of the matter or the difficulty or novelty of the questions raised;
(b) the skill, labour, specialised knowledge and responsibility involved;
(c) the time spent on the business;
(d) the number and importance of the documents prepared or perused, without regard to length;
(e) the place where and the circumstances in which the business or any part thereof is transacted;
(f) the amount or value of any money or property involved;

(g) whether any land involved is registered land within the meaning of the Land Registration Act 2002;
(h) the importance of the matter to the client[3]; and
(i) the approval (express or implied) of the entitled person[3] or the express approval of the testator to:
(i) the solicitor[3] undertaking all or any part of the work giving rise to the costs, or
(ii) the amount of the costs.

[1] The funeral, testamentary and administration expenses are a first charge on the estate of a deceased person, whether this is solvent or insolvent: Administration of Estates Act 1925, s 34(3) and Sch 1.
[2] 'Entitled person' means a client or an entitled third party, and 'entitled third party' means a residuary beneficiary absolutely and immediately (and not contingently) entitled to an inheritance, where a solicitor has charged the estate for his professional costs for acting in the administration of the estate, and the only personal representatives are: (a) solicitors (whether or not acting in a professional capacity); (b) solicitors acting jointly with partners, managers or employees in a professional capacity; (c) employees of a solicitor sole practitioner acting in that capacity; or (d) managers or employees of a recognised body acting in that capacity.
[3] For definitions see the Solicitors' (Non-Contentious Business) Remuneration Order 2009, art 2.

4.274 In determining what is 'fair and reasonable in the circumstances', the sums under art 3 of the Solicitors' (Non-Contentious Business) Remuneration Order 2009 can be cumulative, but there should be no overlapping of allowances. For a large estate, the most important aspect is 'the nature and value of the property involved' and under that heading it is proper to charge as percentages for successive bands of value, the percentage to reduce as the value increases. (*Maltby v DJ Freeman & Co* [1978] 2 All ER 913, [1978] 1 WLR 431: in that case where the estate and number of assets were large, the appropriate bands and percentages suggested were as follows: up to £1¼ million, 1½ per cent; from £¼ million to £1 million, ½ per cent; from £1 million to £2½ million, ⅙ per cent. It was further suggested that in the case of a smaller estate, the first rate of 1½ per cent would be too low.

4.276 The Solicitors' (Non-Contentious Business) Remuneration Order 2009[1], art 4, provides that a solicitor may take security for payment of any costs including an amount for interest. Article 5 makes provision for interest on unpaid costs plus any paid disbursements and value added tax. Unlike the previous Remuneration Order (Solicitors' (Non-Contentious Business) Remuneration Order 1994) the new Remuneration Order does not contain any provision for the entitled person to require the solicitor to obtain a remuneration certificate from the Council of the Law Society. This does not affect the client's or solicitor's right to have the solicitor's bill of costs assessed under ss 70–72 of the Solicitors Act 1974.

[1] See para A5.01.

4.277 Except where the solicitor's costs have been assessed under the Solicitors Act 1974 he must, before bringing proceedings to recover his costs, inform his client in writing of the latter's right.

4.278 *Probates*

Assessment of costs

4.278 Proceedings for the assessment (previously taxation) of a solicitor's bill of costs under the Solicitors Act 1974 must be commenced in the Senior Courts Costs Office[1]: for the practice, see the notes under the Solicitors Act 1974 in Volume 2 of the Civil Procedure Rules.

[1] NCPR 60 excludes assessment in probate matters under the Solicitors Act 1974 from the jurisdiction of district judges or registrars of the Family Division.

Chapter 5

LETTERS OF ADMINISTRATION WITH THE WILL ANNEXED

Note.—This chapter deals only with grants of administration (with will) in cases where the deceased died **domiciled** in England and Wales. For the practice in cases where the deceased died domiciled elsewhere, see Ch 12. For interpretation of wills (including codicils), see Ch 3.

IN WHAT CIRCUMSTANCES GRANTED

Administration (will)

5.01 Where a will is proved by any person other than an executor, a grant of administration (with the will annexed) is made.

In what circumstances granted

5.02 This form of grant is made in the following instances, inter alia:

(a) Where no executor has been appointed;
(b) Where the executor appointed in the will has died in the lifetime of the testator, or after his death without having proved the will;
(c) Where the executor has renounced probate, or has been cited to accept or refuse a grant and has not appeared to the citation;
(d) Where the appointment of an executor is void for uncertainty[1];
(e) Where the court exercises the discretion given to it by s 116 of the Senior Courts Act 1981[2] to pass over the prior right of the executor and order that a grant be made to some other person[3];
(f) Where the executor is incompetent by reason of his minority or lacks capacity to manage his affairs within the meaning of the Mental Capacity Act 2005; or desires to apply through an attorney. In such cases the grant is normally expressed to be for the use and benefit of the executor, and reserves his right to apply for a grant by means of an appropriate limitation;
  (As to grant where the executor is a minor, see paras 11.140 ff; where he lacks capacity within the meaning of the Mental Capacity Act 2005, see paras 11.237 ff, and as to grant to the attorney of an executor, see paras 11.80 ff.)
(g) Where a corporation, association or charitable body etc, not being a trust corporation, is appointed as sole executor, when a grant may be made to a nominee or attorney for its use and benefit (see para 5.233).

[1] See paras 4.25 ff.
[2] See para A1.343.
[3] See para 25.94.

5.08 *Letters of administration with the will annexed*

ORDER OF PRIORITY

Settled land

5.08 It has not been possible to issue a general grant specifically including settled land vested in the deceased since 14 October 1991. In all cases since that date separate grants have been necessary[1].

[1] Secretary's Circular (2), 26 September 1991.

PERSONS INTERESTED IN THE RESIDUARY ESTATE

Persons entitled

Adopted persons

ADOPTIONS ORDERS MADE BEFORE 30 DECEMBER 2005

5.60 The effect of the making of an adoption under the Convention is to confer on the child the same status in England and Wales as that conferred on any other adopted person coming within the scope of Pt IV of the 1976 Act (or the former Sch 1 to the Children Act 1975). Accordingly, from 23 October 1978 adoptions made under the Convention in the several countries who have signed up to the Convention will be recognised in non-contentious probate applications.

ADOPTION ORDERS MADE ON AND AFTER 30 DECEMBER 2005

5.73 The provision in the Act (s 67) that an adopted child is not to be treated as the child of any other person other than the adopter or adopters does not prejudice any qualifying interest or interest expectant on a qualifying interest which the adopted person may have had. A qualifying interest is one vested in possession in the adopted person before the adoption. The effect of this is that a child adopted by his natural parent as a sole adoptive parent acquires any entitlement to property depending on that relationship.

5.78 Section 74 provides exception to the rule for adoptions under s 67 for purposes of marriage or formation of civil partnership with kindred; incest; nationality; immigration; and citizenship.

PERSONS INTERESTED IN THE RESIDUARY ESTATE

Gift to charities

5.88A A gift of residue to 'be taken over by the diocese of Westminster' to hold in trust for the 'Black community of Hackney, Haringey, Islington and Tower Hamlet' was not invalid for the reason that the reference 'Black community' was uncertain. In modern usage the term was another way of saying black people and did not negative the charitable intention of the testatrix. The class of inhabitants did not have to be identified with the same degree of certainty as the beneficiaries of a private trust. The remedy was to remove the reference to colour. Accordingly the disposition took effect as a gift to the diocese on charitable trusts the precise nature of which could be dealt with by a scheme—*Re Harding deceased, Gibbs v Harding* [2007] EWHC 3 (Ch), [2007] 1 All ER 747, [2007] All ER (D) 28 (Jan).

TO WHOM GRANTED

Residuary legatee or devisee

Death by murder or manslaughter

5.187 The court refused to modify the rule where the residuary beneficiary was convicted of manslaughter on the grounds of diminished responsibility. The court took into account the conduct of the offender in having spent large amounts of the deceased's money for his own benefit and not providing formal medical care for the deceased who suffered from dementia. Further the manslaughter verdict had not extinguished the offender's responsibility but merely reduced it[1].

The court has also established that it is not relevant to explore whether the matters relied upon to modify the rule give rise to the partial defence of provocation. A factor to be considered is the consequence of applying or modifying the rule: for example whether the effect of the application of the rule would confer an unexpected windfall on those who stand to inherit and to unfairly deprive the applicant of money to which he or she would have some moral entitlement[2].

1 *Dalton v Latham* [2003] EWHC 796 (Ch), 147 Sol Jo LB 537.
2 *Mack v Lockwood* [2009] EWHC 1524 (Ch).

Persons entitled to share in undisposed-of estate

Where deceased left a surviving spouse or (after 5 December 2005) surviving civil partner

5.192 In considering who is entitled to a grant under this provision, if the deceased left a surviving spouse or surviving civil partner (after 5 December 2005), regard must be had to the provisions of the Administration of Estates Act 1925 (as amended by the Intestates' Estates Act 1952 and the Family Provision Act 1966[1] and Civil Partnership Act 2004)[2]. Where all dispositions in a will fail, the residuary estate is distributed as on a total intestacy (see paras 6.38 ff), but where the will effectively disposes of part of the estate, the provisions of the Administration of Estates Act 1925 apply as modified by s 49 thereof[3].

[1] See para A1.185 ff.

5.192 *Letters of administration with the will annexed*

² See para A1.579 (Sch 4 Pt 2).
³ See para A1.117 and fn 1, para 5.130.

5.193 The statutory legacy in favour of the surviving spouse or surviving civil partner on intestacy varies according to the date of death of the deceased and whether the deceased left issue surviving.

5.193A In 2005 the Department for Constitutional Affairs, now the Ministry of Justice, carried out a full public consultation on the statutory legacy. This review was prompted by complaints from Members of Parliament, lawyers and the public about the current levels of the statutory legacy which was last increased to its current levels in 1991. The response to the consultation paper may be found on the Ministry of Justice website[1]. The outcome of the consultation resulted in a proposal to increase the lower level of the statutory legacy (where issue survive) to £250,000 and the upper level (no issue survive) to £450,000. This proposal has been given effect by the Family Provision (Intestate Succession) Order 2009[2] which came into force on 1 February 2009. The increased limits apply where the deceased died on or after this date.

¹ At http://www.justice.gov.uk/publications/cp1105.htm.
² SI 2009/135.

5.194 Where the death occurred on or after 1 December 1993, the surviving spouse or surviving civil partner after 5 December 2005 is entitled to the first £125,000 (where the deceased left issue also surviving), or £200,000 (where the deceased left no issue), of the net undisposed-of estate[1], *less* any beneficial interests acquired under the will, other than personal chattels specifically bequeathed; such interests being valued as at the date of death[2]. It is only where the value of the net undisposed-of estate does not exceed the appropriate sum, reduced as ff, that it all passes to the surviving spouse or surviving civil partner after 5 December 2005.

¹ The net value of the undisposed-of residuary estate is found, for the present purpose, by the deduction of the value of the personal chattels, debts, funeral expenses, inheritance tax or capital transfer tax, probate fees and costs of the grant, but not costs of administration.
² Administration of Estates Act 1925, s 46(1), as amended by Intestates' Estates Act 1952, s 1, Family Provision Act 1966, s 1 and the Family Provision (Intestate Succession) Orders 1977, 1981, 1987 and 1993 (SIs 1977/415, 1981/255, 1987/799 and 1993/2906).

5.196 Where the death was before 1 January 1953, and the net value of the undisposed-of estate[1] does not exceed £1,000, the whole passes to the surviving spouse; no deduction is made in respect of the amount (if any) which passes to the spouse under the terms of the will.

¹ The net value of the undisposed-of residuary estate is found, for the present purpose, by the deduction of the value of the personal chattels, debts, funeral expenses, inheritance tax or capital transfer tax, probate fees and costs of the grant, but not costs of administration.

5.197 Whatever the date of death is, if the amount of the undisposed-of estate is such that it all passes to the surviving spouse or civil partner, he or she is the only person entitled to a grant under the provision under discussion. As to the position where the spouse or civil partner renounces, see para 5.192.

5.198 If the whole of the undisposed-of estate has vested in a surviving spouse or civil partner who has since died, the grant may be made to his or her personal representative (NCPR 20(d)).

5.199 Where the net value of the undisposed-of estate, arrived at as aforesaid, exceeds the appropriate statutory figure applicable for a death occurring after 1952, or the sum of £1,000 where the death occurred before 1953, a grant may be made to any person entitled to share in the undisposed-of residue[1]. Where the deceased died after 1952 leaving a spouse or (from 5 December 2005) civil partner and issue, or before 1953 leaving a spouse, a life interest arises in these circumstances, and the grant must accordingly be made to not less than two individuals or to a trust corporation with or without an individual, unless the court thinks it expedient in all the circumstances to appoint a sole administrator[2]. (As to grants to trust corporations, see Ch 9.)

[1] This is the wording of the rule, but in practice the normal order of priority would operate, and, for example, a grant would not be made to children of the deceased without clearing off the surviving spouse or civil partner.
[2] Supreme Court Act 1981, s 114(2) (see para A1.341).

5.200 If the surviving spouse or civil partner has since died, administration (with will) may be granted to any other person taking a beneficial interest in the undisposed-of estate[1].

[1] NCPR 20(c).

5.201 If the spouse or civil partner had acquired an absolute interest in the whole of the undisposed-of estate (ie if the testator left no other surviving relative within the degrees mentioned in paras 6.52–6.83, in case of death before 1 January 1953; or no issue, parent, brother or sister of the whole blood or issue of brother or sister of the whole blood in case of death on or after that date), a grant may be made to the personal representative of the spouse or civil partner. In such event the classes who would have been entitled to share with the spouse or civil partner must be specifically cleared off in the oath.

5.202 If the spouse or civil partner and all other persons entitled to share in the undisposed-of estate have since died, a grant may be made to the personal representative of any of them[1], priority being given in practice to the personal representative of the spouse or civil partner unless the spouse's or civil partner's interest in the estate has been wholly satisfied.

[1] NCPR 20(d).

No surviving spouse or civil partner

5.203 Where the residuary estate is wholly or partly undisposed of, or has lapsed, and the deceased died leaving no spouse or civil partner, the order of priority of right to a grant is that applicable in cases of total intestacy (see para 6.30 Table B), and is not affected by the amount of the undisposed-of

5.203 *Letters of administration with the will annexed*

estate. The grant may be made to any person entitled to share in the undisposed-of estate, or, if every such person has since died or is otherwise cleared off, to the personal representative of any such person who has since died. (Form of oath, No 156.)

Failure of gift over: spouse or civil partner residuary legatee for life

5.204 Where a testator's will gives his wife or civil partner a life interest in the residuary estate but there is no gift over or the gift over fails, the provisions of s 46 of the Administration of Estates Act 1925 have, in accordance with s 49 of that Act, to be read into the will. The joint effect of the will and the statute is to give the widow or surviving civil partner a life interest and, subject thereto, the residuary estate stands charged with the immediate payment to her of the statutory legacy under s 46(1)(i) of the Act, there being no warrant for making it a charge in favour of her personal representative only[1]. Except where the date of death was prior to 1 January 1953 or after 1 January 1996, the statutory sum would presumably be reduced by the value of the beneficial interests acquired by the spouse or civil partner under the terms of the will (Administration of Estates Act 1925, s 49(1), as amended).

[1] *Re Bowen-Buscarlet's Will Trusts, Nathan v Bowen-Buscarlet* [1972] Ch 463, [1971] 3 All ER 636, following *Re Douglas's Will Trusts, Lloyds Bank Ltd v Nelson* [1959] 2 All ER 620, [1959] 1 WLR 744, and not following *Re McKee, Public Trustee v McKee* [1931] 2 Ch 145.

5.205 As to the converse case where there is no disposition during the lifetime of the spouse or civil partner, see paras 5.128 ff.

Miscellaneous grants of administration (with will)

Deeds of assignment executed before 1 December 2003

5.249 The Stamp Duty (Exempt Instruments) Regulations 1987 (SI 1987/516) came into force on 1 May 1987 and provide that instruments executed on or after that date of a kind specified in the Schedule to the Regulations and which bear a certificate in a form which satisfies the requirements of the Regulations shall be exempt from payment of duty under certain headings in Sch 1 to the Stamp Act 1891 and ss 83(2) and 84(8) of the Finance Act 1985. The certificate referred to must be in writing and

(a) either be included in the instrument or be endorsed on or physically attached to it;
(b) contain a sufficient description of:
 (i) the instrument concerned where the certificate is separate but physically attached; and
 (ii) the category of the Schedule into which the instrument falls; and
(c) must be signed by the transferor or grantor or by his solicitor or duly authorised agent.

Requirements on obtaining administration (with will) 5.276

Where it is not signed by the transferor or grantor or his solicitor, it must contain a statement by the signatory of the capacity in which he signs, that he is authorised so to sign and that he gives the certificate from his own knowledge of the facts stated in it. Where a deed of assignment is produced on an application for a grant and is supported by a certificate (as indicated above) it is checked in the registry against the above criteria and the exempt categories set out in the Schedule to the Regulations to establish whether the requirements of the Regulations have been satisfied. The court, however, retains the right to require adjudication if in doubt as to the correctness of the certificate[1]. But see para 5.246.

[1] Secretary's Circular, 10 September 1987.

Other grants of administration (with will)

5.258 For the practice in obtaining a grant for the use and benefit of a minor or a person who lacks capacity to manage his or her affairs within the meaning of the Mental Capacity Act 2005, or to the attorney of the person entitled to a grant, see Ch 11; grants in cases where the deceased died domiciled out of England and Wales, see Ch 12; grants in the exercise of the discretionary power of the Court, see Ch 14; grants de bonis non and cessate grants, see Ch 13.

REQUIREMENTS ON OBTAINING ADMINISTRATION (WITH WILL)

Administration (will) oath

Minority or life interest

5.266 Where the residuary estate is not wholly disposed of by the will and the deceased left a surviving spouse, regard must be had to the extent of the spouse's statutory entitlement in respect of the undisposed-of estate in deciding whether or not a life interest arises. The spouse's entitlement of £125,000/£250,000 (where the deceased left issue) or £200,000/£450,000 (where the deceased left no issue)[1] is diminished by the value of any beneficial interests (other than personal chattels specifically bequeathed) acquired by the spouse under the will[2]. Where the date of death was before 1 January 1953 the spouse is entitled to the first £1,000 of the undisposed-of estate, irrespective of any beneficial interest taken under the will. The increased limits, respectively £250,000 and £450,000 mentioned above, apply where the deceased died on or after 1 February 2009 by virtue of the Family Provision (intestate Succession) Order 2009[3].

[1] Or such other sum as is appropriate in case of death prior to 1 December 1993 (see para 5.195 and Administration of Estates Act 1925, s 46).
[2] Administration of Estates Act 1925, s 49(1)(aa): see para A1.117.
[3] SI 2009/135.

5.276 *See Chapter 8 for the HMRC account update.*

Chapter 6
LETTERS OF ADMINISTRATION

Notes.—1. This chapter deals only with grants of administration in cases where the deceased died **domiciled in England and Wales**. For the practice in cases where the deceased died domiciled elsewhere, see Ch 12.

2. Except where otherwise stated, the practice given in this chapter applies where the date of death of the intestate was on or after 1 January 1926.

TO WHOM GRANTED

6.17 The general rule applicable to the grant of letters of administration is that where possible administration is granted to one or more of the persons taking a beneficial interest in the estate of the deceased (see the reference to the probate rules in s 116(1) of the Senior Courts Act 1981[1] and NCPR 22(1)[2]).

[1] See para A2.61.
[2] See para A1.343.

6.18 In the case of death on or after 1 January 1926 the distribution of the residuary estate of an intestate is regulated by Pt IV (ie ss 45–52) of the Administration of Estates Act 1925[1]. This Part of the Act has been amended, as regards deaths occurring on or after 1 January 1953, by the Intestates' Estates Act 1952 and further amended as regards deaths occurring on or after 1 January 1967 by the Family Provision Act 1966. In the case of death on or after 1 January 1970, rights of succession on intestacy were given to illegitimate, as well as legitimate, children of the deceased, and to the natural parents of an illegitimate intestate by Pt II of the Family Law Reform Act 1969[2]. As regards deaths on or after 4 April 1988 illegitimacy is not to be taken into account regarding any of the classes of relations entitled to succeed on intestacy, by reason of s 18 of the Family Law Reform Act 1987[3]. With effect from and in respect of deaths on and after 5 December 2005 rights of succession are given to the surviving civil partners of the deceased by s 46 of the Administration of Estates Act 1925 as amended by the Civil Partnership Act 2004, s 71, Sch 4, Pt 2, para 7 (see para A1.579). The Gender Recognition Act 2004 came into effect on 5 April 2005. The effect of the Act is that where at the date of death of the deceased on or after 5 April 2005 a person has acquired an alternative gender his or her relationship to the deceased is described as of the acquired gender. This does not however apply to the parents of the deceased. Section 12 of this Act provides that a person's acquired gender does not affect his or her status as the father or mother of the child.

[1] See para A1.112–A1.124 ff.
[2] See Senior Courts Act 1981, s 25, para A1.316.
[3] See para A1.431.

Number of administrators. Minority or life interest

6.21 By s 114(1) of the Senior Courts Act 1981[1], the maximum number of persons allowed to take a grant in respect of the same part of the estate[2] is four, and if a minority or a life interest arises under the intestacy, administration must (unless the court in its discretion thinks it expedient in all the circumstances to appoint a sole administrator) be granted to a trust corporation, with or without an individual, or to not less than two individuals[3]. This applies whatever the date of death.

[1] See para A1.341.
[2] *Re Holland's Estate* [1936] 3 All ER 13.
[3] Section 114(2) of the Senior Courts Act 1981 (para A1.341).

Subsequent appointment of additional administrator

6.23 Where a grant has been made to one personal representative other than a trust corporation, or where one of two personal representatives has died and there is a minor beneficiary or a life interest subsists, an additional administrator may be appointed by a district judge or registrar under s 114(4) of the Senior Courts Act 1981. The original grant may be noted with the appointment (without any necessity for a new grant), or it may be impounded or revoked as the circumstances of the case require, or as the district judge or registrar may direct. See NCPR 26 and paras 7.40 ff and 16.32.

Civil partnership

Tables showing the persons entitled to the estate and to a grant in the case of intestacy since January 1926

6.37 Notes.

1. Under s 1(1) of the Law Reform (Succession) Act 1995 (as amended) (see para A1.497) a spouse or (with effect from 5 December 2005) a civil partner of an intestate dying on or after 1 January 1996 must survive the intestate for a period of 28 days beginning with the day on which the intestate died, before the spouse acquires a beneficial interest in the estate under s 46 of the Administration of Estates Act 1925.
2. **The Family Provision (Intestate Succession) Order 2009 came into effect on 1 February 2009. Where the deceased dies on or after that date, the level of the spouse's or civil partner's statutory legacy increases to £250,000 (where the deceased left issue) and £450,000 (where the deceased left no issue).

6.37 *Letters of administration*

A. *Death On or After 1 January 1953 where Deceased left a Surviving Spouse or Civil Partner*[1]

	Intestate leaves	Distribution of estate	Entitled to grant
I.	Husband or widow or civil partner and issue (**net estate not exceeding £250,000;** £125,000 where death on or after 1 December 1993 but before 1 February 2009; £75,000 where death on or after 1 June 1987 but before 1 December 1993, £40,000 where death on or after 1 March 1981 but before 1 June 1987; £25,000 where death after 14 March 1977 but before 1 March 1981; £15,000 where death after 30 June 1972 but before 15 March 1977; £8,750 where death after 31 December 1966 but before 1 July 1972; or £5,000 where death before 1 January 1967)[2]	All to husband or widow or civil partner	Husband or widow or civil partner

To whom granted 6.37

	Intestate leaves	Distribution of estate	Entitled to grant
II.	Husband or widow or civil partner without issue (**net estate not exceeding **£450,000; £200,000 where death on or after 1 December 1993 but before 1 February 2009; £125,000 where death on or after 1 June 1987 but before 1 December 1993; £85,000 where death on or after 1 March 1981 but before 1 June 1987; £55,000 where death after 14 March 1977 but before 1 March 1981; £40,000 where death after 30 June 1972 but before 15 March 1977; £30,000 where death after 31 December 1966 but before 1 July 1972; or £20,000 where death before 1 January 1967)[2]	All to husband or widow or civil partner	Husband or widow or civil partner

39

6.37   *Letters of administration*

	Intestate leaves	Distribution of estate	Entitled to grant
III.	Husband or widow or civil partner and issue (**net estate exceeding **£250,000, £125,000, £75,000, £40,000, £25,000, £15,000, £8,750 or £5,000 (whichever is appropriate: see I above))	Husband or widow or civil partner takes personal chattels, **£250,000, (£125,000 where death on or after 1 December 1993 but before 1 February 2009; (£75,000 where death on or after 1 June 1987 but before 1 December 1993; £40,000 where death on or after 1 March 1981 but before 1 June 1987; £25,000 where death after 14 March 1977 but before 1 March 1981; £15,000 where death after 30 June 1972 but before 15 March 1977; £8,750 where death after 31 December 1966 but before 1 July 1972; or £5,000 where death before 1 January 1967) free of costs and duty, with interest at the appropriate rate[3], and a life interest in half remainder of estate, with reversion to the issue, the other half to the issue absolutely	*Husband or widow or civil partner and a child

To whom granted 6.37

	Intestate leaves	Distribution of estate	Entitled to grant
IV.	Husband or widow or civil partner without issue (**net estate exceeding **£450,000, £200,000, £125,000, £85,000, £55,000, £40,000, £30,000 or £20,000 (whichever is appropriate: see II above))[2]	Husband or widow or civil partner takes personal chattels, **£450,000 (£200,000 where death on and after 1 December 1993 but before 1 February 2009, (£125,000 where death on or after 1 June 1987 but before 1 December 1993; £85,000 where death on or after 1 March 1981 but before 1 June 1987; £55,000 where death after 14 March 1977 but before 1 March 1981; £40,000 where death after 30 June 1972 but before 15 March 1977; £30,000 where death after 31 December 1966 but before 1 July 1972; or £20,000 where death before 1 January 1967) free of costs and duty, with interest at the appropriate rate[3], and one-half of the remainder absolutely. As to the other half, where there are parents[4], to the parents absolutely: where there are no parents, to the brothers and sisters of the whole blood[4] in equal shares, the issue[4] of such as have predeceased the intestate taking per stirpes the share to which their parent would have been entitled.	*Husband or widow or civil partner

41

6.37   *Letters of administration*

	Intestate leaves	Distribution of estate	Entitled to grant
V.	Husband or widow or civil partner without issue, parent, brother or sister of the whole blood or their issue[4] (whatever the amount of the estate)	All to husband or widow or civil partner	Husband or widow or civil partner
*See notes at end of tables. **See note 2 above table.			

[1] References to civil partner apply to deaths on and after 5 December 2006; see para 6.37. As to devolution of the estate of a married woman who has been judicially separated from her husband or of the estate of a civil partner who has been judicially separated from his or her partner, see paras 6.154–6.155 ff.

[2] For method of determining the amount of the 'net estate' for this purpose, see paras 6.102. As to the meaning of 'issue', see note 3 to para 6.45.

[3] The Intestate Succession (Interest and Capitalisation) Order 1977 (Amendment) Order 1983, SI 1983/1374 provides that for the purposes of s 46(1)(i) of the Administration of Estates Act 1925, as it applies both in respect of persons dying before 1953 and in respect of persons dying after 1952, the rate of interest payable on the statutory legacy until it is paid or appropriated shall be 6% per annum with effect from 1 October 1983. The previous rate of interest was 7% per annum for the period commencing on 15 September 1977 (the Intestate Succession (Interest and Capitalisation) Order 1977, SI 1977/1491 which increased the then current rate of 4% per annum or, in the case of persons dying before the coming into operation of the Intestates' Estates Act 1952, 5% per annum). Accordingly, where a statutory legacy remains unpaid for a considerable time, the interest payable on that legacy will need to be calculated at different rates for different periods. For example, where the death occurs after 1952 but before 15 September 1977, the interest to be paid on the statutory legacy will be 4% per annum up to 15 September 1977 and thereafter 7% per annum until 1 October 1983 and thereafter 6% per annum until the legacy is paid or appropriated.

[4] In respect of deaths on or after 4 April 1988 illegitimacy is not to be taken into account: Family Law Reform Act 1987, s 18.

B. *Death On or at any time After 1 January 1926. No Surviving Spouse or Civil Partner*[1]

	Intestate leaves	Distribution of estate	Entitled to grant
I.	Issue only[2]‡	Issue[1] who attain full age or marry under age take equally (children, including illegitimate children when the intestate died on or after 4 April 1988, of predeceasing children taking their parent's share, per stirpes)	*Issue[1]

	Intestate leaves	Distribution of estate	Entitled to grant
II.	Father or mother[2]‡	Father or mother[2]	Father or mother[2]
III.	Father and mother[3]‡	In equal shares	Either or both
IV.	Brothers and sisters of the whole blood, and issue of such as died in the lifetime of the intestate	Brothers and sisters of the whole blood in equal shares, the issue of such as have predeceased the intestate taking their parent's share, per stirpes	*A person or persons entitled to share in the estate
V.	Brothers and sisters of the half blood and issue of such as died in the lifetime of the intestate‡	Brothers and sisters of the half blood in equal shares and issue as in IV	*A person or persons entitled to share in the estate
VI.	Grandparents	Grandparents in equal shares	Grandparent (one or more)
VII.	Uncles and aunts of the whole blood, and issue of such as died in the lifetime of the intestate‡	Uncles and aunts of the whole blood and issue as in IV	*A person or persons entitled to share in the estate
VIII.	Uncles and aunts of the half blood and issue of such as died in the lifetime of the intestate‡	Uncles and aunts of the half blood and issue as in IV	*A person or persons entitled to share in the estate
IX.	No blood relation taking an interest as above	(a) The Crown, (b) Duchy of Lancaster, (c) Duchy of Cornwall	(a) Treasury Solicitor for the use of Her Majesty (b) Solicitor for the Duchy of Lancaster for the use of Her Majesty (c) Solicitor for the affairs of the Duchy of Cornwall
X.	Creditor		†Creditor

*†‡ See notes at end of tables.

6.37 Letters of administration

[1] References to civil partner apply to deaths on and after 5 December 2006; see para 6.37.
[2] Including illegitimate children where the death was on or after 1 January 1970. In the case of deaths prior to this date but after 1926, illegitimate children are entitled only where the deceased left no lawful issue. See also Family Law Reform Act 1987, s 18, para A1.431, in respect of deaths on or after 4 April 1988.
[3] Including natural parents where the death was on or after 1 January 1970. In the case of deaths prior to this date but after 1926 the natural mother but not the natural father is entitled. See also Family Law Reform Act 1987, s 18, para A1.431, in respect of deaths on or after 4 April 1988.

C. Death on or After 1 January 1926, but Before 1 January 1953, where Deceased left a Surviving Spouse[1]

	Intestate leaves	Distribution of estate	Entitled to grant
I.	Husband or widow (**net estate not exceeding £1,000**)[2]	All to husband or widow	Husband or widow
II.	Husband or widow and issue (**net estate exceeding £1,000**)[2]	Husband or widow takes the personal chattels, £1,000 (free of costs and duty) with interest at the appropriate rate[3]. Life interest in half the remainder of estate, with reversion to the issue. As to the other half, to the issue absolutely	*Husband or widow and a child
III.	Husband or widow without issue (**net estate exceeding £1,000**)[2]	Husband or widow takes the personal chattels, £1,000 (free of costs and duty) with interest at the appropriate rate[3], life interest in all the remainder of the estate, with reversion to nearest class of blood relations (see Table B, above)	*Husband or widow and a person entitled to share in the estate
IV.	Husband or widow but no blood relation within the classes entitled to share (see Table B, above) (whatever the amount of the estate)	All to husband or widow	Husband or widow

Distribution of estate where death on or after 1 January 1926 **6.39**

*   In the event of a minority or life interest arising there must normally be two applicants for the grant; the second person should be a person entitled to share, having a vested interest, but if all of these are cleared off the guardian of a minor entitled to share upon attaining full age may be joined as second applicant. See Ch 7, as to the discretionary power vested in the court to appoint a sole administrator where it is expedient to do so in all the circumstances.

†   Upon the renunciation or clearing off of all persons having a prior right to the grant.

‡   As to the interests of legitimated persons, see para 6.192 ff. In respect of deaths on or after 4 April 1988 illegitimacy is not to be taken into consideration in respect of the relationships—see Family Law Reform Act 1987, s 18, para A1.431.

1   As to devolution of the estate of a married woman who has been judicially separated from her husband see paras 6.154 ff.
2   For method of determining the amount of the 'net estate' for this purpose, see para 6.102.
3   Intestate Succession (Interest and Capitalisation) Order 1977 (Amendment) Order 1983 (SI 1983/1374); see also note 3 ante as to the need to calculate the interest payable at different rates for different periods.

DISTRIBUTION OF AN INTESTATE'S ESTATE WHERE THE DEATH HAS OCCURRED ON OR AFTER 1 JANUARY 1926

6.39 Under this Act, where the deceased leaves a surviving spouse or (with effect from 5 December 2005) a civil partner the latter is entitled to a charge on the residuary estate for a fixed net sum. This sum was originally £1,000[1], but was increased, first by the Intestates' Estates Act 1952[2] in relation to deaths occurring on or after 1 January 1953 to £5,000 (where the deceased also left issue surviving) or £20,000 (where the deceased left no issue), and more recently by the Family Provision Act 1966[3] in relation to deaths on or after 1 January 1967 to £8,750 (where the deceased left issue) or £30,000 (where the deceased left no issue). The last-mentioned Act includes power for the Lord Chancellor to specify larger sums than £8,750 and £30,000 respectively by statutory instrument, to be laid before Parliament in draft (s 1) and, in exercise of this power, the sums of £15,000 (where the deceased left issue) and £40,000 (where the deceased left no issue) were specified in the case of persons dying on or after 1 July 1972 by the Family Provision (Intestate Succession) Order 1972; increased to the respective sums of £25,000 and £55,000 in the case of persons dying on or after 15 March 1977; and further increased to the respective sums of £40,000 and £85,000 for deaths on or after 1 March 1981; and further increased to £75,000 and £125,000 for deaths on or after 1 June 1987 and further increased to £125,000 and £200,000 for deaths on or after 1 December 1993 and further increased to £250,000 and £450,000 for deaths on or after 1 February 2009.

Note. *See note 1 in heading before table A in para 6.37 about deaths on or after 1 January 1996*[4] *and note 2 for deaths on or after 1 February 2009.*

1   Administration of Estates Act 1925, s 46(1) (as originally enacted: see para A1.113).
2   See para A1.139 ff.
3   See para A1.185 ff.

6.39   Letters of administration

⁴   SIs 1972/916, 1977/415, 1981/255, 1987/799 and 1993/2906 (see paras A2.01 ff, A2.06 ff, A2.18 ff, A2.38 ff and A2.116 ff).

6.40 The relationships entitled to participate in an intestate's estate were in general restricted to lawful blood relationships, but by virtue of the Legitimacy Acts 1926 and 1959, and the Adoption Acts 1958 to 1968, legitimated persons and adopted persons, and persons related to the deceased through a legitimation or an adoption were, in specified circumstances, given rights on an intestacy. And, in relation to deaths after 31 December 1975, the succession rights of adopted and legitimated persons, including the rights of persons related to the deceased through an adoption or a legitimation, are now generally equated to those arising from a lawful blood relationship: see the Adoption Act 1976[1] and the Legitimacy Act 1976[2]. Limited rights of succession on intestacy between illegitimate children and their parents were introduced by the Legitimacy Act 1926, s 9, and these rights were extended in relation to deaths on or after 1 January 1970 by Pt II of the Family Law Reform Act 1969. Details of these provisions are given later in this chapter. Sections 14, 15 and 17 (in Pt II) of the Family Law Reform Act 1969 were repealed as from 4 April 1988: see s 33(4) of the Family Law Reform Act 1987[3]. In respect of intestates dying on or after 4 April 1988, by virtue of s 18 of the Family Law Reform Act 1987[3] references (however expressed) in Pt IV of the Administration of Estates Act 1925 (which deals with the distribution of the estate of an intestate) to any relationship between two persons are to be construed without regard to whether or not the father and mother of either of them, or the father and mother of any person through whom the relationship is deduced, have or had been married to each other at any time. Consequently, *in respect of an intestate dying on or after 4 April 1988 a blood relation in the relevant class is beneficially entitled to (or to share in) the estate and is entitled to apply for letters of administration whether or not the relationship is lawful.* See also para 6.173. The Human Fertilisation and Embryology Act 2008 received Royal Assent on 13 November 2008. In Pt 2 of the Act, headed 'Parenthood in Cases Involving Assisted Reproduction', various sections extend the meaning of 'mother', 'father' and 'parent' of a child born as a result of assisted reproduction. The effective parts of this Act bring into force amendments to enactments where relationship in the relevant class is construed or determined. For ease of reference Pt 2 of and Sch 6 to the Act are reproduced in Appendix I.

¹   See para A1.286 ff.
²   See para A1.275 ff.
³   See para A1.431.

6.44 This subject is dealt with in Ch 41.

The Law Commission recently published a Consultation Paper entitled Intestacy and Family Provision Claims on Death (*Law Com Consultation Paper no 191*) (*www.lawcom.gov.uk/intestacy.htm*). *The paper sought views on various proposals to amend the law including restoring the rights of issue of the deceased who are subsequently adopted and the extension of classes entitled on intestacy and to apply for family provision. The consultation period ended on 28 February 2010.*

Distribution of estate where death on or after 1 January 1926 **6.45**

Husband or wife or civil partner : (a) Death on or after 1 January 1953[1]

Note.—See note under heading above table A in para 6.37 *about deaths on or after 1 January 1996.*

6.45

(1) If the intestate dies leaving a husband or wife or civil partner, but no issue[2] or parent[3], or brother or sister of the whole blood[4], or issue of brother or sister of the whole blood[4], he or she is entitled to the whole estate, whatever its value.

(2) If the intestate dies leaving a husband or wife or civil partner and issue[2], the husband or wife or civil partner is entitled to the personal chattels absolutely[5] and a charge on the residuary estate for a fixed net sum (£250,000 with effect from 1 February 2009[6]) free of death duties and costs, with interest thereon at the appropriate rate per annum from the date of death until paid or appropriated[7].

(3) If the intestate dies leaving a husband or wife or civil partner and one or more of the following: a parent[3], brother or sister of the whole blood[4], or issue of brother or sister of the whole blood[4], but leaves no issue[2], the husband or wife or civil partner is entitled to the personal chattels and a charge on the residuary estate for a fixed net sum (£450,000 with effect from 1 February 2009[8]), free of death duties and costs, with interest thereon at the rate of 6% per annum from the date of death until paid or appropriated[7].

(4) And as to the residue of the estate the husband or wife or civil partner is entitled to—
   (a) a life interest in one half *where there is issue[2] surviving* (on failure of the statutory trusts[9] as to the issue[2] the residue and any statutory accumulations go as though the intestate had left no issue).
   (b) an absolute interest in one half *where there is no issue[2]*, but there is a parent[3], or brother or sister of the whole blood[4], or issue of a brother or sister of the whole blood[4], surviving.

---

[1] Section 46, Administration of Estates Act 1925, as amended by the Intestates' Estates Act 1952 and the Family Provision Act 1966 and Civil Partnership Act 2004, Sch 4, Pt 2: see paras A1.113 and A1.579.

[2] See para 6.51 ff for meaning of the expression 'issue'.

[3] In relation to deaths occurring on or after 1 January 1970, the expression 'parents' includes natural parents (Family Law Reform Act 1969, s 14: see para A1.198). See also, para 6.70 ff. See also, ss 33 ff as they apply to extend the meaning of 'mother', 'father' and 'parent': para A1.1.

[4] See para 6.40.

[5] Personal chattels mean carriages, horses, stable furniture and effects (not used for business purposes), motor cars and accessories (not used for business purposes), garden effects, domestic animals, plate, plated articles, linen, china, glass, books, pictures, prints, furniture, jewellery, articles of household or personal use or ornament, musical and scientific instruments and apparatus, wines, liquors and consumable stores, but do not include any chattels used at the death of the intestate for business purposes nor money or securities for money (Administration of Estates Act 1925, s 55(1)(x), para A1.127).

[6] See para 6.39 for earlier figures and dates.

[7] Intestate Succession (Interest and Capitalisation) Order 1977 (SI 1977/1491) (Amendment) Order 1983 (SI 1983/1374); but see fn 3 to para 6.37, as to the need to calculate the interest payable at different rates for different periods.

6.45 Letters of administration

⁸ See para 6.39 for earlier figures and dates.
⁹ See 'Statutory trusts for issue', paras 6.63 ff.

Issue of intestate

6.52 If the intestate dies leaving a *husband or a wife or a civil partner* and *issue*, the issue takes half the residue of the estate (other than personal chattels) remaining after satisfying the spouse's or civil partner's statutory legacy (of £250,000, £125,000, £75,000, £40,000, £25,000, £15,000, £8,750, £5,000 or £1,000 according to the date of death), and interest thereon; and succeeds to the other half on the death of the surviving husband or wife or civil partner (both interests being subject to the statutory trusts, see paras 6.63 ff).

Surviving spouse or civil partner. Failure of kin within the classes entitled to share

6.85 Where there is a surviving spouse or civil partner, but no issue, parent, or brother or sister of the whole blood or their issue, where the death occurred on or after 1 January 1953 (or no kin within the degrees mentioned in table B in para 6.37, where the death occurred on or after 1 January 1926, but before 1 January 1953) the estate vests absolutely in the spouse or civil partner (as appropriate to the death of death) no matter what the amount may be. In respect of deaths on or after 4 April 1988 issue, parent and brother and sister of the whole blood or their issue includes those who are not lawfully related to the intestate (Family Law Reform Act 1987, s 18[1]).

[1] See para A1.431.

Failure of statutory trusts

6.86 If the statutory trusts in favour of any class of relatives of the intestate fail by reason that none of them attain an absolutely vested interest, reach the age of majority, or marry under that age, the estate devolves as though the intestate had left no relative of that class[1]. Issue of the deceased who are subsequently adopted do not attain an absolutely vested interest in his estate. From the date of the adoption these are treated in law as if they are not the children of any person other than adopters and as if each is born to the adopters either as a child of the marriage or born to an adopter in wedlock[2].

The Law Commission in its Consultation Paper entitled Intestacy and Family Provision Claims on Death *(Law Com Consultation Paper no 191) invited comments on its proposal that the contingent interest of a child in his deceased parent's estate should not be lost on adoption but should be held on statutory trusts during his/her minority (the paper and related documents may be accessed at www.lawcom.gov.uk/intestacy.htm).*

[1] Administration of Estates Act 1925, s 47(2): see para A1.114.

² Adoption Act 1976, s 39(1) and (2) but subject to (3) and subsequently the Adoption and Children Act 2002, s 67: see para A1.289 and a1.523.

RIGHT TO THE GRANT

Grant to surviving spouse or civil partner

Right of husband or widow or civil partner

6.95 The surviving spouse or (*with effect from 5 December 2005*) a civil partner is entitled to the whole estate:

(a) where the net value of the estate, after making the permitted deductions (see para 6.102) does not exceed:
   (i) *where the deceased dies on or after 1 February 2009*: £250,000 where the deceased left issue, or £450,00 where the deceased left no issue[1];
   (ii) *where the deceased died on or after 1 December 1993*: £125,000 where the deceased left issue, or £200,000 where the deceased left no issue[1];
   (iii) *where the deceased died on or after 1 June 1987*: £75,000 where the deceased left issue, or £125,000 where the deceased left no issue[1];
   (iv) *where the deceased died on or after 1 March 1981*: £40,000 where the deceased left issue, or £85,000 where the deceased left no issue[1];
   (v) *where the deceased died on or after 15 March 1977, but before 1 March 1981*: £25,000 where the deceased left issue, or £55,000 where the deceased left no issue[1];
   (vi) *where the deceased died on or after 1 July 1972 but before 15 March 1977*: £15,000 where the deceased left issue, or £40,000 where the deceased left no issue[1];
   (vii) *where the deceased died after 31 December 1966, but before 1 July 1972*: £8,750 where the deceased left issue, or £30,000 where the deceased left no issue[1];
   (viii) *where the deceased died after 31 December 1952, but before 1 January 1967*: £5,000 where the deceased left issue, or £20,000 where the deceased left no issue;
   (ix) *where the deceased died after 31 December 1925, but before 1 January 1953*: £1,000.
   In these cases, the oath should describe the applicant as 'the lawful husband (*or* lawful widow, *as the case may be*) or lawful civil partner and only person now entitled to the estate'[2]. As to the wording to be included where the gross estate is in excess of the appropriate amount stated above, but the permitted deductions reduce the net estate below this figure, see paras 6.103 ff (Form of oath, No 87);

(b) where the deceased left no kin within the degrees entitled to share with the spouse, ie down to the issue of brothers or sisters of the whole blood, where the death occurred on or after 1 January 1953 (see table A, para 6.37); or down to the issue of uncles or aunts of the half blood

6.95 *Letters of administration*

where the death occurred before 1 January 1953 (see table B, para 6.37). The kin should be specifically cleared off in the oath in such cases. The oath should describe the applicant as 'the lawful husband (*or* lawful widow, *as the case may be*) (*or* lawful civil partner) and only person entitled to the estate'.

[1] In the case of death on or after 1 January 1970 as well as lawful issue, illegitimate children of the intestate and the lawful issue of any who have predeceased the intestate (and, as regards (i) above) in the case of death on or after 4 April 1988 illegitimate as well as lawful issue of any who have predeceased the intestate) are within the definition of 'issue' for this purpose: see fn 2 to para 6.45.

[2] Where the net estate exceeds £125,000, but does not exceed £200,000 (or the corresponding lower figures where the date of death was before 1 December 1993), and the deceased died without issue, the oath should state that the deceased died 'without issue or any other person entitled to share in the estate by virtue of any enactment'. Should these words not be included, the oath will be accepted if the applicant's solicitor is prepared to certify to the effect that he is instructed that the deceased died intestate without issue or any other person entitled to share in the estate by virtue of any enactment (Registrar's Circular, 29 July 1977, as amended).

6.96 Where the deceased died on or after 1 January 1953 leaving a surviving spouse or (*on or after 5 December* 2005) a surviving civil partner, *but no issue*, no life interest arises whatever the amount of the estate, so that, unless the spouse or civil partner or any person entitled to share with the spouse is a minor, a grant may be made to the surviving spouse or civil partner alone. In such cases, where the estate is in excess of £450,000,000 (or the appropriate lower figure where the death was before 1 December 1993), after making the permitted deductions, the applicant should be described as 'the lawful husband *or* "lawful widow" *or* "lawful civil partner" and one of the persons entitled to share in the estate'.

Child 'en ventre sa mère'

6.122 The minority interest will arise only in cases where the surviving spouse or civil partner is not entitled to the whole estate, ie in case of death on or after 1 December 1993, where the net value of the estate is over £125,000 or, in the case of death on or after 1 February 2009, where the net value of the estate is over £250,000 and consequently there will also be a life interest: thus the widow of the deceased cannot normally take a grant alone, although the court has a discretion where it is expedient in all the circumstances to appoint a sole administrator[1].

[1] See s 114(2) of the Supreme Court Act 1981, para A1.341.

Grant to children or other issue

Grant to children or other issue

6.170 Section 18(2) of the Family Law Reform Act 1987 provides:

Right to the grant **6.172**

(2) For the purposes of subsection (1) above and that Part of that Act, a person whose father and mother were not married to each other at the time of his birth shall be presumed not to have been survived by his father, or by any person related to him only through his father, unless the contrary is shown.

Accordingly when the intestate died on or after 4 April 1988 it does not matter as regards succession whether the parents of any child or other issue were married to each other at any time[1] and it is sufficient to refer to any such child as the 'son (daughter) of the intestate and only person (one of the persons) entitled to (share in) the estate' and any such other issue as the 'son (daughter) of C D the son (daughter) of the said deceased who died before the deceased and only person (one of the persons[2]) entitled to (share in) the estate'[2] or as the case may be.

[1] Family Law Reform Act 1987, s 18 (see para A1.431).
[2] Registrar's Direction (1988) 19 April.

6.170A In respect of an intestate dying on or after 1 April 2009 s 18 of the Family Law Reform Act 1987 is amended[1] so as to provide:

[(2A) In the case of a person who has a parent by virtue of section 43 of the Human Fertilisation and Embryology Act 2008 (treatment provided to woman who agrees that second woman to be parent), the second and third references in subsection (2) to the person's father are to be read as references to the woman who is a parent of the person by virtue of that section.]

[1] Human Fertilisation and Embryology Act 2008 (Commencement No 1 and Transitional Provisions) Order 2009, SI 2009/479, art 6(1)(d).

6.171 Under s 21 of the Family Law Reform Act 1987[1], for the purpose of determining the person or persons who would in accordance with probate rules be entitled to a grant of probate or administration in respect of the estate of a deceased person dying on or after 4 April 1988, the deceased is presumed, unless the contrary is shown, not to have been survived by any person related to him whose father and mother were not married to each other at the time of his birth or by any person whose relationship with him is deduced through a person whose father and mother were not married to each other at the time of his birth. In this context references to 'father' are to be treated as references to a woman who is a parent by virtue of s 43 of the Human Fertilisation and Embryology Act 2008. The applicant's title, as sworn to in the oath, will be taken as sufficient to rebut any such presumption[2].

[1] See para A1.434.
[2] Registrar's Direction (1988) 19 April.

6.172 Under s 27 of the Family Law Reform Act 1987, where, on or after 4 April 1988, a child is born in England and Wales as the result of the artificial insemination of a woman who was at the time of the insemination a party to a marriage (being a marriage which had not at that time been dissolved or annulled) and was artificially inseminated with the semen of some person other than the other party to the marriage, then, unless it is proved to the satisfaction of any court by which the matter has to be determined that the

6.172 *Letters of administration*

other party to that marriage did not consent to the insemination, the child is to be treated in law as the child of the parties to that marriage and is not to be treated as the child of any person other than the parties to that marriage[1]. The section does not affect the succession to any dignity or title of honour or render any person capable of succeeding to or transmitting a right to succeed to any such dignity or title[2].

See para 6.221A for a recent ruling on this subject.

[1] See para A1.439.
[2] Family Law Reform Act 1987, s 27(3), see para A1.439.

6.175 A child of an intestate who is subsequently adopted would appear to be divested of his interest in the estate by virtue of the adoption. (*See para 6.86 for the Law Commission's proposal to retain an adopted child's contingent right to the estate of an intestate.*)

Legitimated persons

Children of void marriages

6.221A Where both parties to a purported marriage were female and a child was born by artificial insemination to the 'wife' (C) the Court of Appeal held that the 'husband' (J) was not and never was the child's parent. C was not aware neither at the date of the 'marriage' nor at the date of birth of the child that J was not a male. The marriage had since been declared null and void. Subsequently J obtained recognition under the Gender Recognition Act 2004 that his gender was male and he also obtained a fresh birth certificate giving his sex at birth as male. However the court in applying the Family Law Reform Act 1987 ruled that at the date of the insemination s 28, Human Fertilization and Embryology Act 1990 was not effective. The fact that he had acted as the child's father did not as a matter of law enable him to claim the status of parenthood (*Re C (children) (parent: purported marriage between two women: artificial insemination by donor)* [2006] EWCA Civ 551, [2006] All ER (D) 216 (May)).

Adopted persons

Adoption and Children Act 2002

6.246 The 'Convention' means the Convention on Protection of Children and Co-operation in respect of Intercountry Adoption concluded at the Hague on 29 May 1993[1] and 'Convention adoption order' means an adoption order which, by virtue of regulations under section 1 of the Adoption (Intercountry Aspects) Act 1999 (c 18) (regulations giving effect to the Convention), is made as a Convention adoption order[1]. (For a current list of signatories to the Convention, see para 6.263.)

[1] Adoption and Children Act 2002, s 144(1): see para A1.512.

Grant to a creditor

Administration pending determination of a probate claim or ad colligenda bona

6.369 As to grants of administration pending determination of a probate claim and ad colligenda bona, see paras 11.348 ff and 11.365 ff.

REQUIREMENTS ON OBTAINING ADMINISTRATION

Description of applicant

Death on or after 5 April 1988

6.384 The following persons applying for administration are to be described as follows:

A husband as	'the lawful spouse'[1]
A wife as	'the lawful spouse'[1]
A civil partner as	'the lawful civil partner'[1]

Where the net estate, after allowing the permissible deductions, does not exceed £125,000[2]/£250,000[3] (or £200,000[2]/£450,000[3] if the deceased left no issue) the spouse or civil partner should be further described as 'the only person *now* entitled to the estate' or where it can be sworn that there are no issue nor parent nor brother nor sister of the whole blood nor issue of a brother or sister of the whole blood, the spouse is to be described as 'the only person entitled to the estate'. Applicants in other classes entitled to a grant of administration are described as set out in para 3.370.

[1] Section 46 Administration of Estates Act 1925 as amended with effect from 5 December 2005 by the Civil Partnership Act 2004, Sch 2, art 4.
[2] When the intestate died on or after 1 December 1993. For the relevant amounts for earlier dates of death, see para 6.39.
[3] When the deceased died on or after 1 February 2009.

6.385 Otherwise than as described in para 3.384 persons applying for administration, where the death occurred after 5 April 1988, are to be described as follows[1]:

6.385 *Letters of administration*

A husband	'the lawful husband'
A wife	'the lawful widow and relict (*or* (if she has remarried) the lawful relict)'. (Where the net estate, after allowing the permissible deductions, does not exceed £125,000/£250,000 (or £200,000/£450,000 if the deceased left no issue)[2] the husband or relict should be further described as 'the only person *now* entitled to the estate'. It is only where it can be sworn that there are no kin within the degrees mentioned in the tables in para 6.37 (no issue nor parent nor brother nor sister of the whole blood nor issue of a brother or sister of the whole blood), that the spouse can be described as 'the only person entitled to the estate'.
Issue of marriage *Note: A child or other issue who has acquired an alternative gender under the Gender Recognition Act 2004 at the death of the deceased is described as a child or issue in the acquired gender*	'the son (or daughter), and only person entitled to the estate'; or 'the son (or daughter), and one of the persons entitled to share in the estate'; 'the lawful adopted son *or* daughter' or 'the lawful legitimated son *or* daughter', as the case may be[3]. 'the grandson (or granddaughter), and only person entitled to the estate'; or 'the grandson (or granddaughter), and one of the persons entitled to share in the estate'[4]. (In the case of grandchildren or more remote issue, the oath should establish that the applicant has a beneficial interest, ie it should show either that the deceased died without child, or that the applicant is 'the [*or* lawful adopted *or* lawful legitimated] son (or daughter) of A. B., the [lawful] [*or* natural *or* lawful adopted *or* lawful legitimated] son (or daughter) of the said intestate, who died in the lifetime of the said intestate.')
A father or a mother	'the father (or mother), and only person entitled to the estate'; or 'the father (or mother), and one of the persons entitled to share in the estate.' *Note: a parent who has acquired an alternative gender under the Gender Recognition Act 2004 retains the original status as father or mother of the intestate.*

A brother or a sister	'the brother (or sister) of the whole blood, and only person entitled to the estate'; or 'the brother (or sister) of the whole blood, and one of the persons entitled to share in the estate'. *If there be no brother or sister of the whole blood, nor any issue of such brother or sister*, then the half blood is described as 'the brother (or sister) of the half blood, and' etc. Note: *a sibling who has acquired an alternative gender under the Gender Recognition Act 2004 at the death of death of the deceased is described as a sibling of the acquired gender.*
Issue of a brother or sister	'the nephew, or great-nephew (or niece), of the whole blood, and only person entitled to the estate'; or 'the nephew, or great-nephew (or niece), of the whole blood, and one of the persons entitled to share in the estate'. (The oath must also establish that the applicant has a beneficial interest, in a similar manner to that given under 'Issue of marriage', above.) *If there be no brother or sister of the whole blood, or any issue of such brother or sister*, then the half blood, if entitled to take a beneficial interest in the estate, is described as 'the nephew, or great-nephew (or niece), of the half blood, and' etc. Note: *a person in this class who has acquired an alternative gender under the Gender Recognition Act 2004 at the death of death of the deceased is described as of the acquired gender.*
A grandparent	'the grandfather (or grandmother), and only person entitled to the estate'; or 'the grandfather (or grandmother), and one of the persons entitled to share in the estate'. Note: *A person in this class who has acquired an alternative gender under the Gender Recognition Act 2004 at the date of death of the deceased is described as of the acquired gender.*
An uncle or an aunt	'the uncle (or aunt) of the whole blood, and only person entitled to the estate'; or 'the uncle (or aunt) of the whole blood, and one of the persons entitled to share in the estate'. *If there be no uncle or aunt (being brother or sister of the whole blood of a parent), or any issue of such uncle or aunt*, such person shall be described as 'the uncle (or aunt) of the half blood, and', etc. Note: *a person in this class who has acquired an alternative gender under the Gender Recognition Act 2004 at the death of death of the deceased is described as of the acquired gender.*

6.385 *Letters of administration*

Issue of an uncle or aunt	'the cousin german of the whole blood, and only person entitled to the estate'; or 'the cousin german of the whole blood, and one of the persons entitled to share in the estate'. (The oath must also establish that the applicant has a beneficial interest: see above.) *If there be no uncle or aunt (being brother or sister of the whole blood of a parent), or any issue of such uncle or aunt, such person shall be described as* 'the lawful cousin german of the half blood, and' etc.

1   Following President's Direction (1925) (Non-Contentious Probate).
2   The lower values are applicable when the intestate died on or after 1 December 1993 and the higher values apply when the deceased died on or after 1 February 2009. For the relevant amounts for earlier dates of death, see para 6.39.
3   As to a grant in the case of illegitimacy, adoption or legitimation, see paras 6.186 ff, 6.241 ff and 6.192 ff, respectively.
4   As to the practice under which, on the renunciation of the surviving spouse, the issue or other kin may apply as persons 'who may have a beneficial interest in the estate in the event of an accretion thereto', see para 6.108.

Deaths after 1925 but before 5 April 1988

6.386 Where the death occurred after 1925 but before 5 April 1988 the description of the applicant is given as follows:

A husband

A wife	'the lawful widow and relict (*or* (if she has remarried) the lawful relict)'. (Where the net estate, after allowing the permissible deductions, does not exceed £75,000 (or £125,000 if the deceased left no issue)[2] the husband or relict should be further described as 'the only person *now* entitled to the estate'. It is only where it can be sworn that there are no kin within the degrees mentioned in the tables in para 6.31 (no issue nor parent nor brother nor sister of the whole blood nor issue of a brother or sister of the whole blood), that the spouse can be described as 'the only person entitled to the estate'.

Requirements on obtaining administration **6.386**

Issue of marriage	'the lawful son (or daughter), and only person entitled to the estate'; or 'the son (or daughter), and one of the persons entitled to share in the estate'; 'the lawful adopted son *or* daughter' or 'the lawful legitimated son *or* daughter', as the case may be[3]. 'the lawful grandson (or granddaughter), and only person entitled to the estate'; or 'the lawful grandson (or granddaughter), and one of the persons entitled to share in the estate'[4]. (In the case of grandchildren or more remote issue, the oath should establish that the applicant has a beneficial interest, ie it should show either that the deceased died without child, or that the applicant is 'the [*or* lawful adopted *or* lawful legitimated] son (or daughter) of A. B., the [lawful] [*or* natural *or* lawful adopted *or* lawful legitimated] son (or daughter) of the said intestate, who died in the lifetime of the said intestate.')
A father or a mother	'the lawful [or natural] father (or mother), and only person entitled to the estate'; or 'the father [or natural] father (or mother), and one of the persons entitled to share in the estate.'
A brother or a sister	'the lawful brother (or sister) of the whole blood, and only person entitled to the estate'; or 'the lawful brother (or sister) of the whole blood, and one of the persons entitled to share in the estate'. *If there be no brother or sister of the whole blood, nor any issue of such brother or sister*, then the half blood is described as 'lawful the brother (or sister) of the half blood, and' etc.
Issue of a brother or sister	'the nephew, or great-nephew (or niece), of the whole blood, and only person entitled to the estate'; or 'the nephew, or great-nephew (or niece), of the whole blood, and one of the persons entitled to share in the estate'. (The oath must also establish that the applicant has a beneficial interest, in a similar manner to that given under 'Issue of marriage', above.) *If there be no brother or sister of the whole blood, or any issue of such brother or sister*, then the half blood, if entitled to take a beneficial interest in the estate, is described as 'the nephew, or great-nephew (or niece), of the half blood, and' etc.
A grandparent	'the grandfather (or grandmother), and only person entitled to the estate'; or 'the grandfather (or grandmother), and one of the persons entitled to share in the estate'.

6.386 *Letters of administration*

An uncle or an aunt	'the uncle (or aunt) of the whole blood, and only person entitled to the estate'; or 'the uncle (or aunt) of the whole blood, and one of the persons entitled to share in the estate'. *If there be no uncle or aunt (being brother or sister of the whole blood of a parent), or any issue of such uncle or aunt, such person shall be described as* 'the uncle (or aunt) of the half blood, and', etc.
Issue of an uncle or aunt	'the cousin german of the whole blood, and only person entitled to the estate'; or 'the cousin german of the whole blood, and one of the persons entitled to share in the estate'. (The oath must also establish that the applicant has a beneficial interest: see above.) *If there be no uncle or aunt (being brother or sister of the whole blood of a parent), or any issue of such uncle or aunt, such person shall be described as* 'the lawful cousin german of the half blood, and' etc.

[1] President's Direction (1925) (Non-Contentious Probate).
[2] When the intestate died on or after 1 December 1993. For the relevant amounts for earlier dates of death, see para 6.39.
[3] As to a grant in the case of illegitimacy, adoption or legitimation, see paras 6.186 ff, 6.241 ff and 6.192 ff, respectively.
[4] As to the practice under which, on the renunciation of the surviving spouse, the issue or other kin may apply as persons 'who may have a beneficial interest in the estate in the event of an accretion thereto', see para 6.108.
[5] As to grant to a natural parent, see paras 6.293 ff.

Chapter 7
MINORITY OR LIFE INTERESTS AND SECOND ADMINISTRATORS

WHEN DISTRICT JUDGE'S OR REGISTRAR'S ORDER NOT REQUIRED

7.22 Where the person entitled to the grant lacks capacity within the meaning of the Mental Capacity Act 2005 to manage his/her affairs and there is only one person competent and willing to take a grant for his use and benefit either under r 35(2)(a)—the person authorised by the Court of Protection—or, if there is no person so authorised, under r 35(2)(b)—the lawful attorney of the person who lacks capacity acting under a registered enduring power of attorney or registered lasting power of attorney—or, under r 35(2)(c)—where there is no such attorney entitled to act or if the attorney has renounced administration for the use and benefit of the person who lacks capacity, the person entitled to the residuary estate of the deceased; and a life or minority interest arises, then, unless the district judge or registrar otherwise directs, the person entitled to the grant under either r 35(2)(a) or r 35(2)(b) or r 35(2)(c) may nominate his co-administrator in accordance with r 35(3). For form of oath, see Nos 167–169[1], and for form of nomination, see No 63.

[1] As amended in Appendix VI to this Supplement.

7.23 If it is desired to join a person who does not qualify in one of these ways, application should be made to the district judge or registrar as set out in the preceding paragraph. NCPR 35(4), as amended, allows a district judge or registrar to appoint a person to obtain a grant for the use and benefit of a person who lacks capacity within the meaning of the Mental Capacity Act 2005 to manage his affairs, but this does not override the need for at least two applicants if a minority or life interest arises in the estate.

SURVIVING SPOUSE OR CIVIL PARTNER AND MINOR CHILDREN

7.25 In the case of an intestacy, where the deceased left a surviving spouse and children (all of whom are minors) entitled to share in the estate, if the surviving spouse is the parent of the minors with parental responsibility for them under s 2(1) of the Children Act 1989 and there is no other person or body mentioned in NCPR 32(2) with qualifying parental responsibility for any

7.25 Minority or life interests and second administrators

of them, the surviving spouse may nominate a fit person as co-administrator under NCPR 25(3)(a) and 32(3). The various persons or bodies mentioned in NCPR 32(2) are with the appropriate qualification defined in the rule: parent (including adoptive parent), a person in whose favour the court has made a residence order, step parent, a guardian, a special guardian, an adoption agency or a local authority (see also para 7.29). Equally, a surviving civil partner who is a lawful parent by adoption of a minor child of the deceased may in similar situation nominate a fit person a co-administrator. For form of oath see Form 92 and, for nomination, see No 62. The right to nominate is confined to cases where, for the purpose of a grant, a second administrator is required. It does not extend to cases in which the purpose is other than to facilitate compliance with s 114(2) of the Supreme Court Act 1981.

ONLY ONE CHILD ETC OF FULL AGE

7.28 Where the deceased has left no spouse or civil partner, but several children, of whom only one is of full age, an application without notice under NCPR 25(2), supported by affidavit, should be made to the district judge or registrar for the appointment of the proposed second administrator for the purpose of joining with the child of full age in taking the grant. The consent of the proposed co-administrator may be either exhibited to the affidavit or submitted separately with the affidavit. A person entitled to a grant in his own right will not be appointed on behalf of the minor to enable him to nominate a co-administrator[1].

[1] Registrar's Direction (1955) 7 November.

7.29 The practice given in this section is applicable also in cases where kin other than children of the deceased are beneficially entitled, but it should be particularly noted that:

(a) both parents of a minor child with parental responsibility for him are entitled to apply jointly for a grant on behalf of the child[1];
(b) where there is only one parent with parental responsibility competent and willing to take a grant, that parent may apply with a co-administrator[1];
(c) a step-parent who has acquired parental responsibility under s 4A of the Children Act 1989 may appoint a fit person as co-administrator[1];
(d) where the court has made a residence order in favour of a person that person may apply with a co-administrator[1];
(e) if a minor has a guardian with parental responsibility for him, such guardian has a right to a grant on behalf of the minor[1];
(f) a special guardian of the minor appointed in accordance with s 14A of the Children Act 1989 has a right to a grant on behalf of the minor[1];
(g) an adoption agency which has parental responsibility for a minor by virtue of s 25(2) of the Children Act 1989 has a right to grant on behalf of the minor[1];
(h) a local authority designated in a care order under s 33 of the Children Act 1989[1] may apply with a co-administrator if it is not applying as a trust corporation.

In other cases an application to a district judge or registrar may be necessary[2].

[1] NCPR 32(1) (as amended to include amendments consequential on the Adoption and Children Act 2002, Civil Partnership Act 2004 and the Human Fertilisation and Embryology Act 2008).
[2] NCPR 25(2).

ATTORNEY OF SPOUSE, AND A PERSON JOINED

7.35 Where the attorney of a husband or widow or civil partner of an intestate applies for a grant jointly with a person having a vested interest in the estate of the intestate, the grant is limited for the use and benefit of the donor of the power and until further representation be granted[1], thus the spouse's or civil partner's priority under NCPR 22 is preserved.

[1] Following the principle in *Re Rose* (1940) October.

Chapter 8
INLAND REVENUE ACCOUNTS

CHANGE OF NAME OF INLAND REVENUE TO HER MAJESTY'S REVENUE AND CUSTOMS

Royal Assent for the amalgamation of the Inland Revenue and Her Majesty's Customs and Excise was given on 7 April 2005 and Her Majesty's Revenue and Customs became a legal entity on 18 April 2005. Previous references to the Inland Revenue have been amended to Her Majesty's Revenue and Customs (HMRC) accordingly. The office dealing with inheritance tax and its predecessors, Capital Transfer Tax and Estate Duty, is now known as HMRC Inheritance Tax. The office addresses and telephone numbers remain unchanged.

Previously issued forms and accounts bearing the previous titles for the office will still be accepted.

NATIONAL PROBATE AND INHERITANCE TAX HELPLINE

A local rate number is now available for all probate and inheritance tax enquiries, which replaces the Capital Taxes Helpline numbers for Nottingham, Edinburgh and Belfast. The new number is 0845 30 20 900 and lines are open from 9.00 am to 5.00 pm, Monday to Friday. For information on Probate, visit the Court Service website: www.hmcourts-service.gov.uk. For information on inheritance tax, the new HMRC website may be found at www.hmrc.gov.uk/inheritancetax.

NECESSITY FOR ACCOUNT

8.01 Section 109 of the Senior Courts Act 1981 provides that, subject to arrangements made between the President of the Family Division and the Commissioners of Her Majesty's Revenue and Customs, the High Court shall not make any grant or reseal any grant except on production of an account receipted or certified by the Commissioners of Her Majesty's Revenue and Customs to show that inheritance tax or capital transfer tax payable on

Necessity for account **8.01B**

delivery of that account has been paid or that no tax is payable. New arrangements were introduced in late 1999 to provide that a Form IHT421 suitably completed and, if appropriate, receipted by HMRC Inheritance Tax, would be sufficient evidence to satisfy this necessity. The requirement to deliver an account to the Commissioners is provided by the Inheritance Tax Act 1984 (IHTA 1984), s 216[1].

The new Inland Revenue Account Form IHT400 and all completed appropriate supplementary pages should be sent to the HMRC Inheritance Tax, Ferrers House, PO Box 38, Castle Meadow Road, Nottingham, NG2 1BB *or* DX 701201 Nottingham 4. This office was formerly known as the IR Capital Taxes Office or the Capital Taxes Office and may be shown as such on some forms or accounts. The previous Form IHT200 will only be accepted until 9 June 2009, after which date only the Form IHT400 will be accepted by HMRC Inheritance Tax.

If no tax is payable *and* the deceased was domiciled in the United Kingdom, Form IHT421 should be sent to the Probate Registry at the same time.

[1] See para A1.570. The management and collection of inheritance tax, capital transfer tax and of the former British death duties are by statute vested in the Commissioners of Her Majesty's Revenue and Customs. The business relative to the tax and to these duties is transacted in a special office of Her Majesty's Revenue and Customs called HMRC Inheritance Tax, and enquiries concerning the tax and any of the duties in question should be addressed to the Director of that office at Ferrers House, PO Box 38, Castle Meadow Road, Nottingham, NG2 1BB, Document Exchange: DX 701201 Nottingham 4, Tel: 0845 30 20 900, Fax: 0115 9742432.

For some account of the pre-1894 duties payable to the ecclesiastical courts, see Ch II of Soward and Willan's *Taxation of Capital* (London, 1919).

A brief history of, and the practice relating to, the probate duty payable before 2 August 1894 will be found in earlier editions of this work. The appropriate forms of affidavit were form B where the gross estate did not exceed £300 and form A for all other cases.

The law and practice relating to estate duty will be found in the twenty-fourth edition of this work, while the transitional period between the introduction of capital transfer tax on 27 March 1974 and the abolition of estate duty on and after 13 March 1975 is covered by the second (cumulative) supplement to the twenty-fourth edition. Note: the rate at which interest accrues in respect of unpaid estate duty has been altered from time to time in uniformity with the rates of interest accruing on unpaid inheritance and capital transfer tax chargeable on death: see 'Assessment', paras 8.124 ff.

Solicitor applications

8.01A If tax is payable or the deceased was domiciled outside the United Kingdom, Form IHT421 and any appropriate Inheritance Tax payment should accompany the Form IHT400 to HMRC Inheritance Tax. If all is in order, the Form IHT421 will be authorised in HMRC Inheritance Tax and returned to the Solicitor. It should then be sent to the Probate Registry with any other necessary papers to enable a Grant to issue. The Form IHT 400 will be retained by HMRC Inheritance Tax.

Personal applications

8.01B If tax is payable or the deceased was domiciled outside the United Kingdom, Form IHT421 should firstly be sent with the other necessary papers

8.01B *Inland Revenue accounts*

to the Probate Registry. The Probate Registry will return Form IHT421 with the address of the Registry filled in, with the appointment letter for an interview to the applicant. Form IHT422 should be sent to HMRC Inheritance Tax to obtain a reference and an IHT payslip at least two weeks prior to the submission of Form IHT400. Form IHT400, all the supplementary pages including Form IHT421 and any documents requested should then be sent to HMRC Inheritance Tax. (If the applicant has calculated the tax, the appropriate payment should also be sent in a separate envelope with the reference number and payslip obtained under the IHT422 procedure. If, however, the applicant wishes HMRC Inheritance Tax to calculate the tax, a calculation will then be sent to the applicant.) If payment is to be made by way of the Direct Payment Scheme, Form IHT423 should be sent to the bank or building society at the same time as the submission of the Form IHT400. Once payment is received and all is in order, HMRC Inheritance Tax will complete its part of the Form IHT421 and send it direct to the Probate Registry. The Probate Registry will normally issue the Grant within 10 days of the interview. The Form IHT400 will be retained by HMRC Inheritance Tax. Form IHT400 Calculation should also be submitted if the simple Inheritance Tax calculation on page 11 of the account cannot be used.

8.02 Section 256(1) of the IHTA 1984 (formerly Capital Transfer Tax), which consolidated the Finance Act 1980, s 94(1), empowers the Commissioners of Her Majesty's Revenue and Customs to make regulations inter alia to dispense with this requirement. In pursuance of that power the Capital Transfer Tax (Delivery of Accounts) Regulations 1981[1] as amended[2] provide the concept of the 'excepted estate'.

A revised version of the Form IHT205 is now available in respect of deaths on or after 1 September 2006, known as IHT205[2006]. As with previous versions, the new form covers estates where the deceased had their main home in the United Kingdom and the gross value of their estate was below the appropriate inheritance tax excepted estate limit, or the gross value of the estate was below £1,000,000 and no tax is payable due to spouse, civil partner or charity exemption only. It is important that joint assets passing by survivorship, whether to a spouse, a civil partner or otherwise should be included in the appropriate box. However, there are new questions regarding benefits under a registered pension scheme and also where the deceased was a member of a pension scheme or had a personal pension policy from which, in either case, they had not taken their full retirement benefits before the date of death. These additional questions are as a result of the additional charging provisions contained in s 160 and Sch 22 to the Finance Act 2006. The forms may be completed on screen or printed and subsequently filled in by referring to http://www.hmrc.gov.uk/inheritancetax/iht-probate-forms. An instruction booklet IHT206 (2006) is also available on this website.

The earlier versions of Form IHT205 remain appropriate for deaths prior to 1 September 2005.

For deaths on or after 6 April 2004, the overall cash limit for the previous category of excepted estates is brought in line with the contemporaneous inheritance tax threshold, currently £300,000 (£263,000 as at the date of change on 6 April 2004). The limits for foreign assets, simple lifetime transfers and settled property remain at the 2002 limits.

For deaths on or after 6 April 2003 and before 6 April 2004, the excepted estate gross value limit to fall within the procedures is £240,000. This increase was authorised by SI 2003/1688. The limits for foreign assets, simple lifetime transfers and settled property remain at the 2002 limits.

For deaths on or after 6 April 2002, for a person domiciled in the United Kingdom, the excepted estate gross value limit is £220,000. From that date for the excepted estate procedures to apply, the value of that person's estate must be attributable wholly to property passing under his will or intestacy, or under a nomination of an asset taking effect on his death, or by survivorship in a beneficial joint tenancy or, in Scotland, by survivorship, or additionally under a single settlement in which he was entitled to an interest in possession. Of that property, not more than £100,000 represented value attributable to property which, immediately before that person's death, was settled property, and not more than £75,000 represented value attributable to property which was situate outside the United Kingdom. Also, that person died without having made any chargeable transfers during the period of seven years ending with his death other than specified transfers where the aggregate value transferred did not exceed £100,000. These specified transfers mean cash, quoted shares and securities or an interest in or over land (and furnishings and chattels disposed of at the same time to the same donee and intended to be enjoyed with the land) save to the extent that either ss 102 or 102A(2) of the Finance Act 1986 apply to that transfer or the land (or furnishings or chattels) became settled property on that transfer.

A new category of excepted estate is introduced for deaths on or after 6 April 2004 where the gross value of the estate does not exceed £1m and the net chargeable value, after deduction of liabilities, spouse and/or charity exemption or exemption for a gift for National purposes, does not exceed the inheritance tax threshold. No other exemption or relief can be taken into account for this purpose.

Additionally, the following provisions apply for deaths on or after 6 April 2002 for a person who was never domiciled in the United Kingdom or treated as domiciled in the United Kingdom by virtue of s 267(1) of the 1984 Act. If the value of that person's estate situate in the United Kingdom is wholly attributable to cash or quoted shares or securities passing under his will or intestacy, or by survivorship in a beneficial joint tenancy or, in Scotland, by survivorship, and the gross value of which does not exceed £100,000, the excepted estate provisions also apply.

SI 2002/1733 refers in respect of deaths on or after 6 April 2002.

The provisions of the third category of excepted estate, where the deceased was never domiciled or treated as domiciled in the United Kingdom, remain at the levels appropriate from 2002.

8.02 *Inland Revenue accounts*

The provisions of SI 2002/1733 and SI 2003/1688 are revoked in relation to persons who died on or after 6 April 2004.

Every application for a grant/confirmation where the deceased died on or after 6 April 2004 must now be accompanied by basic information about the estate. In England and Wales and Northern Ireland, this means that every application must be accompanied by a revised Form IHT205. In Scotland, the Inventory must be accompanied by form C5. The appropriate form must be produced to the Board (in accordance with the regulations) by producing it to:

(a) a probate registry in England and Wales;
(b) the sheriff in Scotland;
(c) the Probate and Matrimonial Office in Northern Ireland.

These changes were authorised by SI 2004/2543.

For deaths on or after 6 April 2001, to qualify as an excepted estate, the following limits apply. Earlier figures are provided in the footnotes.

— the total gross value of the estate[3] does not exceed £210,000[4];
— the estate comprises only property which passes by will or intestacy, by nomination, or by survivorship in joint tenancy;
— not more than £50,000[5] consists of property situated outside the United Kingdom; and
— the deceased died domiciled in the United Kingdom having made simple lifetime transfers such as cash or quoted securities not exceeding £75,000;

then the estate is an excepted estate and applicants for a grant of representation are not required to deliver an account or to swear to the exact value of the estate to obtain a grant. Instead they are required to swear in the oath as to the limits within which the estate falls. For the purposes of these limits, it is the value of the deceased's beneficial interest, and not the entirety value, of survivorship property which falls to be taken into account. It should be noted that an estate would not be an excepted estate if the deceased had an interest in settled property or had made lifetime transfers which became chargeable with tax by reason or his or her death within seven years thereafter, or (on or after 18 March 1986) had gifted property subject to a reservation which subsisted up to, or within seven years before, the date of death.

[1] SI 1981/880, which came into operation on 1 August 1981.
[2] Capital Transfer Tax (Delivery of Accounts) (No 3) Regulations 1983, SI 1983/1039 with effect from 1 April 1983; and Inheritance Tax (Delivery of Accounts) Regulations 1987, SI 1987/1127 with effect from 1 April 1987, SI 1989/1078 with effect from 1 April 1989, SI 1990/1110 with effect from 1 April 1990, SI 1991/1248 with effect from 1 April 1991, SI 1995/1461 with effect from 6 April 1995, SI 1996/1470 with effect from 6 April 1996, SI 1998/1431 with effect from 6 April 1998 and SI 2000/967 with effect from 6 April 2000.
[3] Estate for this purpose has the extended meaning as for inheritance tax and capital transfer tax.
[4] £200,000 in the case of a death before 6 April 2000; £180,000 in the case of a death before 6 April 1998; £145,000 in the case of a death before 6 April 1996; £125,000 in the case of a death before 6 April 1995; £115,000 in the case of a death before 1 April 1991;

£100,000 in the case of a death before 1 April 1990; £70,000 in the case of a death before 1 April 1989; £40,000 in the case of a death before 1 April 1987; £25,000 in the case of a death before 1 April 1983.
5   £30,000 in the case of a death before 6 April 1998; £15,000 in the case of a death before 6 April 1996; £10,000 in the case of a death before 1 April 1989; £2,000 in the case of a death before 1 April 1987; £1,000 in the case of a death before 1 April 1983.

8.03 The foregoing procedure may be used in any case where the criterion of an excepted estate is wholly met—not only in the case of first grants which are not limited in nature but also in cases, for example, of applications for grants de bonis non or where a fresh grant is to be made following revocation of an original grant. The Commissioners of Her Majesty's Revenue and Customs retain the right to call for an account by giving notice in writing within 35 days of the date of issue of the first grant other than a limited grant. If a person, having obtained a grant without delivery of an account, later discovers that the estate is not in fact an excepted estate he or she must deliver an account of all the property comprised in the estate within six months of making that discovery. Please note the amendments contained under para 8.34 below regarding interim and second grants.

Scope of the tax

8.06 The efficacy of the tax depends upon a tree of concepts at the root of which is the—undefined—'disposition'. A liability for tax becomes a possibility if a disposition is a 'transfer of value': that is to say it is made by a person and, as a result, the estate of that person is less than it otherwise would have been[1]. The amount by which the value of the estate is so decreased is known as the 'value transferred'[2]. Most dispositions are transfers of value but some are specifically provided not to be[3]. Moreover no account is taken of 'excluded property'[4]. If a transfer of value is made by an individual (as distinct from a person) and is not an 'exempt transfer'[5] or a potentially exempt transfer[6] then it is a 'chargeable transfer' and tax is chargeable[7] upon the value transferred[8]. The 'exempt transfer' needs no elaboration here; but a 'potentially exempt transfer' would become a chargeable transfer upon the death of the transferor within seven years thereafter.

As a result of the changes introduced by s 156 and Sch 20 to the Finance Act 2006, for lifetime transfers made on or after 22 March 2006, a transfer of value will only qualify as a potentially exempt transfer (PET) when it is a transfer to:

(a)   another individual;
(b)   a disabled trust; or
(c)   a bereaved minor's trust on the coming to an end of an immediate post death interest.

With effect from 22 March 2006, all transfers into interest in possession trusts or accumulation and maintenance trusts are no longer regarded as potentially exempt transfers and are immediately chargeable to tax. The only exception to this rule is where the transfer is the payment of a life insurance premium and

8.06 Inland Revenue accounts

the policy was held on interest in possession or accumulation and maintenance trusts which commenced prior to 22 March 2006. Payments of premiums in these circumstances retain their PET treatment (Inheritance Tax Act 1984, ss 46A and 46B).

Where the lifetime transfer is made to an interest in possession or accumulation and maintenance trust created before 22 March 2006, if the trust is not one of the categories above that allow the transfer to qualify for PET treatment, the transfer will be immediately chargeable and tax will be charged as appropriate.

The trust will then contain property that is subject to the original interest in possession or accumulation and maintenance trusts and 'relevant property' that will be subject to ten-year and exit charges.

1   See fn 3 to para 8.02 as to the meaning of 'estate'.
2   IHTA 1984, s 3(1) (FA 1975, s 20(2)).
3   IHTA 1984, ss 10–17 (eg FA 1975, ss 20(4) and 46; FA 1976, ss 89–92).
4   IHTA 1984, s 3(2) (FA 1975, s 20(3)) (see eg IHTA 1984, s 6 (FA 1975, s 24(2) and Sch 7, paras 3(1), 5(1) and 6)).
5   IHTA 1984, ss 18 ff (eg FA 1975, Sch 6).
6   IHTA 1984, s 3A in relation to events on and after 18 March 1986.
7   IHTA 1984, s 2 (FA 1975, s 20).
8   IHTA 1984, s 1 (FA 1975, s 19) (see para A1.557).

8.09 For the purposes of the tax a person's estate is the aggregate of all the property to which he or she is beneficially entitled, except that the estate immediately before death does not include excluded property[1]. It is to be noted that the word 'property' is not limited in any way and is apt to cover both real and personal property, movable and immovable property wherever situate. Similarly, the phrase 'On the death of any person'[2] is wide enough to extend to persons wherever domiciled. However, property outside the United Kingdom is excluded property if the person beneficially entitled to it is domiciled outside the United Kingdom[3]. Excluded property also includes a reversionary interest, unless it was acquired by the deceased (or by a person previously entitled to it) for a consideration in money or money's worth. There are other exceptions[4] but generally speaking inherited reversions are excluded property unless purchased by a predecessor in title.

1   IHTA 1984, s 5(1) (FA 1975, s 23(1)) (para A1.595).
2   IHTA 1984, s 4(1) (FA 1975, s 22(1)).
3   IHTA 1984, s 6(1) (FA 1975, s 24(2)) (para A1.595). The general law of domicile is considered in Ch 12—but there are provisions for 'deeming' a person to be domiciled in the United Kingdom for the purposes of the tax.
4   IHTA 1984, s 48 (FA 1975, s 24(3), FA 1976, s 120, FA 1981, s 104(3)) (para A1.598) and FA 2006, s 157.

8.10 Besides excluded property certain other categories of property are removed from the ambit of the tax. So, for example, growing timber (in certain prescribed circumstances) is to be 'left out of account'[1], and no account shall be taken of any value attributable to the fact that cottages occupied by persons employed solely for agricultural purposes are suitable for the residential purposes of persons not so employed[2]; whilst the charge to tax on death under s 4 of the 1984 Act (FA 1975, s 22) is specifically not to apply in relation to the death of a person who was, broadly speaking, killed in a war[3] and the Act is not to apply at all as respects Apsley House and the Chevening Estate[4]. And there is other such miscellany.

[1] IHTA 1984, s 125 (FA 1975, Sch 9) and see under the sub-heading of 'Reliefs', paras 8.76 ff.
[2] IHTA 1984, s 169 (FA 1975, Sch 10, para 12(1)).
[3] IHTA 1984, s 154 (FA 1975, Sch 7, para 1).
[4] IHTA 1984, s 156 (FA 1981, s 135 and FA 1982, s 100).

8.11 On the other hand, a person is to be treated as beneficially entitled to settled property in which he or she has a beneficial interest in possession[1], and to property over which he or she has a general power of disposition and money which he or she may charge on property, in each case other than settled property. But there is one exception to this exclusion in relation to 'approved' superannuation schemes[2] so that, for example, a death benefit subject to an unexercised or revocable exercised power of nomination forms a part of the deceased's estate. For deaths on or after 6 April 2006, s 160 and Sch 22 to the Finance Act 2006 provide an inheritance tax charge on the death over the age of 75 of a pension scheme member on any assets remaining in the fund that has been used to provide him or her with an Alternatively Secured Pension. Also, a dependant relative who had inherited such a pension fund from a member over 75 is also subject to a charge when the benefit ceases, normally on the survivor's death. Additionally, a person is treated as beneficially entitled to any property being the subject of a 'gift with reservation' if the reservation concerned is still subsisting immediately before his or her death[3]. (A gift with reservation is, broadly speaking, a disposal by way of gift on or after 18 March 1986 which is to any extent subject to a reservation in favour of the donor.)

A person is treated as beneficially entitled:

(a) to settled property in which they have a beneficial interest in[4], except for certain interests under pension schemes[5], or trusts for the benefit of employees under s 86 of the IHTA 1984. For property where the interest in possession began on or after 22 March 2006, s 49(1) only applies to interests in possession where the interest is an immediate post-death interest, disabled person's interest or a transitional serial interest. Further details are provided below;
(b) to a direct interest in the whole (or an appropriate part) of the net assets of an unadministered residuary estate in which they have a beneficial interest;
(c) to unsettled property over which they have a general power[6], except for certain interests under cash options under pension schemes[7], the scope of s 5(2) is extended to settled property in relation to interests under a registered pension scheme[8].
(d) on their death, to gift with reservation property then subject to a reservation[9]. The scope of s 102 of the Finance Act 1986 is extended to interests in possession to which s 49(1) of the IHTA 1984 applies that come to an end on or after 22 March 2006.

8.11 *Inland Revenue accounts*

For deaths before 22 March 2006, the first sentence in (a) above and in para 8.09 remain appropriate. That is to say, a person is to be treated as beneficially entitled to settled property in which he or she has a beneficial interest in possession, and to the property over which he or she has a general power of disposition and money which he or she may charge on property, in each case other than settled property. Accordingly, such property will be aggregated with all other property to which they were beneficially entitled as at their date of death.

However, with effect from 22 March 2006, the inheritance tax treatment of settled property changed in certain specific circumstances which will become more common with the passage of time from that date.

From that date, where a deceased (or transferor) became entitled to an interest in possession on or after 22 March 2006, s 49(1A) of the IHTA 1984 now limits the extent to which a person entitled to an interest in possession is treated as beneficially entitled to the property in which the interest subsists to:

– an immediate post-death interest;
– a disabled person's interest; or
– a transitional serial interest.

Unless a trust qualifies as one of the above interests and the settled property in which the deceased had an interest in possession will accordingly be treated as part of their estate, it will be a relevant property trust and subject to both ten-yearly and exit charges.

An immediate post-death interest[10] is one where:

(i) the settlement was created by will or under intestacy;
(ii) the life tenant became beneficially entitled to the interest in possession on the death of the testator; and
(iii) the settlement is not a bereaved minor's or age 18–25 trust and has never been so since the life tenant became beneficially entitled to the interest in possession.

A disabled person's interest is an interest in possession in settled property to which a person is treated as being beneficially entitled under the existing provisions of s 89(2) of IHTA 1984 and the new provisions of s 89A(4). This latter provision is where a person beneficially entitled to property puts it into a settlement on themselves on or after 22 March 2006 and that person is suffering from a condition that is likely to result in them becoming disabled.

A transitional serial interest[11] is an interest that arises under one of three sets of circumstances. The circumstances are as follows:

(1) Transitional period to 6 April 2008 (IHTA 1984, s 49A):
    (a) the settlement commenced before 22 March 2006;
    (b) immediately before that date, the individual or another person had an interest in possession in the settlement;
    (c) that interest came to an end after 22 March 2006 but before 6 April 2008;

####### Necessity for account 8.11

(d) the individual became beneficially entitled to their interest at this time; and
(e) the settlement is not a bereaved minor's or age 18–25 trust.
(2) Marriage settlements (IHTA 1984, s 49D):
(a) the settlement commenced before 22 March 2006;
(b) immediately before that date the individual's spouse or civil partner had an interest in possession in the settlement;
(c) that interest came to an end on the death of the spouse or civil partner on or after 6 April 2008;
(d) the individual became beneficially entitled to their interest at this time; and
(e) the settlement is not a bereaved minor's or age 18–25 trust.
(3) Life insurance trusts (IHTA 1984, s 49E):
(a) the settlement commenced before 22 March 2006;
(b) immediately before that date, the deceased or another person had an interest in possession in the settlement;
(c) immediately before that date, the settled property consisted of, or included, a contract of life insurance;
(d) that interest came to an end on the death of another person on or before 6 April 2008 (or a succession of interests have come to an end, all on the death of the person concerned and the first death occurred on or after 6 April 2008);
(e) the deceased became beneficially entitled to their interest at this time;
(f) the rights under the contract were comprised in the settlement throughout the period beginning with 22 March 2006 to the date the deceased became entitled to their interest in possession;
(g) the settlement is not a bereaved minor's or age 18–25 trust.

A bereaved minor[12] is a person who has not yet reached the age of 18 and at least one of their parents (or step-parent) has died.

A trust for a bereaved minor[13] is a trust set up under the will or intestacy of a minor's parent (or step-parent) where the bereaved minor will alone receive absolute ownership of the settled property on or before their 18th birthday (including any income accumulated up to that point).

An age 18–25 trust[14] is a trust set up under the will or intestacy of a minor's parent (or step-parent) where the bereaved minor will alone receive absolute ownership of the settled property on or before their 25th birthday. Certain accumulation and maintenance trusts created before 22 March 2006 can also be age 18–25 trusts.

Changes introduced by the Finance Act 2007 provide that all charges arising under ss 151A to 151C are now 'top-slice' charges. This ensures that the nil-rate band is used in priority against the remainder of the estate passing on death first and where a charge does arise on left-over alternatively secured pension funds, this can be settled without reference to the remainder of the estate. Additionally, in order to accommodate the interaction of inheritance tax and the income tax resulting from unauthorised payment pension charges

8.11 *Inland Revenue accounts*

being introduced, where the alternatively secured pension funds on the death of a scheme member are transferred to other scheme members, the inheritance tax charge will now take account of any such income tax that has already been paid before the inheritance tax charge arises.

The Finance Act 2007 also introduced specific provisions for dealing with left-over pension pots on the death of scheme members who were aged over 75 before they were traced by the scheme provider. Any left-over funds on the death of such a scheme member are brought within the inheritance tax framework, but the reporting requirements are altered so that the scheme administrators have six months from the end of the month in which they discovered the scheme member's death to file their return.

The definition of excluded property has also been amended, in this instance by s 157 of the Finance Act 2006. Additionally, with effect from 5 December 2005, settled property situated outside the United Kingdom is not excluded property by virtue of s 48(3) or 48(3A) of the IHTA 1984 if:

(a) a person is, or has been, beneficially entitled to an interest in possession in the property at any time;
(b) the person is, or was, at that time an individual domiciled in the United Kingdom (the deemed domicile rules under s 267 of the IHTA 1984 also apply for this purpose); and
(c) the entitlement arose directly or indirectly as a result of a disposition made on or after 5 December 2005 for a consideration in money or money's worth.

It is immaterial whether the consideration was given by the person or by anyone else. Also, the occasions in which an entitlement arose indirectly as a result of a disposition include any case where the entitlement arose under a will or the law relating to intestacy.

[1] IHTA 1984, s 49(1) (FA 1975, Sch 5, para 3(1)). This means broadly a present right of present enjoyment of the property or the income, if any, produced by it. (In *Pearson v IRC* [1981] AC 753, [1980] 2 All ER 479, HL, it was held that where the trustees of a settlement have a valid power to accumulate income the beneficiaries entitled in default of exercise of that power are nevertheless prevented from having an interest in possession in the settled property for the purposes of the tax.)
[2] IHTA 1984, s 151(4) (FA 1975, Sch 5, para 16(4)).
[3] FA 1986, s 102(3) (para A1.580).
[4] IHTA 1984, s 49(1).
[5] IHTA, s 151(2) and (3)).
[6] IHTA 1984, s 5(2)).
[7] IHTA 1984, s 152).
[8] IHTA 1984, s 151(4).
[9] Finance Act 1986, s 102(3).
[10] IHTA 1984, s 49A.
[11] IHTA 1984, s 49B.
[12] IHTA 1984, s 71C.
[13] IHTA 1984, s 71A.
[14] IHTA 1984, s 71D.

Rates of tax

8.13 Tax is chargeable if the total for rate exceeds the contemporary threshold, presently £312,000. The total for rate is found by aggregating the value transferred by the instant transfer with the cumulative total of the values transferred by any chargeable transfers made by the transferor within the previous seven years[1]. This does not involve a series of fixed seven-year periods but a moving seven-year cumulation period from which successive transfers fall away as time passes. The rate of tax chargeable can be summarised as follows:

(a) For deaths on and after 15 March 1988 the rate of tax on values in excess of the contemporary threshold is 40% but there is a taper relief in the form of a percentage reduction in the tax payable in respect of any chargeable transfer which occurred more than three years but less than seven years before the date of death[2]. If the transfer was a chargeable transfer immediately (as distinct from being a potentially exempt transfer) then any tax paid at that time is allowed as a credit against the tax payable in connection with the death. (A chargeable transfer made before 18 March 1986, however, is chargeble at the death rate only if made within three years before the transferor's death.)

(b) For deaths before 15 March 1988 but on or after 18 March 1986 the position is at (a) save that in place of the flat rate of 40% there was a progressively banded table of rates[3].

(c) For deaths before 18 March 1986 but on or after 10 March 1981 the cumulation period was ten years. There were two rate tables and tax in respect of the deceased's estate and any chargeable transfers made within three years before the death were charged according to the first table[4]. All other lifetime chargeable transfers were chargeable according to the second table. Any tax paid under the second table was allowed as a credit pro tanto against tax payable by reason of the transferor's death within three years after the transfer.

(d) For deaths before 10 March 1981 but on or after 13 March 1975 the position was as at (c) save that instead of a moving cumulation period of ten years there was a fixed period which commenced on 27 March 1974.

(e) Under the provisions of s 10 and Sch 4 to the Finance Act 2008, the transfer of any unused nil rate band of the estate of a spouse or civil partner who died before the deceased (the deceased must have died on or after 9 October 2007) may be made subject to the completion of the claim Form IHT402. The deceased's nil rate band is increased by the percentage of the nil rate band that was unused when his or her spouse or civil partner died. More detailed instructions are incorporated in the notes section on Form IHT402.

[1] IHTA 1984, s 7 as amended by the FA 1986, s 101(1) and Sch 19, para 2 [FA 1975, s 37 as amended by the FA 1981, s 93(1)].
[2] IHTA 1984, s 7 as amended by the FA 1986, Sch 19, para 2.
[3] See Appendix IV, para A4.01.
[4] See Appendix IV, para A4.01.

Grants for provisional amounts only

8.18 It is only in the most exceptional cases that any relaxation of the above rule is conceded and a grant is allowed to issue showing property only 'so far

8.18 *Inland Revenue accounts*

as can at present be ascertained'. But where any particular case is so circumstanced as, in the opinion of the parties, to render it imperative that the grant should issue before full particulars of the deceased's estate can be ascertained, the facts should, in the first instance, be laid before the Director of HMRC Inheritance Tax with an Inland Revenue Account IHT400, as a Form IHT421 disclosing the estate at a provisional figure only will not be accepted by the probate registrars in the absence of the concurrence of the Commissioners of Her Majesty's Revenue and Customs. Such concurrence, as mentioned above, is only given in cases of the most exceptional or urgent type. In such cases the applicant for the grant is required to include their best possible estimate, after making full enquiries, of all taxable property wherever situate and not a *nominal* amount. It is not necessary in any such case to give an undertaking to pay any additional fees which may become due to the Registry.

Exceptions

(3) Property on which tax may be paid by instalments ('Instalment-option property')

8.23 Inheritance Tax accounts provide for the written election to pay tax in instalments to be exercised. It is understood that the Board of Her Majesty's Revenue and Customs will accept payment of tax in full notwithstanding an election to pay by instalments. But it is understood too that if the election is not so exercised and tax is paid in full the option will be spent—so that it will not be possible to obtain a refund of tax paid and switch to payment in instalments. Such a failure to exercise the option to pay in instalments can have unwelcome consequences: certain categories of instalment option property carry interest on tax only from the date the instalment concerned becomes due[1]; and so were such property to be sold during the instalment period, and the option to pay in instalments had not been exercised, interest would be payable on the whole amount of the tax from its due date rather than upon so many of the instalments as might by then have become due.

[1] IHTA 1984, s 234 [FA 1975, Sch 4, para 16].

GRANTS ON CREDIT

Practice as to grants on credit

8.24 The Commissioners of Her Majesty's Revenue and Customs may allow the applicant to postpone the payment of tax on such terms as they think fit where excessive sacrifice would be caused by raising the full tax at once rather than later. In view of the facilities normally available for raising tax, the Commissioners of Her Majesty's Revenue and Customs use these powers sparingly and only after and to the extent that they are fully satisfied that every effort short of excessive sacrifice has been made to raise the tax due. The relief is not given merely because some sacrifice can be shown; the sacrifice envisaged is excessive and must in fact be greater than is customary or normal in prevailing conditions. In such cases application should be made to the Director of HMRC Inheritance Tax. The applicant should give full details of the estate, preferably by way of the Inland Revenue account, relate the steps taken and the difficulties encountered in attempting to raise the tax due, and state the maximum amount raisable irrespective of any sacrifice entailed, preferably in the form of a letter from the bank or other source approached. Should the Commissioners of Her Majesty's Revenue and Customs be willing to postpone the payment of all or part of the tax they will normally require an undertaking as to payment of, and the provision of security for, any postponed tax. Specific proposals for payment within a reasonable time, showing how it is intended to raise the tax, should be made in the application. The availability of the grant obtained after the Commissioners of Her Majesty's Revenue and Customs have exercised their powers of postponement is not usually restricted, at any rate while any undertaking as to payment is duly observed and any security taken remains adequate.

Arrangements are now available for the taxpayer to pay their inheritance tax by the Inheritance Tax Direct Payment Scheme. Under this scheme, participating institutions such as banks and building societies will, on receipt of instructions from the personal representatives, transfer money electronically to HMRC. Further details are provided at para 8.133.

CURRENT FORMS

8.25 Although the forms detailed below may still be accepted by the HMRC Inheritance Tax until 9 June 2009, with the exception of forms IHT205 and Cap A5C these have all been replaced by a new Form IHT400. This account form is a 16-page version with supplementary schedules to be attached as necessary covering the will, gifts, joint and nominated assets, pensions, stocks and shares, life insurance and annuities, household and personal goods, land buildings and interests in land, additional information and a probate summary. The new Form IHT400 encompasses United Kingdom domicile, foreign domicile and sub-threshold estates. For deaths on or after 18 March 1986, the new Form IHT400 replaces all previous references to IHT200, IHT201 and IHT202 in their various applications.

In addition to obtaining forms from HMRC Inheritance Tax by post or by telephone (Tel: 0845 30 20 900), forms may also be obtained via the website (www.inlandrevenue.gov.uk/inheritancetax).

Forms of account	Grants for which applicable
IHT200	Original grant regardless of where the deceased was domiciled including sub-threshold estates
IHT200 (1993)	Original grant where the deceased died domiciled in some part of the United Kingdom
IHT201 (1993)	Original grant where the deceased died domiciled outside the United Kingdom
IHT200	Predecessor of IHT200 (1993). Still acceptable for use

8.26 *Inland Revenue accounts*

Forms of account	*Grants for which applicable*
IHT201	Predecessor of IHT201 (1993). Still acceptable for use
IHT202 (1993)	Original grant where the deceased died domiciled in the United Kingdom and the whole of the estate was situate in the United Kingdom, the deceased had not made any chargeable transfers within 7 years of death and had no interest in settled property, the net estate after exemptions and reliefs does not exceed the inheritance tax threshold at death and the gross estate before exemptions and reliefs does not exceed twice the threshold. [Note: An instructional booklet IHT 210 is available in respect of the above accounts.]
IHT204	For completion at the request of Her Majesty's Revenue and Customs following the issue of an 'excepted estate' grant
Cap A5C	De bonis non, double probate and cessate grants

Form IHT400

8.26 This form is designed to disclose (1) the full name and description of the deceased, together with the dates of birth and death and where it is claimed he or she was domiciled; (2) the full name, address and description of the applicant for the grant; and (3) particulars of the property to be covered by the grant. It then makes provision for the deponent to certify the correctness of the accompanying schedules of the property in respect of which tax is payable (or would be payable if tax were payable on estates however small their principal value) and of its value; and of the schedules of the debts and incumbrances which are deductible in arriving at the amounts, if any, chargeable with tax.

8.27 Any limitation to the grant (or reseal) for which application is made must be indicated in the declaration on page 8 of the IHT400. Details of the boxes of the IHT400 which need to be completed in such circumstances are detailed on pages 4 to 6 of the IHT400 Notes. Examples of relevant limitations are:

(a) pending suit or ad colligenda bona;
(b) limited to prosecuting or defending a specified action;
(c) limited to, or excluding, a particular part of, or type of estate; such as, realty; personalty; immovable; movable; literary estate; estate in Wales; settled land; or exclusive of settled land.

8.28 In the case of an application for a grant of administration *with will* this should be expressly stated in the declaration on page 12 at box 119. No reference to codicils to be proved with a will is necessary.

8.29 With the abolition of resealing as between the constituent countries of the United Kingdom by the Administration of Estates Act 1971[1], applications for grants in respect of the estates of persons dying domiciled in any part of the United Kingdom should be made in the country of domicile. The application should be made for a grant covering the assets in all parts of the United Kingdom. Thus in the case of a person dying domiciled in England and Wales, a grant of representation from the High Court in that part of the United Kingdom by reference to an Inheritance Tax account Form IHT400 will be recognised throughout the United Kingdom of England and Wales, Scotland and Northern Ireland without the necessity for resealing.

[1] See para A1.224.

8.31 Where the deceased has died domiciled in Northern Ireland and no grant of representation has been obtained there, a separate grant may still be extracted in Great Britain limited to that part of Great Britain where application is made[1]. In such a case a separate Inland Revenue account must be delivered to HMRC Inheritance Tax, Belfast.

[1] See Ch 12—Grant where deceased died domiciled out of England and Wales.

Settled land[1]

8.32 If the grant is only required for land which was settled before the death and continues to be settled thereafter, the declaration on page 12 at box 119 should state 'limited to the settled land of which true particulars and value are given'. Schedule IHT418 should not be completed, but Schedule IHT405 should be used instead.

[1] See Ch 10.

No estate (other than trust property)

8.33 IHT400 is also appropriate in the case of a person who left no estate in the jurisdiction (other than property of which he was a trustee only). Boxes 1 to 22 and the declaration on pages 12 and 13 only of the form need to be completed. This applies both to cases where a grant is required in order to deal with trust property, and also to other cases where the grant is sought notwithstanding that the deceased left no estate within the jurisdiction[1]. Where a grant limited to trust property is applied for under the Senior Courts Act 1981, s 113(1)[2], in a case where the deceased had property of their own in the jurisdiction, the form appropriate to the deceased's own estate should be used, and the applicant should give particulars and value thereof to the best of their knowledge and belief, even if they are not accountable for the relative tax.

[1] See Ch 4—'Requirements on proving a will'—paras 4.90 ff.
[2] See para A1.340.

8.34   *Inland Revenue accounts*

Double probate, de bonis non and cessate grants: Cap A5C[1]

Application for a subsequent grant in England and Wales (and Northern Ireland) including use of Cap A5C

8.34   This form is for use in cases whenever the deceased died—at any rate since 1 August 1894—and application is being made for a grant de bonis non, or for a grant of double probate, or for a cessate grant, where the estate to be covered by the new grant was within the operation of the previous grant. If the estate was not within the operation of the previous grant, the form of Inland Revenue account as for an original grant should be used. Among the cases to which Cap A5C is *not* applicable are a full grant following a grant pending suit or ad colligenda bona, a grant caeterorum, and a fresh grant following the revocation of the previous grant.

In view of the different reporting requirements as a result of the changes to the Excepted Estates rules, clarification as to the appropriate forms to be used is provided below.

[1]   Cap A5C is obtainable on application to the Director, HMRC Inheritance Tax, Ferrers House, PO Box 38, Castle Meadow Road, Nottingham NG2 1BB, Telephone 0845 30 20 900.

8.34A   There are two categories of subsequent grant, namely 'second grant' and 'grant following an interim grant'. These are dealt with below.

FIRST CATEGORY: SECOND GRANT

8.34B   The first category is where the first grant was a full grant and then a grant such as a grant de bonis non is applied for. The subsequent grant is a second grant and a reduced fee applies. (The latest figure can be obtained from the appropriate Probate Office.)

A grant of double probate belongs in this category and is where an executor with power reserved wishes to take up office (or unreserve their power reserved). It is possible to have two (or more) grants valid at the same time in these circumstances. (The grant must be a grant of probate and the applicant(s) must be (a) named executor(s) in the will.)

SECOND CATEGORY: GRANT FOLLOWING AN INTERIM GRANT

8.34C   The second category is where the first grant was an interim grant, for example, a grant ad colligenda bona which may have been obtained to sell a house. (An interim grant is specific and limited until a further grant is issued and then is no longer valid.) The subsequent grant is usually a full grant, but not in every case. For example, someone may obtain a further grant ad colligenda bona.

The subsequent grant is *not* called a second grant, and the same fee applies as for the first grant. There is no reduction in the fee.

(Grants ad colligenda bona are expedited through the application process but require agreement from the Probate Registry and HMRC Inheritance Tax. However, the full relevant information is required, eg IHT205 for an excepted estate, IHT400 for a non-excepted estate.)

Revocation

8.34D A grant following the revocation of a previous grant is an anomaly. It is called a second grant for the purpose of the fee payable, but requires full information and so has been included in the tables below with the second category.

Second grant following a 'full' grant:

- grant of administration de bonis non;
- grant of double probate;
- fresh grant following a cessate grant.

First grant	Subsequent grant
Date of Death 02/08/1894–12/03/1975 (Estate Duty)	Sworn Cap A5C
Date of Death 13/03/1975–31/03/1981 (Capital Transfer Tax)	Cap A5C

First grant	Subsequent grant
Date of Death 01/04/1981–17/03/1986 (Capital Transfer Tax)	
Excepted Estate—whether first grant applied for by a personal applicant (IHT205: Short Form for Personal Applicants used) or by a solicitor (no IHT205 used).	If 2nd applicant is a personal applicant: IHT205: Short Form for Personal Applicants. If 2nd applicant is a solicitor: Executor's oath (no IHT205).
Non-excepted Estate (Cap 200 used)	Cap A5C
Date of Death 18/03/1986–05/04/2004 (Inheritance Tax)	

8.34D *Inland Revenue accounts*

First grant	Subsequent grant
Excepted Estate—whether first grant applied for by a personal applicant (IHT205: Short Form for Personal Applicants used) or by a solicitor (no IHT205 used).	If 2nd applicant is a personal applicant: IHT205: Short Form for Personal Applicants. If 2nd applicant is a solicitor: Executor's oath (no IHT205).
Non-excepted Estate (IHT200 or IHT400 used)	Cap A5C
Date of Death 06/04/2004–31/08/2006 (Inheritance Tax)	
Excepted Estate (IHT205: Return of Estate Information used).	Both personal applicants and solicitors: IHT205: Return of Estate Information
Non-excepted Estate (IHT200 or IHT400 used)	Cap A5C
Date of Death 01/09/2006 onwards (Inheritance Tax)	
Excepted Estate (IHT205(2006) used)	Both personal applicants and solicitors: IHT205(2006): Return of Estate Information
Non-excepted Estate (IHT200 or IHT400 used)	Cap A5C

Full grant following an 'interim' grant:

- full grant following a grant pendente lite or ad colligenda bona;
- grant caeterorum;

plus:

- new grant following the **revocation** of a previous grant.

A Cap A5C cannot be used for any of the above.

First grant	Subsequent grant
Date of Death 02/08/1894–12/03/1975 (Estate Duty)	Appropriate 'A' form, eg A-9
Date of Death 13/03/1975–31/03/1981 (Capital Transfer Tax)	Standard form of account, usually IHT400
Date of Death 01/04/1981–17/03/1986 (Capital Transfer Tax)	
Excepted Estate—whether first grant applied for by a personal applicant (IHT205: Short Form for Personal Applicants used) or by a solicitor (no IHT205 used).	If 2nd applicant is a personal applicant: IHT205: Short Form for Personal Applicants. If 2nd applicant is a solicitor: Executor's oath (no IHT205).
Non-excepted Estate (Cap 200 used)	Standard form of account, usually IHT400
Date of Death 18/03/1986–05/04/2004 (Inheritance Tax)	
Excepted Estate—whether first grant applied for by a personal applicant (IHT205: Short Form for Personal Applicants used) or by a solicitor (no IHT205 used).	If 2nd applicant is a personal applicant: IHT205: Short Form for Personal Applicants. If 2nd applicant is a solicitor: Executor's oath (no IHT205).
Non-excepted Estate (IHT200 or IHT400 used)	Standard form of account, usually IHT400

8.34E   *Inland Revenue accounts*

First grant	Subsequent grant
Date of Death 06/04/2004–31/08/2006 (Inheritance Tax)	
Excepted Estate (IHT205: Return of Estate Information used).	Both personal applicants and solicitors: IHT205: Return of Estate Information
Non-excepted Estate (IHT200 or IHT400 used)	Standard form of account, usually IHT400
Date of Death 01/09/2006 onwards (Inheritance Tax)	
Excepted Estate (IHT205(2006) used)	Both personal applicants and solicitors: IHT205(2006): Return of Estate Information
Non-excepted Estate (IHT200 or IHT400 used)	Standard form of account, usually IHT400

CAP A5C/CAP A5N

8.34E   These forms are not available in an electronic format. Supplies of Cap A5C can be obtained from HMRC Inheritance Tax in Nottingham. Supplies of Cap A5N can be obtained from HMRC Inheritance Tax in Belfast.

When a personal applicant has to swear (or affirm) a Cap A5C/Cap A5N for deaths before 13 March 1975, the unsworn document is sent to the Probate Registry and is sworn at the interview.

Other requirements: England and Wales

8.34F   A personal applicant should submit a PA1 with any of the above, plus a sealed copy of the original grant (not a photocopy), and will if applicable. Any queries on this can (and, if from a solicitor, should) be referred to the appropriate Probate Registry.

Reporting procedures: England and Wales

8.34G   Cap A5C or IHT205 (together with other documents required, eg PA1 and copy grant) should be sent to the Probate Registry, who will forward them to HMRC Inheritance Tax.

IHT400 as at present:

(a) personal applicant—PA1 and IHT421 to Probate Registry, then IHT400 and IHT421 to HMRC Inheritance Tax for all but two situations. If the deceased had a foreign domicile or the grant is needed for land which was, and remains, settled property, the IHT400 and D18 should go to HMRC Inheritance Tax first.
(b) solicitor—IHT400 and IHT421 to HMRC Inheritance Tax, then oath and IHT421 to Probate Registry.

Estate Duty 'A' forms to HMRC Inheritance Tax, then to Probate Registry.

Intestacy and next of kin

8.34H Where, for example, children of the deceased have equal rights to apply for a grant, there cannot be more than one valid grant.

Any queries on this subject following the first grant should be referred to the Probate Service.

Minority grant

8.34I When a minority grant has been issued, the estate may not have been fully administered by the time the child reaches the age of 18.

Any queries on this subject following the first grant should be referred to the Probate Service.

Revocation

8.34J Sometimes the Treasury Solicitors take out a grant for an estate when there are no known next of kin, but next of kin may come to light later on. The Treasury Solicitors would revoke their grant, usually through the Principal Probate Office in London.

For a non-excepted estate (with date of death 18/3/1986 onwards) HMRC Inheritance Tax would require an IHT400 and IHT421 from the new executors. If the Treasury Solicitors will not release sufficient information for the new executors to file an account the executors can, in these circumstances, supply an IHT421 (with a covering letter) which contains the gross and net values that were previously declared for Probate (this information is public) which—as long as the Treasury Solicitors are not wanting their money back—HMRC Inheritance Tax will stamp and effectively transfer the payment to that new IHT421. The grant can then be issued by the Probate Service, and the new executors obtain details of the estate and deliver their own IHT400.

Within HMRC Inheritance Tax, the file would keep the same reference number.

8.36 Inland Revenue accounts

8.36 The form, when completed, should be sent directly to the appropriate Probate Registry, without prior reference to HMRC Inheritance Tax. Where the deceased died domiciled in England and Wales or Scotland, the unadministered property situate in the United Kingdom (ie, in Great Britain and Northern Ireland) should be shown in Account 'A', valued at the date of the account. In all other cases, only the unadministered property situate in Great Britain should be shown.

Second or subsequent grants where Cap A5C not applicable

8.38 In cases of second or subsequent grants where Cap A5C is not applicable, but the full tax was duly paid on the application for the first grant, it is necessary, if a second payment of tax is to be avoided, to obtain a transfer of the receipt and stamp from the original to the new account. Application should be made to the Director, HMRC Inheritance Tax by a letter accompanying the new account and setting out the circumstances fully. Where the applicant for the new grant did not themselves pay the tax, either it must be stated, if such be the fact, that the tax was paid out of moneys forming part of the estate, or a consent to the desired transfer, signed by the person who paid the tax (or, if that person is dead, by his or her legal personal representative), must be annexed[1]. Again, references to 'tax' should be read as references to estate duty where the death occurred before 13 March 1975.

[1] This transfer procedure is also appropriate for a first grant when, after an Inheritance Tax account has been receipted, the application is rejected by the Registry and a fresh application is being made.

PRACTICE

Where forms may be obtained

8.44 All current forms of account and the booklet of instruction, IHT 400 Notes, are available from HMRC Inheritance Tax, Ferrers House, PO Box 38, Castle Meadow Road, Nottingham, NG2 1BB, Tel 0845 30 20 900.

Completion of account

8.45 IHT400 should be used for all estates except those properly regarded as 'excepted estates'.

8.46 The declaration on pages 12 and 13 should be considered and completed.

8.47 Where the account of the estate includes property with the instalment option the questions on pages 6, 7 and 11 should be answered to indicate whether or not the legal personal representatives wish to pay by instalments.

Completion of account

8.48 Enquiries are raised on pages 4 and 5 of the form regarding gifts and other lifetime dispositions, settled property in which by virtue of or before his or her death the deceased ceased to have a beneficial interest in possession, nominations and property in beneficial joint ownership. The applicant must disclose everything he or she could reasonably be expected to have ascertained by enquiring of the deceased's relatives, accountants, solicitors, etc and by investigating the deceased's records. Certain transfers of value (all of which would be exempt transfers—see pages 72 and 73 of IHT Notes 'Exemptions and reliefs') need not be reported. Where the answers disclose property on which tax is payable (or would be so payable if tax were payable on estates however small their principal value) such property should be included in the appropriate sections of the form and the relevant Schedules IHT402–420.

It is important that joint assets passing by survivorship are included in the account. Joint assets form part of the deceased's estate for inheritance tax purposes. This includes any assets which pass to a spouse or a civil partner and are exempt, even when these pass by survivorship, for example a house or (in England) bank accounts in joint names. The requirements of HMRC Inheritance Tax differ in this respect from those of the Probate Service. Details of the joint assets should generally be included on Schedule IHT404 and Form IHT400, but will not be counted twice.

8.50 Pages 1, 2 and 3 include all factual details regarding the deceased and any professional agents. An authority for any repayment of overpaid tax is included on page 2.

Pages 4 and 5 cover basic elements regarding the estate and cross-references to supplementary pages which must necessarily be completed and attached to the IHT400.

Pages 6 and 7 cover the deceased's assets.

Pages 8 and 9 cover liabilities plus funeral expenses.

Pages 9 and 10 cover exemptions and reliefs.

Pages 10 and 11 provide a summary of the chargeable estate and bring together details already included in the earlier pages of the IHT400 plus other details from the various schedules.

Page 11 deals with the calculation of the tax. Separate forms IHT400 Calculation and the IHT400 Helpsheet are provided as worksheets to assist.

Pages 12 and 13 relate to the formal declaration together with details and signatures of the intending legal personal representatives.

Page 14 provides a checklist and page 15 provides relevant HMRC addresses and contact details, together with a space for any additional information.

8.51 *Inland Revenue accounts*

8.51 If the deceased died domiciled outside the United Kingdom according to general law (notwithstanding that, by virtue of s 267 of the IHTA 1984 he or she might be treated for the purposes of the tax as having been domiciled in the United Kingdom), Schedule IHT401 must be annexed to the account[1]. An additional statement from one or two individuals who were related to or well acquainted with the deceased and who might speak with authority with regard to any domicile of choice outside the United Kingdom could usefully be furnished where the domicile of origin was in the United Kingdom or the deceased had lived there at the time of or before his or her death. The case of a married woman or civil partner [after 5 December 2005] has no distinguishing features save where a married woman had already acquired—and had retained—a domicile of dependence by reference to her husband's domicile before 1 January 1974[2]. In such a case it would be necessary to indicate the husband's domicile of origin and give brief particulars of his life in addition to those of the deceased married woman since January 1974.

[1] Domicile is explained in Ch 12: ordinary residence outside the United Kingdom is relevant for the 'exclusion' of Government securities: see fn 4, para 8.75.
[2] Domicile and Matrimonial Proceedings Act 1973, s 1: see para A1.238.

8.52 Particulars should similarly be furnished if it is claimed that the deceased was resident or ordinarily resident outside the United Kingdom, using Schedule IHT401.

In certain circumstances it is now possible for a reduced version of this account to be completed. To qualify for the reduced version:

- the deceased must have been domiciled in the United Kingdom at the date of death;
- some assets must pass under the will or intestacy to a United Kingdom domiciled spouse or, on or after 5 December 2005, to a civil partner (either directly or into a trust under which the surviving spouse or civil partner has a right to benefit), and/or directly to a charity that is registered in the United Kingdom, and/or directly to a body listed in Sch 3 to the Inheritance Tax Act 1984, and/or to be held on trusts established in the United Kingdom for charitable purposes only.

If the gross value of any assets passing to beneficiaries other than listed above, plus the value of any other assets chargeable on death, and the chargeable value of any gifts made within seven years of the date of death is less than or equal to the inheritance tax threshold, then the reduced form of account may be used. The account is the standard Form IHT400, but only the following details need to be completed:

- boxes 1 to 28 – in full;
- boxes 29 to 48 – answer all questions, but it may not be necessary to fill in all of the schedules. If the answer to any of boxes 29, 30, 31, 35, 36, 44, 45 or 47 is affirmative, the relevant schedules must be completed, though where an asset passes to an exempt beneficiary, an estimated value may be included;

Practice **8.61**

- pages 6–10 – fill in the appropriate boxes for the various assets and liabilities. Again, where an asset is passing to an exempt beneficiary, an estimate may be included;
- list all assets passing to exempt beneficiaries in boxes 92 and 93 as appropriate. Leave out boxes 109 and 110, but fill in boxes 111 to 117 to make sure no tax is payable;
- leave out box 118 but complete the declaration at box 119;
- use the checklist on page 14.

Valuation

Lifetime gifts on transfers of value

8.57 Questions regarding gifts made by the deceased within seven years of death and gifts with reservation made after 18 March 1986 must be answered and the relevant details included on Schedule IHT403 and box 111 on page 11 of the IHT400 and box 4 on page 1 of the IHT400 Calculation, as appropriate. The value of each gift is calculated as the loss to the estate caused by the transfer.

Assets

8.59 Quoted shares and securities are normally valued at one-quarter up from the lower to the higher of the quotations for the date of death. Where no prices are available for the date of death, the list for the nearest business day, either before or after the death, may be used at the option of the accounting party. If prices are taken from newspapers, it should be borne in mind that morning newspapers usually give the prices for the previous day. If bargains, other than bargains at special prices, are recorded however, the valuation may be based on the price at which business was done, if there is only one price, or a price midway between the lowest and the highest of the different prices. Where quotations are ex-dividend, the dividend should be included separately. Where there is no quotation or record of dealings, the value of the stocks or shares should be estimated on the best evidence available. Units of a unit trust should be valued at the manager's bid price. Stocks, shares and other securities which are quoted (listed in the order of appearance in the official list) or traded on the Unlisted Securities Market should be shown separately from other securities which are not quoted. All such securities should be listed on Schedule IHT411 (quoted) or IHT412 (unlisted or control holdings) and incorporated on page 7 of the IHT400.

8.60 In the case of National Savings Certificates, a letter stating the value should be obtained from the Director of Savings, Savings Certificates Division, Durham. In the absence of such a letter, full details of the certificates should be given.

8.61 IHT407 should be completed in respect of household and personal goods, the details to include individual values of items valued at £500 and

8.61 *Inland Revenue accounts*

over. It is not essential that a professional valuation be obtained, though this may be advisable in respect of any more valuable items. It is essential to complete Schedule IHT420 for any articles for which conditional exemption is claimed as of national, scientific, historic or artistic interest, as to which see para 8.75, in connection with exemptions from tax.

8.63 Benefits payable under superannuation schemes which have been 'approved' for income tax purposes are not normally liable for tax unless the deceased's personal representatives are entitled as of right or the benefit was subject to the deceased's power of nomination and that power had not been exercised irrevocably.

For registered pension schemes, the amendments in the Finance Act 2007, Sch 20 para 20 allow the exemption from inheritance tax charges to operate within the same time frame as permitted by the rules of a registered pension scheme for payment of lump sum benefits following the death of a scheme member.

Under the tax rules operating before 6 April 2006, schemes were allowed a period of up to two years from the date of the member's death in which to pay out the death benefits. HMRC Inheritance Tax recognised this rule, so provided the benefits were paid out within the same time frame, no inheritance tax charges under the relevant property regime arose on the trust property. The pension rules for registered pension schemes have been amended by the Finance Act 2007, Sch 20 para 20 so that the time allowed for payment will run from the date on which the scheme is notified or, if earlier, the date the scheme could have reasonably been aware of the member's death.

This timing will be mirrored for inheritance tax so that provided lump sums are paid within the time allowed by the pension scheme rules on or after 6 April 2006, the scheme funds will not attract charges under ss 64 to 69 of the IHTA 1984. Failure to meet the deadline will have the effect, as before, that the protection from the inheritance tax charges will have ceased at the date of death of the scheme member.

Schedule IHT409 should be completed and the figures transferred to IHT400 box 56 (lump sum benefit) or IHT400 box 106 (alternatively secured pension funds or dependant's pension fund).

Liabilities

8.69 The option to pay tax by instalments has already been considered. Page 11 of the IHT400 makes provision for exercising the option and the appropriate boxes should be completed. Page 3 of IHT400 Calculation provides the facility to invoke the instalment option in respect of some but not all of the property. Details of all real and leasehold property, including any such property which is an asset of a business or partnership, should be given by completing Schedule IHT405. IHT405 provides for inclusion of particulars, such as lettings, which might affect the value of the property concerned.

8.70 If the estate includes a business or an interest in a partnership, trading accounts should be provided, showing the position at the date of death, and supplemented by an inventory and valuation of stock and implements. If the goodwill (if any) of such a business is not to be taken over at a price reached in a bargain struck at arm's length, it should be valued according to the custom of the trade or on the basis of the average profits. If there was no goodwill, or goodwill was valueless, a brief explanatory statement should be appended. IHT413 must be completed.

Foreign property

8.71 In respect of foreign property, particulars should be given on Schedule IHT417. As the value of such property would normally be found in foreign currency and then converted to sterling, the rate of exchange and the source of that rate should be stated.

Other interests including settled property

8.74 Details of assets and liabilities with values should be shown in Schedule IHT418 according to the titles under which they passed on the death of the deceased. The full name of the settlor or testator and the date of the settlement or other instrument and the date of the testator's death in the case of a will trust should be provided, as should brief particulars of any earlier occasion when the instrument concerned was produced to or discussed with HMRC Inheritance Tax. If tax is to be paid on delivery of the account, the funds concerned should be clearly indicated in the appropriate boxes 99 and/or 100 of the IHT400, and here again it is important to complete the appropriate boxes relating to the instalment option. Otherwise the property should be shown in the alternative box 105 of the IHT400 and the names, addresses and references shown of the persons liable for the tax chargeable in respect of those funds (or such persons' solicitors or other professional advisers if known) should be included in the IHT418.

Exemptions from tax

8.75 Where property, which forms part of the estate passing under the grant of probate or administration, is exempt from tax, its value should be included in the Inheritance Tax account, in order that the true value for the purpose of the grant may be shown, and detailed in the spaces provided in the account on pages 9 and 10 as property on which tax is either not payable at all or is not at present payable. In addition to the exemptions in respect of transfers between spouses or civil partners (from 5 December 2005), to charities and political parties, and gifts for national purposes, considered in para 8.12, in connection with lifetime transfers, this applies, inter alia, to the following types of property, which are variously 'exempt', 'conditionally exempt', or 'excluded' from being included for the purpose of ascertaining the tax payable on the rest of the estate—in certain cases with the reservations stated:

8.75   *Inland Revenue accounts*

(a) Heritage property. Objects of national, scientific, historic or artistic interest, land of scenic, historic or scientific interest; and historic buildings with their adjoining land and associated contents. A claim for conditional exemption must be made using Schedule IHT420 and accepted by the Commissioners of Her Majesty's Revenue and Customs[1]. In addition, transfers to approved maintenance fund settlements for certain heritage property are exempt transfers[2].

(b) Gifts of property of any kind to national heritage bodies such as national or local art galleries or museums, local authorities, government departments and universities.

Gifts for public benefit to bodies not run for profit where the Treasury approves exemption. Such gifts are limited to objects and land as at item (a). In addition, a reasonable maintenance fund may be included[3].

(c) Property situate in the United Kingdom by United Kingdom law but treated as situate elsewhere by virtue of a double taxation convention or agreement where the deceased was domiciled outside the United Kingdom.

(d) Certain British Government securities which are excluded property where the deceased was domiciled and ordinarily resident abroad[4].

Under s 161 of the Finance Act 1998 which is effective for transfers on or after 6 April 1998, the excluded Government securities were expanded to include any gilt-edged security issued before 6 April 1998. Such securities are treated as if they were securities issued with the post-1996 Act conditions. The one exception to this exclusion relates to 3½% War Loan 1952 or after.

Under s 154 of the Finance Act 1996, with effect from 29 April 1996, provided the deceased was ordinarily resident outside the United Kingdom, the Treasury was empowered to issue securities which were excluded from the charge to Inheritance Tax. The Domicile qualification previously required for such exclusion was negated for such securities. The securities issued within this qualification are 8% Treasury Stock 2000, Floating Rate Treasury Stock 2001, 7% Treasury Stock 2001, 7% Treasury Stock 2002, 6½% Treasury Stock 2003, 7¼% Treasury Stock 2007, 8% Treasury Stock 2015, 8% Treasury Stock 2021 and 6% Treasury Stock 2028.

Details of the Government securities which were regarded as excluded property for earlier transfers are detailed below.

(e) Property of which the deceased was life tenant is exempt from tax if it would have been exempt from estate duty under the Finance Act 1894, s 5(2), duty having been paid thereon in connection with the death of the deceased's spouse, such death having occurred before 13 November 1974. Any apportionment of income received after his or her death to which the estate may be entitled is treated as covered by the exemption[5].

(f) Reversionary interests which have not been acquired by the deceased or by a person previously entitled to it for a consideration in money or money's worth are excluded property.

[1] Undertakings are required, inter alia, as to maintenance and retention of the objects in the United Kingdom. Reasonable access for the public must also be provided in all cases: IHTA 1984, ss 30 ff [FA 1976, ss 76 ff replacing, in relation to deaths on and after 7 April 1976,

Practice 8.77

FA 1975, ss 31 ff]. Tax will be chargeable when sold (unless the sale is by private treaty to a national heritage body or similar public body) or on failure to observe the terms of the undertaking imposed as a condition of relief. Claims for exemption or enquiries relating thereto are dealt with by HMRC Inheritance Tax. Any claim for exemption is investigated after the issue of the grant, and inspection of the objects by Officers of the National Collections is usually necessary. The objects should therefore not be dispersed before inspection has taken place, without adequate notice to HMRC Inheritance Tax. If any objects were exempted on the ground of national, etc, interest in connection with a previous death, further inspection of those objects may be waived, but the name and date of death of the former owner and, if known, the HMRC Inheritance Tax references to his estate, should be mentioned.

2   IHTA 1984, s 27 (see also Sch 4) [FA 1982, s 95 replacing, in relation to deaths on and after 9 March 1982, the FA 1976, s 84 which applied to deaths on and after 3 May 1976 as amended with effect from 1 August 1980 by the FA 1980, s 88. (See also the FA 1982, ss 93 and 94 and Sch 16 replacing, in relation to deaths on and after 9 March 1982, the FA 1976, s 84, amended as aforesaid)].

3   IHTA 1984, ss 25 and 26 [FA 1975, Sch 6, paras 12 and 13]. There is no limit in value, but, as regards gifts for public benefit, undertakings are required, inter alia, as to maintenance, use or disposal and as to reasonable access for the public.

4   Viz 3½% War Loan; 13% Treasury Stock 1990; 8% Treasury Convertible Stock 1990; 8¼% Treasury Loan 1987–90; 11% Exchequer Loan 1990; 10% Treasury Convertible Stock 1991; 5¾% Funding Loan 1987–91; 2% Index Linked Treasury Stock 1992; 8% Treasury Loan 1992; 10½% Treasury Convertible Loan Stock 1992; 12¾% Treasury Loan 1992; 10% Treasury Loan 1993; 6% Funding Loan 1993; 12½% Treasury Loan 1993; 13¾% Treasury Loan 1993; 9% Treasury Loan 1994; 10% Treasury Loan 1994; 14½% Treasury Loan 1994; 12¾% Treasury Loan 1995; 9% Treasury Loan 1992–96; 13¼% Exchequer Loan 1996; 15¼% Treasury Loan 1996; 8¾% Treasury Loan 1997; 13¼% Treasury Loan 1997; 7% Treasury Convertible Loan 1997; 6¾% Treasury Loan 1995–98; 4⅝% Index-linked Treasury Stock 1998; 7¼% Treasury Stock 1998; 15½% Treasury Loan 1998; 6% Treasury Stock 1999; 9½% Treasury Loan 1999; 8½% Treasury Loan 2000; 9% Conversion Stock 2000; 9½% Conversion Loan 2001; 8% Treasury Stock 2003; 9¾% Conversion Loan 2003; 8% Treasury Loan 2002–06; 4⅜% Index-linked Treasury Stock 2004; 6¾% Treasury Stock 2004; 8½% Treasury Stock 2005; 7½% Treasury Stock 2006; 7¾% Treasury Stock 2006; 8½% Treasury Loan 2007; 9% Treasury Loan 2008; 6¼% Treasury Stock 2010; 9% Conversion Loan 2011; 5½% Treasury Stock 2008–12; 9% Treasury Stock 2012; 8% Treasury Stock 2013; 7¾% Treasury Loan 2012–15; 8¾% Treasury Stock 2017; 2½% Index-Linked Treasury Stock 2024; 4⅛% Index-linked Treasury Stock 2030.

5   IHTA 1984, Sch 6, para 2 [FA 1975, s 22(4)].

Reliefs

8.76 The several relieving provisions operate for the most part in one of two ways. Most reliefs are given against capital: they reduce the value of the property concerned to produce a net figure to reckon towards the total value of the estate for the purpose of charging tax. But two, the reliefs for double taxation and for successive charges, take the form of reducing the amount of tax chargeable. As with exemptions, reliefs against capital should be recorded on pages 9 and 10 of the account. The principal reliefs against capital are as follows.

Relevant business property

8.77 Schedules IHT412 or IHT413, as appropriate, will need to be completed for any claim for business relief, and the results should then be transferred to the appropriate boxes in the IHT400.

8.77   *Inland Revenue accounts*

For deaths on or after 6 April 1996, business relief at a rate of 100% now applies to all qualifying business property [FA 1996, s 184(2) relates]. Relief is still restricted to 50% for land, buildings, machinery and plant used only or mainly by a company of which the deceased had control or by a partnership in which he or she was a partner.

For deaths prior to 6 April 1996, para 1, Sch 14, Finance (No 2) Act 1992 (previously s 104 of the 1984 Act and Sch 10, para 2 of the FA 1976) stipulates the rates of relief for the various categories of relevant business property defined in s105 [para 3] of the 1984 Act. From these provisions it can be said that:

— relief is available at 100% with effect from 10 March 1992—previously 50%—for an interest in a business (which includes a partnership interest), for a control holding in a company[1] and, in the case of a death on or after 17 March 1987[2], for a minority holding in an unquoted company which yields not less than 25% of the voting capacity; and
— relief is available at 50%—30% prior to 10 March 1992—for other minority holdings in unquoted companies, for land, buildings, machinery and plant used only or mainly in a company of which the deceased had control or of a partnership in which he or she was a partner and, in the case of a death on or after 10 March 1981, for those similar assets which, being settled property in which the deceased had a beneficial interest in possession, were used wholly or mainly in a business carried on by the deceased.

[1]   IHTA 1984, s 269 as to 'control'.
[2]   FA 1987, s 58 and Sch 8, para 5.

Agricultural property

8.86   Schedules IHT414 and IHT405 must be completed and the results transferred to the appropriate boxes in the IHT400.

Earlier provisions[1] affording relief for agricultural property were replaced by ss 115 ff of the 1984 Act [FA 1981, s 96 and Sch 14]. Where a transfer of value, including a transfer on death, made after 9 March 1981 is attributable to agricultural property in the United Kingdom, the Channel Islands or the Isle of Man, the value transferred is reduced for tax purposes provided the prescribed conditions are satisfied.

[1]   FA 1975, s 35 and Sch 8, as amended by the FA 1976, s 74. In relation to deaths prior to 10 March 1981 relief is available only in respect of chargeable transfers. The requirements for relief are: (i) the land must comply with the statutory definition of agricultural property, (ii) the deceased must have been a qualifying working farmer (farming alone or in partnership; employed in farming; director of a company whose main activity is farming in the United Kingdom; undergoing full-time education; or, in receipt of not less than 75% of income from engagement in farming in the United Kingdom) during not less than five of the seven years ending with 5 April immediately preceding the death (special rules apply to retired farmers and to property inherited from a spouse), (iii) the deceased must have occupied the land in question for agricultural purposes for two years immediately preceding the transfer (special provision is made in the case of successive transfers within a two-year period), and (iv) the relief must be applied for within two years of the death (Form 220 obtainable from HMRC Inheritance Tax should be used). The relief is limited

Practice **8.101**

to a maximum of 1,000 acres (rough grazing land counting as one-sixth of its actual area as from 7 April 1976) or £250,000 and is calculated by reducing the agricultural value by half. (Prior to 7 April 1976 the agricultural property was valued at 20 times the rent it would fetch if let so far as it was situated in Great Britain.)

8.91 The relief may be given without formal claim, although Schedules IHT414 and IHT405 are generally required to be completed, and where available there will be no entitlement to business relief.

8.92 In the schedule of real and leasehold property (Schedule IHT405) the open market value of any agricultural property (which is relevant for all probate and tax purposes) should be shown.

Variations: changes in the distribution of the estate on death

8.101 *Instruments of variation and disclaimer—s 142.* Provision is made here for a beneficiary to vary or disclaim benefits from the deceased's estate without, in so doing, incurring a charge to tax. This is secured by treating a variation as though it had been effected by the deceased under the original disposition and by treating a disclaimed benefit as though it had never been conferred[1]. Neither the variation nor the disclaimer is a transfer of value[2]. To be eligible for relief a variation may be made within but not more than two years after the date of death[1]. It must be in writing and executed by all the persons who were to benefit under the terms of the original disposition in relation to the property being re-directed[1]. It should be in a form which identifies the original disposition (commonly the deceased's will) and clearly indicates which property is being re-directed and to whom. With effect from 1 August 2002, while there is no longer a need for a formal election to be submitted to the Board of Her Majesty's Revenue and Customs, the instrument of variation must incorporate a statement of intent if the relevant persons want s 142 of the IHTA 1984 to apply to the variation. Additionally, the instrument of variation does not have to be referred to HMRC Inheritance Tax if there is no increase in tax payable as a result of the variation. A new s 218A of the IHTA 1984 places a statutory obligation on the relevant persons to submit the instrument of variation to HMRC Inheritance Tax if the variation results in additional tax becoming payable. An addition to s 245 of the same Act provides a penalty of up to £100 to be charged if the instrument of variation which results in additional tax becoming payable is not sent to HMRC Inheritance Tax within six months. The provision applies to property, including 'excluded property' passing under a will or intestacy. It applies too to property passing by nomination and survivorship, but not to settled property unless the deceased immediately prior to his or her death had a beneficial interest in possession and a general power of appointment which power had been exercised by will[4].

[1] IHTA 1984, s 142(1).
[2] IHTA 1984, s 17(a).
[3] IHTA 1984, s 142(2).
[4] IHTA 1984, s 142(5).

8.109   *Inland Revenue accounts*

Death on active service etc

8.109 Total relief from tax is granted by s 154(1) of the 1984 Act [FA 1975, Sch 7, para 1] in connection with the death of a member of the armed forces of the Crown or any other person subject to the law governing any of those forces by reason of association with or of accompanying any body of those forces including, in relation to any time before 28 July 1981 when the Armed Forces Act 1981[1] was enacted, a member of the women's services. The death must be one which is certified by the appropriate authority[2] as resulting from a wound inflicted, accident occurring or disease contracted at a time when the deceased was on active service against an enemy or on other service of a warlike nature, or which in the opinion of the Treasury involved the same risks as service of a warlike nature, or from a disease contracted at some previous time and due to or hastened by the aggravation of the disease during such period. The usual Inheritance Tax account should be completed, the certificate being attached in support of the claim for exemption.

[1]   Ch 55 (which provided, inter alia, for the assimilation of the women's services).
[2]   Service Personnel and Veterans Agency, Joint Casualty and Compassionate Centre (Attn SO3 Deceased Estates), Innsworth Station, Gloucester, GL3 1HW. It is advisable to enclose the deceased's service number, a copy of the death certificate and any supporting medical evidence such as a post mortem report which might be of relevance. See Ch 4, for probate fees.

Relief from double taxation

8.111 Page 4 of IHT400 Calculation should be completed.

Agreements or conventions for the avoidance of double taxation made with the United States of America[1], South Africa[2], the Netherlands[3], Switzerland[4], Sweden[5], France[6], Italy[7] and the Republic of Ireland[8] provide special rules for determining the situation of property for inheritance tax and capital transfer tax only. Apart from the conventions with the Netherlands and Switzerland, they also provide for credits in respect of overseas tax paid by reference to gifts or on death[9]. They do not affect the situation of property for the purposes of the grant of representation, and the Inland Revenue account should be completed in accordance with the general law regarding the situation of property. Any variation due to the application of an agreement or convention should be made by adjusting the value for tax. Where property of a person domiciled outside the United Kingdom is situate in the United Kingdom under the general law but outside the United Kingdom under an agreement or convention, its value should be deducted as property on which tax is not payable; but if the property is situate outside the United Kingdom under the general law and is taxable only because of the agreement or convention, it should be included in the Inland Revenue account, with an explanatory note. No adjustment is necessary if an asset is taxable or exempt irrespective of its situation.

[1]   SR & O 1946/1351; superseded by SI 1979/1454 in the case of deaths or transfers after 11 November 1979 but with transitional savings.
[2]   SR & O 1947/314, as amended by SI 1955/424; superseded by SI 1979/576 in the case of deaths or transfers after 31 December 1977 but with transitional savings.

³   SI 1950/1197; superseded by SI 1980/706 in the case of deaths or transfers after 16 June 1980 but with transitional savings.
⁴   SI 1957/426: superseded by SI 1994/3214 in the case of deaths or transfers after 6 March 1995.
⁵   SI 1961/578, as amended by SI 1965/599; superseded by SI 1981/840 in the case of deaths or transfers after 19 June 1981.
⁶   SI 1963/1319.
⁷   SI 1968/304.
⁸   SI 1978/1107.
⁹   FA 1975, Sch 7, para 7(6).

8.116 Where an allowance is appropriate, a provisional deduction may be taken in the Inheritance Tax account if accompanied by a reasoned estimate of the amount of duty or tax payable in the country concerned to be included on page 4 of the IHT400 Calculation. The deduction is not to exceed the amount of inheritance tax or capital transfer tax on the property in question.

Relief from successive charges ('quick succession relief')

8.118 Pages 1 and 2 of IHT400 Calculation should be completed.

Where the estate of a person dying after 9 March 1981 has been increased by a chargeable transfer made not more than five years before his death the tax chargeable on the death is reduced by a percentage of the tax charged on the earlier transfer, as follows:

(a)   by 100% if the intervening period was one year or less;
(b)   by 80% if that period was more than one year but not more than two years;
(c)   by 60% if that period was more than two years but not more than three years;
(d)   by 40% if that period was more than three years but not more than four years; and
(e)   by 20% if it exceeds four years[1].

¹   IHTA 1984, s 141 [FA 1975, s 101].

ASSESSMENT, PAYMENT AND DELIVERY

8.122 As already explained, the Inheritance Tax account is arranged to show, in pages 6 and 7, the property in respect of which the grant is to be made. Except for liabilities specifically charged on property with the instalment option or incurred in respect of a business with the instalment option, funeral expenses and debts for which the estate is liable are deducted against the non-instalment option property. If there is a deficit in the non-instalment property, this is deducted against the total of the instalment option property and vice versa.

8.123 For most estates, completing the details for the simple Inheritance Tax calculation on page 11 of the IHT400 or, by following the directions on the

8.123 *Inland Revenue accounts*

pages of the IHT400 Calculation, the value of the property on which the assessment is to be based may be ascertained. The value of the estate in respect of which the grant is to be made may be carried through to Form IHT421. These two amounts are not necessarily the same[1].

[1] See paras 8.126 and 8.127, on assessment as to the calculations which may be necessary where part only of an estate is entitled to relief in respect of gifts to a surviving spouse etc.

ASSESSMENT, PAYMENT AND DELIVERY

Assessment

8.124 As tax must be paid on delivery of the Inheritance Tax account on all property not entitled to the instalment option and any instalments due on instalment option property (in each case for which the personal representatives are liable), the simple Inheritance Tax calculation on page 11 of the IHT400 may be used in most circumstances. For estates that do not fall within the criteria detailed on page 11 of the IHT400, full details must be transferred to Form IHT400 Calculation, and the form should be fully completed to arrive at the correct figures on page 8 of that form.

8.125 [*This paragraph has been deleted.*]

8.126 Where exemption being claimed on pages 9 and/or 10 under one or more of ss 18 and 23 to 26 of the 1984 Act [FA 1975, Sch 6, paras 1 and 10 to 13] (gifts to surviving spouse, civil partner etc) extends to part only of the estate, the calculation of that exemption must have regard to the incidence of the tax. Where the death occurred on or after 7 April 1976[1], 'specific gifts' not bearing their own tax are added together and grossed-up to the tax appropriate to their total value, ignoring all other gifts and residue. If no other part of the estate is chargeable that grossed-up value determines the tax payable. In such circumstances, more detailed information is available on the Inheritance Tax website (www.hmrc.gov.uk/inheritancetax).

[1] Originally, 'specific gifts' (FA 1975, Sch 6, para 23(1)) not bearing their own tax had to be grossed-up at an 'assumed rate' which was the average rate of tax calculated on the basis that no exemption was due. For the same net benefit to a beneficiary this produced a different tax liability as between a legacy which was grossed-up and one which, because it bore its own tax, was not. To ameliorate this, FA 1976, s 96 introduced a different approach.

8.127 [*This paragraph has been deleted.*]

8.128 The foregoing procedure undergoes an additional operation in the case of deaths on and after 18 March 1986 where relief for business or agricultural property (or both) is available and the transfer on death is partly exempt. This operation[1] entails reducing specific gifts of business or agricultural property to their values after relief and reducing other specific gifts to the 'appropriate fraction' of their values. This 'appropriate fraction' is X/Y where X is the value of the estate after the relief concerned less the value after relief of any

Assessment, payment and delivery 8.130

specific gift of business or agricultural property, and Y is the value of the estate before relief less any specific gift also before relief of any business or agricultural property. The grossing procedure is then followed as in paragraph 8.126, but using the reduced figures obtained from the process described in this paragraph. In such circumstances, more information is available on the Inheritance Tax website (www.hmrc.gov.uk/inheritancetax).

[1] IHTA 1984, s 39A as inserted by FA 1986, s 105 with respect to transfers of value on and after 18 March 1986.

8.130 Interest on tax on property not entitled to the 'instalment option' is payable from the end of the sixth month after the date of death to the date of payment. The rates of interest for all outstanding tax and effective periods are tabled below. The adjustments after 1989 until 12 August 2009 were made in accordance with the Finance Act 1989, s 178(1). The Taxes and Duties (Interest Rate) (Amendment) Regulations 2009, SI 2009/2032, took effect on 12 August 2009 and contained provisions that replaced the single rate of interest of Inheritance Tax, Capital Transfer Tax and Estate Duty with one rate for charging interest on unpaid tax and another, lower, rate for the repayment interest supplement that is added to repayments. The interest rates so calculated are linked to the Bank of England base rate and will move with base rate changes announced by the Bank's Monetary Policy Committee (MPC).

Interest rate	Effective dates	Authority
6%	Up to 31 December 1979	FA 1974, Sch 4, para 19
9%	1 January 1980 to 30 November 1982	SI 1979/1688
6%	1 December 1982 to 30 April 1985	SI 1982/1585 and Inheritance Tax Act 1984, s 233
9%	1 May 1985 to 15 December 1986	SI 1985/560
8%	16 December 1986 to 5 June 1987	SI 1986/1944
6%	6 June 1987 to 5 August 1988	SI 1987/887
8%	6 August 1988 to 5 October 1988	SI 1988/1280
9%	6 October 1988 to 5 July 1989	SI 1988/1623
11%	6 July 1989 to 5 March 1991	Board's Order June 1989

8.130 Inland Revenue accounts

Interest rate	Effective dates	Authority
10%	6 March 1991 to 5 May 1991	Board's Order 18 February 1989
9%	6 May 1991 to 5 July 1991	Board's Order April 1991
8%	6 July 1991 to 5 November 1992	Board's Order 21 June 1991
6%	6 November 1992 to 5 December 1992	Board's Order 22 October 1992
5%	6 December 1992 to 5 January 1994	Board's Order 20 November 1992
4%	6 January 1994 to 5 October 1994	Board's Order 15 December 1993
5%	6 October 1994 to 5 March 1999	Board's Order 20 September 1994
4%	6 March 1999 to 5 February 2000	Board's Order 18 February 1999
5%	6 February 2000 to 5 May 2001	Board's Order 20 January 2000
4%	6 May 2001 to 5 November 2001	Board's Order 23 April 2001
3%	6 November 2001 to 5 August 2003	Board's Order 19 October 2001
2%	6 August 2003 to 5 December 2003	Board's Order 21 July 2003
3%	6 December 2003 to 5 September 2004	Board's Order 17 November 2003
4%	6 September 2004 to 5 September 2005	Board's Order 10 August 2004
3%	6 September 2005 to 5 September 2006	Board's Order 5 September 2005
4%	6 September 2006 to 5 August 2007	Revenue and Customs (Interest Rates) Order 2006, dated 22 August 2006
5%	6 August 2007 to 5 January 2008	Revenue and Customs (Interest Rates) Order 2007, dated 20 July 2007

Interest rate	Effective dates	Authority
4%	6 January 2008 until 5 November 2008	Revenue and Customs (Interest Rates) Order 2007, dated 7 December 2007
3%	6 November 2008 until 5 January 2009	Revenue and Customs (Interest Rates) Order (No 2) 2008, dated 21 October 2008
2%	6 January 2009 until 26 January 2009	Revenue and Customs (Interest Rates) Order (No 3) 2008, dated 16 December 2008
1%	27 January 2009 until 23 March 2009	Revenue and Customs (Interest Rates) Order 2009, dated 12 January 2009
0%	24 March 2009 until 28 September 2009	Revenue and Customs (Interest Rates) Order (No 2) 2009, dated 10 March 2009
3% for late payments; 0·5% for overpayments	29 September 2009 onwards	HM Revenue and Customs announcement dated 29 July 2009. Recalculation of interest rates following September Monetary Policy meeting of Bank of England.

Payment of tax

8.133 Where tax is payable, the assessed HMRC account and the Form IHT421 should first be sent to the HMRC Inheritance Tax, Ferrers House, PO Box 38, Castle Meadow Road, Nottingham, NG2 1BB or DX 701202 Nottingham 4 for the Form IHT421 to be receipted and impressed by that office. Cheques or money orders should be crossed and made payable to 'HMRC' or 'Her Majesty's Revenue and Customs' and should be sent separately as detailed below.

Where tax is payable and is being paid by cheque, the assessed HMRC account and the Form IHT421 should first be sent to HMRC Inheritance Tax, PO Box 38, Ferrers House, Castle Meadow Road, Nottingham, NG2 1BB, or DX 701201, Nottingham 4. The cheque and the payslip should be sent in a separate envelope to HMRC, St Mungo's Road, Cumbernauld, Glasgow, G67 1YZ or by DX to HM Revenue & Customs, DX 550100, Cumbernauld 7. The cheque should be made payable to 'HM Revenue and Customs' followed

8.133   *Inland Revenue accounts*

by the Inheritance Tax reference and should be crossed 'Account payee'. The Inheritance Tax reference number may be obtained by contacting HMRC Inheritance Tax, either by telephone to the Inheritance Tax helpline on 0845 30 20 900, or by completing the Form IHT422 which is a supplementary form to the Inheritance Tax account. The Form IHT422 should be submitted to the HMRC Inheritance Tax office at least two weeks before the expected submission of the Form IHT400. The full name of the deceased and the date of death should be written on the back of the cheque.

If payment is being made electronically by BACS Direct Credit, Internet, telephone banking or CHAPS, the account to be used for paying inheritance tax is HMRC Inheritance Tax, account number 12001136 with the sort code of 08-32-10. If a bank giro credit method of payment is being used at the applicant's bank, the cheque should be made payable to 'HM Revenue & Customs' followed by the Inheritance Tax reference and should be accompanied by the payslip. The Inheritance Tax reference number may be obtained as detailed above.

These details for payment are also appropriate for payment of subsequent calculations of tax, or payments on account.

Under a scheme effective from 31 March 2003, a new means is available to the taxpayer to discharge inheritance tax from the deceased's Bank or Building Society account directly to HMRC immediately prior to a Grant of Representation being applied for, providing there are sufficient funds in the account(s). Taxpayers wishing to use this scheme should contact HMRC Inheritance Tax to obtain a reference number, either by telephone to the Inheritance Tax Helpline on 0845 30 20 900, or by completing Form IHT422 which is a new supplementary page to the Inheritance Tax Account. The Form IHT422 indicates which office to use and should be submitted to that Inheritance Tax office at least two weeks before expected date of submission of the Form IHT400. When the Form IHT400 has been completed and the amount of tax that must be paid before the application for a Grant of Representation has been calculated, the Form IHT423 should be fully completed, including the Inheritance Tax reference number, and sent to the Bank or Building Society that will be making the transfer of funds. The Form IHT400, the relevant supplementary pages, the Form IHT421 and any other supporting documents should be sent to the appropriate Inheritance Tax office at the same time. The Bank or Building Society will transfer the relevant amount directly to HMRC and, once notification of payment has been received, details will be linked to the Form IHT400 and, provided all is in order, the Form IHT421 will be stamped and returned. The whole process may take slightly longer than payment by cheque, and some Banks or Building Societies may charge a fee for the service. It is therefore recommended that early contact be made with the appropriate institution to establish their requirements and to identify the Personal Representatives. Section 118 of the Guide to the Form IHT400 Notes provides further details.

It is also possible for Inheritance Tax to be discharged using the deceased's Government Stock. In the first instance, write to the registrars for British

Assessment, payment and delivery **8.136**

Government Stock and let them know that it is desired for funds to be transferred from British Government Stock to pay Inheritance Tax on the deceased's estate and let them know how much it is desired to transfer. The registrars are: Computershare Investor Services plc, PO Box 2411, The Pavilions, Bridgwater Road, Bristol, BS3 9WX. Telephone number 0870 703 0143. E-mail: gilts@computershare.co.uk. Computershare may require the stock reference number to help them find a particular investment. This number appears on the stock certificate and correspondence from the Bank of England. They aim to deal with requests within five days.

Once this has been done, the Form IHT400, the Form IHT421 and a letter stating how much of the tax is to be paid out of the British Government Stock should be sent to HM Revenue & Customs, Ferrers House, PO Box 38, Castle Meadow Road, Nottingham, NG2 1BB. Once this is received, HMRC will contact Computershare and ask for the money to be transferred. This may take up to four weeks. If the amount so transferred is sufficient to cover the tax due, HMRC will then send the receipted Form IHT421 direct to the Probate Registry (personal applicant) or to the practitioner so that a grant can be applied for.

8.134 In small cases, where there is difficulty in raising the money for the tax before the grant by other means, it may be possible to arrange to have the tax paid out of deposits in the National Savings Bank or by encashment of Savings Certificates or Premium Savings Bonds.

8.135 If payment by any of these methods is desired, application should be made by letter to the Director, HMRC Inheritance Tax, accompanied by the Inheritance Tax account and, where appropriate, by the National Savings Bank book, or, in the case of Savings Certificates, by a statement from the Money Order Department of the extent and value of the holding. HMRC Inheritance Tax makes the necessary arrangements or gives instructions. Some delay in the receipting of the account and consequently in the issue of the grant is inevitable[1].

[1] The Commissioners of Her Majesty's Revenue and Customs may, if they think fit, accept in or towards satisfaction of tax, landed property and objects kept in any building where it appears to be desirable for the objects to remain associated with the building; any picture, print, book, manuscript, work of art, scientific object, etc which is considered pre-eminent for its national, scientific, historic or artistic interest. Collections of pictures etc may be treated similarly. (Section 230 of the 1984 Act [FA 1975, Sch, 4, para 17 as amended] is in point.) Tax should be paid in the usual way. The offer or enquiry should be made to the Director, HMRC Inheritance Tax.

Examination of account before the grant and delivery

8.136 Although, to avoid delay in obtaining the grant, generally the full examination of the Inheritance Tax account is deferred until after the issue of the grant has been authorised, nevertheless in the following instances the account must be examined and assessed by HMRC Inheritance Tax before the IHT421 may be authorised:

8.136 *Inland Revenue accounts*

(a) where it is claimed that the deceased died domiciled outside the United Kingdom;
(b) where conditional exemption is claimed in respect of objects of national, scientific, historic or artistic interest or in respect of land or buildings of outstanding interest;
(c) where payment of tax is to be made out of a National Savings Bank deposit, or out of the proceeds of National Savings Certificates or Premium Savings Bonds; and
(d) where the grant is required only in respect of settled land.

8.137 It is particularly important where an English solicitor is acting for individuals overseas in cases where the deceased is claimed to be domiciled outside the United Kingdom that the papers concerned are delivered to HMRC Inheritance Tax at the earliest opportunity—not least to avoid the possibility of 'intermeddling' with the estate. Cases of difficulty may still be sent to that office for advice.

8.138 In correspondence with HMRC Inheritance Tax use of the file number (when known) is always helpful and time-saving, but its absence need cause no special delay to correspondence provided the full name and date of death of the deceased is given.

8.139 A duplicate Inheritance Tax account, if delivered to HMRC Inheritance Tax in Nottingham at the time of payment with a letter of request, will be endorsed with a certificate of payment as on the original.

8.140 Evidence of payment for fiscal purposes abroad can be obtained after the issue of the grant, usually on a certified copy of the Inheritance Tax account, for which a copying fee may be payable.

CORRECTIVE ACCOUNTS

Practice as to corrective accounts

8.141 Where any correction of the tax paid upon an Inheritance Tax account becomes necessary after the grant of representation has issued, details should be provided to the Director of HMRC Inheritance Tax as soon as possible.

Clearance letters

8.142 Under the provisions of s 239 of the IHTA 1984, on being satisfied that all the tax attributable to the value transferred by a chargeable transfer had been paid (or would be paid if, for example, payments were being made by instalments) a certificate of discharge was provided by the Commissioners of Her Majesty's Revenue and Customs following an application by a person liable for the tax.

With effect from 30 April 2007, this practice changed. After that date, a stamped and signed letter will be sent by HMRC Inheritance Tax to provide the necessary confirmation that all enquiries are settled and that either:

(a) no tax is due;
(b) all the tax has been paid; or
(c) all the tax has been paid except for any tax being deferred (eg on timber) or otherwise being paid later (by instalments).

The letter will have exactly the same effect as a formal certificate. So, for example, if the HMRC Inheritance Tax had sent such a closure letter to both the executors and the trustees of a chargeable will trust and the latter discover an additional asset thereby increasing the value of the will trust and consequently the chargeable estate, the executors will still be protected by their letter and no additional tax will be sought from the estate. The letter will be issued at the appropriate time in every estate, whether or not a liability arises. These clearance letters will not apply to lifetime transfers, whether potentially exempt transfers or immediately chargeable transfers, given that a (further) liability may arise should the transferor die within seven years of making the gift.

Gifts with reservation/pre-owned assets

8.143 If property gifted during the lifetime of the transferor was subject to a reservation of benefit in favour of the transferor which still existed at the time of their death, that property is deemed to be property to which they were beneficially entitled immediately before their death (except to the extent that the property forms part of their estate anyway). The property is therefore part of the transferor's estate (unless it was excluded property) and has to be valued at that time.

If the reservation ceases during the transferor's lifetime, the transferor is treated as making a potentially exempt transfer at that time of the property comprised in the gift. this is a deemed potentially exempt transfer and comes into charge on the transferor's death in the same way as any other potentially exempt transfer made within that period. Because of the definition of a gift with reservation, the reservation must have existed within the seven-year charging period for potentially exempt transfers. Because s 102(4) of IHTA 1984 creates a deemed potentially exempt transfer, the annual exemption is not available to set against it.

For certain interests in possession in settled property that come to an end in an individual's lifetime and on or after 22 March 2006, Finance Act 1986, s 102ZA allows the owner of the interest in possession to be treated as making a gift of the underlying property for the purposes of Finance Act 1986, s 102 and Sch 20. Section 102ZA applies to interests in possession to which either an individual became entitled before 22 March 2006 or to interests in possession that are an immediate post-death interest, a disabled person's interest or a transitional serial interest.

8.143 *Inland Revenue accounts*

If the original gift of the property was itself a chargeable transfer when made or was a potentially exempt transfer and the transferor dies within seven years, charges in respect of both a lifetime transfer and a gift with reservation will arise. To prevent a double charge to tax, relief under the Double Charges Regulations may be available.

Schedule 15 to the Finance Act 2004 introduced an income tax charge on pre-owned assets. This was basically an additional measure to prevent people from ostensibly disposing of valuable assets like the family home whilst continuing to benefit from them. It was achieved by imposing an annual income tax charge on the benefit of using the asset. As an alternative to the pre-owned assets income tax charge, the transferor may elect that the property will be treated for inheritance tax purposes as if it were subject to a reservation, and the value of the property will form part of the former owner's taxable estate if they continue to enjoy it up to their death, or if they cease to do so within seven years of their death.

Under s 66 of the Finance Act 2007, a provision is made whereby HMRC Inheritance Tax may accept a late election. The normal filing date for an election will continue to apply (ie 31 January in the tax year following the year of assessment concerned) and there is no change to the date to withdraw the election. This measure is aimed at people who may have been unaware that they were liable to the pre-owned assets charge. Provided they elect as soon as practical after discovering they were liable to the pre-owned assets charge, HMRC Inheritance Tax will normally be able to accept a late election.

Chapter 9
TRUST CORPORATIONS

ADMINISTRATION: CONSENTS REQUIRED

9.37 Similarly, where the trust corporation is not applying as the attorney of some person, where the deceased died intestate, the consents of all persons sharing beneficially in the estate should be obtained and recited in the oath, which must also include the necessary clearings of prior classes as on application by a beneficiary himself. Form of consent, No 58. Form of oath, No 117.

ALL PERSONS ENTITLED UNDER AGE

9.47 A grant to a trust corporation under the above procedure will be limited until one of the minors upon attaining 18 years of age shall obtain a grant or until further representation be granted.

Chapter 11
LIMITED GRANTS

GRANTS TO ATTORNEYS AND CONSULAR OFFICERS

Grants to attorney for the use and benefit of the person entitled

11.31 Rule 31 of the NCPR, as amended with effect from 1 October 2007 by the Mental Capacity Act 2005 (Transitional and Consequential Provisions) Order 2007, SI 2007/1898, is as follows:

'(1) Subject to paragraphs (2) and (3) below, the lawfully constituted attorney of a person entitled to a grant may apply for administration for the use and benefit of the donor, and such grant shall be limited until further representation be granted, or in such other way as the district judge or registrar may direct.

(2) Where the donor referred to in paragraph (1) above is an executor, notice of the application shall be given to any other executor unless such notice is dispensed with by the district judge or registrar.

(3) Where the donor referred to in paragraph (1) above lacks capacity within the meaning of the Mental Capacity Act 2005 and the attorney is acting under an enduring power of attorney or lasting power of attorney, the application shall be made in accordance with rule 35.'

Form of power of attorney

11.40 Forms of power of attorney are given in Appendix VI, Nos 185–188.

11.41 The Mental Capacity Act 2005 replaced enduring powers of attorney with lasting powers of attorney with effect from 1 October 2007. However, the Enduring Powers of Attorney (Prescribed Form) (Amendment) Amendment Regulations 2007, SI 2007/548 extend transitional arrangements by which such enduring powers of attorney that were executed before that date may be registered after that date.

11.41A An enduring power of attorney made and executed in the prescribed form before 1 October 2007 is acceptable (see the Enduring Powers of Attorney (Prescribed Form) Regulations 1990, SI 1990/1376 and the Enduring

Powers of Attorney (Prescribed Form) (Amendment) Regulations 2005, SI 2005/3116 further extended by the Enduring Powers of Attorney (Prescribed Form) (Amendment) Amendment Regulations 2007, SI 2007/548 and the Enduring Powers of Attorney (Welsh Language Prescribed Form) (Amendment) Regulations 2007, SI 2007/549 which together combine to extend the power to execute enduring powers of attorney in the appropriate prescribed form until 30 September 2007; see also para 11.257 ff)). The oath should confirm that the donor remains mentally capable or is not mentally incapable and that the Public Guardian has not registered the power. If the power has been registered the application for the grant must be made under NCPR 35 (see paras 11.257 ff).

11.42 The Enduring Powers of Attorney (Prescribed Form) (Amendment) Regulations 2005 came into force on 5 December 2005 and prescribe a new form of enduring power of attorney however the transitional provision in art 3 of the regulations allows the execution of a power in the form which was replaced until 1 April 2007. The Enduring Powers of Attorney (Prescribed Form) (Amendment) Amendment Regulations 2007 and The Enduring Powers of Attorney (Welsh Language Prescribed Form) (Amendment) Regulations 2007 which came into force on 30 March 2007 extended the transitional arrangements so that enduring powers of attorney could be executed until 30 September 2007 and prescribe a new form of enduring power of attorney. The previous (Amendment) Regulations (2005) in reg 3 of the Regulations allowed the execution of a power in the old form until 1 April 2007.

Note that a form, which has the same effect as the prescribed form but which differs in an immaterial respect or mode of expression or which contain variations according to circumstances or as the Court of Protection or the Public Guardian approves, is acceptable[1].

[1] Lasting Powers of Attorney, Enduring Powers of Attorney and Public Guardian Regulations 2007, art 3. See para 11.42A below.

11.42A The Lasting Powers of Attorney, Enduring Powers of Attorney and Public Guardian Regulations 2007 prescribe forms of lasting powers of attorney (Sch 1, Parts 1 and 2). References to the forms mentioned in the Regulations include a Welsh version of the forms. A donor may execute an instrument intended to create a property and affairs lasting power of attorney or/and an instrument intended to create a personal welfare lasting power of attorney. Of these, only a lasting power of attorney in respect of property and (financial) affairs may be used for the purpose of obtaining a grant for the use and benefit of the donor. The donor of a lasting power of attorney may appoint more than one donee. A lasting power of attorney is not created and therefore unusable until the Public Guardian registers it irrespective of whether the donor lacks capacity within the meaning of the Mental Capacity Act 2005 or not. An application made under NCP Rule 31(1) that relies upon a registered lasting power of attorney should include a statement in the oath that the donor does not lack capacity within the meaning of the Act to manage his property and affairs and that the registered lasting power of attorney has not been revoked nor has the donee disclaimed his appointment. The

11.42A *Limited grants*

registered lasting power of attorney stamped by the Office of the Public Guardian together with a copy should be submitted with the application. The registry returns the original stamped power after inspection. Equally acceptable is an office copy of the registered lasting power or a copy certified on each page pursuant to s 3 of the Powers of Attorney Act 1971.

Substituted attorney

11.65 If the general power of attorney contains a power of substitution, and the attorney has exercised it, the substitute may take the grant[1], and on the substituted power being executed the first attorney drops out until the substituted power is revoked, the appointment of the substituted attorney being filed with the original power.

[1] *Palliser v Ord* (1724) Bunb 166. An attorney appointed by an attorney was accepted, where it was allowed by the law of the deceased's domicile; *Re Abdul Hamid Bey's Goods* (1898) 78 LT 202.

Oath of attorney

11.80 The oath should contain all the particulars which would be necessary in the case of a direct grant to the donor of the power. Additionally an attorney acting under an enduring power must confirm that the power is not registered with the Public Guardian and that the donor remains mentally capable. See para 11.253 ff below for practice where the power is registered. The appropriate limitation must be included. A grant to an attorney is expressed to be for the use and benefit of the donor and the usual limitation required by r 31(1) is 'until further representation be granted' but, under that rule, the district judge or registrar may direct some other form of limitation. The usual form of limitation in a grant allows a further grant to issue not only to the donor of the original power of attorney, or another attorney appointed by him, but to any other person with an equal title to a grant. The district judge or registrar would not normally allow a further grant to issue to anyone other than the original donor, or an attorney appointed by him in substitution for the original attorney, without good reason being given and without the original attorney or donor being given an opportunity to be heard on the matter. Some other possible forms of limitation are dealt with in the following paragraphs. See forms of oath, Nos 120–122, 164 and 171.

GRANTS FOR USE OF MINORS

Grant where person entitled is a minor

11.123 The practice in making grants for the use and benefit of minors is governed by NCPR 32[1]. The Practice Direction of 26 September 1991 (Practice Direction (probate: non-contentious probate: grant on behalf of minor) [1991] 4 All ER 562, [1991] 1 WLR 1069) remains in force so far as it is applicable to the rule. The text of NCPR 32(1) as amended by the

Grants for use of minors **11.124**

Non-Contentious Probate (Amendment) Rules 1998, SI 1998/1903, the Adoption and Children Act 2002 (Consequential Amendments) Order 2005, SI 2005/3504, and the Non-Contentious Probate (Amendment) Rules 2009, SI 2009/1893, consequential upon the Human Fertilisation and Embryology Act 2008 is as follows:

'(1) Where a person to whom a grant would otherwise be made is a minor, administration for his use and benefit, limited until he attains the age of eighteen years, shall, unless otherwise directed, and subject to paragraph (2) of this rule, be granted to

[(a) a parent of the minor who has, or is deemed to have, parental responsibility for him in accordance with—
  [(i) section 2(1), 2(1A), 2(2), 2(2A), 4 or 4ZA of the Children Act 1989,]
   (ii) paragraph 4 or 6 of Schedule 14 to that Act, or
   (iii) an adoption order within the meaning of section 12(1) of the Adoption Act 1976 [or section 46(1) of the Adoption and Children Act 2002], or
[(aa) a person who has, or is deemed to have, parental responsibility for the minor by virtue of section 12(2) of the Children Act 1989 where the court has made a residence order under section 8 of that Act in respect of the minor in favour of that person; or]
[(ab) a step-parent of the minor who has parental responsibility for him in accordance with section 4A of the Children Act 1989; or]
 (b) a guardian of the minor who is appointed, or deemed to have been appointed, in accordance with section 5 of the Children Act 1989 or in accordance with paragraph 12, 13 or 14 of Schedule 14 to that Act]; [or]
[(ba) a special guardian of the minor who is appointed in accordance with section 14A of the Children Act 1989; or
 (bb) an adoption agency which has parental responsibility for the minor by virtue of section 25(2) of the Adoption and Children Act 2002; or]
[(c) a local authority which has, or is deemed to have, parental responsibility for the minor by virtue of section 33(3) of the Children Act 1989 where the court has made a care order under section 31(1)(a) of that Act in respect of the minor and that local authority is designated in that order;]'

1 See Appendix II.

11.124 The Adoption and Children Act 2002 has extended the classes or persons who may have parental responsibility for a minor. In addition the Human Fertilisation and Embryology Act 2008 defines the parent of a child born as a result of placing in a woman an embryo or sperm and eggs or her artificial insemination. Accordingly with effect from 5 December 2005 priority of right to a grant for the use and benefit of a minor is now given by the NCPR 32 equally to a parent (including an adoptive parent and from 6 April 2009 a parent by virtue of the Human Fertilisation and Embryology Act 2008[1]) with parental responsibility for him, a person who has parental responsibility by virtue of a residence order in his favour in respect of the minor, a step-parent who has acquired parental responsibility for the minor, a guardian with parental responsibility for him, a special guardian (appointed by order of the court), an adoption agency authorised to place the minor for adoption or a local authority with parental responsibility for him. In the absence of or in appropriate circumstances in spite of such persons, adoption agency or local authority having parental responsibility, other persons may be appointed by district judge's or registrar's order[2] to obtain administration for the use and benefit of the minor.

11.124 *Limited grants*

¹ Section 2, Children Act 1989 as amended consequential to the Human Fertilisation and Embryology Act 2008.
² NCPR 32(2).

Parents, persons, guardians, special guardians, adoption agency and local authority entitled in priority

11.149 Under NCPR 32(1), as last amended and with effect from 1 October 2009, where the person to whom a grant of administration (with or without will) would otherwise be made is a minor, the persons primarily entitled to a grant on his behalf are a parent or a person in whose favour a residence order is made in respect of the minor or a step-parent or a guardian or special guardian or adoption agency or a local authority all having parental responsibility as mentioned in the rule. This includes the mother of an illegitimate child or the father of an illegitimate child, the father acquiring parental responsibility by being registered as the minor's father¹ or under a court order² or recorded parental responsibility agreement.

¹ Section 4(1)(a), Children Act 1989 as amended by s 111, Adoption and Children Act 2002 with effect from 1 December 2003.
² Ie, of the High Court, a county court or a magistrates' court (see the Children Act 1989, s 5 and Sch 14, paras 12, 13 and 14; paras A1.450, A1.467 ff).

Grant to parents (including adoptive parents)

11.152 NCPR 32(1), as previously amended with effect from 14 October 1991 and further amended with effect from 14 September 1998, 30 December 2005 and most recently from 1 October 2009, no longer requires both parents, if living, to apply jointly for the grant. This change is a consequence of s 2(7) of the Children Act 1989, which provides:

'(7) Where more than one person has parental responsibility for a child, each of them may act alone and without the other (or others) in meeting that responsibility; but nothing in this Part shall be taken to affect the operation of any enactment which requires the consent of more than one person in a matter affecting the child.'

However, where a minority interest arises under a will or an intestacy, a grant may not normally issue to less than two individuals (Senior Courts Act 1981, s 114(2)). Accordingly, where both parents have parental responsibility for the minor, they will normally apply jointly for the grant. If one of them is not competent or is not willing to take a grant (eg because he or she is mentally incapable or has renounced his or her right to take a grant for the use and benefit of the minor) the competent and willing parent normally may nominate any fit and proper person to act jointly with him or her in taking the grant (NCPR 32(3) as amended).

11.159 Where the father of a minor was not married to the mother at the time of the child's birth, but has parental responsibility in accordance with paras 4 or 6 of Sch 14 to the Children Act 1989 either (a) by virtue of an order under s 4(1) of the Family Law Reform Act 1987; or (b) by virtue of an order giving him custody or care and control of the child, in force immediately before the commencement of Pts I and II of the Children Act 1989, the oath must state that he is the father of the minor and a parent having parental responsibility by virtue of such an order which was in force immediately before the commencement of the Children Act 1989. A copy of the order must be produced in each instance[1].

[1] Practice Direction, 26 September 1991 ([1991] 4 All ER 562, [1991] 1 WLR 1069).

11.159A Section 4 of the Children Act 1989 and s 1 of the Family Law Reform Act 1987 are further amended by virtue of ss 42 and 43 of the Human Fertilisation and Embryology Act 2008 so as to confer rights to a woman other than the mother of a child who is treated as the parent of the child. The amendments are reproduced in Appendix I. A man who is treated as the father of a child by virtue of ss 37–40 of the Act (agreed father conditions) acquires parental responsibility under s 4(1)(a) of the Children Act 1989 on being registered as the child's father under the enactments mentioned in that subsection. The Act will be brought into effect in three stages from 6 April 2009 to April 2010.

11.161A The Children Act 1989 is further amended by the Human Fertilisation and Embryology Act 2008 with effect from 6 April 2009 to include amendments to s 2 and the addition of a new s 4ZA (inserted after s 4) to confirm the circumstances when a second female parent has, or may acquire, parental responsibility for a child born as a result of assisted reproduction. The text of the amendments and addition are as follows:

'2(1A) Where a child—

(a) has a parent by virtue of section 42 of the Human Fertilisation and Embryology Act 2008; or
(b) has a parent by virtue of section 43 of that Act and is a person to whom section 1(3) of the Family Law Reform Act 1987 applies,

the child's mother and the other parent shall each have parental responsibility for the child.'

'2(2A) Where a child has a parent by virtue of section 43 of the Human Fertilisation and Embryology Act 2008 and is not a person to whom section 1(3) of the Family Law Reform Act 1987 applies—

(a) the mother shall have parental responsibility for the child;
(b) the other parent shall have parental responsibility for the child if she has acquired it (and has not ceased to have it) in accordance with the provisions of this Act.'

'**4ZA Acquisition of parental responsibility by second female parent**

(1) Where a child has a parent by virtue of section 43 of the Human Fertilisation and Embryology Act 2008 and is not a person to whom section 1(3) of the Family Law Reform Act 1987 applies, that parent shall acquire parental responsibility for the child if—

(a) she becomes registered as a parent of the child under any of the enactments specified in subsection (2);
(b) she and the child's mother make an agreement providing for her to have parental responsibility for the child; or

11.161A *Limited grants*

(c) the court, on her application, orders that she shall have parental responsibility for the child.

(2) The enactments referred to in subsection (1)(a) are—

(a) paragraphs (a), (b) and (c) of section 10(1B) and of section 10A(1B) of the Births and Deaths Registration Act 1953;
(b) paragraphs (a), (b) and (d) of section 18B(1) and sections 18B(3)(a) and 20(1)(a) of the Registration of Births, Deaths and Marriages (Scotland) Act 1965; and
(c) sub-paragraphs (a), (b) and (c) of Article 14ZA(3) of the Births and Deaths Registration (Northern Ireland) Order 1976.

(3) The Secretary of State may by order amend subsection (2) so as to add further enactments to the list in that subsection.

(4) An agreement under subsection (1)(b) is also a "parental responsibility agreement", and section 4(2) applies in relation to such an agreement as it applies in relation to parental responsibility agreements under section 4.

(5) A person who has acquired parental responsibility under subsection (1) shall cease to have that responsibility only if the court so orders.

(6) The court may make an order under subsection (5) on the application—

(a) of any person who has parental responsibility for the child; or
(b) with the leave of the court, of the child himself,

subject, in the case of parental responsibility acquired under subsection (1)(c), to section 12(4).

(7) The court may only grant leave under subsection (6)(b) if it is satisfied that the child has sufficient understanding to make the proposed application.'

Parental responsibility of a minor in these instances is summarised as follows:

- Section 2(1A)(a): If at the time of placing in her of an embryo or the sperm and eggs or her artificial insemination a woman (the mother) was in a civil partnership, the civil partner is treated as a parent of the minor unless it is shown that she did not consent to the placing of the embryo and sperm and eggs or artificial insemination; both the mother and civil partner (the parent) have parental responsibility for the minor.
- Section 2(1A)(b): Where the minor is a person to whom s 1(3) of the Family Law Reform Act 1987 applies and no man is treated as father or no woman is treated as parent at the time of placing in the mother an embryo or the sperm and eggs or of her artificial insemination (the treatment) the agreed parent conditions[1] were met in relation to another woman who remained alive at the time she is treated as a parent; the mother and parent have parental responsibility for the minor.
- Section 2(2A)(a): Where s 1(3) of the Family Law Reform Act 1987 does not apply to the minor the mother has parental responsibility; (b) the parent shall have parental responsibility if she acquires it and does not cease to have it.
- Section 2(4Z) sets out the conditions under which the parent of a child to whom s 1(3) of the Family Law Reform Act 1987 does not apply.

[1] Section 44 of the Human Fertilisation and Embryology Act 2008 (see A1.592L).

Grants for use of persons under disability **11.237A**

Oath and supporting evidence

11.161B The applicant's oath should include details of the residence order. A copy of the order must be produced with the oath together with any will to be proved.

Persons in whose favour a residence order has been made

11.161C Subject to it coming into force, s 12 of the Children Act 1989 (residence orders and parental responsibility) is amended by the insertion of sub-s (1A) which provides that where the court makes a residence order in favour of a woman who is a parent of a child by virtue of s 43 of the Human Fertilisation and Embryology Act 2008, it shall, if that woman would not otherwise have parental responsibility for the child, also make an order under s 4ZA giving her that responsibility.

11.163 Section 12 of the Children Act 1989 is amended by the Human Fertilisation and Embryology Act 2008 by inclusion of sub-s (1A) to allow the court making a residence order in favour of woman who is a parent of the minor by virtue of s 43 of the Human Fertilisation and Embryology Act 2008. Section 12(2) of the Children Act 1989 provides further that where the court makes a residence order in respect of a minor in favour of any person who is not a parent or guardian of the minor, that person shall have parental responsibility for the minor while the order remains in force. The Children Act 1989, s 8 defines 'residence order' as an order settling the arrangements to be made as to the person with whom the child is to live.

GRANTS FOR USE OF PERSONS UNDER DISABILITY

Lack of mental capacity within the meaning of the Mental Capacity Act 2005

11.237 The Mental Capacity Act 2005 received Royal assent on 7 April 2005 and came into force on 1 October 2007. The Act follows extensive consultation flowing from the Law Commission Report (No 231), published in 1995, and the Government's policy statement 'Making Decisions', published in October 1999, which set out proposals to reform the law and clarify the decision-making process for people unable to make decisions for themselves. On the day it came into force the Act replaced Part 7 of the Mental Health Act 1983 and the Enduring Powers of Attorney Act 1985.

11.237A Part 1 of the Mental Capacity Act 2005 sets out among other things the guiding principles to apply the Act, the concept of lasting powers of attorney, the powers of the court to make declarations, appoint deputies and powers in relation to validity and operation of lasting powers of attorney. Section 9 allows a donor of a lasting power of attorney to confer on the donor or donees authority to make decisions about all or any of:

11.237A *Limited grants*

(a) the donor's personal welfare or specified matters concerning his personal welfare; and
(b) the donor's property and affairs or specified matters concerning his property and affairs,

and including authority to make such decisions in circumstances when the donor no longer has capacity.

11.237B The principles set out in s 1 of the Act are:

'(2) A person must be assumed to have capacity unless it is established that he lacks capacity.

(3) A person is not to be treated as unable to make a decision unless all practicable steps to help him to do so have been taken without success.

(4) A person is not to be treated as unable to make a decision merely because he makes an unwise decision.

(5) An act done, or decision made, under this Act for or on behalf of a person who lacks capacity must be done, or made, in his best interests.

(6) Before the act is done, or the decision is made, regard must be had to whether the purpose for which it is needed can be as effectively achieved in a way that is less restrictive of the person's rights and freedom of action.'

11.237C Under s 2 of the Act, a person lacks capacity in relation to a matter if at the material time he is unable to make a decision for himself in relation to the matter because of an impairment of, or a disturbance in the functioning of, the mind or brain. It does not matter whether the impairment or disturbance is temporary or permanent. Under s 16 of the Act, if a person lacks capacity, the court has power to appoint a deputy to make decisions concerning the person's personal welfare or his property or affairs.

11.237D Part 2 of the Act replaces the present Court of Protection with a new Court of Protection, a superior court of record with its own judges and procedures, and appoints a statutory official, the Public Guardian, to support the court and whose functions include the duty to register and maintain a record of lasting powers of attorney and enduring powers of attorney.

11.237E Lasting powers of attorney must be in a prescribed form. Enduring powers of attorney, which exist at the commencement date, will continue to be effective and capable of registration upon mental incapacity of the donor supervening. A document being or purporting to be an office copy of a registered lasting power of attorney or registered enduring power of attorney is in any part of the United Kingdom evidence of the contents of the instrument and the fact that it has been registered (Sch 1, art 16; Sch 4, para 15).

11.237F Where the person entitled to a grant lacks capacity to manage his affairs within the meaning of the Mental Capacity Act 2005, administration

Grants for use of persons under disability **11.240**

may be granted for his use and benefit in accordance with NCPR 35, as amended with effect from 1 October 2007[1].

[1] Mental Capacity Act 2005 (Transitional and Consequential Provisions) Order 2007. The Non-Contentious Probate Rules 1987, SI 1987/2024, as amended, are included in Appendix II of this Supplement.

11.238 NCPR 35 is now as follows:

'(1) Unless a district judge or registrar otherwise directs, no grant shall be made under this rule unless all persons entitled in the same degree as the person who lacks capacity within the meaning of the Mental Capacity Act 2005 referred to in paragraph (2) below have been cleared off.

(2) Where a district judge or registrar is satisfied that a person entitled to a grant is a person who lacks capacity within the meaning of the Mental Capacity Act 2005 to manage his affairs, administration for his use and benefit, limited until further representation be granted or in such other way as the district judge or registrar may direct, may be granted in the following order of priority—

(a) to the person authorised by the Court of Protection to apply for a grant;
(b) where there is no person so authorised, to the lawful attorney of the person who lacks capacity within the meaning of the Mental Capacity Act 2005 acting under a registered enduring power of attorney or lasting power of attorney;
(c) where there is no such attorney entitled to act, or if the attorney shall renounce administration for the use and benefit of the person who lacks capacity within the meaning of the Mental Capacity Act 2005, to the person entitled to the residuary estate of the deceased.

(3) Where a grant is required to be made to not less than two administrators, and there is only one person competent and willing to take a grant under the foregoing provisions of this rule, administration may, unless a district judge or registrar otherwise directs, be granted to such person jointly with any other person nominated by him.

(4) Notwithstanding the foregoing provisions of this rule, administration for the use and benefit of the person who lacks capacity within the meaning of the Mental Capacity Act 2005 may be granted to such other person as the district judge or registrar may by order direct.

(5) Unless the applicant is the person authorised in paragraph 2(a) above notice of an intended application under this rule shall be given to the Court of Protection.'

Other persons having equal right

11.239 Unless otherwise directed by the district judge or registrar, a grant will not be made for the use of a person who lacks capacity to manage his affairs within the meaning of the mental Capacity Act 2005 without clearing off all other persons equally entitled with him. (See NCPR 35(1).)

11.240 Where one of several persons entitled in the same degree lacks capacity within the meaning of the Mental Capacity Act 2005, application for a grant should wherever possible be made by one or more of the capable persons. If such persons do not wish to act and it is desired that a grant should be made for the use and benefit of the person who lacks capacity, the normal

11.240 *Limited grants*

procedure is to obtain the renunciations of the capable persons. If there is some difficulty in clearing off such persons, or if for some reason it is sought to prefer the person representing the person who lacks capacity, the facts should be put before the district judge or registrar for his directions.

11.241 Where one of several executors named in a will lacks capacity within the meaning of the Mental Capacity Act 2005 to manage his affairs, probate is granted to the other executors, power being reserved to the excecutor[1] who lacks capacity. The district judge's or registrar's power under r 35(1) does not enable a grant to be made on behalf of an executor who lacks capacity without clearing off other executors who are sui juris[2].

[1] *Evans v Tyler* (1849) 2 Rob Eccl 128 at 131.
[2] Registrar's Circular, 12 June 1967.

11.242 Where one of two executors lacks capacity to manage his affairs within the meaning of the Mental Capacity Act 2005 and administration (with will) is granted to the other's attorney, it is limited until further representation be granted, leaving it open for the capable executor to obtain probate and for the one who lacks capacity to obtain probate upon recovering his capacity. Form of oath, No 164, suitably adapted.

Foreign domicile

11.243 Where it is sought to obtain a grant in the estate of a person of foreign domicile for the use and benefit of a person who lacks capacity to manage his affairs within the meaning of the Mental Capacity Act 2005, due regard must be had to the general practice with regard to grants of administration where the deceased died domiciled out of England and Wales[1]. If the applicant for the grant is not the person entrusted with the administration of the estate by the court having jurisdiction at the place where the deceased died domiciled, it must be shown how the person who lacks capacity is beneficially entitled to the estate by the law of the place where the deceased died domiciled and how the applicant is entitled to represent the incapable person by that law with the limitation, if any, imposed by that law; alternatively, if the circumstances justify it, the district judge or registrar may order that the grant be made to such person as he thinks fit. In any event, a district judge's or registrar's order must be obtained.

[1] See Ch 12.

Wording of oath

11.244 The oath must state that the person entitled to the grant lacks capacity to manage his affairs within the meaning of the Mental Capacity Act 2005. For forms of oath, see No 134. The date of any relevant order or authorisation (of the Court of Protection) is quoted in the oath, and the order or authorisation must be produced; the usual statements as to minority and life interests and settled land must be included (see paras 6.378 and 6.379). If any minority or life interest arises, the grant will normally be made to not less than two individuals, or to a trust corporation with or without an individual[1]. If a life or minority interest arises and two administrators are required and if there is only one person competent and willing to take a grant, who is either the person authorised by the Court of Protection or the lawful attorney of the incapable person acting under a registered enduring power of attorney or the person entitled to the residuary estate of the deceased, under r 35(2), he may nominate his co-administrator under r 35(3) (Form 63 in this Supplement).

[1] Supreme Court Act 1981, s 114(2) (see para A1.341).

11.245 The limitation 'for the use and benefit of' the person who lacks capacity 'and until further representation be granted' must be included in the oath.

Person authorised by Court of Protection

11.246 The Mental Capacity Act 2005 replaced and reconstituted the former Court of Protection with a superior court of record that is also called the Court of Protection[1]. Where the person entitled to the grant lacks capacity to manage his affairs within the meaning of the Mental Capacity Act 2005, priority of right to a grant is given to the person authorised by the Court of Protection under the provisions of the Act[2] to apply for the grant[3].

[1] Mental Capacity Act 2005, s 45.
[2] Under s 16 of the Mental Capacity Act 2005 (which replaces the Mental Health Act 1983 which in turn replaced the Mental Capacity Act 1959 and the Lunacy Acts 1890 to 1908), the Court of Protection may appoint a deputy to make decisions for a person who lacks capacity in relation to a matter or matters concerning his personal welfare or his property and affairs The powers and duties of a deputy in relation to the welfare, property and affairs of the person who lacks capacity are respectively in ss 17 and 18 of the Mental Capacity Act 2005.
[3] NCPR 35(2)(a).

11.247 The authority of the Court of Protection confers on the person authorised such powers only as are specified in that authority which may include power to apply for a grant in the estate of a deceased person for the use and benefit of the person who lacks capacity. An order appointing a deputy is not accepted unless it embodies authority to apply for a grant. A supplemental order must be obtained where this authority is lacking. The order, under the seal of the Court of Protection, must be produced with the application for the grant.

11.248 The authority of the Court of Protection may contain provision for the appointment of another person (unspecified) as co-administrator with the person named in the event of there being a minority or life interest and the person named in the order can now nominate a second administrator to act with him, unless a district judge or registrar otherwise directs[1].

[1] NCPR 35(3).

11.249 *Limited grants*

Notice to Court of Protection

11.249 In cases where the person entitled to a grant lacks capacity with the meaning of the Act to manage his affairs and no person has been authorised by the Court of Protection to apply for a grant, notice of the intended application must be given by the extracting solicitor or probate practitioner to that Court[1]. It is not necessary to give that court notice where application for representation is made by the person specifically authorised to apply for the grant[2].

[1] NCPR 35(5).
[2] NCPR 35(5).

11.250 The notice should be addressed to: The Court of Protection, Archway House, 2 Junction Road, London N19 5SZ. The e-mail address is: custserve@guardianship.gov.uk and the website is www.guardianship.gov.uk. The telephone number is: 0845 330 2900.

11.251 There is now no requirement for the Court of Protection to return a sealed acknowledgment.

11.252 The prior right given by NCPR 35(2)(a) to a person authorised by the Court of Protection to apply for a grant is sufficiently cleared off by the acknowledgment by that court of the notice of application, unless it indicates that a person has been, or will be, appointed to apply for the grant[1]. Note, however, that with effect from 14 September 1998 the rule does not require that notice be given to the Court of Protection if the applicant is the authorised person.

[1] Registrar's Direction (1956) 16 July.

Proof of a person's lack of capacity to manage his affairs

11.253 In cases where a person who is entitled to grant lacks capacity to manage his affairs within the meaning of the Mental Capacity Act 2005, where the applicant for the grant is not a person authorised by the Court of Protection to apply or an attorney acting under a registered enduring power of attorney, evidence of lack of capacity within the meaning of the Act must be lodged.

11.254 When the person who lacks capacity within the meaning of the Act is a patient who is resident in an institution, the district judges and registrars will normally accept a certificate from the Responsible Medical Officer of the institution in the following terms:

[Name of Institution]

[Name of patient]

I certify that:

The above-named patient, who is now residing in this Institution, suffers from an impairment of, or a disturbance in the functioning of, the mind or brain as a result of which he is unable to make a decision for himself in relation to making an application for a grant representation and administration of the estate of A B and in my opinion he lacks capacity to manage his property and affairs within the meaning of the Mental Capacity Act 2005.

Date:

(Signed)
Responsible Medical Officer.

11.255 If the person who lacks capacity is not resident in an institution the district judges and registrars will normally accept a certificate in similar form by the patient's doctor certifying also the period in which he has attended the patient in respect of the disability.

11.256 If the Responsible Medical Officer, or the patient's doctor, as the case may be, is unable to give such a certificate, the matter should be referred to the district judge or registrar for directions[1].

[1] *Practice Note* [1962] 2 All ER 613, [1962] 1 WLR 738; *Practice Direction (incapacity: evidence of)* [1969] 1 All ER 494, [1969] 1 WLR 301.

Lawful attorney acting under a registered enduring power of attorney

11.257 Where there is no person authorised by the Court of Protection to apply for a grant, the person next entitled to apply for a grant for the use and benefit of the incapable person is his lawful attorney acting under a registered enduring power of attorney. Notice of the application must be given to the Court of Protection as required by NCPR 35(5).

11.258 A registered enduring power of attorney is one which is in the prescribed form (see the Enduring Powers of Attorney (Prescribed Form) Regulations 1990[1], as amended (see para 11.259), which contain saving provisions in respect of powers executed by donors in the forms prescribed by the earlier regulations) and made under the Enduring Powers of Attorney Act 1985 and the Court of Protection (Enduring Powers of Attorney) Rules 2001[2].

[1] SI 1990/1376.
[2] SI 2001/825.

11.259 Limited grants

11.259 The Enduring Powers of Attorney (Prescribed Form) (Amendment) Regulations 2005[1], which took effect on and from 5 December 2005, prescribe a new form of enduring power of attorney. However, the transitional provision in art 3 of the Regulations allows the execution of a power in the (old) form that was replaced until 1 April 2007, at which time it was anticipated that lasting powers of attorney pursuant to the Mental Capacity Act 2005 would become effective. The Enduring Powers of Attorney (Prescribed Form) (Amendment) Amendment Regulations 2007[2] extended the transitional arrangements to enduring powers executed before the Lasting Powers of Attorney, Enduring Powers of Attorney and Public Guardian Regulations 2007[3] came into force on 1 October 2007.

[1] SI 2005/3116.
[2] SI 2007/548.
[3] SI 2007/1253.

11.260 An enduring power of attorney does not cease when the donor becomes incapable but the powers of the attorney are limited until the power of attorney is registered by the Public Guardian.

11.261 The oath should confirm that no one has been authorised by the Court of Protection to apply for a grant. Form of oath, No 135.

11.262 The registered enduring power of attorney, stamped by the Office of the Public Guardian, should be lodged for inspection together with a copy for filing with the application for the grant. The production of the registered power of attorney stamped as such by the Office of the Public Guardian, coupled with a statement in the oath that the incapable donor remains mentally incapable of managing his affairs is accepted as sufficient evidence of the lack of capacity. The registered power of attorney is returned by the registry.

11.263 Unless there is a relevant restriction in the power of attorney, the grant will be limited for the use and benefit of the incapable person and until further representation be granted.

Lawful attorney acting under a registered lasting power of attorney

11.263A On the day it came into force (1 October 2007) the Lasting Powers of Attorney, Enduring Powers of Attorney and Public Guardian Regulations 2007 gave practical effect to s 9 of the Mental Capacity Act 2005 by prescribing the form of lasting powers of attorney in Parts 1 and 2 of Sch 1 to the Regulations.

11.263B A lasting power of attorney allows the donor to confer on the donee(s) authority to make decisions about all or any of the following matters:

Grants for use of persons under disability 11.265

(a) the donor's personal welfare or specified matters concerning his welfare; and
(b) the donor's property and affairs or specified matters concerning the donor's property and affairs.

The power includes authority for the attorney to make decisions in circumstances when the donor no longer has capacity to manage his affairs. The donor may appoint more than one donee. An attorney who appoints more than one person may authorise the donees to act jointly or jointly and severally or jointly in specified matters and severally in other matters.

11.263C In respect of an application for a grant of representation, a lasting power of attorney must give the donee powers to deal with the property and affairs (which include finance) of the donor. A power that is limited to making decisions about the donor's personal affairs, or that does not include specific power to obtain a grant or general power to deal with property and affairs, is not acceptable to allow the attorney to extract a grant for the use and benefit of the donee.

11.263D The registered lasting power of attorney, stamped as such by the Office of the Public Guardian, should be lodged for inspection together with a copy for filing with the application for the grant. Alternatively, an office copy of the registered lasting power issued by the Office of the Public Guardian or a copy of the registered power certified in accordance with s 3 of the Powers of Attorney Act 1971 is acceptable. In addition, a medical certificate confirming the donor's lack of capacity within the meaning of the Act must be filed (see para 11.254). This requirement flows from the fact that a lasting power of attorney may be registered and acted upon before the donor lacks capacity within the meaning of the Act. The registry returns the registered power of attorney after inspection.

11.263E Unless there is a relevant restriction in the power of attorney, the grant will be limited for the use and benefit of the person who lacks capacity and until further representation be granted. For oath, see Form 135 in this Supplement.

Passing over a person who lacks capacity to manage his affairs

11.264 An application to pass over a person who lacks capacity to manage his affairs, as distinct from making a grant for his use and benefit, must be made under s 116 of the Supreme Court Act 1981 (see para A1.343).

Sole executor or residuary legatee or devisee in trust lacks capacity to manage his affairs: grant to residuary legatee

11.265 Where the sole executor or residuary legatee or devisee in trust, as the case may be, is entitled to a grant but lacks capacity to manage his affairs and

11.265   Limited grants

if no person has been appointed by the Court of Protection and there is no lawful attorney acting under a registered enduring power of attorney or registered lasting power of attorney (or any such attorney has renounced administration for the use and benefit of the person who lacks capacity) a grant will be made to the residuary legatee or devisee named in the will, for the use and benefit of the person who lacks capacity and limited until further representation be granted (or otherwise limited as the district judge or registrar may direct). For oath, see Form 169 in this Supplement. If there be no residuary legatee or devisee, a similar grant will be made to the person entitled to the undisposed-of residuary estate of the deceased[1].

[1]   NCPR 35(2)(c).

11.266 If a life or minority interest arises and there is only one residuary legatee or devisee or person entitled to the undisposed-of residuary estate who is competent and willing to take a grant, he may nominate his co-administrator, unless the district judge or registrar otherwise directs, under r 35(3).

11.267 As to the position where there are two or more executors, one of whom is lacks capacity to manage his affairs, see 'Other persons having equal right', paras 11.239–11.242.

Residuary legatee lacks capacity to manage his affairs

11.268 If the sole residuary legatee and devisee lacks capacity to manage his affairs (there being no executor or residuary legatee or devisee in trust), administration (with the will annexed) will be granted for his use and benefit during the period when he lacks capacity (i) to the person authorised by the Court of Protection, or, if none, (ii) to the lawful attorney of the person who lacks capacity acting under a registered enduring power of attorney or registered lasting power of attorney; or, if none, or if such renounces administration for the use and benefit of the person who lacks capacity (iii) to such other person as the district judge or registrar may by order direct[1] (see paras 11.274 ff).

[1]   NCPR 35(4).

11.269 As to the position where the will appoints more than one residuary legatee and devisee, see 'Other persons having equal right', paras 11.239–11.242.

Only person entitled on intestacy lacks capacity to manage his affairs

11.270 In the case of an intestacy, where the only person entitled to the grant lacks capacity to manage his affairs within the meaning of the Mental Capacity Act 2005, administration will be granted for his use and benefit and during his incapacity (i) to the person authorised by the Court of Protection or, if none, (ii) to his lawful attorney acting under a registered enduring power of attorney or registered lasting power of attorney; or, if none, or if such attorney renounces administration for the use and benefit of the person who lacks capacity (iii) to such other person as the district judge or registrar may by order direct (see paras 11.274–11.275). For forms of oath, see Nos 134 to 136.

11.271 As to the position where there is more than one person entitled on an intestacy, see 'Other persons having equal right', paras 11.239–11.242.

When spouse or civil partner of intestate is entitled but lacks capacity

11.272 Where a surviving spouse or civil partner is lacks capacity to manage his/her affairs within the meaning of the Mental Capacity Act 2005, and there is no person authorised by the Court of Protection and no attorney acting under a registered enduring power of attorney or registered lasting power of attorney, a district judge's or registrar's order is required for a grant to issue to such person as the district judge or registrar may by order direct, for the use and benefit of the spouse or civil partner who lacks capacity and usually limited until further representation be granted. In view of the spouse's or civil partner's prior right to a grant under NCPR 22(1), this applies whether or not the whole estate vests in the surviving spouse or civil partner.

11.273 In such a case, notwithstanding that the grantees may themselves have a beneficial interest in the estate, the grant is limited 'for the use and benefit of … (*the spouse/civil partner*) and until further representation be granted' (or in such other way as the district judge or registrar may direct), in order to preserve his or her prior right, under NCPR 22, to a grant in the event of recovery[1].

[1] Registrar's Direction (1956) 16 July.

Grant to persons appointed by district judge or registrar

11.274 When a person entitled in priority to a grant lacks mental capacity within the meaning of the Mental Capacity Act 2005 and no person has been authorised by the Court of Protection, there is no attorney acting under a registered enduring power of attorney or registered lasting power of attorney and there is no other person entitled to the residuary estate capable of taking a grant, the district judge or registrar may by order direct that a grant for the use and benefit of the person who lacks capacity be made to such other person as he thinks fit[1]. The district judge or registrar may also direct that a grant issue to another person where there is a person authorised by the Court of Protection, or an attorney acting under a registered lasting power or registered enduring power of attorney, or a person entitled to the residuary estate, instead of to such of these persons who would otherwise be entitled to a grant, if he considers it appropriate[1]. Form of oath, No 136.

[1] NCPR 35(4).

11.275 Limited grants

11.275 Application for the order of the district judge or registrar is made by lodging an affidavit of the facts at the probate department of the Principal Registry, or if the application for the grant is to be made at a district probate registry, at that registry. Unless it is submitted separately the affidavit should exhibit a medical certificate of the person who lacks capacity as detailed in para 11.254 above. The sealed acknowledgment of the notice given to the Court of Protection (see para 11.249) must also be lodged. The district judge or registrar may direct that the application be made on notice or summons if it becomes apparent that it is being, or likely to be, opposed[1].

[1] NCPR 61(1).

11.276 Instances of circumstances in which such an order is necessary are set out in the following paragraphs.

Only person entitled lacks capacity to manage his affairs

11.277 Where the sole person entitled to the estate of the intestate lacks capacity to manage his property or affairs, a grant may be made, on a district judge's or registrar's order, to a next of kin of the incompetent person for his use and benefit limited until further representation be granted (or in such other way as the district judge or registrar may direct).

Surviving spouse or civil partner lacks capacity; his kin under age; guardian

11.278 Where an intestate's spouse or civil partner lacks capacity, and his sole next of kin is a minor, application may be made for an order for a grant to the parents or guardians of the child, for the use and benefit of the spouse or civil partner and limited until further representation be granted (or in such other way as the district judge or registrar may direct).

To a creditor for the use of person entitled

11.279 If no person has been appointed by the Court of Protection and there is no attorney acting under a registered enduring power of attorney or registered lasting power of attorney, and all other persons interested in the estate renounce, the court may make a grant for the use and benefit of the person who lacks capacity to a creditor[1], or to a stranger[2] by a district judge's or registrar's order.

[1] Cf *Re Penny's Goods* (1846) 1 Rob Eccl 426.
[2] *Re Hastings' Goods* (1877) 4 PD 73; *Re Burrell's Goods* (1858) 1 Sw & Tr 64; *Re Eccles' Goods* (1889) 15 PD 1.

Supervening incapacity after grant issued

11.281 For the procedure in cases where lack of capacity has supervened after probate or administration has been granted, see 'Grounds for revocation', and 'Impounding grants', paras 17.07 ff and 17.67 ff.

Recovery of person who previously lacked capacity

11.282 For practice in obtaining a cessate grant to a person who formerly lacked capacity upon recovering his capacity, see paras 13.111 ff.

ADMINISTRATION PENDING DETERMINATION OF PROBATE CLAIM

Practice

11.356 Unless HMRC Inheritance Tax dispenses with it or if it is an 'excepted' estate, the HMRC account for the whole estate should be submitted to HMRC Inheritance Tax with a request for the transfer of the receipt for the tax (if any) paid on the application for the limited grant. A receipted or stamped IHT421 should be included with the application. A fee of £40 is payable for the grant if the assessed value exceeds £5,000[1].

[1] Non-Contentious Probate Fees Order 2004, Fee 1.

MISCELLANEOUS

Grant limited to a claim

11.358 Where it is necessary for the personal representative of a deceased person to be made a party to legal proceedings (eg a claim by or against the estate of the deceased), but the executors or other persons entitled to obtain a grant will not constitute themselves as personal representatives, application may be made for a grant of administration to a nominee, limited to bringing, defending or being a party to the claim or proceedings in question. The grant will in no case be a general grant[1]. The claim or proceedings must be identified in the oath so far as possible[2] and will be specified in the grant.

[1] *Re Chanter's Goods* (1844) 1 Rob Eccl 273; *Davis v Chanter* (1848) 2 Ph 545; *Re Dawson's Goods, Maclean and Maclean v Dawson* (1859) 1 Sw & Tr 425.
[2] Circular, 14 March 1956; Registrar's Direction (1964) 23 March.

Administration 'ad colligenda bona'

Practice in obtaining grant

11.368 When the order has been made, the papers to lead the grant should be prepared and lodged at the Principal Registry or a district probate registry. The following documents are necessary: administrator's oath (Form No 146); HMRC account summary (IHT421) (if required, see Ch 8); the order appointing the administrator and the supporting affidavits etc.

11.372 *Limited grants*

Subsequent application for full grant

11.372 *For form of HMRC account (if required), see Chapter 8 of this Supplement.*

Chapter 12

GRANT WHERE DECEASED DIED DOMICILED OUT OF ENGLAND AND WALES

SECTION II. ENTITLEMENT TO A GRANT WHERE DECEASED DIED DOMICILED OUT OF ENGLAND AND WALES

Grant to, or on behalf of, executor where will is in English or Welsh language

12.81 *See Chapter 8 of this Supplement for an update on HMRC requirements for inheritance tax accounts.*

Whole or substantially whole of estate in England and Wales immovable property

12.120 *See Chapter 8 of this Supplement for an update on HMRC requirements for inheritance tax accounts.*

SECTION III. APPLICATION FOR DISTRICT JUDGE'S OR REGISTRAR'S ORDER

HMRC account

12.148 *See Chapter 8 of this Supplement for an update on HMRC requirements for inheritance tax accounts.*

Inheritance tax, capital transfer tax or estate duty paid in Scotland or Northern Ireland

12.150 *See Chapter 8 of this Supplement for an update on HMRC requirements for inheritance tax accounts.*

Chapter 13
GRANTS 'DE BONIS NON'—CESSATE GRANTS—DOUBLE PROBATE

PARTICULAR CASES

For the use and benefit of a person who lacks capacity within the meaning of the Mental Capacity Act 2005 to manage his affairs

13.48 If the person entitled to a grant of administration (with or without will) de bonis non lacks capacity to manage his affairs within the meaning of the Mental Capacity Act 2005, administration de bonis non may be granted for his use and benefit to the persons to whom an original grant would have been made in the same circumstances. The lack of capacity of the person for whose use the grant is made should be established in the same manner as in the case of an original grant (see paras 11.249 ff of this Supplement).

Sole grantee lacks capacity to manage affairs

13.49 As to the practice where the sole grantee subsequently lacks capacity to manage his affairs within the meaning of the Mental Capacity Act 2005, see paras 17.64 ff.

Limited administration (with will) 'de bonis non' to legatee

13.52 Under the present practice, however, except by order under s 116 of the Senior Courts Act 1981[1], the court will not grant limited administration without the renunciation or citation of persons entitled to a general grant in priority to the applicant (see NCPR 51(b)).

[1] See para A1.343. For practice on application for such an order, see paras 25.94 ff.

Limited administration 'de bonis non' in respect of legal proceedings

13.53 When the grantee of administration limited to institute or defend legal proceedings dies before the termination of the proceedings, he is considered to have left the estate unadministered, and a further grant may be made to another person by order under s 116 of the Senior Courts Act 1981 (see also para 11.358 ff).

PRACTICE IN GRANTS 'DE BONIS NON'

HMRC account

13.76 *See Chapter 8 of this Supplement for updates in practice for the submission of HMRC accounts.*

Papers required

13.77 The practitioner lodges the oath and HMRC account summary (Form D421) or return of estate (Form IHT205) (if required: see Ch 8) at the probate department at the Principal Registry or at any district probate registry or sub-registry. If the papers are lodged at the Principal Registry or at a district probate registry other than that from which the previous grant was extracted, the previous grant, or an office copy thereof, must also be lodged. Unless 'marked' by the applicant (see paras 13.67–13.70), the former grant or office copy will be returned with the new grant.

CESSATE GRANTS

Grant for use of executor who lacks capacity to manage his affairs

13.92 When administration (with the will annexed) has been granted for the use and benefit of an executor who lacks capacity to manage his affairs within the meaning of the Mental Capacity Act 2005 and it is limited 'for his use and benefit' or as previously 'during his incapacity', it ceases on his recovery; he may then take probate of the will.

13.93

If the administrator should die before the recovery of an executor who lacks capacity to manage his affairs, further administration (with the will annexed) may be granted to some other person for the use and benefit of the executor, the latter's lack of capacity to manage his affairs being established in the same manner as on the occasion of the first grant. The oath should recite:

> 'That on the   day of   20   letters of administration (with the said will annexed) of the estate of the said deceased were granted at the principal (*or as the case may be*) registry, to A B the residuary legatee named in the said will (*or as the case may be*) for the use and benefit of C D the sole executor therein named while he lacks capacity to manage his affairs within the meaning of the Mental Capacity Act 2005 during his incapacity. That the said A B died on the   day of   20   whereby the said letters of administration (with the said will annexed) have ceased and expired. That the said C D continues to lack capacity to manage his affairs within the meaning of the Act'.

13.108 *Grants 'de bonis non'—Cessate grants—Double probate*

Administration (with or without will) for use of minor beneficiary

13.108 If one of the administrators should die before majority is attained by any one of the minors, application may be made, under s 114(4) of the Senior Courts Act 1981[1], for the appointment of an additional administrator (see NCPR 26: for practice see paras 7.40–7.42).

[1] See para A1.341.

Administration to person on recovering capacity to manage his affairs

13.111 Where administration has been granted to a person authorised by the Court of Protection, or to some other person, for a person who lacks capacity to manage his affairs limited while he lacks capacity to manage his affairs, the grant ceases on the recovery of that person, or the death of the administrator; and a cessate grant may be made in the one case to the person who formerly lacked capacity himself, and in the other to a person authorised by a further order of the Court of Protection (see paras 11.242 ff of this Supplement), or some other person, for the use of the person who lacks capacity (as the case may require).

13.112 In the case of the administrator's death, where the original grant was made to a person other than the person authorised by the Court of Protection or an attorney acting under a registered enduring power of attorney or registered lasting power of attorney, evidence must again be adduced as to the lack of capacity of the person for whose use and benefit administration is to be granted.

13.113 The recovery of the person who lacks capacity must be proved:

(a) where administration has been granted to a person authorised by an order of the Court of Protection, by the production of the order of that Court determining the proceedings; or
(b) where administration has been granted to some other person, by an affidavit of the doctor.

Unless the consent of the person who obtained the limited grant is lodged, evidence will be required that notice of the application for a cessate grant has been given to him.

13.114 If the grant for the use and benefit of the person who lacks capacity was limited until further representation be granted, it does not cease on the recovery of the person who formerly lacked capacity. The recovered person may apply for a grant himself, supported by evidence as to his recovery as in the preceding paragraph, and the limited grant ceases on the issue of the new grant.

13.115 If the person who lacks capacity should die, the administration granted for his use comes to an end, and administration de bonis non will be granted to the person entitled to the grant, eg if he was the only person entitled to the estate, to his personal representative.

DOUBLE PROBATE

13.120 Probate may not be granted to more than four persons in respect of the same part of the estate of a deceased person[1].

[1] Senior Courts Act 1981, s 114(1) (see para A1.341).

13.125 As to the practice in cases where the proving executor subsequently lacks capacity to manage his affairs within the meaning of the Mental Capacity Act 2005, see paras 17.64 ff.

Chapter 14

RIGHT OF THE COURT TO SELECT AN ADMINISTRATOR; 'COMMORIENTES'

Dispute between executors

14.13 An executor may object or refuse to be joined with his co-executor, if the latter lacks capacity to manage his affairs; and the court will exclude the latter from the probate, if the objection be proved[1], but power is reserved to him on regaining his capacity; see also 'Other persons having equal right', paras 11.237H ff of this Supplement.

[1] *Evans v Tyler* (1849) 2 Rob Eccl 128 at 131.

Chapter 15
RENUNCIATION AND RETRACTION

RENUNCIATION

By person appointed by Court of Protection

15.43 A person appointed by an order made by the Court of Protection, previously under the Mental Health Act 1983 or now under the Mental Capacity Act 2005, may renounce probate or administration on behalf of a person who lacks capacity to manage his affairs, if specifically authorised so to do (see NCPR 34(1)).

15.44 The nearest of kin of a person who lacks capacity to manage his affairs within the meaning of the Mental Capacity Act 2005 is not allowed to renounce on behalf of that person.

15.45 When no person has been authorised by the Court of Protection, the only way of clearing off such a person who is entitled to a grant is by citation: but in practice it is usual in such a case to apply for a grant for the use and benefit of the person who lacks capacity or, in special circumstances, for a grant under s 116 of the Senior Courts Act 1981, passing over the person who lacks capacity (see paras 25.94 ff). As to grants for the use and benefit of persons who lack capacity within the meaning of the Mental Health Act 2005, see paras 11.237 ff of this Supplement.

By attorney acting under a registered enduring power of attorney or lasting power of attorney

15.46 An attorney acting under a registered enduring power of attorney or lasting power of attorney may renounce administration for the use and benefit of the person who lacks capacity within the meaning of the Mental Health Act 2005 (see NCPR 35(2)(c)).

Chapter 16
AMENDMENT AND NOTATION OF GRANTS

ELECTION BY SPOUSE OR CIVIL PARTNER TO HAVE LIFE INTEREST REDEEMED

Right of surviving spouse or civil partner to redemption

16.36 By s 47A of the Administration of Estates Act 1925[1] (as amended), the surviving husband or wife of an intestate dying on or after 1 January 1953 or with effect from 5 December 2005 the civil partner of the intestate has the right to require the personal representatives to redeem, at a price to be ascertained in accordance with specific rules[2], any life interest to which he or she is entitled in part of the intestate's estate, being property then in possession.

[1] See para A1.115.
[2] See the Intestate Succession (Interest and Capitalisation) Order 1977, SI 1977/1491, the Intestate Succession (Interest and Capitalisation) (Amendment) Order 1983, SI 1983/1374 and the Intestate Succession (Interest and Capitalisation) (Amendment) Order 2008, SI 2008/3162, which is reproduced in Appendix II of this work.

ORDERS FOR PROVISION OUT OF ESTATE OF DECEASED

Practice for recording orders

Principal Registry

16.48 The grant of probate, letters of administration (with will) or letters of administration and a copy of the order are sent to the Principal Registry by the Chancery Master, Family Division district judge or county court district judge, as the case may be. If the grant was made in the Principal Registry a memorandum of the order is prepared by the probate department and photocopied. A copy of the memorandum is attached to the grant, and a further copy is sent to HMRC Inheritance Tax. The order and another copy of the memorandum are sent to the Birmingham Probate Registry for filing at the Probate record Centre with the original will, or if there is no will, with the oath to lead the grant of administration.

ALTERATIONS IN VALUE OF ESTATE

Grant marked by HMRC Inheritance Tax

16.53 It is not the practice of the probate registries to amend the grant or the record where there has been an increase or decrease in the value of the estate. In cases where either the gross or net values of the estate, or the amount of the estate duty[1], have altered, the grant of representation may be lodged with HMRC Inheritance Tax, if it is desired that the amendment be noted thereon.

[1] In the case of a death occurring after 12 March 1975, no statement of the amount of inheritance tax or capital transfer tax paid (if any) appears on the grant of representation following the repeal of s 30 of the Customs and Inland Revenue Act 1881 by the Finance Act 1975, s 59 and Sch 13, Pt I: *Practice Note* [1975] CLY 266.

Further security

16.57 If the grant is one of administration (with or without will) *which issued prior to 1 January 1972*, so that an administration bond was filed, and the gross value of the estate is increased, before such a notation can be made by HMRC Inheritance Tax it is necessary to obtain a certificate from the district judge or registrar of the registry from which the grant issued that the administrator has given sufficient security for due administration of the further assets. This requirement still appears to be operative notwithstanding the abolition of bonds in relation to grants issued on or after 1 January 1972.

Affidavit

16.58 After the amended figures have been agreed by HMRC Inheritance Tax, the administrator makes an affidavit stating the facts as to the grant, the value of the estate then sworn to, and the true value. Form of affidavit, No 27. If the grant was made to more than one administrator, all must join in making the affidavit.

Practice

16.66 The certificate is then returned to the applicant, in order to be transmitted to HMRC Inheritance Tax.

Chapter 17
REVOCATION AND IMPOUNDING OF GRANTS

GROUNDS FOR REVOCATION

2. Supervening defect in grant

17.09 Where a grant has been properly made, but has subsequently become ineffective and useless; or which, if allowed to subsist, would prevent the proper administration of the estate.

Cases for revocation under first head

Cases for revocation under second head

One of two or more grantees subsequently lack capacity to manage his affairs

17.13 Where one of two or more grantees subsequently lacks capacity to manage his affairs within the meaning of the Mental Capacity Act 2007, the grant must be revoked.

17.14 If application for a new grant is made by persons all of whom had a right equal to that of the grantee who lacks capacity (whether they are the other grantees or not) a general grant may be made to them.

17.15 If any of them is in a lower category, the new grant will be in accordance with NCPR 35 (see paras 11.237 ff of this Supplement), for the use and benefit of the person who lacks capacity and limited until further representation be granted[1].

[1] *Registrar's Direction* (1956) 16 July (as modified by NCPR 35).

One of several executors subsequently lacks capacity to manage his affairs

17.16 When two executors prove a will, but one subsequently lacks capacity to manage his affairs within the meaning of the Mental Capacity Act 2005, probate is revoked and a new grant made to the capable executor, power being reserved to the executor who lacks capacity of taking probate again on recovering his capacity[1].

[1] Re Sowerby's Goods (1891) 65 LT 764; Re Shaw's Estate [1905] P 92.

One of several administrators (with or without will) subsequently lacks capacity to manage his affairs

17.17 Where administration (or administration with will annexed) has been granted to two or more persons, of whom one subsequently lacks capacity to manage his affairs within the meaning of the Mental Capacity Act 2005[1], the grant is revoked and a fresh grant made to the capable administrator. If any minority or life interest subsists the further grant will normally be made to not less than two individuals, or to a trust corporation with or without an individual.

[1] Re Newton's Goods (1843) 3 Curt 428; Re Phillips' Goods (1824) 2 Add 335. In the latter case, the committees of the person and estate of the incapable administrator consented.

17.18 If the grantee who lacks capacity had a superior title to that of the capable grantee, the former's right to a grant on recovering his capacity must be reserved by a limitation in the new grant.

17.19 For the practice when the sole grantee subsequently lacks capacity, see paras 17.64 ff below.

Both executors subsequently lack capacity to manage their affairs

17.20 Where there was the clearest evidence that both the surviving executors were of advanced age and suffering from such a degree of physical and mental infirmity as made continuance of their duties impossible, the court revoked the grant of probate and granted letters of administration (with will) de bonis non to a great-nephew of the testator[1].

[1] Re Galbraith's Goods [1951] P 422, [1951] 2 All ER 470n.

INCAPACITY OF SOLE GRANTEE

17.64 Where a sole grantee, or sole surviving grantee, subsequently lacks capacity to manage his affairs, a new grant may be made without revocation of the existing grant. The former practice of impounding the old grant in these circumstances has been abandoned[1].

[1] Registrar's Direction (1985) 9 July.

17.65 *Revocation and impounding of grants*

17.65 The new grant, whether made to a person equally entitled or, in accordance with NCPR 35 (see paras 11.237 ff of this Supplement), to some other person, will be a grant de bonis non and for the use and benefit of the grantee who lacks capacity, limited while he lacks capacity—see para 17.71: except that if the new grantee is an executor to whom power had been reserved, an ordinary grant of double probate (see paras 13.119 ff) will issue, with a note referring to the lack of capacity of the other proving, or sole surviving proving, executor[1].

[1] *Registrar's Direction* (1956) 16 July.

17.66 As to the procedure where one of two or more grantees subsequently lacks capacity, see paras 17.13–17.15 above.

IMPOUNDING GRANTS

When grant impounded

17.67 Where a sole, or sole surviving, grantee subsequently lacks capacity, and a new grant is made, the former practice of impounding the old grant has been abandoned[1].

[1] *Registrar's Direction* (1985) 9 July.

Chapter 18
RESEALING

COLONIAL GRANTS RESEALED IN ENGLAND AND WALES

HMRC account

18.40–18.43 *See Chapter 8 of this Supplement for updates as to procedure in respect of inheritance tax.*

Documents required

18.71 The following documents should be lodged:

(a) The colonial grant, or an officially issued duplicate, copy or exemplification, including, or accompanied by, a duly certified or sealed copy of the will, if any (see also 'Documents which may be resealed', paras 18.55–18.61).

(b) A complete copy of the grant, including a copy of any will, for deposit in accordance with s 2(1) of the Colonial Probates Act 1892. If desired, a photographic copy will be made in the registry, upon payment of a fee of 25p for each page[1].

(c) Where the application is made by some person on behalf of the grantee, the power of attorney, or other document authorising the agent to apply for resealing (see 'Power of attorney etc' paras 18.78 ff).

(d) HMRC account summary Form D241 or Form IHT207 for an 'excepted' estate (see paras 18.40–18.42). The account itself should be submitted to the HMRC Inheritance Tax office for control before the papers are lodged at the registry. That office will endorse Form D18 and return it to the applicant to submit with the other papers.

[1] Secretary's Circular, 17 June 1954: NC Probate Fees Order 1981, Fee 8.

Chapter 20

DEPOSIT AND REGISTRATION OF WILLS OF LIVING PERSONS

DEPOSIT OF WILLS

20.01 Section 126 of the Senior Courts Act 1981[1] requires the provision of 'safe and convenient depositories for the custody of the wills of living persons' under the control and direction of the High Court, in which any person may deposit his will on payment of such prescribed fee and subject to such conditions as may be prescribed by regulations made by the President of the Family Division with the concurrence of the Lord Chancellor.

[1] See para A1.353.

Chapter 21

SEARCHES AND COPIES – EXEMPLIFICATIONS – DUPLICATE GRANTS

SEARCHES AND COPIES

Calendars of grants

21.01 Calendars, or indexes, of all grants of probate or administration issued in the probate registries are available for public search at the Principal Registry and district probate registries[1]. Where a grant of representation was made before 9 November 1998 the details which appear in the calendars are: full name, date of death and last address of the deceased; the type of grant, its date and the registry at which it was made; and the gross value of the estate[2]. As from 9 November 1998, records of all grants of representations issued at the Principal Registry and district probate registries, kept pursuant to s 111 of the Senior Courts Act 1981, are retained in the form of a computer record[3]. The entries for each estate in the annual calendar books will now comprise: the full name of the deceased and any alias names; the last address of the deceased; the date of death and domicile of the deceased; the names and addresses of the executor(s) or administrator(s); the type of grant; the gross and net values of the estate or in the case of an excepted estate the limits within which the estate falls; the name and address of the extracting solicitor or probate practitioner (if any) or the fact that the grant was obtained by way of personal application and the date of the grant and the issuing registry.

[1] See Senior Courts Act 1981, s 111 (see also para A1.338), which provides for the keeping of records in such form and containing such particulars as the President of the Family Division may direct. The calendars are now compiled from weekly lists, produced by computer, of grants issued.
[2] Registrar's Circular, 22 December 1969.
[3] Practice Direction (probate: grants of representation: computer records) [1999] 1 All ER 384, [1998] 1 WLR 1699 which revokes Registrar's Circular, 22 December 1969.

21.02 Once the entry in the calendar has been found, a copy of the grant and will may be ordered or the inspection of the will may be requested.

21.04 *Searches and copies – Exemplifications – Duplicate grants*

Wills proved since 11 January 1858

Searches and copies

21.04 Computer terminals have now been installed in most registries including sub-registries by which the public may search probate records. The Probate Records Centre has begun to comprehensively update the electronic records to include all calendars since 1858.

No fee is payable on a search for a grant in the calendars if it is made personally at the registry, although on inspection of a copy will or any other document (in the presence of an officer of that registry) a fee of £15 is charged[1]. Where application is made in the Principal Registry or a district probate registry either personally or by post for a copy of a grant (other than on the application for the issue of the original grant) a fee of £5 is payable[2]. The fee will include the copying of the will and codicil proved[3]. If additional copies are requested at the same time the fee is £1 for each copy[4]. The NC Probate Fees Order 2004 (Fee 8(c)) makes provision for the supply of copies of documents on computer disk or in other electronic form at the cost of £3 for each copy but facilities are not yet in place to provide such copies.

[1] NC Probate Fees Order 2004, Fee 7.
[2] NC Probate Fees Order 2004, Fee 8(a).
[3] Secretariat Circular 15 April 2004.
[4] NC Probate Fees Order 2004, Fee 8(b).

21.07 Section 125 of the Senior Courts Act 1981 provides that a copy of the whole or any part of a will may be obtained, on payment of the prescribed fee: (i) from the registry in which the will is preserved; or (ii) where the will is preserved in some place other than a registry, from the Principal Registry; or (iii) subject to the approval of the Senior District Judge of the Family Division, from the Principal Registry in any case in which the will was proved in a district probate registry. In practice, following the setting up of a computerised retrieval system, a copy[1] of any will which has been proved may be obtained from either the Principal Registry, any district probate registry or any probate sub-registry which has access to this system. For the time being the sub-registries which are not connected to the system will forward applications for copies to their parent registries. The sub-registries in question are Peterborough, Lincoln, Carlisle and Middlesbrough.

[1] See paras 21.17 and 21.18 as to office copies and sealed and certified copies.

Standing search for grant of representation

Production at other courts of documents filed in Probate Registries

21.33 From time to time requests are made to the probate registries for a proved original will to be produced for the purposes of court proceedings other than in a probate claim (eg criminal proceedings in a magistrates' court or a Crown Court). In such a case, unless production of the original will is requested as a matter of urgency, it is usually transmitted by Document

Exchange post to the probate registry or sub-registry most conveniently situated to the court in which the proceedings are being brought so that an officer of that registry may attend the court with it. As all proved original wills which are under the control of the High Court are required to be deposited and preserved (s 124 of the Senior Courts Act 1981), the officer attending the court with an original will must arrange to retrieve it at the determination of the proceedings and return it to the registry. Should it be necessary to leave the will with the court for the duration of the proceedings, the officer will obtain a written receipt for the will including an undertaking for its return from the appropriate court official[1].

[1] Registrar's Circular, 13 November 1978.

Production of original will for inspection and examination

21.34 Occasionally a request is made to a probate registry for a proved original will to be made available for inspection and forensic examination. Normally, such a request is made by or on behalf of the police authorities. Sometimes, however, the request is made by a solicitor or probate practitioner, acting on behalf of his client in contemplation of bringing a probate claim, or exceptionally a researcher. Where the request is made by a solicitor or probate practitioner or researcher, it will be referred to the district judge or registrar for consideration. Subject to his approval and to such further conditions or restrictions which the district judge or registrar may see fit to impose, it is considered appropriate that any such examination shall normally take place only in a probate registry and that the examination of the will shall be conducted in the presence of a registry official in order that the official may ensure that the will is preserved in its original state and condition. If appropriate, the will may be transmitted by registered post or through the Document Exchange to another probate registry to enable the examination to be made[1]. Exceptionally the district judge or registrar may permit the will to be inspected in the office of a forensic expert subject to an undertaking by the expert not to physically damage or physically interfere with the testamentary paper other than by visual inspection under microscope, photography, photocopy, scanning or application of non-adhesive and non-staining dry substances. The practitioner further undertakes to pay the cost of travel and subsistence of the registry official taking the will to that office or, alternatively, the practitioner arranging for transmission and return of the document by courier and paying of courier fee. A fee of £15 is payable for the inspection[2].

[1] Registrar's Circular, 13 November 1978.
[2] Non-Contentious Probate Fees Order 2004, SI 2004/3120, Fee 7.

Chapter 25

APPLICATIONS TO DISTRICT JUDGE, REGISTRAR OR HIGH COURT JUDGE (NON-CONTENTIOUS BUSINESS)

APPLICATIONS WITHOUT NOTICE

25.12 The following types of application, which are dealt with in other parts of this work in the paragraphs indicated, may be made without notice subject to any requirement to the contrary by the district judge or registrar:

Refusal of probate of a will: paras 3.137–3.142.

Uncontested applications for omission of words from probate or for rectification or interpretation of a will: paras 3.257–3.279.

Application for joinder of a co-administrator having an inferior, or no, title: paras 7.17–7.19.

Preference of 'dead' interest to living interest, or of guardians of an infant to a person of full age: paras 5.127, 6.07–6.10 and 11.128–11.130.

Grant where the deceased died domiciled out of England and Wales: paras 12.126–12.135.

Appointment of persons to obtain administration (with or without will) for use and benefit of minors: paras 11.220–11.227.

Appointment of grantees on behalf of person who lacks capacity to manage his property and affairs within the meaning of the Mental Capacity Act 2005: paras 11.275–11.303.

Direction for grant to person representing person who lacks capacity to manage his property and affairs within the meaning of the Mental Capacity Act 2005 where a person equally entitled is sui juris: paras 11.233–11.235.

Amendment or revocation of grant: paras 16.01–16.28 and 17.01–17.59.

Application for appointment of additional personal representative after issue of grant: paras 7.40–7.42.

Application for leave to retract a renunciation: paras 15.62–15.75.

Grants under s 116 of the Senior Courts Act 1981

Mode of application

25.102 An order for a grant under s 116[1] of the Senior Courts Act 1981 may be made by a district judge of the Principal Registry or a registrar of a district probate registry, irrespective of the value of the estate. The application must be supported by an affidavit setting out the grounds of the application[2]. The applicant, or at least one of the joint applicants for the grant should, save in exceptional circumstances, make the affidavit. All material facts must be disclosed to the court. Failure to do so could result in a grant made under s 116 being revoked[3].

[1] See para A1.343.
[2] NCPR 52.
[3] *Shephard v Wheeler* (2000) Times, 15 February.

Mode of application

25.103 Exceptionally, where a local authority applies as a trust corporation in the circumstances mentioned below the district judge or registrar may dispense with the affidavit in support of the application for order. In these circumstances, the local authority applies by virtue of the Public Trustee (Custodian Trustee) Rules 1975, SI 1975/1189, as amended (see paras 9.05–9.08) on behalf of a person who by age, infirmity or other reason is in need of care and attention and resides in residential accommodation of the authority provided under s 21(1)(a) of the National Assistance Act 1948. The facts are recited fully in the oath and the written consent of the person in care is lodged (Registrar's Direction (1976) 30 June). It should be noted that application for an order under s 116 in these circumstances is an alternative procedure to an application being made under NCPR 31 (see para A2.70) for a grant to an attorney on behalf of the person in care or made under r 35 (see para A2.74) for a grant based on the lack of capacity within the meaning of the Mental Capacity Act 2005 of such a person.

Part II
CONTENTIOUS BUSINESS

Chapter 26

INTRODUCTION

Summary
Contentious business	149
Grants in common form and in solemn form distinguished	150
Jurisdiction of the court	152
The practice: High Court and County Court	154

CONTENTIOUS BUSINESS

Definition of non-contentious or 'common form' business

26.01 By the definition in s 128 of the Supreme Court Act 1981—

' "Non-contentious or common form probate business" means the business of obtaining probate and administration where there is no contention as to the right thereto, including

(a) the passing of probates and administrations through the High Court in contentious cases where the contest has been terminated,
(b) all businesses of a non-contentious nature in matters of testacy and intestacy not being proceedings in any action, and
(c) the business of lodging caveats against the grant of probate or administration.'

Non-contentious probate business extends to the warning of caveats. Although there is no lis pendens until a claim form is issued[1], it is the practice to treat the costs of entering and warning a caveat and of appearing to the warning as costs in the case.

[1] *Moran v Place* [1896] P 214; *Salter v Salter* [1896] P 291.

26.02 Introduction

Contentious business

26.02 By Pt 57.1(2) of the Civil Procedure Rules 1998 a probate claim is defined as:

'a claim

(i) for the grant of probate of the will, or letters of administration of the estate, of a deceased person;
(ii) for the revocation of such a grant; or
(iii) for a decree pronouncing for or against the validity of an alleged will,

not being an claim which is non-contentious (or common form) probate business'.

GRANTS IN COMMON FORM AND IN SOLEMN FORM DISTINGUISHED

26.03 Before treating of the various steps to be taken in a probate claim, it will be useful here to point out the distinction between grants of representation in common form and those in solemn form. A will is proved in 'common form' where its validity is not contested or questioned. The executor, or the person entitled to administration with the will annexed, brings the will into the Principal Registry or a district probate registry, and obtains the grant notwithstanding the absence of other parties interested, upon his own oath and any further affidavits which may be required.

A will is proved in 'solemn form' by the executor, or a person interested under the will, propounding it in an claim to which the persons prejudiced by it have been made parties, and by the court, upon hearing evidence, pronouncing for the validity of the will and ordering the issue of a grant.

As to the effect of probate in common form, see paras 1.18 and 1.19.

Any person whose interest is adversely affected by a probate granted in common form may proceed by claim for revocation to put the person who obtained it, or his representative, to proof of the will in solemn form. This right is not affected by mere lapse of time, by acquiescence, or by the receipt of legacies under the will[1]. Where a defendant after the lapse of four years from the death of the testator elected to put an executor to proof in solemn form, it was said that he was entitled to do so, but that he was not entitled to any indulgence; he was entitled to have the law strictly administered but nothing beyond it[2].

The difference in effect between a probate which has been granted in common form, and a probate which has been granted in solemn form, is that the former is revocable, and the latter, provided proper notice has been given to all persons interested, is, subject to two exceptions, irrevocable[3].

[1] *Hoffman v Norris and White* (1805) 2 Phillim 230n; *Merryweather v Turner* (1844) 3 Curt 802; *Re Topping's Goods* (1853) 2 Rob Eccl 620. But the legatee may be called upon to pay the amount of his legacy into court; see para 27.05.
[2] Per Sir Herbert Jenner Fust in *Blake v Knight* (1843) 3 Curt 547 at 553.

³   *Wytcherley v Andrews* (1871) LR 2 P & D 327; *Young v Holloway* [1895] P 87. The discovery, after the grant in solemn form has issued, of a valid marriage contracted by the testator subsequent to the execution of the will would presumably be a further exception.

Later will

26.04   If the existence of a will of later date is discovered subsequently to the date of the decree, the probate, although granted in solemn form, is liable to be revoked in favour of the later will¹.

¹   Wentworth's *Office of Executors* (14th edn) pp. 111, 112.

Fraud

26.05   The judgment may be set aside if it has been obtained by fraud, and though in most cases a judgment obtained by fraud can be set aside only as against the person who committed or procured the fraud, this limitation does not apply to an action to set aside judgment granting probate of a will, inasmuch as a will must be either good or bad as against all the world¹.

¹   *Birch v Birch* [1902] P 130.

Parties to a probate claim and those privy thereto bound by the result

26.06   With these exceptions probate in solemn form cannot be impeached by any person who has been a party to the claim, or who has been privy thereto. A probate claim is, in a sense, an action in rem, and anyone who is aware of the probate proceedings and has an interest which would have entitled him to intervene, is bound by the decision of the court and cannot start a fresh claim. It matters not that such a party subsequently wishes to claim in a different capacity¹. And it is to be observed that a person having an interest need not be a party to a probate claim to be bound by its results. If he was cognisant of it and had the opportunity of becoming a party, but was content to stand aside while others contested the claim, he is precluded from reopening the case². But if he did not at the time know of his interest and thus of his right to intervene he will not be bound by the action although cognisant of the proceedings³. Should the probate be subsequently called in by a person adversely affected by it, who was not bound by the decision, and be revoked, such revocation will enure to the benefit of parties and those privy to the first action, who were adversely affected by the revoked probate⁴. Use may also be made of CPR 19.8A (see para 28.04) to obtain a direction as to service of notice of a claim, relating to the estate of a deceased, upon any person who is not a party to the claim. The persons served in accordance with the direction are bound by the judgment given in the claim.

¹   *Re Langton's Estate* [1964] P 163, sub nom *Re Langton, Langton v Lloyd's Bank Ltd* [1964] 1 All ER 749.
²   *Newell v Weeks* (1814) 2 Phillim 224; *Ratcliffe v Barnes* (1862) 2 Sw & Tr 486. It should be noted that under NCPR r 45(1) and (2) notice of a probate claim is now given by the Senior District Judge to every person (other than the claimant) who has entered a caveat or who does so while the claim is pending.

26.06 *Introduction*

³ *Ratcliffe v Barnes* (1862) 2 Sw & Tr 486; *Young v Holloway* [1895] P 87.
⁴ *Young v Holloway* [1895] P 87.

Power to set aside judgment

26.07 A party who does not attend a trial and has an order made against him may apply for the judgment to be set aside under CPR 39.3(3). However, this will only be done if he satisfies all the requirements of CPR 39.3(5), namely that he acted promptly when he found out that the court had made an order against him, he had good reason for not attending the trial and had a reasonable prospect of success at the trial. If a defendant has notice of the proceedings but no notice of the trial he is still required to show a reasonable prospect of success at the trial[1].

¹ *Hackney LBC v Driscoll* [2003] EWCA Civ 1037, [2003] 1 WLR 2602.

JURISDICTION OF THE COURT

26.08 The decision of the court, either on the title to probate or on the title to administration, is conclusive in all courts in England and Wales, and where the decision turns upon any particular question, such decision is conclusive upon that question as between the same parties. Thus, if the finding in a claim for a grant of letters of administration turns upon the question which of the parties is next of kin or heir-at-law to the intestate, such finding is conclusive upon that question in an claim for distribution between or succession to the same parties[1]. When a document has been admitted to probate, all courts in England and Wales must treat it as testamentary[2]. Where there is a question whether legacies or devises are cumulative or substitutive, and it is determinable by the circumstances of the bequests or devises having been given by distinct instruments, and probate has issued of 'a will and codicil', the form of the probate is conclusive of the fact of their being distinct instruments, though written on the same paper[3].

To enable the court to exercise jurisdiction, the question must fairly arise out of the suit for probate or administration—the issue involved in the decision must be fairly raised on the pleadings—all the parties whose interest can be affected by the decision should be before the court, and the court should be of opinion that the question it is asked to determine is ready to be and can be conveniently and properly decided between the parties to the pending claim[4]. The court may not only decide on the title to probate but construe the will or make any other declaration normally obtainable in the Chancery Division.

¹ *Barrs v Jackson* (1845) 1 Ph 582; *Bouchier v Taylor* (1776) 4 Bro Parl Cas 708.
² *Re Barrance, Barrance v Ellis* [1910] 2 Ch 419, 103 LT 104.
³ *Baillie v Butterfield* (1787) 1 Cox Eq Cas 392.
⁴ *Re Tharp's Goods, Tharp v Macdonald* (1878) 3 PD 76, in which it was held, on appeal, to be the duty of the court not only to grant probate of the will of a married woman limited to such property as, under the law then in force, she had power to dispose of, but also to decide, so far as the evidence and pleadings would allow, of what such property consisted, and to add to the decree a declaration in accordance with its findings.

Jurisdiction of the court **26.12**

High Court

26.09 Contentious probate business in the High Court is by statute assigned to the Chancery Division[1].

A probate claim in the High Court must be begun by claim form issued out of Chancery Chambers (that is, the offices of the Chancery Division in the Thomas More Building, Royal Courts of Justice, Strand, London WC2A 2LL) or out of one of the Chancery district registries (that is, one of the district registries of Birmingham, Bristol, Cardiff, Leeds, Liverpool, Manchester, Newcastle upon Tyne and Preston)[2].

A probate claim in the High Court may only be transferred to Chancery Chambers or to one of the Chancery district registries[3].

[1] Section 61(1) of the Supreme Court Act 1981 and Sch 1, para 1(h).
[2] CPR 57.3(a) and 57.1(2)(b)(i) and (ii).
[3] CPR 30.2(8).

26.10 It is unusual for a county court to try a probate claim, even when it has jurisdiction. Except where otherwise stated, therefore, this Part deals with contentious probate proceedings in the High Court; and references to the 'court' are references to the master (or, in a district registry, the district judge) or to the judge or to the court officer (as the case may be) at the Chancery Chambers or at the Chancery district registry, wherever the case is proceeding.

26.11 Procedure and case management in the Chancery Division are set out in the Chancery Guide (October 2005). Copies may be obtained from the Fees Room, Room EO1 at the Royal Courts of Justice at the cost of £4.75 a copy. The Guide is also to be found on the court website: www.hmcourts-service.gov.uk.

County court

26.12 The county court has all the jurisdiction of the High Court in respect of any contentious matter arising in connection with the grant or revocation of probate or administration in the following circumstances, namely where:

(a) an application for the grant has been made through the Principal Registry or a district probate registry; and
(b) the value of the net estate (after payment of expenses and debts) does not exceed the county court limit (currently £30,000)[1].

The need for there to have been a prior application in the probate registry and the limit of £30,000 mean that probate claims are rarely commenced or heard in the county court.

Where the county court does have jurisdiction the claim form can only be issued out of a county court in a place where there is also a Chancery District Registry of the High Court[2] (namely Birmingham, Bristol, Cardiff, Leeds,

26.12 *Introduction*

Liverpool, Manchester, Newcastle upon Tyne and Preston). This is because of the specialist Chancery nature of the proceedings (even in the High Court probate claims can only be commenced, if out of London, in one of those registries); and because of the administrative requirements associated with the court staff having to receive and preserve in safekeeping the testamentary documents.

The parties cannot by agreement confer jurisdiction on a county court[3].

Where an order is made by a county court for the grant or revocation of probate or administration the district judge shall transmit to the principal registry of the Family Division or a district probate registry as he thinks convenient, a certificate under the seal of the court certifying that the order has been made and on the application of the party in whose favour the order has been made, probate or administration in compliance with the order shall be issued from the registry to which the certificate was sent, or, as the case may require, the probate or letters of administration previously granted shall be recalled or varied by, as the case may be, a district judge of the Principal Registry of the Family Division or the district probate registrar according to the effect of the order[4].

[1] County Courts Act 1984, s 32; County Courts Jurisdiction Order 1981; see also *Re Thomas, Davies v Davies* [1949] P 336, [1949] 1 All ER 1048.
[2] CPR 57.2(3).
[3] The only power to do so in other cases is conferred by the County Courts Act 1984, ss 18 and 24, neither of which applies to a probate claim.
[4] County Courts Act 1984, s 33.

Procedure in the county court

26.13 Procedure in the county court is also governed by CPR Pt 57. A probate claim is allocated to the multi-track[1].

[1] CPR 57.2(4).

THE PRACTICE: HIGH COURT AND COUNTY COURT

26.14 The practice in relation to contentious probate is regulated (both for the High Court and the county court) by CPR Pt 57 Section I supplemented by the Practice Directions to that Section. Sections II, III and IV of Part 57 do not deal with contentious probate.

Transitional Provisions

26.15 Where the claim form was issued before 15 October 2001 CPR Pt 57 does not apply and the rules in force immediately before that date continue to apply[1].

[1] The Civil Procedure (Amendment No 2) Rules 2001, para 19. The rules in force immediately before 15 October 2001 were contained in the Practice Direction supplementing CPR Pt 49 and they are set out in Appendix II.

Chapter 28

PARTIES TO CLAIMS

Summary
Who may be a party   155
Parties generally   155

WHO MAY BE A PARTY

28.01 The foundation of title to be a party to a probate claim is *interest*—so that whenever it can be shown that it is competent to the court to make a decree in a claim for probate or administration, or for the revocation of probate or of administration, which may affect the interest, or possible interest, of any person, such person has a right to be a party to such a suit[1].

Such was the rule in the Prerogative Court of Canterbury as to the foundation of title to be a party to a cause in that court.

In a claim for the revocation of a grant every person who is or claims to be entitled to administer the estate under that grant must be made a party to the claim[2].

A claim under the Inheritance (Provision for Family and Dependants) Act 1975 was a sufficient interest for the purposes of bringing a probate action. The claimant's motivation for challenging the will was that her Inheritance Act claim would be more likely to succeed on intestacy than under the will[3].

[1] *Kipping and Barlow v Ash* (1845) 1 Rob Eccl 270; *Crispin v Doglioni* (1860) 2 Sw & Tr 17.
[2] CPR 57.6(1).
[3] *O'Brian v Seagrave* [2007] EWHC 1247 (Ch), [2007] 3 All ER 633.

PARTIES GENERALLY

Claimants

28.02 CPR 19.1 provides that any number of claimants (or defendants) may be joined as parties to a claim. CPR 3.1 gives the court wide powers of case

28.02 *Parties to claims*

management including power to consolidate proceedings, to try two or more claims on the same occasion and to direct a separate trial on any issue.

CPR 19.3 (provisions applicable where two or more persons are jointly entitled to a remedy) does not apply to a probate claim[1].

[1] CPR 19.3(3).

Defendants

28.03 CPR 19.1 applies to the joinder of defendants as well as claimants.

It is important in a probate claim to ensure that all persons whose interests may be adversely affected by the relief claimed are either joined as defendants or served with notice of proceedings, in order that such persons may be bound by the decision of the court. When there are a large number of persons who might be affected by an order of the court, eg beneficiaries under two disputed wills, it is not always convenient to join them all as parties. In such circumstances the master or district judge may by using CPR 19.8A direct them to be served thereby allowing them to become parties to the claim and in any event causing them to be bound by the result of the claim (Form CP6).

In certain cases it may be appropriate to apply for a representation order under CPR 19.6 (representation of parties with same interest) or CPR 19.7 (representation of interested parties who cannot be ascertained etc). These are matters to which the master or district judge may also give consideration at a case management conference (see Ch 37).

Adding parties

Court of Probate

28.04 In the Prerogative Court of Canterbury, and subsequently in the Court of Probate, when a suit was pending, a person whose interest might by possibility be affected by the suit was allowed to intervene to protect his interest. He may now apply to the court to be added as a defendant. If, being cognizant of the proceedings and of an interest enabling him to intervene, such a person fails to apply, he will be bound by the proceedings, although not a party[1]. This does not apply where the parties to a suit compromise it and the decree is founded on a compromise to which he is not a party[2]. An interest, acquired after the death of the deceased, by purchase of part of the estate from the administrator, has been held sufficient to entitle a person to intervene in a suit for revocation of letters of administration[3].

[1] *Wytcherley v Andrews* (1871) LR 2 P & D 327; *Young v Holloway* [1895] P 87.
[2] *Wytcherley v Andrews* (1871) LR 2 P & D 327.
[3] *Lindsay v Lindsay* (1873) 42 LJP 32.

Application for permission to be added as a party

28.05 The court's permission is required to add a party unless the claim form has not been served[1]. An application for permission may be made by an existing party or by a person who wishes to become a party[2]. The application is made under CPR Pt 23 by an application notice supported by written evidence[3].

[1] CPR 19.4(1).
[2] CPR 19.4(2).
[3] CPR 19 PD para 1.4.

Chapter 32

STATEMENTS OF CASE GENERALLY

Summary
Practice as to statements of case   158

PRACTICE AS TO STATEMENTS OF CASE

How indorsed and headed

32.01 To start a probate claim the claimant should use Form N1P[1]. The claim form and all subsequent court documents must be marked at the top 'In the estate of [*name*] deceased (Probate)'[2].

The claim form must be headed with the title of the proceedings and the title should state the number of the proceedings, the court or division where they are proceeding, the full name of each party and his status in the proceedings ie claimant or defendant[3].

Where there is more than one claimant and/or more than one defendant the parties should be described in the title as follows:

(1) AB
(2) CD
(3) EF   Claimants
    and
(1) GH
(2) IJ
(3) KL   Defendants[4]

The claim form and, where they are not included in the claim form, the particulars of claim must be verified by a statement of truth in the form '[I believe][the claimant believes] that the facts stated in [this claim form][these particulars of claim] are true'[5]. The party or his litigation friend or the legal representative of the party or his litigation friend may sign the statement of truth[6].

[1] CPR Pt 4; Form N1P is set out in Appendix VI.

2   CPR Pt 57 PD para 1.2.
3   CPR Pt 7 PD para 4.1.
4   CPR Pt 7 PD para 4.2.
5   CPR Pt 7 PD para 7.1; CPR 22.1.
6   CPR Pt 22 PD para 3.1.

Signature

32.02 Statements of case and other documents drafted by a legal representative should bear his or her signature, and if they are drafted by a legal representative as a member or employee of a firm they should be signed in the name of the firm[1].

1   CPR Pt 5 PD para 2.1.

Allegation as to condition of mind

32.03 Where he wishes to rely on them in support of his claim a claimant must specifically set out in his particulars of claim the following matters, namely any allegation of fraud, the fact of any illegality, details of any misrepresentation, notice or knowledge of a fact, and details of unsoundness of mind or undue influence[1].

1   CPR Pt 16 PD para 9.2.

Want of knowledge and approval: particulars to be given

32.04 Any party who contends that at the time when a will was executed the testator did not know of and approve its contents must give particulars of the facts and matters relied on[1].

1   CPR 57.7(3).

Other pleas to be specifically pleaded

32.05 Any party who wishes to contend that:
(a)   a will was not duly executed;
(b)   at the time of the execution of a will the testator was not of sound mind, memory and understanding; or
(c)   the execution of a will was obtained by undue influence or fraud,

must set out the contention specifically and give particulars of the facts and matters relied on[1].

1   CPR 57.7(4).

Statements of interest and denial of interest

32.06 The claim form must contain a statement of the nature of the interest of the claimant and of each defendant in the estate[1]. If a party disputes

32.06 *Statements of case generally*

another party's interest in the estate he must state this in his statement of case and set out his reasons². See also *O'Brian v Seagrave*³.

1   CPR 57.7(1).
2   CPR 57.7(2).
3   [2007] EWHC 1247 (Ch), [2007] 3 All ER 633 – see para 28.01.

Chapter 34

DEFENCE AND COUNTERCLAIM

Summary	
Service of defence	161
Counterclaim	162
Notice of intention merely to cross-examine	163
Precedents of defences:	163
(1) Want of due execution	163
(2) Incapacity	172
(3) Undue influence	175
(4) Fraud	177
(5) Want of knowledge and approval	178
(6) Sham will	182
(7) Revocation	183
(8) Deceased prevented by threats from altering will	193
(9) Estoppel—Laches	194
(10) Minority	194
Interest action	195
Forfeiture	195

SERVICE OF DEFENCE

34.01 A defendant who intends to defend a claim must, unless the court gives leave to the contrary, file a defence before the expiration of 28 days after service of the particulars of claim on him[1].

If the defendant needs more time to prepare his defence he should in the first instance apply to the claimant for further time. The parties may agree a further 28 days, and the defendant must inform the court in writing of any such agreement[2]. No further extension can be agreed and if the defendant needs still more time (as well as in the event that no initial agreement is reached) he will have to apply to the court for an extension under CPR 3.1(2)(a).

[1] CPR 15.4; CPR 57.4(4).
[2] CPR 15.5.

34.02 *Defence and counterclaim*

COUNTERCLAIM

34.02 In a probate claim, a defendant who alleges that he has any claim or is entitled to any relief or remedy in respect of any matter relating to the grant of probate of the will, or letters of administration of the estate, of the deceased must add to his defence a counterclaim in respect of that matter[1]. The alternative of bringing a separate action is not permissible in probate proceedings. If the claimant fails to serve particulars of claim any such defendant may apply for permission to serve a counterclaim and the claim shall proceed on the basis that the counterclaim is the particulars of claim[2].

A defendant who wishes to counterclaim against a person other than the claimant must apply to the court for an order that that person be added as a defendant to the counterclaim. The application may be made without notice and where the court makes an order it will give directions as to the management of the case[3].

It is possible to counterclaim for probate in other proceedings[4]. A probate counterclaim must contain a statement of the nature of the interest of the defendant and the claimant in the estate of the deceased to which the counterclaim relates[5]. If the action is not in the Chancery Division the court will, if necessary of its own motion, transfer the action to the Chancery Division and to either the Royal Courts of Justice or a Chancery district registry (if it is not already proceeding in one of those places)[6]. Application may however be made within seven days after the service of a probate counterclaim for the counterclaim to be dealt with in separate proceedings (under CPR 3.1(2)(e) or to be struck out (under CPR 3.4)[7]. If an order is made that the probate counterclaim be dealt with in separate proceedings the order shall order the transfer of the probate counterclaim (if not already proceeding there) to the Chancery Division and to either the Royal Courts of Justice or to a Chancery District Registry[8].

By s 20 of the Administration of Justice Act 1982 (see para A1.374), if the court is satisfied that a will is expressed in any way that fails to carry out the testator's intentions in consequence of a clerical error or of a failure to understand his instructions it may order that the will shall be rectified so as to carry out those intentions. This can be dealt with by way of a counterclaim in a probate claim or by separate proceedings. Except with leave of the court, proceedings must be taken within six months of the date of the grant of representation. See also paras 3.258 ff and para 41.01.

[1] CPR 57.8(1).
[2] CPR 57.8(2).
[3] CPR Pt 20.5.
[4] CPR 57.9.
[5] CPR 57.9(3).
[6] CPR 57.9(4).
[7] CPR 57.9(4).
[8] CPR 57.9(5).

NOTICE OF INTENTION MERELY TO CROSS-EXAMINE

34.03 A defendant may in his defence give notice that he merely insists upon the will of the deceased being proved in solemn form of law and only intends to cross-examine the witnesses produced in support of the will.

When such notice has been given, then, unless the court is of opinion that there was no reasonable ground for opposing the will, no order will be made for the costs of the other side to be paid by him[1]. (Form of notice, CP 8.)

The notice must be given in the defence[2]. It may be conditional upon both witnesses being called[3], and includes questions as to the testator's knowledge and approval of the contents of the will. It does not follow, because a defendant fails, that there was no reasonable ground for opposing the will[4].

This rule does not apply to the case of a party applying for revocation of a grant[5]; and a plea of undue influence or fraud is inconsistent with the notice, but questions may be asked as to testamentary capacity[6].

If the opposing party is merely put to proof of due execution, but the notice is *not* given, witnesses to negative due execution may be called[7].

[1] CPR 57.7(5).
[2] See CPR 57.7(5).; and *Bone v Whittle* (1866) LR 1 P & D 249.
[3] *Leeman v George* (1868) LR 1 P & D 542.
[4] *Davies v Jones* [1899] P 161.
[5] *Tomalin v Smart* [1904] P 141.
[6] *Ireland v Rendall* (1866) LR 1 P & D 194; *Cleare and Forster v Cleare* (1869) LR 1 P & D 655; *Harrington v Bowyer* (1871) LR 2 P & D 264.
[7] *Patrick v Hevercroft* (1920) 123 LT 201.

PRECEDENTS OF DEFENCES

34.04 The following are examples of the more usual defences in probate claims.

(1) WANT OF DUE EXECUTION

Form of defence:

34.05

> 'That the said will and codicil of the deceased were not duly executed according to the provisions of the Wills Act 1837.'

Any party who wishes to contend that a will was not duly executed must set out the contention specifically and give particulars of the facts and matters relied on[1].

[1] CPR 57.7(4)

34.06 *Defence and counterclaim*

Onus of proof

34.06 The onus of proving that the will propounded was executed as required by law is on the claimant or party propounding it. The onus is a shifting one. It is for the person propounding the will to establish a prima facie case by proving due execution. If the will is not irrational, and was not drawn by the person propounding it and benefiting under it, the onus is discharged unless or until, by cross-examination of the witnesses, or by pleading and evidence, the issue of testamentary capacity or want of knowledge and approval is raised. The onus on these points is then again on the person propounding. As to other allegations the onus is, generally speaking, on the party making them.

As to the burden of proof and right to begin, see also para 39.10.

Form of defence

34.07 The burden of proof being on the party propounding the will, it may be sufficient simply to put him to proof that s 9 of the Wills Act 1837[1] has been complied with; but where substantive allegations against due execution, supported by evidence, are to be made, the allegations must be pleaded[2], eg:

(a) That on the face of the paper, what purports to be the signature or mark of the testator dying before 1 January 1983 is not placed at the foot or end of the will—nor so placed as to come within the requirements of the Wills Act Amendment Act 1852[3]. (It should be noted that this requirement is relaxed for *deaths on or after 1 January 1983* by the Administration of Justice Act 1982: see para A1.371.)
(b) That such signature or mark was not made by the testator himself, nor by any one for him, nor in his presence, nor by his direction.
(c) That it was neither so made nor acknowledged by the testator as his signature in the presence of two witnesses present at the same time.
(d) That the two witnesses subsequently to the making or acknowledgment of the testator's signature did not subscribe, or acknowledge, their signatures to the will in the presence of the testator.

[1] See para A1.04.
[2] CPR 16.5 and 57.7(4).
[3] See para A1.34.

34.08 For form of defence pleading want of due execution, see CP 32.

Forgery

34.09 The charge that the signature or mark of the testator is a forgery is also raised by this plea, but forgery itself must also be specifically pleaded[1].

[1] CPR 16.5 and 57.7(4).

Notice under CPR 57.7(5)

34.10 Where it is proposed merely to put the executors to proof and only to cross-examine their witnesses, the notice as to such cross-examination must be given in the defence.

Pleas against validity other than under Wills Act 1837, s 9

34.11 The will propounded may be alleged to be invalid also either:

(a) Under the provisions of Lord Kingsdown's Act[1]; see also para 33.06.
(b) Under the foreign laws of the place of domicil; see para 33.12.
(c) In the case of death on or after 1 January 1964 under the Wills Act 1963: see para 33.21 ff. For precedent of defence, see CP 43.
(d) As the will of a soldier, sailor or airman, under s 11 of the Wills Act 1837[2], and the Wills (Soldiers and Sailors) Act 1918[3]. For precedent of defence, see CP 44.

[1] See para A1.38.
[2] See para A1.07.
[3] See para A1.59.

Summary of reported cases as to due execution

34.12 See also Part I, paras 3.57–3.132 and note the relaxation of the formalities of execution under s 9 of the Wills Act 1837, as substituted by the Administration of Justice Act 1982, s 17 (see para A1.04) in respect of testators dying on or after 1 January 1983. See also paras 27.08 and 27.09.

A Form of signature

34.13

(a) *By mark* (*Baker v Dening* (1838) 8 Ad & El 94; *Re Field's Goods* (1843) 2 Curt 752); without name of testator beside it (*Re Bryce's Goods* (1839) 2 Curt 325); with correct name beside it, but testator wrongly described in will (*Re Douce's Goods* (1862) 2 Sw & Tr 593); with wrong name beside it (*Re Clarke's Goods* (1858) 1 Sw & Tr 22); by wrong or assumed name (to be treated as a mark) (*Re Glover's Goods* (1847) 5 Notes of Cases 553; *Re Redding's Goods* (1850) 2 Rob Eccl 339). By uncompleted signature—due to weakness (*Re Chalcraft, Chalcraft v Giles* [1948] P 222, [1948] 1 All ER 700). See also paras 3.70 ff.
(b) *By a seal* (inscribed with testator's initials) (*Re Emerson's Goods* (1882) 9 LR Ir 443).
(c) *By a thumb mark* (*Re Finn's Estate*) (1935) 154 LT 242; *Re Parsons* [2002] WTLR 237.
(d) *Undecipherable scrawls* (treated as mark) *Re Kieran* [1933] IR 222.

34.13 *Defence and counterclaim*

(e) *By an impressed stamp* (*Jenkins v Gaisford and Thring, Re Jenkin's Goods* (1863) 3 Sw & Tr 93).
(f) *By initials* (*Re Christian's Goods* (1849) 2 Rob Eccl 110).
(g) *By another person at testator's direction* (signing either his own or testator's name) *Re Clark's Goods* (1839) 2 Curt 239; but a testator cannot adopt or acknowledge a signature pencilled beforehand by another person as an indication (*Reeves v Grainger* (1908) 52 Sol Jo 355).
(h) *By one of the attesting witnesses* (*Re Bailey's Goods* (1838) 1 Curt 914).
(i) *By the person who drew the will* (*Re Elcock's Goods* (1869) 20 LT 757; *Smith v Harris* (1845) 1 Rob Eccl 262).
(j) *By wrong or assumed name* (*Re Glover's Goods* (1847) 5 Notes of Cases 553; *Re Redding's Goods* (1850) 2 Rob Eccl 339).
(k) *By the words 'your loving mother'* (will held to be duly signed (*Re Cook's Estate, Murison v Cook* [1960] 1 All ER 689, [1960] 1 WLR 353)).

B Position of signature

34.14 NB *In respect of wills of testators* dying on or after 1 January 1983, s 9 of the Wills Act 1837, as substituted by the Administration of Justice Act 1982, s 17 (see para A1.04), *no longer requires the testator to have signed the will 'at the foot or end thereof'*.

(a) *In testimonium clause* (*Re Mann's Goods* (1858) 28 LJP & M 19).
(b) *In the attestation clause Re Huckvale's Goods* (1867) LR 1 P & D 375; *Re Pearn's Goods* (1875) 1 PD 70; *Re Walker's Goods* (1862) 2 Sw & Tr 354; *Re Casmore's Goods* (1869) LR 1 P & D 653; signature on second page, all dispositions being on first page and not visible to witnesses (*Re Moore's Goods* [1901] P 44); testator's signature below those of the witnesses (*Re Puddephatt's Goods* (1870) LR 2 P & D 97).
(c) *Signatures held to be under, beside, or opposite the end of the will*—Entirely above last line with exception of one letter which touched it (*Re Woodley's Goods* (1864) 3 Sw & Tr 429); along lower part of edge of paper (*Re Jones' Goods* (1865) 4 Sw & Tr 1); see also *Re Wright's Goods* (1865) 4 Sw & Tr 35; on second of three pages, crossways (*Re Coombs's Goods* (1866) LR 1 P & D 302; see *Royle v Harris* [1895] P 163); beside last lines of will (*Re Ainsworth's Goods* (1870) LR 2 P & D 151); on third page opposite end of will on second page (*Re Williams' Goods* (1865) LR 1 P & D 4). In margin (*Re Roberts's Estate* [1934] P 102). In an oblong space drawn on right-hand side of the sheet and among the dispositive words (*Re Hornby* [1946] P 171, [1946] 2 All ER 150).
(d) *Signature on page containing no part of the will* (*Re Wright's Goods* (1865) 4 Sw & Tr 35; *Re Williams' Goods* (1865) LR 1 P & D 4; *Re Coombs' Goods* (1866) LR 1 P & D 302; *Re Fuller's Goods* [1892] P 377); signature in attestation clause (*Re Moore's Goods* [1901] P 44).
(e) *Signature on separate sheet of paper attached to will*—Signature pasted on will (*Re Gausden's Goods* (1862) 2 Sw & Tr 362; *Cook v Lambert*

Want of due execution **34.14**

(1863) 3 Sw & Tr 46); attached to will by string (*Re Horsford's Goods* (1874) LR 3 P & D 211); sheets held together by testator at time of execution (*Lewis v Lewis* [1908] P 1; *Re Little, Foster v Cooper* [1960] 1 All ER 387, [1960] 1 WLR 495). Where a will is written on several sheets, only the last of which is signed and attested, there is a prima facie presumption (rebuttable by evidence) that all formed part of the will at the time of execution, even though the witnesses only observed the page they signed (*Gregory v Queen's Proctor* (1846) 4 Notes of Cases 620; *Rees v Rees* (1873) LR 3 P & D 84). Where a will was signed by the testator but the witnesses signed a duplicate, probate was refused (*Re Hatton's Goods* (1881) 6 PD 204).

(f) *Signature on envelope in which will enclosed*—A secret will, enclosed in a sealed envelope which was indorsed as to its contents and signed by the testator and witnesses, was accepted as valid under the Wills Act 1837 so as to pass real estate in England, on the footing that the two documents were sufficiently 'attached' to each other to constitute one document. It was valid by the law of the (Peruvian) domicil, and there were special circumstances (*Re Nicholls, Hunter v Nicholls* [1921] 2 Ch 11); in *Re Almosnino's Goods* (1859) 1 Sw & Tr 508, followed, though in that case the decision appears to have been based on the principle of incorporation. On envelope, signed by testatrix, the will being then signed by the witnesses and placed in the envelope (*Re Mann's Goods* [1942] P 146, [1942] 2 All ER 193). Held insufficient where spaces in printed indorsement on envelope were filled in by testator, including his name, but he did not indicate that it was intended to be his signature to the will, or that the envelope was part of it; the will was then signed by the witnesses whilst the envelope was lying on the table, visible to them (*Re Bean's Estate* [1944] P 83, [1944] 2 All ER 348).

(g) *Signature in middle of will not necessarily good execution even of the part that precedes it* (*Sweetland v Sweetland* (1865) 4 Sw & Tr 6: all pages signed except the last; *Margary v Robinson* (1886) 12 PD 8); unless the court is satisfied that the second page was incorporated by reference, or could be regarded as being in fact the first page of the will (*Re Anstee's Goods* [1893] P 283); but when a will was written on a printed form and the signature was on first page and will on following pages, it has been held that the signature was really on the last page and that will was duly executed (*Re Wotton's Goods* (1874) LR 3 P & D 159); see also *Royle v Harris* [1895] P 163; distinguishing *Wotton*; *Re Gilbert's Goods* (1898) 78 LT 762; *Re Coombs's Goods* (1866) LR 1 P & D 302; *Re Powell's Goods* (1865) 4 Sw & Tr 34 (will written on first two sides and part of third side of sheet of notepaper; attestation clause and signatures at bottom of second side, but testator's signature projected slightly on to third side. All three pages admitted to proof on the basis that paper was spread open at time of execution: if not spread open signature might only have referred to second side); and see *Re Smith's Goods* [1931] P 225 (but this case has not been followed). In special circumstances, where a codicil, which had been begun near the bottom of a page of the will, was continued and signed in a space immediately above its commencement, the words that were in fact

34.14 *Defence and counterclaim*

below the signature were admitted (*Re Kimpton's Goods* (1864) 3 Sw & Tr 427); where the whole of the dispositions were on the second page, the front page being confined to the appointment of executors and the execution, whilst all the facts and the appearance of the document justified the presumption that the will began on the second page and was continued on the first—the whole was admitted (*Re Long's Estate* [1936] P 166, [1936] 1 All ER 435); see also *Re Staniforth's Estate, Gilbert v Heining* (1965) 109 Sol Jo 112. Words following signature may be included in probate if they can be regarded as interlineations or incorporated by reference in the will (*Re Birt's Goods* (1871) LR 2 P & D 214; *Re Greenwood's Goods* [1892] P 7; *Re Watkins's Goods* (1865) LR 1 P & D 19; *Re Dallow's Goods* (1866) LR 1 P & D 189; *Palin v Ponting* [1930] P 185); but in a will signed only at the foot of the first page, the mere fact that an uncompleted sentence, at the end of the first page, is completed on the second page, is not sufficient to justify admission of any part of the second page, in the absence of any reference, asterisk or other mark that can be deemed to constitute incorporation—even though it be established that the whole was written before execution (*Re Gee's Goods* (1898) 78 LT 843; *Royle v Harris* [1895] P 163); an unattested signature, subsequently witnessed under the words 'signed again in the presence', etc., the testator having then signed, was held a good acknowledgment of the earlier signature (*Re Pattison's Goods, Henderson v Priestman* [1918] 2 IR 90); but a will on one sheet with signature at the top was held invalid (*Re Stalman, Stalman v Jones* (1931) 145 LT 339, CA, followed in *Re Harris, Murray v Everard* [1952] P 319, [1952] 2 All ER 409— signature at top of right-hand margin; *Re Bercovitz's Estate, Canning v Enever* [1962] 1 All ER 552, [1962] 1 WLR 321, witnesses held to have attested a signature at head of will, not that at foot or end: will not duly executed; but cf *Re Usborne's Goods* (1909) 25 TLR 519; *Re Roberts's Estate* [1934] P 102; signature in margin—*Stalman* distinguished). In *Re Beadle, Mayes v Beadle* [1974] 1 All ER 493, [1974] 1 WLR 417 a will was signed in the presence of one witness and inserted in an envelope. The envelope was signed on one side by the testator and a certificate by the two witnesses indorsed on the back. The court pronounced against the will. In *Wood v Smith* [1993] Ch 90, [1992] 3 All ER 556 it was held by the Court of Appeal that where the testator's signature was written earlier than the rest of the will, the will was nevertheless valid because the signature on the facts of that case was written as part of one transaction with the rest of the will. See also *Weatherhill v Pearce* [1995] 2 All ER 492, [1995] 1 WLR 592: name of testatrix in attestation clause in her own handwriting held a sufficient signature. See also paras 3.70–3.90.

C Acknowledgment of signature by testator

34.15 Witnesses must see or have an opportunity of seeing the signature (*Hudson v Parker* (1844) 1 Rob Eccl 14 at 40; *Re Gunstan's (or Gunston) Goods, Blake v Blake* (1882) 7 PD 102), or part of the signature (*Re Glass'*

Estate, Hosking v Hutchings (1961) 105 Sol Jo 612); if signature was there, and witnesses had opportunity of seeing it, it does not matter that they did not actually see it (*Blake v Knight* (1843) 3 Curt 547; *Daintree v Butcher and Fasulo* (1888) 13 PD 67; on appeal 13 PD 102, CA); there is no acknowledgment within s 9 of the Wills Act 1837 if will is folded up inside testator's coat pocket when he asks witnesses to sign, even though later each separately saw the signature when signing the will (*Re Groffman, Groffman and Block v Groffman* [1969] 2 All ER 108, [1969] 1 WLR 733); in the absence of proof as to existence of signature at time of execution probate may be refused (*Ilott v Genge* (1842) 3 Curt 160; *Fischer v Popham* (1875) LR 3 P & D 246); but as to absence of direct proof, see *Re Huckvale's Goods* (1867) LR 1 P & D 375. See also *Wright v Sanderson* (1884) 9 PD 149, CA. It is not necessary that a witness should know that the document signed is a will (*Re Benjamin's Estate* (1934) 150 LT 417).

34.16 *Acknowledgment may be verbal* (*Gaze v Gaze* (1843) 3 Curt 451; *Blake v Knight* (1843) 3 Curt 547; *Ilott v Genge* (1842) 3 Curt 160 at 172); or by gestures (*Re Davies' Goods* (1850) 2 Rob Eccl 337); or nodding head (*Re Hadler's Estate, Goodall v Hadler* (1960) Times, 20 October, cf. *Re Holtam's Estate, Gillett v Rogers* (1913) 108 LT 732); or by demeanour (*Faulds v Jackson* (1845) 6 Notes of Cases Supp i; *Inglesant v Inglesant* (1874) LR 3 P & D 172; *Re Jones' Goods* (1855) Dea & Sw 3; *Cooke v Henry* [1932] IR 574); or by proffering document as will (*Weatherhill v Pearce* [1995] 2 All ER 492, [1995] 1 WLR 592). See also paras 3.91 and 3.92.

D *Presence of witnesses and testator*

34.17 Signature must be made or acknowledged in the joint presence of witnesses (*Faulds v Jackson* (1845) 6 Notes of Cases Supp i); and before either of them has signed as witnesses (*Faulds v Jackson*; *Cooper v Bockett* (1846) 4 Moo PCC 419; *Hindmarsh v Charlton* (1861) 8 HL Cas 160; *Re Davies' Estate, Russell v Delaney* [1951] 1 All ER 920; *Re Linley, McDonnell v Linley* (1949) 207 LT Jo 372); the witnesses must both sign in the presence of the testator *(first three cases above)*; but need not do so in the presence of each other (*Faulds v Jackson*); for what constitutes 'presence' of the testator, see *Re Colman's Goods* (1842) 3 Curt 118; *Brown v Skirrow* [1902] P 3; *Jenner v Ffinch* (1879) 5 PD 106; *Carter v Seaton* (1901) 85 LT 76; it is not sufficient for testator to be corporeally present, he must be mentally aware of what is taking place when witnesses attest his signature (*Right v Price* (1779) 1 Doug KB 241; *Re Killick's Goods* (1864) 3 Sw & Tr 578). It is not essential that the testator should actually see the witnesses sign; it is enough if he might have seen them had he chosen to look. A will attested in an office while testatrix was outside in her carriage was upheld, because she might have seen what occurred through the office window (*Casson v Dade* (1781) 1 Bro CC 99); but where the witnesses left the room in which testator had signed and subscribed their names in an adjoining room, the door being open but testator not being in a position where he could see the witnesses, there was no due execution (*Doe d Wright v Manifold* (1813) 1 M & S 294; *Jenner v Ffinch*

34.17 *Defence and counterclaim*

(1879) 5 PD 106). See also *Weatherhill v Pearce* [1995] 2 All ER 492, [1995] 1 WLR 592 where, in the absence of contrary evidence and on limited evidence about the configuration of the rooms of the house, the court presumed that the testatrix and the witnesses had been present together at the same time. See also *Couser v Couser* [1996] 3 All ER 256, [1996] 1 WLR 1301—will validly executed where testator signed will in absence of witnesses and acknowledged signature to one witness and then acknowledged signature to second witness, the first witness being present in the same room. See also paras 3.101 and 3.102.

E Subscription by witnesses

34.18 NB *In respect of wills of testators* dying on or after 1 January 1983, s 9 *of the Wills Act 1837, as substituted by the Administration of Justice Act 1982, s 17 (see* para A1.04), *now allows a witness to acknowledge his earlier signature.*

May be by mark (*Re Ashmore's Goods* (1843) 3 Curt 756; *Re Amiss' Goods* (1849) 2 Rob Eccl 116); see also *Hindmarsh v Charlton* (1861) 8 HL Cas 160; or by description of himself (*Re Duggins' Goods* (1870) 39 LJP & M 24; *Re Sperling's Goods* (1863) 3 Sw & Tr 272); but not by signing the name of another person (*Re Leverington's Goods* (1886) 11 PD 80); another person may write name or mark of witness so long as he holds the pen (*Lewis v Lewis* (1861) 2 Sw & Tr 153; *Bell v Hughes* (1880) 5 LR Ir 407); but another person cannot subscribe for witness at his desire (*Re Cope's Goods* (1850) 2 Rob Eccl 335; *Re Duggins' Goods*); nor is it sufficient if witness's name is affixed by means of a rubber stamp affixed by the other witness in his presence but without any physical act or participation on his part (*Re Bulloch's Estate* [1968] NI 96, applying dictum in *Bell v Hughes*); signature of witness cannot be acknowledged afterwards by any means as can that of a testator, nor is it sufficient to re-write, with a dry pen, a signature written before acknowledgment by the testator in the presence of *both* witnesses (*Re Maddock's Goods* (1874) LR 3 P & D 169; *Hindmarsh v Charlton*; *Horne v Featherstone* (1895) 73 LT 32); if witness is unable to complete signature the execution is invalid (*Re Maddock's Goods* (1874) LR 3 P & D 169; *McConville v McCreesh* (1879) 13 ILTR 35); the signatures of the witnesses need not appear on any particular part of the instrument (*Re Davis' Goods* (1843) 3 Curt 748; *Re Chamney's Goods* (1849) 1 Rob Eccl 757; *Roberts v Phillips* (1855) 4 E & B 450); but if not on same sheet as signature of testator, the sheets must be physically connected at time of execution (*Re Braddock's Goods* (1876) 1 PD 433); and the court must be satisfied that witnesses intended to attest the signature of the testator (*Re Streatley's Goods* [1891] P 172; *Re Taylor's Goods* (1851) 2 Rob Eccl 411; *Phipps v Hale* (1874) LR 3 P D 166; *Re Denning, Harnett v Elliott* [1958] 2 All ER 1, [1958] 1 WLR 462 (signatures of witnesses upside down on reverse of paper on which will written: see also para 3.103)); the signature of third person at end of will may be omitted from probate upon proof that it was not written for purpose of attesting (*Re Sharman's Goods* (1869) LR 1 P & D 661): see also paras 3.104–3.106. See also *Re White, Barker v Gribble* [1991] Ch 1, [1990] 3 All ER 1 (witnesses only attested alterations). An attesting witness may validly sign a will at the direction of the testator and as attesting witness without signing a second time when it is clear that the witness had intended to perform the dual function of both signing the will on behalf of the testator and of witnessing the direction to do so (*Re Elsie Marsden Deceased* LTL 21/3/2006, an appeal from the Registrar's refusal to admit the will to probate).

F *Presumption of due execution*

34.19 If document is ex facie duly executed the court may pronounce for it although the evidence of attesting witnesses is adverse (*Cooper v Bockett* (1846) 4 Moo PCC 419; *Lloyd v Roberts* (1858) 12 Moo PCC 158; see also *Neal v Denston* (1932) 147 LT 460), or though the witness could not speak as to what writing was on the will when executed (*Wright v Sanderson* (1884) 9 PD 149, CA; *Re Coghlan, Briscoe v Broughton* [1948] 2 All ER 68), or although for 20 years no step was taken to prove the will (*Re Musgrove's Estate, Davis v Mayhew* [1927] P 264, CA); for the maxim *omnia praesumuntur rite esse acta* applies (*Woodhouse v Balfour* (1887) 13 PD 2; *Dayman v Dayman* (1894) 71 LT 699; *Wright v Sanderson* (1884) 9 PD 149; *Kavanagh v Fegan* [1932] IR 566); the presumption applies, but with less force, where attestation clause is incomplete (*Vinnicombe v Butler* (1864) 3 Sw & Tr 580); see also *Re Peverett's Goods* [1902] P 205; *Re Denning, Harnett v Elliot* [1958] 2 All ER 1, [1958] 1 WLR 462; and *Re Strong's Estate, Strong v Hadden* [1915] P 211, distinguishing *Peverett*. In *Re Puddephatt's Goods* (1870) LR 2 P & D 97, a will in which the testator's signature appeared below those of the witnesses was pronounced for although no evidence was available from the witnesses or other person present, on the presumption of due execution arising from the wording of the attestation clause. The force of the presumption varies with all the circumstances. It may be very strong if the document is entirely regular in form, but where it is irregular and unusual in form the maxim cannot apply with the same force (*Re Bercovitz's Estate, Canning v Enever* [1961] 2 All ER 481, [1961] 1 WLR 892). As to the presumption, see also *Harris v Knight* (1890) 15 PD 170 at 179. In *Sherrington v Sherrington* [2005] WTLR 587 it was held that where there was a presumption of due execution arising from an attestation clause the court had to be satisfied on 'the strongest evidence' that the presumption had been rebutted. See also paras 3.114–3.136, and *Burgoyne v Showler* (1844) 1 Rob Eccl 5.

G *Who else may prove execution*

34.20 Evidence of a person present but not a witness (*Mackay v Rawlinson* (1919) 35 TLR 223).

34.21 *Defence and counterclaim*

(2) INCAPACITY

Form of defence

34.21

'That the deceased, at the time the said will and codicil respectively purport to have been executed, was not of sound mind, memory and understanding.'

Particulars required

34.22 A party who wishes to contend that at the time of the execution of a will the testator was not of sound mind, memory and understanding must set out that contention specifically and give particulars of the facts and matters relied on[1].

[1] CPR 57.7(4).

Classes of persons incapacitated from making a will

34.23 In the textbooks and reported cases, insanity is divided into two kinds, general insanity and partial insanity.

General insanity

34.24 General insanity exists where the mind is unsound on multifarious matters, so as to indicate that it is diseased throughout.

A person whose mind is generally unsound is held to be incapable of making a valid will whilst such unsoundness continues.

Partial insanity

34.25 Partial insanity exists in the case of a monomaniac who has insane delusions, limited to a particular subject.

For precedent of defence, see Form CP 33.

Summary of reported cases

Presumption of sanity

34.26 A duly executed will, rational on the face of it, is presumed, in the absence of evidence to the contrary, to be that of a person of competent understanding (*Symes v Green* (1859) 1 Sw & Tr 401; *Sutton v Sadler* (1857) 3 CBNS 87). Sanity must be presumed until the contrary is shown (*Burrows v Burrows* (1827) 1 Hag Ecc 109).

Burden of proof

34.27 Where unsoundness of mind is alleged, the burden of proof rests upon those who set up the will, and, a fortiori, when it has already appeared that there was, in some particular, undoubtedly unsoundness of mind, that burden is considerably increased (*Smee v Smee* (1879) 5 PD 84 at 91; but see *Dew v Clark and Clark* (1826) 3 Add 79; *Wheeler and Batsford v Alderson* (1831) 3 Hag Ecc 574 at 598; and *Waring v Waring* (1848) 6 Moo PCC 341). So also where the will is not rational on the face of it (*Arbery v Ashe* (1828) 1 Hag Ecc 214). So where a testator has been found lunatic by inquisition the onus probandi must be upon him who asserts complete or partial recovery (*Prinsep and East India Co v Dyce Sombre, Troup and Solaroli* (1856) 10 Moo PCC 232 at 244; and *Boughton v Knight* (1873) LR 3 P & D 64 (unsoundness of mind extending over many years)).

Foreign domicil

34.28 The general rule is that the testator's capacity is to be determined by the law of his domicil, but as to burden of proof the English court, if conducting the enquiry de novo and not merely giving effect to probate or its equivalent granted abroad, must follow its own lex fori (*Re Fuld's Estate (No 3), Re Hartley v Fuld* [1968] P 675, [1965] 3 All ER 776).

What is testamentary capacity?

34.29 The testator must understand the nature of the act and effect; the extent of the property of which he is disposing; the claims to which he ought to give effect; and, with a view to the latter object; no disorder of the mind must poison his affections, pervert his sense of right or prevent the exercise of his natural faculties, and no insane delusion must influence his will in disposing of his property, and bring about a disposal of it which, if the mind had been sound, would not have been made (*Banks v Goodfellow* (1870) LR 5 QB 549 at 565; *Harwood v Baker* (1840) 3 Moo PCC 282; *Re Belliss, Polson v Parrott* (1929) 141 LT 245). See also *Boughton v Knight* (1873) LR 3 P & D 64 at 72, note (1). For a borderline case, see *d'Eye v Avery* [2001] WTLR 227. Testamentary capacity was established on the facts in *Re Parsons* [2002] WTLR 237 and *Hoff v Atherton* [2005] WTLR 99 but not in *Brown v Deacy* [2002] WTLR 782 and *Tchilingiran v Ouzouhian* [2003] WTLR 709. In *Abbot and Help the Aged v Richardson* LTL 12 May 2006, it was held that the testator did not have testamentary capacity but had knowledge of the contents of the will and approved them.

Partial insanity and delusion

34.30 Monomania, that a brother had administered poison (*Greenwood v Greenwood* (1790) 3 Curt App 1 xxxi). An insane antipathy to an only daughter (*Dew v Clark and Clark* (1822) 1 Add 279; (1824) 2 Add 102;

34.30 *Defence and counterclaim*

(1826) 3 Add 79. See also *Smith v Tebbitt* (1867) LR 1 P & D 398). Testator a paranoid psychopath—delusion affected one disposition only (*Re Bohrmann's Estate, Caesar and Watmough v Bohrmann* [1938] 1 All ER 271, 158 LT 180). A repulsion to children or others having natural claims on testator's bounty may amount to a delusion (*Boughton v Knight* (1873) LR 3 P & D 64). If such repulsion be proved, the party setting up the will must prove that it was not operative at the time of execution, and the court must regard the contents of the will and the surrounding circumstances (*Boughton v Knight*). Where a delusion has had, or is calculated to have had, an influence on the testamentary disposition it must be held to be fatal to its validity. But where the delusion must be taken neither to have had any influence on the provisions of the will, nor to have been capable of having had any, such delusion does not destroy the capacity to make the will (*Banks v Goodfellow* (1870) LR 5 QB 549; *Boughton v Knight* (1873) LR 3 P & D 64).

Old age or illness

34.31 Testamentary incapacity may arise from old age or illness. As to what constitutes a sound disposing mind, see *Harwood v Baker* (1840) 3 Moo PCC 282 at 290; *Combes' Case* (1604) Moore KB 759; and *Marsh v Tyrrell and Harding* (1828) 2 Hag Ecc 84 at 122. If a testator was of complete capacity when he gave instructions for a will, a very slight degree of capacity at the time of its execution suffices (*Harwood v Baker*; *Parker v Felgate* (1883) 8 PD 171; *Clancy v Clancy* [2002] WTLR 1097). But not if the instructions were given by a third party on the testator's behalf (*Battan Singh v Amirchand* [1948] AC 161, [1948] 1 All ER 152). As to capacity as to part of a will see *Thomas v Jones* [1928] P 162. In *Hoff v Atherton* [2005] WTLR 99 testamentary capacity was established despite the testatrix having suffered from moderate dementia. It was pointed out that the requirements of testamentary capacity and want of knowledge and approval are conceptually different. It would be absurd for the law to insist upon proof of actual understanding of the nature of the act of making a will in every case where testamentary capacity was challenged. Given the simplicity of the will and her knowledge of her assets the correct test was whether the testatrix was able to understand the nature and act of making a will.

In *Re Loxton Deceased, Abbott v Richardson* [2006] WTLR 1567, the elderly testatrix was held to have lacked testamentary capacity as she was unable to recall or focus on all the persons she might reasonably wish to benefit and arrive at a rational decision as to which of them should benefit and in what way. She was, however, held to have known and approved the contents of the will.

In *Sharp v Adam* [2006] WTLR 1059, the impairment of cognitive functions caused by multiple sclerosis led to the testator lacking the capacity to arrive at a rational judgment.

See also *Re Barker-Benfield, Hansen v Barker-Benfield* [2006] WTLR 1141. In that case it was held that the elderly testator lacked capacity but undue influence was not established.

Drunkenness

34.32 When a man is drunk, or under the influence of excessive drinking, he is incapable of making a will; but where, although an habitual drunkard, he is not under the excitement of liquor, he is not incapable of making a will (*Billinghurst v Vickers (formerly Leonard)* (1810) 1 Phillim 187 at 193; *Ayrey v Hill* (1824) 2 Add 206 at 210). For drunkenness to vitiate a will it must have such an effect on the testator that he does not know the nature and quality of the act he is carrying out (*Chana v Chana* [2001] WTLR 205).

Paralysis

34.33 Indication of wishes by nodding, etc. (*Re Holtam's Estate, Gillett v Rogers* (1913) 108 LT 732). See also para 34.53.

(3) UNDUE INFLUENCE

Form of defence

34.34

> 'That the execution of the said will and codicil was obtained by the undue influence of the claimant (and of others acting with him whose names are at present unknown to the defendant).'

Any party who wishes to contend that the execution of a will was obtained by undue influence must set out the contention specifically and give particulars of the facts and matters relied on[1].

For precedent of defence, see Form CP 34.

A plea of undue influence ought never to be put forward unless the person who pleads it has reasonable grounds on which to support it[2]. Nor may the plea be used as a screen behind which to make veiled charges of fraud and dishonesty[3].

[1] CPR 57.7(4).
[2] *Spiers v English* [1907] P 122 at 124.
[3] *Low v Guthrie* [1909] AC 278.

Summary of reported cases

What constitutes undue influence

34.35 To be undue influence there must be coercion (*Wingrove v Wingrove* (1885) 11 PD 81); or fraud (*Boyse v Rossborough* (1857) 6 HL Cas 2 at 45; *Williams v Goude* (1828) 1 Hag Ecc 577 at 581); a testator may be led but not driven; his will must be the offspring of his own volition and not the record of

34.35 *Defence and counterclaim*

someone else's (*Hall v Hall* (1868) LR 1 P & D 481). See also *Mountain v Bennet* (1787) 1 Cox Eq Cas 353 at 355.

What is not undue influence

34.36 Appeals to affection, ties of kindred, gratitude for past services, or pity for future destitution are legitimate; but not pressure if so exerted as to overpower the volition without convincing the judgment (*Hall v Hall* (1868) LR 1 P & D 481). Even immoral considerations do not amount to undue influence unless the testator is in such a condition that if he could speak his wishes to the last, he would say, 'This is not my wish, but I must do it' (*Baudains v Richardson* [1906] AC 169 at 184).

As to part of a will

34.37 Where only part of a will was obtained by undue influence, the remainder may be admitted, provided that the omissions do not upset the whole tenor of what remains (*Rhodes v Rhodes* (1882) 7 App Cas 192); and similarly where words were included without the instruction or knowledge of the testator (*Re Duane's Goods* (1862) 2 Sw & Tr 590); but the court cannot add or substitute words. See para 34.51.

The burden of proof

34.38 This is cast upon the person propounding a will and is in general discharged by proof of capacity and the fact of execution (*Barry v Butlin* (1838) 2 Moo PCC 480), together with proof of knowledge and approval if the prima facie case is met, see paras 34.06 and 34.50. When this is discharged the burden of proving that a will was executed under undue influence is on the party who alleges it (*Boyse v Rossborough* (1857) 6 HL Cas 2 at 45). Although undue influence will not be presumed, strong proof may be required of intention (*Billinghurst v Vickers* (1810) 1 Phillim 187 at 194), as when the suspicion and vigilance of the court are excited, eg by the fact that the will was drawn or prepared by an exceptionally interested party (*Barry v Butlin* (1838) 2 Moo PCC 480; *Greville v Tylee* (1851) 7 Moo PCC 320; *Low v Guthrie* [1909] AC 278; *Spiers v English* [1907] P 122 at 124). See also *Re Liver, Scott v Woods* (1955) 106 L Jo 75; *Wintle v Nye* [1959] 1 All ER 552, [1959] 1 WLR 284, HL; even if the power to overbear the will of the testator is admitted, it must be shown that such power was exercised, and that the circumstances of the execution are inconsistent with any other view but undue influence (*Craig v Lamoureux* [1920] AC 349). An allegation of undue influence succeeded in *Killick v Poutney* [2000] WTLR 41 but the defendants did not defend the proceedings.

Nature of evidence necessary to establish undue influence

34.39 *Boyse v Rossborough* (1857) 6 HL Cas 2 at 45. See also *Radford v Risdon* (1912) 28 TLR 342, as to evidence of a statement of a deceased person.

Foreign domicil

34.40 The question of undue influence is part of the substantive law of wills and therefore the law of the domicil should be followed, though not blindly: the English court will refuse to apply a law which outrages its sense of justice or decency, but it must consider the foreign law as a whole (*Re Fuld's Estate (No 3), Re Hartley v Fuld* [1968] P 675, [1965] 3 All ER 776).

(4) FRAUD

Form of defence

34.41

> 'That the execution of the said will and codicil was obtained by the fraud of the claimant, such fraud, so far as is within the defendant's present knowledge, being [*state the nature of the fraud*].'

Any party who wishes to contend that the execution of a will was obtained by fraud must set out the contention specifically and give particulars of the facts and matters relied on[1].

(See Form CP 35.)

Whenever fraud is relied upon, the necessary particulars must be included in the pleading.

1   CPR 57.7(4).

Summary of reported cases

Nature of plea

34.42 Fraud and imposition upon weakness is a sufficient ground to set aside a will (*Lord Donegal's Case* (1751) 2 Ves Sen 408). False representations as to character of person to induce testator to revoke a bequest to him are fraud (*Allen v M'Pherson* (1847) 1 HL Cas 191 at 207). So too are false representations to prevent testator from benefiting his relatives or other persons (*Boyse v Rossborough* (1857) 6 HL Cas 2 at 49). The question of fraud may depend to some extent on that of the capacity of the testator (*Marsh v Tyrrell and Harding* (1828) 2 Hag Ecc 84 at 123).

34.43 *Defence and counterclaim*

Fraud must pleaded specifically (Order 18, r 8(1))

34.43 Evidence of fraud will not be let in by a plea of undue influence (*White v White and Cato* (1862) 2 Sw & Tr 504); leave to amend by alleging fraud may, however, be granted during the hearing (*White v White and Cato* (1862) 2 Sw & Tr 504), even though the case of the party, on whom lay the onus of proof, has been closed (*Riding v Hawkins* (1889) 14 PD 56). In an action in which knowledge and approval are in issue, and no allegation of fraud is made in the pleadings, it is permissible to cross-examine a party to show that if the testator did not know and approve of the contents of the will, it was because that party was fraudulent (*Wintle v Nye* [1959] 1 All ER 552, [1959] 1 WLR 284, HL).

Part of will obtained by fraud

34.44 If part of a will has been obtained by fraud, probate ought to be refused of that part and granted of the rest (*Allen v M'Pherson* (1847) 1 HL Cas 191 at 207, 208).

Probate in solemn form revoked

34.45 A decree pronouncing for a will in solemn form may be set aside if it be proved that the decree was obtained by fraud (*Birch v Birch* [1902] P 130, CA; see also *Priestman v Thomas* (1884) 9 PD 210); but evidence of fraud discovered since the decree must be adduced and be sufficient to raise a reasonable probability of the success of the action (*Birch v Birch*).

(5) WANT OF KNOWLEDGE AND APPROVAL

Form of defence

34.46

'The deceased at the time of the execution of the said will and codicil did not know and approve of the contents thereof [*or*] of the contents of the residuary clause in the said will [*as the case may be*].'

34.47 Any party who contends that at the time when a will was executed the testator did not know of and approve its contents must give particulars of the facts and matters relied on[1].

For precedent of defence, see Form CP 36.

[1] CPR 57.7(3).

Summary of reported cases

Knowledge and approval essential

34.48 It is essential to the validity of a will that the testator should know and approve of its contents (*Hastilow v Stobie* (1865) LR 1 P & D 64; *Guardhouse v Blackburn* (1866) LR 1 P & D 109; but see *Parker v Felgate* (1883) 8 PD 171; *Battan Singh v Amirchand* [1948] AC 161, [1948] 1 All ER 152).

Presumption of law

34.49 Unless suspicion attaches to the document, the testator's execution is sufficient evidence of his knowledge and approval (*Guardhouse v Blackburn* (1866) LR 1 P & D 109). Where there is no question of fraud, the fact that a will has been read over to or by a capable testator, or the contents brought to his knowledge in some other way, is (*as a rule*) conclusive evidence that he knew and approved of the contents of it (*Guardhouse v Blackburn* (1866) LR 1 P & D 109; *Atter v Atkinson* (1869) LR 1 P & D 665 at 670). (N.B. The words 'as a rule' above are introduced owing to the case of *Fulton v Andrew* (1875) LR 7 HL 448, where Lord Cairns comments on the two cases cited, and rather questions the unyielding nature of the above proposition of law.) See also *Re Crerar, Rushforth v Rushforth* (1956) 106 L Jo 694; *Wintle v Nye* [1959] 1 All ER 552, [1959] 1 WLR 284; *Re Morris, Lloyds Bank Ltd v Peake* [1971] P 62, [1970] 1 All ER 1057, in which it was held that the rule in *Guardhouse v Blackburn*, no longer survives. But if the way in which the will was read over is called in question, the above presumption may be rebutted (*Garnett-Botfield v Garnett-Botfield* [1901] P 335), but only by the clearest evidence (*Gregson v Taylor* [1917] P 256). If knowledge and approval are clearly established at the time of giving instructions for a will, or drafting it, very little evidence of the position at the time of execution is required (*Re Wallace's Estate, Solicitor of the Duchy of Cornwall v Batten* [1952] 2 TLR 925).

Burden of proof

34.50 The burden of proof of the testator's knowledge and approval lies on the party setting up the will (*Barry v Butlin* (1838) 2 Moo PCC 480 at 482; *Cleare and Forster v Cleare* (1869) LR 1 P & D 655), and the burden is discharged prima facie by proof of capacity and due execution (*Barry v Butlin*; *Cleare v Cleare*); but where this prima facie presumption is met by the cross-examination of the witnesses, the party propounding must prove affirmatively that the testator knew and approved of the contents (*Cleare and Forste v Cleare*); *Atter v Atkinson* (1869) LR 1 P & D 665 at 668). Where a will is prepared in suspicious circumstances the onus is cast upon the person propounding it to remove such suspicion, and to prove that the testator knew and approved of its contents (*Tyrrell v Painton* [1894] P 151 at 157, CA, followed in *Re Scott, Huggett v Reichman* (1966) 110 Sol Jo 852). So where a

34.50 Defence and counterclaim

person propounds a will prepared by himself and under which he takes benefit, he must give clear proof that the testator knew and approved of that part under which he takes a benefit (*Hegarty v King* (1880) 5 LR Ir 249; affd (1880) 7 LR Ir 18, CA). See also *Re Liver, Scott v Woods* (1955) 106 L Jo 75. This plea refers to the circumstances attending the preparation and execution of the will itself, and not to extraneous matters (*Re R* [1951] P 10, [1950] 2 All ER 117). A person who is instrumental in preparing a will under which he is a beneficiary has to satisfy the court on the balance of probabilities that the testator knew and approved the contents, and while the amount of suspicion would vary depending on the circumstances there is no basis for imposing a burden beyond reasonable doubt. The question is not whether the court approves of the circumstances in which the will was executed but whether it is satisfied that it truly represents the testator's testamentary intentions (*Fuller v Strum* [2001] EWCA Civ 1897, [2002] 1 WLR 1097, *Hart v Dabbs* [2001] WTLR 527).

In *Buckenham v Dickinson* [2000] WTLR 1083 the testator was very deaf and partially blind and it was held that further affirmative evidence of knowledge and approval is required when the testator is deaf or blind, and to establish a will where the testator is blind or nearly so it must be shown to the satisfaction of the court that the will was read over in the presence of witnesses or the testator otherwise knew its contents. In that case, while the testator was of sound mind the evidence of communication was lacking. The court reiterated that the will of an old or infirm person should be witnessed by a medical practitioner. For a case where suspicious circumstances existed but the burden of proof was discharged see *Re Good decd, Carapeto v Good* [2002] WTLR 801 and *Shuck v Loveridge* [2005] EWHC 72 (Ch), [2005] All ER (D) 306 (Jan).

It is not the law that in no circumstances can a solicitor or other person who has prepared a will for a testator take a benefit under it; but that fact creates a suspicion that must be removed by the person propounding the will. In all cases the court must be vigilant and jealous. The degree of suspicion will vary with the circumstances of the case. It may be slight and easily dispelled; it may, on the other hand, be so grave that it can hardly be removed (*Wintle v Nye* [1959] 1 All ER 552, [1959] 1 WLR 284, HL). A solicitor beneficiary under a will has a personal obligation to see that the testator was separately advised before he could benefit (*Re a Solicitor* [1975] QB 475, [1974] 3 All ER 853). When a testator is elderly and infirm his will should be witnessed and approved by, a medical practitioner who satisfies himself as to the capacity and understanding of the testator and who records his examination and findings (*Re Simpson, Schaniel v Simpson* (1977) 121 Sol Jo 224).

In *Franks v Sinclair* [2007] WTLR 439, the son, who was a solicitor and had drafted the will, read it to the testatrix but the court was not satisfied that she understood it. The court held that the burden was not discharged.

See also *Cattermole v Prisk* [2006] 1 FLR 693 where it was held that the burden was discharged. The golden rule that the will of an old and infirm person should be witnessed and approved by a medical practitioner (who

Want of knowledge and approval **34.52**

satisfied himself as to the capacity and understanding of the testator, and made a record of his examination) is not itself a touchstone of validity. It merely provided guidance how disputes should be avoided or minimised and was not a substitute for the established tests of capacity and knowledge and approval.

The will of a 92-year-old testatrix was held to be valid in *Re Wilkes, Wilkes v Wilkes* [2006] WTLR 1087. The testatrix had capacity, knew and approved the contents of her will and was not unduly influenced by her son, who was the sole beneficiary out of five children.

Mistake

34.51 Where words have been inserted in a will by the mistake of the draftsman, and the will is not read to the testator, such words may be omitted from the probate (*Morrell v Morrell* (1882) 7 PD 68; *Re Walkeley's Goods* (1893) 69 LT 419; *Re Boehm's Goods* [1891] P 247; *Re Reade's Goods* [1902] P 75; *Vaughan v Clerk* (1902) 87 LT 144; *Re White's Estate* (1961) 105 Sol Jo 259 (omission from codicil of words mistakenly confirming an earlier will which had been revoked by a later one)). But where the draftsman has made the mistake owing to misunderstanding the intentions of the testator, or by the language used fails to give effect to them, the mistake must stand (*Harter v Harter* (1873) LR 3 P & D 11; *Collins v Elstone* [1893] P 1.) (But see also *Re Swords' Goods* [1952] P 368, [1952] 2 All ER 281). The court cannot supply words omitted from the will by mistake, or correct an obvious mistake (*Guardhouse v Blackburn* (1866) LR 1 P & D 109 at 114; *Morrell v Morrell* (1882) 7 PD 68 at 70; and see *Re Schott's Goods* [1901] P 190 at 192 where Jeune J deals with decisions of Butt J to the contrary in *Re Bushell's Goods* (1887) 13 PD 7, and *Re Huddleston's Goods* (1890) 63 LT 255). See also *Re Horrocks, Taylor v Kershaw* [1939] P 198, [1939] 1 All ER 579, CA (word 'or' said to have been inserted by mistake for 'and'; no jurisdiction to alter words chosen by testator, *Re Boehm* [1891] P 247 and *Re Schott* [1901] P 190 distinguished). See also paras 3.257 ff.

Rectification

34.52 In respect of a will of a testator dying on or after 1 January 1983, the court has power by virtue of s 20 of the Administration of Justice Act 1982 to rectify the will in certain limited instances (see para 41.01). For earlier deaths, it has been held in a case in which the testator is not bound by a draftsman's error that the Probate Court has power to rectify the matter so far as it can, but has no power to do so by adding words. Where the testator's intention was to revoke clauses 3 and 7(iv) of her will (clause 7 containing a large number of legacies each preceded by a roman numeral) but by mistake the codicil as drafted and executed revoked clauses 3 and 7, it was held that the testator's intentions would be most nearly met by excluding the numeral '7' so that the clause containing the revocation would read 'I revoke clauses 3 and ... of my said will'. The court of construction might then deduce from the

34.52 *Defence and counterclaim*

documents that the intention was to revoke clause 7(iv), or might decide that the gift in the codicil to the particular beneficiary was in substitution for that in clause 7(iv) of the will (*Re Morris, Lloyds Bank Ltd v Peake* [1971] P 62, [1970] 1 All ER 1057).

See also *Re Phelan* [1972] Fam 33, [1971] 3 All ER 1256; and *Re Reynette-James, Wightman v Reynette-James* [1975] 3 All ER 1037, [1976] 1 WLR 161.

Deaf mutes and paralytics

34.53 A will prepared in conformity with instructions made by signs by a testator who was deaf and dumb was proved on an affidavit setting forth the signs by which the testator signified that he understood and approved the provisions of the will (*Re Geale's Goods* (1864) 3 Sw & Tr 431); where testatrix could not speak or write owing to apoplectic stroke (*Re Owston's Goods* (1862) 2 Sw & Tr 461; *Re Holtam's Estate, Gillett v Rogers* (1913) 108 LT 732); where testatrix was paralysed.

Blind or illiterate

34.54 The court must always be satisfied that such testators knew and approved the contents of the will. If the will is proved to be in conformity with instructions of the testator, that will suffice, even though the will may not have been read to the testator (*Fincham v Edwards* (1842) 3 Curt 63). See also *Buckenham v Dickinson* [2000] WTLR 1083.

Foreign domicil

34.55 The court must decide whether the instruments propounded express the intentions of a free and capable testator. The whole point of the rule is evidential: in certain cases it requires of the court vigilant care and circumspection in investigating the facts (see, eg, *Wintle v Nye* [1959] 1 All ER 552, [1959] 1 WLR 284, HL). The rule must therefore be applied by the English court as part of its lex fori (*Re Fuld's Estate (No 3), Hartley v Fuld* [1968] P 675, [1965] 3 All ER 776).

(6) SHAM WILL

Form of defence

34.56

'That the said alleged will is not a testamentary document.'

The necessary particulars must be given. For form of defence, see CP 37.

Summary of reported cases

Will not made animo testandi

34.57 (1) Upon proof that a document, though testamentary on the face of it, was not executed with intention to effect disposition of property after death, probate of it will be refused (*Lister v Smith* (1863) 3 Sw & Tr 282; *Nichols v Nichols* (1814) 2 Phillim 180); (2) but if a document is clearly testamentary the court cannot look to the effect of it (*King's Proctor v Daines* (1830) 3 Hag Ecc 218). (3) If the wrong document is executed by mistake, probate of the whole must be refused even though some of the testamentary dispositions contained in it were intended by the testator (*Re Meyer's Estate* [1908] P 353). (4) If a document appears on the face of it not to be testamentary, or if its purport be equivocal, the onus of showing that it was made animo testandi is upon the party setting it up (*King's Proctor v Daines* (document appearing to be donatio inter vivos); *Griffin and Amos v Ferard* (1835) 1 Curt 97 (a declaration to his executors that a sum of money standing in deceased's name was held by him in trust); *Coventry v Williams* (1844) 3 Curt 787 (document setting out terms of codicil which deceased intended to execute); *Thorncroft and Clarke v Lashmar* (1862) 2 Sw & Tr 479 (the offer of an appointment at a salary with expression of wish that it should continue after the death)). A document on the face of it not testamentary may be shown to be so by extrinsic evidence (*cases cited above*). See also *Re Berger* [1990] Ch 118, [1989] 1 All ER 591, CA in which a tzava'ah (Hebrew will) in an English translation was admitted to probate. But if a document is executed in accordance with the requirements of the Wills Act 1837 there is a prima facie presumption that it is intended to be testamentary (*Re Meynell* (1949) 93 Sol Jo 466). See also *Corbett v Newey* [1998] Ch 57, [1996] 2 All ER 914 where a will was held invalid that had been executed with the intention (not expressed in the will itself) that it should take effect as a testamentary document a only subject to the fulfilment of a condition (which condition was later fulfilled). It was held that it would be contrary to the Wills Act 1837 to allow extrinsic evidence of the testatrix's intentions to be used to write a condition into the will which she had neither stated in writing nor signed. See also paras 3.22–3.32.

(7) REVOCATION

34.58 As to revocation of wills in cases where the testator died on or after 1 January 1964 see Wills Act 1963. This Act does not alter the internal law of England and Wales as contained in the Wills Act 1837, as to modes of revocation, but provides that in the circumstances specified revocation by other methods is effective.

(i) By marriage or the formation of a civil partnership or in effect by their annulment or dissolution

34.59 By s 18 of the Administration of Justice Act 1982, substituting a new s 18 to the Wills Act 1837, it is provided that a will (including codicils) *made*

34.59 *Defence and counterclaim*

on or after 1 January 1983 shall be revoked by the testator's subsequent marriage, subject to certain exceptions referred to in the section. As regards wills (and codicils) *made before 1 January 1983*, similar provision is contained in the former s 18 to the 1837 Act and s 177 of the Law of Property Act 1925 (see paras A1.13, A1.86). For an analysis of these exceptions, see Part I, Ch 3, paras 3.36 ff. Schedule 4, para 1 of the Civil Partnership Act 2004 inserts a new s 18B into the Wills Act 1837 to provide that a will shall be revoked by a civil partnership between the testator and another person.

Revocation of a will by marriage of testator or the formation of a civil partnership with another person. Form of defence

34.60

'That the deceased, subsequently to the execution of the will, contracted a marriage valid by the law of England/entered into a civil partnership with another person valid by the law of England.'

Particulars of the date and place of marriage/civil partnership should be included in the defence.

Revocation in effect by annulment or dissolution of marriage or civil partnership

34.61 If a will appoints a spouse as sole executor and sole beneficiary, the subsequent annulment or dissolution of the testator's marriage to that spouse brings about an intestacy (if such will is not then replaced) by virtue of s 18A of the Wills Act 1837 (see *Re Sinclair, Lloyds Bank plc v Imperial Cancer Research Fund* [1985] Ch 446, [1985] 1 All ER 1066) although the ineffective will still has to be proved as the last will. A new s 18A has been substituted by s 3(1) of the Law Reform (Succession) Act 1995 in respect of a will made by a person dying on or after 1 January 1996 (see Law Reform (Succession) Act 1995, s 3(2)). A new s 18C has been added by Sch 4, para 1 of the Civil Partnership Act 2004 to provide that if a testator makes a will and a court of civil jurisdiction in England and Wales dissolves his civil partnership or makes a nullity order in respect of it, or his civil partnership is dissolved or annulled and the dissolution or annulment is entitled to recognition in England and Wales by virtue of Chapter 3 of Part 5 of the Civil Partnership Act 2004 (dealing with civil partnerships dissolved abroad) then, except in so far as a contrary intention appears in the will, the provisions in the will take effect as if the former civil partner had died on the date of dissolution or annulment.

(ii) **By subsequent will**

Revocation by subsequent testamentary papers. Form of defence

34.62

'That the said will was revoked by a will or other testamentary paper of later date.'

The defence should include the date of the later will, which should be propounded in the counterclaim.

(iii) By destruction

Revocation by destruction. Form of defence

34.63

'That the said will was revoked by the same having been burnt, torn, or otherwise destroyed, by the testator, or by some person in his presence and by his direction, with the intention to revoke the same.'

The defence should include particulars of when, how, and by whom the will was destroyed or, if such be the case, that the defendant will rely on the presumption of law that, the will not being forthcoming on the death, it was destroyed by the testator animo revocandi.

For precedent of defence, see Form CP 40.

(A) Partial revocation (s 21, Wills Act 1837[1])

34.64 A will may be revoked in part by a duly executed obliteration, interlineation or other alteration, or by such an alteration as renders the former words or effect of the will no longer apparent.

[1] See para A1.18.

(B) Dependent relative, or conditional, revocation

34.65 A will though revoked by the testator may be held good by the doctrine of dependent relative revocation.

'A revocation grounded on an assumption of fact which is false takes effect unless, as a matter of construction, the truth of the fact is the condition of the revocation, or, in other words, unless the revocation is contingent upon the facts being true.'

This definition was adopted in *Re Faris, Goddard v Overend (No 2)* [1911] 1 IR 469 at 472 and approved by the Court of Appeal in *Re Southerden's Estate, Adams v Southerden* [1925] P 177.

Summary of reported cases

I. By the marriage of the testator (s 18, Wills Act 1837[1])

34.66 But see s 177 of the Law of Property Act 1925[2].

[1] See para A1.14.
[2] See para A1.86.

34.67 *Defence and counterclaim*

34.67 NB. The following decisions under this heading 'By the marriage of the Testator' are based on s 18 of the Wills Act 1837 prior to its replacement by s 18 of the Administration of Justice Act 1982 (see para A1.372). These decisions continue to apply in respect of wills *made before 1 January 1983*. However, in respect of wills *made on or after 1 January 1983*, those decisions must be considered in the light of the revised s 18 (and in light also of the amendments to s 18A made by s 3 of the Law Reform (Succession) Act 1995 in relation to deaths on or after 1 January 1996).

34.68 The will is not revoked by a marriage which is invalid by the law of England (*Mette v Mette* (1859) 1 Sw &Tr 416; *Warter v Warter* (1890) 15 PD 152). A marriage which may be voidable is effective to revoke a will (*Re Roberts, Roberts v Roberts* [1978] 3 All ER 225, [1978] 1 WLR 653, CA). The section does not affect wills of persons domiciled in countries where subsequent marriage does not revoke a will (*Re Reid's Goods* (1866) LR 1 P & D 74); but see *Re Martin, Loustalan v Loustalan* [1900] P 211, CA. The marriage must be valid by English law and contracted by or with a husband who was then domiciled in England. This statement should now be considered in the light of s 1 of the Domicile and Matrimonial Proceedings Act 1973 under which, as from 1 January 1974, a married woman is capable of having a domicil other than that of her husband. See also Dicey and Morris, *Conflict of Laws*, 11th edition. Subsequent marriage does not revoke such portion of a will as may have exercised a power of appointment, save as provided in s 18 of the Wills Act 1837 (*Re Fitzroy's Goods* (1858) 1 Sw & Tr 133; *Re Russell's Goods* (1890) 15 PD 111; *Re Paul, Public Trustee v Pearce* [1921] 2 Ch 1). Subsequent marriage does not revoke such portion of a will as may have exercised a power of appointment if the property would not pass to the *widow* and kin in default of appointment (*Re Gilligan* [1950] P 32, [1949] 2 All ER 401). A soldier's will is not excepted from the general rule (*Re Wardrop's Estate* [1917] P 54); nor, it would appear, is a mutual will (*Re Hey's Estate, Walker v Gaskill* [1914] P 192). As to presumption in favour of marriage where no certificate or other confirmation is produced, see *Rumsey v Sterne* (1967) 111 Sol Jo 113. But a will made on or since 1 January 1926, if expressed to be made in contemplation of a marriage, is not revoked by the marriage contemplated: s 177, Law of Property Act 1925[1]. The marriage contemplated must be identified in the will (*Sallis v Jones* [1936] P 43 (will pronounced against)). A duly executed indorsement on an envelope containing a will revoked by marriage stating that 'The herein named is now my lawful wife' was held to revive the will (*Re Davis' Estate* [1952] P 279, [1952] 2 All ER 509). See also paras 3.36 and 35.06. The section does not require that the testator should set out that the will is made because he contemplates marriage: it is sufficient if there is a practical expression of his contemplation of marriage to a particular person. A gift to 'my fiancée' (whom the testator afterwards married) was held to be sufficient (*Re Langston's Estate* [1953] P 100, [1953] 1 All ER 928): see *Pilot v Gainfort* [1931] P 103. It is sufficient if one can collect from the words of the will themselves the fact that the marriage which later took place was mentally in view of the testator at the time when he made the will (*Re Gray's Estate* (1963) 107 Sol Jo 156). The will, not merely some gifts in it, must be in contemplation of marriage (*Re Coleman, Coleman v Coleman* [1976] Ch 1, [1975] 1 All ER 675).

1   See para A1.86.

II. By another will or codicil (s 20, Wills Act 1837[1])

34.69

(i)   *Containing express words of revocation.* The expression, 'This is my last will and testament' need not, standing alone, revoke all former testamentary papers (*Cutto v Gilbert* (1854) 9 Moo PCC 131), neither need the words, 'This is the last and only will of me', etc. (*Simpson v Foxon* [1907] P 54). General words of revocation revoke a will exercising a general or special power of appointment (*Sotheran v Dening* (1881) 20 Ch D 99; *Re Kingdon, Wilkins v Pryer* (1886) 32 Ch D 604), unless there is cogent evidence to the contrary (*Lowthorpe-Lutwidge v Lowthorpe-Lutwidge* [1935] P 151 (*Smith v Thompson* (1931) 47 TLR 603, distinguished)). Cf. *Re Wayland's Estate* [1951] 2 All ER 1041. In *Jones v Treasury Solicitor* (1932) 49 TLR 75, CA, the word 'ungultig' substituted by the word 'cancelled' was held to revoke an earlier will. Revocation of a will does not involve revocation of a codicil to such will (*Black v Jobling* (1869) LR 1 P & D 685; see also *Re Savage's Goods* (1870) LR 2 P & D 78; *Re Turner's Goods* (1872) LR 2 P & D 403; *Gardiner v Courthope* (1886) 12 PD 14; *Farrer v St Catherine's College, Cambridge* (1873) LR 16 Eq 19). Words of revocation inserted per incuriam and without the knowledge of the testator may be omitted from the probate (*Re Moore's Goods* [1892] P 378; *Re Oswald's Goods* (1874) LR 3 P & D 162), but if the testator's mind was directed to the words, even if he did not intend them, they will operate as a revocation (*Collins v Elstone* [1893] P 1; *Re Hope-Brown's Goods* [1942] P 136, sub nom *Re Brown's Goods*, [1942] 2 All ER 176). See also *Re Cocke's Goods* [1960] 2 All ER 289, [1960] 1 WLR 491: two wills both appointed the same executor; the later will contained a revocation clause but the residuary clause was inchoate. Both wills admitted to proof, omitting the revocation clause in later will and clauses in the earlier will inconsistent with the later will. In the case of a lost will, prepared hurriedly by a solicitor who was unable to recollect any of its contents, no copy being available, the judge drew the inference that a solicitor-drawn will would contain a revocation clause, and found that all previous wills were revoked (*Re Hampshire's Estate* [1951] WN 174). But a contrary view was taken in *Re Wyatt* [1952] 1 All ER 1030. See further, as to revocation, paras 3.34 ff.

1   See para A1.17.

(ii) *Inconsistent wills.* In considering what documents constitute the will, the whole question is one of intention (*Methuen v Methuen* (1817) 2 Phillim 416; see also *Chichester v Quatrefages* [1895] P 186 at 188). Where different testamentary documents are co-extensive and in such terms that probate cannot be granted of both, probate will be granted

34.69 *Defence and counterclaim*

of the latest in date (*O'Leary v Douglass* (1879) 3 LR Ir 323). Where the priority of two wills (both containing express words of revocation) is uncertain, and their terms are so inconsistent that they cannot stand together, neither will be admitted to probate, but they revoke a previous will (*Re Howard, Howard v Treasury Solicitor* [1944] P 39); if neither contains express words of revocation, the court will, if possible, so construe them that they can both stand as together being the will of the testator (*Townsend v Moore* [1905] P 66, CA). If there is no real inconsistency and no revocation, any number of documents may be admitted as the last will (*Deakin v Garvie* (1919) 36 TLR 122, CA). If the intention of the testator remains in doubt on the face of the two documents, evidence of the surrounding circumstances may be admitted (*Re Bryan's Estate* [1907] P 125), and parol evidence of the testator's intention is admissible (*Thorne v Rooke* (1841) 2 Curt 799; *Jenner v Ffinch* (1879) 5 PD 106). Where the later will is only partly inconsistent the former is only revoked in part, and both are entitled to probate (*Lemage v Goodban* (1865) LR 1 P & D 57): *Re Cocke's Goods*, above. Although the first will disposes of the whole of the property, and a later will contains no words of revocation, and leaves the residue undisposed of, yet the earlier will may be held to be revoked by the later one (*Re Bryan's Estate* [1907] P 125). If a later will partly revoked an earlier will and is in its turn revoked, such revocation will not effect a revival of the revoked portion of the earlier will (*Re Hodgkinson's Goods* [1893] P 339, CA). The general bequest by a later testamentary document, inconsistent with the exercise of a power of appointment by an earlier will, will revoke such will (*Cadell v Wilcocks* [1898] P 21; see also *Wrigley v Lowndes* [1908] P 348; *Re Gibbes' Settlement, White v Randolf* (1887) 37 Ch D 143, but see *Smith v Thompson* (1931) 47 TLR 603 (exercise of power of appointment in first will not revoked by revocatory clause in second)). This case was distinguished in *Lowthorpe-Lutwidge v Lowthorpe-Lutwidge* [1935] P 151. A codicil headed 'codicil' but beginning 'This is the last will and testament', and not referring to the will but effecting a substantial difference in the disposition of the property, was proved with the will (*Kitcat v King* [1930] P 266). See also *Re Mardon's Estate* [1944] P 109, [1944] 2 All ER 397, as to partial revocation, and *Re Swords' Goods* [1952] P 368, [1952] 2 All ER 281, as to exclusion of a revocation clause inserted, in error, in a codicil: *Re White's Estate* (1961) 105 Sol Jo 259 (omission from codicil of words mistakenly confirming a will revoked by one later in date).

(iii) '*By some writing declaring an intention to revoke*' (*s 20, Wills Act 1837*). A document executed and attested as a will, containing a request to destroy a will, has been held to revoke that will (*Re Spracklan's Estate* [1938] 2 All ER 345, CA). The intention need not be express (*Ford v de Pontés* (1861) 30 Beav 572; *Re Hicks' Goods* (1869) LR 1 P & D 683; *Re Durance's Goods* (1872) LR 2 P & D 406); and, in the absence of any other testamentary directions, the written declaration need not be annexed to the grant (*Toomer v Sobinska* [1907] P

106; *Re Eyre's Goods* [1905] 2 IR 540) (see para 6.06, as to practice). See also *Re Brennan's Goods* [1932] IR 633 (instructions for new will admitted to probate).

III. *By burning, tearing, or otherwise destroying (s 20, Wills Act 1837[1])*

34.70 (i) *Generally:*

(a) *Intention to revoke.* The intention to revoke must accompany the act (*Bibb v Thomas* (1775) 2 Wm Bl 1043; *Clarke v Scripps* (1852) 2 Rob Eccl 563 at 567; *Giles v Warren* (1872) LR 2 P & D 401). Therefore a person of unsound mind cannot revoke his will by destruction (*Brunt v Brunt* (1873) LR 3 P & D 37 at 38; *Re Taylor's Estate, National and Provincial and Union Bank of England v Taylor* (1919) 64 Sol Jo 148). As to standard of capacity required, see *Re Sabatini* (1969) 114 Sol Jo 35. Where the destruction is not with consent of the testator, he cannot subsequently ratify such destruction so as to effect a revocation (*Mills v Millward* (1889) 15 PD 20; *Gill v Gill* [1909] P 157), and subsequent acquiescence does not constitute revocation (*Re Booth, Booth v Booth* [1926] P 118). If there is an express revocation clause in a later will which is not in accord with the testator's instructions there is no rule of law that the testator is bound by the draftsman's mistake. The burden of proving on the balance of probabilities that the testator had not intended to revoke the earlier will is on the party seeking to prevent the express clause having effect. The standard of proof is no higher then the usual balance of proof, but the existence of the revocation clause is strong evidence that needs to be overcome (*Lamothe v Lamothe* [2006] WTLR 1431). For a later lost will to revoke an earlier will there must be clear, stringent and conclusive evidence that there was either a revocation clause in the lost will or that its provisions were inconsistent with those of the earlier will (*Broadway v Fernandes* [2007] EWHC 684 (Ch), [2007] All ER (D) 485 (Mar)).

(b) *Presumption as to will not forthcoming at testator's death.* Where a will is traced into the testator's custody, and there is no evidence of its having subsequently left his custody, and it is not forthcoming at his death—this will be prima facie evidence of its destruction by him animo revocandi (*Patten v Poulton* (1858) 1 Sw & Tr 55; *Welch v Phillips* (1836) 1 Moo PCC 299 at 302), and it is not necessary for those alleging revocation to show how, in fact, it was lost or destroyed (*Patten v Poulton* (1858) 1 Sw & Tr 55). The presumption may be rebutted by surrounding circumstances, eg declaration of unchanged affection or intention (*Patten v Poulton* (1858) 1 Sw & Tr 55; *Welch v Phillips* (1836) 1 Moo PCC 299 at 302; *Re Mackenzie's Estate* [1909] P 305; *Re Sykes, Drake v Sykes* (1906) 22 TLR 741; affd (1907) 23 TLR 747, CA); *Re Wilson's Estate, Walker v Treasury Solicitor* (1961) 105 Sol Jo 531. The strongest proof of the improbability of revocation by destruction arises from the contents of the document itself (*Saunders v Saunders* (1848) 6 Notes of Cases 518 at 522). Where a will which has been in the custody of a testator at a time when he has been of unsound mind as well as of sound mind, is found torn, or is not forthcoming at

34.70 *Defence and counterclaim*

his death, the burden of showing that it was revoked by him while of sound mind lies on the party who sets up the revocation (*Harris v Berrall* (1858) 1 Sw & Tr 153). See also *Sprigge v Sprigge* (1868) LR 1 P & D 608 (the presumption of destruction animo revocandi does not apply where the testator became of unsound mind after execution of the will and continued so until his death. The burden of showing that the will was revoked before he became of unsound mind lies on the party asserting revocation); *Re Yule's Estate* (1965) 109 Sol Jo 317 (the presumption of destruction animo revocandi and the contrary presumption, in the case where the testator had lost testamentary capacity, that the will was destroyed unintentionally, were not intended to be rigid rules but as indications of the inferences which would always be drawn from a given state of evidence. But the court was not entitled to depart from *Sprigge v Sprigge*, above). In *Re Dickson* [1984] LS Gaz R 3012, CA; [2002] WTLR 1395 the presumption that a missing will had been destroyed animo revocandi was rebutted where the only reasonable inference from declarations by the testator and other evidence was that he had intended the missing will to be effective and had intended to benefit the beneficiaries thereunder. If the deceased has passed the will to a third party for safe custody no presumption arises (*Chana v Chana* [2001] WTLR 205). In *Rowe v Clarke* [2006] WTLR 347 the presumption was rebutted on the facts, which pointed to the testator having lost or destroyed the will in his lifetime without intending to revoke it. In *Wren v Wren* [2007] WTLR 531, the will was not found at death, however, the deceased's clear post-will testamentary declarations rebutted the presumption of revocation.

(c) *Revocation by partial destruction.* Where a testator signed his name, which was attested by both the witnesses, on each of the sheets of his will, and at his death only two of the middle sheets were found among his papers, it was held that the will must be presumed to be revoked (*Re Gullan's Goods* (1858) 1 Sw & Tr 23); so, too, where the testator had replaced the three middle sheets of his will (consisting of five sheets) by three other sheets, and the original sheets could not be found (*Treloar v Lean* (1889) 14 PD 49); see also *Clarke v Scripps* (1852) 2 Rob Eccl 563 (the question is whether the portion destroyed is so important as to raise a presumption that the remainder cannot have been intended to stand without it, or whether it is unimportant and independent of the remainder of the will); *Leonard v Leonard* [1902] P 243. Where part of a will is destroyed, but the part preserved contains the signatures of testator and the witnesses, the onus is normally on the party alleging revocation to prove the necessary animus. But if the part preserved is so mutilated as to be unworkable as a testamentary instrument this raises a presumption that the testator could not have intended it to stand as his will (*Re Green's Estate, Ward v Bond* (1962) 106 Sol Jo 1034). In *Re Adams* [1990] Ch 601, [1990] 2 All ER 97 it was held that the obliteration of his signature by the testator, so that it could not be read with a magnifying glass was by itself sufficient evidence of intention to revoke the whole will.

(d) *Revocation of duplicate wills.* Where a will is executed in duplicate the revocation of one is the revocation of both (*Boughey v Moreton* (1758)

3 Hag Ecc 191). But there must be evidence that the will was, in fact, executed in duplicate—subsequent declarations by the testator to this effect are inadmissible (*Atkinson v Morris* [1897] P 40, CA; *Eyre v Eyre* [1903] P 131 at 137). See para 3.209.

1   See para A1.17.

34.71 (*ii*) *Burning*. There must be actual burning, not merely an attempt to burn (*Doe d Reed v Harris* (1837) 6 Ad & El 209); but this may be slight, if done with the intention of revoking (*Bibb v Thomas* (1775) 2 Wm Bl 1043).

34.72 (*iii*) *Tearing (including cutting)*. The tearing need not divide the instrument in two if done with the intention of revoking (*Bibb v Thomas* (1775) 2 Wm Bl 1043; *Elms v Elms* (1858) 1 Sw & Tr 155 at 157); but the process of tearing must be completed. Where the testator was stopped in course of tearing his will and there was evidence of change of intention, it was held that there was no revocation (*Doe d Perkes v Perkes* (1820) 3 B & Ald 489); see also *Elms v Elms* (1858) 1 Sw & Tr 155; in similar circumstances the court may refuse to decree probate on motion (*Re Colberg's Goods* (1841) 2 Curt 832); the tearing must be accompanied by intention to revoke (*Giles v Warren* (1872) LR 2 P & D 401); see *Re Thornton's Goods* (1889) 14 PD 82; *Re Cowling, Jinkin v Cowling* [1924] P 113; cutting away the signature or the signature of either of the attesting witnesses may effect a revocation (*Hobbs v Knight* (1838) 1 Curt 768; *Re Dallow's Goods, Evans v Dallow* (1862) 31 LJPM & A 128; *Bell v Fothergill* (1870) LR 2 P & D 148; though not necessarily, if the piece is preserved (*Re Wheeler's Goods* (1879) 49 LJP 29), for as the intention of the testator is relevant, it must be considered whether he did this for some other purpose, eg in an attempt to prevent forfeiture of a legacy to the witness or his spouse; scratching out the signature with a knife (which is lateral cutting) will revoke, but only if carried out by the testator to the extent of making his signature illegible) (*Re Godfrey's Goods* (1893) 69 LT 22); cutting away signature to a will may, on proof of intention, also operate as revocation of a codicil executed on the same paper (*Re Bleckley's Goods* (1883) 8 PD 169); cutting away of portions of a will may operate merely as revocation of such portion (*Clarke v Scripps* (1852) 2 Rob Eccl 563; *Re Nunn's Estate* [1936] 1 All ER 555).

34.73 (*iv*) *Otherwise destroying*, must be ejusdem generis as burning or tearing (per Sir H Jenner in *Stephens v Taprell* (1840) 2 Curt 458); see also *Cheese v Lovejoy* (1877) 2 PD 251; cancellation is not such 'otherwise destroying' (*Stephens v Taprell* (1840) 2 Curt 458).

34.74 (*v*) *In the presence of the testator*. If not effected by the testator, the destruction at his direction must take place in his presence; otherwise there is no revocation (*Re Dadds' Goods* (1857) Dea & Sw 290; *Re De Kremer's Estate, Lundbeck v De Kremer* (1965) 110 Sol Jo 18).

34.75 *Defence and counterclaim*

A Partial revocation

34.75

(a) *By duly executed obliteration, interlineation, or other alteration.*
(b) *By such an alteration as will render the former words or effect of the will no longer apparent.* Such obliteration must be complete. If the portion can be read by any means other than physical interference with the document it is not revoked (*Ffinch v Combe* [1894] P 191; *Re Brasier's Goods* [1899] P 36). (See further re obliterations, paras 3.248–3.255.)

B Dependent relative, or conditional, revocation

34.76 *Dependent relative revocation.* Will destroyed in belief that thereby an earlier will would be revived (*Powell v Powell* (1866) LR 1 P & D 209; *Cossey v Cossey* (1900) 82 LT 203); part of will destroyed in belief that its place would be taken by an unexecuted memorandum (*Dancer v Crabb* (1873) LR 3 P & D 98); document destroyed in belief that later will (unexecuted) would take its place (*Re Irvin's Estate* (1908) 25 TLR 41; and *West v West* [1921] 2 IR 34; see also *Dixon v Treasury Solicitor* [1905] P 42); will destroyed in belief that a later will (in fact pronounced against) was properly executed (*Re Bunn, Durber v Bunn* (1926) 134 LT 669); destruction of earlier will after execution of later will in belief later will valid (*Re Davies' Estate, Russell v Delaney* [1951] 1 All ER 920); will mutilated on expressed intention—not fulfilled—of making another (*Re Botting's Estate, Botting v Botting* [1951] 2 All ER 997; *Re Addison's Estate* (1964) 108 Sol Jo 504: testator took will from solicitor's office saying he wanted to make a new will because of his wife's death. No will was found on his death nine months later. The proper inference was that he destroyed the will intending to make a new one. There was no revocation and the will, as contained in a copy, was admitted). See also *Re Bridgewater's Estate* [1965] 1 All ER 717, [1965] 1 WLR 416 (three wills, each with a revocation clause. Testator wrote to solicitor saying he had deposited second will at a bank, having destroyed the third. On his death only the earliest will was found. Held, the letter was admissible as evidence of intention to destroy the third will with a view to reviving the second, and as evidence of the destruction. The third will, as contained in a copy, was admitted); lapse of time immaterial if intention at date of destruction was clear (*Re Bromham's Estate, Wass v Treasury Solicitor* [1952] 1 All ER 110n); will revoked in mistaken belief that certain legatees were dead (*Campbell v French* (1797) 3 Ves 321); a printed form of will, with revocation clause, executed with blanks which were subsequently filled in—probate refused, it being held that the revocation was dependent on another will being made (*Re Irvine's Goods* [1919] 2 IR 485); destruction in mistaken belief as to distribution on intestacy (*Re Southerden's Estate, Adams v Southerden* [1925] P 177, CA). Where a second will which was incomplete revoked the first, both wills were admitted with the revocatory clause excluded (*Re Hope-Brown's Goods*, sub nom *Re Brown's Goods* [1942] P 136, [1942] 2 All ER 176: followed in *Re Allen* (1962) 106 Sol Jo 115 (all dispositions in a later will, executed on a printed form which included a revocation clause, were proved to have been added after execution. The revocation clause was held to be conditional upon the later will being effective: the earlier will was therefore not revoked)). See also *Re Cocke's Goods* [1960] 2 All ER 289, [1960] 1 WLR 491 (two inconsistent wills, the later having a revocation clause but no effective residuary gift: both wills admitted, the revocation clause in the second, and clauses in the first will inconsistent with those in the second, being omitted). When a testator destroyed a will under belief that he no longer had anything to leave the revocation was held to be conditional and the will admitted to probate (*Re Carey* (1977) 121 Sol Jo 173).

In the absence of evidence of any direct connection between the destruction of an earlier will and the purported execution of a later will the doctrine was held not applicable (*Re Green's Estate, Ward v Bond* (1962) 106 Sol Jo 1034) and *Re Jones, Evans v Harries* [1976] Ch 200, [1976] 1 All ER 593. Revocation in part of earlier will held not to have been conditional in *Re Feis, Guillaume v Ritz-Remorf* [1964] Ch 106, [1963] 3 All ER 303. See also paras 3.244–3.255.

In *Re Finnemore* [1992] 1 All ER 800, [1991] 1 WLR 793, an intention to devise a house gathered from two previous wills was held to give a conditional (and therefore a distributive) effect to a revocation clause contained in the third will. Thus the clause did not destroy the devise in the first or second will, even though the similar devise in the third will was ineffective (that will being witnessed by the husband of the devisee). The clause did, however, operate to revoke the remainder of the earlier wills.

(8) DECEASED PREVENTED BY THREATS FROM ALTERING WILL

Form of defence

34.77

'That the deceased was prevented by threats on the part of the claimants from making a fresh will or altering the will propounded.'

This was a defence permitted under the Judicature Act 1873, and if established it entitles the court to declare the executors of the will propounded to be trustees for the parties intended to have been benefited by another will[1].

Plea allowed by Hannen P,

'that after making the said alleged will of May, 1853, the deceased was prevented by force and threats from executing a further will prepared by and under his instructions whereby the plaintiff would have been deprived of his interest under the said alleged will.'

Where a testator has in a will given a legacy to A. B., and by the threats or undue influence or fraud of the residuary legatee of a subsequent will, has been induced to omit the legacy from the said will, A. B. may plead the fact

34.77 *Defence and counterclaim*

and ask the court to declare the executors of the last will to be trustees for him of a part of the estate equivalent to the amount of the legacy.

For precedent of defence, see CP 42.

[1] *Betts v Doughty* (1879) 5 PD 26.

(9) ESTOPPEL—LACHES

Form of defence

34.78

'The claimant is estopped by reason of [as the case maybe].'

The defence should include particulars of the previous action and judgment.

Summary of reported cases

34.79 A claimant may be estopped from setting up a will by a previous judgment on the same issue between the same parties (*Priestman v Thomas* (1884) 9 PD 210, CA). Even where the matter was not definitely held to be res judicata, a claimant was estopped from prosecuting a claim for a grant of administration as next of kin, where she had practically acquiesced in Chancery proceedings four years before, in which her title as next of kin was involved, and where the property had been distributed by order of the court, it being held that the claimant had been guilty of such laches as to disentitle her to maintain her suit (*Mohan v Broughton* [1899] P 211; affd [1900] P 56, CA). As to the binding effect of probate in solemn form, see also para 26.06.

As to laches, see also *Mahon v Quinn* [1904] 2 IR 267; *David v Frowd* (1833) 1 My & K 200; and *Sawyer v Birchmore* (1837) 1 Keen 825. The fact that an executor, who is also next of kin, has taken probate, does not estop him from afterwards taking proceedings for a pronouncement against the will (*Williams v Evans* [1911] P 175). A certain amount of delay on the part of such a person, even though he had all along had full knowledge of the facts, in instituting proceedings for revocation of probate does not necessarily amount to laches on his part (*Williams v Evans*).

(10) MINORITY

Form of defence

34.80

'That the said alleged will is invalid by reason of the fact that the deceased was under the age of eighteen years at the time the said will purports to have been executed.'

By s 7 of the Wills Act 1837[1], no will made by any person under the age of 21 years is valid. By the Family Law Reform Act 1969, s 3(1), the age of 18 years is substituted for 21 years under s 7 of the Wills Act 1837 and ss 1 and 3(1) of the Wills (Soldiers and Sailors) Act 1918. For exceptions in the case of soldiers, sailors or airmen being in actual military service, or of mariners or seamen being at sea, see paras 3.338–3.342, and paras 33.27 ff.

For precedent of defence, see CP 38.

[1] See para A1.03.

INTEREST ACTION

34.81 Form of defence, CP 46.

FORFEITURE

34.82 See para 33.60.

Chapter 39

TRIAL

Summary
Place of trial 196
Lists and duration 196
The hearing 197
Matters following judgment 200

PLACE OF TRIAL

39.01 A probate claim will normally be tried at the place where the claim was commenced (ie in London at the Royal Courts of Justice or in one of the Chancery district registries of the High Court in Birmingham, Bristol, Caenarfon, Cardiff, Leeds, Liverpool, Manchester, Mold, Newcastle upon Tyne, Preston) or, rarely, in the county court in one of those places.

If a probate claim has been commenced in the High Court in London it can be transferred to one of the Chancery district registries[1] (or rarely and exceptionally, and if the county court has jurisdiction – see Ch 26 para 26.09 – to the county court). The transfer will normally be ordered at the case management conference.

[1] CPR 30.2(8).

LISTS AND DURATION

Lists

39.02 There are now three Chancery lists; the trial list (for cases with witnesses); the interim hearing lists (interim applications and appeals from Masters) and the general list (for cases without witnesses). The former short probate list no longer exists.

Day-to-day management of Chancery listing in the Royal Courts of Justice. is dealt with by the Chancery Listing Office (Room WG4 Royal Courts of Justice).

39.03 The procedure for Chancery cases in the Royal Courts of Justice is that at an early stage the court will give directions fixing the period during which the case will be heard (the trial window).

The court will direct that one party, normally the claimant, makes an appointment to attend on the Listing Officer to fix a trial date within the trial window, by such date as may be specified in the order and give notice of the appointment to all other parties. In determining the trial window the court will have regard to the listing constraints created by the existing court list and will determine a trial window which provides the parties with enough time to complete the preparation for trial. A list of current trial windows is published on the HMCS website[1].

[1] Chancery Guide Ch 6 para 6.8. As to the listing appointment see Chancery Guide Ch 6 para 6.9.

Estimate of duration

39.04 If after a case is listed in the Royal Courts of Justice the estimated length of the hearing is varied, or if the case is settled, withdrawn or discontinued, the solicitors for the parties must forthwith inform the Chancery Listing Officer in writing. Failure to do so may result in an adverse costs order being made[1].

Seven days before the date for the hearing, the claimant's solicitors must inform the Chancery Listing Officer whether there is any variation in the estimate of duration, and, in particular, whether the case is likely to be disposed of in some summary way[2].

[1] Chancery Guide Ch 6 para 6.13.
[2] Chancery Guide Ch 6 para 6.14.

Daily list of cases

39.05 This is available on www.hmcourts-service.gov.uk/cms/cause.htm.

Time limits

39.06 The court may, either at the outset of the trial or at any other time thereafter fix time limits for oral submissions, speeches and the examination and cross-examination of witnesses[1].

[1] Chancery Guide Ch 8 para 8.3.

THE HEARING

Opening oral submissions

39.07 Generally the claimant opens, unless the burden of proof of all issues in the case lies on the defendant, in which case the defendant has the right to

39.07 *Trial*

begin. In general and subject to any direction to the contrary by the trial judge there should be a short opening statement on behalf of the claimant, at the conclusion of which the judge will invite short opening statements on behalf of the other parties[1]. Unless notified otherwise advocates should assume that the judge will have read the skeleton arguments and the principal documents referred to in the reading list lodged in advance of the hearing. The judge will state at an early stage how much he or she has read and what arrangements are to be made about reading documents not already read. If additional documents need to be read by the judge a list should be provided during the opening[2].

[1] Chancery Guide Ch 8 para 8.4.
[2] Chancery Guide Ch 8 para 8.5.

Witness statements

39.08 Appendix 4 of the Chancery Guide lays down guidelines for the preparation of witness statements. Unless the court otherwise orders, a witness statement stands as the witness's evidence-in-chief if he is called and confirms that its contents are true[1]. A witness may be allowed to supplement his statement in chief if the Judge is satisfied that there are good reasons[2].

Witnesses are expected to have re-read their witness statements shortly before they are called to give evidence[3]. Where a party decides not to call a witness whose statement has been served, prompt notice must be given to the other parties, making it clear whether that party proposes to seek to put in the statement as hearsay evidence. If he does not any other party may put it in as hearsay evidence[4].

[1] Chancery Guide Ch 8 para 8.10.
[2] Chancery Guide Ch 8 para 8.11.
[3] Chancery Guide Ch 8 para 8.12.
[4] Chancery Guide Ch 8 para 8.13.

Evidence

39.09 At the hearing the court will have to be satisfied by the party propounding the will that it was duly executed, that the testator was of testamentary capacity, and that he knew and approved the contents of the will. The general rule is that any fact which needs to be proved by the evidence of witnesses is to be proved at the trial by their oral evidence given in public.

This is subject to any order of the court[1]. When a will and codicil or codicils are being propounded evidence must of course be called in respect of each document. If a decree pronouncing against a will is sought evidence must be produced to justify such a decree eg that the will was not duly executed or at the time of execution the deceased was not of sound mind.

It is the usual practice to have any later will pronounced against, but when proceedings are undefended and evidence has been adduced in favour of an earlier will the court may pronounce for the earlier will without pronouncing against the later will provided it is satisfied that everyone interested under the later will has been served or had proper notice[2].

A grant may be made to the next of kin when the executors and persons interested under the alleged will have not appeared or taken any part in the proceedings. In such circumstances it is not necessary to have the will pronounced against[3].

[1] CPR 32.2.
[2] *Re Morton's Goods, Morton v Thorpe* (1863) 3 SW & Tr 179.
[3] *Re Quick's Goods, Quick v Quick* [1899] P 187.

Closing oral submissions

39.10 After the evidence is concluded, and subject to contrary directions by the judge, the claimant will make closing oral submissions followed by the defendant(s) in the order they appear on the claim form, followed by a reply on behalf of the claimant[1]. This differs from the traditional order of speeches where the defendant made his submissions before the claimant. In a lengthy and complex case each party should provide written summaries of their closing submissions. The court may require the written summaries to set out the principal findings of fact for which a party contends[2].

[1] Chancery Guide Ch 8 para 8.7.
[2] Chancery Guide Ch 8 para 8.8.

Burden of proof

39.11 In a probate claim there may well be shifts in the burden of proof, but in broad outline, where the issues raised in the claim include those arising out of the alleged condition, act or omission of the testator (eg lack of testamentary capacity, want of knowledge and approval or lack of due execution) the burden of proof on those issues is primarily upon the party propounding the will, and it lies with that party to begin[1]. If, however, the validity of the will is not attacked and the sole issue is revocation, it is for the party alleging the revocation of a will to begin[2]. If the party opposing a will should not appear at the trial, the party propounding it should proceed to prove it in solemn form.

The burden of proving affirmative allegations impeaching the will where the fault does not lie with the testator (eg undue influence or fraud) is upon the party making them, and if they are pleaded without including the issues referred to above it lies with that party to begin[3]. This applies notwithstanding that the party propounding the will has the burden of satisfying the court as to due execution, for this remains an essential whatever other issues may be raised in the claim[4]. Should there be more than one will before the court it may often be convenient for the defendant to begin when he is setting up the last will in point of time[5].

39.11 Trial

The same considerations apply in a revocation action[6].

1. *Hutley v Grimstone* (1879) 5PD 24.
2. *North v North* (1909) 25 TLR 322.
3. *Hutley v Grimstone* (1879) 5PD 24; *Tate v Tate* (1890) 63 LT 112.
4. *Hutley v Grimstone* (1879) 5PD 24.
5. *Re Parry's Estate, Parry v Fraser* [1977]1 All ER 309, [1977] 1WLR 93n.
6. *Cross v Cross* (1864) 3 SW & Tr 292.

Admission of further evidence while judgment reserved

39.12 While judgment is reserved a judge can accede in his discretion to an application to adduce further evidence which was not available at the trial[1].

1. *Acosta v Longworth, Jones and Turton* [1965] 1 WLR 107, PC applying *Sugden v Lord St Leonards* (1876) 1 PD 154; the action was for proof of a lost will, and the evidence was not merely to credit but also to the terms of the will.

MATTERS FOLLOWING JUDGMENT

Application for grant following judgment

39.13 A copy of the court's sealed order should be obtained for production to the probate registry.

Unless the court orders otherwise, if a testamentary document is held by the court (whether lodged by a party or previously held at a probate registry) when the claim has been disposed of the court will send it to the Leeds District Probate Registry[1].

Unless an application is pending at the Leeds District Probate registry it appears that the original will will be handed back to the solicitors of the party entitled to apply for a grant.

As to the wording of the oath and the procedure on application for a grant see para 4.178 ff. As to procedure where a grant pending determination of the claim has previously issued see paras 11.353 and 11.354.

Under NC Probate Rules 45(4), upon application for a grant by the person shown to be entitled thereto by the decision of the court in the claim, any caveat entered by the claimant in the claim and any caveat in respect of which notice of the action was given ceases to have effect (see para 23.16).

1. CPR Pt 57 PD para 3.1.

Handing out of a confirmed grant

39.14 Where a grant of representation has previously issued in common form, if the will previously proved is pronounced for in solemn form, or the title to the grant is confirmed by the judgment, the latter should include a direction that the grant be handed out to the grantee or his solicitor.

Matters following judgment 39.14

In the case of a will, the grant is marked as follows: 'The force and validity of the will, a copy whereof is hereunto annexed, was pronounced for in an action entitled AB against CD on the   day of   20   '. This notation is signed by the authorised officer.

The probate records at Leeds will be noted, and the copy grant released to the extracting solicitor either from the Chancery Court, or if there has to be any notations made to the original probate records, from Leeds.

Chapter 40
COSTS

Summary
General rules	202
Costs of parties propounding a testamentary document	203
Costs of parties opposing probate	206
Costs of particular parties	211
More than one set of costs allowed	213
Apportionment of costs	213

GENERAL RULES

Costs are in the discretion of the court

40.01 The question of costs of probate claims has always been in the discretion of the court, whether under the practice of the Prerogative Court, under the former Contentious Probate Rules, or under the Judicature Acts and the Rules of the Supreme Court.

By s 51(1) of the Supreme Court Act 1981:

'Subject to the provisions of this or any other Act, and to rules of court, the costs of and incidental to the proceedings in the civil division of the Court of Appeal and in the High Court, including the administration or estates and trusts, shall be in the discretion of the court, and the court shall have full powers to determine by whom and to what extent the costs are to be paid.'

Rules as to costs

40.02 The rules as to costs are continued in CPR Pts 43 to 48. (The Civil Procedure Rules do not however apply to non-contentious or common form probate proceedings by virtue of CPR 2.1.)

The court has discretion as to whether costs are to be payable by one party to another, the amount of those costs and when they are to be paid. If the court decides to make an order about costs, the general rule is that the unsuccessful party will be ordered to pay the costs of the successful party, but the court can make a different order. CPR 44.3 sets out the circumstances the court should take into account.

CPR 44.14 makes provision as to costs arising from misconduct or neglect and provides that a legal representative may be ordered to pay costs personally. CPR 48.7 applies to the court's power under s 51(6) of the Supreme Court Act 1981 to disallow or order a legal representative to meet wasted costs.

Restriction of discretion as to costs

40.03 In a probate claim where a defendant has in his defence given notice that he requires the will to be proved in solemn form the court will not make an order for costs against the defendant unless it appears that there were no reasonable grounds for opposing the will[1].

[1] CPR Pt 44 PD para 8.2.

Exceptions to the rule that costs follow the event

40.04 Although the general rule is that costs follow the event[1], and should be asked for at the trial[2], there are certain substantial exceptions, and these are dealt with in the following pages.

[1] See *Twist v Tye* [1902] P 92.
[2] *Re Elmsley's Goods, Dyke v Williams* (1871) LR 2 P & D 239.

COSTS OF PARTIES PROPOUNDING A TESTAMENTARY DOCUMENT

(i) Executors

An executor proving a will in solemn form is entitled to take his costs out of the estate

40.05 An executor who proves a will in solemn form is, as a rule, entitled to have his costs out of the estate[1], and this applies whether he has done so of his own motion, or has been put on proof of the will by parties interested. It is unnecessary for him to make any application to the court for them, as he has a right to take them out of the estate without an order of court[2]. This right would seem to flow as a consequence from the ancient rule that all the expenses incidental to proving a will are a charge upon the estate of the testator, and that the party who takes probate is entitled to recoup himself out of the estate for the costs he may have incurred in obtaining such probate.

Even when an executor propounds a will and codicil, and the court pronounces for the will but against the codicil, he is entitled (unless he is shown to have acted unreasonably) to have his costs out of the estate[3].

40.05 *Costs*

1. *Headington v Holloway* (1830) 3 Hag Ecc 280 at 282.
2. It was pointed out by Karminski J that the executor is better off without an order for costs out of the estate, for such an order necessitates taxation of his costs (*Re Cole's Estate, Barclays Bank Ltd v Cole* (1962) 106 Sol Jo 837).
3. *Re Plant's Estate, Wild v Plant* [1926] P 139, CA.

Executor may be ordered to pay costs

40.06 But an executor is not bound to propound a will unless he chooses[1]. If therefore he puts forward a document, and it be proved that he must have known that it could not be supported, he will as a general rule be condemned in costs[2]. If one of two executors is found to have exercised undue influence and the other is exonerated, the action may none the less be dismissed with costs against both[3]. Even if the executor is not guilty of a breach of duty, the court may order him to pay costs[4]. But if an executor had good reason for supposing that a testator was of sound mind and capable of managing his own affairs, he will be allowed his costs out of the estate, even though the will be pronounced against on the ground of the testator's incapacity[5].

If an executor who is also a beneficiary elects to propound a will he does so at risk as to costs[6].

Where executors had obtained a verdict in favour of the validity of a will, and a new trial was granted to parties who had appeared but had not originally pleaded, the court made an order for the executors to have the costs of the first trial out of the estate, up to the time of the ruling for the new trial being made absolute[7].

Where executors, who had proved a will and two codicils, insisted on a third codicil being propounded, they were condemned in the costs[8]; and an executor who insists on asking for probate of clauses found not to be testamentary may be condemned in costs[9].

Where an executrix, who (through carelessness) had lost a will, proved a draft of it in solemn form, she was allowed only such costs as she would have incurred in proving the original will in solemn form, and was condemned in the costs of the defendant[10].

1. *Rennie v Massie* (1866) LR 1 P & D 118 at 119.
2. *Rennie v Massie* (1866) LR 1 P & D 118; see also *Boughton v Knight* (1873) LR 3 P & D 64 at 77; *Rogers v Le Cocq* (1896) 65 LJP 68; *Page v Williamson* (1902) 87 LT 146; *Re Benham's Estate, Saint v Tuckfield* (1961) 105 Sol Jo 511.
3. *Re Barlow's Estate, Haydon v Pring* [1919] P 131, CA.
4. *Re Jeffries, Hill v Jeffries* (1916) 33 TLR 80, CA.
5. *Boughton v Knight* (1873) LR 3 P & D 64 at 79.
6. *Re Scott, Huggett v Reichman* (1966) 110 Sol Jo 852: the court, not being satisfied that the suspicion aroused by the circumstances had been dispelled, or that the testator knew and approved the contents of a will under which the executor was a beneficiary, ordered him to pay the costs. See also *Re Persse's Estate, O'Donnell v Bruce and Dawson* (1962) 106 Sol Jo 432: executors (a solicitor and his clerk) who were also the principal beneficiaries had opportunities of observing the testatrix at a time when, because of their fiduciary relationship with her, it was their duty to exercise the utmost vigilance in her interest.

Although they claimed they had been led to believe she was of testamentary capacity by correspondence purporting to come from her which was in fact written by her companion they were condemned in costs.

7   Boulton v Boulton (1867) LR 1 P & D 456.
8   Re Speke's Estate, Speke v Deakin (1913) 109 LT 719. See also Wilkinson v Corfield (1881) 6 PD 27.
9   Thomas v Jones [1928] P 162.
10 Burls v Burls (1868) LR 1 P & D 472.

(ii) Beneficiaries

When costs allowed out of the estate

40.07 A beneficiary under a will who propounds it in solemn form and obtains a decree in favour of such will, is entitled to have his costs paid out of the estate[1]. But he has not, like an executor, a right to take them ex officio, unless he becomes administrator with the will annexed. When the court pronounces for a will propounded by an executor, the executor takes probate of it himself and is put in possession of the fund out of which he may recoup himself for the expenses he has incurred in the suit. But when the court pronounces for a will propounded by a residuary legatee or a legatee, the residuary legatee or legatee is not always of right entitled to letters of administration with the will annexed. If the will is pronounced for, it is competent to an executor, if he has not renounced (even though he has been cited to propound it and has not done so), to come in and take probate in the usual way, or, if he is cleared off, it is competent to a non-litigant residuary legatee to take letters of administration with the will annexed in preference to the specific legatee who propounded the will[2].

1   Williams v Goude (1828) 1 Hag Ecc 577 at 610; Sutton v Drax (1815) 2 Phillim 323.
2   Bewsher v Williams and Ball (1861) 3 Sw & Tr 62.

Where a legatee propounded a codicil

40.08 A legatee, who has propounded and established a codicil, is entitled to the same costs as an executor in similar circumstances. In a case in which the court awarded a legatee party and party costs against the executor who unsuccessfully opposed the codicil, it further ordered that the legatee should have such sum as the registrar should consider sufficient to cover his extra costs[1]. But where a legatee, who had successfully propounded a codicil, had been guilty of unwise delay in producing it, the court refused to allow him costs out of the estate[2].

1   Bewsher v Williams (1861) 3 Sw & Tr 62.
2   Headington v Holloway (1830) 3 Hag Ecc 280.

Application should be made to the court. Order for costs has been made subsequently to decree

40.09 Should a person having a prior title to the grant take it in priority to the party who has established the will, the latter is without control over the

40.09 *Costs*

estate of the testator, and therefore without power to recoup himself for the expenses incurred by him in obtaining the decree. The most convenient mode of his securing payment of his costs is by applying to the court to include in the decree pronouncing for the will an order that his costs be paid out of the estate. The application should be made on the court pronouncing for the validity of the will. But where no order had been made as to costs when the decree was pronounced, the court has subsequently ordered the costs to be paid out of the estate[1].

[1] *Wilkinson v Corfield* (1880) 6 PD 27.

Scale of costs

40.10 The costs will be assessed on the standard basis unless the judge orders otherwise. On an assessment on this basis the court will only allow costs which are proportionate to the matters in issue and will resolve any doubt which it may have as to whether the costs were reasonably incurred or proportionate in favour of the paying party[1].

Where costs are to be paid to a party, either by another party or out of any fund, the court may in any case in which it thinks fit to do so order them to be assessed on the indemnity basis. On the indemnity basis the court will resolve any doubt which it may have as to whether costs were reasonably incurred or were reasonable in amount in favour of the receiving party[2].

Where a person is a party to proceedings as a trustee or personal representative the general rule is that where he is entitled to be paid his costs out of the fund those costs shall be assessed on the indemnity basis, but the court may order otherwise if a trustee or personal representative has acted for a benefit other than the fund[3].

An appropriate case for indemnity costs was in *Franks v Sinclair (Costs)* [2007] WTLR 785, where the conduct of the parties or the circumstances of the case were such as to take the situation out of the norm. The claimant, a solicitor, had sought to propound a will executed by his mother that he knew to be invalid and had not been truthful in giving evidence. This was a sufficient basis for an order for indemnity costs as was also the rejection of two offers of settlement.

[1] CPR 44.4(2).
[2] CPR 44.4(3).
[3] CPR 48.4.

COSTS OF PARTIES OPPOSING PROBATE

40.11 Probate of a will may be opposed by any person entitled to share in the estate in the event of an intestacy, or by any person interested under another will.

(i) Costs of parties successfully opposing probate

40.12 If a party who successfully opposes probate is entitled to, and obtains, a grant either of letters of administration or of probate of another will, he may recoup himself out of the estate for his costs. He should proceed for recovery of his costs from any party condemned to pay them.

If, however, the successful party is not entitled to, or fails to obtain, a grant, he can only proceed as to his costs under the order of the court. The court may give him his costs either out of the estate or against the unsuccessful party[1]. In the latter case he can only obtain payment of his costs from the party who has been condemned as to them[2] and to the extent of the scale of costs ordered.

1   *Critchell v Critchell* (1863) 3 Sw & Tr 41; *Bewsher v Williams and Ball* (1861) 3 Sw & Tr 62.
2   *Nash v Yelloly* (1862) 3 Sw & Tr 59.

(ii) Costs of parties unsuccessfully opposing probate

40.13 As has been stated above, the general rule is that costs follow the event. Two main principles have, however, been laid down as to the circumstances which justify the court in departing from this rule[1]. These are (1) that where the testator, or those interested in the residue, have been the cause of the litigation, the costs of unsuccessfully opposing probate may be ordered to be paid out of the estate, and (2) that if the circumstances led reasonably to an investigation in regard to a propounded document the costs may be left to be borne by those who respectively incurred them.

These principles are not to be regarded as exact rules, for it is not in the nature of discretion that its exercise should be adjusted by exact rules[2], nor are they exhaustive[3]. However, since the year 1863[4], when they were first enunciated, they have been almost universally acted upon. Decisions as to costs before that date are not as a rule to be relied upon. Whether a probate litigant challenging the validity (as a will) of the whole or part of a testamentary paper should, if unsuccessful, receive his costs out of the estate was a matter for the judge's discretion. The Court of Appeal so held and that the judge was not bound in deciding whether the challenge was reasonable and proper by *Orton v Smith*[5] which laid down no principle as to what was reasonable and proper[6].

Jarrom & Anr v Sellars [2007] WTLR 1219 was a case where special circumstances justified the exceptional course of no order as to costs. The executors were entitled to their costs out of the estate but no order was made against the person challenging the will as the executors had not taken up repeated suggestions of a meeting.

Somewhat different considerations apply when the opposing party has given notice merely to cross-examine under CPR 57.7(5), or where undue influence or fraud has been unsuccessfully pleaded. These will be considered separately below.

40.13 *Costs*

1. *Spiers v English* [1907] P 122; *Twist v Tye* [1902] P 92 at 94; *Mitchell and Mitchell v Gard and Kingwell* (1863) 3 Sw & Tr 275 at 278; *Re Cutcliffe's Estate, Le Duc v Veness* [1959] P 6, [1958] 3 All ER 642, CA
2. Per Sir J. P. Wilde in *Mitchell and Mitchell v Gard* (1863) 3 Sw & Tr 275 at 277.
3. *Spiers v English* [1907] P 122.
4. Ie since the decision in *Mitchell v Gard*. As to the principles which prevailed in the Court of Probate, and in the ecclesiastical courts before 1863, see the note to *Summerell v Clements* (1862) 3 Sw & Tr 35, 32 LJPM & A 33, where several decisions are collected.
5. (1873) LR 3 P & D 23.
6. See *Fanshawe's Estate* (1983) Times, 17 November.

(a) Where the litigation has been caused by the testator, or those interested in the residuary estate

Where testator has himself caused the litigation

40.14 If the litigation be caused by the state in which the deceased left his testamentary papers, the costs of both parties will be ordered to be paid out of the estate[1].

So, too, where the testator by his own conduct and habits and mode of life has given reasonable ground for questioning his testamentary capacity, the costs of those opposing probate of his will will be ordered to be paid out of the estate[2], as will also be the case where the testator's statements, to the parties unsuccessfully opposing probate, led them to plead undue influence[3].

But although it is not possible to limit the circumstances in which a testator can be said to have brought about the litigation by leaving his affairs in confusion, they should not extend to cases where the testator has misled other people by his words, written or spoken, and perhaps inspired false hopes that they might benefit on his death[4].

In *Rowe v Clarke* [2006] EWHC 1292 (Ch), [2006] All ER (D) 124 (May) the testator disorganised and probably lost or destroyed the will through carelessness. The costs of all parties were awarded out of estate.

1. *Lemage v Goodban* (1865) LR 1 P & D 57 at 63; *Davies v Gregory* (1873) LR 3 P & D 28; *Mitchell and Mitchell v Gard and Kingwell* (1863) 3 Sw & Tr 275; *Jenner v Ffinch* (1879) 5 PD 106; *Re Hall-Dare, Le Marchant v Lee Warner* [1916] 1 Ch 272, 114 LT 559 (Chancery).
2. *Davies v Gregory* (1873) LR 3 P & D 28.
3. *Cousins v Tubb* (1891) 65 LT 716.
4. *Re Cutcliffe's Estate, Le Duc v Veness* [1959] P 6, [1958] 3 All ER 642, CA.

Where conduct of beneficiary under the will caused the litigation

40.15 Where a party had taken out administration after enquiry, made of the residuary legatee of a will, whether there was a will, to which enquiry he received no answer, and a will was twelve months afterwards produced and proved in solemn form, the court held that the administrator, who was the defendant in the suit, was entitled to have his costs out of the estate, including the costs of taking out administration[1].

An unsuccessful party is usually given his costs where one of the principal beneficiaries under a will has been actively engaged in its preparation, and has not shown by disinterested evidence that its dispositions were read over or explained to and approved of by the testator before its execution[2].

The omission to annex to or mention in the affidavit of scripts the instructions for a will is no ground for allowing out of the estate the costs of an unsuccessful opposition to the will, if such opposition is not founded on the absence of instructions[3].

1   *Smith v Smith* (1865) 4 Sw & Tr 3; see also *Williams v Henery* (1864) 3 Sw & Tr 471.
2   *Dale v Murrell* (March 1879, unreported). See also *Orton v Smith* (1873) LR 3 P & D 23; and *Wilson v Bassil* [1903] P 239.
3   *Foxwell v Poole* (1862) 3 Sw & Tr 5.

(b) **Where the circumstances lead reasonably to an investigation**

40.16 The losing party will not be condemned in costs if there be a sufficient and reasonable ground, looking to his knowledge and means of knowledge, for him to question either the execution of the will or the capacity of the testator[1]. Thus, where the attesting witnesses gave conflicting accounts as to the due execution of the will[2], or the judge was satisfied with a verdict establishing a will, but would not have been dissatisfied with a contrary verdict[3], or where a next of kin, who had unsuccessfully opposed a will upon information given to him by one of the attesting witnesses, the testator's medical attendant, to the effect that when the will was read over the testator signified his approval of it by gesture only, and that he could not swear that the testator was of sound mind[4], the court refused to condemn the unsuccessful party in costs.

Where the principal beneficiary took instructions for the will himself, and the solicitor who drew the will did not see the testator, it was held that the circumstances so far invited enquiry as to justify the court in refusing to condemn in costs the party opposing the will[5].

1   *Mitchell and Mitchell v Gard and Kingwell* (1863) 3 Sw & Tr 275 at 278; *Spiers v English* [1907] P 122 at 123. In a probate action in which there was a conflict of evidence on the issues of knowledge and approval and incapacity, the widow, who unsuccessfully contested the will, had been supplied with proofs of the evidence of the other side's witnesses before the action was brought. She was ordered to pay one-third of the costs (*Re Coe's Estate* [1957] CLY 3736).
2   *Ferrey v King* (1861) 3 Sw & Tr 51.
3   *Bramley v Bramley* (1864) 3 Sw & Tr 430.
4   *Tippett v Tippett* (1865) LR 1 P & D 54.
5   *Aylwin v Aylwin* [1902] P 203.

(c) **Where the opposing party gives notice to cross-examine under CPR 57.7(5)**

40.17 Under CPR 57.7(5), in probate claims the party opposing a will may give notice in his defence that he does not raise any positive case but insists on the will being proved in solemn form and, for that purpose, will cross-examine

40.17 *Costs*

the witnesses who attested the will. If a defendant gives such a notice, the court will not make an order for costs against him unless it considers there was no reasonable ground for opposing the will. It does not follow, because a defendant fails, that there was no reasonable ground for opposing the will[1].

The notice may be a conditional one to the effect that if both attesting witnesses to the will are called, it is merely intended to cross examine them[2]. The protection offered by the rule may be relied on if it be pleaded that the deceased did not know or approve of the contents of the will, and the opposing parties may be put to proof of testamentary capacity[3], but it is lost if undue influence or fraud is pleaded[4].

[1] *Davies v Jones* [1899] P 161 at 164. For a case under the rule where it was held that there had been no reasonable ground for opposing the will, see *Re Spicer, Spicer v Spicer* [1899] P 38. See also *Perry v Dixon* (1899) 80 LT 297.
[2] *Leeman v George* (1868) LR 1 P & D 542.
[3] *Cleare and Forster v Cleare* (1869) LR 1 P & D 655. See also *Re Sanders' Estate, Riches and Woodey v Sanders* (1961) 105 Sol Jo 324; the plaintiff not having complied with a request for information of the evidence of the person who arranged for the preparation and execution of a will propounded by him, the judge although pronouncing for the will refused to condemn the defendant in costs.
[4] *Ireland v Rendall* (1866) LR 1 P & D 194.

Parties not protected by the rule

40.18 A party who seeks to call in and obtain revocation of a probate is not within the rule, and a notice given thereunder by such a party is bad[1].

[1] *Tomalin v Smart* [1904] P 141. See also *Patrick v Hevercroft* (1920) 123 LT 201.

(d) Where undue influence or fraud has been unsuccessfully pleaded

40.19 Where an unsuccessful party has pleaded undue influence or fraud it must be shown that he had reasonable and sufficient ground for so doing, or he will be condemned in the costs of the other side[1].

If there be reasonable ground for putting such a plea forward, costs may be allowed out of the estate, or the unsuccessful party may be ordered to bear his own costs only, according to the circumstances of the case (see paras 40.14–40.16).

A party may be condemned in the costs of the other side in respect of his plea of undue influence, and allowed his costs out of the estate in respect of the other pleas put forward by him against the will[2].

Where an order was made allowing costs to a party who had unsuccessfully pleaded undue influence it was held on appeal that, where there are any grounds on which a judge can base such a special order, there is no jurisdiction to interfere with it[3].

1   Mitchell and Mitchell v Gard and Kingwell (1863) 3 Sw & Tr 275 at 278; Spiers v English [1907] P 122 at 123; Levy v Leo (1909) 25 TLR 717; Re Cutcliffe's Estate, Le Duc v Veness [1959] P 6, [1958] 3 All ER 642.
2   Levy v Leo (1909) 25 TLR 717.
3   Cummins v Murray [1906] 2 IR 509.

COSTS OF PARTICULAR PARTIES

40.20 The position as to costs of executors or beneficiaries under a will, and of the persons interested on an intestacy, has been discussed above, but a few words should be added as to the position of certain other particular parties.

(i) Defendants intervening

40.21 Where a defendant intervening in a probate action pleads separately, he will not, as a rule, be allowed separate costs, even though he be successful[1], unless his interest is different from those of the other parties to the action[2]. If his interest is the same as that of another party who has already pleaded, he should adopt the pleadings of such party[3]. The next of kin intervening, on a question as to the due execution of a will, in order to take the opinion of the court as to alterations which appeared in the will enhancing their interests, were (although the alterations were pronounced invalid) allowed their costs out of the estate[4]. But where the executor, in his affidavit of scripts, in effect denied the validity of a legacy to a person who intervened, but, subsequently, by his plea, admitted its validity, and such intervener appeared by counsel at the hearing of the cause, the court refused to allow him his costs out of the estate[5].

1   Twist v Tye [1902] P 92 at 98.
2   Bagshaw v Pimm [1900] P 148.
3   Twist v Tye [1902] P 92 at 98; Colvin v Fraser (1829) 2 Hag Ecc 266 at 368.
4   Burgoyne v Showler (1844) 1 Rob Eccl 5. See also Cross v Cross (1864) 3 Sw & Tr 292.
5   Shawe and Dickens v Marshall (1858) 1 Sw & Tr 129.

(ii) Parties to an interest suit

40.22 A party who fails to prove his case in an interest suit is, except in special circumstances, condemned in costs[1].

1   Wiseman v Wiseman (1866) LR 1 P & D 351.

(iii) Trustees, personal representatives, etc

40.23 A person who is or has been a party to any proceedings in the capacity of trustee, personal representative or mortgagee is, unless otherwise ordered, entitled to the costs of those proceedings, in so far as they are not recovered from or paid by any other person, out of the fund held by the trustee or personal representative or the mortgaged property, as the case may be. The court may otherwise order only on the ground that he has acted unreasonably

40.23 *Costs*

or, in the case of a trustee or personal representative, has in substance acted for his own benefit rather than for the benefit of the fund[1].

[1] CPR 48.4. See also *Re Dallaway* [1982] 3 All ER 118, [1982] 1 WLR 756.

(iv) Creditors

40.24 A creditor who obtains a grant may reimburse himself out of the estate for the expense he has been put to in obtaining it.

The costs of a creditor of obtaining the appointment of an administrator pending suit may be allowed out of the estate[1].

[1] *Tichborne v Tichborne, ex p Norris* (1869) LR 1 P & D 730.

(v) The Official Solicitor[1]

40.25 To entitle the Official Solicitor to costs as against any other party on other than a standard basis, the order as to costs must specifically direct taxation on an indemnity basis[2].

[1] See *White v Duvernay* [1891] P 290; *Gill v Gill* [1909] P 157.
[2] *Eady v Elsdon* [1901] 2 KB 460.

(vi) The Treasury Solicitor

40.26 Where the Treasury Solicitor unsuccessfully contested a will on behalf of the Crown, he could not, prior to the Administration of Justice (Miscellaneous Provisions) Act 1933, be condemned in the costs[1], but s 7 of that Act gives the court discretion in the matter of such costs.

[1] *Atkinson v Queen's Proctor* (1871) LR 2 P & D 255.

(vii) Legally aided parties

40.27 Legal Aid under the Legal Aid Act 1988 has been replaced by community funding under the Access to Justice Act 1999. The 1988 Act and regulations continue to apply to Legal Aid cases started before 1 April 2000. Under the 1999 Act the Legal Services Commission is responsible for drawing up plans for funding and the code of criteria deciding which individual cases should be funded.

MORE THAN ONE SET OF COSTS ALLOWED

Two sets of costs

40.28 Separate sets of costs may be allowed in exceptional circumstances where there is a sufficient divergency of interest between the parties appearing on the same side[1].

[1] See *Bagshaw v Pimm* [1900] P 148, CA; *Jenner v Ffinch* (1879) 5 PD 106.

APPORTIONMENT OF COSTS

40.29 The court is empowered, when ordering costs in a probate action to be paid out of the estate, to direct out of what portion or portions of the estate they are to be paid, by virtue of the general discretion as to costs conferred on the court by the Supreme Court Act 1981, s 51[1].

Orders have been made, under the predecessor section, that the costs of both plaintiff and defendant be charged on, and paid out of, the corpus of certain real estate devised by the will to successive life tenants[2]; that the costs of all parties be paid out of that portion of the residuary estate passing under the will to four out of six defendants[3], and that the costs of all parties should come out of that portion of the estate which was bequeathed to the persons whose conduct had been the cause of the enquiry, although they had been successful in the litigation[4].

[1] See para A1.323. See also Order 62, r 2(4).
[2] *Dean v Bulmer* [1905] P 1.
[3] *Harrington v Butt* [1905] P 3n.
[4] *Re Osment's Estate, Child and Jarvis v Osment* [1914] P 129.

Chapter 41

ASSOCIATED ACTIONS

REMOVAL OF A PERSONAL REPRESENTATIVE

41.02 As an alternative to a beneficiary bringing an administration action or a personal representative or a beneficiary applying for the appointment of a judicial trustee, s 50 of the Administration of Justice Act 1985 introduced an action for the removal of a personal representative with or without his substitution.

Claims under s 50 must be brought in the High Court and are assigned to the Chancery Division[1]. Every personal representative of the estate must be joined as a party[2].

Under s 50, if substitution is not requested, the appointment of a sole personal representative cannot be terminated, for it would leave the estate unrepresented. Terminations alone can thus not be requested in respect of all personal representatives. To achieve this substitution must be sought. The court may treat any application for substitution or termination as an application for the appointment of a judicial trustee under the Judicial Trustee Act 1896.

The claim form must be accompanied by a sealed or certified copy of the grant of probate or letters of administration and written evidence containing the grounds of the claim and, so far as it is known to the claimant, brief details of the property comprised in the estate, with an approximate estimate of its capital value and any income that is received from it, and brief details of the liabilities of the estate, the names and address of the persons who are in possession of the documents relating to the estate, the names of the beneficiaries and their respective interests in the estate and the name, address and occupation of any proposed substituted personal representative[3]. If the claim is for the appointment of a substituted personal representative, the claim form must be accompanied by a signed or (in the case of the Public Trustee or a corporation) sealed consent to act, and written evidence as to the fitness of the proposed substituted personal representative, if an individual, to act[4].

On the hearing of the claim the personal representative must produce to the Court the grant of representation to the deceased's estate[5]. If an order is made substituting or removing a personal representative, the grant (together with a sealed copy of the order) must be sent to and remain in the custody of the Principal Registry of the Family Division until a memorandum of the order has been endorsed on or permanently annexed to the grant[6]. The date of an order under s 50 is the effective date of appointment of any new personal representative appointed thereby; and he may be authorised to charge remuneration[7].

There is nothing in the wording of s 50 to preclude an application for the removal (or substitution) of an executor before a grant has issued[8]; but equally there is nothing in that wording[9] to allow such an application in respect of an administrator (who, before a grant, ex hypothesi does not exist). This distinction is reflected in CPR Pt 57 PD 13 and 14. A person beneficially entitled under the doctrine of mutual wills cannot apply under s 50[10].

[1] CPR 57 r 13(2).
[2] CPR 57 r 13(3).
[3] CPR Pt 57 PD para 13.1.
[4] CPR Pt 57 PD para 13.2.
[5] CPR Pt 57 PD para 14.1.
[6] CPR Pt 57 PD para 14.2.
[7] Administration of Justice Act 1985, s 50(3).
[8] *Pace* an observation obiter in *Perotti v Watson* [2001] EWCA Civ 116, [2001] All ER (D) 26 (Feb).
[9] Or in the definition of 'administrator' and 'personal representative' in Administration of Estates Act 1925, s 55.
[10] See *Thomas and Agnes Carvel Foundation v Carvel* [2007] EWHC 1314 (Ch), [2007] 4 All ER 81. Such a person may, however, apply under s 1 of the Judicial Trustees Act 1896—see above).

Appendix I
STATUTES

APPENDIX I SUMMARY

	Para
Part I–Non-Contentious Business	
Colonial Probates Act 1892	A1.45
Trustee Act 1925	A1.79
Administration of Estates Act 1925	A1.127
Law of Property (Amendment) Act 1926	A1.130
Consular Conventions Act 1949	A1.137
Intestates' Estates Act 1952	A1.147
Births and Deaths Registration Act 1953	A1.148
Public Records Act 1958	A1.155
Perpetuities and Accumulations Act 1964	A1.173
Administration of Estates Act 1971	A1.223
Domicile and Matrimonial Proceedings Act 1973	A1.240
Legitimacy Act 1976	A1.281
Adoption Act 1976	A1.297
[Senior Courts Act 1981]	A1.309
Administration of Justice Act 1982	A1.377
Mental Health Act 1983	A1.387
County Courts Act 1984	A1.393
Family Law Act 1986	A1.416
Family Law Reform Act 1987	A1.424
Children Act 1989	A1.448
Access to Health Records Act 1990	A1.469
Courts and Legal Services Act 1990	A1.480A
Adoption and Children Act 2002	A1.517
Gender Recognition Act 2004	A1.548A
Civil Partnership Act 2004	A1.567
Mental Capacity Act 2005	A1.583
Human Fertilisation and Embryology Act 2008	A1.592A
Part II—Finance Acts etc.	
Inheritance Tax Act 1984	A1.595
Finance Act 1986	A1.616

Appendix I
STATUTES

Note.
The following text contains extracts from Acts of Parliament having a bearing on the probate practice. In general, those enactments, since repealed, which remain applicable in relation to cases where death occurred prior to the relevant date of repeal have been retained for the purpose of reference.

PART I—PROBATE BUSINESS

COLONIAL PROBATES ACT 1892

For a list of places to which this Act has been applied, see para 18.39; see also the Colonial Probates (Protected States and Mandated Territories) Act 1927 (para A1.131), the powers under which were preserved by the Mandated and Trust Territories Act 1947.

(55 & 56 VICT C 6)

A1.45

2 Sealing in United Kingdom of colonial probates and letters of administration

(1) Where a court of probate in a British possession to which this Act applies has granted probate or letters of administration in respect of the estate of a deceased person [then (subject to section [109 of the [Senior Courts Act 1981]], section 42 of the Probate and Legacy Duties Act 1808 and section 99A of the Probates and Letters of Administration Act (Ireland) 1857)] the probate or letters so granted may, on being produced to, and a copy thereof deposited with, a court of probate in the United Kingdom, be sealed with the seal of that court, and, thereupon, shall be of the like force and effect, and have the same operation in the United Kingdom, as if granted by that court.

(2) Provided that the court shall, before sealing a probate or letters of administration under this section, be satisfied—

 (a) < ... >

A1.45 *Statutes*

(b) in the case of letters of administration, that security has been given in a sum sufficient in amount to cover the property (if any) in the United Kingdom to which letters of administration relate;

and may require such evidence, if any, as it thinks fit as to the domicile of the deceased person.

(3) The court may also, if it thinks fit, on the application of any creditor, require, before sealing, that adequate security be given for the payment of debts due from the estate to creditors residing in the United Kingdom.

(4) For the purposes of this section, a duplicate of any probate or letters of administration sealed with the seal of the court granting the same, or a copy thereof certified as correct by or under the authority of the court granting the same, shall have the same effect as the original.

(5) Rules of court may be made for regulating the procedure and practice, including fees and costs, in courts of the United Kingdom, on and incidental to an application for sealing a probate or letters of administration granted in a British possession to which this Act applies < ... >

Sub-s (1): words from 'then (subject to' to 'Probates and Letters of Administration Act (Ireland) 1857)' in square brackets inserted by the Finance Act 1975, s 52(1), Sch 12, paras 2, 4.

Sub-s (1): words in square brackets beginning with the words '109 of the' substituted by the Supreme Court Act 1981, ss 152(1), 153(4), Sch 5.

Sub-s (1): words 'Senior Courts Act 1981' in square brackets substituted by the Constitutional Reform Act 2005, s 59(5), Sch 11, Pt 1, para 1(2). Date in force: 1 October 2009: see SI 2009/1604, art 2(d).

Sub-ss (2), (5): words omitted repealed by the Finance Act 1975, ss 52(2), 59(5), Sch 13, Part I.

TRUSTEE ACT 1925

(15 & 16 GEO 5, C 19)

A1.79

36 Power of appointing new or additional trustees

(1) Where a trustee, either original or substituted, and whether appointed by a court or otherwise, is dead, or remains out of the United Kingdom for more than twelve months, or desires to be discharged from all or any of the trusts or powers reposed in or conferred on him, or refuses or is unfit to act therein, or is incapable of acting therein, or is an infant, then, subject to the restrictions imposed by this Act on the number of trustees,—

(a) the person or persons nominated for the purpose of appointing new trustees by the instrument, if any, creating the trust; or
(b) if there is no such person, or no such person able and willing to act, then the surviving or continuing trustees or trustee for the time being, or the personal representatives of the last surviving or continuing trustee;

may, by writing, appoint one or more other persons (whether or not being the persons exercising the power) to be a trustee or trustees in the place of the trustee so deceased remaining out of the United Kingdom, desiring to be discharged, refusing, or being unfit or being incapable, or being an infant, as aforesaid.

Trustee Act 1925 A1.79

(2) Where a trustee has been removed under a power contained in the instrument creating the trust, a new trustee or new trustees may be appointed in the place of the trustee who is removed, as if he were dead, or, in the case of a corporation, as if the corporation desired to be discharged from the trust, and the provisions of this section shall apply accordingly, but subject to the restrictions imposed by this Act on the number of trustees.

(3) Where a corporation being a trustee is or has been dissolved, either before or after the commencement of this Act, then, for the purposes of this section and of any enactment replaced thereby, the corporation shall be deemed to be and to have been from the date of the dissolution incapable of acting in the trusts or powers reposed in or conferred on the corporation.

(4) The power of appointment given by subsection (1) of this section or any similar previous enactment to the personal representatives of a last surviving or continuing trustee shall be and shall be deemed always to have been exercisable by the executors for the time being (whether original or by representation) of such surviving or continuing trustee who have proved the will of their testator or by the administrators for the time being of such trustee without the concurrence of any executor who has renounced or has not proved.

(5) But a sole or last surviving executor intending to renounce, or all the executors where they all intend to renounce, shall have and shall be deemed always to have had power, at any time before renouncing probate, to exercise the power of appointment given by this section, or by any similar previous enactment, if willing to act for that purpose and without thereby accepting the office of executor.

[(6) Where, in the case of any trust, there are not more than three trustees—]

(a) the person or persons nominated for the purpose of appointing new trustees by the instrument, if any, creating the trust; or
(b) if there is no such person, or no such person able and willing to act, then the trustee or trustees for the time being;

may, by writing appoint another person or other persons to be an additional trustee or additional trustees, but it shall not be obligatory to appoint any additional trustee, unless the instrument, if any, creating the trust, or any statutory enactment provides to the contrary, nor shall the number of trustees be increased beyond four by virtue of any such appointment.

[(6A) A person who is either—

(a) both a trustee and attorney for the other trustee (if one other), or for both of the other trustees (if two others), under a registered power; or
(b) attorney under a registered power for the trustee (if one) or for both or each of the trustees (if two or three),

may, if subsection (6B) of this section is satisfied in relation to him, make an appointment under subsection (6)(b) of this section on behalf of the trustee or trustees.

(6B) This subsection is satisfied in relation to an attorney under a registered power for one or more trustees if (as attorney under the power)—

(a) he intends to exercise any function of the trustee or trustees by virtue of section 1(1) of the Trustee Delegation Act 1999; or
(b) he intends to exercise any function of the trustee or trustees in relation to any land, capital proceeds of a conveyance of land or income from land by virtue of its delegation to him under section 25 of this Act or the instrument (if any) creating the trust.

(6C) In subsections (6A) and (6B) of this section 'registered power' means [an enduring power of attorney or lasting power of attorney registered under the Mental Capacity Act 2005].

(6D) Subsection (6A) of this section—

(a) applies only if and so far as a contrary intention is not expressed in the instrument creating the power of attorney (or, where more than one, any of them) or the instrument (if any) creating the trust; and

(b) has effect subject to the terms of those instruments.]

(7) Every new trustee appointed under this section as well before as after all the trust property becomes by law, or by assurance, or otherwise, vested in him, shall have the same powers, authorities, and discretions, and may in all respects act as if he had been originally appointed a trustee by the instrument, if any, creating the trust.

(8) The provisions of this section relating to a trustee who is dead include the case of a person nominated trustee in a will but dying before the testator, and those relative to a continuing trustee include a refusing or retiring trustee, if willing to act in the execution of the provisions of this section.

[(9) Where a trustee [lacks capacity to exercise] his functions as trustee and is also entitled in possession to some beneficial interest in the trust property, no appointment of a new trustee in his place shall be made by virtue of paragraph (b) of subsection (1) of this section unless leave to make the appointment has been given by [the Court of Protection].]

Subsection (6): words in square brackets substituted by the Trusts of Land and Appointment of Trustees Act 1996, s 25(1), Sch 3, para 3(11); for savings see para A1.509.

Subsections (6A)–(6D): inserted by the Trustee Delegation Act 1998, s 8 as from 1 March 2000 (in relation to powers created after that date): see SI 2000/216, art 2.

Sub-s (6C): words from 'an enduring power' to 'Mental Capacity Act 2005' in square brackets substituted by the Mental Capacity Act 2005, s 67(1), Sch 6, para 3(1), (2)(a). Date in force: 1 October 2007: see SI 2007/1897, art 2(1)(d).

Subsection (9) substituted by Mental Health Act 1959, s 149(1) and Sch 7.

Sub-s (9): words 'lacks capacity to exercise' in square brackets substituted by the Mental Capacity Act 2005, s 67(1), Sch 6, para 3(1), (2)(b)(i). Date in force: 1 October 2007: see SI 2007/1897, art 2(1)(d).

Sub-s (9): words 'the Court of Protection' in square brackets substituted by the Mental Capacity Act 2005, s 67(1), Sch 6, para 3(1), (2)(b)(ii). Date in force: 1 October 2007: see SI 2007/1897, art 2(1)(d).

ADMINISTRATION OF ESTATES ACT 1925

(15 & 16 GEO 5, C 23)

An Act to consolidate Enactments relating to the Administration of the Estates of Deceased Persons

[9th April 1925]

A1.115

[47A   Right of surviving spouse to have his own life interest redeemed]

[(1) Where a surviving [spouse or civil partner] is entitled to the interest in part of the residuary estate, and so elects, the personal representative shall purchase or redeem the life interest by paying the capital value thereof to the tenant for life, or the persons deriving title under the tenant for life, and the costs of the transaction; and thereupon the residuary estate of the intestate may be dealt with and distributed free from the life interest.

(2)   < ... >

(3) An election under this section shall only be exercisable if at the time of the election the whole of the said part of the residuary estate consists of property in possession, but, for the purposes of this section, a life interest in property partly in possession and partly not in possession shall be treated as consisting of two separate life interests in those respective parts of the property.

[(3A) The capital value shall be reckoned in such manner as the Lord Chancellor may by order direct, and an order under this subsection may include transitional provisions.

(3B) The power to make orders under subsection (3A) above shall be exercisable by statutory instrument subject to annulment in pursuance of a resolution of either House of Parliament; and any such order may be varied or revoked by a subsequent order made under the power.]

(4)   < ... >

(5) An election under this section shall be exercisable only within the period of twelve months from the date on which representation with respect to the estate of the intestate is first taken out:

Provided that if the surviving [spouse or civil partner] satisfies the court that the limitation to the said period of twelve months will operate unfairly—

(a) in consequence of the representation first taken out being probate of a will subsequently revoked on the ground that the will was invalid, or
(b) in consequence of a question whether a person had an interest in the estate, or as to the nature of an interest in the estate, not having been determined at the time when representation was first taken out, or
(c) in consequence of some other circumstances affecting the administration or distribution of the estate,

the court may extend the said period.

(6) An election under this section shall be exercisable, except where the tenant for life is the sole personal representative, by notifying the personal representative (or, where there are two or more personal representatives of whom one is the tenant for life, all of

A1.115 Statutes

them except the tenant for life) in writing; and a notification in writing under this subsection shall not be revocable except with the consent of the personal representative.

(7) Where the tenant for life is the sole personal representative an election under this section shall not be effective unless written notice thereof is given to the [[Senior Registrar] of the Family Division of the High Court] within the period within which it must be made; and provision may be made by probate rules for keeping a record of such notices and making that record available to the public.

In this subsection the expression "probate rules" means rules [of court made under section 127 of the [Senior Courts Act 1981]].

(8) An election under this section by a tenant for life who is an infant shall be as valid and binding as it would be if the tenant for life were of age; but the personal representative shall, instead of paying the capital value of the life interest to the tenant for life, deal with it in the same manner as with any other part of the residuary estate to which the tenant for life is absolutely entitled.

(9) In considering for the purposes of the foregoing provisions of this section the question when representation was first taken out, a grant limited to settled land or to trust property shall be left out of account and a grant limited to real estate or to personal estate shall be left out of account unless a grant limited to the remainder of the estate has previously been made or is made at the same time.]

Sub-s (1): words 'spouse or civil partner' in square brackets substituted by the Civil Partnership Act 2004, s 71, Sch 4, Pt 2, para 9. Date in force: 5 December 2005: see SI 2005/3175, art 2(1), Sch 1.
Sub-ss (2), (4): repealed by the Administration of Justice Act 1977, ss 28(2), 32(4), Sch 5, Pt VI.
Sub-ss (3A), (3B): inserted by the Administration of Justice Act 1977, s 28(3).
Sub-s (5): in the proviso words 'spouse or civil partner' in square brackets substituted by the Civil Partnership Act 2004, s 71, Sch 4, Pt 2, para 9. Date in force: 5 December 2005: see SI 2005/3175, art 2(1), Sch 1.
Sub-s (7): words in square brackets ending with the words 'the High Court' substituted by the Administration of Justice Act 1970, s 1(6), Sch 2, para 4.
Sub-s (7): words 'Senior Registrar' in square brackets substituted by the Supreme Court Act 1981, s 152(1), Sch 5.
Sub-s (7): words in square brackets beginning with the words 'of court made' substituted by the Supreme Court Act 1981, s 152(1), Sch 5.
Sub-s (7): words 'Senior Courts Act 1981' in square brackets substituted by the Constitutional Reform Act 2005, s 59(5), Sch 11, Pt 1, para 1(2). Date in force: 1 October 2009: see SI 2009/1604, art 2(d).

A1.127

55 Definitions

In this Act, unless the context otherwise requires, the following expressions have the meanings hereby assigned to them respectively, that is to say:—

(1)

(i) 'Administration' means, with reference to the real and personal estate of a deceased person, letters of administration whether general or limited, or with the will annexed or otherwise:

(ii) 'Administrator' means a person to whom administration is granted:

Administration of Estates Act 1925   A1.127

(iii) 'Conveyance' includes a mortgage, charge by way of legal mortgage, lease, assent, vesting, declaration, vesting instrument, disclaimer, release and every other assurance of property or of an interest therein by any instrument, except a will, and 'convey' has a corresponding meaning, and 'disposition' includes a 'conveyance' also a devise bequest and an appointment of property contained in a will, and 'dispose of' has a corresponding meaning:

[(iiiA) 'the County Court limit', in relation to any enactment contained in this Act, means the amount for the time being specified by an Order in Council under section 145 of the County Courts Act 1984 as the county court limit for the purposes of that enactment (or, where no such Order in Council has been made, the corresponding limit specified by Order in Council under section 192 of the County Courts Act 1959);]

(iv) 'the Court' means the High Court and also the county court, where that court has jurisdiction ...

(v) 'Income' includes rents and profits:

(vi) 'Intestate' includes a person who leaves a will but dies intestate as to some beneficial interest in his real or personal estate:

[(via) 'Land' has the same meaning as in the Law of Property Act 1925;]

(vii) 'Legal estates' mean the estates charges and interests in or over land (subsisting or created at law) which are by statute authorised to subsist or to be created at law; and 'equitable interests' mean all other interests and charges in or over land ...:

(viii) ...

(ix) 'Pecuniary legacy' includes an annuity, a general legacy, a demonstrative legacy so far as it is not discharged out of the designated property, and any other general direction by a testator for the payment of money, including all death duties free from which any devise, bequest, or payment is made to take effect:

(x) 'Personal chattels' mean carriages, horses, stable furniture and effects (not used for business purposes), motor cars and accessories (not used for business purposes), garden effects, domestic animals, plate, plated articles, linen, china, glass, books, pictures, prints, furniture, jewellery, articles of household or personal use or ornament, musical and scientific instruments and apparatus, wines, liquors and consumable stores, but do not include any chattels used at the death of the intestate for business purposes nor money or securities for money:

(xi) 'Personal representative' means the executor, original or by representation, or administrator for the time being of a deceased person, and as regards any liability for the payment of death duties includes any person who takes possession of or intermeddles with the property of a deceased person without the authority of the personal representatives or the court, and 'executor' includes a person deemed to be appointed executor as respects settled land:

(xii) 'Possession' includes the receipt of rents and profits or the right to receive the same, if any:

(xiii) 'Prescribed' means prescribed by rules of court ...:

(xiv) 'Probate' means the probate of a will:

(xv), (xvi) < ... >:

(xvii) 'Property' includes a thing in action and any interest in real or personal property:

A1.127 *Statutes*

(xviii) 'Purchaser' means a lessee, mortgagee, or other person who in good faith acquires an interest in property for valuable consideration, also an intending purchaser and 'valuable consideration' includes marriage, [and formation of a civil partnership,] but does not include a nominal consideration in money:

(xix) 'Real estate' save as provided in Part IV of this Act means real estate, including chattels real, which by virtue of Part I of this Act devolves on the personal representative of a deceased person:

(xx) 'Representation' means the probate of a will and administration, and the expression 'taking out representation' refers to the obtaining of the probate of a will or of the grant of administration:

(xxi) 'Rent' includes a rent service or a rentcharge, or other rent, toll, duty, or annual or periodical payment in money or money's worth, issuing out of or charged upon land, but does not include mortgage interest; and 'rentcharge' includes a fee farm rent:

(xxii) ...

(xxiii) 'Securities' include stocks, funds, or shares:

(xxiv) 'Tenant for life,' 'statutory owner,' ... 'settled land,' 'settlement,' 'trustees of the settlement,' 'term of years absolute,' 'death duties,' and 'legal mortgage,' have the same meanings as in the Settled Land Act 1925, and 'entailed interest' and 'charge by way of legal mortgage' have the same meanings as in the Law of Property Act 1925:

(xxv) 'Treasury solicitor' means the solicitor for the affairs of His Majesty's Treasury, and includes the solicitor for the affairs of the Duchy of Lancaster:

(xxvi) 'Trust corporation' means the public trustee or a corporation either appointed by the court in any particular case to be a trustee or entitled by rules made under subsection (3) of section four of the Public Trustee Act 1906, to act as custodian trustee:

(xxvii) ...

(xxviii) 'Will' includes codicil.

(2) References to a child or issue living at the death of any person include child or issue en ventre sa mere at the death.

(3) References to the estate of a deceased person include property over which the deceased exercises a general power of appointment (including the statutory power to dispose of entailed interests) by his will.

Subsection (1):

Para (iiiA) inserted by the County Courts Act 1984, s 148(1), Sch 2, Part III, para 15.

Remainder of para (iv) repealed by Courts Act 1971, s 56 and Sch 11, Pt II.

Para (via) inserted by the Trusts of Land and Appointment of Trustees Act 1996, s 25(1), Sch 3, para 6(1), (5); for savings see s 25(4), (5) (para A1.509).

Para (vii): words omitted repealed by the Trusts of Land and Appointment of Trustees Act 1996, s 25(2), Sch 4; for savings see s 25(4), (5) (para A1.509).

Para (viii) repealed by the Mental Capacity Act 2005, s 67(1), Sch 6, para 5(1), (3), Sch 7. Date in force: 1 October 2007: see SI 2007/1897, art 2(1)(d).

Para (x): a collection of clocks and watches is included in the definition of 'personal chattels' (*Re Crispin's Will Trusts* [1975] Ch 245 at 248, [1974] 3 All ER 772).

Para (xiii): words in brackets repealed by Supreme Court Act 1981, s 152(4) and Sch 7.

Para (xxiv) word omitted repealed by the Trusts of Land and Appointment of Trustees Act 1996, s 25(2), Sch 4; for savings see s 25(4), (5) (para A1.509).

Para (xxvi): definition extended by Law of Property (Amendment) Act 1926 (see also paras 9.05–9.07).

LAW OF PROPERTY (AMENDMENT) ACT 1926

(16 & 17 GEO 5, C 11)

A1.130

3 Meaning of 'trust corporation'

(1) For the purposes of the Law of Property Act 1925, the Settled Land Act 1925, the Trustee Act 1925, the Administration of Estates Act 1925, and the [Senior Courts Act 1981], the expression 'Trust Corporation' includes the Treasury Solicitor, the Official Solicitor and any person holding any other official position prescribed by the Lord Chancellor, and, in relation to the property of a bankrupt and property subject to a deed of arrangement, includes the trustee in bankruptcy and the trustee under the deed respectively, and, in relation to charitable ecclesiastical and public trusts, also includes any local or public authority so prescribed, and any other corporation constituted under the laws of the United Kingdom or any part thereof which satisfies the Lord Chancellor that it undertakes the administration of any such trusts without remuneration, or that by its constitution it is required to apply the whole of its net income after payment of outgoings for charitable ecclesiastical or public purposes, and is prohibited from distributing, directly or indirectly, any part thereof by way of profits amongst any of its members, and is authorised by him to act in relation to such trusts as a trust corporation.

(2) For the purposes of this provision, the expression 'Treasury Solicitor' means the solicitor for the affairs of His Majesty's Treasury, and includes the solicitor for the affairs of the Duchy of Lancaster.

Sub-s (1): words 'Senior Courts Act 1981' in square brackets substituted by the Constitutional Reform Act 2005, s 59(5), Sch 11, Pt 1, para 1(2). Date in force: 1 October 2009: see SI 2009/1604, art 2(d).

CONSULAR CONVENTIONS ACT 1949

(12, 13 & 14 GEO 6, C 29)

[26 April 1949]

A1.137

6 Application of sections 1, 2 and 4

(1) His Majesty may by Order in Council direct that sections one and two ... of this Act shall apply to any foreign State specified in the Order, being a State with which a consular convention providing for matters for which provision is made by those sections has been concluded by His Majesty.

Sub-s (1): words omitted repealed by the Consular Relations Act 1968, s 16(3), (4).

INTESTATES' ESTATES ACT 1952

(15 & 16 GEO 6 & 1 ELIZ 2, C 64)

[30th October 1952]

A1.147

1 (1) Subject to the provisions of this Schedule, where the residuary estate of the intestate comprises of interest in a dwelling-house in which the surviving [spouse or civil partner] was resident at the time of the intestate's death, the surviving [spouse or civil partner] may require the personal representative in exercise of the power conferred by section forty-one of the principal Act (and with due regard to the requirements of that section as to valuation) to appropriate the said interest in the dwelling-house in or towards satisfaction of any absolute interest of the surviving [spouse or civil partner] in the real and personal estate of the intestate.

(2) The right conferred by this paragraph shall not be exercisable where the interest is—

(a) a tenancy which at the date of the death of the intestate was a tenancy which would determine within the period of two years from that date; or
(b) a tenancy which the landlord by notice given for that date could determine within the remainder of that period.

(3) Nothing in subsection (5) of section forty-one of the principal Act (which requires the personal representative, in making an appropriation to any person under that section, to have regard to the rights of others) shall prevent the personal representative from giving effect to the right conferred by this paragraph.

(4) The reference in this paragraph to an absolute interest in the real and personal estate of the intestate includes a reference to the capital value of a life interest which the surviving [spouse or civil partner] has under this Act elected to have redeemed.

(5) Where part of a building was, at the date of the death of the intestate, occupied as a separate dwelling, that dwelling shall for the purposes of this Schedule be treated as a dwelling-house.

2 Where—

(a) the dwelling-house forms part of a building and an interest in the whole of the building is comprised in the residuary estate; or
(b) the dwelling-house is held with agricultural land and an interest in the agricultural land is comprised in the residuary estate; or
(c) the whole or part of the dwelling-house was at the time of the intestate's death used as a hotel or lodging house; or
(d) a part of the dwelling-house was at the time of the intestate's death used for purposes other than domestic purposes,

the right conferred by paragraph 1 of this Schedule shall not be exercisable unless the court, on being satisfied that the exercise of that right is not likely to diminish the value of assets in the residuary estate (other than the said interest in the dwelling-house) or make them more difficult to dispose of, so orders.

3 (1) The right conferred by paragraph 1 of this Schedule.

(a) shall not be exercisable after the expiration of twelve months from the first taking out of representation with respect to the intestate's estate;
(b) shall not be exercisable after the death of the surviving [spouse or civil partner];

(c) shall be exercisable, except where the surviving [spouse or civil partner] is the sole personal representative, by notifying the personal representative (or, where there are two or more personal representatives of whom one is the surviving [spouse or civil partner], all of them except the surviving [spouse or civil partner]) in writing.

(2) A notification in writing under paragraph (c) of the foregoing sub-paragraph shall not be revocable except with the consent of the personal representative; but the surviving [spouse or civil partner] may require the personal representative to have the said interest in the dwelling-house valued in accordance with section forty-one of the principal Act and to inform him or her of the result of that valuation before he or she decides whether to exercise the right.

(3) Subsection (9) of the section forty-seven A added to the principal Act by section two of this Act shall apply for the purposes of the construction of the reference in this paragraph to the first taking out of representation, and the promise to subsection (5) of that section shall apply for the purpose of enabling the surviving [spouse or civil partner] to apply for an extension of the period of twelve months mentioned in this paragraph.

4 (1) During the period of twelve months mentioned in paragraph 3 of this Schedule the personal representative shall not without the written consent of the surviving [spouse or civil partner] sell or otherwise dispose of the said interest in the dwelling-house except in the course of administration owing to want of other assets.

(2) An application to the court under paragraph 2 of this Schedule may be made by the personal representative as well as by the surviving [spouse or civil partner], and if, on an application under that paragraph, the court does not order that the right conferred by paragraph 1 of this Schedule shall be exercisable by the surviving [spouse or civil partner], the court may authorise the personal representative to dispose of the said interest in the dwelling-house within the said period of twelve months.

(3) Where the court under sub-paragraph (3) of paragraph 3 of this Schedule extends the said period of twelve months, the court may direct that this paragraph shall apply in relation to the extended period as it applied in relation to the original period of twelve months.

(4) This paragraph shall not apply where the surviving [spouse or civil partner] is the sole personal representative or one of two or more personal representatives.

(5) Nothing in this paragraph shall confer any right on the surviving [spouse or civil partner] as against a purchaser from the personal representative.

5 (1) Where the surviving [spouse or civil partner] is one of two or more personal representatives, the rule that a trustee may not be a purchaser of trust property shall not prevent the surviving [spouse or civil partner] from purchasing out of the estate of the intestate an interest in a dwelling-house in which the surviving [spouse or civil partner] was resident at the time of the intestate's death.

(2) The power of appropriation under section forty-one of the principal Act shall include power to appropriate an interest in a dwelling-house in which the surviving [spouse or civil partner] was resident at the time of the intestate's death partly in satisfaction of an interest of the surviving [spouse or civil partner] in the real and personal estate of the intestate and partly in return for a payment of money by the surviving [spouse or civil partner] to the personal representative.

6 [(1) Where the surviving spouse or civil partner lacks capacity (within the meaning of the Mental Capacity Act 2005) to make a requirement or give a consent under this Schedule, the requirement or consent may be made or given by a deputy appointed by the Court of Protection with power in that respect or, if no deputy has that power, by that court.]

(2) A requirement or consent made or given under this Schedule by a surviving [spouse or civil partner] who is an infant shall be as valid and binding as it would be if he or she were of age, and, as respects an appropriation in pursuance of paragraph 1 of this Schedule, the provisions of section forty-one of the principal Act as to obtaining the consent of the infant's parent or guardian, or of the court on behalf of the infant, shall not apply.

7 (1) Except where the context otherwise requires, references in this Schedule to a dwelling-house include references to any garden or portion of ground attached to and usually occupied with the dwelling-house or otherwise required for the amenity or convenience of the dwelling-house.

(2) This Schedule shall be construed as one with Part IV of the principal Act.

Para 1: in sub-paras (1), (4) words 'spouse or civil partner' in square brackets in each place they occur substituted by the Civil Partnership Act 2004, s 71, Sch 4, Pt 2, para 13(1), (2). Date in force: 5 December 2005: see SI 2005/3175, art 2(1), Sch 1.

Para 3: words 'spouse or civil partner' in square brackets in each place they occur substituted by the Civil Partnership Act 2004, s 71, Sch 4, Pt 2, para 13(1), (2). Date in force: 5 December 2005: see SI 2005/3175, art 2(1), Sch 1.

Para 4: in sub-paras (1), (2), (4), (5) words 'spouse or civil partner' in square brackets in each place they occur substituted by the Civil Partnership Act 2004, s 71, Sch 4, Pt 2, para 13(1), (2). Date in force: 5 December 2005: see SI 2005/3175, art 2(1), Sch 1.

Para 5: words 'spouse or civil partner' in square brackets in each place they occur substituted by the Civil Partnership Act 2004, s 71, Sch 4, Pt 2, para 13(1), (2). Date in force: 5 December 2005: see SI 2005/3175, art 2(1), Sch 1.

Para 6: sub-para (1) substituted by the Mental Capacity Act 2005, s 67(1), Sch 6, para 8. Date in force: 1 October 2007: see SI 2007/1897, art 2(1)(d).

Para 6: words 'spouse or civil partner' in square brackets in both places they occur substituted by the Civil Partnership Act 2004, s 71, Sch 4, Pt 2, para 13(1), (2). Date in force: 5 December 2005: see SI 2005/3175, art 2(1), Sch 1.

BIRTHS AND DEATHS REGISTRATION ACT 1953

(1 & 2 ELIZ 2, C 20)

[14th July 1953]

A1.148

[10 Registration of father where parents not married or of second female parent where parents not civil partners]

[(1) *Notwithstanding anything in the foregoing provisions of this Act* [*and subject to section 10ZA of this Act*], *in the case of a child whose father and mother were not married to each other at the time of his birth, no person shall as father of the child be required to give information concerning the birth of the child, and the registrar* [In the case of a child whose father and mother were not married to each other at the time of the child's birth, no person shall as father of the child be required to give information concerning the birth of the child except by virtue of regulations under section 2C or 2E, and the registrar] shall not enter in the register the name of any person as father of the child except—

Births and Deaths Registration Act 1953 **A1.148**

(a) at the joint request of the mother and the person stating himself to be the father of the child (in which case that person shall sign the register together with the mother); or
(b) at the request of the mother on production of—
  (i) a declaration in the prescribed form made by the mother stating that that person is the father of the child; and
  (ii) a statutory declaration made by that person stating himself to be the father of the child; or
  [(ii) a declaration in the prescribed form which is made by that person, states himself to be the father of the child, and is countersigned by a prescribed person; or]
(c) at the request of that person on production of—
  (i) a declaration in the prescribed form by that person stating himself to be the father of the child; and
  (ii) a statutory declaration made by the mother stating that that person is the father of the child; or
  [(ii) a declaration in the prescribed form which is made by the mother, states that that person is the father of the child, and is countersigned by a prescribed person; or]
[(d) at the request of the mother or that person on production of—
  (i) a copy of [any agreement made between them under section 4(1)(b) of the Children Act 1989 in relation to the child]; and
  (ii) a declaration in the prescribed form by the person making the request stating that the agreement was made in compliance with section 4 of [that Act] and has not been brought to an end by an order of a court; or
(e) at the request of the mother or that person on production of—
  (i) a certified copy of an order under section 4 of the Children Act 1989 giving that person parental responsibility for the child; and
  (ii) a declaration in the prescribed form by the person making the request stating that the order has not been brought to an end by an order of a court; or
(f) at the request of the mother or that person on production of—
  (i) a certified copy of an order under paragraph 1 of Schedule 1 to the Children Act 1989 which requires that person to make any financial provision for the child and which is not an order falling within paragraph 4(3) of that Schedule; and
  (ii) a declaration in the prescribed form by the person making the request stating that the order has not been discharged by an order of a court; or
(g) at the request of the mother or that person on production of—
  (i) a certified copy of any of the orders which are mentioned in subsection (1A) of this section which has been made in relation to the child; and
  (ii) a declaration in the prescribed form by the person making the request stating that the order has not been brought to an end or discharged by an order of a court]; [or
(h) in accordance with regulations made under section 2C (confirmation of parentage information given by mother), section 2D (declaration before registration by person claiming to be other parent) or section 2E (scientific tests)].

[(1A) The orders are—

(a) an order under section 4 of the Family Law Reform Act 1987 that that person shall have all the parental rights and duties with respect to the child;

A1.148 *Statutes*

    (b) an order that that person shall have custody or care and control or legal custody of the child made under section 9 of the Guardianship of Minors Act 1971 at a time when such an order could only be made in favour of a parent;
    (c) an order under section 9 or 11B of that Act which requires that person to make any financial provision in relation to the child;
    (d) an order under section 4 of the Affiliation Proceedings Act 1957 naming that person as putative father of the child.]

[(1B) *Notwithstanding anything in the foregoing provisions of this Act and subject to section 10ZA of this Act, in the case of a child to whom section 1(3) of the Family Law Reform Act 1987 does not apply no woman shall as a parent of the child by virtue of section 43 of the Human Fertilisation and Embryology Act 2008 be required to give information concerning the birth of the child, and the registrar shall not enter in the register the name of any woman as a parent of the child by virtue of that section* [In the case of a child to whom section 1(3) of the Family Law Reform Act 1987 does not apply, no woman shall as parent of the child by virtue of section 43 of the Human Fertilisation and Embryology Act 2008 be required to give information concerning the birth of the child except by virtue of regulations under section 2C, and the registrar shall not enter the name of any woman as a parent of the child by virtue of that section] except—

    (a) at the joint request of the mother and the person stating herself to be the other parent of the child (in which case that person shall sign the register together with the mother); or
    (b) at the request of the mother on production of—
        (i) a declaration in the prescribed form made by the mother stating that the person to be registered ('the woman concerned') is a parent of the child by virtue of section 43 of the Human Fertilisation and Embryology Act 2008; and
        (ii) a statutory declaration made by the woman concerned stating herself to be a parent of the child by virtue of section 43 of that Act; or
        [(ii) a declaration in the prescribed form which is made by the woman concerned, states herself to be a parent of the child by virtue of section 43 of that Act, and is countersigned by a prescribed person; or]
    (c) at the request of the woman concerned on production of—
        (i) a declaration in the prescribed form made by the woman concerned stating herself to be a parent of the child by virtue of section 43 of the Human Fertilisation and Embryology Act 2008; and
        (ii) a statutory declaration made by the mother stating that the woman concerned is a parent of the child by virtue of section 43 of that Act; or
        [(ii) a declaration in the prescribed form which is made by the mother, states that the woman concerned is a parent of the child by virtue of section 43 of that Act, and is countersigned by a prescribed person; or]
    (d) at the request of the mother or the woman concerned on production of—
        (i) a copy of any agreement made between them under section 4ZA(1)(b) of the Children Act 1989 in relation to the child; and
        (ii) a declaration in the prescribed form by the person making the request stating that the agreement was made in compliance with section 4ZA of that Act and has not been brought to an end by an order of a court; or
    (e) at the request of the mother or the woman concerned on production of—
        (i) a certified copy of an order under section 4ZA of the Children Act 1989 giving the woman concerned parental responsibility for the child; and
        (ii) a declaration in the prescribed form by the person making the request stating that the order has not been brought to an end by an order of a court; or
    (f) at the request of the mother or the woman concerned on production of—

(i) a certified copy of an order under paragraph 1 of Schedule 1 to the Children Act 1989 which requires the woman concerned to make any financial provision for the child and which is not an order falling within paragraph 4(3) of that Schedule; and
(ii) a declaration in the prescribed form by the person making the request stating that the order has not been discharged by an order of a court; [or
(g) in accordance with regulations made under section 2C (confirmation of parentage information given by mother) or section 2D (declaration before registration by person claiming to be other parent)].]

[(1C) Subsections (1) and (1B) have effect subject to section 10ZA.]

(2) Where, in the case of a child whose father and mother were not married to each other at the time of his birth, a person stating himself to be the father of the child makes a request to the registrar in accordance with paragraph (c) [to (g)] of subsection (1) of this section—

(a) he shall be treated as a qualified informant concerning the birth of the child for the purposes of this Act; and
(b) the giving of information concerning the birth of the child by that person and the signing of the register by him in the presence of the registrar shall act as a discharge of any duty of any other qualified informant under *section 2* [section 2A] of this Act.

[(2A) Where, in the case of a child to whom section 1(3) of the Family Law Reform Act 1987 does not apply, a person stating herself to be a parent of the child by virtue of section 43 of the Human Fertilisation and Embryology Act 2008 makes a request to the registrar in accordance with any of paragraphs (c) to (f) of subsection (1B)—

(a) she shall be treated as a qualified informant concerning the birth of the child for the purposes of this Act; and
(b) the giving of information concerning the birth of the child by that person and the signing of the register by her in the presence of the registrar shall act as a discharge of any duty of any other qualified informant under *section 2* [section 2A] of this Act.]

(3) *In this section and section 10A of this Act references to a child whose father and mother were not married to each other at the time of his birth shall be construed in accordance with section 1 of the Family Law Reform Act 1987 < ... >.*]
Substituted by the Family Law Reform Act 1987, s 24.
Section heading: substituted by the Human Fertilisation and Embryology Act 2008, s 56, Sch 6, Pt 1, para 5(1), (2). Date in force (for certain purposes): 6 April 2009: see SI 2009/479, art 6(1)(e). Date in force (for remaining purposes): 1 September 2009: see SI 2009/479, art 6(2).
Sub-s (1): words from 'Notwithstanding anything in' to 'and the registrar' in italics repealed and subsequent words in square brackets substituted by the Welfare Reform Act 2009, s 56, Sch 6, Pt 1, paras 1, 11(1), (2)(a). Date in force: to be appointed: see the Welfare Reform Act 2009, s 61(3)–(5).
Sub-s (1): words 'and subject to section 10ZA of this Act' in square brackets inserted by the Human Fertilisation and Embryology (Deceased Fathers) Act 2003, s 2(1), Schedule, para 2. Date in force: 1 December 2003: see SI 2003/3095, art 2; for retrospective, transitional and transitory provision see the Human Fertilisation and Embryology (Deceased Fathers) Act 2003, s 3(1).
Sub-s (1): para (b)(ii) substituted by the Welfare Reform Act 2009, s 56, Sch 6, Pt 1, paras 1, 11(1), (2)(b). Date in force: to be appointed: see the Welfare Reform Act 2009, s 61(3)–(5).
Sub-s (1): para (c)(ii) substituted by the Welfare Reform Act 2009, s 56, Sch 6, Pt 1, paras 1, 11(1), (2)(c). Date in force: to be appointed: see the Welfare Reform Act 2009, s 61(3)–(5).
Sub-s (1): paras (d)–(g) substituted by the Children Act 1989, s 108(4), Sch 12, para 6.
Sub-s (1): in para (d)(i) words from 'any agreement made' to 'to the child' in square brackets substituted by the Adoption and Children Act 2002, s 139(1), Sch 3, para 6(a). Date in force: 1 December 2003: see SI 2003/3079, art 2(2)(b).

A1.148 *Statutes*

Sub-s (1): in para (d)(ii) words 'that Act ' in square brackets substituted by the Adoption and Children Act 2002, s 139(1), Sch 3, para 6(b). Date in force: 1 December 2003: see SI 2003/3079, art 2(2)(b).
Sub-s (1): para (h) and word 'or' immediately preceding it inserted by the Welfare Reform Act 2009, s 56, Sch 6, Pt 1, paras 1, 11(1), (2)(d). Date in force: to be appointed: see the Welfare Reform Act 2009, s 61(3)–(5).
Sub-s (1B): inserted by the Human Fertilisation and Embryology Act 2008, s 56, Sch 6, Pt 1, para 5(1), (3). Date in force (for certain purposes): 6 April 2009: see SI 2009/479, art 6(1)(e). Date in force (for remaining purposes): 1 September 2009: see SI 2009/479, art 6(2).
Sub-s (1B): words from 'Notwithstanding anything in' to 'of that section' in italics repealed and subsequent words in square brackets substituted by the Welfare Reform Act 2009, s 56, Sch 6, Pt 1, paras 1, 11(1), (3)(a). Date in force: to be appointed: see the Welfare Reform Act 2009, s 61(3)–(5).
Sub-s (1B): para (b)(ii) substituted by the Welfare Reform Act 2009, s 56, Sch 6, Pt 1, paras 1, 11(1), (3)(b). Date in force: to be appointed: see the Welfare Reform Act 2009, s 61(3)–(5).
Sub-s (1B): para (c)(ii) substituted by the Welfare Reform Act 2009, s 56, Sch 6, Pt 1, paras 1, 11(1), (3)(c). Date in force: to be appointed: see the Welfare Reform Act 2009, s 61(3)–(5).
Sub-s (1B): para (g) and word 'or' immediately preceding it inserted by the Welfare Reform Act 2009, s 56, Sch 6, Pt 1, paras 1, 11(1), (4). Date in force: to be appointed: see the Welfare Reform Act 2009, s 61(3)–(5).
Sub-s (1C): inserted by the Welfare Reform Act 2009, s 56, Sch 6, Pt 1, paras 1, 11(1), (4). Date in force: to be appointed: see the Welfare Reform Act 2009, s 61(3)–(5).
Sub-s (2): words 'to (g)' in square brackets substituted by the Children Act 1989, s 108(4), Sch 12, para 6(4).
Sub-s (2): in para (b) words 'section 2' in italics repealed and subsequent words in square brackets substituted by the Welfare Reform Act 2009, s 56, Sch 6, Pt 1, paras 1, 11(1), (5). Date in force: to be appointed: see the Welfare Reform Act 2009, s 61(3)–(5).
Sub-s (2A): inserted by the Human Fertilisation and Embryology Act 2008, s 56, Sch 6, Pt 1, para 5(1), (4). Date in force (for certain purposes): 6 April 2009: see SI 2009/479, art 6(1)(e). Date in force (for remaining purposes): 1 September 2009: see SI 2009/479, art 6(2).
Sub-s (2A): in para (b) words 'section 2' in italics repealed and subsequent words in square brackets substituted by the Welfare Reform Act 2009, s 56, Sch 6, Pt 1, paras 1, 11(1), (5). Date in force: to be appointed: see the Welfare Reform Act 2009, s 61(3)–(5).
Sub-s (3): repealed by the Welfare Reform Act 2009, ss 56, 58(1), Sch 6, Pt 1, paras 1, 11(1), (6), Sch 7, Pt 5. Date in force: to be appointed: see the Welfare Reform Act 2009, s 61(3)–(5).
Sub-s (3): words omitted repealed by the Adoption and Children Act 2002, s 139(1), (3), Sch 3, para 6(c), Sch 5. Date in force: 1 December 2003: see SI 2003/3079, art 2(2)(b).

A1.148A

[10ZA   Registration of father or second female parent by virtue of certain provisions of Human Fertilisation and Embryology Act 2008]

[(1)   Notwithstanding anything in the foregoing provisions of this Act, the registrar shall not enter in the register—

(a) as the father of a child, the name of a man who is to be treated for that purpose as the father of the child by virtue of section 39(1) or 40(1) or (2) of the Human Fertilisation and Embryology Act 2008 (circumstances in which man to be treated as father of child for purposes of registration of birth where fertility treatment undertaken after his death); or
(b) as a parent of the child, the name of a woman who is to be treated for that purpose as a parent of the child by virtue of section 46(1) or (2) of that Act (circumstances in which woman to be treated as parent of child for purposes of registration of birth where fertility treatment undertaken after her death),

unless the condition in subsection (2) below is satisfied.

(2)   The condition in this subsection is satisfied if—

(a) the mother requests the registrar to make such an entry in the register and produces the relevant documents; or
(b) in the case of the death or inability of the mother, the relevant documents are produced by some other person who is a qualified informant.

(3) In this section "the relevant documents" means—
(a) the consent in writing and election mentioned in section 39(1), 40(1) or (2) or 46(1) or (2) (as the case requires) of the Human Fertilisation and Embryology Act 2008;
(b) a certificate of a registered medical practitioner as to the medical facts concerned; and
(c) such other documentary evidence (if any) as the registrar considers appropriate.]

Substituted by the Human Fertilisation and Embryology Act 2008, s 56, Sch 6, Pt 1, para 6. Date in force (for certain purposes): 6 April 2009: see SI 2009/479, art 6(1)(e). Date in force (for remaining purposes): 1 September 2009: see SI 2009/479, art 6(2).

A1.149

[10A Re-registration where parents neither married nor civil partners]

[(1) Where there has been registered under this Act the birth of a child whose father and mother were not married to each other at the time of the birth, but no person has been registered as the father of the child [(or as a parent of the child by virtue of section 42, 43 or 46(1) or (2) of the Human Fertilisation and Embryology Act 2008)], the registrar shall re-register the birth so as to show a person as the father—

(a) at the joint request of the mother and that person; or
(b) at the request of the mother on production of—
  (i) a declaration in the prescribed form made by the mother stating that that person is the father of the child; and
  (ii) a statutory declaration made by that person stating himself to be the father of the child; or
  [(ii) a declaration in the prescribed form which is made by that person, states himself to be the father of the child, and is countersigned by a prescribed person; or]
(c) at the request of that person on production of—
  (i) a declaration in the prescribed form by that person stating himself to be the father of the child; and
  (ii) a statutory declaration made by the mother stating that that person is the father of the child; or
  [(ii) a declaration in the prescribed form which is made by the mother, states that that person is the father of the child, and is countersigned by a prescribed person; or]
[(d) at the request of the mother or that person on production of—
  (i) a copy of [any agreement made between them under section 4(1)(b) of the Children Act 1989 in relation to the child]; and
  (ii) a declaration in the prescribed form by the person making the request stating that the agreement was made in compliance with section 4 of [that Act] and has not been brought to an end by an order of a court; or
(e) at the request of the mother or that person on production of—
  (i) a certified copy of an order under section 4 of the Children Act 1989 giving that person parental responsibility for the child; and
  (ii) a declaration in the prescribed form by the person making the request stating that the order has not been brought to an end by an order of a court; or

A1.149 *Statutes*

    (f) at the request of the mother or that person on production of—
        (i) a certified copy of an order under paragraph 1 of Schedule 1 to the Children Act 1989 which requires that person to make any financial provision for the child and which is not an order falling within paragraph 4(3) of that Schedule; and
        (ii) a declaration in the prescribed form by the person making the request stating that the order has not been discharged by an order of a court; or
[(ff) in the case of a man who is to be treated as the father of the child by virtue of section 39(1) or 40(1) or (2) of the Human Fertilisation and Embryology Act 2008, if the condition in section 10ZA(2) of this Act is satisfied; or]
    (g) at the request of the mother or that person on production of—
        (i) a certified copy of any of the orders which are mentioned in subsection (1A) of this section which has been made in relation to the child; and
        (ii) a declaration in the prescribed form by the person making the request stating that the order has not been brought to an end or discharged by an order of a court.]

but no birth shall be re-registered under this section except in the prescribed manner and with the authority of the Registrar General.

[(1A) The orders are—
    (a) an order under section 4 of the Family Law Reform Act 1987 that that person shall have all the parental rights and duties with respect to the child;
    (b) an order that that person shall have custody or care and control or legal custody of the child made under section 9 of the Guardianship of Minors Act 1971 at a time when such an order could only be made in favour of a parent;
    (c) an order under section 9 or 11B of that Act which requires that person to make any financial provision in relation to the child;
    (d) an order under section 4 of the Affiliation Proceedings Act 1957 naming that person as putative father of the child.]

[(1B) Where there has been registered under this Act the birth of a child to whom section 1(3) of the Family Law Reform Act 1987 does not apply, but no person has been registered as a parent of the child by virtue of section 42, 43 or 46(1) or (2) of the Human Fertilisation and Embryology Act 2008 (or as the father of the child), the registrar shall re-register the birth so as to show a woman ('the woman concerned') as a parent of the child by virtue of section 43 or 46(1) or (2) of that Act—

    (a) at the joint request of the mother and the woman concerned; or
    (b) at the request of the mother on production of—
        (i) a declaration in the prescribed form made by the mother stating that the woman concerned is a parent of the child by virtue of section 43 of the Human Fertilisation and Embryology Act 2008; and
        (ii) a statutory declaration made by the woman concerned stating herself to be a parent of the child by virtue of section 43 of that Act; or
     [(ii) a declaration in the prescribed form which is made by the woman concerned, states herself to be a parent of the child by virtue of section 43 of that Act, and is countersigned by a prescribed person; or]
    (c) at the request of the woman concerned on production of—
        (i) a declaration in the prescribed form made by the woman concerned stating herself to be a parent of the child by virtue of section 43 of the Human Fertilisation and Embryology Act 2008; and
        (ii) a statutory declaration made by the mother stating that the woman concerned is a parent of the child by virtue of section 43 of that Act; or
     [(ii) a declaration in the prescribed form which is made by the mother, states

Births and Deaths Registration Act 1953 **A1.149**

        that the woman concerned is a parent of the child by virtue of section 43 of that Act, and is countersigned by a prescribed person; or]
- (d) at the request of the mother or the woman concerned on production of—
  - (i) a copy of an agreement made between them under section 4ZA(1)(b) of the Children Act 1989 in relation to the child; and
  - (ii) a declaration in the prescribed form by the person making the request stating that the agreement was made in compliance with section 4ZA of that Act and has not been brought to an end by an order of a court; or
- (e) at the request of the mother or the woman concerned on production of—
  - (i) a certified copy of an order under section 4ZA of the Children Act 1989 giving the woman concerned parental responsibility for the child; and
  - (ii) a declaration in the prescribed form by the person making the request stating that the order has not been brought to an end by an order of a court; or
- (f) at the request of the mother or the woman concerned on production of—
  - (i) a certified copy of an order under paragraph 1 of Schedule 1 to the Children Act 1989 which requires the woman concerned to make any financial provision for the child and which is not an order falling within paragraph 4(3) of that Schedule; and
  - (ii) a declaration in the prescribed form by the person making the request stating that the order has not been discharged by an order of a court; or
- (g) in the case of a woman who is to be treated as a parent of the child by virtue of section 46(1) or (2) of the Human Fertilisation and Embryology Act 2008, if the condition in section 10ZA(2) of this Act is satisfied.]

(2) On the re-registration of a birth under this section—
- (a) the registrar shall sign the register;
- [(b) in the case of any of the following requests—
  - (i) a request under subsection (1)(a) or (b) or subsection (1B)(a) or (b);
  - (ii) a request under subsection (1)(d), (e), (f) or (g) or subsection (1B)(d), (e) or (f) made by the mother of the child,

the mother shall also sign the register;
- (bb) in a case within subsection (1)(ff) or (1B)(g), the mother or (as the case may be) the qualified informant shall also sign the register;
- (c) in the case of a request made under subsection (1)(a) or (c) or a request made under subsection (1)(d), (e), (f) or (g) by the person requesting to be registered as the father of the child, that person shall also sign the register;
- (cc) in the case of a request made under subsection (1B)(a) or (c) or a request made under subsection (1B)(d), (e) or (f) by a woman requesting to be registered as a parent of the child by virtue of section 43 of the Human Fertilisation and Embryology Act 2008, that woman shall also sign the register; *and*]
- (d) if the re-registration takes place more than three months after the birth, the superintendent registrar shall also sign the register.]

Inserted by the Children Act 1975, s 93(2).
Substituted by the Family Law Reform Act 1987, s 25.
Section heading: substituted by the Human Fertilisation and Embryology Act 2008, s 56, Sch 6, Pt 1, para 7(1), (2). Date in force (for certain purposes): 6 April 2009: see SI 2009/479, art 6(1)(e). Date in force (for remaining purposes): 1 September 2009: see SI 2009/479, art 6(2).
Sub-s (1): words from '(or as a' to 'Human Fertilisation and Embryology Act 2008)' in square brackets inserted by the Human Fertilisation and Embryology Act 2008, s 56, Sch 6, Pt 1, para 7(1), (3)(a). Date in force (for certain purposes): 6 April 2009: see SI 2009/479, art 6(1)(e). Date in force (for remaining purposes): 1 September 2009: see SI 2009/479, art 6(2).
Sub-s (1): para (b)(ii) substituted by the Welfare Reform Act 2009, s 56, Sch 6, Pt 1, paras 1, 12(1), (2)(a). Date in force: to be appointed: see the Welfare Reform Act 2009, s 61(3)–(5).
Sub-s (1): para (c)(ii) substituted by the Welfare Reform Act 2009, s 56, Sch 6, Pt 1, paras 1, 12(1), (2)(b). Date in force: to be appointed: see the Welfare Reform Act 2009, s 61(3)–(5).
Sub-s (1): paras (d)–(g) substituted by the Children Act 1989, s 108(4), Sch 12, para 6.

Sub-s (1): in para (d)(i) words from 'any agreement made' to 'to the child' in square brackets substituted by the Adoption and Children Act 2002, s 139(1), Sch 3, para 7(a). Date in force: 1 December 2003: see SI 2003/3079, art 2(2)(b).
Sub-s (1): in para (d)(ii) words 'that Act' in square brackets substituted by the Adoption and Children Act 2002, s 139(1), Sch 3, para 7(b). Date in force: 1 December 2003: see SI 2003/3079, art 2(2)(b).
Sub-s (1): para (ff) substituted by the Human Fertilisation and Embryology Act 2008, s 56, Sch 6, Pt 1, paras 7(1), (3)(b). Date in force (for certain purposes): 6 April 2009: see SI 2009/479, art 6(1)(e). Date in force (for remaining purposes): 1 September 2009: see SI 2009/479, art 6(2).
Sub-s (1A): inserted by the Children Act 1989, s 108(4), Sch 12, para 6(3).
Sub-s (1B): inserted by the Human Fertilisation and Embryology Act 2008, s 56, Sch 6, Pt 1, paras 7(1), (4). Date in force (for certain purposes): 6 April 2009: see SI 2009/479, art 6(1)(e). Date in force (for remaining purposes): 1 September 2009: see SI 2009/479, art 6(2).
Sub-s (1B): para (b)(ii) substituted by the Welfare Reform Act 2009, s 56, Sch 6, Pt 1, paras 1, 12(1), (3)(a). Date in force: to be appointed: see the Welfare Reform Act 2009, s 61(3)–(5).
Sub-s (1B): para (c)(ii) substituted by the Welfare Reform Act 2009, s 56, Sch 6, Pt 1, paras 1, 12(1), (3)(b). Date in force: to be appointed: see the Welfare Reform Act 2009, s 61(3)–(5).
Sub-s (2): paras (b), (bb), (c), (cc) substituted, for paras (b), (bb), (c) as previously enacted, by the Human Fertilisation and Embryology Act 2008, s 56, Sch 6, Pt 1, paras 7(1), (5). Date in force (for certain purposes): 6 April 2009: see SI 2009/479, art 6(1)(e). Date in force (for remaining purposes): 1 September 2009: see SI 2009/479, art 6(2).
Sub-s (2): para (d) and word 'and' immediately preceding it repealed by the Welfare Reform Act 2009, ss 56, 58(1), Sch 6, Pt 1, paras 1, 12(1), (4), Sch 7, Pt 5. Date in force: to be appointed: see the Welfare Reform Act 2009, s 61(3)–(5).

A1.149A

[10B Re-registration after sole registration: information provided by other parent and confirmed by mother]

[(1) The Minister may by regulations make provision for the re-registration of a birth to show a person as the father of a relevant child, on the basis of information given by that person after the birth is registered and confirmed by the mother.

(2) In this section a 'relevant child' means a child—

(a) whose father and mother were not married to each other at the time of the child's birth, and
(b) whose birth has been registered before or after the commencement of this section without any person being registered as the father of the child (or as a parent of the child by virtue of section 42, 43 or 46(1) or (2) of the Human Fertilisation and Embryology Act 2008).

(3) Regulations under subsection (1) may—

(a) enable a person who believes himself to be the father of a relevant child to make a declaration to that effect to the registrar,
(b) enable or require the registrar by notice to require the mother to state whether or not she acknowledges that the person is the father of the child, and
(c) where the mother acknowledges that the person is the father, require the registrar to re-register the birth so as to show the person as the father.

(4) In the case of a child who has a parent by virtue of section 43 of the Human Fertilisation and Embryology Act 2008, references in subsections (1) and (3) to the father are to be read as references to the woman who is a parent by virtue of that section.

(5) Regulations under this section may—

(a) require anything to be done in a prescribed form or manner or in the presence of the registrar,

Births and Deaths Registration Act 1953 **A1.149B**

(b) make provision as to the time within which anything is required or authorised to be done.

(6) Regulations under this section may not provide for any birth to be re-registered except with the authority of the Registrar General.

(7) In this section 'prescribed' means prescribed by regulations made under this section by the Minister.]

Inserted by the Welfare Reform Act 2009, s 56, Sch 6, Pt 1, paras 1, 13. Date in force: to be appointed: see the Welfare Reform Act 2009, s 61(3)–(5).

A1.149B

[10C   Re-registration after sole registration: information provided by mother and confirmed by other parent]

[(1) The Minister may by regulations make provision for the re-registration of a birth to show a person as the father of a relevant child, on the basis of information given by the mother after the birth is registered and confirmed by that person.

(2) In this section a 'relevant child' means a child—

(a) whose father and mother were not married to each other at the time of the child's birth, and
(b) whose birth has been registered before or after the commencement of this section without any person being registered as the father of the child (or as a parent of the child by virtue of section 42, 43 or 46(1) or (2) of the Human Fertilisation and Embryology Act 2008).

(3) Regulations under subsection (1) may—

(a) enable the mother of a relevant child to make a declaration to the registrar stating that a specified person ('the alleged father') is the father of the child,
(b) enable or require the registrar by notice to require the alleged father to state whether or not he acknowledges that he is the father of the child,
(c) where the alleged father acknowledges that he is the father of the child, require the alleged father to give prescribed information to the registrar, and
(d) where the alleged father gives that information to the registrar, require the registrar to re-register the birth so as to show the alleged father as the father.

(4) In the case of a child who has a parent by virtue of section 43 of the Human Fertilisation and Embryology Act 2008, references in subsections (1) and (3) to the father are to be read as references to the woman who is a parent by virtue of that section (and references to the alleged father have a corresponding meaning).

(5) Regulations under this section may—

(a) require anything to be done in a prescribed form or manner or in the presence of the registrar,
(b) make provision as to the time within which anything is required or authorised to be done.

(6) Regulations under this section may not provide for any birth to be re-registered except with the authority of the Registrar General.

(7) In this section 'prescribed' means prescribed by regulations made under this section by the Minister.]

Inserted by the Welfare Reform Act 2009, s 56, Sch 6, Pt 1, paras 1, 13. Date in force: to be appointed: see the Welfare Reform Act 2009, s 61(3)–(5).

A1.150 Statutes

A1.150

14 Re-registration of births of legitimated persons

(1) Where, in the case of any person whose birth has been registered in England or Wales, evidence is produced to the Registrar General which appears to him to be satisfactory that that person has become a legitimated person < ... > the Registrar General may authorise at any time the re-registration of that person's birth, and the re-registration shall be effected in such manner and at such place as may be prescribed:
Provided that, except where—

(a) the name of a person [stating] himself to be the father of the legitimated person[, or herself to be a parent of the legitimated person by virtue of section 43 of the Human Fertilisation and Embryology Act 2008,] has been entered in the register in pursuance of section ten [or 10A] of this Act; or

(b) the paternity of the legitimated person [(or, as the case may be, the parentage of the legitimated person by virtue of section 43 of that Act),] has been established < ... > by a decree of a court of competent jurisdiction; or

(c) a declaration of the legitimacy of the legitimated person has been made under section seventeen of the Matrimonial Causes Act 1950 [or section 56 of the Family Law Reform Act 1987],

the Registrar General shall not authorise the re-registration unless information with a view to obtaining it is furnished by both parents.

(2) Where the Registrar General believes any person to have become a legitimated person < ... > on the marriage of his parents [or on their becoming civil partners of each other], and the parents or either of them fail to furnish within a period of three months from the date of the marriage [or of the formation of the civil partnership] such information, if any, as may be necessary to enable the Registrar General to authorise the re-registration of that person's birth, the Registrar General may at any time after the expiration of the said period require the parents or either of them to give him such information concerning the matter as he may consider necessary, verified in such manner as he may direct, and for that purpose to attend personally either at a registrar's office or at any other place appointed by him within such time, not being less than seven days after the receipt of the notice, as may be specified in the notice.

(3) < ... >

(4) This section shall apply with the prescribed modifications in relation to births at sea of which a return is sent to the Registrar General.

[(5) This section shall apply and be deemed always to have applied in relation to all persons recognised by the law of England and Wales as having been legitimated by the subsequent marriage of their parents whether or not their legitimation or the recognition thereof was effected under any enactment.]

Sub-s (1): words omitted repealed by the Legitimation (Registration of Birth) Act 1957, s 1(2); in para (a) first word in square brackets substituted by the Family Law Reform Act 1987, s 33(1), Sch 2, para 16(a), Sch 3, para 1, second words in square brackets inserted by the Children Act 1975, s 108(1)(a), Sch 3, para 13; in para (b) words omitted repealed by the Family Law Reform Act 1987, s 33(1), Sch 2, para 16(b), Sch 3, para 1; in para (c) words in square brackets inserted by the Family Law Reform Act 1987, s 33(1), Sch 2, para 16(c), Sch 3, para 1.

Sub-s (2): words omitted repealed by the Legitimation (Registration of Birth) Act 1957, s 1(2).

Sub-s (3): repealed by SI 1968/1242, art 4(1), Sch 2.

Sub-s (5): inserted by the Legitimacy Act 1976, s 11(1), Sch 1.

Sub-s (1): in para (a) words from ', or herself to' to 'Human Fertilisation and Embryology Act 2008,' in square brackets inserted by the Human Fertilisation and Embryology Act 2008, s 56, Sch 6, Pt 1, para 9(1), (2)(a). Date in force (for certain purposes): 6 April 2009: see SI 2009/479, art 6(1)(e). Date in force (for remaining purposes): 1 September 2009: see SI 2009/479, art 6(2).

Sub-s (1): words from '(or, as the' to 'of that Act),' in square brackets inserted by the Human Fertilisation and Embryology Act 2008, s 56, Sch 6, Pt 1, para 9(1), (2)(b). Date in force (for certain purposes): 6 April 2009: see SI 2009/479, art 6(1)(e). Date in force (for remaining purposes): 1 September 2009: see SI 2009/479, art 6(2).

Sub-s (2): words 'or on their becoming civil partners of each other' in square brackets inserted by the Human Fertilisation and Embryology Act 2008, s 56, Sch 6, Pt 1, para 9(1), (3)(a). Date in force (for certain purposes): 6 April 2009: see SI 2009/479, art 6(1)(e). Date in force (for remaining purposes): 1 September 2009: see SI 2009/479, art 6(2).

Sub-s (2): words 'or of the formation of the civil partnership' in square brackets inserted by the Human Fertilisation and Embryology Act 2008, s 56, Sch 6, Pt 1, para 9(1), (3)(b). Date in force (for certain purposes): 6 April 2009: see SI 2009/479, art 6(1)(e). Date in force (for remaining purposes): 1 September 2009: see SI 2009/479, art 6(2).

PUBLIC RECORDS ACT 1958

(6 & 7 ELIZ 2, C 5L)

[23rd July 1958]

A1.155

8 Court records

(1) The Lord Chancellor shall be responsible for the public records of every court of record or magistrates' court which are not in the Public Record Office or a place of deposit appointed by him under this Act and shall have power to determine in the case of any such records [other than records of the Supreme Court,] the officer in whose custody they are for the time being to be:

...

[(1A) Records of the Supreme Court for which the Lord Chancellor is responsible under subsection (1) shall be in the custody of the chief executive of that court.]

(2), (3)   < ... >

(4) Where any private documents have remained in the custody of a court in England or Wales for more than fifty years without being claimed, the Keeper of Public Records may, with the approval of the Master of the Rolls, require the documents to be transferred to the Public Record Office and thereupon the documents shall become public records for the purposes of this Act.

(5) Section three of this Act shall not apply to such of the records of ecclesiastical courts described in paragraph (n) of sub-paragraph (1) of paragraph 4 of the First Schedule to this Act as are not held in any office of the [Senior Courts] or in the Public Record Office, but, if the Lord Chancellor after consulting the President of the [Family Division] so directs as respects any of those records, those records shall be transferred to such place of deposit as may be appointed by the Lord Chancellor and shall thereafter be in the custody of such officer as may be so appointed.

(6) The public records which at the commencement of this Act are in the custody of the University of Oxford and which are included in the index a copy of which was transmitted to the principal probate registrar under section two of the Oxford University Act 1860 shall not be required to be transferred under the last foregoing subsection but the Lord Chancellor shall make arrangements with the University of Oxford as to the conditions under which those records may be inspected by the public.

A1.155 *Statutes*

Sub-s (1): words 'other than records of the Supreme Court,' in square brackets inserted by the Constitutional Reform Act 2005, s 56(1), (2)(a). Date in force: 1 October 2009: see SI 2009/1604, art 2(b).
Sub-s (1): words omitted repealed by the Courts Act 1971, s 56(4), Sch 11, Pt II.
Sub-s (1A): inserted by the Constitutional Reform Act 2005, s 56(1), (2)(b). Date in force: 1 October 2009: see SI 2009/1604, art 2(b).
Sub-s (2): repealed by the Supreme Court Act 1981, s 152(4), Sch 7.
Sub-s (3): repealed by the Administration of Justice Act 1969, ss 27(2), 35(2), Sch 2.
Sub-s (5): words 'Senior Courts' in square brackets substituted by the Constitutional Reform Act 2005, s 59(5), Sch 11, Pt 2, para 4(1), (3). Date in force: 1 October 2009: see SI 2009/1604, art 2(d).
Sub-s (5): words 'Family Division' in square brackets substituted by the Administration of Justice Act 1970, s 1(6), Sch 2, para 19.

SCHEDULE 1
DEFINITION OF PUBLIC RECORDS

Section 10

* * * * *

Records of courts and tribunals

A1.157

1   The provisions of this Schedule shall have effect for determining what are public records for the purposes of this Act.

* * * * *

4   (1) Subject to the provisions of this paragraph, records of the following descriptions shall be public records for the purposes of this Act:—

[(za) records of the Supreme Court;]
(a) records of, or held in any department of, the [Senior Courts] (including any court held under a commission of assize);

* * * * *

(n) records of ecclesiastical courts when exercising the testamentary and matrimonial jurisdiction removed from them by the Court of Probate Act 1857 and the Matrimonial Causes Act 1857 respectively;

* * * * *

(3) In this paragraph 'records' includes records of any proceedings in the court or tribunal in question and includes rolls, writs, books, decrees, bills, warrants and accounts of, or in the custody of, the court or tribunal in question.

Interpretation

8   It is hereby declared that any description of government department, court, tribunal or other body or establishment in this Schedule by reference to which a class of public records is framed extends to a government department, court, tribunal or other body or establishment, as the case may be, which has ceased to exist, whether before or after the passing of this Act.

Para 4: sub-para (1)(za) inserted by the Constitutional Reform Act 2005, s 56(1), (3). Date in force: 1 October 2009: see SI 2009/1604, art 2(b).
Para 4: in sub-para (1)(a) words 'Senior Courts' in square brackets substituted by the Constitutional Reform Act 2005, s 59(5), Sch 11, Pt 2, para 4(1), (3). Date in force: 1 October 2009: see SI 2009/1604, art 2(d).

PERPETUITIES AND ACCUMULATIONS ACT 1964

(1964, C 55)

[16 July 1964]

A1.173

15 Short title, interpretation and extent

(1) This Act may be cited as the Perpetuities and Accumulations Act 1964.

(2) In this Act—

'disposition' includes the conferring of a power of appointment and any other disposition of an interest in or right over property, and references to the interest disposed of shall be construed accordingly;
'in being' means living or en ventre sa mere;
'power of appointment' includes any discretionary power to transfer a beneficial interest in property without the furnishing of valuable consideration;
'will' includes a codicil;

and for the purposes of this Act a disposition contained in a will shall be deemed to be made at the death of the testator.

(3) For the purposes of this Act a person shall be treated as a member of a class if in his case all the conditions identifying a member of the class are satisfied, and shall be treated as a potential member if in his case some only of those conditions are satisfied but there is a possibility that the remainder will in time be satisfied.

(4) Nothing in this Act shall affect the operation of the rule of law rendering void for remoteness certain dispositions under which property is limited to be applied for purposes other than the benefit of any person or class of persons in cases where the property may be so applied after the end of the perpetuity period.

(5) The foregoing sections of this Act shall apply (except as provided in section 8 (2) above) only in relation to instruments taking effect after the commencement of this Act, and in the case of an instrument made in the exercise of a special power of appointment shall apply only where the instrument creating the power takes effect after that commencement;

Provided that section 7 above shall apply in all cases for construing the foregoing reference to a special power of appointment.

[(5A) The foregoing sections of this Act shall not apply in relation to an instrument taking effect on or after the day appointed under section 22(2) of the Perpetuities and Accumulations Act 2009 (commencement), but this shall not prevent those sections applying in relation to an instrument so taking effect if—

(a) it is a will executed before that day, or
(b) it is an instrument made in the exercise of a special power of appointment, and the instrument creating the power took effect before that day.

(5B) Subsection (5A) above shall not affect the operation of sections 4(6) and 11(2) above.]

(6) This Act shall apply in relation to a disposition made otherwise than by an instrument as if the disposition had been contained in an instrument taking effect when the disposition was made.

A1.173 *Statutes*

(7) This Act binds the Crown.

(8) Except in so far as the contrary intention appears, any enactment of the Parliament of Northern Ireland passed for purposes similar to the purposes of this Act shall bind the Crown.

(9) This Act shall not extend to Scotland or (apart from subsection (8) above) to Northern Ireland.

Sub-ss (5A), (5B): inserted by the Perpetuities and Accumulations Act 2009, s 16. Date in force: 6 April 2010: see SI 2010/37, art 2.

ADMINISTRATION OF ESTATES ACT 1971

(1971, C 25)

[12 May 1971]

Miscellaneous and supplemental

A1.223

11 Sealing of Commonwealth and Colonial grants

(1) The following provisions of section 2 of the Colonial Probates Act 1892, that is to say—

(a) subsection (2)(b) (which makes it a condition precedent to sealing in the United Kingdom letters of administration granted in certain overseas countries and territories that a sufficient security has been given to cover property in the United Kingdom); and

(b) subsection (3) (power of the court in the United Kingdom to require that adequate security is given for the payment of debts due to creditors residing in the United Kingdom);

shall not apply to the sealing of letters of administration by the High Court in England and Wales under that section, and the following provisions of this section shall apply instead.

(2) A person to whom letters of administration have been granted in a country or territory to which the said Act of 1892 applies shall on their being sealed by the High Court in England and Wales under the said section 2 have the like duties with respect to the estate of the deceased which is situated in England and Wales and the debts of the deceased which fall to be paid there as are imposed by section 25(a) and (b) of the Administration of Estates Act 1925 on a person to whom a grant of administration has been made by that court.

(3) As a condition of sealing letters of administration granted in any such country or territory, the High Court in England and Wales may, in cases to which [section 120 of the [Senior Courts Act 1981]] (power to require administrators to produce sureties) applies and subject to the following provisions of this section and subject to and in accordance with probate rules < ... > require one or more sureties, in such amount as the court thinks fit, to guarantee that they will make good, within any limit imposed by the court on the total liability of the surety or sureties, any loss which any person interested in the administration of the estate of the deceased in England and Wales may suffer in consequence of a breach by the administrator of his duties in administering it there.

(4) A guarantee given in pursuance of any such requirement shall enure for the benefit of every person interested in the administration of the estate in England and Wales as if contained in a contract under seal made by the surety or sureties with every such person and, where there are two or more sureties, as if they had bound themselves jointly or severally.

(5) No action shall be brought on any such guarantee without the leave of the High Court.

(6) Stamp duty shall not be chargeable on any such guarantee.

(7) Subsections (2) to (6) above apply to the sealing by the High Court in England and Wales of letters of administration granted by a British court in a foreign country as they apply to the sealing of letters of administration granted in a country or territory to which the Colonial Probates Act 1892 applies.

(8) In this section—

> 'letters of administration' and 'British court in a foreign country' have the same meaning as in the Colonial Probates Act 1892; and
> ['probate rules' means rules of court made under section 127 of the [Senior Courts Act 1981]].

Sub-s (3): words in square brackets beginning with the words 'section 120 of' substituted by the Supreme Court Act 1981, s 152(1), Sch 5.
Sub-s (3): words 'Senior Courts Act 1981' in square brackets substituted by the Constitutional Reform Act 2005, s 59(5), Sch 11, Pt 1, para 1(2). Date in force: 1 October 2009: see SI 2009/1604, art 2(d).
Sub-s (3): words omitted repealed by the Supreme Court Act 1981, s 152(4), Sch 7.
Sub-s (8): definition 'probate rules' substituted by the Supreme Court Act 1981, s 152(1), Sch 5.
Sub-s (8): in definition 'probate rules' words 'Senior Courts Act 1981' in square brackets substituted by the Constitutional Reform Act 2005, s 59(5), Sch 11, Pt 1, para 1(2). Date in force: 1 October 2009: see SI 2009/1604, art 2(d).

DOMICILE AND MATRIMONIAL PROCEEDINGS ACT 1973

(1973, C 45)

[25 July 1973]

A1.240

4 Dependent domicile of child not living with his father

(1) Subsection (2) of this section shall have effect with respect to the dependent domicile of a child as at any time after the coming into force of this section when his father and mother are alive but living apart.

(2) The child's domicile as at that time shall be that of his mother if—

(a) he then has his home with her and has no home with his father; or
(b) he has at any time had her domicile by virtue of paragraph (a) above and has not since had a home with his father.

A1.240 *Statutes*

(3) As at any time after the coming into force of this section, the domicile of a child whose mother is dead shall be that which she last had before she died if at her death he had her domicile by virtue of subsection (2) above and he has not since had a home with his father.

(4) Nothing in this section prejudices any existing rule of law as to the cases in which a child's domicile is regarded as being, by dependence, that of his mother.

(5) In this section, 'child' means a person incapable of having an independent domicile; ...

(6) This section extends to England and Wales, Scotland and Northern Ireland.
Repealed, in relation to Scotland, by the Family Law (Scotland) Act 2006, s 45(2), Sch 3. Date in force: 4 May 2006: see SSI 2006/212, art 2.
Sub-s (5): words omitted repealed by the Children Act 1975, s 108(1)(b), Sch 4, Part I.

LEGITIMACY ACT 1976

(1976, C 31)

[22nd July 1976]

A1.281

9   Re-registration of birth of legitimated persons

(1) It shall be the duty of the parents of a legitimated person or, in cases where re-registration can be effected on information furnished by one parent and one of the parents is dead, of the surviving parent to furnish to the Registrar General information with a view to obtaining the re-registration of the birth of that person within 3 months after the date of the marriage [or of the formation of the civil partnership] by virtue of which he was legitimated.

(2) The failure of the parents of either of them to furnish information as required by subsection (1) above in respect of any legitimated person shall not affect the legitimation of that person.

(3) This section does not apply in relation to a person who was legitimated otherwise than by virtue of the subsequent marriage [or civil partnership] of his parents.

(4) Any parent who fails to give information as required by this section shall be liable on summary conviction to a fine not exceeding [level 1 on the standard scale].
Sub-s (1): words 'or of the formation of the civil partnership' in square brackets inserted by the Human Fertilisation and Embryology Act 2008, s 56, Sch 6, Pt 1, para 18(a). Date in force (for certain purposes): 6 April 2009: see SI 2009/479, art 6(1)(e). Date in force (for remaining purposes): 1 September 2009: see SI 2009/479, art 6(2).
Sub-s (3): words 'or civil partnership' in square brackets inserted by the Human Fertilisation and Embryology Act 2008, s 56, Sch 6, Pt 1, para 18(b). Date in force (for certain purposes): 6 April 2009: see SI 2009/479, art 6(1)(e). Date in force (for remaining purposes): 1 September 2009: see SI 2009/479, art 6(2).
Sub-s (4): maximum fine increased and converted to a level on the standard scale by the Criminal Justice Act 1982, ss 37, 38, 46.

A1.282

10 Interpretation

(1) In this Act, except where the context otherwise requires,—

'disposition' includes the conferring of a power of appointment and any other disposition of an interest in or right over property;
'existing', in relation to an instrument, means one made before 1st January 1976;
'legitimated person' means a person legitimated or recognised as legitimated—
  (a) under section 2[, 2A] or 3 above; or
  (b) under section 1 or 8 of the Legitimacy Act 1926; or
  (c) except in section 8, by a legitimation (whether or not by virtue of the subsequent marriage of his parents) recognised by the law of England and Wales and effected under the law of any other country;
and cognate expressions shall be construed accordingly;
'power of appointment' includes any discretionary power to transfer a beneficial interest in property without the furnishing of valuable consideration;
'void marriage' means a marriage, not being voidable only, in respect of which the High Court has or had jurisdiction to grant a decree of nullity, or would have or would have had such jurisdiction if the parties were domiciled in England and Wales.

(2) For the purposes of this Act 'legitimated person' includes, where the context admits, a person legitimated, or recognised as legitimated, before the passing of the Children Act 1975.

(3) For the purpose of this Act, except where the context otherwise requires,—

(a) the death of the testator is the date at which a will or codicil is to be regarded as made;
(b) an oral disposition of property shall be deemed to be contained in an instrument made when the disposition was made.

(4) < ... >

(5) Except in so far as the context otherwise requires, any reference in this Act to an enactment shall be construed as a reference to that enactment as amended by or under any other enactment, including this Act.

Sub-s (1): in definition 'legitimated person' in para (a) reference to ', 2A' in square brackets inserted by the Human Fertilisation and Embryology Act 2008, s 56, Sch 6, Pt 1, para 19. Date in force (for certain purposes): 6 April 2009: see SI 2009/479, art 6(1)(e). Date in force (for remaining purposes): 1 September 2009: see SI 2009/479, art 6(2).
Sub-s (4): repealed by the Trusts of Land and Appointment of Trustees Act 1996, s 25(2), Sch 4; for savings in relation to entailed interests created before the commencement of that Act, and savings consequential upon the abolition of the doctrine of conversion, see s 25(4), (5) thereof.

A1.297 *Statutes*

ADOPTION ACT 1976

(1976, C 36)

[22nd July 1976]

PART IV
STATUS OF ADOPTED CHILDREN

A1.297

47   Miscellaneous enactments

(1)   Section 39 does not apply for the purposes of [section 1 of and Schedule 1 to the Marriage Act 1949 or Schedule 1 to the Civil Partnership Act 2004 (prohibited degrees of kindred and affinity),] [or sections 64 and 65 of the Sexual Offences Act 2003 (sex with an adult relative)].

(2)   … , section 39 does not apply for the purposes of any provision of—

(a)   [the British Nationality Act 1981],
(b)   the Immigration Act 1971,
(c)   any instrument having effect under an enactment within paragraph (a) or (b), or
(d)   any other provision of the law for the time being in force which determines [British citizenship, [British overseas territories citizenship] [, the status of a British National (Overseas)] or British Overseas citizenship].

(3)–(5)   < … >

This section derived from the Children Act 1975, Sch 1, para 7.
Sub-s (1): words from 'or sections 64' to 'an adult relative)' in square brackets substituted by the Criminal Justice and Immigration Act 2008, s 73(c), Sch 15, para 7.
Date in force: 8 July 2008: see the Criminal Justice and Immigration Act 2008, s 153(2)(e).
Sub-s (2): words omitted repealed by the British Nationality Act, s 52(8), Sch 9.
Sub-s (2): in para (a) words 'the British Nationality Act 1981' in square brackets substituted by the British Nationality Act 1981, s 52(6), Sch 7.
Sub-s (2): in para (d) words from 'British citizenship,' to 'British Overseas citizenship' in square brackets substituted by the British Nationality Act 1981, s 52(6), Sch 7.
Sub-s (2): in para (d) words 'British overseas territories citizenship' in square brackets substituted by virtue of the British Overseas Territories Act 2002, s 2(3).
Date in force: this amendment came into force on 26 February 2002 (date of Royal Assent of the British Overseas Territories Act 2002) in the absence of any specific commencement provision.
Sub-s (2): in para (d) words ', the status of a British National (Overseas)' in square brackets inserted by SI 1986/948, art 8, Schedule.
Sub-s (3): repealed by the Social Security Act 1986, s 86, Sch 11.
Sub-ss (4), (5): repealed by the Social Security Act 1988, s 16, Sch 5.
Modified, in relation to parental orders under the Human Fertilisation and Embryology Act 1990, s 30, by the Parental Orders (Human Fertilisation and Embryology) Regulations 1994, SI 1994/2767, reg 2, Sch 1.

[SENIOR COURTS ACT 1981]

(1981, C 54)

[28th July 1981]

Words 'Senior Courts Act 1981' in square brackets substituted by the Constitutional Reform Act 2005, s 59(5), Sch 11, Pt 1, para 1. Date in force: 1 October 2009: see SI 2009/1604, art 2(d).

PART I
CONSTITUTION OF [SENIOR COURTS]

Part heading: words 'Senior Courts' in square brackets substituted by the Constitutional Reform Act 2005, s 59(5), Sch 11, Pt 4, para 26(1), (2). Date in force: 1 October 2009: see SI 2009/1604, art 2(d).

The [Senior Courts]

Cross-heading: words 'Senior Courts' in square brackets substituted by the Constitutional Reform Act 2005, s 59(5), Sch 11, Pt 4, para 26(1), (2). Date in force: 1 October 2009: see SI 2009/1604, art 2(d).

A1.309

1 The [Senior Courts]

(1) The [Senior Courts] of England and Wales shall consist of the Court of Appeal, the High Court of Justice and the Crown Court, each having such jurisdiction as is conferred on it by or under this or any other Act.

(2) ...

Section heading: words 'Senior Courts' in square brackets substituted by the Constitutional Reform Act 2005, s 59(5), Sch 11, Pt 4, para 26(1), (2). Date in force: 1 October 2009: see SI 2009/1604, art 2(d).
Sub-s (1): words 'Senior Courts' in square brackets substituted by the Constitutional Reform Act 2005, s 59(5), Sch 11, Pt 4, para 26(1), (2). Date in force: 1 October 2009: see SI 2009/1604, art 2(d).
Sub-s (2): repealed by the Constitutional Reform Act 2005, ss 7(5), 146, Sch 18, Pt 2. Date in force: 3 April 2006: see SI 2006/1014, art 2(a), Sch 1, paras 5, 29, 30(b).The High Court

PART II
JURISDICTION

THE COURT OF APPEAL

* * * * *

A1.312

16 Appeals from High Court

(1) Subject as otherwise provided by this or any other Act (and in particular to the provision in section 13(2)(a) of the Administration of Justice Act 1969 excluding appeals to the Court of Appeal in cases where leave to appeal from the High Court directly to the [Supreme Court] is granted under Part II of that Act), [or as provided by any order made by the Lord Chancellor under section 56(1) of the Access to Justice Act 1999,] the Court of Appeal shall have jurisdiction to hear and determine appeals from any judgment or order of the High Court.

A1.312 *Statutes*

(2) An appeal from a judgment or order of the High Court when acting as a prize court shall not be to the Court of Appeal, but shall be to Her Majesty in Council in accordance with the Prize Acts 1864 to 1944.

Sub-s (1): words 'Supreme Court' in square brackets substituted by the Constitutional Reform Act 2005, s 40(4), Sch 9, Pt 1, para 36(1), (3). Date in force: 1 October 2009: see SI 2009/1604, art 2(d).

Sub-s (1): words from 'or as provided' to 'Justice Act 1999,' in square brackets inserted by SI 2000/1071, art 7. Date in force: 2 May 2000 (with savings in relation to a person who has filed a notice of appeal or applied for permission to appeal before that date): see SI 2000/1071, arts 1(1), 6.

Other particular fields of jurisdiction

A1.317

31 Application for judicial review

(1) An application to the High Court for one or more of the following forms of relief, namely—

- [(a) a mandatory, prohibiting or quashing order;]
- (b) a declaration or injunction under subsection (2); or
- (c) an injunction under section 30 restraining a person not entitled to do so from acting in an office to which that section applies,

shall be made in accordance with rules of court by a procedure to be known as an application for judicial review.

(2) A declaration may be made or an injunction granted under this subsection in any case where an application for judicial review, seeking that relief, has been made and the High Court considers that, having regard to—

- (a) the nature of the matters in respect of which relief may be granted by [mandatory, prohibiting or quashing orders];
- (b) the nature of the persons and bodies against whom relief may be granted by such orders; and
- (c) all the circumstances of the case,

it would be just and convenient for the declaration to be made or of the injunction to be granted, as the case may be.

(3) No application for judicial review shall be made unless the leave of the High Court has been obtained in accordance with rules of court; and the court shall not grant leave to make such an application unless it considers that the applicant has a sufficient interest in the matter to which the application relates.

[(4) On an application for judicial review the High Court may award to the applicant damages, restitution or the recovery of a sum due if—

- (a) the application includes a claim for such an award arising from any matter to which the application relates; and
- (b) the court is satisfied that such an award would have been made if the claim had been made in an action begun by the applicant at the time of making the application.]

[(5) If, on an application for judicial review, the High Court quashes the decision to which the application relates, it may in addition—

- (a) remit the matter to the court, tribunal or authority which made the decision, with a direction to reconsider the matter and reach a decision in accordance with the findings of the High Court, or

[Senior Courts Act 1981] **A1.329**

(b) substitute its own decision for the decision in question.

(5A) But the power conferred by subsection (5)(b) is exercisable only if—
- (a) the decision in question was made by a court or tribunal,
- (b) the decision is quashed on the ground that there has been an error of law, and
- (c) without the error, there would have been only one decision which the court or tribunal could have reached.

(5B) Unless the High Court otherwise directs, a decision substituted by it under subsection (5)(b) has effect as if it were a decision of the relevant court or tribunal.]

(6) Where the High Court considers that there has been undue delay in making an application for judicial review, the court may refuse to grant—
- (a) leave for the making of the application; or
- (b) any relief sought on the application,

if it considers that the granting of the relief sought would be likely to cause substantial hardship to, or substantially prejudice the rights of, any person or would be detrimental to good administration.

(7) Subsection (6) is without prejudice to any enactment or rule of court which has the effect of limiting the time within which an application for judicial review may be made.

This section derived from the Rules of the Supreme Court 1965, SI 1965/1776, Order 53, rr 1(1), (2), 3(1), (7), 4(1), 7(1), 9(4).
Sub-s (1): para (a) substituted by SI 2004/1033, arts 2, 4(a). Date in force: 1 May 2004: see SI 2004/1033, art 1.
Sub-s (2): in para (a) words 'mandatory, prohibiting or quashing orders' in square brackets substituted by SI 2004/1033, arts 2, 4(b). Date in force: 1 May 2004: see SI 2004/1033, art 1.
Sub-s (4): substituted by SI 2004/1033, arts 2, 4(c). Date in force: 1 May 2004: see SI 2004/1033, art 1.
Sub-ss (5), (5A), (5B): substituted, for sub-s (5) as originally enacted, by the Tribunals, Courts and Enforcement Act 2007, s 141. Date in force: 6 April 2008: see SI 2008/749, art 2.

RULES OF COURT

A1.329

84 Power to make rules of court

(1) Rules of court may be made for the purpose of regulating and prescribing[, except in relation to any criminal cause or matter,] the practice and procedure to be followed in the [Crown Court ...].

(2) Without prejudice to the generality of subsection (1), the matters about which rules of court may be made under this section include all matters of practice and procedure in the [Senior Courts] which were regulated or prescribed by rules of court immediately before the commencement of this Act.

(3) No provision of this or any other Act, or contained in any instrument made under any Act, which—
- (a) authorises or requires the making of rules of court about any particular matter or for any particular purpose; or
- (b) provides (in whatever words) that the power to make rules of court under this section is to include power to make rules about any particular matter or for any particular purpose,

shall be taken as derogating from the generality of subsection (1).

A1.329 *Statutes*

(4) ...

[(5) Special rules may apply—

(a) any rules made under this section, ...
(b) Civil Procedure Rules,
[(c) Criminal Procedure Rules, or
(d) Family Procedure Rules,]

to proceedings to which the special rules apply.

(5A) Rules made under this section may apply—

(a) any special rules, ...
(b) Civil Procedure Rules,
[(c) Criminal Procedure Rules, or
(d) Family Procedure Rules,]

to proceedings to which rules made under this section apply.

(6) Where rules may be applied under subsection (5) or (5A), they may be applied—

(a) to any extent,
(b) with or without modification, and
(c) as amended from time to time.]

(7) No rule which may involve an increase of expenditure out of public funds may be made under this section except with the concurrence of the Treasury, but the validity of any rule made under this section shall not be called in question in any proceedings in any court either by the court or by any party to the proceedings on the ground only that it was a rule as to the making of which the concurrence of the Treasury was necessary and that the Treasury did not concur or are not expressed to have concurred.

(8) ...

(9) In this section 'special rules' means rules applying to proceedings of any particular kind in the [Senior Courts], being rules made by an authority other than the [Civil Procedure Rule Committee][, the Family Procedure Rule Committee, the Criminal Procedure Rule Committee,] or the Crown Court Rule Committee under any provision of this or any other Act which (in whatever words) confers on that authority power to make rules in relation to proceedings of that kind in the [Senior Courts].

Sub-s (1): words ', except in relation to any criminal cause or matter,' in square brackets inserted by SI 2004/2035, art 3, Schedule, paras 11, 15(1), (2)(a). Date in force: 1 September 2004: see SI 2004/2035, art 2(1); for effect see art 2(2) thereof.

Sub-s (1): words in square brackets beginning with the words 'Crown Court' substituted by the Civil Procedure Act 1997, s 10, Sch 2, para 1(4)(a). Date in force: 26 April 1999: see SI 1999/1009, art 3(b).

Sub-s (1): words omitted repealed by SI 2004/2035, art 3, Schedule, paras 11, 15(1), (2)(b). Date in force: 1 September 2004: see SI 2004/2035, art 2(1); for effect see art 2(2) thereof.

Sub-s (2): words 'Senior Courts' in square brackets substituted by the Constitutional Reform Act 2005, s 59(5), Sch 11, Pt 4, para 26(1), (2). Date in force: 1 October 2009: see SI 2009/1604, art 2(d).

Sub-s (4): repealed by the Civil Procedure Act 1997, s 10, Sch 2, para 1(4)(b). Date in force: 26 April 1999: see SI 1999/1009, art 3(b).

Sub-ss (5), (5A), (6): substituted, for sub-ss (5), (6) as originally enacted, by the Civil Procedure Act 1997, s 10, Sch 2, para 1(4)(c).

Sub-s (5): in para (a) word omitted repealed by SI 2004/2035, art 3, Schedule, paras 11, 15(1), (3)(a). Date in force: 1 September 2004: see SI 2004/2035, art 2(1); for effect see art 2(2) thereof.

Sub-s (5): paras (c), (d) inserted by SI 2004/2035, art 3, Schedule, paras 11, 15(1), (3)(b). Date in force: 1 September 2004: see SI 2004/2035, art 2(1); for effect see art 2(2) thereof.

Sub-s (5A): in para (a) word omitted repealed by SI 2004/2035, art 3, Schedule, paras 11, 15(1), (3)(a). Date in force: 1 September 2004: see SI 2004/2035, art 2(1); for effect see art 2(2) thereof.
Sub-s (5A): paras (c), (d) inserted by SI 2004/2035, art 3, Schedule, paras 11, 15(1), (3)(b). Date in force: 1 September 2004: see SI 2004/2035, art 2(1); for effect see art 2(2) thereof.
Sub-s (8): repealed by the Constitutional Reform Act 2005, ss 15(1), 146, Sch 4, Pt 1, paras 114, 136, Sch 18, Pt 2. Date in force: 3 April 2006: see SI 2006/1014, art 2(a), Sch 1, paras 10, 11(p), 29, 30(b).
Sub-s (9): words 'Senior Courts' in square brackets in both places they occur substituted by the Constitutional Reform Act 2005, s 59(5), Sch 11, Pt 4, para 26(1), (2). Date in force: 1 October 2009: see SI 2009/1604, art 2(d).
Sub-s (9): words 'Civil Procedure Rule Committee' in square brackets substituted by the Civil Procedure Act 1997, s 10, Sch 2, para 1(4)(d). Date in force: 26 April 1999: see SI 1999/1009, art 3(b).
Sub-s (9): words ', the Family Procedure Rule Committee, the Criminal Procedure Rule Committee,' in square brackets inserted by SI 2004/2035, art 3, Schedule, paras 11, 15(1), (4). Date in force: 1 September 2004: see SI 2004/2035, art 2(1); for effect see art 2(2) thereof.

PART VI
MISCELLANEOUS AND SUPPLEMENTARY
Miscellaneous provisions

A1.357

132 Proof of documents bearing seal or stamp of [Senior Courts] or any office thereof

Every document purporting to be sealed or stamped with the seal or stamp of the [Senior Courts] or of any office of the [Senior Courts] shall be received in evidence in all parts of the United Kingdom without further proof.

Section heading: words 'Senior Courts' in square brackets substituted by the Constitutional Reform Act 2005, s 59(5), Sch 11, Pt 4, para 26(1), (2). Date in force: 1 October 2009: see SI 2009/1604, art 2(d).
Words 'Senior Courts' in square brackets in both places they occur substituted by the Constitutional Reform Act 2005, s 59(5), Sch 11, Pt 4, para 26(1), (2). Date in force: 1 October 2009: see SI 2009/1604, art 2(d).

A1.358

134 Powers of attorney deposited before October 1971

(1) This section applies to any instrument creating, or verifying the execution of, a power of attorney which was deposited in the Central Office of the [Senior Courts] before 1st October 1971.

(2) A separate file of such instruments shall continue to be kept and, subject to payment of [the fee prescribed by an order under section 92 of the Courts Act 2003 (fees)]—

(a) any person may search that file, and may inspect any such instrument; and
(b) an office copy of any such instrument shall be issued to any person on request.

(3) A document purporting to be an office copy of any such instrument shall, in any part of the United Kingdom, without further proof be sufficient evidence of the contents of the instrument and of its having been deposited as mentioned in subsection (1).

Sub-s (1): words 'Senior Courts' in square brackets substituted by the Constitutional Reform Act 2005, s 59(5), Sch 11, Pt 4, para 26(1), (2). Date in force: 1 October 2009: see SI 2009/1604, art 2(d).

A1.358 *Statutes*

Sub-s (2): words 'the fee prescribed by an order under section 92 of the Courts Act 2003 (fees)' in square brackets substituted by virtue of the Courts Act 2003, s 109(1), Sch 8, para 262(c). Date in force: 1 April 2005: see SI 2005/910, art 3(y).

A1.359

136 Production of documents filed in, or in custody of, [Senior Courts]

(1) [Rules may be made in accordance with Part 1 of Schedule 1 to the Constitutional Reform Act 2005] for providing that, in any case where a document filed in, or in the custody of, any office of the [Senior Courts] is required to be produced to any court or tribunal (including an umpire or arbitrator) sitting elsewhere than at the Royal Courts of Justice—

(a) it shall not be necessary for any officer, whether served with a subpoena in that behalf or not, to attend for the purpose of producing the document; but
(b) the document may be produced to the court or tribunal by sending it to the court or tribunal, in the manner prescribed in the rules, together with a certificate, in the form so prescribed, to the effect that the document has been filed in, or is in the custody of, the office;

and any such certificate shall be prima facie evidence of the facts stated in it.

(2) Rules under this section may contain—

(a) provisions for securing the safe custody and return to the proper office of the [Senior Courts] of any document sent to a court or tribunal in pursuance of the rules; and
(b) such incidental and supplementary provisions as appear to the [person making the rules] to be necessary or expedient.

(3) ...

Section heading: words 'Senior Courts' in square brackets substituted by the Constitutional Reform Act 2005, s 59(5), Sch 11, Pt 4, para 26(1), (2). Date in force: 1 October 2009: see SI 2009/1604, art 2(d).
Sub-s (1): words 'Rules may be made in accordance with Part 1 of Schedule 1 to the Constitutional Reform Act 2005' in square brackets substituted by the Constitutional Reform Act 2005, s 12(2), Sch 1, Pt 2, paras 11, 13(1), (2). Date in force: 3 April 2006: see SI 2006/1014, art 2(a), Sch 1, para 7.
Sub-s (1): words 'Senior Courts' in square brackets substituted by the Constitutional Reform Act 2005, s 59(5), Sch 11, Pt 4, para 26(1), (2). Date in force: 1 October 2009: see SI 2009/1604, art 2(d).
Sub-s (2): in para (a) words 'Senior Courts' in square brackets substituted by the Constitutional Reform Act 2005, s 59(5), Sch 11, Pt 4, para 26(1), (2). Date in force: 1 October 2009: see SI 2009/1604, art 2(d).
Sub-s (2): in para (b) words 'person making the rules' in square brackets substituted by the Constitutional Reform Act 2005, s 12(2), Sch 1, Pt 2, paras 11, 13(1), (3). Date in force: 3 April 2006: see SI 2006/1014, art 2(a), Sch 1, para 7.
Sub-s (3): repealed by the Constitutional Reform Act 2005, ss 12(2), 146, Sch 1, Pt 2, paras 11, 13(1), (4), Sch 18, Pt 1. Date in force: 3 April 2006: see SI 2006/1014, art 2(a), Sch 1, paras 7, 29, 30(a).

A1.360

151 Interpretation of this Act, and rules of construction for other Acts and documents

(1) In this Act, unless the context otherwise requires—

'action' means any civil proceedings commenced by writ or in any other manner prescribed by rules of court;

'appeal', in the context of appeals to the civil division of the Court of Appeal, includes—
    (a) an application for a new trial, and
    (b) an application to set aside a verdict, finding or judgment in any cause or matter in the High Court which has been tried, or in which any issue has been tried, by a jury;

['arbitration agreement' has the same meaning as it has in [Part I of the Arbitration Act 1996;]]

'cause' means any action or any criminal proceedings;

'Division', where it appears with a capital letter, means a division of the High Court;

'judgment' includes a decree;

'jurisdiction' includes powers;

'matter' means any proceedings in court not in a cause;

'party', in relation to any proceedings, includes any person who pursuant to or by virtue of rules of court or any other statutory provision has been served with notice of, or has intervened in, those proceedings;

'prescribed' means—
    (a) except in relation to fees, prescribed by rules of court; ...
    (b) ...

['senior judge', where the reference is to the senior judge of a Division, means the president of that Division;]

'solicitor' means a solicitor of the [Senior Courts];

'statutory provision' means any enactment, whenever passed, or any provision contained in subordinate legislation (as defined in section 21(1) of the Interpretation Act 1978), whenever made;

'this or any other Act' includes an Act passed after this Act.

(2) Section 128 contains definitions of expressions used in Part V and in the other provisions of this Act relating to probate causes and matters.

(3) Any reference in this Act to rules of court under section 84 includes a reference to rules of court [in relation to the [Senior Courts]] under any provision of this or any other Act which confers on the [Civil Procedure Rule Committee] or the Crown Court Rule Committee power to make rules of court.

(4) Except where the context otherwise requires, in this or any other Act—

    ...
    ...

'divisional court' (with or without capital letters) means a divisional court constituted under section 66;

'judge of the [Senior Courts]' means—
    (a) a judge of the Court of Appeal other than an ex-officio judge within paragraph (b) or (c) of section 2(2), or
    (b) a judge of the High Court,
and accordingly does not include, as such, a judge of the Crown Court;

'official referees' business' has the meaning given by section 68(6);

    ...

(5) The provisions of Schedule 4 (construction of references to superseded courts and officers) shall have effect.

Sub-s (1): definition 'arbitration agreement' inserted by the Courts and Legal Services Act 1990, s 125(3), Sch 18, para 41.

Sub-s (1): in definition 'arbitration agreement' words 'Part I of the Arbitration Act 1996;' in square brackets substituted by the Arbitration Act 1996, s 107(1), Sch 3, para 37(3).

A1.360 *Statutes*

Sub-s (1): in definition 'prescribed' para (b) and word omitted immediately preceding it repealed by the Courts Act 2003, s 109(1), (3), Sch 8, para 265, Sch 10. Date in force: 1 April 2005: see SI 2005/910, art 3(y), (aa).

Sub-s (1): definition 'senior judge' substituted by the Constitutional Reform Act 2005, s 15(1), Sch 4, Pt 1, paras 114, 146. Date in force: 3 April 2006: see SI 2006/1014, art 2(a), Sch 1, paras 10, 11(q).

Sub-s (1): in definition 'solicitor' words 'Senior Courts' in square brackets substituted by the Constitutional Reform Act 2005, s 59(5), Sch 11, Pt 4, para 26(1), (2). Date in force: 1 October 2009: see SI 2009/1604, art 2(d).

Sub-s (3): words in square brackets beginning with the words 'in relation to' inserted by the Civil Procedure Act 1997, s 10, Sch 2, para 1(7)(a). Date in force: 26 April 1999: see SI 1999/1009, art 3(e).

Sub-s (3): words 'Senior Courts' in square brackets substituted by the Constitutional Reform Act 2005, s 59(5), Sch 11, Pt 4, para 26(1), (2). Date in force: 1 October 2009: see SI 2009/1604, art 2(d).

Sub-s (3): words 'Civil Procedure Rule Committee' in square brackets substituted by the Civil Procedure Act 1997, s 10, Sch 2, para 1(7)(a). Date in force: 26 April 1999: see SI 1999/1009, art 3(e).

Sub-s (4): definition 'Criminal Appeal Rules' (omitted) repealed by SI 2004/2035, art 3, Schedule, paras 11, 18. Date in force: 1 September 2004: see SI 2004/2035, art 2(1); for effect see art 2(2) thereof.

Sub-s (4): definition 'Crown Court Rules' (omitted) repealed by SI 2004/2035, art 3, Schedule, paras 11, 18. Date in force: 1 September 2004: see SI 2004/2035, art 2(1); for effect see art 2(2) thereof.

Sub-s (4): in definition 'judge of the Senior Courts' words 'Senior Courts' in square brackets substituted by the Constitutional Reform Act 2005, s 59(5), Sch 11, Pt 4, para 26(1), (2). Date in force: 1 October 2009: see SI 2009/1604, art 2(d).

Sub-s (4): definition 'Rules of Supreme Court' (omitted) repealed by the Civil Procedure Act 1997, s 10, Sch 2, para 1(7)(b). Date in force: 26 April 1999: see SI 1999/1009, art 3(e).

A1.362

153 Citation, commencement and extent

(1) This Act may be cited as the [Senior Courts Act 1981].

(2) This Act, except the provisions mentioned in subsection (3), shall come into force on 1st January 1982; and references to the commencement of this Act shall be construed as references to the beginning of that day.

(3) Sections 72, 143 and 152(2) and this section shall come into force on the passing of this Act.

(4) In this Act—
  (a) the following provisions extend to Scotland, namely—
    section 80(3);
    section 152(4) and Schedule 7, so far as they relate to the Admiralty Court Act 1861;
  (b) the following provisions extend to Northern Ireland so far as they relate to the Northern Ireland Assembly Disqualification Act 1975, namely—
    section 152(1) and Schedule 5;
    section 152(3) and paragraph 3(1) of Schedule 6;
  (c) the following provisions extend to Scotland and Northern Ireland, namely—
    section 36;
    sections 132 and 134(3);
    section 152(1) and Schedule 5, so far as they amend—
      (i) references to section 49 of the [Senior Courts] of Judicature (Consolidation) Act 1925,
      (ii) the House of Commons Disqualification Act 1975, and

(iii) section 4 of the Evidence (Proceedings in Other Jurisdictions) Act 1975;
section 152(3) and paragraph 3(1) of Schedule 6, so far as they relate to the House of Commons Disqualification Act 1975;
section 152(4) and Schedule 7, so far as they relate to—
(i) provisions of the [Senior Courts] of Judicature (Consolidation) Act 1925 which extend throughout the United Kingdom,
(ii) the Evidence and Powers of Attorney Act 1940, and
(iii) section 57(3)(a) of the Courts Act 1971;
(d) section 145 extends to any place to which the Courts-Martial (Appeals) Act 1968 extends, and section 152(1) and (4) and Schedules 5 and 7, so far as they relate to any of the following enactments, namely—
Army Act 1955,
Air Force Act 1955,
section 9(2) of, and Part II of Schedule 1 to, the Criminal Appeal Act 1966,
Courts-Martial (Appeals) Act 1968,
Hovercraft Act 1968,
< ... >
extend to any place to which that enactment extends;
but, save as aforesaid, the provisions of this Act, other than those mentioned in subsection (5), extend to England and Wales only.

(5) The provisions of this Act whose extent is not restricted by subsection (4) are—
section 27;
section 150;
section 151(1);
section 152(4) and Schedule 7 as far as they relate to the Naval Prize Act 1864, the Prize Courts Act 1915 and section 56 of the Administration of Justice Act 1956;
this section;
paragraph 1 of Schedule 4.

Sub-s (1): words 'Senior Courts Act 1981' in square brackets substituted by the Constitutional Reform Act 2005, s 59(5), Sch 11, Pt 1, para 1(2). Date in force: 1 October 2009: see SI 2009/1604, art 2(d).
Sub-s (4): in para (c) words 'Senior Courts' in square brackets in both places they occur substituted by the Constitutional Reform Act 2005, s 59(5), Sch 11, Pt 4, para 26(1), (2). Date in force: 1 October 2009: see SI 2009/1604, art 2(d).
Sub-s (4): in para (d) words omitted repealed by the Merchant Shipping Act 1995, s 314(1), Sch 12.

SCHEDULE 1
DISTRIBUTION OF BUSINESS IN HIGH COURT

Section 61(1), (3)

A1.363

Chancery Division

1   To the Chancery Division are assigned all causes and matters relating to—
* * * * *

(d) the administration of the estates of deceased persons;
* * * * *

(h) probate business, other than non-contentious or common form business;

A1.363 *Statutes*

Family Division

3   To the Family Division are assigned—

* * * * *

(b) all causes and matters (whether at first instance or on appeal) relating to—
(i) legitimacy;
[(ii) the exercise of the inherent jurisdiction of the High Court with respect to minors, the maintenance of minors and any proceedings under the Children Act 1989, except proceedings solely for the appointment of a guardian of a minor's estate;]
(iii) ... adoption;
(iv) non-contentious or common form probate business;

* * * * *

Para 3: in sub-para (b)(iii) words omitted repealed by the Family Law Reform Act 1987, s 33(4), Sch 4.

ADMINISTRATION OF JUSTICE ACT 1982

(1982, C 53)

[28th October 1982]

A1.377

23   Deposit and registration of wills of living persons

(1) The following, namely—

(a) the Principal Registry of the Family Division of the High Court of Justice;
(b) the Keeper of the Registers of Scotland; and
(c) the Probate and Matrimonial Office of the [Court of Judicature] of Northern Ireland,

shall be registering authorities for the purposes of this section.

(2) Each registering authority shall provide and maintain safe and convenient depositories for the custody of the wills of living persons.

(3) Any person may deposit his will in such a depository in accordance with regulations under section 25 below and on payment of the prescribed fee.

(4) It shall be the duty of a registering authority to register in accordance with regulations under section 25 below—

(a) any will deposited in a depository maintained by the authority; and
(b) any other will whose registration is requested under Article 6 of the Registration Convention.

(5) A will deposited in a depository provided—

(a) under section 172 of the Supreme Court of Judicature (Consolidation) Act 1925 or section 126 of the [Senior Courts Act 1981]; or
(b) under Article 27 of the Administration of Estates (Northern Ireland) Order 1979,

260

shall be treated for the purposes of this section as if it had been deposited under this section.

(6) In this section 'prescribed' means—

(a) in the application of this section to England and Wales, prescribed by an order under [section 92 of the Courts Act 2003];
(b) in its application to Scotland, prescribed by an order under section 26 below; and
(c) in its application to Northern Ireland, prescribed by an order under section 116 of the Judicature (Northern Ireland) Act 1978.

Sub-s (1): in para (c) words 'Court of Judicature' in square brackets substituted by the Constitutional Reform Act 2005, s 59(5), Sch 11, Pt 4, para 27(1), (2)(a). Date in force: 1 October 2009: see SI 2009/1604, art 2(d).
Sub-s (5): in para (a) words 'Senior Courts Act 1981' in square brackets substituted by the Constitutional Reform Act 2005, s 59(5), Sch 11, Pt 1, para 1(2). Date in force: 1 October 2009: see SI 2009/1604, art 2(d).
Sub-s (6): in para (a) words 'section 92 of the Courts Act 2003' in square brackets substituted by the Courts Act 2003, s 109(1), Sch 8, para 270. Date in force: 1 April 2005: see SI 2005/910, art 3(y).

A1.379

25 Regulations as to deposit and registration of wills

(1) Regulations may make provision—

(a) as to the conditions for the deposit of a will;
(b) as to the manner of and procedure for—
   (i) the deposit and registration of a will; and
   (ii) the withdrawal of a will which has been deposited; and
   (iii) the cancellation of the registration of a will; and
(c) as to the manner in which the Principal Registry of the Family Division is to perform its functions as the national body under the Registration Convention.

(2) Regulations under this section may contain such incidental or supplementary provisions as the authority making the regulations considers appropriate.

(3) Any such regulations are to be made—

(a) for England and Wales, by the President of the Family Division of the High Court of Justice, with the concurrence of the Lord Chancellor;
(b) for Scotland, by the Secretary of State after consultation with the Lord President of the Court of Session; and
(c) for Northern Ireland, by the Northern Ireland [Court of Judicature] Rules Committee, with the concurrence of the Lord Chancellor.

(4) Regulations made by virtue of subsection (1)(c) above shall be made by the Lord Chancellor [after consulting the Lord Chief Justice of England and Wales].

(5) Subject to subsection (6) below, regulations under this section shall be made by statutory instrument and shall be laid before Parliament after being made.

(6) Regulations for Northern Ireland shall be statutory rules for the purposes of the Statutory Rules (Northern Ireland) Order 1979; and any such statutory rule shall be laid before Parliament after being made in like manner as a statutory instrument and section 4 of the Statutory Instruments Act 1946 shall apply accordingly.

(7) The Statutory Instruments Act 1946 shall apply to a statutory instrument containing regulations made in accordance with subsection (3)(a) or (c) above as if the regulations had been made by a Minister of the Crown.

A1.379 *Statutes*

(8) Any regulations made under section 172 of the Supreme Court of Judicature (Consolidation) Act 1925 or section 126 of the [Senior Courts Act 1981] shall have effect for the purposes of this Part of this Act as they have effect for the purposes of the enactment under which they were made.

[(9) The Lord Chief Justice may nominate a judicial office holder (as defined in section 109(4) of the Constitutional Reform Act 2005) to exercise his functions under subsection (4).]

Sub-s (3): in para (c) words 'Court of Judicature' in square brackets substituted by the Constitutional Reform Act 2005, s 59(5), Sch 11, Pt 4, para 27(1), (2)(b). Date in force: 1 October 2009: see SI 2009/1604, art 2(d).

Sub-s (4): words 'after consulting the Lord Chief Justice of England and Wales' in square brackets inserted by the Constitutional Reform Act 2005, s 15(1), Sch 4, Pt 1, paras 147, 148(1), (2). Date in force: 3 April 2006: see SI 2006/1014, art 2(a), Sch 1, paras 10, 11(q).

Sub-s (8): words 'Senior Courts Act 1981' in square brackets substituted by the Constitutional Reform Act 2005, s 59(5), Sch 11, Pt 1, para 1(2). Date in force: 1 October 2009: see SI 2009/1604, art 2(d).

Sub-s (9): inserted by the Constitutional Reform Act 2005, s 15(1), Sch 4, Pt 1, paras 147, 148(1), (3). Date in force: 3 April 2006: see SI 2006/1014, art 2(a), Sch 1, paras 10, 11(q).

A1.383

76 Commencement

(1) The provisions of this Act specified in subsection (2) below shall come into operation on such day as the Lord Chancellor may by order appoint.

(2) The provisions of this Act mentioned in subsection (1) above are—

- (a) section 6;
- (b) Part III;
- (c) sections 34 and 35;
- (d) sections 38 to 47;
- (e) section 54;
- (f) section 57;
- (g) section 69;
- (h) section 73(8);
- (j) section 75, so far as it relates—
    - (i) to the Judicial Trustees Act 1896;
    - (ii) to section 17 of the Law Reform (Miscellaneous Provisions) Act (Northern Ireland) 1937;
    - (iii) to the Prevention of Fraud (Investments) Act 1958;
    - (iv) to sections 99(3), 168 to 174A and 176 of the County Courts Act 1959;
    - (v) to sections 1 to 16 of the Administration of Justice Act 1965 and Schedule 1 to that Act;
    - (vi) to the Administration of Justice Act 1977; and
    - (vii) to the Judicature (Northern Ireland) Act 1978;
- (k) paragraph 10 of Schedule 6; and
- (l) paragraphs 6 to 8 of Schedule 8.

(3) The provisions of this Act specified in subsection (4) below shall come into operation on such day as the Secretary of State may by order appoint.

(4) The provisions of this Act mentioned in subsection (3) above are—

- (a) section 12;
- (b) section 14(2);
- (c) section 48; and
- (d) section 75 above, so far as it relates to the Damages (Scotland) Act 1976.

(5) The provisions of this Act specified in subsection (6) below shall come into operation on such day as the Lord Chancellor and the Secretary of State may by order jointly appoint.

(6) The provisions of this Act mentioned in subsection (5) above are—
- (a) sections 23 to 25;
- (b) sections 27 and 28;
- (c) section 75, so far as it relates—
  - (i) to section 126 of the [Senior Courts Act 1981]; and
  - (ii) to Article 27 of the Administration of Estates (Northern Ireland) Order 1979.

(7) Any order under this section shall be made by statutory instrument.

(8) Any such order may appoint different days for different provisions and for different purposes.

(9) The provisions of this Act specified in subsection (10) below shall come into operation on the day this Act is passed.

(10) The provisions of this Act mentioned in subsection (9) above are—
- (a) section 32;
- (b) section 36;
- (c) section 52;
- (d) section 60;
- (e) section 64;
- (f) section 65;
- (g) this section;
- (h) section 77; and
- (i) section 78.

(11) Subject to the foregoing provisions of this section, this Act shall come into operation on 1st January 1983.

Sub-s (6): in para (c)(i) words 'Senior Courts Act 1981' in square brackets substituted by the Constitutional Reform Act 2005, s 59(5), Sch 11, Pt 1, para 1(2). Date in force: 1 October 2009: see SI 2009/1604, art 2(d).

MENTAL HEALTH ACT 1983

(1983, C 20)

[9th May 1983]

PART VII
MANAGEMENT OF PROPERTY AND AFFAIRS OF PATIENTS

A1.387–A1.391

94–98 ...

...

Repealed by the Mental Capacity Act 2005, ss 66(1)(a), (2), 67(2), Sch 7.
Date in force: 1 October 2007: see SI 2007/1897, art 2(1)(c), (d); see the Mental Capacity Act 2005, s 68(1); for transitional provisions and savings see s 66(4), Sch 5, Pt I thereof.

A1.393 *Statutes*

COUNTY COURTS ACT 1984

(1984, C 28)

[26 June 1984]

PART II
FAMILY PROVISION PROCEEDINGS

PROBATE PROCEEDINGS

A1.393

[32   Contentious probate jurisdiction]

[(1) Where—

(a) an application for the grant or revocation of probate or administration has been made through the principal registry of the Family Division or a district probate registry under section 105 of the [Senior Courts Act 1981]; and
(b) it is shown to the satisfaction of a county court that the value at the date of the death of the deceased of his net estate does not exceed the county court limit,

the county court shall have the jurisdiction of the High Court in respect of any contentious matter arising in connection with the grant or revocation.

(2)   In subsection (1) 'net estate', in relation to a deceased person, means the estate of that person exclusive of any property he was possessed of or entitled to as a trustee and not beneficially, and after making allowances for funeral expenses and for debts and liabilities.]

Substituted by the Administration of Justice Act 1985, s 51(1).
Sub-s (1): in para (a) words 'Senior Courts Act 1981' in square brackets substituted by the Constitutional Reform Act 2005, s 59(5), Sch 11, Pt 1, para 1(2). Date in force: 1 October 2009: see SI 2009/1604, art 2(d).

A1.394

33   Effect of order of judge in probate proceedings

Where an order is made by a ... county court for the grant or revocation of probate or administration, in pursuance of any jurisdiction conferred upon [the court] by section 32—

(a) the [district judge] of the county court shall transmit to the principal registry of the Family Division or a district probate registry, as he thinks convenient, a certificate under the seal of the court certifying that the order has been made; and
(b) on the application of a party in favour of whom the order has been made, probate or administration in compliance with the order shall be issued from the registry to which the certificate was sent or, as the case may require, the probate or letters of administration previously granted shall be recalled or varied by, as the case may be, a [district judge] of the principal registry of the Family Division or the district probate registrar according to the effect of the order.

Words omitted repealed by the Administration of Justice Act 1985, s 67, Sch 7, para 7.
Words 'the court' in square brackets substituted by the Administration of Justice Act 1985, s 67, Sch 7, para 7, Sch 8, Pt III.

In para (a) words 'district judge' in square brackets substituted by the Courts and Legal Services Act 1990, s 74(1)(a), (3). Date in force: 1 January 1991.
In para (b) words 'district judge' in square brackets substituted by the Courts and Legal Services Act 1990, s 74(2). Date in force: 1 January 1991.

A1.396

41   Transfer to High Court by Order of High Court

(1)   If at any stage in proceedings commenced in a county court or transferred to a county court under section 40, the High Court thinks it desirable that the proceedings, or any part of them, should be heard and determined in the High Court, it may order the transfer to the High Court of the proceedings or, as the case may be, of that part of them.

(2)   The power conferred by subsection (1) is without prejudice to section 29 of the [Senior Courts Act 1981] (power of High Court to issue prerogative orders) [but shall be exercised in relation to family proceedings (within the meaning of Part V of the Matrimonial and Family Proceedings Act 1984) in accordance with any directions given under section 37 of that Act (directions as to distribution and transfer of family business and proceedings)].

[(3)   The power conferred by subsection (1) shall be exercised subject to any provision made—

(a)   under section 1 of the Courts and Legal Services Act 1990; or
(b)   by or under any other enactment.]

Sub-s (2): words 'Senior Courts Act 1981' in square brackets substituted by the Constitutional Reform Act 2005, s 59(5), Sch 11, Pt 1, para 1(2). Date in force: 1 October 2009: see SI 2009/1604, art 2(d).
Sub-s (2): words from 'but shall be' to 'business and proceedings)' in square brackets inserted by the Matrimonial and Family Proceedings Act 1984, s 46(1), Sch 1, para 30. Sub-s (3): inserted by the Courts and Legal Services Act 1990, s 2(2).

FAMILY LAW ACT 1986

(1986, C 55)

[7 November 1986]

PART III
DECLARATIONS OF STATUS

A1.416

[56   **Declarations of parentage, legitimacy or legitimation**]

[(1)   Any person may apply to [the High Court or a county court] for a declaration—

(a)   < ... >
(b)   that he is the legitimate child of his parents.

(2)   Any person may apply to [the High Court or a county court] for one (or for one or, in the alternative, the other) of the following declarations, that is to say—

(a)   a declaration that he has become a legitimated person;

(b) a declaration that he has not become a legitimated person.

(3) A court shall have jurisdiction to entertain an application under this section if, the applicant—
- (a) is domiciled in England and Wales on the date of the application; or
- (b) has been habitually resident in England and Wales throughout the period of one year ending with that date.

(4) Where a declaration is made [by a court] on an application under subsection (1) above, the prescribed officer of the court shall notify the Registrar General, in such a manner and within such period as may be prescribed, of the making of that declaration.

(5) In this section 'legitimated person' means a person legitimated or recognised as legitimated—
- (a) under section 2[, 2A] or 3 of the Legitimacy Act 1976;
- (b) under section 1 or 8 of the Legitimacy Act 1926; or
- (c) by a legitimation (whether or not by virtue of the subsequent marriage of his parents) recognised by the law of England and Wales and effected under the law of another country.]

Substituted by the Family Law Reform Act 1987, s 22.
Sub-ss (1), (2): words 'the High Court or a county court' in square brackets substituted by the Child Support, Pensions and Social Security Act 2000, s 83(5), Sch 8, paras 3, 5(a). Date in force: 1 April 2001 (except in relation to proceedings pursuant to an application under sub-s (1)(a) above which are pending immediately before that date): see the Child Support, Pensions and Social Security Act 2000, s 83(6)(a) and SI 2001/774, art 2(b), (c).
Sub-s (1): para (a) repealed by the Child Support, Pensions and Social Security Act 2000, s 85, Sch 9, Pt IX. Date in force: 1 April 2001: see SI 2001/774, art 2(d).
Sub-s (4): words 'by a court' in square brackets inserted by the Child Support, Pensions and Social Security Act 2000, s 83(5), Sch 8, paras 3, 5(b). Date in force: 1 April 2001 (except in relation to proceedings pursuant to an application under sub-s (1)(a) above which are pending immediately before that date): see the Child Support, Pensions and Social Security Act 2000, s 83(6)(a) and SI 2001/774, art 2(b), (c).
Sub-s (5): in para (a) reference to ', 2A' in square brackets inserted by the Human Fertilisation and Embryology Act 2008, s 56, Sch 6, Pt 1, para 23. Date in force (for certain purposes): 6 April 2009: see SI 2009/479, art 6(1)(e). Date in force (for remaining purposes): 1 September 2009: see SI 2009/479, art 6(2).

FAMILY LAW REFORM ACT 1987

(1987 C 42)

[15 May 1987]

PART I
GENERAL PRINCIPLE

A1.424

1   General principle

(1)   In this Act and enactments passed and instruments made after the coming into force of this section, references (however expressed) to any relationship between two persons shall, unless the contrary intention appears, be construed without regard to whether or not the father and mother of either of them, or the father and mother of any person through whom the relationship is deduced, have or had been married to each other at any time.

(2)   In this Act and enactments passed after the coming into force of this section, unless the contrary intention appears—

- (a)   references to a person whose father and mother were married to each other at the time of his birth include; and
- (b)   references to a person whose father and mother were not married to each other at the time of his birth do not include,

references to any person to whom subsection (3) below applies, and cognate references shall be construed accordingly.

(3)   This subsection applies to any person who—

- (a)   is treated as legitimate by virtue of section 1 of the Legitimacy Act 1976;
- (b)   is a legitimated person within the meaning of section 10 of that Act;
- [(ba) has a parent by virtue of section 42 of the Human Fertilisation and Embryology Act 2008 (which relates to treatment provided to a woman who is at the time of treatment a party to a civil partnership or, in certain circumstances, a void civil partnership);
- (bb)   has a parent by virtue of section 43 of that Act (which relates to treatment provided to woman who agrees that second woman to be parent) who—
  - (i)   is the civil partner of the child's mother at the time of the child's birth, or
  - (ii)   was the civil partner of the child's mother at any time during the period beginning with the time mentioned in section 43(b) of that Act and ending with the child's birth;]
- [(c)   is an adopted person within the meaning of Chapter 4 of Part 1 of the Adoption and Children Act 2002]; or
- (d)   is otherwise treated in law as legitimate.

(4)   For the purpose of construing references falling within subsection (2) above, the time of a person's birth shall be taken to include any time during the period beginning with—

- (a)   the insemination resulting in his birth; or
- (b)   where there was no such insemination, his conception,

and (in either case) ending with his birth.

[(5)   A child whose parents are parties to a void civil partnership shall, subject to subsection (6), be treated as falling within subsection (3)(bb) if at the time when the

A1.424 *Statutes*

parties registered as civil partners of each other both or either of the parties reasonably believed that the civil partnership was valid.

(6) Subsection (5) applies only where the woman who is a parent by virtue of section 43 was domiciled in England and Wales at the time of the birth or, if she died before the birth, was so domiciled immediately before her death.

(7) Subsection (5) applies even though the belief that the civil partnership was valid was due to a mistake as to law.

(8) It shall be presumed for the purposes of subsection (5), unless the contrary is shown, that one of the parties to a void civil partnership reasonably believed at the time of the formation of the civil partnership that the civil partnership was valid.]

Sub-s (3): paras (ba), (bb) inserted by the Human Fertilisation and Embryology Act 2008, s 56, Sch 6, Pt 1, paras 24(1), (2). Date in force: 6 April 2009: see SI 2009/479, art 6(1)(d).
Sub-s (3): para (c) substituted by the Adoption and Children Act 2002, s 139(1), Sch 3, paras 50, 51. Date in force: 30 December 2005: see SI 2005/2213, art 2(o).
Sub-ss (5)–(8): inserted by the Human Fertilisation and Embryology Act 2008, s 56, Sch 6, Pt 1, para 24(3). Date in force: 6 April 2009: see SI 2009/479, art 6(1)(d).

PART II
RIGHTS AND DUTIES OF PARENTS ETC.

Parental rights and duties: general

A1.425

2 Construction of enactments relating to parental rights and duties

(1) In the following enactments, namely—

(a) < ... >
(b) section 6 of the Family Law Reform Act 1969;
(c) the Guardianship of Minors Act 1971 (in this Act referred to as 'the 1971 Act');
(d) Part I of the Guardianship Act 1973 (in this Act referred to as 'the 1973 Act');
(e) Part II of the Children Act 1975;
(f) the Child Care Act 1980 except Part I and sections 13, 24, 64 and 65;
(g) < ... >

references (however expressed) to any relationship between two persons shall be construed in accordance with section 1 above.

(2) < ... >

Sub-s (1): para (a) repealed by the Health and Social Care Act 2008, s 166, Sch 15, Pt 5. Date in force (in relation to England): 6 April 2009: see SI 2009/462, art 4(c). Date in force (in relation to Wales): 6 April 2009: see SI 2009/631, art 2(c). Date in force (in relation to England): to be appointed: see the Health and Social Care Act 2008, s 170(3).
Sub-s (1): para (g) repealed by the Social Security (Consequential Provisions) Act 1992, s 3, Sch 1.
Sub-s (2): amends the Guardianship Act 1973, s 1(7).

PART III
PROPERTY RIGHTS

A1.431

18 Succession on intestacy

(1) In Part IV of the Administration of Estates Act 1925 (which deals with the distribution of the estate of an intestate), references (however expressed) to any relationship between two persons shall be construed in accordance with section 1 above.

Family Law Reform Act 1987 **A1.434**

(2) For the purposes of subsection (1) above and that Part of that Act, a person whose father and mother were not married to each other at the time of his birth shall be presumed not to have been survived by his father, or by any person related to him only through his father, unless the contrary is shown.

[(2A) In the case of a person who has a parent by virtue of section 43 of the Human Fertilisation and Embryology Act 2008 (treatment provided to woman who agrees that second woman to be parent), the second and third references in subsection (2) to the person's father are to be read as references to the woman who is a parent of the person by virtue of that section.]

(3) In [section 50(1) of the Administration of Estates Act 1925] (which relates to the construction of documents), the reference to Part IV of that Act, or to the foregoing provisions of that Part, shall in relation to an instrument inter vivos made, or a will or codicil coming into operation, after the coming into force of this section (but not in relation to instruments inter vivos made or wills or codicils coming into operation earlier) be construed as including references to this section.

(4) This section does not affect any rights under the intestacy of a person dying before the coming into force of this section.

Sub-s (2A): inserted by the Human Fertilisation and Embryology Act 2008, s 56, Sch 6, Pt 1, para 25(1), (2). Date in force: 6 April 2009: see SI 2009/479, art 6(1)(d).

Sub-s (3): words 'section 50(1) of the Administration of Estates Act 1925' in square brackets substituted by the Human Fertilisation and Embryology Act 2008, s 56, Sch 6, Pt 1, para 25(1), (3). Date in force: 6 April 2009: see SI 2009/479, art 6(1)(d).

A1.434

21   Entitlement to grant of probate etc

(1) For the purpose of determining the person or persons who would in accordance with probate rules be entitled to a grant of probate or administration in respect of the estate of a deceased person, the deceased shall be presumed, unless the contrary is shown, not to have been survived—

(a) by any person related to him whose father and mother were not married to each other at the time of his birth; or

(b) by any person whose relationship with him is deduced through such a person as is mentioned in paragraph (a) above.

(2) In this section 'probate rules' means rules of court made under section 127 of the [Senior Courts Act 1981].

(3) This section does not apply in relation to the estate of a person dying before the coming into force of this section.

Sub-s (2): words 'Senior Courts Act 1981' in square brackets substituted by the Constitutional Reform Act 2005, s 59(5), Sch 11, Pt 1, para 1(2). Date in force: 1 October 2009: see SI 2009/1604, art 2(d).

A1.448 *Statutes*

CHILDREN ACT 1989

(1989, C 41)

[16th November 1989]

PART I
INTRODUCTORY

A1.448

2   Parental responsibility for children

(1) Where a child's father and mother were married to each other at the time of his birth, they shall each have parental responsibility for the child.

[(1A) Where a child—

(a) has a parent by virtue of section 42 of the Human Fertilisation and Embryology Act 2008; or
(b) has a parent by virtue of section 43 of that Act and is a person to whom section 1(3) of the Family Law Reform Act 1987 applies,

the child's mother and the other parent shall each have parental responsibility for the child.]

(2) Where a child's father and mother were not married to each other at the time of his birth—

(a) the mother shall have parental responsibility for the child;
(b) the father [shall have parental responsibility for the child if he has acquired it (and has not ceased to have it)] in accordance with the provisions of this Act.

[(2A) Where a child has a parent by virtue of section 43 of the Human Fertilisation and Embryology Act 2008 and is not a person to whom section 1(3) of the Family Law Reform Act 1987 applies—

(a) the mother shall have parental responsibility for the child;
(b) the other parent shall have parental responsibility for the child if she has acquired it (and has not ceased to have it) in accordance with the provisions of this Act.]

(3) References in this Act to a child whose father and mother were, or (as the case may be) were not, married to each other at the time of his birth must be read with section 1 of the Family Law Reform Act 1987 (which extends their meaning).

(4) The rule of law that a father is the natural guardian of his legitimate child is abolished.

(5) More than one person may have parental responsibility for the same child at the same time.

(6) A person who has parental responsibility for a child at any time shall not cease to have that responsibility solely because some other person subsequently acquires parental responsibility for the child.

(7) Where more than one person has parental responsibility for a child, each of them may act alone and without the other (or others) in meeting that responsibility; but nothing in this Part shall be taken to affect the operation of any enactment which requires the consent of more than one person in a matter affecting the child.

Children Act 1989 **A1.450A**

(8) The fact that a person has parental responsibility for a child shall not entitle him to act in any way which would be incompatible with any order made with respect to the child under this Act.

(9) A person who has parental responsibility for a child may not surrender or transfer any part of that responsibility to another but may arrange for some or all of it to be met by one or more persons acting on his behalf.

(10) The person with whom any such arrangement is made may himself be a person who already has parental responsibility for the child concerned.

(11) The making of any such arrangement shall not affect any liability of the person making it which may arise from any failure to meet any part of his parental responsibility for the child concerned.

Sub-s (1A): inserted by the Human Fertilisation and Embryology Act 2008, s 56, Sch 6, Pt 1, para 26(1), (2). Date in force (for certain purposes): 6 April 2009: see SI 2009/479, art 6(1)(e). Date in force (for remaining purposes): 1 September 2009: see SI 2009/479, art 6(2).

Sub-s (2): in para (b) words 'shall have parental responsibility for the child if he has acquired it (and has not ceased to have it)' in square brackets substituted by the Adoption and Children Act 2002, s 111(5). Date in force: 1 December 2003: see SI 2003/3079, art 2(2)(a).

Sub-s (2A): inserted by the Human Fertilisation and Embryology Act 2008, s 56, Sch 6, Pt 1, para 26(1), (3). Date in force (for certain purposes): 6 April 2009: see SI 2009/479, art 6(1)(e). Date in force (for remaining purposes): 1 September 2009: see SI 2009/479, art 6(2).

A1.450A

[4ZA Acquisition of parental responsibility by second female parent]

[(1) Where a child has a parent by virtue of section 43 of the Human Fertilisation and Embryology Act 2008 and is not a person to whom section 1(3) of the Family Law Reform Act 1987 applies, that parent shall acquire parental responsibility for the child if—

(a) [except where subsection (3A) applies,] she becomes registered as a parent of the child under any of the enactments specified in subsection (2);
(b) she and the child's mother make an agreement providing for her to have parental responsibility for the child; or
(c) the court, on her application, orders that she shall have parental responsibility for the child.

(2) The enactments referred to in subsection (1)(a) are—

(a) paragraphs (a), (b) and (c) of section 10(1B) and of section 10A(1B) of the Births and Deaths Registration Act 1953;
[(aa) regulations under section 2C, 2D, 10B or 10C of the Births and Deaths Registration Act 1953;]
(b) paragraphs (a), (b) and (d) of section 18B(1) and sections 18B(3)(a) and 20(1)(a) of the Registration of Births, Deaths and Marriages (Scotland) Act 1965; and
(c) sub-paragraphs (a), (b) and (c) of Article 14ZA(3) of the Births and Deaths Registration (Northern Ireland) Order 1976.

(3) The Secretary of State may by order amend subsection (2) so as to add further enactments to the list in that subsection.

[(3A) A person who is a parent of a child by virtue of section 43 of the Human Fertilisation and Embryology Act 2008 does not acquire parental responsibility by virtue of subsection (1)(a) if, before she became registered as a parent of the child under the enactment in question—

A1.450A *Statutes*

(a) the court considered an application by her for an order under subsection (1)(c) in relation to the child but did not make such an order, or
(b) in a case where she had previously acquired parental responsibility for the child, the court ordered that she was to cease to have that responsibility.]

(4) An agreement under subsection (1)(b) is also a 'parental responsibility agreement', and section 4(2) applies in relation to such an agreement as it applies in relation to parental responsibility agreements under section 4.

(5) A person who has acquired parental responsibility under subsection (1) shall cease to have that responsibility only if the court so orders.

(6) The court may make an order under subsection (5) on the application—

(a) of any person who has parental responsibility for the child; or
(b) with the leave of the court, of the child himself,

subject, in the case of parental responsibility acquired under subsection (1)(c), to section 12(4).

(7) The court may only grant leave under subsection (6)(b) if it is satisfied that the child has sufficient understanding to make the proposed application.]
Inserted by the Human Fertilisation and Embryology Act 2008, s 56, Sch 6, Pt 1, para 27. Date in force (for certain purposes): 6 April 2009: see SI 2009/479, art 6(1)(e). Date in force (for remaining purposes): 1 September 2009: see SI 2009/479, art 6(2).
Sub-s (1): in para (a) words 'except where subsection (3A) applies,' in square brackets inserted by the Welfare Reform Act 2009, s 56, Sch 6, Pt 2, para 22(1), (2). Date in force: to be appointed: see the Welfare Reform Act 2009, s 61(3), (4).
Sub-s (2): para (aa) inserted by the Welfare Reform Act 2009, s 56, Sch 6, Pt 2, para 22(1), (3). Date in force: to be appointed: see the Welfare Reform Act 2009, s 61(3), (4).
Sub-s (3A): inserted by the Welfare Reform Act 2009, s 56, Sch 6, Pt 2, para 22(1), (4). Date in force: to be appointed: see the Welfare Reform Act 2009, s 61(3), (4).

PART II
ORDERS WITH RESPECT TO CHILDREN IN FAMILY PROCEEDINGS
General

A1.455

12 Residence orders and parental responsibility

(1) Where the court makes a residence order in favour of the father of a child it shall, if the father would not otherwise have parental responsibility for the child, also make an order under section 4 giving him that responsibility.

[(1A) Where the court makes a residence order in favour of a woman who is a parent of a child by virtue of section 43 of the Human Fertilisation and Embryology Act 2008 it shall, if that woman would not otherwise have parental responsibility for the child, also make an order under section 4ZA giving her that responsibility.]

(2) Where the court makes a residence order in favour of any person who is not the parent or guardian of the child concerned that person shall have parental responsibility for the child while the residence order remains in force.

(3) Where a person has parental responsibility for a child as a result of subsection (2), he shall not have the right—

(a) < ... >
(b) to agree, or refuse to agree, to the making of an adoption order, or an order under [section 84 of the Adoption and Children Act 2002], with respect to the child; or

(c) to appoint a guardian for the child.

(4) Where subsection (1) [or (1A)] requires the court to make an order under section 4 [or 4ZA] in respect of the *father* [parent] of a child, the court shall not bring that order to an end at any time while the residence order concerned remains in force.

[(5) < ... >

(6) < ... >]

Sub-s (1A): inserted by the Human Fertilisation and Embryology Act 2008, s 56, Sch 6, Pt 1, para 28(1), (2). Date in force (for certain purposes): 6 April 2009: see SI 2009/479, art 6(1)(e). Date in force (for remaining purposes): 1 September 2009: see SI 2009/479, art 6(2).
Sub-s (3): para (a) repealed by the Adoption and Children Act 2002, s 139(1), (3), Sch 3, paras 54, 57(a), Sch 5. Date in force: 30 December 2005: see SI 2005/2213, art 2(o).
Sub-s (3): in para (b) words 'section 84 of the Adoption and Children Act 2002' in square brackets substituted by the Adoption and Children Act 2002, s 139(1), Sch 3, paras 54, 57(b). Date in force: 30 December 2005: see SI 2005/2213, art 2(o).
Sub-s (4): words 'or (1A)' in square brackets inserted by the Human Fertilisation and Embryology Act 2008, s 56, Sch 6, Pt 1, para 28(1), (3)(a). Date in force (for certain purposes): 6 April 2009: see SI 2009/479, art 6(1)(e). Date in force (for remaining purposes): 1 September 2009: see SI 2009/479, art 6(2).
Sub-s (4): words 'or 4ZA' in square brackets inserted by the Human Fertilisation and Embryology Act 2008, s 56, Sch 6, Pt 1, para 28(1), (3)(b). Date in force (for certain purposes): 6 April 2009: see SI 2009/479, art 6(1)(e). Date in force (for remaining purposes): 1 September 2009: see SI 2009/479, art 6(2).
Sub-s (4): word 'father' in italics repealed and subsequent word in square brackets substituted by the Human Fertilisation and Embryology Act 2008, s 56, Sch 6, Pt 1, para 28(1), (3)(c). Date in force (for certain purposes): 6 April 2009: see SI 2009/479, art 6(1)(e). Date in force (for remaining purposes): 1 September 2009: see SI 2009/479, art 6(2).
Sub-ss (5), (6): inserted by the Adoption and Children Act 2002, s 114(1). Date in force: 30 December 2005: see SI 2005/2213, art 2(k).
Sub-ss (5), (6): repealed by the Children and Young Persons Act 2008, ss 37(2), 42, Sch 4. Date in force (in relation to Wales): 1 September 2009: see SI 2009/1921, art 2(b). Date in force (in relation to England): 1 September 2009: see SI 2009/2273, art 2(2)(k).

PART XII
MISCELLANEOUS AND GENERAL

* * * * *

Adoption

A1.459

88 Amendments of adoption legislation

(1) ...

* * * * *

Sub-s (1): repealed by the Adoption and Children Act 2002, s 139(1), (3), Sch 3, paras 54, 67, Sch 5. Date in force: 30 December 2005: see SI 2005/2213, art 2(o).

Effect and duration of orders etc

A1.460

91 Effect and duration of orders etc

(1) The making of a residence order with respect to a child who is the subject of a care order discharges the care order.

(2) The making of a care order with respect to a child who is the subject of any section 8 order discharges that order.

[(2A) Where a contact activity direction has been made as regards contact with a child, the making of a care order with respect to the child discharges the direction.]

(3) The making of a care order with respect to a child who is the subject of a supervision order discharges that other order.

(4) The making of a care order with respect to a child who is a ward of court brings that wardship to an end.

(5) The making of a care order with respect to a child who is the subject of a school attendance order made under [section 437 of the Education Act 1996] discharges the school attendance order.

[(5A) The making of a special guardianship order with respect to a child who is the subject of—

(a) a care order; or
(b) an order under section 34,

discharges that order.]

(6) Where an emergency protection order is made with respect to a child who is in care, the care order shall have effect subject to the emergency protection order.

(7) Any order made under section 4(1), [4ZA(1),] [4A(1)] or 5(1) shall continue in force until the child reaches the age of eighteen, unless it is brought to an end earlier.

(8) Any—

(a) agreement under section 4[, 4ZA] [or 4A]; or
(b) appointment under section 5(3) or (4),

shall continue in force until the child reaches the age of eighteen, unless it is brought to an end earlier.

(9) An order under Schedule 1 has effect as specified in that Schedule.

(10) A section 8 order [other than a residence order] shall, if it would otherwise still be in force, cease to have effect when the child reaches the age of sixteen, unless it is to have effect beyond that age by virtue of section 9(6) [< ... >].

(11) Where a section 8 order has effect with respect to a child who has reached the age of sixteen, it shall, if it would otherwise still be in force, cease to have effect when he reaches the age of eighteen.

(12) Any care order, other than an interim care order, shall continue in force until the child reaches the age of eighteen, unless it is brought to an end earlier.

(13) Any order made under any other provision of this Act in relation to a child shall, if it would otherwise still be in force, cease to have effect when he reaches the age of eighteen.

(14) On disposing of any application for an order under this Act, the court may (whether or not it makes any other order in response to the application) order that no application for an order under this Act of any specified kind may be made with respect to the child concerned by any person named in the order without leave of the court.

(15) Where an application ('the previous application') has been made for—

(a) the discharge of a care order;
(b) the discharge of a supervision order;
(c) the discharge of an education supervision order;

(d) the substitution of a supervision order for a care order; or
(e) a child assessment order,

no further application of a kind mentioned in paragraphs (*a*) to (*e*) may be made with respect to the child concerned, without leave of the court, unless the period between the disposal of the previous application and the making of the further application exceeds six months.

(16) Subsection (15) does not apply to applications made in relation to interim orders.

(17) Where—

(a) a person has made an application for an order under section 34;
(b) the application has been refused; and
(c) a period of less than six months has elapsed since the refusal,

that person may not make a further application for such an order with respect to the same child, unless he has obtained the leave of the court.

Sub-s (2A): inserted by the Children and Adoption Act 2006, s 15(1), Sch 2, paras 7, 9. Date in force: 8 December 2008: see SI 2008/2870, art 2(2)(e).
Sub-s (5): words in square brackets substituted by the Education Act 1996, s 582(1), Sch 37, para 90.
Sub-s (5A): inserted by the Adoption and Children Act 2002, s 139(a), Sch 3, paras 54, 68(a). Date in force: 30 December 2005: see SI 2005/2213, art 2(o).
Sub-s (7): reference to '4ZA(1),' in square brackets inserted by the Human Fertilisation and Embryology Act 2008, s 56, Sch 6, Pt 1, para 29(a). Date in force (for certain purposes): 6 April 2009: see SI 2009/479, art 6(1)(e). Date in force (for remaining purposes): 1 September 2009: see SI 2009/479, art 6(2).
Sub-s (7): reference to '4A(1)' in square brackets inserted by the Adoption and Children Act 2002, s 139(1), Sch 3, paras 54, 68(b). Date in force: 30 December 2005: see SI 2005/2213, art 2(o).
Sub-s (8): in sub-para (a) reference to ', 4ZA' in square brackets inserted by the Human Fertilisation and Embryology Act 2008, s 56, Sch 6, Pt 1, para 29(b). Date in force (for certain purposes): 6 April 2009: see SI 2009/479, art 6(1)(e). Date in force (for remaining purposes): 1 September 2009: see SI 2009/479, art 6(2).
Sub-s (8): in para (a) words 'or 4A' in square brackets inserted by the Adoption and Children Act 2002, s 139(1), Sch 3, paras 54, 68(c). Date in force: 30 December 2005: see SI 2005/2213, art 2(o).
Sub-s (10): words 'other than a residence order' in square brackets inserted by the Children and Young Persons Act 2008, s 37(3)(a). Date in force (in relation to Wales): 1 September 2009: see SI 2009/1921, art 2(b). Date in force (in relation to England): 1 September 2009: see SI 2009/2273, art 2(2)(k).
Sub-s (10): words 'or 12(5)' in square brackets inserted by the Adoption and Children Act 2002, s 114(3). Date in force: 30 December 2005: see SI 2005/2213, art 2(k).
Sub-s (10): words omitted repealed by the Children and Young Persons Act 2008, ss 37(3)(b), 42, Sch 4. Date in force (in relation to Wales): 1 September 2009: see SI 2009/1921, art 2(b). Date in force (in relation to England): 1 September 2009: see SI 2009/2273, art 2(2)(k).

A1.463

105 Interpretation

(1) In this Act—

'adoption agency' means a body which may be referred to as an adoption agency by virtue of [section 2 of the Adoption and Children Act 2002];
['appropriate children's home' has the meaning given by section 23;]
'bank holiday' means a day which is a bank holiday under the Banking and Financial Dealings Act 1971;
['care home' has the same meaning as in the Care Standards Act 2000;]

'care order' has the meaning given by section 31(11) and also includes any order which by or under any enactment has the effect of, or is deemed to be, a care order for the purposes of this Act; and any reference to a child who is in the care of an authority is a reference to a child who is in their care by virtue of a care order;

'child' means, subject to paragraph 16 of Schedule 1, a person under the age of eighteen;

'child assessment order' has the meaning given by section 43(2);

'child minder' has the meaning given by section 71;

['child of the family', in relation to parties to a marriage, or to two people who are civil partners of each other, means—
   (a) a child of both of them, and
   (b) any other child, other than a child placed with them as foster parents by a local authority or voluntary organisation, who has been treated by both of them as a child of their family;]

['children's home' has the meaning given by section 23;]

['children's home' has the same meaning as it has for the purposes of the Care Standards Act 2000 (see section 1 of that Act);]

'community home' has the meaning given by section 53;

['contact activity condition' has the meaning given by section 11C;]

['contact activity direction' has the meaning given by section 11A;]

'contact order' has the meaning given by section 8(1);

'day care' [(except in Part XA)] has the same meaning as in section 18;

'disabled', in relation to a child, has the same meaning as in section 17(11);

< ... >

'domestic premises' has the meaning given by section 71(12);

['dwelling-house' includes—
   (a) any building or part of a building which is occupied as a dwelling;
   (b) any caravan, house-boat or structure which is occupied as a dwelling;
and any yard, garden, garage or outhouse belonging to it and occupied with it;]

'education supervision order' has the meaning given in section 36;

'emergency protection order' means an order under section 44;

['enforcement order' has the meaning given by section 11J;]

'family assistance order' has the meaning given in section 16(2);

'family proceedings' has the meaning given by section 8(3);

'functions' includes powers and duties;

'guardian of a child' means a guardian (other than a guardian of the estate of a child) appointed in accordance with the provisions of section 5;

'harm' has the same meaning as in section 31(9) and the question of whether harm is significant shall be determined in accordance with section 31(10);

< ... >

'health service hospital' [means a health service hospital within the meaning given by the National Health Service Act 2006 or the National Health Service (Wales) Act 2006];

'hospital' [(except in Schedule 9A)] has the same meaning as in the Mental Health Act 1983, except that it does not include a *special hospital within the meaning of that Act* [hospital at which high security psychiatric services within the meaning of that Act are provided];

'ill-treatment' has the same meaning as in section 31(9);

['income-based jobseeker's allowance' has the same meaning as in the Jobseekers Act 1995;]

['income-related employment and support allowance' means an income-related allowance under Part 1 of the Welfare Reform Act 2007 (employment and support allowance);]

['independent hospital' has the same meaning as in the Care Standards Act 2000;]

'independent school' has the same meaning as in [the Education Act 1996];

'local authority' means, in relation to England < ... > , the council of a county, a metropolitan district, a London Borough or the Common Council of the City of London[, in relation to Wales, the council of a county or a county borough] and, in relation to Scotland, a local authority within the meaning of section 1(2) of the Social Work (Scotland) Act 1968;
'local authority foster parent' has the same meaning as in section 23(3);
['local authority foster parent' has the meaning given in section 22C(12);]
'local education authority' has the same meaning as in [the Education Act 1996];
['Local Health Board' means a Local Health Board established under section 11 of the National Health Service (Wales) Act 2006;]
'local housing authority' has the same meaning as in the Housing Act 1985;
< ... >
< ... >
['officer of the Service' has the same meaning as in the Criminal Justice and Court Services Act 2000;]
'parental responsibility' has the meaning given in section 3;
'parental responsibility agreement' has the meaning given in [sections 4(1)[, 4ZA(4)] and 4A(2)];
'prescribed' means prescribed by regulations made under this Act;
['private children's home' means a children's home in respect of which a person is registered under Part II of the Care Standards Act 2000 which is not a community home or a voluntary home;]
['Primary Care Trust' means a Primary Care Trust established under [section 18 of the National Health Service Act 2006];]
'privately fostered child' and 'to foster a child privately' have the same meaning as in section 66;
'prohibited steps order' has the meaning given by section 8(1);
< ... >
< ... >
'registered pupil' has the same meaning as in [the Education Act 1996];
'relative', in relation to a child, means a grandparent, brother, sister, uncle or aunt (whether of the full blood or half blood or [by marriage or civil partnership)] or step-parent;
'residence order' has the meaning given by section 8(1);
< ... >
'responsible person', in relation to a child who is the subject of a supervision order, has the meaning given in paragraph 1 of Schedule 3;
'school' has the same meaning as in [the Education Act 1996] or, in relation to Scotland, in the Education (Scotland) Act 1980;
['section 31A plan' has the meaning given by section 31A(6);]
'service', in relation to any provision made under Part III, includes any facility;
'signed', in relation to any person, includes the making by that person of his mark;
'special educational needs' has the same meaning as in [the Education Act 1996];
['special guardian' and 'special guardianship order' have the meaning given by section 14A;]
['Special Health Authority' means a Special Health Authority established under [section 28 of the National Health Service Act 2006 or section 22 of the National Health Service (Wales) Act 2006,];]
'specific issue order' has the meaning given by section 8(1);
['Strategic Health Authority' means a Strategic Health Authority established under [section 13 of the National Health Service Act 2006];]
'supervision order' has the meaning given by section 31(11);
'supervised child' and 'supervisor', in relation to a supervision order or an education supervision order, mean respectively the child who is (or is to be) under supervision and the person under whose supervision he is (or is to be) by virtue of the order;

A1.463 *Statutes*

'upbringing', in relation to any child, includes the care of the child but not his maintenance;

'voluntary home' has the meaning given by section 60;

'voluntary organisation' means a body (other than a public or local authority) whose activities are not carried on for profit;

['Welsh family proceedings officer' has the meaning given by section 35 of the Children Act 2004].

(2) References in this Act to a child whose father and mother were, or (as the case may be) were not, married to each other at the time of his birth must be read with section 1 of the Family Law Reform Act 1987 (which extends the meaning of such references).

(3) References in this Act to—

(a) a person with whom a child lives, or is to live, as the result of a residence order; or

(b) a person in whose favour a residence order is in force,

shall be construed as references to the person named in the order as the person with whom the child is to live.

(4) References in this Act to a child who is looked after by a local authority have the same meaning as they have (by virtue of section 22) in Part III.

(5) References in this Act to accommodation provided by or on behalf of a local authority are references to accommodation so provided in the exercise of functions [of that or any other local authority which are social services functions within the meaning of] the Local Authority Social Services Act 1970.

[(5A) References in this Act to a child minder shall be construed—

(a) < ... >;
(b) in relation to < ... > Wales, in accordance with section 79A.]

[(5B) References in this Act to acting as a child minder and to a child minder shall be construed, in relation to Scotland, in accordance with section 2(17) of the Regulation of Care (Scotland) Act 2001 (asp 8).]

(6) In determining the 'ordinary residence' of a child for any purpose of this Act, there shall be disregarded any period in which he lives in any place—

(a) which is a school or other institution;
(b) in accordance with the requirements of a supervision order under this Act < ... >
[(ba) in accordance with the requirements of a youth rehabilitation order under Part 1 of the Criminal Justice and Immigration Act 2008; or]
(c) while he is being provided with accommodation by or on behalf of a local authority.

(7) References in this Act to children who are in need shall be construed in accordance with section 17.

(8) Any notice or other document required under this Act to be served on any person may be served on him by being delivered personally to him, or being sent by post to him in a registered letter or by the recorded delivery service at his proper address.

(9) Any such notice or other document required to be served on a body corporate or a firm shall be duly served if it is served on the secretary or clerk of that body or a partner of that firm.

(10) For the purposes of this section, and of section 7 of the Interpretation Act 1978 in its application to this section, the proper address of a person—

Children Act 1989 **A1.463**

(a) in the case of a secretary or clerk of a body corporate, shall be that of the registered or principal office of that body;
(b) in the case of a partner of a firm, shall be that of the principal office of the firm; and
(c) in any other case, shall be the last known address of the person to be served.

Sub-s (1): in defintion 'adoption agency' words 'section 2 of the Adoption and Children Act 2002' in square brackets substituted by the Adoption and Children Act 2002, s 139(1), Sch 3, paras 54, 70(a). Date in force: 30 December 2005: see SI 2005/2213, art 2(o).

Sub-s (1): definition 'appropriate children's home' inserted by the Care Standards Act 2000, s 116, Sch 4, para 14(1), (23)(a)(i). Date in force (in relation to England): 1 April 2002: see SI 2001/4150, art 3(3)(a); for transitional provisions see SI 2001/4150, arts 3(2), 4(1), (3), (4) and SI 2002/1493, art 4 (as amended by SI 2002/1493, art 6). Date in force (in relation to Wales): 1 April 2002: see SI 2002/920, art 3(3)(d); for transitional provisions see arts 2, 3(2), (4), (6)–(10), Sch 1 thereto.

Sub-s (1): definition 'appropriate children's home' repealed by the Children and Young Persons Act 2008, ss 8(2), 42, Sch 1, para 3(1), (2), Sch 4. Date in force: to be appointed: see the Children and Young Persons Act 2008, s 44(3), (4), (5)(a).

Sub-s (1): definition 'care home' inserted by the Care Standards Act 2000, s 116, Sch 4, para 14(1), (23)(a)(ii). Date in force (in relation to England): 1 April 2002: see SI 2001/4150, art 3(3)(a); for transitional provisions see SI 2001/4150, arts 3(2), 4(1), (3), (4) and SI 2002/1493, art 4 (as amended by SI 2002/1493, art 6). Date in force (in relation to Wales): 1 April 2002: see SI 2002/920, art 3(3)(d); for transitional provisions see arts 2, 3(2), (4), (6)–(10), Sch 1 thereto.

Sub-s (1): definition 'child minder' repealed by the Care Standards Act 2000, s 117(2), Sch 6. Date in force (in relation to Wales): 1 April 2002: see SI 2002/920, art 3(3)(g)(vi); for transitional provisions see arts 2, 3(2), (5)–(10), Schs 1, 2 thereto. Date in force (in relation to England): to be appointed: see the Care Standards Act 2000, s 122.

Sub-s (1): definition 'child of the family' substituted by the Civil Partnership Act 2004, s 75(1), (3). Date in force: 5 December 2005: see SI 2005/3175, art 2(1), Sch 1.

Sub-s (1): definition 'children's home' substituted by the Care Standards Act 2000, s 116, Sch 4, para 14(1), (23)(a)(iii). Date in force (in relation to England): 1 April 2002: see SI 2001/4150, art 3(3)(a); for transitional provisions see SI 2001/4150, arts 3(2), 4(1), (3), (4) and SI 2002/1493, art 4 (as amended by SI 2002/1493, art 6). Date in force (in relation to Wales): 1 April 2002: see SI 2002/920, art 3(3)(d); for transitional provisions see arts 2, 3(2), (4), (6)–(10), Sch 1 thereto.

Sub-s (1): definition 'children's home' further substituted by the Children and Young Persons Act 2008, s 8(2), Sch 1, para 3(1), (3). Date in force: to be appointed: see the Children and Young Persons Act 2008, s 44(3), (4), (5)(a).

Sub-s (1): definition 'contact activity condition' inserted by the Children and Adoption Act 2006, s 15(1), Sch 2, paras 7, 11. Date in force: 8 December 2008: see SI 2008/2870, art 2(2)(e).

Sub-s (1): definition 'contact activity direction' inserted by the Children and Adoption Act 2006, s 15(1), Sch 2, paras 7, 11. Date in force: 8 December 2008: see SI 2008/2870, art 2(2)(e).

Sub-s (1): in definition 'day care' words '(except in Part XA)' in square brackets inserted by the Care Standards Act 2000, s 116, Sch 4, para 14(1), (23)(a)(iv). Date in force (in relation to England): 2 July 2001: see SI 2001/2041, art 2(1)(d)(ii). Date in force (in relation to Wales): 1 April 2002: see SI 2002/920, art 3(3)(d); for transitional provisions see arts 2, 3(2), (4), (6)–(10), Schs 1, 2 thereto.

Sub-s (1): definition 'district health authority' (omitted) repealed by the Health Authorities Act 1995, ss 2(1), 5(1), Sch 1, para 118(10)(a), Sch 3.

Sub-s (1): definition 'dwelling house' inserted by the Family Law Act 1996, s 52, Sch 6, para 5. Date in force: 1 October 1997: see SI 1997/1892, art 3(1)(a).

Sub-s (1): definition 'enforcement order' inserted by the Children and Adoption Act 2006, s 15(1), Sch 2, paras 7, 11. Date in force: 8 December 2008: see SI 2008/2870, art 2(2)(e).

Sub-s (1): definition 'Health Authority' (omitted) repealed by the National Health Service (Consequential Provisions) Act 2006, s 2, Sch 1, paras 124, 125(a). Date in force: 1 March 2007: see the National Health Service (Consequential Provisions) Act 2006, s 8(2).

Sub-s (1): in definition 'health service hospital' words from 'means a health' to 'National Health Service (Wales) Act 2006' in square brackets substituted by the National Health Service (Consequential Provisions) Act 2006, s 2, Sch 1, paras 124, 125(b). Date in force: 1 March 2007: see the National Health Service (Consequential Provisions) Act 2006, s 8(2).

Sub-s (1): in definition 'hospital' words '(except in Schedule 9A)' in square brackets inserted by the Care Standards Act 2000, s 116, Sch 4, para 14(1), (23)(a)(v). Date in force (in relation to

A1.463 *Statutes*

England): 2 July 2001: see SI 2001/2041, art 2(1)(d)(ii). Date in force (in relation to Wales): 1 April 2002: see SI 2002/920, art 3(3)(d); for transitional provisions see arts 2, 3(2), (4), (6)–(10), Schs 1, 2 thereto.
Sub-s (1): in definition 'hospital' words 'special hospital within the meaning of that Act' in italics repealed and subsequent words in square brackets substituted, in relation to England and Wales only, by SI 2000/90, arts 2(1), 3(2), Sch 2, para 5. Date in force: 1 April 2000: see SI 2000/90, art 1.
Sub-s (1): definition 'income-based jobseeker's allowance' inserted by the Jobseekers Act 1995, s 41(4), Sch 2, para 19(4).
Sub-s (1): definition 'income-related employment and support allowance' inserted, in relation to England and Wales, by the Welfare Reform Act 2007, s 28(1), Sch 3, para 6(1), (5). Date in force: 27 October 2008: see SI 2008/787, art 2(4)(b), (f).
Sub-s (1): definition 'independent hospital' inserted by the Care Standards Act 2000, s 116, Sch 4, para 14(1), (23)(a)(vi). Date in force (in relation to England): 1 April 2002: see SI 2001/4150, art 3(3)(a); for transitional provisions see SI 2001/4150, arts 3(2), 4(1), (3), (4) and SI 2002/1493, art 4 (as amended by SI 2002/1493, art 6). Date in force (in relation to Wales): 1 April 2002: see SI 2002/920, art 3(3)(d); for transitional provisions see arts 2, 3(2), (4), (6)–(10), Sch 1 thereto.
Sub-s (1): in definitions 'independent school', 'local education authority', 'registered pupil', 'school' and 'special educational needs' words 'the Education Act 1996' in square brackets substituted by the Education Act 1996, s 582(1), Sch 37, para 91.
Sub-s (1): in definition 'local authority' words omitted repealed by the Local Government (Wales) Act 1994, ss 22(4), 66(8), Sch 10, para 13, Sch 18.
Sub-s (1): in definition 'local authority' words ', in relation to Wales, the council of a county or a county borough' in square brackets inserted by the Local Government (Wales) Act 1994, ss 22(4), 66(8), Sch 10, para 13.
Sub-s (1): definition 'local authority foster parent' substituted by the Children and Young Persons Act 2008, s 8(2), Sch 1, para 3(1), (4). Date in force: to be appointed: see the Children and Young Persons Act 2008, s 44(3), (4), (5)(a).
Sub-s (1): definition 'Local Health Board' inserted by SI 2007/961, art 3, Schedule, para 20(1), (3). Date in force: 1 April 2007: see SI 2007/961, art 1(1).
Sub-s (1): definition 'mental nursing home' (omitted) repealed by the Care Standards Act 2000, s 117(2), Sch 6. Date in force (in relation to England): 1 April 2002: see SI 2001/4150, art 3(3)(c)(viii); for transitional provisions see SI 2001/4150, arts 3(2), 4(1)–(3), (5) and SI 2002/1493, art 4 (as amended by SI 2002/1493, art 6). Date in force (in relation to Wales): 1 April 2002: see SI 2002/920, art 3(3)(g)(vi); for transitional provisions see arts 2, 3(2), (5)–(10), Sch 1 thereto.
Sub-s (1): definition 'nursing home' (omitted) repealed by the Care Standards Act 2000, s 117(2), Sch 6. Date in force (in relation to England): 1 April 2002: see SI 2001/4150, art 3(3)(c)(viii); for transitional provisions see SI 2001/4150, arts 3(2), 4(1)–(3), (5) and SI 2002/1493, art 4 (as amended by SI 2002/1493, art 6). Date in force (in relation to Wales): 1 April 2002: see SI 2002/920, art 3(3)(g)(vi); for transitional provisions see arts 2, 3(2), (5)–(10), Sch 1 thereto.
Sub-s (1): definition 'officer of the Service' inserted by the Criminal Justice and Court Services Act 2000, s 74, Sch 7, Pt II, paras 87, 95. Date in force: 1 April 2001: see SI 2001/919, art 2(f)(ii).
Sub-s (1): in definition 'parental responsibility agreement' words 'sections 4(1) and 4A(2)' in square brackets substituted by the Adoption and Children Act 2002, s 139(1), Sch 3, paras 54, 70(c). Date in force: 30 December 2005: see SI 2005/2213, art 2(o).
Sub-s (1): in definition 'parental responsibility agreement' reference to ', 4ZA(4)' in square brackets inserted by the Human Fertilisation and Embryology Act 2008, s 56, Sch 6, Pt 1, para 31. Date in force (for certain purposes): 6 April 2009: see SI 2009/479, art 6(1)(e). Date in force (for remaining purposes): 1 September 2009: see SI 2009/479, art 6(2).
Sub-s (1): definition 'private children's home' inserted by the Care Standards Act 2000, s 116, Sch 4, para 14(1), (23)(a)(vii). Date in force (in relation to England): 1 April 2002: see SI 2001/4150, art 3(3)(a); for transitional provisions see SI 2001/4150, arts 3(2), 4(1), (3), (4) and SI 2002/1493, art 4 (as amended by SI 2002/1493, art 6). Date in force (in relation to Wales): 1 April 2002: see SI 2002/920, art 3(3)(d); for transitional provisions see arts 2, 3(2), (4), (6)–(10), Sch 1 thereto.
Sub-s (1): definition 'Primary Care Trust' inserted, in relation to England and Wales only, by SI 2000/90, arts 2(1), 3(1), Sch 1, para 24(1), (10). Date in force: 8 February 2000: see SI 2000/90, art 1.
Sub-s (1): in definition 'Primary Care Trust' words 'section 18 of the National Health Service Act 2006' in square brackets substituted by the National Health Service (Consequential

Provisions) Act 2006, s 2, Sch 1, paras 124, 125(c). Date in force: 1 March 2007: see the National Health Service (Consequential Provisions) Act 2006, s 8(2).

Sub-s (1): definition 'protected child' (omitted) repealed by the Adoption and Children Act 2002, s 139(1), (3), Sch 3, paras 54, 70(d), Sch 5. Date in force: 30 December 2005: see SI 2005/2213, art 2(o).

Sub-s (1): definition 'registered children's home' (omitted) repealed by the Care Standards Act 2000, s 117(2), Sch 6. Date in force (in relation to England): 1 April 2002: see SI 2001/4150, art 3(3)(c)(viii); for transitional provisions see SI 2001/4150, arts 3(2), 4(1)–(3), (5) and SI 2002/1493, art 4 (as amended by SI 2002/1493, art 6). Date in force (in relation to Wales): 1 April 2002: see SI 2002/920, art 3(3)(g)(vi); for transitional provisions see arts 2, 3(2), (5)–(10), Schs 1, 3 thereto.

Sub-s (1): in definition 'relative' words 'by marriage or civil partnership)' in square brackets substituted by the Civil Partnership Act 2004, s 75(1), (4). Date in force: 5 December 2005: see SI 2005/3175, art 2(1), Sch 1.

Sub-s (1): definition 'residential care home' (omitted) repealed by the Care Standards Act 2000, s 117(2), Sch 6. Date in force (in relation to England): 1 April 2002: see SI 2001/4150, art 3(3)(c)(viii); for transitional provisions see SI 2001/4150, arts 3(2), 4(1)–(3), (5) and SI 2002/1493, art 4 (as amended by SI 2002/1493, art 6). Date in force (in relation to Wales): 1 April 2002: see SI 2002/920, art 3(3)(g)(vi); for transitional provisions see arts 2, 3(2), (5)–(10), Sch 1 thereto.

Sub-s (1): definition 'section 31A plan' inserted by the Adoption and Children Act 2002, s 139(1), Sch 3, paras 54, 70(b). Date in force: 30 December 2005: see SI 2005/2213, art 2(o).

Sub-s (1): definition 'special guardian' and 'special guardianship order' inserted by the Adoption and Children Act 2002, s 139(1), Sch 3, paras 54, 70(e). Date in force: 30 December 2005: see SI 2005/2213, art 2(o).

Sub-s (1): definition 'Special Health Authority' substituted by the Health Authorities Act 1995, ss 2(1), 5(1), Sch 1, para 118(10)(c).

Sub-s (1): in definition 'Special Health Authority' words from 'section 28 of' to 'National Health Service (Wales) Act 2006,' in square brackets substituted by the National Health Service (Consequential Provisions) Act 2006, s 2, Sch 1, paras 124, 125(d). Date in force: 1 March 2007: see the National Health Service (Consequential Provisions) Act 2006, s 8(2).

Sub-s (1): definition 'Strategic Health Authority' inserted by SI 2002/2469, reg 4, Sch 1, Pt 1, para 16(1), (3). Date in force: 1 October 2002: see SI 2002/2469, reg 1.

Sub-s (1): in definition 'Strategic Health Authority' words 'section 13 of the National Health Service Act 2006' in square brackets substituted by the National Health Service (Consequential Provisions) Act 2006, s 2, Sch 1, paras 124, 125(e). Date in force: 1 March 2007: see the National Health Service (Consequential Provisions) Act 2006, s 8(2).

Sub-s (1): definition 'Welsh family proceedings officer' inserted by the Children Act 2004, s 40, Sch 3, paras 5, 11. Date in force: 1 April 2005: by virtue of SI 2005/700, art 2(2).

Sub-s (5): words from 'of that or any other' to 'within the meaning of' in square brackets substituted by the Local Government Act 2000, s 107, Sch 5, para 22. Date in force (in relation to England): 26 October 2000: see SI 2000/2849, art 2(f). Date in force (in relation to Wales): 28 July 2001 (unless the National Assembly for Wales by order provides for this amendment to come into force before that date): see the Local Government Act 2000, s 108(4), (6)(b).

Sub-s (5A): inserted by the Care Standards Act 2000, s 116, Sch 4, para 14(1), (23)(b). Date in force (in relation to England): 2 July 2001: see SI 2001/2041, art 2(1)(d)(ii). Date in force (in relation to Wales): 1 April 2002: see SI 2002/920, art 3(3)(d); for transitional provisions see arts 2, 3(2), (4), (6)–(10), Schs 1, 2 thereto.

Sub-s (5A): para (a) repealed, in relation to Scotland, by the Regulation of Care (Scotland) Act 2001, s 79, Sch 3, paras 15(1), (2)(a). Date in force: 1 April 2002: see the Regulation of Care (Scotland) Act 2001, s 81(2) and SSI 2002/162, arts 1(2), 2(f), (h); for transitional provisions see SSI 2002/162, arts 3, 4(6), (9), (10), 7, 8(c), 12, 13.

Sub-s (5A): in para (b) words omitted repealed by the Childcare Act 2006, s 103, Sch 2, para 17, Sch 3, Pt 2. Date in force: 1 September 2008: see SI 2008/2261, art 2; for transitional provisions and savings see arts 3, 4, Schs 1, 2 thereto.

Sub-s (5B): inserted, in relation to Scotland, by the Regulation of Care (Scotland) Act 2001, s 79, Sch 3, paras 15(1), (2)(b). Date in force: 1 April 2002: see the Regulation of Care (Scotland) Act 2001, s 81(2) and SSI 2002/162, arts 1(2), 2(f), (h); for transitional provisions see SSI 2002/162, arts 3, 4(6), (9), (10), 7, 8(c), 12, 13.

Sub-s (6): in para (b) words omitted repealed by the Criminal Justice and Immigration Act 2008, ss 6(2), 149, Sch 4, Pt 1, paras 33, 36(a), Sch 28, Pt 1. Date in force: 30 November 2009: see

A1.463 *Statutes*

SI 2009/3074, art 2(f), (k), (l), (p)(v), (t)(i), (u)(xi); for transitional provisions and savings see the Criminal Justice and Immigration Act 2008, s 148(2), Sch 27, Pt 1, paras 1(1), 5.
Sub-s (6): para (ba) inserted by the Criminal Justice and Immigration Act 2008, s 6(2), Sch 4, Pt 1, paras 33, 36(b). Date in force: 30 November 2009: see SI 2009/3074, art 2(f), (k), (p)(v), (t)(i); for transitional provisions and savings see the Criminal Justice and Immigration Act 2008, s 148(2), Sch 27, Pt 1, paras 1(1), 5.

ACCESS TO HEALTH RECORDS ACT 1990

(1990 C 23)

[13th July 1990]

Preliminary

A1.469

1 'Health record' and related expressions

(1) In this Act 'health record' means a record which—

   (a) consists of information relating to the physical or mental health of an individual who can be identified from that information, or from that and other information in the possession of the holder of the record; and

   (b) has been made by or on behalf of a health professional in connection with the care of that individual ...

(2) In this Act 'holder', in relation to a health record, means—

   [(a) in the case of a record made by a health professional performing primary medical services under a general medical services contract made with a Primary Care Trust or Local Health Board, the person or body who entered into the contract with the Trust or Board (or, in a case where more than one person so entered into the contract, any such person);

   (aa) in the case of a record made by a health professional performing such services in accordance with arrangements under [section 92 or 107 of the National Health Service Act 2006, or section 50 or 64 of the National Health Service (Wales) Act 2006,] with a Primary Care Trust, Strategic Health Authority or Local Health Board, the person or body which made the arrangements with the Trust, Authority or Board (or, in a case where more than one person so made the arrangements, any such person);]

   (b) in the case of a record made by a health professional for purposes connected with the provision of health services by a health service body [(and not falling within paragraph (aa) above)], the health service body by which or on whose behalf the record is held;

   (c) in any other case, the health professional by whom or on whose behalf the record is held.

(3) In this Act 'patient', in relation to a health record, means the individual in connection with whose care the record has been made.

Sub-s (1): words omitted repealed with savings by the Data Protection Act 1998, s 74(2), Sch 16, Pt I; for savings see Sch 14, para 17 thereto. Date in force: 1 March 2000: see SI 2000/183, art 2(1).
Sub-s (2): paras (a), (aa) substituted in relation to England and Wales, for para (a) as originally enacted, by the Health and Social Care (Community Health and Standards) Act 2003, s 184,

Sch 11, para 57(1), (2), (6); a corresponding amendment has been made in relation to Scotland by SSI 2004/167, art 2, Schedule, para 3(1), (2). Date in force (in relation to England): 1 April 2004: see SI 2004/288, art 5(1), (2)(v). Date in force (in relation to Scotland): 1 April 2004: see SSI 2004/167, art 1. Date in force (in relation to Wales): 1 April 2004: see SI 2004/480, art 4(1), (2)(z).

Sub-s (2): in para (aa) words from 'section 92 or 107' to 'National Health Service (Wales) Act 2006,' in square brackets substituted by the National Health Service (Consequential Provisions) Act 2006, s 2, Sch 1, paras 134, 135. Date in force: 1 March 2007: see the National Health Service (Consequential Provisions) Act 2006, s 8(2).

Sub-s (2): in para (b) words '(and not falling within paragraph (aa) above)' in square brackets inserted in relation to England and Wales by the Health and Social Care (Community Health and Standards) Act 2003, s 184, Sch 11, para 57(1), (3), (6) and in relation to Scotland by SSI 2004/167, art 2, Schedule, para 3(1), (3). Date in force (in relation to England): 1 April 2004: see SI 2004/288, art 5(1), (2)(v). Date in force (in relation to Scotland): 1 April 2004: see SSI 2004/167, art 1. Date in force (in relation to Wales): 1 April 2004: see SI 2004/480, art 4(1), (2)(z).

Sub-s (2)(a) modified, during the existence of default contracts entered into pursuant to the General Medical Services (Transitional and Other Ancillary Provisions) (Scotland) Order 2004, SSI 2004/142, art 13, by the General Medical Services and Section 17C Agreements (Transitional and other Ancillary Provisions) (Scotland) Order 2004, SSI 2004/163, art 96(1), (2)(a).

See further, in relation to England, the General Medical Services and Personal Medical Services Transitional and Consequential Provisions Order 2004, SI 2004/865, art 109(1), (2)(c), which provides that until such time as default contracts entered into pursuant to the Health and Social Care (Community Health and Standards) Act 2003, s 176(3) cease to exist, any reference to a general medical services contract shall include a reference to a default contract.

See further, in relation to Wales, the General Medical Services Transitional and Consequential Provisions (Wales) (No 2) Order 2004, SI 2004/1016, art 85(1), (2)(c), which provides that until such time as default contracts entered into pursuant to the Health and Social Care (Community Health and Standards) Act 2003, s 176(3) cease to exist, any reference to a general medical services contract shall include a reference to a default contract.

Supplemental

A1.479

11   Interpretation

In this Act—

'application' means an application in writing and 'apply' shall be construed accordingly;
'care' includes examination, investigation, diagnosis and treatment;
...
['general medical services contract' means a contract under section 84 of the National Health Service Act 2006 or section 42 of the National Health Service (Wales) Act 2006];]
...
[...]
'Health Board' has the same meaning as in the National Health Service (Scotland) Act 1978;
'health service body' means—
- [(a) [a Strategic Health Authority, Health Authority] *or Special Health Authority* [, Special Health Authority or Primary Care Trust];]
- (b) a Health Board;
- (c) ... ..
- (d) a National Health Service trust first established under section 5 of the National Health Service and Community Care Act 1990[, section 25 of the National Health Service Act 2006 or section 18 of the National Health Service (Wales) Act 2006] or section 12A of the National Health Service (Scotland) Act 1978;

A1.479 *Statutes*

[(e) an NHS foundation trust;]
'information', in relation to a health record, includes any expression of opinion about the patient;
['Local Health Board' means a Local Health Board established under section 11 of the National Health Service (Wales) Act 2006;]
'make', in relation to such a record, includes compile;
…
['Primary Care Trust' means a Primary Care Trust established under [section 18 of the National Health Service Act 2006];]
['Special Health Authority' means a Special Health Authority established under [section 28 of the National Health Service Act 2006 or section 22 of the National Health Service (Wales) Act 2006];]
['Strategic Health Authority' means a Strategic Health Authority established under [section 13 of the National Health Service Act 2006]].

Definition 'child' (omitted) repealed with savings by the Data Protection Act 1998, s 74(2), Sch 16, Pt I; for savings see Sch 14, para 17 thereto. Date in force: 1 March 2000: see SI 2000/183, art 2(1).

Definition 'general medical services contract' inserted in relation to England and Wales by the Health and Social Care (Community Health and Standards) Act 2003, s 184, Sch 11, para 57(1), (5)(a), (6); a corresponding amendment has been made in relation to Scotland by SSI 2004/167, art 2, Schedule, para 3(1), (5)(a). Date in force (in relation to England): 1 April 2004: see SI 2004/288, art 5(1), (2)(v). Date in force (in relation to Scotland): 1 April 2004: see SSI 2004/167, art 1. Date in force (in relation to Wales): 1 April 2004: see SI 2004/480, art 4(1), (2)(z).

In definition 'general medical services contract' words from 'section 84 of' to 'National Health Service (Wales) Act 2006' in square brackets substituted by the National Health Service (Consequential Provisions) Act 2006, s 2, Sch 1, paras 134, 136(a). Date in force: 1 March 2007: see the National Health Service (Consequential Provisions) Act 2006, s 8(2).

Definition 'general practitioner' (omitted) repealed in relation to England and Wales by the Health and Social Care (Community Health and Standards) Act 2003, ss 184, 196, Sch 11, para 57(1), (5)(b), (6), Sch 14, Pt 4 and in relation to Scotland by SSI 2004/167, art 2, Schedule, para 3(1), (5)(b). Date in force (in relation to England): 1 April 2004: see SI 2004/288, arts 5(1), (2)(v), 6(1), (2)(j). Date in force (in relation to Scotland): 1 April 2004: see SSI 2004/167, art 1. Date in force (in relation to Wales): 1 April 2004: see SI 2004/480, arts 4(1), (2)(z), 5(1), (2)(j) (as amended by SI 2004/1019, art 2(4)).

Definitions 'Health Authority' (omitted), 'Special Health Authority' inserted by the Health Authorities Act 1995, s 2(1), Sch 1, para 119(4).

Definition 'Health Authority' (omitted) repealed by the National Health Service (Consequential Provisions) Act 2006, ss 2, 6, Sch 1, paras 134, 136(b), Sch 4.
Date in force: 1 March 2007: see the National Health Service (Consequential Provisions) Act 2006, s 8(2).

In definition 'health service body' para (a) substituted by the Health Authorities Act 1995, s 2(1), Sch 1, para 119(4).

In definition 'health service body' in para (a) words 'a Strategic Health Authority, Health Authority' in square brackets substituted by SI 2002/2469, reg 4, Sch 1, Pt 1, para 17(a). Date in force: 1 October 2002: see SI 2002/2469, reg 1.

In definition 'health service body' in para (a) words 'or Special Health Authority' in italics repealed and subsequent words in square brackets substituted, in relation to England and Wales only, by SI 2000/90, arts 2(1), 3(1), Sch 1, para 25(a). Date in force: 8 February 2000: see SI 2000/90, art 1.

In definition 'health service body' para (c) repealed by the Mental Health (Care and Treatment) (Scotland) Act 2003, s 331(2), Sch 5, Pt 1. Date in force: 5 October 2005: see SSI 2005/161, art 3.

In definition 'health service body' in para (c) word omitted repealed by the Health and Social Care (Community Health and Standards) Act 2003, ss 34, 196, Sch 4, paras 87, 88, Sch 14, Pt 1. Date in force: 1 April 2004: see SI 2004/759, arts 2, 12.

In definition 'health service body' in para (d) words from ', section 25 of' to 'National Health Service (Wales) Act 2006' in square brackets inserted by the National Health Service (Consequential Provisions) Act 2006, s 2, Sch 1, paras 134, 136(c). Date in force: 1 March 2007: see the National Health Service (Consequential Provisions) Act 2006, s 8(2).

In definition 'health service body' para (e) inserted by the Health and Social Care (Community Health and Standards) Act 2003, s 34, Sch 4, paras 87, 88. Date in force: 1 April 2004: see SI 2004/759, art 2.
Definition 'Local Health Board' inserted by SI 2007/961, art 3, Schedule, para 21(1), (2)(b). Date in force: 1 April 2007: see SI 2007/961, art 1(1).
Definition 'parental responsibility' (omitted) repealed with savings by the Data Protection Act 1998, s 74(2), Sch 16, Pt I; for savings see Sch 14, para 17 thereto. Date in force: 1 March 2000: see SI 2000/183, art 2(1).
Definition 'Primary Care Trust' inserted, in relation to England and Wales only, by SI 2000/90, arts 2(1), 3(1), Sch 1, para 25(b). Date in force: 8 February 2000: see SI 2000/90, art 1.
In definition 'Primary Care Trust' words 'section 18 of the National Health Service Act 2006' in square brackets substituted by the National Health Service (Consequential Provisions) Act 2006, s 2, Sch 1, paras 134, 136(d). Date in force: 1 March 2007: see the National Health Service (Consequential Provisions) Act 2006, s 8(2).
In definition 'Special Health Authority' words from 'section 28 of' to 'National Health Service (Wales) Act 2006' in square brackets substituted by the National Health Service (Consequential Provisions) Act 2006, s 2, Sch 1, paras 134, 136(e). Date in force: 1 March 2007: see the National Health Service (Consequential Provisions) Act 2006, s 8(2).
Definition 'Strategic Health Authority' inserted by SI 2002/2469, reg 4, Sch 1, Pt 1, para 17(b). Date in force: 1 October 2002: see SI 2002/2469, reg 1.
In definition 'Strategic Health Authority' words 'section 13 of the National Health Service Act 2006' in square brackets substituted by the National Health Service (Consequential Provisions) Act 2006, s 2, Sch 1, paras 134, 136(f). Date in force: 1 March 2007: see the National Health Service (Consequential Provisions) Act 2006, s 8(2).

COURTS AND LEGAL SERVICES ACT 1990

(1990, C 41)

[1 November 1990]

Part II
Legal Services

Licensed conveyancers

A1.480A

53 The Council for Licensed Conveyancers

(1) Subject to subsection (2), the Council for Licensed Conveyancers shall have the powers necessary to enable it to become—

(a) an authorised body for the purposes of granting rights of audience under section 27(2)(a);
(b) an authorised body for the purposes of granting rights to conduct litigation under section 28(2)(a); and
(c) an approved body for the purposes of granting, in accordance with section 55, exemption from the provisions of section 23(1) of the Solicitors Act 1974 (preparation of probate papers).

(2) The Council may exercise the powers given to it by this section only with respect to persons who are licensed conveyancers.

(3) Where the Council—

A1.480A *Statutes*

(a) becomes an authorised body for the purposes of section 27 and grants any right of audience;
(b) becomes an authorised body for the purposes of section 28 and grants any right to conduct litigation; or
(c) becomes an approved body for the purposes of section 55 and grants an exemption under that section,

it shall do so by issuing a licence to the licensed conveyancer to whom the right or exemption is being granted.

[(1) The Council for Licensed Conveyancers has the powers necessary to enable it to become designated as an approved regulator in relation to one or more of the reserved legal activities within subsection (1A).

(1A) The reserved legal activities to which this subsection applies are—

(a) the exercise of a right of audience;
(b) the conduct of litigation;
(c) probate activities.

(2) If the Council becomes an approved regulator in relation to one or more of those activities, it may, in that capacity, authorise a person to carry on a relevant activity only if the person is a licensed conveyancer.

(3) Where the Council authorises a licensed conveyancer to carry on a relevant activity, it is to do so by issuing a licence to the licensed conveyancer.]

(4) Any such licence may be granted as a separate licence or as part of a composite licence comprising the licensed conveyancer's licence issued under Part II of the Administration of Justice Act 1985 and any other licence which the Council may grant to the licensed conveyancer concerned.

(5) *The Council's general duty shall include the duty to ensure that the standards of competence and professional conduct among licensed conveyancers who are granted rights of audience, rights to conduct litigation or an exemption under section 55 are sufficient to secure adequate protection for consumers, and that the advocacy, litigation or (as the case may be) probate services provided by such persons are provided both economically and efficiently.*

(6) *Where the Council exercises any of its powers in connection with—*

(a) an application under [Schedule 4] for authorisation or an application under Schedule 9 for approval; or
(b) the granting of any right of audience or right to conduct litigation or of an exemption under section 55,

it shall do so subject to any requirements to which it is subject in accordance with the provisions of this Act relating to the grant of any such right or exemption.

[(6) Where the Council exercises any of its powers in connection with—

(a) an application for designation as an approved regulator in relation to a reserved legal activity within subsection (1A), or
(b) the authorising of a person to carry on a relevant activity,

it is to do so subject to any requirements to which it is subject in accordance with the provisions of the Legal Services Act 2007.]

(7) Schedule 8 makes further provision in connection with the powers given to the Council by this section and the provision made by the Act of 1985 in relation to licensed conveyancers, including amendments of Part II of that Act.

(8) The [Lord Chancellor] may by order make such—

Courts and Legal Services Act 1990 **A1.480A**

(a) amendments of, or modifications to, the provisions of Part II of the Act of 1985; or
(b) transitional or consequential provision,

as he considers necessary or expedient in connection with the provision made by this section and Schedule 8.

(9) Subject to any provision made by this section, Schedule 8 or any order made by the [Lord Chancellor] under subsection (8), the provisions of Part II of the Act of 1985 shall, with the necessary modifications, apply with respect to—

(a) any application for an advocacy, litigation or probate licence;
(b) any such licence;
(c) the practice of any licensed conveyancer which is carried on by virtue of any such licence;
(d) rules made by the Council under Schedule 8;
(e) < ... >
(f) any other matter dealt with by this section or Schedule 8,

as they apply with respect to the corresponding matters dealt with by Part II of that Act.

[(10) For the purposes of this section—

(a) 'right of audience', 'conduct of litigation', 'probate activities' and 'reserved legal activity' have the same meaning as in the Legal Services Act 2007;
(b) references to designation as an approved regulator are to designation as an approved regulator—
 (i) by Part 1 of Schedule 4 to the Legal Services Act 2007, by virtue of an order under paragraph 5 of Schedule 22 to that Act, or
 (ii) under Part 2 of Schedule 4 to that Act;
(c) 'relevant activity' means an activity which is a reserved legal activity—
 (i) which is within subsection (1A), and
 (ii) in relation to which the Council is designated as an approved regulator by Part 1 of Schedule 4 to that Act (by virtue of an order under paragraph 5 of Schedule 22 to that Act) or under Part 2 of that Schedule.]

Sub-ss (1)–(3): substituted, by subsequent sub-ss (1), (1A), (2), (3), by the Legal Services Act 2007, s 182, Sch 17, Pt 2, paras 33, 34(1), (2). Date in force: to be appointed: see the Legal Services Act 2007, s 211(2).
Sub-s (5): repealed by the Legal Services Act 2007, ss 182, 210, Sch 17, Pt 2, paras 33, 34(1), (3), Sch 23. Date in force: to be appointed: see the Legal Services Act 2007, s 211(2).
Sub-s (6): substituted by the Legal Services Act 2007, s 182, Sch 17, Pt 2, paras 33, 34(1), (4). Date in force: to be appointed: see the Legal Services Act 2007, s 211(2).
Sub-s (6): in para (a) words 'Schedule 4' in square brackets substituted by the Access to Justice Act 1999, s 43, Sch 6, paras 4, 8. Date in force: 1 January 2000: see SI 1999/3344, art 2(a).
Sub-s (8): words 'Lord Chancellor' in square brackets substituted by the Legal Services Act 2007, s 182, Sch 17, Pt 2, paras 33, 34(1), (5). Date in force: 31 March 2009: see SI 2009/503, art 2(c)(ii).
Sub-s (9): words 'Lord Chancellor' in square brackets substituted by the Legal Services Act 2007, s 182, Sch 17, Pt 2, paras 33, 34(1), (6)(a). Date in force: 31 March 2009: see SI 2009/503, art 2(c)(ii).
Sub-s (9): para (e) repealed by the Legal Services Act 2007, ss 182, 210, Sch 17, Pt 2, paras 33, 34(1), (6)(b), Sch 23. Date in force: 31 March 2009: see SI 2009/503, art 2(c)(ii).
Sub-s (10): inserted by the Legal Services Act 2007, s 182, Sch 17, Pt 2, paras 33, 34(1), (7). Date in force: to be appointed: see the Legal Services Act 2007, s 211(2).

A1.483 *Statutes*

A1.483

56   Administration of oaths etc by justices in certain probate business

(1) Every justice shall have power to administer any oath or take any affidavit which is required for the purposes of an application for a grant of probate or letters of administration made in any non-contentious or common form probate business.

(2) A justice before whom any oath or affidavit is taken or made under this section shall state in the jurat or attestation at what place and on what date the oath or affidavit is taken or made.

(3) No justice shall exercise the powers conferred by this section in any proceedings in which he is interested.

(4) A document purporting to be signed by a justice administering an oath or taking an affidavit shall be admitted in evidence without proof of the signature and without proof that he is a justice.

(5) In this section—

'affidavit' has the same meaning as in the Commissioners for Oaths Act 1889;
'justice' means a justice of the peace;
'letters of administration' includes all letters of administration of the effects of deceased persons, whether with or without a will annexed, and whether granted for general, special or limited purposes; and
'non-contentious or common form probate business' has the same meaning as in section 128 of the [Senior Courts Act 1981].

Sub-s (5): in definition 'non-contentious or common form probate business' words 'Senior Courts Act 1981' in square brackets substituted by the Constitutional Reform Act 2005, s 59(5), Sch 11, Pt 1, para 1(2). Date in force: 1 October 2009: see SI 2009/1604, art 2(d).

A1.485

125   Short title, minor and consequential amendments, transitionals and repeals

(1) This Act may be cited as the Courts and Legal Services Act 1990.

(2) The minor amendments set out in Schedule 17 shall have effect.

(3) The consequential amendments set out in Schedule 18 shall have effect.

(4) The [Lord Chancellor] may by order make such amendments or repeals in relevant enactments as appear to him to be necessary or expedient in consequence of any provision made by Part II with respect to advocacy, litigation, conveyancing or probate services.

[(5) In subsection (4)—

(a) 'relevant enactments' means such enactments or instruments passed or made before or in the same Session as the Legal Services Act 2007 was passed as may be specified in the order, and
(b) the reference to Part 2 is a reference to that Part as amended by that Act or any enactment or instruments passed or made before or in the same Session as that Act was passed.]

(6) The transitional provisions and savings set out in Schedule 19 shall have effect.

(7) The repeals set out in Schedule 20 (which include repeals of certain enactments that are spent or of no further practical utility) shall have effect.

Sub-s (4): words 'Lord Chancellor' in square brackets substituted by the Legal Services Act 2007, s 208(1), Sch 21, paras 83, 99(a). Date in force: 31 March 2009: see SI 2009/503, art 2(d).

Sub-s (5): substituted by the Legal Services Act 2007, s 208(1), Sch 21, paras 83, 99(b). Date in force: 31 March 2009: see SI 2009/503, art 2(d).

SCHEDULE 17
MINOR AMENDMENTS

A1.487

* * * * *

The Powers of Attorney Act 1971 (c.27)

4 In section 3 of the Powers of Attorney Act 1971 *(proof of instruments creating powers of attorney)*—

(a) in subsection (1)(b), after the word 'solicitor' there shall be inserted 'duly certificated notary public' and
(b) in subsection (3), after the word 'section' there shall be inserted ' "duly certificated notary public" has the same meaning as it has in the Solicitors Act 1974 by virtue of section 87(1) of that Act and'.

* * * * *

The [Senior Courts Act 1981] (c.54)

* * * * *

13 In section 36(4) of that Act (witness not to be punished for failing to appear if he is not offered payment of his reasonable expenses of attending), for the words from 'the expenses', to the end, there shall be substituted '—

(a) the expenses of coming and attending to give evidence and of returning from giving evidence; and
(b) any other reasonable expenses which he has asked to be defrayed in connection with his evidence,

was tendered to him at the time when the writ was served upon him.'

Para 4: repealed by the Legal Services Act 2007, s 210, Sch 23. Date in force: to be appointed: see the Legal Services Act 2007, s 211(2).
Para 13: words 'Senior Courts Act 1981' in square brackets substituted by the Constitutional Reform Act 2005, s 59(5), Sch 11, Pt 1, para 1. Date in force: 1 October 2009: see SI 2009/1604, art 2(d).

Statutes

ADOPTION AND CHILDREN ACT 2002

(2002, C 38)

[7th November 2002]

Chapter 3
Placement for Adoption and Adoption Orders

The making of adoption orders

51 Adoption by one person

(1) An adoption order may be made on the application of one person who has attained the age of 21 years and is not married [or a civil partner].

(2) An adoption order may be made on the application of one person who has attained the age of 21 years if the court is satisfied that the person is the partner of a parent of the person to be adopted.

(3) An adoption order may be made on the application of one person who has attained the age of 21 years and is married if the court is satisfied that—

 (a) the person's spouse cannot be found,
 (b) the spouses have separated and are living apart, and the separation is likely to be permanent, or
 (c) the person's spouse is by reason of ill-health, whether physical or mental, incapable of making an application for an adoption order.

[(3A) An adoption order may be made on the application of one person who has attained the age of 21 years and is a civil partner if the court is satisfied that—

 (a) the person's civil partner cannot be found,
 (b) the civil partners have separated and are living apart, and the separation is likely to be permanent, or
 (c) the person's civil partner is by reason of ill-health, whether physical or mental, incapable of making an application for an adoption order.]

(4) An adoption order may not be made on an application under this section by the mother or the father of the person to be adopted unless the court is satisfied that—

 (a) the other natural parent is dead or cannot be found,
 [(b) by virtue of the provisions specified in subsection (5), there is no other parent, or]
 (c) there is some other reason justifying the child's being adopted by the applicant alone,

and, where the court makes an adoption order on such an application, the court must record that it is satisfied as to the fact mentioned in paragraph (a) or (b) or, in the case of paragraph (c), record the reason.

[(5) The provisions referred to in subsection (4)(b) are—

 (a) section 28 of the Human Fertilisation and Embryology Act 1990 (disregarding subsections (5A) to (5I) of that section), or
 (b) sections 34 to 47 of the Human Fertilisation and Embryology Act 2008 (disregarding sections 39, 40 and 46 of that Act).]

Sub-s (1): words 'or a civil partner' in square brackets inserted by the Civil Partnership Act 2004, s 79(1), (4). Date in force: 30 December 2005: see SI 2005/3175, art 2(9).

Sub-s (3A): inserted by the Civil Partnership Act 2004, s 79(1), (5). Date in force: 30 December 2005: see SI 2005/3175, art 2(9).
Sub-s (4): para (b) substituted by the Human Fertilisation and Embryology Act 2008, s 56, Sch 6, Pt 1, para 39(1), (2). Date in force (for certain purposes): 6 April 2009: see SI 2009/479, art 6(1)(e). Date in force (for remaining purposes): 1 September 2009: see SI 2009/479, art 6(2).
Sub-s (5): inserted by the Human Fertilisation and Embryology Act 2008, s 56, Sch 6, Pt 1, para 39(1), (3). Date in force (for certain purposes): 6 April 2009: see SI 2009/479, art 6(1)(e). Date in force (for remaining purposes): 1 September 2009: see SI 2009/479, art 6(2).

Placement and adoption: general

A1.518

52 Parental etc consent

(1) The court cannot dispense with the consent of any parent or guardian of a child to the child being placed for adoption or to the making of an adoption order in respect of the child unless the court is satisfied that—

(a) the parent or guardian cannot be found or [lacks capacity (within the meaning of the Mental Capacity Act 2005) to give consent], or
(b) the welfare of the child requires the consent to be dispensed with.

(2) The following provisions apply to references in this Chapter to any parent or guardian of a child giving or withdrawing—

(a) consent to the placement of a child for adoption, or
(b) consent to the making of an adoption order (including a future adoption order).

(3) Any consent given by the mother to the making of an adoption order is ineffective if it is given less than six weeks after the child's birth.

(4) The withdrawal of any consent to the placement of a child for adoption, or of any consent given under section 20, is ineffective if it is given after an application for an adoption order is made.

(5) 'Consent' means consent given unconditionally and with full understanding of what is involved; but a person may consent to adoption without knowing the identity of the persons in whose favour the order will be made.

(6) 'Parent' (except in subsections (9) and (10) below) means a parent having parental responsibility.

(7) Consent under section 19 or 20 must be given in the form prescribed by rules, and the rules may prescribe forms in which a person giving consent under any other provision of this Part may do so (if he wishes).

(8) Consent given under section 19 or 20 must be withdrawn—

(a) in the form prescribed by rules, or
(b) by notice given to the agency.

(9) Subsection (10) applies if—

(a) an agency has placed a child for adoption under section 19 in pursuance of consent given by a parent of the child, and
(b) at a later time, the other parent of the child acquires parental responsibility for the child.

(10) The other parent is to be treated as having at that time given consent in accordance with this section in the same terms as those in which the first parent gave consent.

Sub-s (1): in para (a) words in square brackets substituted by the Mental Capacity Act 2005, s 67(1), Sch 6, para 45. Date in force: 1 October 2007: see SI 2007/1897, art 2(1)(d).
See further, the application of this section, with modifications, in relation to an external adoption order effected within the period of six months of the making of the adoption, and in respect of adoptions under the 1993 Hague Convention on Protection of Children and Co-operation in respect of Intercountry Adoption: the Adoptions with a Foreign Element Regulations 2005, SI 2005/392, regs 11(1)(p), 52, 55.

CHAPTER 5
THE REGISTERS

Adopted Children Register etc

A1.534

78 Searches and copies

(1) The Registrar General must continue to maintain at the General Register Office an index of the Adopted Children Register.

(2) Any person may—
   (a) search the index,
   (b) have a certified copy of any entry in the Adopted Children Register.

(3) But a person is not entitled to have a certified copy of an entry in the Adopted Children Register relating to an adopted person who has not attained the age of 18 years unless the applicant has provided the Registrar General with the prescribed particulars.
   'Prescribed' means prescribed by regulations made by the Registrar General with the approval of [the Secretary of State].

(4) The terms, conditions and regulations as to payment of fees, and otherwise, applicable under the Births and Deaths Registration Act 1953 (c 20), and the Registration Service Act 1953 (c 37), in respect of—
   (a) searches in the index kept in the General Register Office of certified copies of entries in the registers of live-births,
   (b) the supply from that office of certified copies of entries in those certified copies,

also apply in respect of searches, and supplies of certified copies, under subsection (2).
Sub-s (3): words 'the Secretary of State' in square brackets substituted by SI 2008/678, arts 3(1), 5, Sch 1, para 12(a), Sch 2, para 12(a). Date in force: 3 April 2008: see SI 2008/678, art 1(2); for transitional provisions see art 4 thereof.

SCHEDULE 3
MINOR AND CONSEQUENTIAL AMENDMENTS

Section 139

A1.547

The Marriage Act 1949 (c 76)

1 Section 3 of the Marriage Act 1949 (marriage of person aged under eighteen) is amended as follows.

2 In subsection (1), for 'person or persons specified in subsection (1A) of this section' there is substituted 'appropriate persons'.

3   For subsection (1A) there is substituted—

'(1A)   The appropriate persons are—
   (a)   if none of paragraphs (b) to (h) apply, each of the following—
       (i)   any parent of the child who has parental responsibility for him; and
       (ii) any guardian of the child;
   (b)   where a special guardianship order is in force with respect to a child, each of the child's special guardians, unless any of paragraphs (c) to (g) applies;
   (c)   where a care order has effect with respect to the child, the local authority designated in the order, and each parent, guardian or special guardian (in so far as their parental responsibility has not been restricted under section 33(3) of the Children Act 1989), unless paragraph (e) applies;
   (d)   where a residence order has effect with respect to the child, the persons with whom the child lives, or is to live, as a result of the order, unless paragraph (e) applies;
   (e)   where an adoption agency is authorised to place the child for adoption under section 19 of the Adoption and Children Act 2002, that agency or, where a care order has effect with respect to the child, the local authority designated in the order;
   (f)   where a placement order is in force with respect to the child, the appropriate local authority;
   (g)   where a child has been placed for adoption with prospective adopters, the prospective adopters (in so far as their parental responsibility has not been restricted under section 25(4) of the Adoption and Children Act 2002), in addition to those persons specified in paragraph (e) or (f);
   (h)   where none of paragraphs (b) to (g) apply but a residence order was in force with respect to the child immediately before he reached the age of sixteen, the persons with whom he lived, or was to live, as a result of the order.'

4   For subsection (1B) there is substituted—

'(1B)   In this section—
   "guardian of a child", "parental responsibility", "residence order", "special guardian", "special guardianship order" and "care order" have the same meaning as in the Children Act 1989;
   "adoption agency", "placed for adoption", "placement order" and "local authority" have the same meaning as in the Adoption and Children Act 2002;
   "appropriate local authority" means the local authority authorised by the placement order to place the child for adoption.'

5   In subsection (2), for 'The last foregoing subsection' there is substituted 'Subsection (1)'.

The Births and Deaths Registration Act 1953 (c 20)

6   In section 10 of the Births and Deaths Registration Act 1953 (registration of father where parents not married)—
   (a)   in subsection (1)(d)(i), for 'a parental responsibility agreement made between them in relation to the child' there is substituted 'any agreement made between them under section 4(1)(b) of the Children Act 1989 in relation to the child',
   (b)   in subsection (1)(d)(ii), for 'the Children Act 1989' there is substituted 'that Act',
   (c)   in subsection (3), the words following 'the Family Law Reform Act 1987' are omitted.

7   In section 10A of the Births and Deaths Registration Act 1953 (re-registration of father where parents not married)—

(a) in subsection (1)(d)(i), for 'a parental responsibility agreement made between them in relation to the child' there is substituted 'any agreement made between them under section 4(1)(b) of the Children Act 1989 in relation to the child',
(b) in subsection (1)(d)(ii), for 'the Children Act 1989' there is substituted 'that Act'.

The Sexual Offences Act 1956 (c 69)

8   In section 28 of the Sexual Offences Act 1956 (causing or encouraging prostitution of, intercourse with, or indecent assault on, girl under sixteen), in subsection (4), the 'or' at the end of paragraph (a) is omitted, and after that paragraph there is inserted—

'(aa) a special guardianship order under that Act is in force with respect to her and he is not her special guardian; or'.

The Health Services and Public Health Act 1968 (c 46)

9   The Health Services and Public Health Act 1968 is amended as follows.

10   In section 64 (financial assistance by the Secretary of State to certain voluntary organisations), in subsection (3)(a)(xviii), for 'the Adoption Act 1976' there is substituted 'the Adoption and Children Act 2002'.

11   In section 65 (financial and other assistance by local authorities to certain voluntary organisations), in subsection (3)(b), for 'the Adoption Act 1976' there is substituted 'the Adoption and Children Act 2002'.

The Local Authority Social Services Act 1970 (c 42)

12   The Local Authority Social Services Act 1970 is amended as follows.

13   In section 7D (default powers of Secretary of State as respects social services functions of local authorities), in subsection (1), after 'the Children Act 1989' there is inserted 'section 1 or 2(4) of the Adoption (Intercountry Aspects) Act 1999 or the Adoption and Children Act 2002'.

14   In Schedule 1 (enactments conferring functions assigned to social services committee)—

(a) the entry relating to the Adoption Act 1976 is omitted,
(b) in the entry relating to the Children Act 1989, after 'Consent to application for residence order in respect of child in care' there is inserted 'Functions relating to special guardianship orders',
(c) in the entry relating to the Adoption (Intercountry Aspects) Act 1999—
    (i) in the first column, for 'Section' there is substituted 'Sections 1 and',
    (ii) in the second column, for 'Article 9(a) to (c) of' there is substituted 'regulations made under section 1 giving effect to' and at the end there is inserted 'and functions under Article 9(a) to (c) of the Convention',

and at the end of the Schedule there is inserted—

| 'Adoption and Children Act 2002 | Maintenance of Adoption Service; functions of local authority as adoption agency.' |

The Immigration Act 1971 (c 77)

15   In section 33(1) of the Immigration Act 1971 (interpretation)—

Adoption and Children Act 2002 **A1.547**

(a) in the definition of 'Convention adoption', after '1978' there is inserted 'or in the Adoption and Children Act 2002',

(b) in the definition of 'legally adopted', for 'section 72(2) of the Adoption Act 1976' there is substituted 'section 87 of the Adoption and Children Act 2002'.

The Legitimacy Act 1976 (c 31)

16 The Legitimacy Act 1976 is amended as follows.

17 In section 4 (legitimation of adopted child)—

(a) in subsection (1), after '1976' there is inserted 'or section 67 of the Adoption and Children Act 2002',

(b) in subsection (2)—

(i) in paragraph (a), after '39' there is inserted 'or subsection (3)(b) of the said section 67',

(ii) in paragraph (b), after '1976' there is inserted 'or section 67, 68 or 69 of the Adoption and Children Act 2002'.

18 In section 6 (dispositions depending on date of birth), at the end of subsection (2) there is inserted 'or section 69(2) of the Adoption and Children Act 2002'.

The Adoption Act 1976 (c 36)

19 In section 38 of the Adoption Act 1976 (meaning of 'adoption' in Part 4), in subsection (2), after '1975' there is inserted 'but does not include an adoption of a kind mentioned in paragraphs (c) to (e) of subsection (1) effected on or after the day which is the appointed day for the purposes of Chapter 4 of Part 1 of the Adoption and Children Act 2002'.

...

20–35

...

The Magistrates' Courts Act 1980 (c 43)

36 The Magistrates' Courts Act 1980 is amended as follows.

37 In section 65 (meaning of family proceedings), in subsection (1), for paragraph (h) there is substituted—

'(h) the Adoption and Children Act 2002;'.

38 In section 69 (sitting of magistrates' courts for family proceedings), in subsections (2) and (3), for 'the Adoption Act 1976' there is substituted 'the Adoption and Children Act 2002'.

39 In section 71 (newspaper reports of family proceedings)—

(a) in subsection (1), '(other than proceedings under the Adoption Act 1976)' is omitted,

(b) in subsection (2)—

(i) for 'the Adoption Act 1976' there is substituted 'the Adoption and Children Act 2002',

(ii) the words following '(a) and (b)' are omitted.

40 In Part 1 of Schedule 6 (fees to be taken by justices' chief executives), in the entry relating to family proceedings—

A1.547 *Statutes*

- (a) for 'the Adoption Act 1976, except under section 21 of that Act', there is substituted 'the Adoption and Children Act 2002, except under section 23 of that Act',
- (b) in paragraph (c), for 'section 21 of the Adoption Act 1976' there is substituted 'section 23 of the Adoption and Children Act 2002'.

The Mental Health Act 1983 (c 20)

41 In section 28 of the Mental Health Act 1983 (nearest relative of minor under guardianship, etc), in subsection (3), after "guardian" there is inserted 'includes a special guardian (within the meaning of the Children Act 1989), but'.

The Child Abduction Act 1984 (c 37)

42 (1) Section 1 of the Child Abduction Act 1984 (offence of abduction of child by parent, etc) is amended as follows.

(2) In subsection (2), after paragraph (c) there is inserted—

'(ca) he is a special guardian of the child; or'.

(3) In subsection (3)(a), after sub-paragraph (iii) there is inserted—
'(iiia)any special guardian of the child;'.

(4) In subsection (4), for paragraphs (a) and (b) there is substituted—

- '(a) he is a person in whose favour there is a residence order in force with respect to the child, and he takes or sends the child out of the United Kingdom for a period of less than one month; or
- (b) he is a special guardian of the child and he takes or sends the child out of the United Kingdom for a period of less than three months.'

(5) In subsection (5A), the 'or' at the end of sub-paragraph (i) of paragraph (a) is omitted, and after that sub-paragraph there is inserted—
'(ia) who is a special guardian of the child; or'.

(6) In subsection (7)(a), after "guardian of a child," there is inserted "special guardian,".

43 (1) The Schedule to that Act (modifications of section 1 for children in certain cases) is amended as follows.

(2) In paragraph 3 (adoption and custodianship), for sub-paragraphs (1) and (2) there is substituted—

'(1) This paragraph applies where—

- (a) a child is placed for adoption by an adoption agency under section 19 of the Adoption and Children Act 2002, or an adoption agency is authorised to place the child for adoption under that section; or
- (b) a placement order is in force in respect of the child; or
- (c) an application for such an order has been made in respect of the child and has not been disposed of; or
- (d) an application for an adoption order has been made in respect of the child and has not been disposed of; or
- (e) an order under section 84 of the Adoption and Children Act 2002 (giving parental responsibility prior to adoption abroad) has been made in respect of the child, or an application for such an order in respect of him has been made and has not been disposed of.

(2) Where this paragraph applies, section 1 of this Act shall have effect as if—

- (a) the reference in subsection (1) to the appropriate consent were—

(i) in a case within sub-paragraph (1)(a) above, a reference to the consent of each person who has parental responsibility for the child or to the leave of the High Court;
(ii) in a case within sub-paragraph (1)(b) above, a reference to the leave of the court which made the placement order;
(iii) in a case within sub-paragraph (1)(c) or (d) above, a reference to the leave of the court to which the application was made;
(iv) in a case within sub-paragraph (1)(e) above, a reference to the leave of the court which made the order or, as the case may be, to which the application was made;
(b) subsection (3) were omitted;
(c) in subsection (4), in paragraph (a), for the words from 'in whose favour' to the first mention of 'child' there were substituted 'who provides the child's home in a case falling within sub-paragraph (1)(a) or (b) of paragraph 3 of the Schedule to this Act'; and
(d) subsections (4A), (5), (5A) and (6) were omitted.'

(3) In paragraph 5 (interpretation), in sub-paragraph (a), for the words from 'and 'adoption order" to the end there is substituted ', 'adoption order', 'placed for adoption by an adoption agency' and 'placement order' have the same meaning as in the Adoption and Children Act 2002; and'.

...

44 ...

The Child Abduction and Custody Act 1985 (c 60)

45 In Schedule 3 to the Child Abduction and Custody Act 1985 (custody orders), in paragraph 1, the 'and' at the end of paragraph (b) is omitted and after that paragraph there is inserted—

'(bb) a special guardianship order (within the meaning of the Act of 1989); and',

and paragraph (c)(v) is omitted.

The Family Law Act 1986 (c 55)

46 The Family Law Act 1986 is amended as follows.

47 In section 1 (orders to which Part 1 applies), in subsection (1), after paragraph (a) there is inserted—

'(aa) a special guardianship order made by a court in England and Wales under the Children Act 1989;
(ab) an order made under section 26 of the Adoption and Children Act 2002 (contact), other than an order varying or revoking such an order'.

48 In section 2 (jurisdiction: general), after subsection (2) there is inserted—

'(2A) A court in England and Wales shall not have jurisdiction to make a special guardianship order under the Children Act 1989 unless the condition in section 3 of this Act is satisfied.

(2B) A court in England and Wales shall not have jurisdiction to make an order under section 26 of the Adoption and Children Act 2002 unless the condition in section 3 of this Act is satisfied.'

49 In section 57 (declarations as to adoptions effected overseas)—

(a) for subsection (1)(a) there is substituted—

A1.547 *Statutes*

'(a) a Convention adoption, or an overseas adoption, within the meaning of the Adoption and Children Act 2002, or',

(b) in subsection (2)(a), after '1976' there is inserted 'or section 67 of the Adoption and Children Act 2002'.

The Family Law Reform Act 1987 (c 42)

50 The Family Law Reform Act 1987 is amended as follows.

51 In section 1 (general principle), for paragraph (c) of subsection (3) there is substituted—

'(c) is an adopted person within the meaning of Chapter 4 of Part 1 of the Adoption and Children Act 2002'.

52 In section 19 (dispositions of property), in subsection (5), after '1976' there is inserted 'or section 69 of the Adoption and Children Act 2002'.

The Adoption (Northern Ireland) Order 1987 (SI 1987/2203 (NI 22))

53 In Article 2(2) (interpretation), in the definition of 'prescribed', for 'Articles 54' there is substituted 'Articles 53(3B) and (3D), 54'.

The Children Act 1989 (c 41)

54 The Children Act 1989 is amended as follows.

55 In section 8 (residence, contact and other orders with respect to children), in subsection (4), for paragraph (d) there is substituted—

'(d) the Adoption and Children Act 2002;'.

56 In section 10 (power of court to make section 8 orders)—

(a) in subsection (4)(a), for 'or guardian' there is substituted ', guardian or special guardian',
(b) after subsection (4)(a) there is inserted—
'(aa) any person who by virtue of section 4A has parental responsibility for the child;',
(c) after subsection (5) there is inserted—

'(5A) A local authority foster parent is entitled to apply for a residence order with respect to a child if the child has lived with him for a period of at least one year immediately preceding the application.',

(d) after subsection (7) there is inserted—

'(7A) If a special guardianship order is in force with respect to a child, an application for a residence order may only be made with respect to him, if apart from this subsection the leave of the court is not required, with such leave.'

57 In section 12 (residence orders and parental responsibility), in subsection (3)—

(a) paragraph (a) is omitted,
(b) in paragraph (b), for 'section 55 of the Act of 1976' there is substituted 'section 84 of the Adoption and Children Act 2002'.

58 In section 16 (family assistance orders), in subsection (2)(a), for 'or guardian' there is substituted ', guardian or special guardian'.

59 In section 20 (provision of accommodation for children: general), in subsection (9), the 'or' at the end of paragraph (a) is omitted and after that paragraph there is inserted—

'(aa) who is a special guardian of the child; or'.

60 In section 24 (persons qualifying for advice and assistance)—

(a) for subsection (1) there is substituted—

'(1) In this Part "a person qualifying for advice and assistance" means a person to whom subsection (1A) or (1B) applies.

(1A) This subsection applies to a person—

- (a) who has reached the age of sixteen but not the age of twenty-one;
- (b) with respect to whom a special guardianship order is in force (or, if he has reached the age of eighteen, was in force when he reached that age); and
- (c) who was, immediately before the making of that order, looked after by a local authority.

(1B) This subsection applies to a person to whom subsection (1A) does not apply, and who—

- (a) is under twenty-one; and
- (b) at any time after reaching the age of sixteen but while still a child was, but is no longer, looked after, accommodated or fostered.',

(b) in subsection (2), for 'subsection (1)(b)' there is substituted 'subsection (1B)(b)',

(c) in subsection (5), before paragraph (a) there is inserted—

'(za) in the case of a person to whom subsection (1A) applies, a local authority determined in accordance with regulations made by the Secretary of State;'.

61 In section 24A (advice and assistance for qualifying persons)—

- (a) in subsection (2)(b), after 'a person' there is inserted 'to whom section 24(1A) applies, or to whom section 24(1B) applies and',
- (b) in subsection (3)(a), after 'if' there is inserted 'he is a person to whom section 24(1A) applies, or he is a person to whom section 24(1B) applies and'.

62 In section 24B (assistance with employment, education and training), in each of subsections (1) and (3)(b), after 'of' there is inserted 'section 24(1A) or'.

63 In section 33 (effect of care order)—

- (a) in subsection (3)(b), for 'a parent or guardian of the child' there is substituted '—
    - (i) a parent, guardian or special guardian of the child; or
    - (ii) a person who by virtue of section 4A has parental responsibility for the child,',
- (b) in subsection (5), for 'a parent or guardian of the child who has care of him' there is substituted 'a person mentioned in that provision who has care of the child',
- (c) in subsection (6)(b)—
    - (i) sub-paragraph (i) is omitted,
    - (ii) in sub-paragraph (ii), for 'section 55 of the Act of 1976' there is substituted 'section 84 of the Adoption and Children Act 2002',
- (d) in subsection (9), for 'a parent or guardian of the child' there is substituted 'a person mentioned in that provision'.

64 In section 34 (parental contact etc with children in care)—

- (a) in subsection (1)(b), after 'guardian' there is inserted 'or special guardian', and
- (b) after subsection (1)(b) there is inserted—

'(ba) any person who by virtue of section 4A has parental responsibility for him;'.

A1.547 *Statutes*

65 In section 80 (inspection of children's homes by persons authorised by Secretary of State), in subsection (1), paragraphs (e) and (f) are omitted.

66 In section 81 (inquiries), in subsection (1), paragraph (b) is omitted.

67 In section 88 (amendments of adoption legislation), subsection (1) is omitted.

68 In section 91 (effect and duration of orders, etc)—

(a) after subsection (5) there is inserted—

'(5A) The making of a special guardianship order with respect to a child who is the subject of—

(a) a care order; or
(b) an order under section 34,

discharges that order.',

(b) in subsection (7), after '4(1)' there is inserted '4A(1)',
(c) in subsection (8)(a), after '4' there is inserted 'or 4A'.

69 In section 102 (power of constable to assist in exercise of certain powers to search for children or inspect premises), in subsection (6), paragraph (c) is omitted.

70 In section 105 (interpretation), in subsection (1)—

(a) in the definition of 'adoption agency', for 'section 1 of the Adoption Act 1976' there is substituted 'section 2 of the Adoption and Children Act 2002',
(b) at the appropriate place there is inserted—
"section 31A plan' has the meaning given by section 31A(6);',
(c) in the definition of 'parental responsibility agreement', for 'section 4(1)' there is substituted 'sections 4(1) and 4A(2)',
(d) the definition of 'protected child' is omitted,
(e) after the definition of 'special educational needs' there is inserted—
"special guardian' and 'special guardianship order' have the meaning given by section 14A;'.

71 In Schedule 1 (financial provision for children)—

(a) in paragraph 1 (orders for financial relief against parents)—
  (i) in sub-paragraph (1), for 'or guardian' there is substituted ', guardian or special guardian', and
  (ii) in sub-paragraph (6), after 'order' there is inserted 'or a special guardianship order',
(b) in paragraph 6 (variation etc of orders for periodical payments), in sub-paragraph (8), after 'guardian' there is inserted 'or special guardian',
(c) in paragraph 8 (financial relief under other enactments), in sub-paragraph (1) and in sub-paragraph (2)(b), after 'residence order' there is inserted 'or a special guardianship order',
(d) in paragraph 14 (financial provision for child resident in country outside England and Wales), in sub-paragraph (1)(b), after 'guardian' there is inserted 'or special guardian'.

72 In Schedule 2, in paragraph 19 (arrangements by local authorities to assist children to live abroad)—

(a) in sub-paragraph (4) (arrangements to assist children to live abroad), after 'guardian,' there is inserted 'special guardian,',
(b) in sub-paragraph (6), for the words from the beginning to 'British subject)' there is substituted 'Section 85 of the Adoption and Children Act 2002 (which imposes restrictions on taking children out of the United Kingdom)',
(c) after sub-paragraph (8) there is inserted—

'(9) This paragraph does not apply to a local authority placing a child for adoption with prospective adopters.'

73   In Schedule 8 (privately fostered children), in paragraph 5, for sub-paragraphs (a) and (b) there is substituted

'he is placed in the care of a person who proposes to adopt him under arrangements made by an adoption agency within the meaning of—

(a)   section 2 of the Adoption and Children Act 2002;
(b)   section 1 of the Adoption (Scotland) Act 1978; or
(c)   Article 3 of the Adoption (Northern Ireland) Order 1987'.

74   Part 1 of Schedule 10 is omitted.

75   In Schedule 11 (jurisdiction), in paragraphs 1 and 2, for the words 'the Adoption Act 1976', wherever they occur, there is substituted 'the Adoption and Children Act 2002'.

The Human Fertilisation and Embryology Act 1990 (c 37)

76   The Human Fertilisation and Embryology Act 1990 is amended as follows.

77   In section 27 (meaning of mother), in subsection (2), for 'child of any person other than the adopter or adopters' there is substituted 'woman's child'.

78   In section 28 (meaning of father), in subsection (5)(c), for 'child of any person other than the adopter or adopters' there is substituted 'man's child'.

79   In section 30 (parental orders in favour of gamete donors), in subsection (10) for 'Adoption Act 1976' there is substituted 'Adoption and Children Act 2002'.

The Courts and Legal Services Act 1990 (c 41)

80   In section 58A of the Courts and Legal Services Act 1990 (conditional fee agreements: supplementary), in subsection (2), for paragraph (b) there is substituted—

'(b)   the Adoption and Children Act 2002;'.

The Child Support Act 1991 (c 48)

81   In section 26 of the Child Support Act 1991 (disputes about parentage), in subsection (3), after '1976' there is inserted 'or Chapter 4 of Part 1 of the Adoption and Children Act 2002'.

The Children (Scotland) Act 1995 (c 36)

82   Section 86 of the Children (Scotland) Act 1995 (parental responsibilities order: general) is amended as follows.

83   In subsection (3), in paragraph (a), for 'section 18 (freeing for adoption) or 55 (adoption abroad) of the Adoption Act 1976' there is substituted 'section 19 (placing children with parental consent) or 84 (giving parental responsibility prior to adoption abroad) of the Adoption and Children Act 2002'.

84   ...

The Family Law Act 1996 (c 27)

85   The Family Law Act 1996 is amended as follows.

86   In section 62 (meaning of 'relevant child' etc)—

A1.547 *Statutes*

(a) in subsection (2), in paragraph (b), after 'the Adoption Act 1976' there is inserted ', the Adoption and Children Act 2002',
(b) in subsection (5), for the words from 'has been freed' to '1976' there is substituted 'falls within subsection (7)'.

87   At the end of that section there is inserted—

'(7) A child falls within this subsection if—

(a) an adoption agency, within the meaning of section 2 of the Adoption and Children Act 2002, has power to place him for adoption under section 19 of that Act (placing children with parental consent) or he has become the subject of an order under section 21 of that Act (placement orders), or
(b) he is freed for adoption by virtue of an order made—
   (i) in England and Wales, under section 18 of the Adoption Act 1976,
   (ii) in Scotland, under section 18 of the Adoption (Scotland) Act 1978, or
   (iii) in Northern Ireland, under Article 17(1) or 18(1) of the Adoption (Northern Ireland) Order 1987.'

88   In section 63 (interpretation of Part 4)—

(a) in subsection (1), for the definition of 'adoption order', there is substituted—
"adoption order' means an adoption order within the meaning of section 72(1) of the Adoption Act 1976 or section 46(1) of the Adoption and Children Act 2002;',
(b) in subsection (2), after paragraph (h) there is inserted—
'(i) the Adoption and Children Act 2002.'

The Housing Act 1996 (c 52)

89   Section 178 of the Housing Act 1996 (meaning of associated person) is amended as follows.

90   In subsection (2), for the words from 'has been freed' to '1976' there is substituted 'falls within subsection (2A)'.

91   After that subsection there is inserted—

'(2A) A child falls within this subsection if—

(a) an adoption agency, within the meaning of section 2 of the Adoption and Children Act 2002, is authorised to place him for adoption under section 19 of that Act (placing children with parental consent) or he has become the subject of an order under section 21 of that Act (placement orders), or
(b) he is freed for adoption by virtue of an order made—
   (i) in England and Wales, under section 18 of the Adoption Act 1976,
   (ii) in Scotland, under section 18 of the Adoption (Scotland) Act 1978, or
   (iii) in Northern Ireland, under Article 17(1) or 18(1) of the Adoption (Northern Ireland) Order 1987.'

92   In subsection (3), for the definition of 'adoption order', there is substituted—

"adoption order' means an adoption order within the meaning of section 72(1) of the Adoption Act 1976 or section 46(1) of the Adoption and Children Act 2002;'.

...

93   ...

The Protection of Children Act 1999 (c 14)

94 In section 2B of the Protection of Children Act 1999 (*individuals named in the findings of certain inquiries*), in subsection (7), after paragraph (a) there is inserted—

'(vi) section 17 of the Adoption and Children Act 2002;'.

The Adoption (Intercountry Aspects) Act 1999 (c 18)

95 The following provisions of the Adoption (Intercountry Aspects) Act 1999 cease to have effect in relation to England and Wales: sections 3, 6, 8, 9 and 11 to 13.

96 Section 2 of that Act (*accredited bodies*) is amended as follows.

97 In subsection (2A)—

(a) for the words from the beginning to '2000' there is substituted 'A registered adoption society',
(b) for 'agency' there is substituted 'society'.

98 For subsection (5) there is substituted—

'(5) In this section, "registered adoption society" has the same meaning as in section 2 of the Adoption and Children Act 2002 (*basic definitions*); and expressions used in this section in its application to England and Wales which are also used in that Act have the same meanings as in that Act.'

99 In subsection (6)—

(a) the words 'in its application to Scotland' are omitted,
(b) after 'expressions' there is inserted 'used in this section in its application to Scotland'.

100 Section 14 (*restriction on bringing children into the United Kingdom for adoption*) is omitted.

101 In section 16(1) (*devolution: Wales*), the words ', or section 17 or 56A of the 1976 Act,' are omitted.

The Access to Justice Act 1999 (c 22)

102 In Schedule 2 to the Access to Justice Act 1999 (*Community Legal Service: excluded services*), in paragraph 2(3)(c)—

(a) for 'section 27 or 28 of the Adoption Act 1976' there is substituted 'section 36 of the Adoption and Children Act 2002',
(b) for 'an order under Part II or section 29 or 55' there is substituted 'a placement order or adoption order (within the meaning of the Adoption and Children Act 2002) or an order under section 41 or 84'.

The Care Standards Act 2000 (c 14)

103 The Care Standards Act 2000 is amended as follows.

104 In section 4 (*basic definitions*), in subsection (7), for 'the Adoption Act 1976' there is substituted 'the Adoption and Children Act 2002'.

105 At the end of section 5 (*registration authorities*) there is inserted—

'(2) This section is subject to section 36A.'

106 In section 11 (*requirement to register*), in subsection (3), for 'reference in subsection (1) to an agency does' there is substituted 'references in subsections (1) and (2) to an agency do'.

107   In section 14 (2) (offences conviction of which may result in cancellation of registration), for paragraph (d) there is substituted—

'(d) an offence under regulations under section 1(3) of the Adoption (Intercountry Aspects) Act 1999,
(e) an offence under the Adoption and Children Act 2002 or regulations made under it'.

108   In section 16(2) (power to make regulations providing that no application for registration may be made in respect of certain agencies which are unincorporated bodies), 'or a voluntary adoption agency' is omitted.

109   In section 22(10) (disapplication of power to make regulations in the case of voluntary adoption agencies), at the end there is inserted 'or adoption support agencies'.

110   In section 23 (standards), at the end of subsection (4)(d) there is inserted 'or proceedings against a voluntary adoption agency for an offence under section 9(4) of the Adoption Act 1976 or section 9 of the Adoption and Children Act 2002'.

111   In section 31 (inspections by authorised persons), in subsection (3)(b), for 'section 9(2) of the Adoption Act 1976' there is substituted 'section 9 of the Adoption and Children Act 2002'.

112   In section 43 (introductory), in subsection (3)(a)—

(a) for 'the Adoption Act 1976' there is substituted 'the Adoption and Children Act 2002',
(b) after 'children' there is inserted 'or the provision of adoption support services (as defined in section 2(6) of the Adoption and Children Act 2002)'.

113   In section 46 (inspections: supplementary), in subsection (7)(c), for 'section 9(3) of the Adoption Act 1976' there is substituted 'section 9 of the Adoption and Children Act 2002'.

114   In section 48 (regulation of fostering functions), at the end of subsection (1) there is inserted—

'(f) as to the fees or expenses which may be paid to persons assisting local authorities in making decisions in the exercise of such functions'.

115   In section 55(2)(b) (definition of 'social care worker'), for 'or a voluntary adoption agency' there is substituted ', a voluntary adoption agency or an adoption support agency'.

116   In section 121 (general interpretation)—

(a) in subsection (1), in the definition of 'voluntary organisation', for 'the Adoption Act 1976' there is substituted 'the Adoption and Children Act 2002',
(b) in subsection (13), in the appropriate place in the table there is inserted—

'Adoption support agency   Section 4'.

117   In Schedule 4 (minor and consequential amendments), paragraph 27(b) is omitted.

The Criminal Justice and Court Services Act 2000 (c 43)

118   In section 12(5) of the Criminal Justice and Court Services Act 2000 (meaning of 'family proceedings' in relation to CAFCASS), paragraph (b) (supervision orders under the 1989 Act) and the preceding 'and' are omitted.

Para 20: repealed by the National Health Service (Consequential Provisions) Act 2006, s 6, Sch 4. Date in force: 1 March 2007: see the National Health Service (Consequential Provisions) Act 2006, s 8(2).
Paras 21–35: repealed by the Adoption and Children (Scotland) Act 2007, s 120(2), Sch 3. Date in force: 28 September 2009: see SSI 2009/267, arts 1(2), 2.
Para 44: repealed by the Courts Act 2003, s 109(3), Sch 10. Date in force: 1 April 2005: see SI 2005/910, art 3(aa); for transitional provisions see SI 2005/911, arts 2–5.
Para 84: repealed by the Adoption and Children (Scotland) Act 2007, s 120(2), Sch 3. Date in force: 28 September 2009: see SSI 2009/267, arts 1(2), 2.
Para 93: repealed by the Serious Organised Crime and Police Act 2005, s 174(2), Sch 17, Pt 2. Date in force: 6 April 2006: see SI 2006/378, art 7(f)(vii).
Para 94: repealed by the Safeguarding Vulnerable Groups Act 2006, s 63(2), Sch 10. Date in force: to be appointed: see the Safeguarding Vulnerable Groups Act 2006, s 65.

SCHEDULE 6
GLOSSARY

Section 147

A1.548

In this Act, the expressions listed in the left-hand column below have the meaning given by, or are to be interpreted in accordance with, the provisions of this Act or (where stated) of the 1989 Act listed in the right-hand column.

Expression	Provision
the 1989 Act	section 2(5)
Adopted Children Register	section 77
Adoption and Children Act Register	section 125
adoption (in relation to Chapter 4 of Part 1)	section 66
adoption agency	section 2(1)
adoption agency placing a child for adoption	section 18(5)
Adoption Contact Register	section 80
adoption order	section 46(1)
Adoption Service	section 2(1)
adoption society	section 2(5)
adoption support agency	section 8
adoption support services	section 2(6)
appointed day (in relation to Chapter 4 of Part 1)	section 66(2)
appropriate Minister	section 144
Assembly	section 144
body	section 144
by virtue of	section 144
care order	section 105(1) of the 1989 Act
child	sections 49(5) and 144
child assessment order	section 43(2) of the 1989 Act
child in the care of a local authority	section 105(1) of the 1989 Act
child looked after by a local authority	section 22 of the 1989 Act
child placed for adoption by an adoption agency	section 18(5)
child to be adopted, adopted child	section 49(5)
consent (in relation to making adoption orders or placing for adoption)	section 52

A1.548 *Statutes*

the Convention	section 144
Convention adoption	section 66(1)(c)
Convention adoption order	section 144
Convention country	section 144
couple	section 144(4)
court	section 144
disposition (in relation to Chapter 4 of Part 1)	section 73
enactment	section 144
fee	section 144
guardian	section 144
information	section 144
interim care order	section 38 of the 1989 Act
local authority	section 144
local authority foster parent	*section 23(3)* [22C(12)] of the 1989 Act
Northern Irish adoption agency	section 144
Northern Irish adoption order	section 144
notice	section 144
notice of intention to adopt	section 44(2)
overseas adoption	section 87
parental responsibility	section 3 of the 1989 Act
partner, in relation to a parent of a child	section 144(7)
placement order	section 21
placing, or placed, for adoption	sections 18(5) and 19(4)
prohibited steps order	section 8(1) of the 1989 Act
records (in relation to Chapter 5 of Part 1)	section 82
registered adoption society	section 2(2)
registers of live-births (in relation to Chapter 5 of Part 1)	section 82
registration authority (in Part 1)	section 144
regulations	section 144
relative	section 144, read with section 1(8)
residence order	section 8(1) of the 1989 Act
rules	section 144
Scottish adoption agency	section 144(3)
Scottish adoption order	section 144
specific issue order	section 8(1) of the 1989 Act
subordinate legislation	section 144
supervision order	section 31(11) of the 1989 Act
unitary authority	section 144
voluntary organisation	section 2(5)

In entry relating to 'local authority foster parent' reference to '23(3)' in italics repealed and subsequent reference in square brackets substituted by the Children and Young Persons Act 2008, s 8(2), Sch 1, para 14. Date in force: to be appointed: see the Children and Young Persons Act 2008, s 44(3), (4), (5)(a).

GENDER RECOGNITION ACT 2004

2004 CHAPTER 7

An Act to make provision for and in connection with change of gender.

[1st July 2004]

Be it enacted by the Queen's most Excellent Majesty, by and with the advice and consent of the Lords Spiritual and Temporal, and Commons, in this present Parliament assembled, and by the authority of the same, as follows:—

Applications for gender recognition certificate

A1.548A

1 Applications

(1) A person of either gender who is aged at least 18 may make an application for a gender recognition certificate on the basis of—

    (a) living in the other gender, or
    (b) having changed gender under the law of a country or territory outside the United Kingdom.

(2) In this Act 'the acquired gender', in relation to a person by whom an application under subsection (1) is or has been made, means—

    (a) in the case of an application under paragraph (a) of that subsection, the gender in which the person is living, or
    (b) in the case of an application under paragraph (b) of that subsection, the gender to which the person has changed under the law of the country or territory concerned.

(3) An application under subsection (1) is to be determined by a Gender Recognition Panel.

(4) Schedule 1 (Gender Recognition Panels) has effect.
Appointment: 4 April 2005: see SI 2005/54, art 2.

A1.548B

2 Determination of applications

(1) In the case of an application under section 1(1)(a), the Panel must grant the application if satisfied that the applicant—

    (a) has or has had gender dysphoria,
    (b) has lived in the acquired gender throughout the period of two years ending with the date on which the application is made,
    (c) intends to continue to live in the acquired gender until death, and
    (d) complies with the requirements imposed by and under section 3.

(2) In the case of an application under section 1(1)(b), the Panel must grant the application if satisfied—

    (a) that the country or territory under the law of which the applicant has changed gender is an approved country or territory, and

A1.548B *Statutes*

(b) that the applicant complies with the requirements imposed by and under section 3.

(3) The Panel must reject an application under section 1(1) if not required by subsection (1) or (2) to grant it.

(4) In this Act 'approved country or territory' means a country or territory prescribed by order made by the Secretary of State after consulting the Scottish Ministers and the Department of Finance and Personnel in Northern Ireland.
Appointment: 4 April 2005: see SI 2005/54, art 2.

A1.548C

3 Evidence

(1) An application under section 1(1)(a) must include either—

(a) a report made by a registered medical practitioner practising in the field of gender dysphoria and a report made by another registered medical practitioner (who may, but need not, practise in that field), or
(b) a report made by a chartered psychologist practising in that field and a report made by a registered medical practitioner (who may, but need not, practise in that field).

(2) But subsection (1) is not complied with unless a report required by that subsection and made by—

(a) a registered medical practitioner, or
(b) a chartered psychologist,

practising in the field of gender dysphoria includes details of the diagnosis of the applicant's gender dysphoria.

(3) And subsection (1) is not complied with in a case where—

(a) the applicant has undergone or is undergoing treatment for the purpose of modifying sexual characteristics, or
(b) treatment for that purpose has been prescribed or planned for the applicant,

unless at least one of the reports required by that subsection includes details of it.

(4) An application under section 1(1)(a) must also include a statutory declaration by the applicant that the applicant meets the conditions in section 2(1)(b) and (c).

(5) An application under section 1(1)(b) must include evidence that the applicant has changed gender under the law of an approved country or territory.

(6) Any application under section 1(1) must include—

(a) a statutory declaration as to whether or not the applicant is married [or a civil partner],
(b) any other information or evidence required by an order made by the Secretary of State, and
(c) any other information or evidence which the Panel which is to determine the application may require,

and may include any other information or evidence which the applicant wishes to include.

(7) The Secretary of State may not make an order under subsection (6)(b) without consulting the Scottish Ministers and the Department of Finance and Personnel in Northern Ireland.

(8) If the Panel which is to determine the application requires information or evidence under subsection (6)(c) it must give reasons for doing so.
Appointment: 4 April 2005: see SI 2005/54, art 2.
Sub-s (6): in para (a) words 'or a civil partner' in square brackets inserted by the Civil Partnership Act 2004, s 250(1), (2)(a). Date in force: 5 December 2005: see SI 2005/3175, art 3, Sch 2.

A1.548D

4   Successful applications

(1) If a Gender Recognition Panel grants an application under section 1(1) it must issue a gender recognition certificate to the applicant.

(2) Unless the applicant is married [or a civil partner], the certificate is to be a full gender recognition certificate.

(3) If the applicant is married [or a civil partner], the certificate is to be an interim gender recognition certificate.

(4) Schedule 2 (annulment or dissolution of marriage after issue of interim gender recognition certificate) has effect.

(5) The Secretary of State may, after consulting the Scottish Ministers and the Department of Finance and Personnel in Northern Ireland, specify the content and form of gender recognition certificates.
Appointment: 4 April 2005: see SI 2005/54, art 2.
Sub-s (2): words 'or a civil partner' in square brackets inserted by the Civil Partnership Act 2004, s 250(1), (2)(b). Date in force: 5 December 2005: see SI 2005/3175, art 3, Sch 2.
Sub-s (3): words 'or a civil partner' in square brackets inserted by the Civil Partnership Act 2004, s 250(1), (2)(b). Date in force: 5 December 2005: see SI 2005/3175, art 3, Sch 2.

A1.548E

[5   **Issue of full certificates where applicant has been married**]

(1) A court which—

(a) makes absolute a decree of nullity granted on the ground that an interim gender recognition certificate has been issued to a party to the marriage, or
(b) (in Scotland) grants a decree of divorce on that ground,

must, on doing so, issue a full gender recognition certificate to that party and send a copy to the Secretary of State.

(2) If an interim gender recognition certificate has been issued to a person and either—

(a) the person's marriage is dissolved or annulled (otherwise than on the ground mentioned in subsection (1)) in proceedings instituted during the period of six months beginning with the day on which it was issued, or
(b) the person's spouse dies within that period,

the person may make an application for a full gender recognition certificate at any time within the period specified in subsection (3) (unless the person is again married [or is a civil partner]).

(3) That period is the period of six months beginning with the day on which the marriage is dissolved or annulled or the death occurs.

A1.548E *Statutes*

(4) An application under subsection (2) must include evidence of the dissolution or annulment of the marriage and the date on which proceedings for it were instituted, or of the death of the spouse and the date on which it occurred.

(5) An application under subsection (2) is to be determined by a Gender Recognition Panel.

(6) The Panel—

  (a) must grant the application if satisfied that the applicant [is neither married nor a civil partner], and
  (b) otherwise must reject it.

(7) If the Panel grants the application it must issue a full gender recognition certificate to the applicant.

Appointment: 4 April 2005: see SI 2005/54, art 2.
Section heading: substituted by the Civil Partnership Act 2004, s 250(1), (3)(c). Date in force: 5 December 2005: see SI 2005/3175, art 3, Sch 2.
Sub-s (2): words 'or is a civil partner' in square brackets inserted by the Civil Partnership Act 2004, s 250(1), (3)(a). Date in force: 5 December 2005: see SI 2005/3175, art 3, Sch 2.
Sub-s (6): in para (a) words 'is neither married nor a civil partner' in square brackets substituted by the Civil Partnership Act 2004, s 250(1), (3)(b). Date in force: 5 December 2005: see SI 2005/3175, art 3, Sch 2.

A1.548F

[5A **Issue of full certificates where applicant has been a civil partner**]

[(1) A court which—

  (a) makes final a nullity order made on the ground that an interim gender recognition certificate has been issued to a civil partner, or
  (b) (in Scotland) grants a decree of dissolution on that ground,

must, on doing so, issue a full gender recognition certificate to that civil partner and send a copy to the Secretary of State.

(2) If an interim gender recognition certificate has been issued to a person and either—

  (a) the person's civil partnership is dissolved or annulled (otherwise than on the ground mentioned in subsection (1)) in proceedings instituted during the period of six months beginning with the day on which it was issued, or
  (b) the person's civil partner dies within that period,

the person may make an application for a full gender recognition certificate at any time within the period specified in subsection (3) (unless the person is again a civil partner or is married).

(3) That period is the period of six months beginning with the day on which the civil partnership is dissolved or annulled or the death occurs.

(4) An application under subsection (2) must include evidence of the dissolution or annulment of the civil partnership and the date on which proceedings for it were instituted, or of the death of the civil partner and the date on which it occurred.

(5) An application under subsection (2) is to be determined by a Gender Recognition Panel.

(6) The Panel—

  (a) must grant the application if satisfied that the applicant is neither a civil partner nor married, and

(b) otherwise must reject it.

(7) If the Panel grants the application it must issue a full gender recognition certificate to the applicant.]
Inserted by the Civil Partnership Act 2004, s 250(1), (4). Date in force: 5 December 2005: see SI 2005/3175, art 3, Sch 2.

A1.548G

6   Errors in certificates

(1) Where a gender recognition certificate has been issued to a person, the person or the Secretary of State may make an application for a corrected certificate on the ground that the certificate which has been issued contains an error.

(2) If the certificate was issued by a court the application is to be determined by the court but in any other case it is to be determined by a Gender Recognition Panel.

(3) The court or Panel—

  (a) must grant the application if satisfied that the gender recognition certificate contains an error, and
  (b) otherwise must reject it.

(4) If the court or Panel grants the application it must issue a corrected gender recognition certificate to the applicant.
Appointment: 4 April 2005: see SI 2005/54, art 2.

A1.548H

7   Applications: supplementary

(1) An application to a Gender Recognition Panel under section 1(1), 5(2)[, 5A(2)] or 6(1) must be made in a form and manner specified by the Secretary of State after consulting the Scottish Ministers and the Department of Finance and Personnel in Northern Ireland.

(2) The applicant must pay to the Secretary of State a non-refundable fee of an amount prescribed by order made by the Secretary of State unless the application is made in circumstances in which, in accordance with provision made by the order, no fee is payable; and fees of different amounts may be prescribed for different circumstances.
Appointment: 4 April 2005: see SI 2005/54, art 2.
Sub-s (1): reference to ', 5A(2)' in square brackets inserted by the Civil Partnership Act 2004, s 250(1), (5)(a). Date in force: 5 December 2005: see SI 2005/3175, art 3, Sch 2.

A1.548I

8   Appeals etc

(1) An applicant to a Gender Recognition Panel under section 1(1), 5(2)[, 5A(2)] or 6(1) may appeal to the High Court or Court of Session on a point of law against a decision by the Panel to reject the application.

(2) An appeal under subsection (1) must be heard in private if the applicant so requests.

(3) On such an appeal the court must—

  (a) allow the appeal and issue the certificate applied for,

A1.548I *Statutes*

(b) allow the appeal and refer the matter to the same or another Panel for re-consideration, or

(c) dismiss the appeal.

(4) If an application under section 1(1) is rejected, the applicant may not make another application before the end of the period of six months beginning with the date on which it is rejected.

(5) If an application under section 1(1), 5(2)[, 5A(2)] or 6(1) is granted but the Secretary of State considers that its grant was secured by fraud, the Secretary of State may refer the case to the High Court or Court of Session.

(6) On a reference under subsection (5) the court—

(a) must either quash or confirm the decision to grant the application, and

(b) if it quashes it, must revoke the gender recognition certificate issued on the grant of the application and may make any order which it considers appropriate in consequence of, or otherwise in connection with, doing so.

Appointment: 4 April 2005: see SI 2005/54, art 2.
Sub-s (1): reference to ', 5A(2)' in square brackets inserted by the Civil Partnership Act 2004, s 250(1), (5)(b). Date in force: 5 December 2005: see SI 2005/3175, art 3, Sch 2.
Sub-s (5): reference to ', 5A(2)' in square brackets inserted by the Civil Partnership Act 2004, s 250(1), (5)(b). Date in force: 5 December 2005: see SI 2005/3175, art 3, Sch 2.

Consequences of issue of gender recognition certificate etc

A1.548J

9 General

(1) Where a full gender recognition certificate is issued to a person, the person's gender becomes for all purposes the acquired gender (so that, if the acquired gender is the male gender, the person's sex becomes that of a man and, if it is the female gender, the person's sex becomes that of a woman).

(2) Subsection (1) does not affect things done, or events occurring, before the certificate is issued; but it does operate for the interpretation of enactments passed, and instruments and other documents made, before the certificate is issued (as well as those passed or made afterwards).

(3) Subsection (1) is subject to provision made by this Act or any other enactment or any subordinate legislation.

Appointment: 4 April 2005: see SI 2005/54, art 2.

A1.548K

10 Registration

(1) Where there is a UK birth register entry in relation to a person to whom a full gender recognition certificate is issued, the Secretary of State must send a copy of the certificate to the appropriate Registrar General.

(2) In this Act 'UK birth register entry', in relation to a person to whom a full gender recognition certificate is issued, means—

(a) an entry of which a certified copy is kept by a Registrar General, or

(b) an entry in a register so kept,

containing a record of the person's birth or adoption (or, if there would otherwise be more than one, the most recent).

(3) 'The appropriate Registrar General' means whichever of—

(a) the Registrar General for England and Wales,
(b) the Registrar General for Scotland, or
(c) the Registrar General for Northern Ireland,

keeps a certified copy of the person's UK birth register entry or the register containing that entry.

(4) Schedule 3 (provisions about registration) has effect.
Appointment: 4 April 2005: see SI 2005/54, art 2.

A1.548L

11 Marriage

Schedule 4 (amendments of marriage law) has effect.
Appointment: 4 April 2005: see SI 2005/54, art 2.

A1.548M

12 Parenthood

The fact that a person's gender has become the acquired gender under this Act does not affect the status of the person as the father or mother of a child.
Appointment: 4 April 2005: see SI 2005/54, art 2.

A1.548N

13 Social security benefits and pensions

Schedule 5 (entitlement to benefits and pensions) has effect.
Appointment: 4 April 2005: see SI 2005/54, art 2.

A1.548O

14 Discrimination

Schedule 6 (amendments of Sex Discrimination Act 1975 (c 65) and Sex Discrimination (Northern Ireland) Order 1976 (SI 1976/1042 (NI 15))) has effect.
Appointment: 4 April 2005: see SI 2005/54, art 2.

A1.548P

15 Succession etc

The fact that a person's gender has become the acquired gender under this Act does not affect the disposal or devolution of property under a will or other instrument made before the appointed day.
Appointment: 4 April 2005: see SI 2005/54, art 2.

A1.548Q

16 Peerages etc

The fact that a person's gender has become the acquired gender under this Act—

A1.548Q *Statutes*

    (a)   does not affect the descent of any peerage or dignity or title of honour, and

    (b)   does not affect the devolution of any property limited (expressly or not) by a will or other instrument to devolve (as nearly as the law permits) along with any peerage or dignity or title of honour unless an intention that it should do so is expressed in the will or other instrument.

Appointment: 4 April 2005: see SI 2005/54, art 2.

A1.548R

17   Trustees and personal representatives

(1) A trustee or personal representative is not under a duty, by virtue of the law relating to trusts or the administration of estates, to enquire, before conveying or distributing any property, whether a full gender recognition certificate has been issued to any person or revoked (if that fact could affect entitlement to the property).

(2) A trustee or personal representative is not liable to any person by reason of a conveyance or distribution of the property made without regard to whether a full gender recognition certificate has been issued to any person or revoked if the trustee or personal representative has not received notice of the fact before the conveyance or distribution.

(3) This section does not prejudice the right of a person to follow the property, or any property representing it, into the hands of another person who has received it unless that person has purchased it for value in good faith and without notice.

Appointment: 4 April 2005: see SI 2005/54, art 2.

A1.548S

18   Orders where expectations defeated

(1) This section applies where the disposition or devolution of any property under a will or other instrument (made on or after the appointed day) is different from what it would be but for the fact that a person's gender has become the acquired gender under this Act.

(2) A person may apply to the High Court or Court of Session for an order on the ground of being adversely affected by the different disposition or devolution of the property.

(3) The court may, if it is satisfied that it is just to do so, make in relation to any person benefiting from the different disposition or devolution of the property such order as it considers appropriate.

(4) An order may, in particular, make provision for—

    (a)   the payment of a lump sum to the applicant,
    (b)   the transfer of property to the applicant,
    (c)   the settlement of property for the benefit of the applicant,
    (d)   the acquisition of property and either its transfer to the applicant or its settlement for the benefit of the applicant.

(5) An order may contain consequential or supplementary provisions for giving effect to the order or for ensuring that it operates fairly as between the applicant and the other person or persons affected by it; and an order may, in particular, confer powers on trustees.

Appointment: 4 April 2005: see SI 2005/54, art 2.

A1.548T

19 Sport

(1) A body responsible for regulating the participation of persons as competitors in an event or events involving a gender-affected sport may, if subsection (2) is satisfied, prohibit or restrict the participation as competitors in the event or events of persons whose gender has become the acquired gender under this Act.

(2) This subsection is satisfied if the prohibition or restriction is necessary to secure—

    (a) fair competition, or
    (b) the safety of competitors,

at the event or events.

(3) 'Sport' means a sport, game or other activity of a competitive nature.

(4) A sport is a gender-affected sport if the physical strength, stamina or physique of average persons of one gender would put them at a disadvantage to average persons of the other gender as competitors in events involving the sport.

(5) This section does not affect—

    (a) section 44 of the Sex Discrimination Act 1975 (c 65) (exception from Parts 2 to 4 of that Act for acts related to sport), or
    (b) Article 45 of the Sex Discrimination (Northern Ireland) Order 1976 (SI 1976/1042 (NI 15)) (corresponding provision for Northern Ireland).

Appointment: 4 April 2005: see SI 2005/54, art 2.

A1.548U

20 Gender-specific offences

(1) Where (apart from this subsection) a relevant gender-specific offence could be committed or attempted only if the gender of a person to whom a full gender recognition certificate has been issued were not the acquired gender, the fact that the person's gender has become the acquired gender does not prevent the offence being committed or attempted.

(2) An offence is a 'relevant gender-specific offence' if—

    (a) either or both of the conditions in subsection (3) are satisfied, and
    (b) the commission of the offence involves the accused engaging in sexual activity.

(3) The conditions are—

    (a) that the offence may be committed only by a person of a particular gender, and
    (b) that the offence may be committed only on, or in relation to, a person of a particular gender,

and the references to a particular gender include a gender identified by reference to the gender of the other person involved.

Appointment: 4 April 2005: see SI 2005/54, art 2.

A1.548V

21 Foreign gender change and marriage

(1) A person's gender is not to be regarded as having changed by reason only that it has changed under the law of a country or territory outside the United Kingdom.

A1.548V   *Statutes*

(2)   Accordingly, a person is not to be regarded as being married by reason of having entered into a foreign post-recognition marriage.

(3)   But if a full gender recognition certificate is issued to a person who has entered into a foreign post-recognition marriage, after the issue of the certificate the marriage is no longer to be regarded as being void on the ground that (at the time when it was entered into) the parties to it were not respectively male and female.

(4)   However, subsection (3) does not apply to a foreign post-recognition marriage if a party to it has entered into a later (valid) marriage [or civil partnership] before the issue of the full gender recognition certificate.

(5)   For the purposes of this section a person has entered into a foreign post-recognition marriage if (and only if)—

   (a)   the person has entered into a marriage in accordance with the law of a country or territory outside the United Kingdom,
   (b)   before the marriage was entered into the person had changed gender under the law of that or any other country or territory outside the United Kingdom,
   (c)   the other party to the marriage was not of the gender to which the person had changed under the law of that country or territory, and
   (d)   by virtue of subsection (1) the person's gender was not regarded as having changed under the law of any part of the United Kingdom.

(6)   Nothing in this section prevents the exercise of any enforceable Community right.
Appointment: 4 April 2005: see SI 2005/54, art 2.
Sub-s (4): words 'or civil partnership' in square brackets inserted by the Civil Partnership Act 2004, s 250(1), (6). Date in force: 5 December 2005: see SI 2005/3175, art 3, Sch 2.

Supplementary

A1.548W

22   Prohibition on disclosure of information

(1)   It is an offence for a person who has acquired protected information in an official capacity to disclose the information to any other person.

(2)   'Protected information' means information which relates to a person who has made an application under section 1(1) and which—

   (a)   concerns that application or any application by the person under section 5(2)[, 5A(2)] or 6(1), or
   (b)   if the application under section 1(1) is granted, otherwise concerns the person's gender before it becomes the acquired gender.

(3)   A person acquires protected information in an official capacity if the person acquires it—

   (a)   in connection with the person's functions as a member of the civil service, a constable or the holder of any other public office or in connection with the functions of a local or public authority or of a voluntary organisation,
   (b)   as an employer, or prospective employer, of the person to whom the information relates or as a person employed by such an employer or prospective employer, or
   (c)   in the course of, or otherwise in connection with, the conduct of business or the supply of professional services.

(4)   But it is not an offence under this section to disclose protected information relating to a person if—

   (a)   the information does not enable that person to be identified,

(b) that person has agreed to the disclosure of the information,
(c) the information is protected information by virtue of subsection (2)(b) and the person by whom the disclosure is made does not know or believe that a full gender recognition certificate has been issued,
(d) the disclosure is in accordance with an order of a court or tribunal,
(e) the disclosure is for the purpose of instituting, or otherwise for the purposes of, proceedings before a court or tribunal,
(f) the disclosure is for the purpose of preventing or investigating crime,
(g) the disclosure is made to the Registrar General for England and Wales, the Registrar General for Scotland or the Registrar General for Northern Ireland,
(h) the disclosure is made for the purposes of the social security system or a pension scheme,
(i) the disclosure is in accordance with provision made by an order under subsection (5), or
(j) the disclosure is in accordance with any provision of, or made by virtue of, an enactment other than this section.

(5) The Secretary of State may by order make provision prescribing circumstances in which the disclosure of protected information is not to constitute an offence under this section.

(6) The power conferred by subsection (5) is exercisable by the Scottish Ministers (rather than the Secretary of State) where the provision to be made is within the legislative competence of the Scottish Parliament.

(7) An order under subsection (5) may make provision permitting—

(a) disclosure to specified persons or persons of a specified description,
(b) disclosure for specified purposes,
(c) disclosure of specified descriptions of information, or
(d) disclosure by specified persons or persons of a specified description.

(8) A person guilty of an offence under this section is liable on summary conviction to a fine not exceeding level 5 on the standard scale.
Appointment: 4 April 2005: see SI 2005/54, art 2.
Sub-s (2): in para (a) reference to ', 5A(2)' in square brackets inserted by the Civil Partnership Act 2004, s 250(1), (5)(c). Date in force: 5 December 2005: see SI 2005/3175, art 3, Sch 2.

A1.548X

23 Power to modify statutory provisions

(1) The Secretary of State may by order make provision for modifying the operation of any enactment or subordinate legislation in relation to—

(a) persons whose gender has become the acquired gender under this Act, or
(b) any description of such persons.

(2) The power conferred by subsection (1) is exercisable by the Scottish Ministers (rather than the Secretary of State) where the provision to be made is within the legislative competence of the Scottish Parliament.

(3) The appropriate Northern Ireland department may by order make provision for modifying the operation of any enactment or subordinate legislation which deals with a transferred matter in relation to—

(a) persons whose gender has become the acquired gender under this Act, or
(b) any description of such persons.

(4) In subsection (3)—

A1.548X *Statutes*

> 'the appropriate Northern Ireland department', in relation to any enactment or subordinate legislation which deals with a transferred matter, means the Northern Ireland department which has responsibility for that matter,
> 'deals with' is to be construed in accordance with section 98(2) and (3) of the Northern Ireland Act 1998 (c 47), and
> 'transferred matter' has the meaning given by section 4(1) of that Act.

(5) Before an order is made under this section, appropriate consultation must be undertaken with persons likely to be affected by it.
Royal Assent: 1 July 2004: (no specific commencement provision).
Sub-ss (3), (4) apply to Northern ireland only: see s 28(4)(a).

A1.548Y

24 Orders and regulations

(1) Any power of the Secretary of State ..., the Scottish Ministers or a Northern Ireland department to make an order under this Act includes power to make any appropriate incidental, supplementary, consequential or transitional provision or savings.

(2) Any power of the Secretary of State ... or the Scottish Ministers to make an order under this Act, and any power of the Registrar General for England and Wales or the Registrar General for Scotland to make regulations under this Act, is exercisable by statutory instrument.

(3) No order may be made under section 2 ... unless a draft of the statutory instrument containing the order has been laid before, and approved by a resolution of, each House of Parliament.

(4) A statutory instrument containing an order made by the Secretary of State under section 7, 22 or 23 is subject to annulment in pursuance of a resolution of either House of Parliament.

(5) A statutory instrument containing an order made by the Scottish Ministers under section 22 or 23 is subject to annulment in pursuance of a resolution of the Scottish Parliament.

(6) Any power of a Northern Ireland department to make an order or regulations under this Act is exercisable by statutory rule for the purposes of the Statutory Rules (Northern Ireland) Order 1979 (SI 1979/1573 (NI 12)).

(7) Orders and regulations made by a Northern Ireland department under this Act are subject to negative resolution (within the meaning of section 41(6) of the Interpretation Act (Northern Ireland) 1954 (c 33 (NI))).
Royal Assent: 1 July 2004: (no specific commencement provision).
Sub-s (5) applies to Scotland only: see s 28(2)(a).
Sub-ss (6), (7) apply to Northern Ireland only: see s 28(4)(b).
Sub-s (1): words omitted repealed by the Legislative and Regulatory Reform Act 2006, Schedule. Date in force: 8 January 2007: see the Legislative and Regulatory Reform Act 2006, s 33.
Sub-s (2): words omitted repealed by the Legislative and Regulatory Reform Act 2006, s 30(1), Schedule. Date in force: 8 January 2007: see the Legislative and Regulatory Reform Act 2006, s 33.
Sub-s (3): words omitted repealed by the Legislative and Regulatory Reform Act 2006, s 30(1), Schedule. Date in force: 8 January 2007: see the Legislative and Regulatory Reform Act 2006, s 33.

A1.548Z

25 Interpretation

In this Act—

'the acquired gender' is to be construed in accordance with section 1(2),
'approved country or territory' has the meaning given by section 2(4),
'the appointed day' means the day appointed by order under section 26,
'chartered psychologist' means a person for the time being listed in the British Psychological Society's Register of Chartered Psychologists,
'enactment' includes an enactment contained in an Act of the Scottish Parliament or in any Northern Ireland legislation,
'full gender recognition certificate' and 'interim gender recognition certificate' mean the certificates issued as such under section 4[, 5 or 5A] and 'gender recognition certificate' means either of those sorts of certificate,
'gender dysphoria' means the disorder variously referred to as gender dysphoria, gender identity disorder and transsexualism,
'Gender Recognition Panel' (and 'Panel') is to be construed in accordance with Schedule 1,
'subordinate legislation' means an Order in Council, an order, rules, regulations, a scheme, a warrant, bye-laws or any other instrument made under an enactment, and
'UK birth register entry' has the meaning given by section 10(2).

Royal Assent: 1 July 2004: (no specific commencement provision).
In definition ' "full gender recognition certificate" and "interim gender recognition certificate" ' words ', 5 or 5A' in square brackets substituted by the Civil Partnership Act 2004, s 250(1), (7). Date in force: 5 December 2005: see SI 2005/3175, art 3, Sch 2.

A1.548ZA

26 Commencement

Apart from sections 23 to 25, this section and sections 28 and 29, this Act does not come into force until such day as the Secretary of State may appoint by order made after consulting the Scottish Ministers and the Department of Finance and Personnel in Northern Ireland.

Royal Assent: 1 July 2004: (no specific commencement provision).

CIVIL PARTNERSHIP ACT 2004

(2004, C 33)

An Act to make provision for and in connection with civil partnership.

[18th November 2004]

Be it enacted by the Queen's most Excellent Majesty, by and with the advice and consent of the Lords Spiritual and Temporal, and Commons, in this present Parliament assembled, and by the authority of the same, as follows:—

A1.567

213 Specified relationships

(1) A specified relationship is a relationship which is specified for the purposes of section 212 by Schedule 20.

(2) The [Lord Privy Seal] may by order amend Schedule 20 by—

(a) adding a relationship,
(b) amending the description of a relationship, or
(c) omitting a relationship.

(3) No order may be made under this section without the consent of the Scottish Ministers and the Department of Finance and Personnel.

(4) The power to make an order under this section is exercisable by statutory instrument.

(5) An order which contains any provision (whether alone or with other provisions) amending Schedule 20 by—

(a) amending the description of a relationship, or
(b) omitting a relationship,

may not be made unless a draft of the statutory instrument containing the order is laid before, and approved by a resolution of, each House of Parliament.

(6) A statutory instrument containing any other order under this section is subject to annulment in pursuance of a resolution of either House of Parliament.

Sub-s (2): words 'Lord Privy Seal' in square brackets substituted by SI 2007/2914, art 8, Schedule, para 14. Date in force: 12 October 2007: see SI 2007/2914, art 1(2).

MENTAL CAPACITY ACT 2005

2005 CHAPTER 9

An Act to make new provision relating to persons who lack capacity; to establish a superior court of record called the Court of Protection in place of the office of the Supreme Court called by that name; to make provision in connection with the Convention on the International Protection of Adults signed at the Hague on 13th January 2000; and for connected purposes.

[7th April 2005]

Be it enacted by the Queen's most Excellent Majesty, by and with the advice and consent of the Lords Spiritual and Temporal, and Commons, in this present Parliament assembled, and by the authority of the same, as follows:—

Lasting powers of attorney

A1.583

11 Lasting powers of attorney: restrictions

(1) A lasting power of attorney does not authorise the donee (or, if more than one, any of them) to do an act that is intended to restrain P, unless three conditions are satisfied.

(2) The first condition is that P lacks, or the donee reasonably believes that P lacks, capacity in relation to the matter in question.

(3) The second is that the donee reasonably believes that it is necessary to do the act in order to prevent harm to P.

(4) The third is that the act is a proportionate response to—

   (a) the likelihood of P's suffering harm, and
   (b) the seriousness of that harm.

(5) For the purposes of this section, the donee restrains P if he—

   (a) uses, or threatens to use, force to secure the doing of an act which P resists, or
   (b) restricts P's liberty of movement, whether or not P resists,

or if he authorises another person to do any of those things.

(6) ...

(7) Where a lasting power of attorney authorises the donee (or, if more than one, any of them) to make decisions about P's personal welfare, the authority—

   (a) does not extend to making such decisions in circumstances other than those where P lacks, or the donee reasonably believes that P lacks, capacity,
   (b) is subject to sections 24 to 26 (advance decisions to refuse treatment), and
   (c) extends to giving or refusing consent to the carrying out or continuation of a treatment by a person providing health care for P.

(8) But subsection (7)(c)—

   (a) does not authorise the giving or refusing of consent to the carrying out or continuation of life-sustaining treatment, unless the instrument contains express provision to that effect, and
   (b) is subject to any conditions or restrictions in the instrument.

A1.583 *Statutes*

Sub-s (6): repealed by the Mental Health Act 2007, ss 50(1), (4)(b), 55, Sch 11, Pt 10. Date in force: 1 April 2009: see SI 2009/139, art 2(b); for transitional provisions see art 3, Schedule thereto.

A1.586A

[16A   Section 16 powers: Mental Health Act patients etc]

[(1) If a person is ineligible to be deprived of liberty by this Act, the court may not include in a welfare order provision which authorises the person to be deprived of his liberty.

(2) If—

  (a) a welfare order includes provision which authorises a person to be deprived of his liberty, and
  (b) that person becomes ineligible to be deprived of liberty by this Act,

the provision ceases to have effect for as long as the person remains ineligible.

(3) Nothing in subsection (2) affects the power of the court under section 16(7) to vary or discharge the welfare order.

(4) For the purposes of this section—

  (a) Schedule 1A applies for determining whether or not P is ineligible to be deprived of liberty by this Act;
  (b) 'welfare order' means an order under section 16(2)(a).]

Inserted by the Mental Health Act 2007, s 50(1), (3). Date in force: 1 April 2009: see SI 2009/139, art 2(b); for transitional provisions see art 3, Schedule thereto.

SCHEDULE 4
PROVISIONS APPLYING TO EXISTING ENDURING POWERS OF ATTORNEY

Section 66(3)

A1.591

PART 1
ENDURING POWERS OF ATTORNEY

Enduring power of attorney to survive mental incapacity of donor

1   (1) Where an individual has created a power of attorney which is an enduring power within the meaning of this Schedule—

  (a) the power is not revoked by any subsequent mental incapacity of his,
  (b) upon such incapacity supervening, the donee of the power may not do anything under the authority of the power except as provided by sub-paragraph (2) unless or until the instrument creating the power is registered under paragraph 13, and
  (c) if and so long as paragraph (b) operates to suspend the donee's authority to act under the power, section 5 of the Powers of Attorney Act 1971 (c 27) (protection of donee and third persons), so far as applicable, applies as if the power had been revoked by the donor's mental incapacity,

and, accordingly, section 1 of this Act does not apply.

(2) Despite sub-paragraph (1)(b), where the attorney has made an application for registration of the instrument then, until it is registered, the attorney may take action under the power—

(a) to maintain the donor or prevent loss to his estate, or
(b) to maintain himself or other persons in so far as paragraph 3(2) permits him to do so.

(3) Where the attorney purports to act as provided by sub-paragraph (2) then, in favour of a person who deals with him without knowledge that the attorney is acting otherwise than in accordance with sub-paragraph (2)(a) or (b), the transaction between them is as valid as if the attorney were acting in accordance with sub-paragraph (2)(a) or (b).

Characteristics of an enduring power of attorney

2 (1) Subject to sub-paragraphs (5) and (6) and paragraph 20, a power of attorney is an enduring power within the meaning of this Schedule if the instrument which creates the power—

(a) is in the prescribed form,
(b) was executed in the prescribed manner by the donor and the attorney, and
(c) incorporated at the time of execution by the donor the prescribed explanatory information.

(2) In this paragraph, 'prescribed' means prescribed by such of the following regulations as applied when the instrument was executed—

(a) the Enduring Powers of Attorney (Prescribed Form) Regulations 1986 (SI 1986/126),
(b) the Enduring Powers of Attorney (Prescribed Form) Regulations 1987 (SI 1987/1612),
(c) the Enduring Powers of Attorney (Prescribed Form) Regulations 1990 (SI 1990/1376),
(d) the Enduring Powers of Attorney (Welsh Language Prescribed Form) Regulations 2000 (SI 2000/289).

(3) An instrument in the prescribed form purporting to have been executed in the prescribed manner is to be taken, in the absence of evidence to the contrary, to be a document which incorporated at the time of execution by the donor the prescribed explanatory information.

(4) If an instrument differs in an immaterial respect in form or mode of expression from the prescribed form it is to be treated as sufficient in point of form and expression.

(5) A power of attorney cannot be an enduring power unless, when he executes the instrument creating it, the attorney is—

(a) an individual who has reached 18 and is not bankrupt, or
(b) a trust corporation.

(6) A power of attorney which gives the attorney a right to appoint a substitute or successor cannot be an enduring power.

(7) An enduring power is revoked by the bankruptcy of the donor or attorney.

(8) But where the donor or attorney is bankrupt merely because an interim bankruptcy restrictions order has effect in respect of him, the power is suspended for so long as the order has effect.

(9) An enduring power is revoked if the court—

(a) exercises a power under sections 16 to 20 in relation to the donor, and
(b) directs that the enduring power is to be revoked.

A1.591 *Statutes*

(10) No disclaimer of an enduring power, whether by deed or otherwise, is valid unless and until the attorney gives notice of it to the donor or, where paragraph 4(6) or 15(1) applies, to the Public Guardian.

Scope of authority etc of attorney under enduring power

3 (1) If the instrument which creates an enduring power of attorney is expressed to confer general authority on the attorney, the instrument operates to confer, subject to—

(a) the restriction imposed by sub-paragraph (3), and
(b) any conditions or restrictions contained in the instrument,

authority to do on behalf of the donor anything which the donor could lawfully do by an attorney at the time when the donor executed the instrument.

(2) Subject to any conditions or restrictions contained in the instrument, an attorney under an enduring power, whether general or limited, may (without obtaining any consent) act under the power so as to benefit himself or other persons than the donor to the following extent but no further—

(a) he may so act in relation to himself or in relation to any other person if the donor might be expected to provide for his or that person's needs respectively, and
(b) he may do whatever the donor might be expected to do to meet those needs.

(3) Without prejudice to sub-paragraph (2) but subject to any conditions or restrictions contained in the instrument, an attorney under an enduring power, whether general or limited, may (without obtaining any consent) dispose of the property of the donor by way of gift to the following extent but no further—

(a) he may make gifts of a seasonal nature or at a time, or on an anniversary, of a birth, a marriage or the formation of a civil partnership, to persons (including himself) who are related to or connected with the donor, and
(b) he may make gifts to any charity to whom the donor made or might be expected to make gifts,

provided that the value of each such gift is not unreasonable having regard to all the circumstances and in particular the size of the donor's estate.

PART 2
ACTION ON ACTUAL OR IMPENDING INCAPACITY OF DONOR

Duties of attorney in event of actual or impending incapacity of donor

4 (1) Sub-paragraphs (2) to (6) apply if the attorney under an enduring power has reason to believe that the donor is or is becoming mentally incapable.

(2) The attorney must, as soon as practicable, make an application to the Public Guardian for the registration of the instrument creating the power.

(3) Before making an application for registration the attorney must comply with the provisions as to notice set out in Part 3 of this Schedule.

(4) An application for registration—

(a) must be made in the prescribed form, and
(b) must contain such statements as may be prescribed.

(5) The attorney—

(a) may, before making an application for the registration of the instrument, refer to the court for its determination any question as to the validity of the power, and

(b) must comply with any direction given to him by the court on that determination.

(6) No disclaimer of the power is valid unless and until the attorney gives notice of it to the Public Guardian; and the Public Guardian must notify the donor if he receives a notice under this sub-paragraph.

(7) A person who, in an application for registration, makes a statement which he knows to be false in a material particular is guilty of an offence and is liable—

(a) on summary conviction, to imprisonment for a term not exceeding 12 months or a fine not exceeding the statutory maximum or both;

(b) on conviction on indictment, to imprisonment for a term not exceeding 2 years or a fine or both.

(8) In this paragraph, 'prescribed' means prescribed by regulations made for the purposes of this Schedule by the Lord Chancellor.

PART 8
INTERPRETATION

23 (1) In this Schedule—

'enduring power' is to be construed in accordance with paragraph 2,

'mentally incapable' or 'mental incapacity', except where it refers to revocation at common law, means in relation to any person, that he is incapable by reason of mental disorder (*within the meaning of the Mental Health Act*) of managing and administering his property and affairs and 'mentally capable' and 'mental capacity' are to be construed accordingly,

'notice' means notice in writing, and

'prescribed', except for the purposes of paragraph 2, means prescribed by regulations made for the purposes of this Schedule by the Lord Chancellor.

[(1A) In sub-paragraph (1), 'mental disorder' has the same meaning as in the Mental Health Act but disregarding the amendments made to that Act by the Mental Health Act 2007.]

(2) Any question arising under or for the purposes of this Schedule as to what the donor of the power might at any time be expected to do is to be determined by assuming that he had full mental capacity at the time but otherwise by reference to the circumstances existing at that time.

Para 23: in sub-para (1) in definition ' "mentally incapable" and "mental incapacity" ' words '(within the meaning of the Mental Health Act)' in italics repealed by the Mental Health Act 2007, ss 1(4), 55, Sch 1, Pt 2, para 23(1), (2), Sch 11, Pt 1. Date in force: 3 November 2008: see SI 2008/1900, art 2(a), (p); for transitional provisions and savings see the Mental Health Act 2007, s 53, Sch 10, paras 1, 2(1)–(3), (4)(a), (g).

Para 23: sub-para (1A) inserted by the Mental Health Act 2007, s 1(4), Sch 1, Pt 2, para 23(1), (3). Date in force: 3 November 2008: see SI 2008/1900, art 2(a); for transitional provisions and savings see the Mental Health Act 2007, s 53, Sch 10, paras 1, 2(1)–(3), (4)(a).

A1.592A *Statutes*

HUMAN FERTILISATION AND EMBRYOLOGY ACT 2008

2008 CHAPTER 22

An Act to amend the Human Fertilisation and Embryology Act 1990 and the Surrogacy Arrangements Act 1985; to make provision about the persons who in certain circumstances are to be treated in law as the parents of a child; and for connected purposes.

[13th November 2008]

Be it enacted by the Queen's most Excellent Majesty, by and with the advice and consent of the Lords Spiritual and Temporal, and Commons, in this present Parliament assembled, and by the authority of the same, as follows:—

PART 2
PARENTHOOD IN CASES INVOLVING ASSISTED REPRODUCTION

Meaning of 'mother'

A1.592A

33   Meaning of 'mother'

(1) The woman who is carrying or has carried a child as a result of the placing in her of an embryo or of sperm and eggs, and no other woman, is to be treated as the mother of the child.

(2) Subsection (1) does not apply to any child to the extent that the child is treated by virtue of adoption as not being the woman's child.

(3) Subsection (1) applies whether the woman was in the United Kingdom or elsewhere at the time of the placing in her of the embryo or the sperm and eggs.

Application of sections 35 to 47

A1.592B

34   Application of sections 35 to 47

(1) Sections 35 to 47 apply, in the case of a child who is being or has been carried by a woman (referred to in those sections as 'W') as a result of the placing in her of an embryo or of sperm and eggs or her artificial insemination, to determine who is to be treated as the other parent of the child.

(2) Subsection (1) has effect subject to the provisions of sections 39, 40 and 46 limiting the purposes for which a person is treated as the child's other parent by virtue of those sections.

Meaning of 'father'

A1.592C

35   Woman married at time of treatment

(1) If—

(a) at the time of the placing in her of the embryo or of the sperm and eggs or of her artificial insemination, W was a party to a marriage, and
(b) the creation of the embryo carried by her was not brought about with the sperm of the other party to the marriage,

then, subject to section 38(2) to (4), the other party to the marriage is to be treated as the father of the child unless it is shown that he did not consent to the placing in her of the embryo or the sperm and eggs or to her artificial insemination (as the case may be).

(2) This section applies whether W was in the United Kingdom or elsewhere at the time mentioned in subsection (1)(a).

A1.592D

36 Treatment provided to woman where agreed fatherhood conditions apply

If no man is treated by virtue of section 35 as the father of the child and no woman is treated by virtue of section 42 as a parent of the child but—

(a) the embryo or the sperm and eggs were placed in W, or W was artificially inseminated, in the course of treatment services provided in the United Kingdom by a person to whom a licence applies,
(b) at the time when the embryo or the sperm and eggs were placed in W, or W was artificially inseminated, the agreed fatherhood conditions (as set out in section 37) were satisfied in relation to a man, in relation to treatment provided to W under the licence,
(c) the man remained alive at that time, and
(d) the creation of the embryo carried by W was not brought about with the man's sperm,

then, subject to section 38(2) to (4), the man is to be treated as the father of the child.

A1.592E

37 The agreed fatherhood conditions

(1) The agreed fatherhood conditions referred to in section 36(b) are met in relation to a man ('M') in relation to treatment provided to W under a licence if, but only if,—

(a) M has given the person responsible a notice stating that he consents to being treated as the father of any child resulting from treatment provided to W under the licence,
(b) W has given the person responsible a notice stating that she consents to M being so treated,
(c) neither M nor W has, since giving notice under paragraph (a) or (b), given the person responsible notice of the withdrawal of M's or W's consent to M being so treated,
(d) W has not, since the giving of the notice under paragraph (b), given the person responsible—
  (i) a further notice under that paragraph stating that she consents to another man being treated as the father of any resulting child, or
  (ii) a notice under section 44(1)(b) stating that she consents to a woman being treated as a parent of any resulting child, and
(e) W and M are not within prohibited degrees of relationship in relation to each other.

(2) A notice under subsection (1)(a), (b) or (c) must be in writing and must be signed by the person giving it.

A1.592F *Statutes*

(3) A notice under subsection (1)(a), (b) or (c) by a person ('S') who is unable to sign because of illness, injury or physical disability is to be taken to comply with the requirement of subsection (2) as to signature if it is signed at the direction of S, in the presence of S and in the presence of at least one witness who attests the signature.

A1.592F

38 Further provision relating to sections 35 and 36

(1) Where a person is to be treated as the father of the child by virtue of section 35 or 36, no other person is to be treated as the father of the child.

(2) In England and Wales and Northern Ireland, sections 35 and 36 do not affect any presumption, applying by virtue of the rules of common law, that a child is the legitimate child of the parties to a marriage.

(3) In Scotland, sections 35 and 36 do not apply in relation to any child who, by virtue of any enactment or other rule of law, is treated as the child of the parties to a marriage.

(4) Sections 35 and 36 do not apply to any child to the extent that the child is treated by virtue of adoption as not being the man's child.

A1.592G

39 Use of sperm, or transfer of embryo, after death of man providing sperm

(1) If—
- (a) the child has been carried by W as a result of the placing in her of an embryo or of sperm and eggs or her artificial insemination,
- (b) the creation of the embryo carried by W was brought about by using the sperm of a man after his death, or the creation of the embryo was brought about using the sperm of a man before his death but the embryo was placed in W after his death,
- (c) the man consented in writing (and did not withdraw the consent)—
  - (i) to the use of his sperm after his death which brought about the creation of the embryo carried by W or (as the case may be) to the placing in W after his death of the embryo which was brought about using his sperm before his death, and
  - (ii) to being treated for the purpose mentioned in subsection (3) as the father of any resulting child,
- (d) W has elected in writing not later than the end of the period of 42 days from the day on which the child was born for the man to be treated for the purpose mentioned in subsection (3) as the father of the child, and
- (e) no-one else is to be treated—
  - (i) as the father of the child by virtue of section 35 or 36 or by virtue of section 38(2) or (3), or
  - (ii) as a parent of the child by virtue of section 42 or 43 or by virtue of adoption,

then the man is to be treated for the purpose mentioned in subsection (3) as the father of the child.

(2) Subsection (1) applies whether W was in the United Kingdom or elsewhere at the time of the placing in her of the embryo or of the sperm and eggs or of her artificial insemination.

(3) The purpose referred to in subsection (1) is the purpose of enabling the man's particulars to be entered as the particulars of the child's father in a relevant register of births.

(4) In the application of this section to Scotland, for any reference to a period of 42 days there is substituted a reference to a period of 21 days.

A1.592H

40   Embryo transferred after death of husband etc who did not provide sperm

(1) If—
- (a) the child has been carried by W as a result of the placing in her of an embryo,
- (b) the embryo was created at a time when W was a party to a marriage,
- (c) the creation of the embryo was not brought about with the sperm of the other party to the marriage,
- (d) the other party to the marriage died before the placing of the embryo in W,
- (e) the other party to the marriage consented in writing (and did not withdraw the consent)—
  - (i) to the placing of the embryo in W after his death, and
  - (ii) to being treated for the purpose mentioned in subsection (4) as the father of any resulting child,
- (f) W has elected in writing not later than the end of the period of 42 days from the day on which the child was born for the man to be treated for the purpose mentioned in subsection (4) as the father of the child, and
- (g) no-one else is to be treated—
  - (i) as the father of the child by virtue of section 35 or 36 or by virtue of section 38(2) or (3), or
  - (ii) as a parent of the child by virtue of section 42 or 43 or by virtue of adoption,

then the man is to be treated for the purpose mentioned in subsection (4) as the father of the child.

(2) If—
- (a) the child has been carried by W as a result of the placing in her of an embryo,
- (b) the embryo was not created at a time when W was a party to a marriage or a civil partnership but was created in the course of treatment services provided to W in the United Kingdom by a person to whom a licence applies,
- (c) a man consented in writing (and did not withdraw the consent)—
  - (i) to the placing of the embryo in W after his death, and
  - (ii) to being treated for the purpose mentioned in subsection (4) as the father of any resulting child,
- (d) the creation of the embryo was not brought about with the sperm of that man,
- (e) the man died before the placing of the embryo in W,
- (f) immediately before the man's death, the agreed fatherhood conditions set out in section 37 were met in relation to the man in relation to treatment proposed to be provided to W in the United Kingdom by a person to whom a licence applies,
- (g) W has elected in writing not later than the end of the period of 42 days from the day on which the child was born for the man to be treated for the purpose mentioned in subsection (4) as the father of the child, and
- (h) no-one else is to be treated—
  - (i) as the father of the child by virtue of section 35 or 36 or by virtue of section 38(2) or (3), or

A1.592I *Statutes*

(ii) as a parent of the child by virtue of section 42 or 43 or by virtue of adoption,

then the man is to be treated for the purpose mentioned in subsection (4) as the father of the child.

(3) Subsections (1) and (2) apply whether W was in the United Kingdom or elsewhere at the time of the placing in her of the embryo.

(4) The purpose referred to in subsections (1) and (2) is the purpose of enabling the man's particulars to be entered as the particulars of the child's father in a relevant register of births.

(5) In the application of this section to Scotland, for any reference to a period of 42 days there is substituted a reference to a period of 21 days.

A1.592I

41   Persons not to be treated as father

(1) Where the sperm of a man who had given such consent as is required by paragraph 5 of Schedule 3 to the 1990 Act (consent to use of gametes for purposes of treatment services or non-medical fertility services) was used for a purpose for which such consent was required, he is not to be treated as the father of the child.

(2) Where the sperm of a man, or an embryo the creation of which was brought about with his sperm, was used after his death, he is not, subject to section 39, to be treated as the father of the child.

(3) Subsection (2) applies whether W was in the United Kingdom or elsewhere at the time of the placing in her of the embryo or of the sperm and eggs or of her artificial insemination.

Cases in which woman to be other parent

A1.592J

42   Woman in civil partnership at time of treatment

(1) If at the time of the placing in her of the embryo or the sperm and eggs or of her artificial insemination, W was a party to a civil partnership, then subject to section 45(2) to (4), the other party to the civil partnership is to be treated as a parent of the child unless it is shown that she did not consent to the placing in W of the embryo or the sperm and eggs or to her artificial insemination (as the case may be).

(2) This section applies whether W was in the United Kingdom or elsewhere at the time mentioned in subsection (1).

A1.592K

43   Treatment provided to woman who agrees that second woman to be parent

If no man is treated by virtue of section 35 as the father of the child and no woman is treated by virtue of section 42 as a parent of the child but—

(a) the embryo or the sperm and eggs were placed in W, or W was artificially inseminated, in the course of treatment services provided in the United Kingdom by a person to whom a licence applies,

(b) at the time when the embryo or the sperm and eggs were placed in W, or W was artificially inseminated, the agreed female parenthood conditions (as set out in section 44) were met in relation to another woman, in relation to treatment provided to W under that licence, and
(c) the other woman remained alive at that time,

then, subject to section 45(2) to (4), the other woman is to be treated as a parent of the child.

A1.592L

44   The agreed female parenthood conditions

(1) The agreed female parenthood conditions referred to in section 43(b) are met in relation to another woman ('P') in relation to treatment provided to W under a licence if, but only if,—

(a) P has given the person responsible a notice stating that P consents to P being treated as a parent of any child resulting from treatment provided to W under the licence,
(b) W has given the person responsible a notice stating that W agrees to P being so treated,
(c) neither W nor P has, since giving notice under paragraph (a) or (b), given the person responsible notice of the withdrawal of P's or W's consent to P being so treated,
(d) W has not, since the giving of the notice under paragraph (b), given the person responsible—
   (i) a further notice under that paragraph stating that W consents to a woman other than P being treated as a parent of any resulting child, or
   (ii) a notice under section 37(1)(b) stating that W consents to a man being treated as the father of any resulting child, and
(e) W and P are not within prohibited degrees of relationship in relation to each other.

(2) A notice under subsection (1)(a), (b) or (c) must be in writing and must be signed by the person giving it.

(3) A notice under subsection (1)(a), (b) or (c) by a person ('S') who is unable to sign because of illness, injury or physical disability is to be taken to comply with the requirement of subsection (2) as to signature if it is signed at the direction of S, in the presence of S and in the presence of at least one witness who attests the signature.

A1.592M

45   Further provision relating to sections 42 and 43

(1) Where a woman is treated by virtue of section 42 or 43 as a parent of the child, no man is to be treated as the father of the child.

(2) In England and Wales and Northern Ireland, sections 42 and 43 do not affect any presumption, applying by virtue of the rules of common law, that a child is the legitimate child of the parties to a marriage.

(3) In Scotland, sections 42 and 43 do not apply in relation to any child who, by virtue of any enactment or other rule of law, is treated as the child of the parties to a marriage.

(4) Sections 42 and 43 do not apply to any child to the extent that the child is treated by virtue of adoption as not being the woman's child.

A1.592N

46 Embryo transferred after death of civil partner or intended female parent

(1) If—
- (a) the child has been carried by W as the result of the placing in her of an embryo,
- (b) the embryo was created at a time when W was a party to a civil partnership,
- (c) the other party to the civil partnership died before the placing of the embryo in W,
- (d) the other party to the civil partnership consented in writing (and did not withdraw the consent)—
  - (i) to the placing of the embryo in W after the death of the other party, and
  - (ii) to being treated for the purpose mentioned in subsection (4) as the parent of any resulting child,
- (e) W has elected in writing not later than the end of the period of 42 days from the day on which the child was born for the other party to the civil partnership to be treated for the purpose mentioned in subsection (4) as the parent of the child, and
- (f) no one else is to be treated—
  - (i) as the father of the child by virtue of section 35 or 36 or by virtue of section 45(2) or (3), or
  - (ii) as a parent of the child by virtue of section 42 or 43 or by virtue of adoption,

then the other party to the civil partnership is to be treated for the purpose mentioned in subsection (4) as a parent of the child.

(2) If—
- (a) the child has been carried by W as the result of the placing in her of an embryo,
- (b) the embryo was not created at a time when W was a party to a marriage or a civil partnership, but was created in the course of treatment services provided to W in the United Kingdom by a person to whom a licence applies,
- (c) another woman consented in writing (and did not withdraw the consent)—
  - (i) to the placing of the embryo in W after the death of the other woman, and
  - (ii) to being treated for the purpose mentioned in subsection (4) as the parent of any resulting child,
- (d) the other woman died before the placing of the embryo in W,
- (e) immediately before the other woman's death, the agreed female parenthood conditions set out in section 44 were met in relation to the other woman in relation to treatment proposed to be provided to W in the United Kingdom by a person to whom a licence applies,
- (f) W has elected in writing not later than the end of the period of 42 days from the day on which the child was born for the other woman to be treated for the purpose mentioned in subsection (4) as the parent of the child, and
- (g) no one else is to be treated—
  - (i) as the father of the child by virtue of section 35 or 36 or by virtue of section 45(2) or (3), or
  - (ii) as a parent of the child by virtue of section 42 or 43 or by virtue of adoption,

then the other woman is to be treated for the purpose mentioned in subsection (4) as a parent of the child.

(3) Subsections (1) and (2) apply whether W was in the United Kingdom or elsewhere at the time of the placing in her of the embryo.

(4) The purpose referred to in subsections (1) and (2) is the purpose of enabling the deceased woman's particulars to be entered as the particulars of the child's other parent in a relevant register of births.

(5) In the application of subsections (1) and (2) to Scotland, for any reference to a period of 42 days there is substituted a reference to a period of 21 days.

A1.592O

47 Woman not to be other parent merely because of egg donation

A woman is not to be treated as the parent of a child whom she is not carrying and has not carried, except where she is so treated—

(a) by virtue of section 42 or 43, or
(b) by virtue of section 46 (for the purpose mentioned in subsection (4) of that section), or
(c) by virtue of adoption.

Effect of sections 33 to 47

A1.592P

48 Effect of sections 33 to 47

(1) Where by virtue of section 33, 35, 36, 42 or 43 a person is to be treated as the mother, father or parent of a child, that person is to be treated in law as the mother, father or parent (as the case may be) of the child for all purposes.

(2) Where by virtue of section 33, 38, 41, 45 or 47 a person is not to be treated as a parent of the child, that person is to be treated in law as not being a parent of the child for any purpose.

(3) Where section 39(1) or 40(1) or (2) applies, the deceased man—

(a) is to be treated in law as the father of the child for the purpose mentioned in section 39(3) or 40(4), but
(b) is to be treated in law as not being the father of the child for any other purpose.

(4) Where section 46(1) or (2) applies, the deceased woman—

(a) is to be treated in law as a parent of the child for the purpose mentioned in section 46(4), but
(b) is to be treated in law as not being a parent of the child for any other purpose.

(5) Where any of subsections (1) to (4) has effect, references to any relationship between two people in any enactment, deed or other instrument or document (whenever passed or made) are to be read accordingly.

(6) In relation to England and Wales and Northern Ireland, a child who—

(a) has a parent by virtue of section 42, or
(b) has a parent by virtue of section 43 who is at any time during the period beginning with the time mentioned in section 43(b) and ending with the time of the child's birth a party to a civil partnership with the child's mother,

A1.592Q *Statutes*

is the legitimate child of the child's parents.

(7) In relation to England and Wales and Northern Ireland, nothing in the provisions of section 33(1) or sections 35 to 47, read with this section—

(a) affects the succession to any dignity or title of honour or renders any person capable of succeeding to or transmitting a right to succeed to any such dignity or title, or

(b) affects the devolution of any property limited (expressly or not) to devolve (as nearly as the law permits) along with any dignity or title of honour.

(8) In relation to Scotland—

(a) those provisions do not apply to any title, coat of arms, honour or dignity transmissible on the death of its holder or affect the succession to any such title, coat of arms or dignity or its devolution, and

(b) where the terms of any deed provide that any property or interest in property is to devolve along with a title, coat of arms, honour or dignity, nothing in those provisions is to prevent that property or interest from so devolving.

References to parties to marriage or civil partnership

A1.592Q

49 Meaning of references to parties to a marriage

(1) The references in sections 35 to 47 to the parties to a marriage at any time there referred to—

(a) are to the parties to a marriage subsisting at that time, unless a judicial separation was then in force, but

(b) include the parties to a void marriage if either or both of them reasonably believed at that time that the marriage was valid; and for the purposes of those sections it is to be presumed, unless the contrary is shown, that one of them reasonably believed at that time that the marriage was valid.

(2) In subsection (1)(a) 'judicial separation' includes a legal separation obtained in a country outside the British Islands and recognised in the United Kingdom.

A1.592R

50 Meaning of references to parties to a civil partnership

(1) The references in sections 35 to 47 to the parties to a civil partnership at any time there referred to—

(a) are to the parties to a civil partnership subsisting at that time, unless a separation order was then in force, but

(b) include the parties to a void civil partnership if either or both of them reasonably believed at that time that the civil partnership was valid; and for the purposes of those sections it is to be presumed, unless the contrary is shown, that one of them reasonably believed at that time that the civil partnership was valid.

(2) The reference in section 48(6)(b) to a civil partnership includes a reference to a void civil partnership if either or both of the parties reasonably believed at the time when they registered as civil partners of each other that the civil partnership was valid; and for this purpose it is to be presumed, unless the contrary is shown, that one of them reasonably believed at that time that the civil partnership was valid.

Human Fertilisation and Embryology Act 2008 **A1.592U**

(3) In subsection (1)(a), 'separation order' means—

(a) a separation order under section 37(1)(d) or 161(1)(d) of the Civil Partnership Act 2004 (c 33),
(b) a decree of separation under section 120(2) of that Act, or
(c) a legal separation obtained in a country outside the United Kingdom and recognised in the United Kingdom.

Further provision about registration by virtue of section 39, 40 or 46

A1.592S

51   Meaning of 'relevant register of births'

For the purposes of this Part a 'relevant register of births', in relation to a birth, is whichever of the following is relevant—

(a) a register of live-births or still-births kept under the Births and Deaths Registration Act 1953 (c 20),
(b) a register of births or still-births kept under the Registration of Births, Deaths and Marriages (Scotland) Act 1965 (c 49), or
(c) a register of live-births or still-births kept under the Births and Deaths Registration (Northern Ireland) Order 1976 (SI 1976/1041 (NI 14)).

A1.592T

52   Late election by mother with consent of Registrar General

(1) The requirement under section 39(1), 40(1) or (2) or 46(1) or (2) as to the making of an election (which requires an election to be made either on or before the day on which the child was born or within the period of 42 or, as the case may be, 21 days from that day) is nevertheless to be treated as satisfied if the required election is made after the end of that period but with the consent of the Registrar General under subsection (2).

(2) The Registrar General may at any time consent to the making of an election after the end of the period mentioned in subsection (1) if, on an application made to him in accordance with such requirements as he may specify, he is satisfied that there is a compelling reason for giving his consent to the making of such an election.

(3) In this section 'the Registrar General' means the Registrar General for England and Wales, the Registrar General of Births, Deaths and Marriages for Scotland or (as the case may be) the Registrar General for Northern Ireland.

Interpretation of references to father etc where woman is other parent

A1.592U

53   Interpretation of references to father etc

(1) Subsections (2) and (3) have effect, subject to subsections (4) and (6), for the interpretation of any enactment, deed or any other instrument or document (whenever passed or made).

(2) Any reference (however expressed) to the father of a child who has a parent by virtue of section 42 or 43 is to be read as a reference to the woman who is a parent of the child by virtue of that section.

A1.592V *Statutes*

(3) Any reference (however expressed) to evidence of paternity is, in relation to a woman who is a parent by virtue of section 42 or 43, to be read as a reference to evidence of parentage.

(4) This section does not affect the interpretation of the enactments specified in subsection (5) (which make express provision for the case where a child has a parent by virtue of section 42 or 43).

(5) Those enactments are—

- (a) the Legitimacy Act (Northern Ireland) 1928 (c 5 (NI)),
- (b) the Schedule to the Population (Statistics) Act 1938 (c 12),
- (c) the Births and Deaths Registration Act 1953 (c 20),
- (d) the Registration of Births, Deaths and Marriages (Special Provisions) Act 1957 (c 58),
- (e) Part 2 of the Registration of Births, Deaths and Marriages (Scotland) Act 1965 (c 49),
- (f) the Congenital Disabilities (Civil Liability) Act 1976 (c 28),
- (g) the Legitimacy Act 1976 (c 31),
- (h) the Births and Deaths Registration (Northern Ireland) Order 1976 (SI 1976/1041 (NI 14)),
- (i) the British Nationality Act 1981 (c 61),
- (j) the Family Law Reform Act 1987 (c 42),
- (k) Parts 1 and 2 of the Children Act 1989 (c 41),
- (l) Part 1 of the Children (Scotland) Act 1995 (c 36),
- (m) section 1 of the Criminal Law (Consolidation) (Scotland) Act 1995 (c 39), and
- (n) Parts 2, 3 and 14 of the Children (Northern Ireland) Order 1995 (SI 1995/755 (NI 2)).

(6) This section does not affect the interpretation of references that fall to be read in accordance with section 1(2)(a) or (b) of the Family Law Reform Act 1987 or Article 155(2)(a) or (b) of the Children (Northern Ireland) Order 1995 (references to a person whose father and mother were, or were not, married to each other at the time of the person's birth).

Parental orders

A1.592V

54 **Parental orders**

(1) On an application made by two people ('the applicants'), the court may make an order providing for a child to be treated in law as the child of the applicants if—

- (a) the child has been carried by a woman who is not one of the applicants, as a result of the placing in her of an embryo or sperm and eggs or her artificial insemination,
- (b) the gametes of at least one of the applicants were used to bring about the creation of the embryo, and
- (c) the conditions in subsections (2) to (8) are satisfied.

(2) The applicants must be—

- (a) husband and wife,
- (b) civil partners of each other, or
- (c) two persons who are living as partners in an enduring family relationship and are not within prohibited degrees of relationship in relation to each other.

(3) Except in a case falling within subsection (11), the applicants must apply for the order during the period of 6 months beginning with the day on which the child is born.

(4) At the time of the application and the making of the order—

(a) the child's home must be with the applicants, and
(b) either or both of the applicants must be domiciled in the United Kingdom or in the Channel Islands or the Isle of Man.

(5) At the time of the making of the order both the applicants must have attained the age of 18.

(6) The court must be satisfied that both—

(a) the woman who carried the child, and
(b) any other person who is a parent of the child but is not one of the applicants (including any man who is the father by virtue of section 35 or 36 or any woman who is a parent by virtue of section 42 or 43),

have freely, and with full understanding of what is involved, agreed unconditionally to the making of the order.

(7) Subsection (6) does not require the agreement of a person who cannot be found or is incapable of giving agreement; and the agreement of the woman who carried the child is ineffective for the purpose of that subsection if given by her less than six weeks after the child's birth.

(8) The court must be satisfied that no money or other benefit (other than for expenses reasonably incurred) has been given or received by either of the applicants for or in consideration of—

(a) the making of the order,
(b) any agreement required by subsection (6),
(c) the handing over of the child to the applicants, or
(d) the making of arrangements with a view to the making of the order,

unless authorised by the court.

(9) For the purposes of an application under this section—

(a) in relation to England and Wales, section 92(7) to (10) of, and Part 1 of Schedule 11 to, the Children Act 1989 (c 41) (jurisdiction of courts) apply for the purposes of this section to determine the meaning of 'the court' as they apply for the purposes of that Act and proceedings on the application are to be 'family proceedings' for the purposes of that Act,
(b) in relation to Scotland, 'the court' means the Court of Session or the sheriff court of the sheriffdom within which the child is, and
(c) in relation to Northern Ireland, 'the court' means the High Court or any county court within whose division the child is.

(10) Subsection (1)(a) applies whether the woman was in the United Kingdom or elsewhere at the time of the placing in her of the embryo or the sperm and eggs or her artificial insemination.

(11) An application which—

(a) relates to a child born before the coming into force of this section, and
(b) is made by two persons who, throughout the period applicable under subsection (2) of section 30 of the 1990 Act, were not eligible to apply for an order under that section in relation to the child as husband and wife,

may be made within the period of six months beginning with the day on which this section comes into force.

A1.592W *Statutes*

A1.592W

55   Parental orders: supplementary provision

(1)   The Secretary of State may by regulations provide—

- (a) for any provision of the enactments about adoption to have effect, with such modifications (if any) as may be specified in the regulations, in relation to orders under section 54, and applications for such orders, as it has effect in relation to adoption, and applications for adoption orders, and
- (b) for references in any enactment to adoption, an adopted child or an adoptive relationship to be read (respectively) as references to the effect of an order under section 54, a child to whom such an order applies and a relationship arising by virtue of the enactments about adoption, as applied by the regulations, and for similar expressions in connection with adoption to be read accordingly.

(2)   The regulations may include such incidental or supplemental provision as appears to the Secretary of State to be necessary or desirable in consequence of any provision made by virtue of subsection (1)(a) or (b).

(3)   In this section 'the enactments about adoption' means—

- (a) the Adoption (Scotland) Act 1978 (c 28),
- (b) the Adoption and Children Act 2002 (c 38),
- (c) the Adoption and Children (Scotland) Act 2007 (asp 4), and
- (d) the Adoption (Northern Ireland) Order 1987 (SI 1987/2203 (NI 22)).

Amendments of enactments

A1.592X

56   Amendments relating to parenthood in cases involving assisted reproduction

Schedule 6 contains amendments related to the provisions of this Part.

General

A1.592Y

57   Repeals and transitional provision relating to Part 2

(1)   Sections 33 to 48 have effect only in relation to children carried by women as a result of the placing in them of embryos or of sperm and eggs, or their artificial insemination (as the case may be), after the commencement of those sections.

(2)   Sections 27 to 29 of the 1990 Act (which relate to status) do not have effect in relation to children carried by women as a result of the placing in them of embryos or of sperm and eggs, or their artificial insemination (as the case may be), after the commencement of sections 33 to 48.

(3)   Section 30 of the 1990 Act (parental orders in favour of gamete donors) ceases to have effect.

(4)   Subsection (3) does not affect the validity of any order made under section 30 of the 1990 Act before the coming into force of that subsection.

A1.592Z

58 Interpretation of Part 2

(1) In this Part 'enactment' means an enactment contained in, or in an instrument made under—

(a) an Act of Parliament,
(b) an Act of the Scottish Parliament,
(c) a Measure or Act of the National Assembly for Wales, or
(d) Northern Ireland legislation.

(2) For the purposes of this Part, two persons are within prohibited degrees of relationship if one is the other's parent, grandparent, sister, brother, aunt or uncle; and in this subsection references to relationships—

(a) are to relationships of the full blood or half blood or, in the case of an adopted person, such of those relationships as would subsist but for adoption, and
(b) include the relationship of a child with his adoptive, or former adoptive, parents,

but do not include any other adoptive relationships.

(3) Other expressions used in this Part and in the 1990 Act have the same meaning in this Part as in that Act.

Initial commencement: To be appointed: see s 68(2).

SCHEDULE 6
AMENDMENTS RELATING TO PARENTHOOD IN CASES INVOLVING ASSISTED REPRODUCTION

Section 56

A1.592AA

PART 1
GENERAL

Population (Statistics) Act 1938 (c 12)

1 (1) In the Schedule to the Population (Statistics) Act 1938 (particulars which may be required), in paragraph 1 (which relates to the registration of a birth)—

(a) in paragraph (b), after 'child,' insert 'or as a parent of the child by virtue of section 42 or 43 of the Human Fertilisation and Embryology Act 2008,', and
(b) in paragraph (c)—
  (i) in sub-paragraph (i), after 'marriage' insert 'or of their formation of a civil partnership', and
  (ii) at the beginning of each of sub-paragraphs (ii) and (iii) insert 'where the parents are married,'.

(2) Sub-paragraph (1)(b)(ii) does not extend to Scotland.

Births and Deaths Registration Act 1953 (c 20)

2 In section 1 of the Births and Deaths Registration Act 1953 (particulars of births to be registered) after subsection (2) insert—

'(3) In the case of a child who has a parent by virtue of section 42 or 43 of the Human Fertilisation and Embryology Act 2008, the reference in subsection (2)(a) to the father of the child is to be read as a reference to the woman who is a parent by virtue of that section.'

3 In section 2 of the Births and Deaths Registration Act 1953 (information concerning birth to be given to registrar within 42 days), renumber the existing provision as subsection (1) of the section and at the end insert—

'(2) In the case of a child who has a parent by virtue of section 42 or 43 of the Human Fertilisation and Embryology Act 2008, the references in subsection (1) to the father of the child are to be read as references to the woman who is a parent by virtue of that section.'

4 In section 9(4) of the Births and Deaths Registration Act 1953 (giving of information to a person other than the registrar), after 'that section,' insert 'or under paragraph (b), (c) or (d) of subsection (1B) of that section,'.

5 (1) Section 10 of the Births and Deaths Registration Act 1953 (registration of father where parents not married) is amended as follows.

(2) For the heading to the section substitute 'Registration of father where parents not married or of second female parent where parents not civil partners'.

(3) After subsection (1A) insert—

'(1B) Notwithstanding anything in the foregoing provisions of this Act and subject to section 10ZA of this Act, in the case of a child to whom section 1(3) of the Family Law Reform Act 1987 does not apply no woman shall as a parent of the child by virtue of section 43 of the Human Fertilisation and Embryology Act 2008 be required to give information concerning the birth of the child, and the registrar shall not enter in the register the name of any woman as a parent of the child by virtue of that section except—

(a) at the joint request of the mother and the person stating herself to be the other parent of the child (in which case that person shall sign the register together with the mother); or
(b) at the request of the mother on production of—
  (i) a declaration in the prescribed form made by the mother stating that the person to be registered ("the woman concerned") is a parent of the child by virtue of section 43 of the Human Fertilisation and Embryology Act 2008; and
  (ii) a statutory declaration made by the woman concerned stating herself to be a parent of the child by virtue of section 43 of that Act; or
(c) at the request of the woman concerned on production of—
  (i) a declaration in the prescribed form made by the woman concerned stating herself to be a parent of the child by virtue of section 43 of the Human Fertilisation and Embryology Act 2008; and
  (ii) a statutory declaration made by the mother stating that the woman concerned is a parent of the child by virtue of section 43 of that Act; or
(d) at the request of the mother or the woman concerned on production of—
  (i) a copy of any agreement made between them under section 4ZA(1)(b) of the Children Act 1989 in relation to the child; and
  (ii) a declaration in the prescribed form by the person making the request stating that the agreement was made in compliance with section 4ZA of that Act and has not been brought to an end by an order of a court; or
(e) at the request of the mother or the woman concerned on production of—
  (i) a certified copy of an order under section 4ZA of the Children Act 1989 giving the woman concerned parental responsibility for the child; and

(ii) a declaration in the prescribed form by the person making the request stating that the order has not been brought to an end by an order of a court; or
(f) at the request of the mother or the woman concerned on production of—
(i) a certified copy of an order under paragraph 1 of Schedule 1 to the Children Act 1989 which requires the woman concerned to make any financial provision for the child and which is not an order falling within paragraph 4(3) of that Schedule; and
(ii) a declaration in the prescribed form by the person making the request stating that the order has not been discharged by an order of a court.'

(4) After subsection (2) insert—

'(2A) Where, in the case of a child to whom section 1(3) of the Family Law Reform Act 1987 does not apply, a person stating herself to be a parent of the child by virtue of section 43 of the Human Fertilisation and Embryology Act 2008 makes a request to the registrar in accordance with any of paragraphs (c) to (f) of subsection (1B)—

(a) she shall be treated as a qualified informant concerning the birth of the child for the purposes of this Act; and
(b) the giving of information concerning the birth of the child by that person and the signing of the register by her in the presence of the registrar shall act as a discharge of any duty of any other qualified informant under section 2 of this Act.'

6 For section 10ZA of the Births and Deaths Registration Act 1953 substitute—

'**10ZA Registration of father or second female parent by virtue of certain provisions of Human Fertilisation and Embryology Act 2008**

(1) Notwithstanding anything in the foregoing provisions of this Act, the registrar shall not enter in the register—

(a) as the father of a child, the name of a man who is to be treated for that purpose as the father of the child by virtue of section 39(1) or 40(1) or (2) of the Human Fertilisation and Embryology Act 2008 (circumstances in which man to be treated as father of child for purposes of registration of birth where fertility treatment undertaken after his death); or
(b) as a parent of the child, the name of a woman who is to be treated for that purpose as a parent of the child by virtue of section 46(1) or (2) of that Act (circumstances in which woman to be treated as parent of child for purposes of registration of birth where fertility treatment undertaken after her death),

unless the condition in subsection (2) below is satisfied.

(2) The condition in this subsection is satisfied if—

(a) the mother requests the registrar to make such an entry in the register and produces the relevant documents; or
(b) in the case of the death or inability of the mother, the relevant documents are produced by some other person who is a qualified informant.

(3) In this section 'the relevant documents' means—

(a) the consent in writing and election mentioned in section 39(1), 40(1) or (2) or 46(1) or (2) (as the case requires) of the Human Fertilisation and Embryology Act 2008;
(b) a certificate of a registered medical practitioner as to the medical facts concerned; and
(c) such other documentary evidence (if any) as the registrar considers appropriate.'

A1.592AA *Statutes*

7 (1) Section 10A of the Births and Deaths Registration Act 1953 (re-registration where parents not married) is amended as follows.

(2) For the heading to the section substitute 'Re-registration where parents neither married nor civil partners'.

(3) In subsection (1)—

(a) after 'as the father of the child' insert '(or as a parent of the child by virtue of section 42, 43 or 46(1) or (2) of the Human Fertilisation and Embryology Act 2008)', and
(b) for paragraph (ff) substitute—
'(ff) in the case of a man who is to be treated as the father of the child by virtue of section 39(1) or 40(1) or (2) of the Human Fertilisation and Embryology Act 2008, if the condition in section 10ZA(2) of this Act is satisfied; or'.

(4) After subsection (1A) insert—

'(1B) Where there has been registered under this Act the birth of a child to whom section 1(3) of the Family Law Reform Act 1987 does not apply, but no person has been registered as a parent of the child by virtue of section 42, 43 or 46(1) or (2) of the Human Fertilisation and Embryology Act 2008 (or as the father of the child), the registrar shall re-register the birth so as to show a woman ("the woman concerned") as a parent of the child by virtue of section 43 or 46(1) or (2) of that Act—

(a) at the joint request of the mother and the woman concerned; or
(b) at the request of the mother on production of—
  (i) a declaration in the prescribed form made by the mother stating that the woman concerned is a parent of the child by virtue of section 43 of the Human Fertilisation and Embryology Act 2008; and
  (ii) a statutory declaration made by the woman concerned stating herself to be a parent of the child by virtue of section 43 of that Act; or
(c) at the request of the woman concerned on production of—
  (i) a declaration in the prescribed form made by the woman concerned stating herself to be a parent of the child by virtue of section 43 of the Human Fertilisation and Embryology Act 2008; and
  (ii) a statutory declaration made by the mother stating that the woman concerned is a parent of the child by virtue of section 43 of that Act; or
(d) at the request of the mother or the woman concerned on production of—
  (i) a copy of an agreement made between them under section 4ZA(1)(b) of the Children Act 1989 in relation to the child; and
  (ii) a declaration in the prescribed form by the person making the request stating that the agreement was made in compliance with section 4ZA of that Act and has not been brought to an end by an order of a court; or
(e) at the request of the mother or the woman concerned on production of—
  (i) a certified copy of an order under section 4ZA of the Children Act 1989 giving the woman concerned parental responsibility for the child; and
  (ii) a declaration in the prescribed form by the person making the request stating that the order has not been brought to an end by an order of a court; or
(f) at the request of the mother or the woman concerned on production of—
  (i) a certified copy of an order under paragraph 1 of Schedule 1 to the Children Act 1989 which requires the woman concerned to make any financial provision for the child and which is not an order falling within paragraph 4(3) of that Schedule; and
  (ii) a declaration in the prescribed form by the person making the request stating that the order has not been discharged by an order of a court; or

(g) in the case of a woman who is to be treated as a parent of the child by virtue of section 46(1) or (2) of the Human Fertilisation and Embryology Act 2008, if the condition in section 10ZA(2) of this Act is satisfied.'

(5) In subsection (2), for paragraphs (b) to (c) substitute—

'(b) in the case of any of the following requests—
  (i) a request under subsection (1)(a) or (b) or subsection (1B)(a) or (b);
  (ii) a request under subsection (1)(d), (e), (f) or (g) or subsection (1B)(d), (e) or (f) made by the mother of the child,
the mother shall also sign the register;
(bb) in a case within subsection (1)(ff) or (1B)(g), the mother or (as the case may be) the qualified informant shall also sign the register;
(c) in the case of a request made under subsection (1)(a) or (c) or a request made under subsection (1)(d), (e), (f) or (g) by the person requesting to be registered as the father of the child, that person shall also sign the register;
(cc) in the case of a request made under subsection (1B)(a) or (c) or a request made under subsection (1B)(d), (e) or (f) by a woman requesting to be registered as a parent of the child by virtue of section 43 of the Human Fertilisation and Embryology Act 2008, that woman shall also sign the register; and'.

8   In section 13 of the Births and Deaths Registration Act 1953 (registration of name of child or alteration of name) after subsection (1) insert—

'(1ZA)   In the case of a child who has a parent by virtue of section 42 or 43 of the Human Fertilisation and Embryology Act 2008, the reference in subsection (1)(b) to the father of the child is to be read as a reference to the woman who is a parent of the child by virtue of that section.'

9   (1) Section 14 of the Births and Deaths Registration Act 1953 (re-registration of births of legitimated persons) is amended as follows.

(2) In subsection (1), in the proviso—

(a) in paragraph (a), after 'legitimated person' insert ', or herself to be a parent of the legitimated person by virtue of section 43 of the Human Fertilisation and Embryology Act 2008,', and
(b) in paragraph (b), after 'the paternity of the legitimated person' insert '(or, as the case may be, the parentage of the legitimated person by virtue of section 43 of that Act),'.

(3) In subsection (2)—

(a) after 'the marriage of his parents' insert 'or on their becoming civil partners of each other', and
(b) after 'the date of the marriage' insert 'or of the formation of the civil partnership'.

10   (1) Section 29A of the Births and Deaths Registration Act 1953 (alternative procedure for certain corrections) is amended as follows.

(2) In subsection (1) for the words from 'the father' to the end substitute

'—

(a) the father of the person to whose birth or death the entry relates; or
(b) a parent of that person (having been so registered on the basis of being such a parent by virtue of 42, 43 or 46(1) or (2) of the Human Fertilisation and Embryology Act 2008).'

(3) In subsection (3), after 'not the father' insert 'or, as the case may be, that the person shown as a parent was not such a parent by virtue of 42, 43 or 46(1) or (2) of the Human Fertilisation and Embryology Act 2008'.

A1.592AA *Statutes*

Registration of Births, Deaths and Marriages (Special Provisions) Act 1957 (c 58)

11   (1)   Section 3A of the Births, Deaths and Marriages (Special Provisions) Act 1957 (alternative procedure for certain corrections) is amended as follows.

(2)   In subsection (1) for the words from 'the father' to the end substitute '—

(a) the father of the person to whose birth or death the entry relates, or
(b) a parent of that person (having been so registered on the basis of being such a parent by virtue of 42, 43 or 46(1) or (2) of the Human Fertilisation and Embryology Act 2008).'

(3)   In subsection (3), after 'not the father' insert 'or, as the case may be, that the person shown as a parent was not such a parent by virtue of 42, 43 or 46(1) or (2) of the Human Fertilisation and Embryology Act 2008'.

12   At the end of section 5 of the Registration of Births, Deaths and Marriages (Special Provisions) Act 1957 (registration of births of legitimated persons in the service departments registers) insert—

'(3)   In relation to a person who has a parent by virtue of section 43 of the Human Fertilisation and Embryology Act 2008—

(a) any reference to the person's father is a reference to the woman who is a parent by virtue of that section,
(b) the reference in subsection (1) to the subsequent marriage of the person's parents is a reference to their subsequent formation of a civil partnership, and
(c) the reference in that subsection to paternity is a reference to parentage by virtue of section 43 of that Act.'

Family Law Reform Act 1969 (c 46)

13   In section 25 of the Family Law Reform Act 1969 (interpretation of Part 3), in the definition of 'excluded'—

(a) for 'and to' substitute ', to', and
(b) after '1990' insert 'and to sections 33 to 47 of the Human Fertilisation and Embryology Act 2008'.

Congenital Disabilities (Civil Liability) Act 1976 (c 28)

14   In section 1 of the Congenital Disabilities (Civil Liability) Act 1976 (civil liability to child born disabled), after subsection (4) insert—

'(4A)   In the case of a child who has a parent by virtue of section 42 or 43 of the Human Fertilisation and Embryology Act 2008, the reference in subsection (4) to the child's father includes a reference to the woman who is a parent by virtue of that section.'

15   In section 4 of the Congenital Disabilities (Civil Liability) Act 1976 (interpretation and other supplementary provisions), at the end of subsection (4A) insert 'or sections 33 to 47 of the Human Fertilisation and Embryology Act 2008.'

Legitimacy Act 1976 (c 31)

16   After section 2 of the Legitimacy Act 1976 (legitimation by subsequent marriage of parents) insert—

'2A   **Legitimation by subsequent civil partnership of parents**

Subject to the following provisions of this Act, where—

Human Fertilisation and Embryology Act 2008 **A1.592AA**

(a) a person ("the child") has a parent ("the female parent") by virtue of section 43 of the Human Fertilisation and Embryology Act 2008 (treatment provided to woman who agrees that second woman to be parent),
(b) at the time of the child's birth, the female parent and the child's mother are not civil partners of each other,
(c) the female parent and the child's mother subsequently enter into a civil partnership, and
(d) the female parent is at the date of the formation of the civil partnership domiciled in England and Wales,

the civil partnership shall render the child, if living, legitimate from the date of the formation of the civil partnership.'

17 In section 3 of the Legitimacy Act 1976 (legitimation by extraneous law), renumber the existing provision as subsection (1) of the section and at the end insert—

'(2) Subject to the following provisions of this Act, where—

(a) a person ("the child") has a parent ("the female parent") by virtue of section 43 of the Human Fertilisation and Embryology Act 2008 (treatment provided to woman who agrees that second woman to be parent),
(b) at the time of the child's birth, the female parent and the child's mother are not civil partners of each other,
(c) the female parent and the child's mother subsequently enter into a civil partnership, and
(d) the female parent is not at the time of the formation of the civil partnership domiciled in England and Wales but is domiciled in a country by the law of which the child became legitimated by virtue of the civil partnership,

the child, if living, shall in England and Wales be recognised as having been so legitimated from the date of the formation of the civil partnership notwithstanding that, at the time of the child's birth, the female parent was domiciled in a country the law of which did not permit legitimation by subsequent civil partnership.'

18 In section 9 of the Legitimacy Act 1976 (re-registration of birth of legitimated persons)—

(a) in subsection (1), after 'marriage' insert 'or of the formation of the civil partnership', and
(b) in subsection (3), after 'marriage' insert 'or civil partnership'.

19 In section 10 of the Legitimacy Act 1976 (interpretation), in the definition of 'legitimated person', in paragraph (a), after 'section 2' insert ', 2A'.

Magistrates' Courts Act 1980 (c 43)

20 In section 65 of the Magistrates' Courts Act 1980 (meaning of family proceedings), in subsection (1), for paragraph (na) substitute—

'(na) section 54 of the Human Fertilisation and Embryology Act 2008;'.

[Senior Courts Act 1981] (c 54)

21 In Schedule 1 to the [Senior Courts Act 1981] (distribution of business in High Court), in paragraph 3(f), for sub-paragraph (iv) substitute—
    '(iv) section 54 of the Human Fertilisation and Embryology Act 2008;'.

British Nationality Act 1981 (c 61)

22 In section 50 of the British Nationality Act 1981 (interpretation) in subsection (9A) (a child's father) for paragraphs (b) and (c) substitute—

A1.592AA *Statutes*

'(b) where a person is treated as the father of the child under section 28 of the Human Fertilisation and Embryology Act 1990 or section 35 or 36 of the Human Fertilisation and Embryology Act 2008, that person, or

(ba) where a person is treated as a parent of the child under section 42 or 43 of the Human Fertilisation and Embryology Act 2008, that person, or

(c) where none of paragraphs (a) to (ba) applies, a person who satisfies prescribed requirements as to proof of paternity.'

Family Law Act 1986 (c 55)

23 In section 56 of the Family Law Act 1986 (declarations of parentage, legitimacy or legitimation), in subsection (5)(a), after 'section 2' insert ', 2A'.

Family Law Reform Act 1987 (c 42)

24 (1) Section 1 of the Family Law Reform Act 1987 (general principle) is amended as follows.

(2) In subsection (3) (children whose father and mother are to be taken to have been married to each other at the time of the child's birth) after paragraph (b) insert—

'(ba) has a parent by virtue of section 42 of the Human Fertilisation and Embryology Act 2008 (which relates to treatment provided to a woman who is at the time of treatment a party to a civil partnership or, in certain circumstances, a void civil partnership);

(bb) has a parent by virtue of section 43 of that Act (which relates to treatment provided to woman who agrees that second woman to be parent) who—
  (i) is the civil partner of the child's mother at the time of the child's birth, or
  (ii) was the civil partner of the child's mother at any time during the period beginning with the time mentioned in section 43(b) of that Act and ending with the child's birth;'.

(3) After subsection (4) insert—

'(5) A child whose parents are parties to a void civil partnership shall, subject to subsection (6), be treated as falling within subsection (3)(bb) if at the time when the parties registered as civil partners of each other both or either of the parties reasonably believed that the civil partnership was valid.

(6) Subsection (5) applies only where the woman who is a parent by virtue of section 43 was domiciled in England and Wales at the time of the birth or, if she died before the birth, was so domiciled immediately before her death.

(7) Subsection (5) applies even though the belief that the civil partnership was valid was due to a mistake as to law.

(8) It shall be presumed for the purposes of subsection (5), unless the contrary is shown, that one of the parties to a void civil partnership reasonably believed at the time of the formation of the civil partnership that the civil partnership was valid.'

25 (1) Section 18 of the Family Law Reform Act 1987 (succession on intestacy) is amended as follows.

(2) After subsection (2) insert—

'(2A) In the case of a person who has a parent by virtue of section 43 of the Human Fertilisation and Embryology Act 2008 (treatment provided to woman who agrees that second woman to be parent), the second and third references in subsection (2) to the person's father are to be read as references to the woman who is a parent of the person by virtue of that section.'

(3) In subsection (3), for 'section 50(1) of that Act' substitute 'section 50(1) of the Administration of Estates Act 1925'.

Children Act 1989 (c 41)

26 (1) Section 2 of the Children Act 1989 (parental responsibility for children) is amended as follows.

(2) After subsection (1) insert—

'(1A) Where a child—

(a) has a parent by virtue of section 42 of the Human Fertilisation and Embryology Act 2008; or
(b) has a parent by virtue of section 43 of that Act and is a person to whom section 1(3) of the Family Law Reform Act 1987 applies,

the child's mother and the other parent shall each have parental responsibility for the child.'

(3) After subsection (2) insert—

'(2A) Where a child has a parent by virtue of section 43 of the Human Fertilisation and Embryology Act 2008 and is not a person to whom section 1(3) of the Family Law Reform Act 1987 applies—

(a) the mother shall have parental responsibility for the child;
(b) the other parent shall have parental responsibility for the child if she has acquired it (and has not ceased to have it) in accordance with the provisions of this Act.'

27 After section 4 of the Children Act 1989 insert—

'**4ZA Acquisition of parental responsibility by second female parent**

(1) Where a child has a parent by virtue of section 43 of the Human Fertilisation and Embryology Act 2008 and is not a person to whom section 1(3) of the Family Law Reform Act 1987 applies, that parent shall acquire parental responsibility for the child if—

(a) she becomes registered as a parent of the child under any of the enactments specified in subsection (2);
(b) she and the child's mother make an agreement providing for her to have parental responsibility for the child; or
(c) the court, on her application, orders that she shall have parental responsibility for the child.

(2) The enactments referred to in subsection (1)(a) are—

(a) paragraphs (a), (b) and (c) of section 10(1B) and of section 10A(1B) of the Births and Deaths Registration Act 1953;
(b) paragraphs (a), (b) and (d) of section 18B(1) and sections 18B(3)(a) and 20(1)(a) of the Registration of Births, Deaths and Marriages (Scotland) Act 1965; and
(c) sub-paragraphs (a), (b) and (c) of Article 14ZA(3) of the Births and Deaths Registration (Northern Ireland) Order 1976.

(3) The Secretary of State may by order amend subsection (2) so as to add further enactments to the list in that subsection.

(4) An agreement under subsection (1)(b) is also a 'parental responsibility agreement', and section 4(2) applies in relation to such an agreement as it applies in relation to parental responsibility agreements under section 4.

(5) A person who has acquired parental responsibility under subsection (1) shall cease to have that responsibility only if the court so orders.

(6) The court may make an order under subsection (5) on the application—

(a) of any person who has parental responsibility for the child; or
(b) with the leave of the court, of the child himself,

subject, in the case of parental responsibility acquired under subsection (1)(c), to section 12(4).

(7) The court may only grant leave under subsection (6)(b) if it is satisfied that the child has sufficient understanding to make the proposed application.'

28 (1) Section 12 of the Children Act 1989 (residence orders and parental responsibility) is amended as follows.

(2) After subsection (1) insert—

'(1A) Where the court makes a residence order in favour of a woman who is a parent of a child by virtue of section 43 of the Human Fertilisation and Embryology Act 2008 it shall, if that woman would not otherwise have parental responsibility for the child, also make an order under section 4ZA giving her that responsibility.'

(3) In subsection (4)—

(a) after '(1)' insert 'or (1A)',
(b) after '4' insert 'or 4ZA', and
(c) for 'father' substitute 'parent'.

29 In section 91 of the Children Act 1989 (effect and duration of orders)—

(a) in subsection (7), after '4(1),' insert '4ZA(1),', and
(b) in subsection (8)(a), after '4' insert ', 4ZA'.

30 In section 104 of the Children Act 1989 (regulations and orders)—

(a) in subsection (2), after '4(1B),' insert '4ZA(3),', and
(b) in subsection (3), after '4(1B)' insert ', 4ZA(3)'.

31 In section 105 of the Children Act 1989 (interpretation), in subsection (1), in the definition of 'parental responsibility agreement', after 'sections 4(1)' insert ', 4ZA(4)'.

32 (1) Schedule 1 to the Children Act 1989 (financial provision for children) is amended as follows.

(2) At the end of paragraph 4 insert—

'(5) In the case of a child who has a parent by virtue of section 42 or 43 of the Human Fertilisation and Embryology Act 2008, any reference in sub-paragraph (2), (3) or (4) to the child's father is a reference to the woman who is a parent of the child by virtue of that section.'

(3) At the end of paragraph 10 insert—

'(8) In the case of a child who has a parent by virtue of section 42 or 43 of the Human Fertilisation and Embryology Act 2008, the reference in sub-paragraph (1)(a) to the child's father is a reference to the woman who is a parent of the child by virtue of that section.'

Human Fertilisation and Embryology Act 1990 (c 37)

33 (1) Section 32 of the 1990 Act (information to be provided to Registrar General) is amended as follows.

(2) In subsection (1)—

(a) for 'man' substitute 'person', and
(b) for 'father' substitute 'parent'.

(3) In subsection (2), for the words from 'that the man' to 'section 28 of this Act' substitute 'that the person may be a parent of the child by virtue of any of the relevant statutory provisions'.

(4) After subsection (2) insert—

'(2A) In subsection (2) "the relevant statutory provisions" means—

(a) section 28 of this Act, and
(b) sections 35 to 47 of the Human Fertilisation and Embryology Act 2008.'

34 In section 34 of the 1990 Act (disclosure in the interests of justice), in subsection (1), after 'of this Act' insert 'or sections 33 to 47 of the Human Fertilisation and Embryology Act 2008'.

35 (1) Section 35 of the 1990 Act (disclosure of information in the interests of justice: congenital disabilities etc) is amended as follows.

(2) In subsections (1) and (2), for 'sections 27 to 29 of this Act' substitute 'the relevant statutory provisions'.

(3) After subsection (2) insert—

'(2A) In subsections (1) and (2) 'the relevant statutory provisions' means—

(a) sections 27 to 29 of this Act, and
(b) sections 33 to 47 of the Human Fertilisation and Embryology Act 2008.'

Child Support Act 1991 (c 48)

36 In section 26 of the Child Support Act 1991 (disputes about parentage), in subsection (2), for Cases B and B1 substitute—

'CASE B

Where the alleged parent is a parent of the child in question by virtue of an order under section 30 of the Human Fertilisation and Embryology Act 1990 or section 54 of the Human Fertilisation and Embryology Act 2008 (parental orders).

CASE B1

Where the Secretary of State is satisfied that the alleged parent is a parent of the child in question by virtue of section 27 or 28 of the Human Fertilisation and Embryology Act 1990 or any of sections 33 to 46 of the Human Fertilisation and Embryology Act 2008 (which relate to children resulting from assisted reproduction).'

Family Law Act 1996 (c 27)

37 In section 63 of the Family Law Act 1996 (definition of family proceedings), in subsection (2), for paragraph (h) substitute—

'(h) section 54 of the Human Fertilisation and Embryology Act 2008;'.

Access to Justice Act 1999 (c 22)

38 In Schedule 2 to the Access to Justice Act 1999 (community legal services: excluded services), in paragraph 2(3), for paragraph (f) substitute—

'(f) under section 54 of the Human Fertilisation and Embryology Act 2008,'.

A1.592AA *Statutes*

Adoption and Children Act 2002 (c 38)

39 (1) Section 51 of the Adoption and Children Act 2002 (adoption by one person) is amended as follows.

(2) In subsection (4), for paragraph (b) substitute—

'(b) by virtue of the provisions specified in subsection (5), there is no other parent, or'.

(3) After subsection (4) insert—

'(5) The provisions referred to in subsection (4)(b) are—

(a) section 28 of the Human Fertilisation and Embryology Act 1990 (disregarding subsections (5A) to (5I) of that section), or
(b) sections 34 to 47 of the Human Fertilisation and Embryology Act 2008 (disregarding sections 39, 40 and 46 of that Act).'

Mental Capacity Act 2005 (c 9)

40 In section 27 of the Mental Capacity Act 2005 (family relationships), in subsection (1), after paragraph (h) insert—

'(i) giving a consent under the Human Fertilisation and Embryology Act 2008.'

Paras 1–12, 16–19, 23, 26–32, 39: Appointment (for certain purposes): 6 April 2009: see SI 2009/479, art 6(1)(e).
Paras 1–12, 16–19, 23, 26–32, 39: Appointment (for remaining purposes): 1 September 2009: see SI 2009/479, art 6(2).
Paras 13–15, 22, 24, 25, 33–35, 40: Appointment: 6 April 2009: see SI 2009/479, art 6(1)(d).
Para 21: words 'Senior Courts Act 1981' in square brackets substituted by the Constitutional Reform Act 2005, s 59(5), Sch 11, Pt 1, para 1(2). Date in force: 1 October 2009: see SI 2009/1604, art 2(d).
Para 36: Appointment (in so far as it substitutes the Child Support Act 1991, s 26, Case B1): 6 April 2009: see SI 2009/479, art 6(1)(d).

PART 2
ENACTMENTS RELATING ONLY TO SCOTLAND

Children and Young Persons (Scotland) Act 1937 (c 37)

41 In section 110(1) of the Children and Young Persons (Scotland) Act 1937 (interpretation), in the definition of 'parental responsibilities'—

(a) the words from 'a father' to the end become paragraph (a), and
(b) after that paragraph insert—
'(b) a second female parent would have as a parent but for the operation of section 3(1)(d) of that Act.'

Registration of Births, Deaths and Marriages (Scotland) Act 1965 (c 49)

42 In section 14 of the Registration of Births, Deaths and Marriages (Scotland) Act 1965 (duty to give information of particulars of birth), after subsection (4) insert—

'(4A) In the case of a child who has a parent by virtue of section 42 of the Human Fertilisation and Embryology Act 2008, the references in subsections (1) and (2) to the father of the child are to be read as references to the woman who is a parent by virtue of that section.'

43 For section 18ZA of the Registration of Births, Deaths and Marriages (Scotland) Act 1965 substitute—

'18ZA   Registration of father or second female parent by virtue of certain provisions of the Human Fertilisation and Embryology Act 2008

(1)   The registrar shall not enter in the register—

(a) as the father of a child the name of a man who is to be treated for that purpose as the father of the child by virtue of section 39(1) or 40(1) or (2) of the Human Fertilisation and Embryology Act 2008 (circumstances in which man to be treated as father of child for purpose of registration of birth where fertility treatment undertaken after his death); or
(b) as a parent of the child, the name of a woman who is to be treated for that purpose as a parent of the child by virtue of section 46(1) or (2) of that Act (circumstances in which woman to be treated as parent of child for purposes of registration of birth where fertility treatment undertaken after her death),

unless the condition in subsection (2) below is satisfied.

(2)   The condition in this subsection is satisfied if—

(a) the mother requests the registrar to make such an entry in the register and produces the relevant documents; or
(b) in the case of the death or inability of the mother, the relevant documents are produced by some other person who is a qualified informant.

(3)   In this section "the relevant documents" means—

(a) the consent in writing and election mentioned in section 39(1), 40(1) or (2) or 46(1) or (2) (as the case requires) of the Human Fertilisation and Embryology Act 2008;
(b) a certificate of a registered medical practitioner as to the medical facts concerned; and
(c) such other documentary evidence (if any) as the registrar considers appropriate.'

44   After section 18A of the Registration of Births, Deaths and Marriages (Scotland) Act 1965 insert—

'18B   Births of children where second female parent by virtue of section 43 of the Human Fertilisation and Embryology Act 2008

(1) No woman shall as a parent of a child by virtue of section 43 of the Human Fertilisation and Embryology Act 2008 ("the woman concerned") be required, as a parent of the child, to give information concerning the birth of the child and, save as provided in section 20 of this Act, the district registrar for the registration district shall not enter in the birth registration form concerning the birth the name and surname of any woman as a parent of the child by virtue of section 43 of that Act of 2008 except—

(a) at the joint request of the mother and the woman concerned (in which case the woman concerned shall attest, in the prescribed manner, the birth registration form together with the mother); or
(b) at the request of the mother on production of—
  (i) a declaration in the prescribed form made by the mother stating that the woman concerned is a parent of the child by virtue of section 43 of the Human Fertilisation and Embryology Act 2008; and
  (ii) a statutory declaration made by the woman concerned acknowledging herself to be a parent of the child by virtue of section 43 of that Act; or
(c) at the request of the mother on production of a decree by a competent court finding or declaring the woman concerned to be a parent of the child by virtue of section 43 of that Act; or

A1.592AA *Statutes*

  (d) at the request of the woman concerned on production of—
     (i) a declaration in the prescribed form made by the woman concerned acknowledging herself to be a parent of the child by virtue of section 43 of that Act; and
     (ii) a statutory declaration made by the mother stating that the woman concerned is a parent of the child by virtue of section 43 of that Act.

(2) Where a person acknowledging herself to be a parent of the child by virtue of section 43 of the Human Fertilisation and Embryology Act 2008 makes a request to the district registrar for the registration district in accordance with paragraph (d) of subsection (1) of this section, she shall be treated as a qualified informant concerning the birth of the child for the purposes of this Act; and the giving of information concerning the birth of the child by that person and the attesting of the birth registration form concerning the birth by her in the presence of the registrar shall act as a discharge of any duty of any other qualified informant under section 14 of this Act.

(3) In any case where the name and surname of a woman who is a parent of a child by virtue of section 43 of the Human Fertilisation and Embryology Act 2008 has not been entered in the birth registration form concerning the birth, the Registrar General may record that name and surname by causing an appropriate entry to be made in the Register of Corrections Etc.—
  (a) if there is produced to him a declaration and a statutory declaration such as are mentioned in paragraph (b) or (d) of subsection (1) of this section; or
  (b) if, where the mother is dead or cannot be found or is incapable of making a request under subsection (1)(b) or (c) of this section, or a declaration under subsection (1)(b)(i) or a statutory declaration under subsection (1)(d)(ii) of this section, the Registrar General is ordered so to do by the sheriff upon application made to the sheriff by the person acknowledging herself to be a parent of the child by virtue of section 43 of the Human Fertilisation and Embryology Act 2008.'

45   In section 20 of the Registration of Births, Deaths and Marriages (Scotland) Act 1965—
  (a) after subsection (1)(c) insert
', or
  (d) the entry relating to the child in the register of births has been made so as to imply that the person, other than the mother, recorded as a parent of the child is so by virtue of section 43 of the Human Fertilisation and Embryology Act 2008 and the mother and that person have subsequently become parties to a civil partnership with each other and subject to subsection (1B) below,', and
  (b) in subsection (1B)—
     (i) after '(c)' insert 'or (d)',
     (ii) after 'paternity' insert 'or parentage', and
     (iii) after '18' insert 'or 18B'.

Family Law (Scotland) Act 1985 (c 37)

46   In section 9(1)(c)(ii) of the Family Law (Scotland) Act 1985 (court to consider burden of caring for child following dissolution of civil partnership), after 'family' insert 'or in respect of whom they are, by virtue of sections 33 and 42 of the Human Fertilisation and Embryology Act 2008, the parents'.

47   In section 27(1) of the Family Law (Scotland) Act 1985 (interpretation), in the definition of 'family', at the end insert 'or in respect of whom they are, by virtue of sections 33 and 42 of the Human Fertilisation and Embryology Act 2008, the parents;'.

Children (Scotland) Act 1995 (c 36)

48 In section 1(1) of the Children (Scotland) Act 1995 (parental responsibilities), after '3(1)(b)' insert ', and (d)'.

49 In section 2(1) of the Children (Scotland) Act 1995 (parental rights), after '3(1)(b)' insert ', and (d)'.

50 (1) Section 3 of the Children (Scotland) Act 1995 (provisions relating both to parental responsibilities and parental rights) is amended as follows.

(2) After subsection (1)(b), insert—

'(c) without prejudice to any arrangements which may be made under subsection (5) below, where a child has a parent by virtue of section 42 of the Human Fertilisation and Embryology Act 2008, that parent has parental responsibilities and parental rights in relation to the child;

(d) without prejudice to any arrangements which may be made under subsection (5) below and subject to any agreement which may be made under section 4A(1) of this Act, where a child has a parent by virtue of section 43 of the Human Fertilisation and Embryology Act 2008, that parent has parental responsibilities and parental rights in relation to the child if she is registered as a parent of the child under any of the enactments mentioned in subsection (3A).'

(3) After subsection (3), insert—

'(3A) Those enactments are—

(a) paragraphs (a), (b) and (d) of section 18B(1) and section 18B(3)(a) of the Registration of Births, Deaths and Marriages (Scotland) Act 1965;

(b) paragraphs (a), (b) and (c) of section 10(1B) and of section 10A(1B) of the Births and Deaths Registration Act 1953;

(c) sub-paragraphs (a), (b) and (c) of Article 14ZA(3) of the Births and Deaths Registration (Northern Ireland) Order 1976.'

(4) In subsection (5), for 'section 4(1)' substitute 'sections 4(1) and 4A(1)'.

51 After section 4 of the Children (Scotland) Act 1995 insert—

'**4A Acquisition of parental responsibilities and parental rights by second female parent by agreement with mother**

(1) Where—

(a) a child's mother has not been deprived of some or all of the parental responsibilities and parental rights in relation to the child; and

(b) the child has a parent by virtue of section 43 of the Human Fertilisation and Embryology Act 2008 and that parent is not registered as such under any of the enactments mentioned in section 3(3A),

the mother and the other parent may by agreement provide that, as from the appropriate date, the other parent shall have the parental responsibilities and rights (in the absence of any order under section 11 of this Act affecting responsibilities and rights) as if the other parent were treated as a parent by virtue of section 42 of that Act of 2008.

(2) Section 4(2), (3) and (4) applies in relation to an agreement under subsection (1) of this section as it applies in relation to an agreement under subsection (1) of section 4.'

52 (1) Section 11 of the Children (Scotland) Act 1995 (court orders relating to parental responsibilities) is amended as follows.

A1.592AA *Statutes*

(2) In subsection (4)(c)—

(a) for 'subsection (9) of section 30 of the Human Fertilisation and Embryology Act 1990 (provision for enactments about adoption to have effect with modifications)' substitute 'section 55(1) of the Human Fertilisation and Embryology Act 2008 (parental orders: supplementary provision)', and
(b) for 'subsection (1) of that section' substitute 'section 54 of that Act'.

(3) In subsection (11), after '4(2)' insert 'or 4A(2)'.

53   In section 12(4)(b) of the Children (Scotland) Act 1995 (meaning of 'child of the family' in civil partnership cases)—

(a) the words from 'who' to the end become sub-paragraph (i), and
(b) after that sub-paragraph insert
'; or
(ii) whose parents are the partners (being parents by virtue of sections 33 and 42 of the Human Fertilisation and Embryology Act 2008).'

54   In section 15(1) of the Children (Scotland) Act 1995 (interpretation of Part 1), in the definition of 'parent'—

(a) after '1990' insert 'and Part 2 of the Human Fertilisation and Embryology Act 2008', and
(b) for 'subsection (9) of the said section 30' substitute 'section 55(1) of that Act of 2008'.

Criminal Law (Consolidation) (Scotland) Act 1995 (c 39)

55   In section 1(1) of the Criminal Law (Consolidation) (Scotland) Act 1995 (offence of incest), at the end of the table set out at the end of that subsection insert—

'3 Relationships by virtue of Part 2 of the Human Fertilisation and Embryology Act 2008
Mother   Father
Daughter   Son
Second female parent by virtue of
section 42 or 43 of that Act'

Adoption and Children (Scotland) Act 2007 (asp 4)

56   (1) Section 30 of the Adoption and Children (Scotland) Act 2007 (adoption by one person) is amended as follows.

(2) In subsection (7), for paragraph (c) substitute—

'(c) by virtue of the provisions specified in subsection (7A), there is no other parent, or'.

(3) After subsection (7) insert—

'(7A) The provisions referred to in subsection (7)(c) are—

(a) section 28 of the Human Fertilisation and Embryology Act 1990 (disregarding subsections (5A) to (5I) of that section), or
(b) sections 34 to 47 of the Human Fertilisation and Embryology Act 2008 (disregarding sections 39, 40 and 46 of that Act).'

Appointment (for certain purposes): 6 April 2009: see SI 2009/479, art 6(1)(e).
Appointment (for remaining purposes): 1 September 2009: see SI 2009/479, art 6(2).

Human Fertilisation and Embryology Act 2008 **A1.592AA**

PART 3
ENACTMENTS RELATING ONLY TO NORTHERN IRELAND

Legitimacy Act (Northern Ireland) 1928 (c 5 (NI))

57 (1) Section 1 of the Legitimacy Act (Northern Ireland) 1928 (legitimation by subsequent marriage of parents) is amended as follows.

(2) In the heading, after 'marriage' insert 'or civil partnership'.

(3) After subsection (1) insert—

'(1A) Subject to subsection (3), where—
   (a) a person ("the child") has a parent ("the female parent") by virtue of section 43 of the Human Fertilisation and Embryology Act 2008 (treatment provided to woman who agrees that second woman to be parent);
   (b) at the time of the child's birth, the female parent and the child's mother are not civil partners of each other;
   (c) the female parent and the child's mother subsequently enter into a civil partnership; and
   (d) the female parent is at the date of the formation of the civil partnership domiciled in Northern Ireland,

the civil partnership shall render the child, if living, legitimate from the date of the formation of the civil partnership.'

58 (1) Section 8 of the Legitimacy Act (Northern Ireland) 1928 (provisions as to persons legitimated by extraneous law) is amended as follows.

(2) After subsection (1) insert—

'(1A) Where—
   (a) a person ("the child") has a parent ("the female parent") by virtue of section 43 of the Human Fertilisation and Embryology Act 2008 (treatment provided to woman who agrees that second woman to be parent);
   (b) at the time of the child's birth, the female parent and the child's mother are not civil partners of each other;
   (c) the female parent and the child's mother subsequently enter into a civil partnership; and
   (d) the female parent is at the time of the formation of the civil partnership domiciled in a country, other than Northern Ireland, by the law of which the child became legitimated by virtue of the civil partnership;

the child, if living, shall in Northern Ireland be recognised as having been so legitimated from the date of the formation of the civil partnership notwithstanding that, at the time of the child's birth, the female parent was not domiciled in a country the law of which permitted legitimation by subsequent civil partnership.'

59 In section 11 of the Legitimacy Act (Northern Ireland) 1928 (interpretation), in the definition of 'date of legitimation', after 'date of the marriage' insert 'or of the formation of the civil partnership'.

Births and Deaths Registration (Northern Ireland) Order 1976 (SI 1976/1041 (NI 14))

60 (1) Article 10 of the Births and Deaths Registration (Northern Ireland) Order 1976 (registration of births) is amended as follows.

(2) In paragraph (4) for 'Article 14' substitute 'Articles 14 and 14ZA'.

(3) After paragraph (4) insert—

A1.592AA *Statutes*

'(4A) In the case of a child who has a parent by virtue of section 42 or 43 of the Human Fertilisation and Embryology Act 2008, the references in paragraphs (3)(a) and (4) to the father of the child are to be read as references to the woman who is a parent by virtue of that section.'

61 After Article 14 of the Births and Deaths Registration (Northern Ireland) Order 1976 insert—

'**14ZA Registration of second female parent where parents not civil partners**

(1) This Article applies, subject to Article 14A, in the case of a child who—

(a) has a parent by virtue of section 43 of the Human Fertilisation and Embryology Act 2008; but

(b) is a person to whom Article 155(3) of the Children (Northern Ireland) Order 1995 (persons to be covered by references to a person whose mother and father were married to each other at the time of the person's birth) does not apply.

(2) The woman who is a parent by virtue of section 43 of the Human Fertilisation and Embryology Act 2008 shall not as such be under any duty to give any information under this Part concerning the birth of the child.

(3) A registrar shall not enter the name of any person as a parent of the child by virtue of that section unless—

(a) the mother and the person stating herself to be the other parent of the child jointly request the registrar to do so and in that event the mother and that person shall sign the register in the presence of each other; or

(b) the mother requests the registrar to do so and produces—

(i) a declaration in the prescribed form made by her stating that the person to be registered ("the woman concerned") is a parent of the child by virtue of section 43 of the Human Fertilisation and Embryology Act 2008; and

(ii) a statutory declaration made by the woman concerned stating herself to be a parent of the child by virtue of section 43 of that Act; or

(c) the woman concerned requests the registrar to do so and produces—

(i) a declaration in the prescribed form made by the woman concerned stating herself to be a parent of the child by virtue of section 43 of the Human Fertilisation and Embryology Act 2008; and

(ii) a statutory declaration made by the mother stating that the woman concerned is a parent of the child by virtue of section 43 of that Act; or

(d) the mother or the woman concerned requests the registrar to do so and produces—

(i) a copy of a parental responsibility agreement made between them in relation to the child; and

(ii) a declaration in the prescribed form by the person making the request stating that the agreement was made in compliance with Article 7 of the Children (Northern Ireland) Order 1995 and has not been brought to an end by an order of a court; or

(e) the mother or the woman concerned requests the registrar to do so and produces—

(i) a certified copy of an order under Article 7 of the Children (Northern Ireland) Order 1995 giving the woman concerned parental responsibility for the child; and

(ii) a declaration in the prescribed form by the person making the request stating that the order has not been brought to an end by an order of a court; or

(f) the mother or the woman concerned requests the registrar to do so and produces—
   (i) a certified copy of an order under paragraph 2 of Schedule 1 to the Children (Northern Ireland) Order 1995 which requires the woman concerned to make any financial provision for the child and which is not an order falling within paragraph 5(3) of that Schedule; and
   (ii) a declaration in the prescribed form by the person making the request stating that the order has not been discharged by an order of a court.

(4) Where, in the case of a child to whom Article 155(3) of the Children (Northern Ireland) Order 1995 does not apply, a person stating herself to be a parent of the child by virtue of section 43 of the Human Fertilisation and Embryology Act 2008 makes a request to the registrar in accordance with any of sub-paragraphs (c) to (f) of paragraph (3)—

(a) she shall be treated as a qualified informant concerning the birth of the child for the purposes of this Part; and
(b) on the giving of the required information concerning the birth of the child by that person and the signing of the register by her in the presence of the registrar every other qualified informant shall cease to be under the duty imposed by Article 10(4).'

62 For Article 14A of the Births and Deaths Registration (Northern Ireland) Order 1976 substitute—

'**14A   Registration of father or second female parent by virtue of certain provisions of Human Fertilisation and Embryology Act 2008**

(1) A registrar shall not enter in the register—

(a) as the father of a child, the name of a man who is to be treated for that purpose as the father of the child by virtue of section 39(1) or 40(1) or (2) of the Human Fertilisation and Embryology Act 2008 (circumstances in which man to be treated as father of child for purposes of registration of birth where fertility treatment undertaken after his death); or
(b) as a parent of the child, the name of a woman who is to be treated for that purpose as a parent of the child by virtue of section 46(1) or (2) of that Act (circumstances in which woman to be treated as parent of child for purposes of registration of birth where fertility treatment undertaken after her death);

unless the condition in paragraph (2) below is satisfied.

(2) The condition in this paragraph is satisfied if—

(a) the mother requests the registrar to make such an entry in the register and produces the relevant documents; or
(b) in the case of the death or inability of the mother, the relevant documents are produced by some other person who is a qualified informant.

(3) In this Article 'the relevant documents' means—

(a) the consent in writing and election mentioned in section 39(1), 40(1) or (2) or 46(1) or (2) (as the case requires) of the Human Fertilisation and Embryology Act 2008;
(b) a certificate of a registered medical practitioner as to the medical facts concerned; and
(c) such other documentary evidence (if any) as the registrar considers appropriate.'

63 (1) Article 18 of the Births and Deaths Registration (Northern Ireland) Order 1976 (re-registration of births) is amended as follows.

A1.592AA *Statutes*

(2) In paragraph (1)—

(a) in sub-paragraph (b), after 'child' insert 'who has a father and',

(b) after sub-paragraph (b) insert—

'(ba) in the case of a child who has a parent by virtue of section 43 of the Human Fertilisation and Embryology Act 2008 and to whom Article 155(3) of the Children (Northern Ireland) Order 1995 does not apply—

(i) the birth was registered as if Article 155(3) of that Order did apply to the child; or

(ii) no particulars relating to a parent of the child by virtue of section 42, 43 or 46(1) or (2) of that Act have been entered in the register; or', and

(c) for sub-paragraph (c) substitute—

'(c) in the case of a person who is to be treated—

(i) as the father of the child by virtue of section 39(1) or 40(1) or (2) of the Human Fertilisation and Embryology Act 2008; or

(ii) as a parent of the child by virtue of section 46(1) or (2) of that Act;

the condition in Article 14A(2) is satisfied.'

(3) At the end of paragraph (1A) insert 'and re-registration under sub-paragraph (ba)(ii) shall not be authorised otherwise than in accordance with Article 14ZA(3)'.

64 (1) Article 19 of the Births and Deaths Registration (Northern Ireland) Order 1976 (re-registration of births of legitimated persons) is amended as follows.

(2) In paragraph (3)—

(a) after sub-paragraph (a) insert—

'(aa) the name of a person acknowledging herself to be a parent of the legitimated person by virtue of section 43 of the Human Fertilisation and Embryology Act 2008 has been entered in the register in pursuance of Article 14ZA or 18 of this Order; or', and

(b) after sub-paragraph (b) insert—

'(ba) the parentage by virtue of section 43 of the Human Fertilisation and Embryology Act 2008 of the legitimated person has been established by a decree of a court of competent jurisdiction; or'.

(3) In paragraph (4), after 'marriage' insert 'or the formation of the civil partnership'.

(4) In paragraph (5)—

(a) after 'marriage' insert 'or civil partnership', and

(b) after 'date of the marriage' insert 'or the formation of the civil partnership'.

65 In Article 20 of the Births and Deaths Registration (Northern Ireland) Order 1976 (registration of births of legitimated person), in paragraph (2), for 'sub-paragraph (a)' substitute 'sub-paragraphs (a) and (aa)'.

66 In Article 37 of the Births and Deaths Registration (Northern Ireland) Order 1976 (registration or alteration of child's name), in paragraph (7)—

(a) after sub-paragraph (a) insert—

'(aa) in the case of a child who has a parent by virtue of section 42 or 43 of the Human Fertilisation and Embryology Act 2008, the mother and other parent of the child if Article 155(3) of the Children (Northern Ireland) Order 1995 applies to the child or if it does not apply but the other parent has parental responsibility for the child;', and

(b) for sub-paragraph (b) substitute—

'(b) the mother of the child if—

(i) in the case of a child who has a father, the child's parents were not married to each other at the time of the birth and the father does not have parental responsibility for the child; and

(ii) in the case of a child who has a parent by virtue of section 43 of the Human Fertilisation and Embryology Act 2008, Article 155(3) of the Children (Northern Ireland) Order 1995 does not apply to the child and the parent by virtue of that section of that Act does not have parental responsibility for the child;'.

Family Law Reform (Northern Ireland) Order 1977 (SI 1977/1250 (NI 17))

67   In Article 13 of the Family Law Reform (Northern Ireland) Order 1977 (interpretation of Part 3), in the definition of 'excluded', after '1990' insert 'and to sections 33 to 47 of the Human Fertilisation and Embryology Act 2008'.

Adoption (Northern Ireland) Order 1987 (SI 1987/2203 (NI 22))

68   (1) Article 15 of the Adoption (Northern Ireland) Order 1987 (adoption by one person) is amended as follows.

(2) In paragraph (3)(a), for the words from 'or, by virtue of' to 'other parent' substitute 'or, by virtue of the provisions specified in paragraph (3A), there is no other parent'.

(3) After paragraph (3) insert—

'(3A) The provisions referred to in paragraph (3)(a) are—

(a) section 28 of the Human Fertilisation and Embryology Act 1990 (disregarding subsections (5A) to (5I) of that section), or

(b) sections 34 to 47 of the Human Fertilisation and Embryology Act 2008 (disregarding sections 39, 40 and 46 of that Act).'

Child Support (Northern Ireland) Order 1991 (SI 1991/2628 (NI 23))

69   In Article 27 of the Child Support (Northern Ireland) Order 1991 (disputes about parentage), in paragraph (2), for Cases B and B1 substitute—

'CASE B

Where the alleged parent is a parent of the child in question by virtue of an order under section 30 of the Human Fertilisation and Embryology Act 1990 or section 54 of the Human Fertilisation and Embryology Act 2008 (parental orders).

CASE B1

Where the Department is satisfied that the alleged parent is a parent of the child in question by virtue of section 27 or 28 of the Human Fertilisation and Embryology Act 1990 or any of sections 33 to 46 of the Human Fertilisation and Embryology Act 2008 (which relate to children resulting from assisted reproduction).'

Children (Northern Ireland) Order 1995 (SI 1995/755 (NI 2))

70   In Article 2 of the Children (Northern Ireland) Order 1995, in paragraph (2), in the definition of 'parental responsibility agreement', for 'Article 7(1)(b)' substitute 'Article 7(1ZB)'.

71   (1) Article 5 of the Children (Northern Ireland) Order 1995 (parental responsibility for children) is amended as follows.

(2) After paragraph (1) insert—

'(1A) Where a child—

A1.592AA *Statutes*

    (a) has a parent by virtue of section 42 of the Human Fertilisation and Embryology Act 2008; or

    (b) has a parent by virtue of section 43 of that Act and is a person to whom Article 155(3) applies,

the child's mother and the other parent shall each have parental responsibility for the child.'

(3) After paragraph (2) insert—

'(2A) Where a child has a parent by virtue of section 43 of the Human Fertilisation and Embryology Act 2008 and is not a person to whom Article 155(3) applies—

    (a) the mother shall have parental responsibility for the child;

    (b) the other parent shall have parental responsibility for the child if she has acquired it (and has not ceased to have it) in accordance with the provisions of this Order.'

72 (1) Article 7 of the Children (Northern Ireland) Order 1995 (acquisition of parental responsibility) is amended as follows.

(2) In paragraph (1)(b), omit '(a "parental responsibility agreement")'.

(3) After paragraph (1) insert—

'(1ZA) Where a child has a parent by virtue of section 43 of the Human Fertilisation and Embryology Act 2008 and is not a person to whom Article 155(3) applies, that parent shall acquire parental responsibility for the child if—

    (a) she becomes registered as a parent of the child;

    (b) she and the child's mother make an agreement providing for her to have parental responsibility for the child; or

    (c) the court, on her application, orders that she shall have parental responsibility for the child.

(1ZB) An agreement under paragraph (1)(b) or (1ZA)(b) is known as a 'parental responsibility agreement'.'

(4) After paragraph (2) insert—

'(2A) In paragraph (1)(a) 'registered' means registered under—

    (a) Article 14(3)(a), (b) or (c) of the Births and Deaths Registration (Northern Ireland) Order 1976;

    (b) paragraph (a), (b) or (c) of section 10(1) or 10A(1) of the Births and Deaths Registration Act 1953; or

    (c) paragraph (a), (b)(i) or (c) of section 18(1) of the Registration of Births, Deaths and Marriages (Scotland) Act 1965.

(2B) In paragraph (1ZA)(a) 'registered' means registered under—

    (a) Article 14ZA(3)(a), (b) or (c) of the Births and Deaths Registration (Northern Ireland) Order 1976;

    (b) paragraph (a), (b) or (c) of section 10(1B) and of section 10A(1B) of the Births and Deaths Registration Act 1953; or

    (c) paragraph (a), (b) or (d) of section 18B(1) of, or sections 18B(3)(a) and 20(1)(a) of, the Registration of Births, Deaths and Marriages (Scotland) Act 1965.'

(5) In paragraph (3), omit the words from 'and 'registered'' to the end.

(6) In paragraph (3A), after 'paragraph (1)' insert ', (1ZA)'.

(7) In paragraph (4)—

(a) for 'the father' substitute 'a parent', and
(b) after 'paragraph (1)(c)' insert 'or (1ZA)(c)'.

73 In Article 8 of the Children (Northern Ireland) Order 1995 (residence, contact and other orders with respect to children), in paragraph (4), for sub-paragraph (g) substitute—

'(g) section 54 of the Human Fertilisation and Embryology Act 2008;'.

74 (1) Article 12 of the Children (Northern Ireland) Order 1995 (residence orders and parental responsibility) is amended as follows.

(2) After paragraph (1) insert—

'(1A) Where the court makes a residence order in favour of a person who is a parent of a child by virtue of section 43 of the Human Fertilisation and Embryology Act 2008 it shall, if that person would not otherwise have parental responsibility for the child, also make an order under Article 7(1ZA) giving her that responsibility.'

(3) In paragraph (4)—
(a) after '(1)' insert 'or (1A)', and
(b) for 'father' substitute 'parent'.

75 (1) Article 155 of the Children (Northern Ireland) Order 1995 (parents not being married to each other to have no effect in law on relationships) is amended as follows.

(2) In paragraph (3), after sub-paragraph (b) insert—

(ba) has a parent by virtue of section 42 of the Human Fertilisation and Embryology Act 2008 (which relates to treatment provided to a woman who is at the time of treatment a party to a civil partnership or, in certain circumstances, a void civil partnership);
(bb) has a parent by virtue of section 43 of that Act (which relates to treatment provided to woman who agrees that second woman to be parent) who—
 (i) is the civil partner of the child's mother at the time of the child's birth, or
 (ii) was the civil partner of the child's mother at any time during the period beginning with the time mentioned in section 43(b) of that Act and ending with the child's birth;'.

(3) After paragraph (4) insert—

'(4A) A child whose parents are parties to a void civil partnership shall, subject to paragraph (4B), be treated as falling within paragraph (3)(bb) if at the time when the parties registered as civil partners of each other both or either of the parties reasonably believed that the civil partnership was valid.

(4B) Paragraph (4A) applies only where the woman who is a parent by virtue of section 43 was domiciled in Northern Ireland at the time of the birth or, if she died before the birth, was so domiciled immediately before her death.

(4C) Paragraph (4A) applies even though the belief that the civil partnership was valid was due to a mistake as to law.

(4D) It shall be presumed for the purposes of paragraph (4A), unless the contrary is shown, that one of the parties to a void civil partnership reasonably believed at the time of the formation of the civil partnership that the civil partnership was valid.'

76 In Article 179 of the Children (Northern Ireland) Order 1995 (effect and duration of orders etc), in paragraph (7), after '7(1)' insert ', (1ZA)'.

77 (1) Schedule 1 to the Children (Northern Ireland) Order 1995 (financial provision for children) is amended as follows.

A1.592AA *Statutes*

(2) At the end of paragraph 5 insert—

'(5) In the case of a child who has a parent by virtue of section 42 or 43 of the Human Fertilisation and Embryology Act 2008, any reference in sub-paragraph (2), (3) or (4) to the child's father is a reference to the woman who is a parent of the child by virtue of that section.'

(3) At the end of paragraph 12 insert—

'(8) In the case of a child who has a parent by virtue of section 42 or 43 of the Human Fertilisation and Embryology Act 2008, the reference in sub-paragraph (1)(a) to the child's father is a reference to the woman who is a parent of the child by virtue of that section.'

78 (1) Paragraph 1 of Schedule 6 to the Children (Northern Ireland) Order 1995 (succession on intestacy where parents not married to each other) is amended as follows.

(2) At the end of sub-paragraph (2) insert—

'(2A) In the case of a person who has a parent by virtue of section 43 of the Human Fertilisation and Embryology Act 2008 (treatment provided to woman who agrees that second woman to be parent), the second and third references in paragraph (2) to the person's father are to be read as references to the woman who is a parent of the person by virtue of that section.'

(3) In sub-paragraph (3) for 'section 19(1) of that Act' substitute 'section 19(1) of the Administration of Estates Act (Northern Ireland) 1955'.

Family Homes and Domestic Violence (Northern Ireland) Order 1998 (SI 1998/1071 (NI 6))

79 In Article 2 of the Family Homes and Domestic Violence (Northern Ireland) Order 1998 (interpretation), in paragraph (3), for sub-paragraph (f) substitute—

'(f) section 54 of the Human Fertilisation and Embryology Act 2008;'.

Paras 57–59, 67: Appointment: 6 April 2009: see SI 2009/479, art 6(1)(d).
Paras 60–66, 68, 70–72, 74–78: Appointment (for remaining purposes): 1 September 2009: see SI 2009/479, art 6(2).
Paras 60–66, 68, 70–72, 74–78: Appointment (for certain purposes): 6 April 2009: see SI 2009/479, art 6(1)(e).
Para 69: Appointment (in so far as it substitutes the Child Support (Northern Ireland) Order 1991, art 27, Case B1): 6 April 2009: see SI 2009/479, art 6(1)(d).

PART II—FINANCE ACTS ETC.

INHERITANCE TAX ACT 1984

(1984, C 51)

[31 July 1984]

A1.595

5 Meaning of estate

(1) For the purposes of this Act a person's estate is the aggregate of all the property to which he is beneficially entitled, [except that—

(a) the estate of a person—
　(i) does not include an interest in possession in settled property to which section 71A or 71D below applies, and
　(ii) does not include an interest in possession that falls within subsection (1A) below, and
(b) the] estate of a person immediately before his death does not include excluded property [or a foreign-owned work of art which is situated in the United Kingdom for one or more of the purposes of public display, cleaning and restoration (and for no other purpose)].

[(1A) An interest in possession falls within this subsection if—

(a) it is an interest in possession in settled property,
(b) the settled property is not property to which section 71A or 71D below applies,
(c) the person is beneficially entitled to the interest in possession,
(d) the person became beneficially entitled to the interest in possession on or after 22nd March 2006, and
(e) the interest in possession is—
　(i) not an immediate post-death interest,
　(ii) not a disabled person's interest, and
　(iii) not a transitional serial interest.]

(2) A person who has a general power which enables him, or would if he were sui juris enable him, to dispose of any property other than settled property, or to charge money on any property other than settled property, shall be treated as beneficially entitled to the property or money; and for this purpose "general power" means a power or authority enabling the person by whom it is exercisable to appoint or dispose of property as he thinks fit.

(3) In determining the value of a person's estate at any time his liabilities at that time shall be taken into account, except as otherwise provided by this Act.

(4) The liabilities to be taken into account in determining the value of a transferor's estate immediately after a transfer of value include his liability for inheritance tax on the value transferred but not his liability (if any) for any other tax or duty resulting from the transfer.

(5) Except in the case of a liability imposed by law, a liability incurred by a transferor shall be taken into account only to the extent that it was incurred for a consideration in money or money's worth.

Sub-s (1): words from 'except that— (a)' to 'and (b) the' in square brackets substituted by the Finance Act 2006, s 156, Sch 20, Pt 3, para 10(1), (2). Date in force: 22 March 2006: see the Finance Act 2006, s 156, Sch 20, Pt 3, para 7.

A1.595 *Statutes*

Sub-s (1): in para (b) words from 'or a foreign-owned' to 'no other purpose)' in square brackets inserted by SI 2009/730, art 13(1), (2). Date in force: this amendment has effect in relation to deaths occurring on or after 6 April 2009: see SI 2009/730, arts 1, 13(5).
Sub-s (1A): inserted by the Finance Act 2006, s 156, Sch 20, Pt 3, para 10(1), (3). Date in force: 22 March 2006: see the Finance Act 2006, s 156, Sch 20, Pt 3, para 7.

A1.596

6 Excluded property

(1) Property situated outside the United Kingdom is excluded property if the person beneficially entitled to it is an individual domiciled outside the United Kingdom.

[(1A) A holding in an authorised unit trust and a share in an open-ended investment company is excluded property if the person beneficially entitled to it is an individual domiciled outside the United Kingdom.]

[(1B) A decoration or other award is excluded property if—

(a) it was awarded for valour or gallant conduct, and
(b) it has never been the subject of a disposition for a consideration in money or money's worth.

(1C) In subsection (1B) the reference to a disposition of the decoration or other award includes—

(a) a reference to a disposition of part of it, and
(b) a reference to a disposition of an interest in it (or in part of it).]

(2) Where securities have been issued by the Treasury subject to a condition authorised by section 22 of the Finance (No 2) Act 1931 (or section 47 of the Finance (No 2) Act 1915) for exemption from taxation so long as the securities are in the beneficial ownership of persons [of a description specified in the condition], the securities are excluded property if they are in the beneficial ownership of such a person.

(3) Where the person beneficially entitled to the rights conferred by any of the following, namely—

(a) war savings certificates;
(b) national savings certificates (including Ulster savings certificates);
(c) premium savings bonds;
(d) deposits with the National Savings Bank or with a trustee savings bank;
(e) a [certified SAYE savings arrangement] within the meaning of [section 703(1) of the Income Tax (Trading and Other Income) Act 2005];

is domiciled in the Channel Islands or the Isle of Man, the rights are excluded property.

(4) Property to which this subsection applies by virtue of section 155(1) below is excluded property.

Sub-s (1A): inserted by the Finance Act 2003, s 186(2). Date in force: this amendment has effect in relation to transfers of value or other events occurring on or after 16 October 2002: see the Finance Act 2003, s 186(8).
Sub-ss (1B), (1C): inserted by SI 2009/730, art 14(1). Date in force: this amendment has effect in relation to transfers of value or other events occurring on or after 6 April 2009: see SI 2009/730, arts 1, 14(2).
Sub-s (2): words in square brackets substituted, in relation to income tax as respects the year 1996–97 and subsequent years of assessment, and in relation to corporation tax as respects accounting periods ending on or after 31 March 1996, by the Finance Act 1996, s 154, Sch 28.
Sub-s (3): in para (e) words 'certified SAYE savings arrangement' in square brackets substituted by the Income Tax (Trading and Other Income) Act 2005, s 882(1), Sch 1, Pt 2, paras 393, 394(a). Date in force: this amendment has effect, for the purposes of income tax for the year 2005–06 and

subsequent tax years, and for the purposes of corporation tax for accounting periods ending after 5 April 2005: see the Income Tax (Trading and Other Income) Act 2005, s 883(1).
Sub-s (3): in para (e) words 'section 703(1) of the Income Tax (Trading and Other Income) Act 2005' in square brackets substituted by the Income Tax (Trading and Other Income) Act 2005, s 882(1), Sch 1, Pt 2, paras 393, 394(b). Date in force: this amendment has effect, for the purposes of income tax for the year 2005–06 and subsequent tax years, and for the purposes of corporation tax for accounting periods ending after 5 April 2005: see the Income Tax (Trading and Other Income) Act 2005, s 883(1).

* * * * *

Rates

A1.597

7 Rates

(1) [Subject to subsections (2), (4) and (5) below] the tax charged on the value transferred by a chargeable transfer made by any transferor shall be charged at the following rate or rates, that is to say—

(a) if the transfer is the first chargeable transfer made by that transferor in the period of [seven years] ending with the date of the transfer, at the rate or rates applicable to that value under the < ... > Table in Schedule 1 to this Act;

(b) in any other case, at the rate or rates applicable under that Table to such part of the aggregate of—
   (i) that value, and
   (ii) the values transferred by previous chargeable transfers made by him in that period,
as is the highest part of that aggregate and is equal to that value.

[(2) Except as provided by subsection (4) below, the tax charged on the value transferred by a chargeable transfer made before the death of the transferor shall be charged at one half of the rate or rates referred to in subsection (1) above.]

(3) In [the Table] in Schedule 1 to this Act any rate shown in the third column is that applicable to such portion of the value concerned as exceeds the lower limit shown in the first column but does not exceed the upper limit (if any) shown in the second column.

[(4) Subject to subsection (5) below, subsection (2) above does not apply in the case of a chargeable transfer made at any time within the period of seven years ending with the death of the transferor but, in the case of a chargeable transfer made within that period but more than three years before the death, the tax charged on the value transferred shall be charged at the following percentage of the rate or rates referred to in subsection (1) above—

(a) where the transfer is made more than three but not more than four years before the death, 80 per cent;
(b) where the transfer is made more than four but not more than five years before the death, 60 per cent;
(c) where the transfer is made more than five but not more than six years before the death, 40 per cent; and
(d) where the transfer is made more than six but not more than seven years before the death, 20 per cent.

(5) If, in the case of a chargeable transfer made before the death of the transferor, the tax which would fall to be charged in accordance with subsection (4) above is less than the tax which would have been chargeable (in accordance with subsection (2) above) if

A1.597 Statutes

the transferor had not died within the period of seven years beginning with the date of the transfer, subsection (4) above shall not apply in the case of that transfer.]

Subsection (1): first words in square brackets inserted, second words in square brackets substituted, and word omitted repealed, by the Finance Act 1986, ss 101(1),(3), 114(6), Sch 19, Part I, para 2, Sch 23, Part X, with respect to transfers of value made, and other events occurring, on or after 18 March 1986.

Subsection (2): substituted by the Finance Act 1986, s 101(1),(3), Sch 19, Part I, para 2, with respect to transfers of value made, and other events occurring, on or after 18 March 1986.

Subsection (3): words in square brackets substituted by the Finance Act 1986, s 101(1),(3), Sch 19, Part I, para 2, with respect to transfers of value made, and other events occurring, on or after 18 March 1986.

Subsection (4), (5): inserted by the Finance Act 1986, s 101(1),(3), Sch 19, Part I, para 2, with respect to transfers of value made, and other events occurring, on or after 18 March 1986.

* * * * *

PART III
SETTLED PROPERTY

CHAPTER I
PRELIMINARY

* * * * *

A1.598

48   Excluded property

(1)   A reversionary interest is excluded property unless—

    (a)   it has at any time been acquired (whether by the person entitled to it or by a person previously entitled to it) for a consideration in money or money's worth, or

    (b)   it is one to which either the settlor or his spouse [or civil partner] is or has been beneficially entitled, or

    (c)   it is the interest expectant on the determination of a lease treated as a settlement by virtue of section 43 (3) above.

(2)   In relation to a reversionary interest under a settlement made before 16 April 1976, subsection (1) above shall have effect with the omission of paragraph (b); and, if the person entitled to a reversionary interest under a settlement made on or after 16 April 1976 acquired the interest before 10 March 1981, that subsection shall have effect with the omission of the words 'or has been' in paragraph (b).

Sub-s (1): in para (b) words 'or civil partner' in square brackets inserted by SI 2005/3229, regs 3, 12. Date in force: 5 December 2005: see SI 2005/3229, reg 1(1).

A1.601

200   Transfer on death

(1)   The persons liable for the tax on the value transferred by a chargeable transfer made (under section 4 above) on the death of any person are [(subject to subsection (1A) below)]—

    (a)   so far as the tax is attributable to the value of property which either—

        (i)   was not immediately before the death comprised in a settlement, or

        (ii)   was so comprised and consists of land in the United Kingdom which devolves upon or vests in the deceased's personal representatives,

the deceased's personal representatives;

(b) so far as the tax is attributable to the value of property which, immediately before the death, was comprised in a settlement, the trustees of the settlement;
(c) so far as the tax is attributable to the value of any property, any person in whom the property is vested (whether beneficially or otherwise) at any time after the death, or who at any such time is beneficially entitled to an interest in possession in the property;
(d) so far as the tax is attributable to the value of any property which, immediately before the death, was comprised in a settlement, any person for whose benefit any of the property or income from it is applied after the death.

[(1A) The person liable for tax chargeable by virtue of section 151A or 151C above in relation to any registered pension scheme is the scheme administrator of the pension scheme.]

(2) A purchaser of property, and a person deriving title from or under such a purchaser, shall not by virtue of subsection (1)(c) above be liable for tax attributable to the value of the property unless the property is subject to an Inland Revenue charge.

(3) For the purposes of subsection (1) above a person entitled to part only of the income of any property shall, notwithstanding anything in section 50 above, be deemed to be entitled to an interest in the whole of the property.

(4) Subsections (4) and (5) of section 199 above shall have effect for the purposes of this section as they have effect for the purposes of that section.

Sub-s (1): words '(subject to subsection (1A) below)' in square brackets inserted by the Finance Act 2006, s 160(1), Sch 22, paras 1, 5(1), (2). Date in force: 6 April 2006: see the Finance Act 2006, s 160(2).

Sub-s (1A): inserted by the Finance Act 2006, s 160(1), Sch 22, paras 1, 5(1), (3). Date in force: 6 April 2006: see the Finance Act 2006, s 160(2).

Accounts and information

A1.606

216 Delivery of accounts

(1) Except as otherwise provided by this section or by regulations under section 256 below, the personal representatives of a deceased person and every person who—

(a) is liable as transferor for tax on the value transferred by a chargeable transfer, or would be so liable if tax were chargeable on that value, or
(b) is liable as trustee of a settlement for tax on the value transferred by a transfer of value, or would be so liable if tax were chargeable on that value, or
[(bb) is liable under section 199(1)(b) above for tax on the value transferred by a potentially exempt transfer which proves to be a chargeable transfer, or would be so liable if tax were chargeable on that value, or
(bc) is liable under section 200(1)(c) above for tax on the value transferred by a chargeable transfer made on death, so far as the tax is attributable to the value of property which, apart from section 102(3) of the Finance Act 1986, would not form part of the deceased's estate, or would be so liable if tax were chargeable on the value transferred on the death, or]
[(bca)is liable under section 200(1A) or 210(2) above for tax in respect of any amount, or would be so liable if tax were chargeable in respect of that amount, or]
[(bd)is liable under section 201(1)(b), (c) or (d) above for tax on the value transferred by a potentially exempt transfer which is made under section 52 above and which proves to be a chargeable transfer, or would be so liable if tax were chargeable on that value, or]

(c) is liable as trustee of a settlement for tax on an occasion on which tax is chargeable under Chapter III of Part III of this Act (apart from section 79), or would be so liable if tax were chargeable on the occasion,

shall deliver to the Board an account specifying to the best of his knowledge and belief all appropriate property and the value of that property.

(2) Where in the case of the estate of a deceased person no grant of representation or confirmation has been obtained in the United Kingdom before the expiration of the period of twelve months from the end of the month in which the death occurred—

(a) every person in whom any of the property forming part of the estate vests (whether beneficially or otherwise) on or at any time after the deceased's death or who at any such time is beneficially entitled to an interest in possession in any such property, and

(b) where any of the property is at any such time comprised in a settlement and there is no person beneficially entitled to an interest in possession in that property, every person for whose benefit any of that property (or income from it) is applied at any such time,

shall deliver to the Board an account specifying to the best of his knowledge and belief the appropriate property vested in him, in which he has an interest or which (or income from which) is applicable for his benefit and the value of that property.

[(3) Subject to subsections (3A) and (3B) below, where an account is to be delivered by personal representatives (but not where it is to be delivered by a person who is an executor of the deceased only in respect of settled land in England and Wales), the appropriate property is—

(a) all property which formed part of the deceased's estate immediately before his death [(or would do apart from section 151A(3)(b) or 151C(3)(b) above)], other than property which would not, apart from section 102(3) of the Finance Act 1986, form part of his estate; and

(b) all property to which was attributable the value transferred by any chargeable transfers made by the deceased within seven years of his death.

(3A) If the personal representatives, after making the fullest enquiries that are reasonably practicable in the circumstances, are unable to ascertain the exact value of any particular property, their account shall in the first instance be sufficient as regards that property if it contains—

(a) a statement to that effect;
(b) a provisional estimate of the value of the property; and
(c) an undertaking to deliver a further account of it as soon as its value is ascertained.

(3B) The Board may from time to time give such general or special directions as they think fit for restricting the property to be specified in pursuance of subsection (3) above by any class of personal representatives.]

(4) Where subsection (3) above does not apply the appropriate property is any property to the value of which the tax is or would be attributable [(or would be apart from section 151A(3)(b), 151C(3)(b) or 151B(4) above)].

(5) Except in the case of an account to be delivered by personal representatives, a person shall not be required to deliver an account under this section with respect to any property if a full and proper account of the property, specifying its value, has already been delivered to the Board by some other person who—

(a) is or would be liable for the tax attributable to the value of the property, and
(b) is not or would not be liable with him jointly as trustee;

Inheritance Tax Act 1984 **A1.606**

and a person within subsection (2) above shall not be required to deliver an account under that subsection if he or another person within that subsection has satisfied the Board that an account will in due course be delivered by the personal representatives.

(6) An account under the preceding provisions of this section shall be delivered—

(a) in the case of an account to be delivered by personal representatives, before the expiration of the period of twelve months from the end of the month in which the death occurs, or, if it expires later, the period of three months beginning with the date on which the personal representatives first act as such;

[(aa) in the case of an account to be delivered by a person within subsection (1)(bb) [or (bd)] above, before the expiration of the period of twelve months from the end of the month in which the death of the transferor occurs;

(ab) in the case of an account to be delivered by a person within subsection (1)(bc) above, before the expiration of the period of twelve months from the end of the month in which the death occurs]

[(ac) in the case of an account to be delivered by the scheme administrator of a registered pension scheme [otherwise than by reason of a liability to tax under section 210(3)], before the expiration of the period of twelve months from the end of the month in which the death occurs[, the scheme administrator becomes aware of the death] or the person ceases to be a relevant dependant of the member [(depending on which occasions the charge)];]

(b) in the case of an account to be delivered by a person within subsection (2) above, before the expiration of the period of three months from the time when he first has reason to believe that he is required to deliver an account under that subsection;

(c) in the case of an account to be delivered by any other person, before the expiration of the period of twelve months from the end of the month in which the transfer is made or, if it expires later, the period of three months beginning with the date on which he first becomes liable for tax.

(7) A person liable for tax under section 32, [32A,] 79[, 126 or 151D] above or under Schedule 5 to this Act shall deliver an account under this section before the expiration of the period of six months from the end of the month in which the event by reason of which the tax is chargeable occurs.

Subsection (1): paras (bb), (bc) inserted by the Finance Act 1986, s 101, Sch 19, Part I, para 29, in relation to transfers of value made, and other events occurring, on or after 18 March 1986; para (bd) inserted by the Finance (No 2) Act 1987, s 96, Sch 7, para 4(2), in relation to transfers of value made, and other events occurring, on or after 17 March 1987.

Sub-s (1): para (bca) inserted by the Finance Act 2006, s 160(1), Sch 22, paras 1, 7(1), (2). Date in force: 6 April 2006: see the Finance Act 2006, s 160(2).

Sub-ss (3)–(3B): substituted, for subsection (3) as originally enacted, by the Finance Act 1999, s 105(1). This amendment has effect in relation to deaths occuring on or after 9 March 1999: see the Finance Act 1999, s 105(2).

Sub-s (3): in para (a) words '(or would do apart from section 151A(3)(b) or 151C(3)(b) above)' in square brackets inserted by the Finance Act 2006, s 160(1), Sch 22, paras 1, 7(1), (3). Date in force: 6 April 2006: see the Finance Act 2006, s 160(2).

Sub-s (4): words '(or would be apart from section 151A(3)(b), 151C(3)(b) or 151B(4) above)' in square brackets inserted by the Finance Act 2006, s 160(1), Sch 22, paras 1, 7(1), (4). Date in force: 6 April 2006: see the Finance Act 2006, s 160(2).

Subsection (6): paras (aa),(ab) inserted by the Finance Act 1986, s 101, Sch 19, Part I, para 29, in relation to transfers of value made, and other events occurring, on or after 18 March 1986; words in square brackets in para (aa) inserted by the Finance (No 2) Act 1987, s 96, Sch 7, para 4(3), in relation to transfers of value made, and other events occurring, on or after 17 March 1987.

Sub-s (6): para (ac) inserted by the Finance Act 2006, s 160(1), Sch 22, paras 1, 7(1), (5). Date in force: 6 April 2006: see the Finance Act 2006, s 160(2).

Sub-s (6): in para (ac) words from 'otherwise than by' to 'under section 210(3)' in square brackets inserted by the Finance Act 2008, s 91, Sch 28, paras 12(1), (3). Date in force: this amendment has effect in relation to deaths occurring on or after 6 April 2008: see the Finance Act 2008, s 91, Sch 28, para 15(3).

A1.606 *Statutes*

Sub-s (6): in para (ac) words ', the scheme administrator becomes aware of the death' in square brackets inserted by the Finance Act 2007, s 69, Sch 19, paras 19, 24(a). Date in force: this amendment has effect in relation to deaths, cases where scheme administrators become aware of deaths and cessations of dependency occurring on or after 6 April 2007: see the Finance Act 2007, s 69, Sch 19, para 29(8).

Sub-s (6): in para (ac) words '(depending on which occasions the charge)' in square brackets inserted by the Finance Act 2007, s 69, Sch 19, paras 19, 24(b). Date in force: this amendment has effect in relation to deaths, cases where scheme administrators become aware of deaths and cessations of dependency occurring on or after 6 April 2007: see the Finance Act 2007, s 69, Sch 19, para 29(8).

Subsection (7): number in square brackets inserted by the Finance Act 1985, s 94, Sch 26, para 11, in relation to events on or after 19 March 1985.

Sub-s (7): words ', 126 or 151D' in square brackets substituted by the Finance Act 2008, s 91, Sch 28, paras 6, 12(1), (4). Date in force: this amendment has effect in relation to deaths occurring on or after 6 April 2008: see the Finance Act 2008, s 91, Sch 28, para 15(3).

Penalties

A1.608

[(1) This section applies where a person ('the taxpayer') fails to deliver an account under section 216 or 217 above.

(2) The taxpayer shall be liable—

  (a) to a penalty [of] £100; and
  (b) to a further penalty not exceeding £60 for every day after the day on which the failure has been declared by a court or the [tribunal] and before the day on which the account is delivered.

* * * * *

Substituted, together with s 245A, for s 245 as originally enacted, by the Finance Act 1999, s 108(1). Date in force: this amendment does not have effect in relation to a failure by any person to deliver an account under section 216 or 217 of the Inheritance Tax Act 1984, to make a return under section 218 of that Act, or to comply with a notice under section 219 of that Act, where the period within which the person is required to perform the obligation in question expires before 27 July 1999: see the Finance Act 1999, s 108(3).

Sub-s (2): word 'or' in square brackets substituted by the Finance Act 2004, s 295(1), (2)(a). Date in force: this amendment has effect in relation to a failure by any person to deliver an account under ss 216 or 217 hereof where the period under ss 216(6), (7) or 217 hereof (whichever is applicable) within which the person is required to deliver the account expires after 22 January 2005: see the Finance Act 2004, s 295(5).

Sub-s (2): in para (b) word 'tribunal' in square brackets substituted by SI 2009/56, art 3(1), Sch 1, paras 108, 120. Date in force: 1 April 2009: see SI 2009/56, art 1(2); for transitional and savings provisions see art 6, Sch 3, paras 1, 6–8, 12, 13 thereto.

A1.609

[245A Failure to provide information etc]

[(1) A person who fails to make a return under section 218 above shall be liable—

  (a) to a penalty not exceeding £300; and< ... >
  (b) to a further penalty not exceeding £60 for every day after the day on which the failure has been declared by a court or the [tribunal] and before the day on which the return is made.

[(1A) A person who fails to comply with the requirements of section 218A above shall be liable—

  (a) to a penalty not exceeding £100; and

(b) to a further penalty not exceeding £60 for every day after the day on which the failure has been declared by a court or the [tribunal] and before the day on which the requirements are complied with.]

[(1B) Without prejudice to any penalties under subsection (1A) above, if a person continues to fail to comply with the requirements of section 218A after the anniversary of the end of the period of six months referred to in section 218A(1), he shall be liable to a penalty of an amount not exceeding £3,000.]

(2) *A person who fails to comply with a notice under section 219 above shall be liable*—

(a) to a penalty not exceeding £300; and
(b) to a further penalty not exceeding £60 for every day after the day on which the failure has been declared by a court or the [tribunal] and before the day on which the notice is complied with.

(3) *A person who fails to comply with a notice under section 219A(1) or (4) above shall be liable*—

(a) to a penalty not exceeding £50; and
(b) to a further penalty not exceeding £30 for every day after the day on which the failure has been declared by a court or the [tribunal] and before the day on which the notice is complied with.

(4) A person shall not be liable to a penalty under subsection (1)(b), [(1A)(b),] (2)(b) or (3)(*b*) [or (1A)(b)] above if—

(a) he makes the return required by section 218 above, [or]
[(aa) he complies with the requirements of section 218A above,]
(b) he complies with the notice under section 219 above, or
(c) he complies with the notice under section 219A(1) or (4) above,

before proceedings in which the failure could be declared are commenced.

(5) A person who has a reasonable excuse for failing to make a return[, *to comply with the requirements of section 218A*] or to comply with a notice [or to comply with the requirements of section 218A] shall not be liable by reason of that failure to a penalty under this section, unless he fails to make the return[, *to comply with the requirements of section 218A*] or to comply with the notice [or to comply with those requirements] without unreasonable delay after the excuse has ceased.]

Substituted, together with new s 245, for s 245 as originally enacted, by the Finance Act 1999, s 108(1). Date in force: this amendment does not have effect in relation to a failure by any person to deliver an account under section 216 or 217 of the Inheritance Tax Act 1984, to make a return under section 218 of that Act, or to comply with a notice under section 219 of that Act, where the period within which the person is required to perform the obligation in question expires before 27 July 1999: see the Finance Act 1999, s 108(3).
Sub-s (1): in para (b) word 'tribunal' in square brackets substituted by SI 2009/56, art 3(1), Sch 1, paras 108, 121. Date in force: 1 April 2009: see SI 2009/56, art 1(2); for transitional and savings provisions see art 6, Sch 3, paras 1, 6–8, 12, 13 thereto.
Sub-s (1A): inserted by the Finance Act 2002, s 120(3)(a). Date in force: this amendment applies in relation to instruments made on or after 1 August 2002: see the Finance Act 2002, s 120(4).
Sub-s (1A): in para (b) word 'tribunal' in square brackets substituted by SI 2009/56, art 3(1), Sch 1, paras 108, 121. Date in force: 1 April 2009: see SI 2009/56, art 1(2); for transitional and savings provisions see art 6, Sch 3, paras 1, 6–8, 12, 13 thereto.
Sub-s (1B): inserted by the Finance Act 2004, s 295(1), (3)(a). Date in force: for the effect of this amendment see the Finance Act 2004, s 295(7).
Sub-ss (2), (3): repealed by SI 2009/3054, art 3, Schedule, para 2(1), (4)(a). Date in force: 1 April 2010: see SI 2009/3054, art 1; for savings see art 4(b) thereof.
Sub-s (2): in para (b) word 'tribunal' in square brackets substituted by SI 2009/56, art 3(1), Sch 1, paras 108, 121. Date in force: 1 April 2009: see SI 2009/56, art 1(2); for transitional and savings provisions see art 6, Sch 3, paras 1, 6–8, 12, 13 thereto.

A1.609 *Statutes*

Sub-s (3): in para (b) word 'tribunal' in square brackets substituted by SI 2009/56, art 3(1), Sch 1, paras 108, 121. Date in force: 1 April 2009: see SI 2009/56, art 1(2); for transitional and savings provisions see art 6, Sch 3, paras 1, 6–8, 12, 13 thereto.
Sub-s (4): words ', (1A)(b), (2)(b) or (3)(b)' in italics repealed and subsequent words in square brackets substituted by SI 2009/3054, art 3, Schedule, para 2(1), (4)(b)(i). Date in force: 1 April 2010: see SI 2009/3054, art 1; for savings see art 4(b) thereof.
Sub-s (4): reference to '(1A)(b),' in square brackets and para (aa) inserted by the Finance Act 2002, s 120(3)(b). Date in force: this amendment applies in relation to instruments made on or after 1 August 2002: see the Finance Act 2002, s 120(4).
Sub-s (4): in para (a) word 'or' in square brackets inserted by SI 2009/3054, art 3, Schedule, para 2(1), (4)(b)(ii). Date in force: 1 April 2010: see SI 2009/3054, art 1; for savings see art 4(b) thereof.
Sub-s (4): paras (b), (c) repealed by SI 2009/3054, art 3, Schedule, para 2(1), (4)(b)(iii). Date in force: 1 April 2010: see SI 2009/3054, art 1; for savings see art 4(b) thereof.
Sub-s (5): words ', to comply with the requirements of section 218A' in square brackets in both places they occur inserted by the Finance Act 2004, s 295(1), (3)(b). Date in force: this amendment has effect in relation to a failure to comply with the requirements of s 218A hereof where the period of six months referred to in s 218A(1) expires after 22 July 2004: see the Finance Act 2004, s 295(8).
Sub-s (5): words from ', to comply with' to 'with a notice' in italics repealed and subsequent words in square brackets substituted by SI 2009/3054, art 3, Schedule, para 2(1), (4)(c)(i). Date in force: 1 April 2010: see SI 2009/3054, art 1; for savings see art 4(b) thereof.
Sub-s (5): words from ', to comply with' to 'with the notice' in italics repealed and subsequent words in square brackets substituted by SI 2009/3054, art 3, Schedule, para 2(1), (4)(c)(ii). Date in force: 1 April 2010: see SI 2009/3054, art 1; for savings see art 4(b) thereof.

Miscellaneous

* * * * *

A1.610

256   Regulations about accounts, etc

(1)   The Board may make regulations—

(a) dispensing with the delivery of accounts under section 216 above in such cases as may be specified [or determined under] in the regulations;

[(aa) requiring persons who by virtue of regulations under paragraph (a) above are not required to deliver accounts under section 216 above to produce to the Board, in such manner as may be specified in or determined under the regulations, such information or documents as may be so specified or determined;]

(b) discharging, subject to such restrictions as may be so specified [or determined], property from an Inland Revenue charge and persons from further claims for tax in cases other than those mentioned in section 239 above;

(c) < ... >

(d) modifying section 264(8) below in cases where the delivery of an account has been dispensed with under the regulations.

[(1A)   Regulations under subsection (1)(aa) may in particular—

(a) provide that information or documents must be produced to the Board by producing it or them to—
  (i) a probate registry in England and Wales;
  (ii) the sheriff in Scotland;
  (iii) the Probate and Matrimonial Office in Northern Ireland;
(b) provide that information or documents produced as specified in paragraph (a) is or are to be treated for any or all purposes of this Act as produced to the Board;

(c) provide for the further transmission to the Board of information or documents produced as specified in paragraph (a).]

(2) < ... >

(3) Regulations under this section may contain such supplementary or incidental provisions as the Board think fit [and may make different provision for different cases].

[(3A) Regulations under this section may only be made—

(a) in relation to England and Wales, after consulting the Lord Chancellor;
(b) in relation to Scotland, after consulting the Scottish Ministers;
(c) in relation to Northern Ireland, after consulting the Lord Chief Justice of Northern Ireland.

(3B) The Lord Chief Justice of Northern Ireland may nominate any of the following to exercise his functions under subsection (3A)—

(a) the holder of one of the offices listed in Schedule 1 to the Justice (Northern Ireland) Act 2002;
(b) a Lord Justice of Appeal (as defined in section 88 of that Act).]

(4) The power to make regulations under this section shall be exercisable by statutory instrument, which shall be subject to annulment in pursuance of a resolution of the House of Commons.

Sub-s (1): in para (a) words 'or determined under' in square brackets inserted by the Finance Act 2004, s 293(1), (2)(a). Date in force: this amendment came into force on 22 July 2004 (date of Royal Assent of the Finance Act 2004) in the absence of any specific commencement provision.
Sub-s (1): para (aa) inserted by the Finance Act 2004, s 293(1), (2)(b). Date in force: this amendment came into force on 22 July 2004 (date of Royal Assent of the Finance Act 2004) in the absence of any specific commencement provision.
Sub-s (1): in para (b) words 'or determined' in square brackets inserted by the Finance Act 2004, s 293(1), (2)(c). Date in force: this amendment came into force on 22 July 2004 (date of Royal Assent of the Finance Act 2004) in the absence of any specific commencement provision.
Sub-s (1): para (c) repealed by the Finance Act 2004, ss 293(1), (2)(d), 326, Sch 42, Pt 4(1). Date in force: this repeal came into force on 22 July 2004 (date of Royal Assent of the Finance Act 2004).
Sub-s (1A): inserted by the Finance Act 2004, s 293(1), (3). Date in force: this amendment came into force on 22 July 2004 (date of Royal Assent of the Finance Act 2004) in the absence of any specific commencement provision.
Sub-s (2): repealed by the Finance Act 2004, ss 293(1), (4), 326, Sch 42, Pt 4(1). Date in force: this repeal came into force on 22 July 2004 (date of Royal Assent of the Finance Act 2004).
Sub-s (3): words 'and may make different provision for different cases' in square brackets inserted by the Finance Act 2004, s 293(1), (5). Date in force: this amendment came into force on 22 July 2004 (date of Royal Assent of the Finance Act 2004) in the absence of any specific commencement provision.
Sub-ss (3A), (3B): substituted, for sub-s (3A) as inserted by the Finance Act 2004, s 293(1), (6), by the Constitutional Reform Act 2005, s 15(1), Sch 4, Pt 1, paras 175, 176. Date in force: 3 April 2006: see SI 2006/1014, art 2(a), Sch 1, paras 10, 11(r).

A1.611

257 Form etc of accounts

(1) All accounts and other documents required for the purposes of this Act shall be in such form and shall contain such particulars as may be prescribed by the Board.

(2) All accounts to be delivered to the Board under this Act shall be supported by such books, papers and other documents, and verified (whether on oath or otherwise) in such manner, as the Board may require.

A1.611 *Statutes*

(3) For the purposes of this Act, an account delivered to a probate registry pursuant to arrangements made between the President of the Family Division and the Board or delivered to the Probate and Matrimonial Office in Northern Ireland pursuant to arrangements made between the [Lord Chief Justice of Northern Ireland] and the Board shall be treated as an account delivered to the Board.

[(4) The Lord Chief Justice of Northern Ireland may nominate any of the following to exercise his functions under subsection (3)—

(a) the holder of one of the offices listed in Schedule 1 to the Justice (Northern Ireland) Act 2002;
(b) a Lord Justice of Appeal (as defined in section 88 of that Act).]

Sub-s (3): words 'Lord Chief Justice of Northern Ireland' in square brackets substituted by the Constitutional Reform Act 2005, s 15(1), Sch 4, Pt 1, paras 175, 177(1), (2). Date in force: 3 April 2006: see SI 2006/1014, art 2(a), Sch 1, paras 10, 11(r).

Sub-s (4): inserted by the Constitutional Reform Act 2005, s 15(1), Sch 4, Pt 1, paras 175, 177(1), (3). Date in force: 3 April 2006: see SI 2006/1014, art 2(a), Sch 1, paras 10, 11(r).

FINANCE ACT 1986

(1986, C 41)

[25 July 1986]

A1.616

102 Gifts with reservation

(1) Subject to subsections (5) and (6) below, this section applies where, on or after 18th March 1986, an individual disposes of any property by way of gift and either—

(a) possession and enjoyment of the property is not bona fide assumed by the donee at or before the beginning of the relevant period; or
(b) at any time in the relevant period the property is not enjoyed to the entire exclusion, or virtually to the entire exclusion, of the donor and of any benefit to him by contract or otherwise;

and in this section 'the relevant period' means a period ending on the date of the donor's death and beginning seven years before that date or, if it is later, on the date of the gift.

(2) If and so long as—

(a) possession and enjoyment of any property is not bona fide assumed as mentioned in subsection (1)(a) above, or
(b) any property is not enjoyed as mentioned in subsection (1)(b) above,

the property is referred to (in relation to the gift and the donor) as property subject to a reservation.

(3) If, immediately before the death of the donor, there is any property which, in relation to him, is property subject to a reservation then, to the extent that the property would not, apart from this section, form part of the donor's estate immediately before his death, that property shall be treated for the purposes of the 1984 Act as property to which he was beneficially entitled immediately before his death.

Finance Act 1986 **A1.616**

(4) If, at a time before the end of the relevant period, any property ceases to be property subject to a reservation, the donor shall be treated for the purposes of the 1984 Act as having at that time made a disposition of the property by a disposition which is a potentially exempt transfer.

(5) This section does not apply if or, as the case may be, to the extent that the disposal of property by way of gift is an exempt transfer by virtue of any of the following provisions of Part II of the 1984 Act,—

- (a) section 18 (transfers between spouses [or civil partners])[, except as provided by subsections (5A) and (5B) below];
- (b) section 20 (small gifts);
- (c) section 22 (gifts in consideration of marriage [or civil partnership]);
- (d) section 23 (gifts to charities);
- (e) section 24 (gifts to political parties);
- [(ee) section 24A (gifts to housing associations);]
- (f) section 25 (gifts for national purposes, etc);
- (g) < ... >
- (h) section 27 (maintenance funds for historic buildings); and
- (i) section 28 (employee trusts).

[(5A) Subsection (5)(a) above does not prevent this section from applying if or, as the case may be, to the extent that—

- (a) the property becomes settled property by virtue of the gift,
- (b) by reason of the donor's spouse [or civil partner] ('the relevant beneficiary') becoming beneficially entitled to an interest in possession in the settled property, the disposal is or, as the case may be, is to any extent an exempt transfer by virtue of section 18 of the 1984 Act in consequence of the operation of section 49 of that Act (treatment of interests in possession),
- (c) at some time after the disposal, but before the death of the donor, the relevant beneficiary's interest in possession comes to an end, and
- (d) on the occasion on which that interest comes to an end, the relevant beneficiary does not become beneficially entitled to the settled property or to another interest in possession in the settled property.

(5B) If or, as the case may be, to the extent that this section applies by virtue of subsection (5A) above, it has effect as if the disposal by way of gift had been made immediately after the relevant beneficiary's interest in possession came to an end.

(5C) For the purposes of subsections (5A) and (5B) above—

- (a) section 51(1)(b) of the 1984 Act (disposal of interest in possession treated as coming to end of interest) applies as it applies for the purposes of Chapter 2 of Part 3 of that Act; and
- (b) references to any property or to an interest in any property include references to part of any property or interest.]

(6) This section does not apply if the disposal of property by way of gift is made under the terms of a policy issued in respect of an insurance made before 18th March 1986 unless the policy is varied on or after that date so as to increase the benefits secured or to extend the term of the insurance; and, for this purpose, any change in the terms of the policy which is made in pursuance of an option or other power conferred by the policy shall be deemed to be a variation of the policy.

(7) If a policy issued as mentioned in subsection (6) above confers an option or other power under which benefits and premiums may be increased to take account of increases in the retail prices index (as defined in section 8(3) of the 1984 Act) or any similar index specified in the policy, then, to the extent that the right to exercise that

A1.616 Statutes

option or power would have been lost if it had not been exercised on or before 1st August 1986, the exercise of that option or power before that date shall be disregarded for the purposes of subsection (6) above.

(8) Schedule 20 to this Act has effect for supplementing this section.

Sub-s (5): in para (a) words 'or civil partners' in square brackets inserted by SI 2005/3229, regs 43, 44(1), (2)(a). Date in force: 5 December 2005: see SI 2005/3229, reg 1(1).

Sub-s (5): in para (a) words ', except as provided by subsections (5A) and (5B) below' in square brackets inserted by the Finance Act 2003, s 185(1), (2). Date in force: this amendment has effect in relation to disposals made on or after 20 June 2003: see the Finance Act 2003, s 185(4).

Sub-s (5): in para (c) words 'or civil partnership' in square brackets inserted by SI 2005/3229, regs 43, 44(1), (2)(b). Date in force: 5 December 2005: see SI 2005/3229, reg 1(1).

Sub-s (5): para (ee) inserted, in relation to transfers of value made on or after 14 March 1989, by the Finance Act 1989, s 171(5), (6).

Sub-s (5): para (g) repealed by the Finance Act 1998, s 165, Sch 27, Pt IV. Date in force: this repeal has effect in relation to any disposal on or after 17 March 1998: see the Finance Act 1998, Sch 27, Pt IV.

Sub-ss (5A)–(5C): inserted by the Finance Act 2003, s 185(1), (3). Date in force: this amendment has effect in relation to disposals made on or after 20 June 2003: see the Finance Act 2003, s 185(4).

Sub-s (5A): in para (b) words 'or civil partner' in square brackets inserted by SI 2005/3229, regs 43, 44(1), (3). Date in force: 5 December 2005: see SI 2005/3229, reg 1(1).

Appendix II
RULES, ORDERS AND REGULATIONS

APPENDIX II SUMMARY

		Para
Part 1–Non-Contentious Business		
SI 1977/1491	Intestate Succession (Interest and Capitalisation) Order 1977	A2.07A
SI 1981/880	The Inheritance Tax (Delivery of Accounts) Regulations 1981	A2.20
SI 1982/379	The District Probate Registries Order 1982	A2.28
SI 1987/2024	The Non-Contentious Probate Rules 1987	A2.40
SI 1991/1478	The Parental Responsibility Agreement Regulations 1991	A2.112
SI 2004/2543	Inheritance Tax (Delivery of Accounts) (Excepted Estates) Regulations 2004	A2.118
SI 2007/1253	Lasting Powers of Attorney, Enduring Powers of Attorney and Public Guardian Regulations 2007	A2.135A
SI 2009/135	Family Provision (Intestate Succession) Order 2009	A2.135U
Part II–Contentious Business		
	CPR Part 57 – Probate Claims Rectification of Wills, Substitution and Removal of Personal Representatives	A2.153
	Practice Direction 57 – Probate	A2.169

Appendix II

RULES, ORDERS AND REGULATIONS

PART I—NON-CONTENTIOUS BUSINESS

INTESTATE SUCCESSION (INTEREST AND CAPITALISATION) ORDER 1977

SI 1977/1491

A2.07A

1 Citation and Interpretation

(1) This Order may be cited as the Intestate Succession (Interest and Capitalisation) Order 1977 and shall come into operation on 15th September 1977.

(2) The Interpretation Act 1889 shall apply to the interpretation of this Order as it applies to the interpretation of an Act of Parliament.
Specified date: 15 September 1977: see para (1) above.

A2.07B

2 Interest of Statutory Legacy

For the purposes of section 46(1)(i) of the Administration of Estates Act 1925, as it applies both in respect of persons dying before 1953 and in respect of persons dying after 1952, the specified rate of interest shall be [6] per cent, per annum.
Specified date: 15 September 1977: see art 1(1).
Number '6' in square brackets substituted by SI 1983/1374, art 2. Date in force: 1 October 1983: see SI 1983/1374, art 1.

A2.07C

3 Capitalisation of Life Interests

(1) Where after the coming into operation of this Order an election is exercised in accordance with subsection (6) or (7) of section 47A of the Administration of Estates

A2.07C *Rules, Orders and Regulations*

Act 1925, the capital value of the life interest of the surviving spouse [or civil partner] shall be reckoned in accordance with the following provisions of this article.

(2) There shall be ascertained, by reference to the index compiled by the Financial Times, The Institute of Actuaries and the Faculty of Actuaries, the ... gross redemption yield on ... fifteen-year Government Stocks at the date on which the election was exercised or, if the index was not compiled on that date, by reference to the index on the last date before that date on which it was compiled; and the column which corresponds to that yield in whichever of the Tables set out in the Schedule hereto is applicable to the sex of the surviving spouse [or civil partner] shall be the appropriate column for the purposes of paragraph (3) of this article.

(3) The capital value for the purposes of paragraph (1) of this article is the product of the part of the residuary estate (whether or not yielding income) in respect of which the election was exercised and the multiplier shown in the appropriate column opposite the age which the surviving spouse [or civil partner] had attained at the date on which the election was exercised.

Specified date: 15 September 1977: see art 1(1).
Words 'or civil partner' in square brackets in each place they occur inserted by SI 2005/2114, art 2(6), Sch 6, para 1(1), (2). Date in force: 5 December 2005: see SI 2005/2114, art 1.
Para (2): first word omitted revoked by SI 2008/3162, art 2(1)(a). Date in force: 1 February 2009: see SI 2008/3162, art 1.
Para (2): second words omitted revoked by SI 2008/3162, art 2(1)(b). Date in force: 1 February 2009: see SI 2008/3162, art 1.

SCHEDULE

A2.07D
Table 1

Multiplier to be applied to the part of the residuary estate in respect of which the election is exercised to obtain the capital value of the life interest of a surviving husband or a surviving male civil partner when the gross redemption yield on fifteen year Government Stocks is at the rate shown.

Age last birthday of husband or male civil partner	Less than 2.5%	2.5% or between 2.5% and 3.5%	3.5% or between 3.5% and 4.5%	4.5% or between 4.5% and 5.5%	5.5% or between 5.5% and 6.5%	6.5% or between 6.5% and 7.5%	7.5% or between 7.5% and 8.5%	8.5% or between 8.5% and 9.5%	9.5% or between 9.5% and 10.5%	10.5% or between 10.5% and 11.5%	11.5% or more
16	0.630	0.761	0.836	0.881	0.907	0.922	0.932	0.938	0.942	0.944	0.946
17	0.625	0.756	0.833	0.878	0.905	0.921	0.931	0.937	0.941	0.944	0.945
18	0.620	0.752	0.829	0.875	0.903	0.920	0.930	0.936	0.941	0.943	0.945
19	0.615	0.747	0.825	0.872	0.901	0.918	0.929	0.936	0.940	0.943	0.945
20	0.610	0.743	0.822	0.870	0.899	0.917	0.928	0.935	0.939	0.942	0.945
21	0.604	0.738	0.818	0.867	0.896	0.915	0.927	0.934	0.939	0.942	0.944
22	0.599	0.733	0.814	0.863	0.894	0.913	0.925	0.933	0.938	0.941	0.944
23	0.594	0.728	0.809	0.860	0.891	0.911	0.924	0.932	0.937	0.941	0.943
24	0.588	0.723	0.805	0.857	0.889	0.909	0.922	0.931	0.936	0.940	0.943
25	0.582	0.717	0.801	0.853	0.886	0.907	0.921	0.930	0.936	0.940	0.942
26	0.577	0.712	0.796	0.849	0.883	0.905	0.919	0.928	0.935	0.939	0.942
27	0.571	0.706	0.791	0.846	0.880	0.903	0.917	0.927	0.934	0.938	0.941
28	0.565	0.701	0.786	0.842	0.877	0.900	0.915	0.926	0.932	0.937	0.940
29	0.559	0.695	0.781	0.837	0.874	0.898	0.913	0.924	0.931	0.936	0.940
30	0.553	0.689	0.776	0.833	0.870	0.895	0.911	0.922	0.930	0.935	0.939

A2.07D Rules, Orders and Regulations

31	0.546	0.683	0.771	0.829	0.867	0.892	0.909	0.920	0.928	0.934	0.938
32	0.540	0.676	0.765	0.824	0.863	0.889	0.907	0.918	0.927	0.933	0.937
33	0.533	0.670	0.759	0.819	0.859	0.886	0.904	0.916	0.925	0.931	0.936
34	0.527	0.663	0.753	0.814	0.854	0.882	0.901	0.914	0.923	0.930	0.935
35	0.520	0.657	0.747	0.809	0.850	0.879	0.898	0.912	0.922	0.928	0.933
36	0.514	0.650	0.741	0.803	0.845	0.875	0.895	0.909	0.919	0.927	0.932
37	0.507	0.643	0.734	0.798	0.841	0.871	0.892	0.907	0.917	0.925	0.931
38	0.500	0.636	0.728	0.792	0.836	0.867	0.888	0.904	0.915	0.923	0.929
39	0.493	0.628	0.721	0.785	0.830	0.862	0.885	0.901	0.912	0.921	0.927
40	0.485	0.621	0.714	0.779	0.825	0.858	0.881	0.897	0.910	0.918	0.925
41	0.478	0.613	0.706	0.773	0.819	0.853	0.877	0.894	0.907	0.916	0.923
42	0.471	0.605	0.699	0.766	0.813	0.847	0.872	0.890	0.903	0.913	0.921
43	0.463	0.597	0.691	0.759	0.807	0.842	0.867	0.886	0.900	0.910	0.918
44	0.456	0.589	0.683	0.751	0.800	0.836	0.863	0.882	0.896	0.907	0.916
45	0.448	0.580	0.675	0.744	0.794	0.830	0.857	0.877	0.893	0.904	0.913
46	0.440	0.572	0.666	0.736	0.786	0.824	0.852	0.873	0.888	0.900	0.910
47	0.432	0.563	0.658	0.728	0.779	0.817	0.846	0.868	0.884	0.896	0.906
48	0.424	0.554	0.649	0.719	0.771	0.811	0.840	0.862	0.879	0.892	0.903
49	0.416	0.545	0.640	0.711	0.763	0.803	0.834	0.856	0.874	0.888	0.899
50	0.408	0.536	0.630	0.702	0.755	0.796	0.827	0.850	0.869	0.883	0.895
51	0.400	0.526	0.621	0.692	0.746	0.788	0.820	0.844	0.863	0.878	0.890
52	0.392	0.517	0.611	0.683	0.738	0.780	0.812	0.837	0.857	0.873	0.885
53	0.383	0.507	0.601	0.673	0.728	0.771	0.804	0.830	0.851	0.867	0.880
54	0.375	0.497	0.591	0.663	0.719	0.762	0.796	0.823	0.844	0.861	0.875
55	0.366	0.487	0.580	0.653	0.709	0.753	0.788	0.815	0.837	0.855	0.869
56	0.357	0.477	0.569	0.642	0.698	0.743	0.779	0.807	0.829	0.848	0.863
57	0.349	0.467	0.558	0.631	0.688	0.733	0.769	0.798	0.821	0.840	0.856
58	0.340	0.456	0.547	0.620	0.677	0.723	0.759	0.789	0.813	0.833	0.849
59	0.331	0.445	0.536	0.608	0.665	0.712	0.749	0.779	0.804	0.824	0.841
60	0.322	0.435	0.524	0.596	0.654	0.701	0.738	0.769	0.795	0.816	0.833
61	0.313	0.424	0.512	0.584	0.641	0.689	0.727	0.759	0.785	0.806	0.825
62	0.304	0.413	0.500	0.571	0.629	0.677	0.716	0.748	0.774	0.797	0.815

63	0.295	0.401	0.488	0.558	0.616	0.664	0.704	0.736	0.764	0.786	0.806
64	0.286	0.390	0.475	0.545	0.603	0.651	0.691	0.724	0.752	0.776	0.796
65	0.277	0.379	0.462	0.532	0.590	0.638	0.678	0.712	0.740	0.765	0.785
66	0.268	0.367	0.450	0.519	0.576	0.624	0.665	0.699	0.728	0.753	0.774
67	0.259	0.356	0.437	0.505	0.562	0.610	0.651	0.685	0.715	0.740	0.762
68	0.250	0.344	0.424	0.491	0.547	0.596	0.637	0.671	0.701	0.727	0.750
69	0.240	0.333	0.410	0.476	0.533	0.581	0.622	0.657	0.687	0.714	0.737
70	0.231	0.321	0.397	0.462	0.517	0.565	0.606	0.642	0.673	0.699	0.723
71	0.222	0.309	0.383	0.447	0.502	0.549	0.590	0.626	0.657	0.684	0.708
72	0.213	0.297	0.369	0.432	0.486	0.533	0.574	0.610	0.641	0.669	0.693
73	0.204	0.285	0.355	0.417	0.470	0.516	0.557	0.593	0.624	0.652	0.677
74	0.195	0.273	0.341	0.401	0.453	0.499	0.540	0.575	0.607	0.635	0.660
75	0.186	0.261	0.327	0.385	0.436	0.482	0.522	0.557	0.589	0.617	0.642
76	0.177	0.249	0.313	0.370	0.419	0.464	0.503	0.539	0.570	0.598	0.624
77	0.168	0.237	0.299	0.354	0.402	0.446	0.485	0.519	0.551	0.579	0.604
78	0.159	0.225	0.284	0.337	0.385	0.427	0.465	0.500	0.531	0.559	0.585
79	0.150	0.214	0.270	0.321	0.367	0.409	0.446	0.480	0.510	0.538	0.564
80	0.142	0.202	0.256	0.305	0.349	0.390	0.426	0.459	0.490	0.517	0.543
81	0.133	0.191	0.242	0.289	0.332	0.371	0.406	0.439	0.468	0.496	0.521
82	0.125	0.179	0.228	0.273	0.314	0.352	0.386	0.418	0.447	0.473	0.498
83	0.117	0.168	0.215	0.257	0.297	0.333	0.366	0.397	0.425	0.451	0.475
84	0.109	0.157	0.201	0.242	0.279	0.314	0.346	0.376	0.403	0.429	0.453
85	0.102	0.147	0.188	0.227	0.262	0.296	0.326	0.355	0.381	0.406	0.429
86	0.095	0.137	0.176	0.212	0.246	0.278	0.307	0.334	0.360	0.384	0.406
87	0.088	0.127	0.164	0.198	0.230	0.260	0.288	0.314	0.339	0.362	0.384
88	0.081	0.118	0.152	0.185	0.215	0.243	0.270	0.295	0.318	0.340	0.362
89	0.075	0.110	0.142	0.172	0.200	0.227	0.252	0.276	0.299	0.320	0.340
90	0.070	0.102	0.132	0.160	0.187	0.212	0.236	0.259	0.280	0.301	0.320
91	0.065	0.094	0.122	0.149	0.174	0.198	0.221	0.242	0.263	0.282	0.301
92	0.060	0.088	0.114	0.139	0.162	0.185	0.207	0.227	0.247	0.265	0.283
93	0.056	0.082	0.106	0.130	0.152	0.173	0.194	0.213	0.231	0.249	0.266
94	0.052	0.076	0.099	0.121	0.142	0.162	0.181	0.200	0.217	0.234	0.251

A2.07D *Rules, Orders and Regulations*

95	0.048	0.071	0.092	0.113	0.133	0.152	0.170	0.188	0.204	0.221	0.236
96	0.045	0.066	0.086	0.106	0.124	0.143	0.160	0.176	0.192	0.208	0.223
97	0.042	0.062	0.081	0.099	0.117	0.134	0.150	0.166	0.181	0.196	0.210
98	0.039	0.058	0.075	0.093	0.109	0.125	0.141	0.156	0.170	0.184	0.198
99	0.037	0.054	0.071	0.087	0.102	0.118	0.132	0.146	0.160	0.173	0.186
100 and over	0.034	0.050	0.066	0.081	0.096	0.110	0.124	0.137	0.150	0.163	0.175]

Substituted by SI 2008/3162, art 2(2), Schedule. Date in force: 1 February 2009: see SI 2008/3162, art 1.

[Table 2]

Multiplier to be applied to the part of the residuary estate in respect of which the election is exercised to obtain the capital value of the life interest of a surviving wife or a surviving female civil partner when the gross redemption yield on fifteen year Government Stocks is at the rate shown.

Age last birthday of wife or female civil partner	Less than 2.5%	2.5% or between 2.5% and 3.5%	3.5% or between 3.5% and 4.5%	4.5% or between 4.5% and 5.5%	5.5% or between 5.5% and 6.5%	6.5% or between 6.5% and 7.5%	7.5% or between 7.5% and 8.5%	8.5% or between 8.5% and 9.5%	9.5% or between 9.5% and 10.5%	10.5% or between 10.5% and 11.5%	11.5% or more
16	0.650	0.779	0.851	0.892	0.916	0.929	0.937	0.942	0.944	0.946	0.947
17	0.645	0.775	0.848	0.890	0.914	0.928	0.936	0.941	0.944	0.946	0.947
18	0.640	0.771	0.845	0.888	0.912	0.927	0.936	0.941	0.944	0.946	0.947
19	0.636	0.767	0.842	0.885	0.911	0.926	0.935	0.940	0.944	0.946	0.947
20	0.631	0.762	0.838	0.883	0.909	0.925	0.934	0.940	0.943	0.945	0.947
21	0.626	0.758	0.835	0.880	0.907	0.923	0.933	0.939	0.943	0.945	0.947
22	0.621	0.753	0.831	0.878	0.905	0.922	0.932	0.938	0.942	0.945	0.946
23	0.615	0.749	0.828	0.875	0.903	0.921	0.931	0.938	0.942	0.944	0.946
24	0.610	0.744	0.824	0.872	0.901	0.919	0.930	0.937	0.941	0.944	0.946
25	0.605	0.739	0.820	0.869	0.899	0.917	0.929	0.936	0.941	0.944	0.946
26	0.599	0.734	0.816	0.866	0.897	0.916	0.928	0.935	0.940	0.943	0.945
27	0.594	0.729	0.812	0.863	0.894	0.914	0.926	0.934	0.939	0.943	0.945
28	0.588	0.724	0.807	0.859	0.892	0.912	0.925	0.933	0.939	0.942	0.945
29	0.582	0.719	0.803	0.856	0.889	0.910	0.924	0.932	0.938	0.942	0.944
30	0.577	0.713	0.798	0.852	0.886	0.908	0.922	0.931	0.937	0.941	0.944
31	0.571	0.708	0.794	0.848	0.883	0.906	0.920	0.930	0.936	0.940	0.943
32	0.565	0.702	0.789	0.844	0.880	0.903	0.919	0.929	0.935	0.940	0.943
33	0.559	0.696	0.784	0.840	0.877	0.901	0.917	0.927	0.934	0.939	0.942
34	0.552	0.690	0.778	0.836	0.874	0.898	0.915	0.926	0.933	0.938	0.941

A2.07D *Rules, Orders and Regulations*

35	0.546	0.684	0.773	0.832	0.870	0.896	0.913	0.924	0.932	0.937	0.941
36	0.540	0.678	0.767	0.827	0.866	0.893	0.910	0.922	0.930	0.936	0.940
37	0.533	0.671	0.762	0.822	0.862	0.890	0.908	0.920	0.929	0.935	0.939
38	0.527	0.664	0.756	0.817	0.858	0.886	0.905	0.918	0.927	0.934	0.938
39	0.520	0.658	0.750	0.812	0.854	0.883	0.902	0.916	0.926	0.932	0.937
40	0.513	0.651	0.743	0.807	0.849	0.879	0.900	0.914	0.924	0.931	0.936
41	0.506	0.644	0.737	0.801	0.845	0.875	0.896	0.911	0.922	0.929	0.935
42	0.499	0.636	0.730	0.795	0.840	0.871	0.893	0.909	0.920	0.927	0.933
43	0.492	0.629	0.723	0.789	0.835	0.867	0.890	0.906	0.917	0.926	0.932
44	0.485	0.621	0.716	0.783	0.829	0.862	0.886	0.903	0.915	0.924	0.930
45	0.477	0.613	0.708	0.776	0.823	0.858	0.882	0.899	0.912	0.921	0.928
46	0.470	0.605	0.701	0.769	0.817	0.852	0.878	0.896	0.909	0.919	0.926
47	0.462	0.597	0.693	0.762	0.811	0.847	0.873	0.892	0.906	0.916	0.924
48	0.454	0.589	0.685	0.754	0.805	0.841	0.868	0.888	0.902	0.913	0.922
49	0.447	0.580	0.676	0.747	0.798	0.835	0.863	0.883	0.899	0.910	0.919
50	0.439	0.572	0.668	0.739	0.791	0.829	0.858	0.879	0.895	0.907	0.916
51	0.431	0.563	0.659	0.730	0.783	0.823	0.852	0.874	0.891	0.903	0.913
52	0.422	0.553	0.650	0.722	0.775	0.816	0.846	0.868	0.886	0.899	0.910
53	0.414	0.544	0.640	0.713	0.767	0.808	0.839	0.863	0.881	0.895	0.906
54	0.406	0.534	0.631	0.703	0.758	0.800	0.832	0.857	0.876	0.890	0.902
55	0.397	0.525	0.620	0.694	0.749	0.792	0.825	0.850	0.870	0.885	0.897
56	0.388	0.515	0.610	0.684	0.740	0.784	0.817	0.843	0.864	0.880	0.893
57	0.379	0.504	0.600	0.673	0.730	0.775	0.809	0.836	0.857	0.874	0.888
58	0.371	0.494	0.589	0.663	0.720	0.765	0.800	0.828	0.850	0.868	0.882
59	0.361	0.483	0.577	0.652	0.709	0.755	0.791	0.820	0.843	0.861	0.876
60	0.352	0.472	0.566	0.640	0.698	0.745	0.782	0.811	0.835	0.854	0.869
61	0.343	0.461	0.554	0.628	0.687	0.734	0.771	0.802	0.826	0.846	0.862
62	0.334	0.450	0.542	0.616	0.675	0.722	0.761	0.792	0.817	0.837	0.854
63	0.324	0.438	0.529	0.603	0.662	0.710	0.749	0.781	0.807	0.828	0.846
64	0.315	0.427	0.517	0.590	0.649	0.698	0.737	0.770	0.797	0.819	0.837
65	0.305	0.415	0.504	0.577	0.636	0.685	0.725	0.758	0.786	0.808	0.828
66	0.295	0.403	0.490	0.563	0.622	0.671	0.712	0.746	0.774	0.797	0.817

Intestate Succession (Interest and Capitalisation) Order 1977 A2.07D

Age											
67	0.806	0.786	0.761	0.732	0.698	0.657	0.608	0.549	0.477	0.391	0.286
68	0.795	0.773	0.748	0.719	0.684	0.642	0.593	0.534	0.463	0.378	0.276
69	0.782	0.760	0.734	0.704	0.669	0.627	0.578	0.519	0.449	0.366	0.266
70	0.769	0.746	0.720	0.689	0.653	0.611	0.562	0.504	0.435	0.353	0.256
71	0.754	0.731	0.704	0.673	0.637	0.595	0.545	0.488	0.420	0.340	0.246
72	0.739	0.715	0.688	0.656	0.620	0.578	0.529	0.472	0.405	0.327	0.236
73	0.723	0.698	0.671	0.639	0.602	0.560	0.512	0.455	0.390	0.314	0.226
74	0.706	0.681	0.653	0.621	0.584	0.542	0.494	0.439	0.375	0.301	0.216
75	0.688	0.662	0.634	0.602	0.565	0.524	0.476	0.422	0.359	0.288	0.206
76	0.669	0.643	0.614	0.582	0.546	0.504	0.457	0.404	0.344	0.275	0.196
77	0.649	0.623	0.594	0.562	0.526	0.485	0.439	0.387	0.328	0.262	0.186
78	0.628	0.602	0.573	0.541	0.505	0.465	0.420	0.369	0.312	0.248	0.176
79	0.606	0.580	0.551	0.519	0.484	0.444	0.400	0.351	0.296	0.235	0.166
80	0.583	0.557	0.529	0.497	0.462	0.424	0.381	0.334	0.281	0.222	0.156
81	0.560	0.534	0.506	0.474	0.440	0.403	0.361	0.316	0.265	0.209	0.147
82	0.536	0.510	0.482	0.451	0.418	0.382	0.342	0.298	0.250	0.197	0.138
83	0.511	0.485	0.458	0.428	0.396	0.361	0.322	0.280	0.234	0.184	0.129
84	0.486	0.461	0.434	0.405	0.374	0.340	0.303	0.263	0.219	0.172	0.120
85	0.460	0.436	0.410	0.382	0.352	0.320	0.284	0.246	0.205	0.160	0.111
86	0.435	0.411	0.386	0.359	0.330	0.299	0.266	0.230	0.191	0.149	0.103
87	0.410	0.387	0.363	0.337	0.309	0.280	0.248	0.214	0.177	0.138	0.095
88	0.385	0.363	0.340	0.315	0.289	0.261	0.230	0.198	0.164	0.127	0.088
89	0.361	0.340	0.318	0.294	0.269	0.242	0.214	0.184	0.152	0.118	0.081
90	0.338	0.318	0.297	0.274	0.251	0.225	0.199	0.170	0.140	0.109	0.075
91	0.317	0.297	0.277	0.256	0.233	0.210	0.184	0.158	0.130	0.100	0.069
92	0.297	0.278	0.259	0.238	0.217	0.195	0.171	0.146	0.120	0.093	0.063
93	0.278	0.260	0.242	0.222	0.202	0.181	0.159	0.136	0.111	0.086	0.059
94	0.260	0.243	0.226	0.207	0.189	0.169	0.148	0.126	0.103	0.079	0.054
95	0.244	0.228	0.211	0.194	0.176	0.157	0.137	0.117	0.096	0.073	0.050

A2.07D *Rules, Orders and Regulations*

96	0.046	0.068	0.089	0.109	0.128	0.146	0.164	0.181	0.197	0.213	0.228
97	0.043	0.063	0.083	0.101	0.119	0.137	0.153	0.169	0.185	0.200	0.214
98	0.040	0.059	0.077	0.094	0.111	0.127	0.143	0.158	0.173	0.187	0.201
99	0.037	0.055	0.071	0.088	0.104	0.119	0.134	0.148	0.162	0.175	0.188
100 and over	0.034	0.051	0.066	0.082	0.097	0.111	0.125	0.138	0.152	0.164	0.177]

Substituted by SI 2008/3162, art 2(2), Schedule. Date in force: 1 February 2009: see SI 2008/3162, art 1.

THE INHERITANCE TAX (DELIVERY OF ACCOUNTS) REGULATIONS 1981

SI 1981/880

A2.20

Note.
Inheritance Tax: except in relation to a liability to tax arising before 25 July 1986 capital transfer tax is to be known as inheritance tax and the Capital Transfer Tax Act 1984 may be cited as the Inheritance Tax Act 1984, by virtue of the Finance Act 1986, s 100. Accordingly references to capital transfer tax have been changed to references to inheritance tax throughout these Regulations.
Following the consolidation of the Finance Act 1980, s 94(1), these Regulations have effect as if made under the Inheritance Tax Act 1984, s 256(1). The Regulations, as amended, have equal application to inheritance tax on and after 25 July 1986 by virtue of the Finance Act 1986, s 100. This SI is revoked in relation to deaths occurring on or after 6 April 2002: see SI 2002/1733, reg 9, Schedule.

THE DISTRICT PROBATE REGISTRIES ORDER 1982

SI 1982/379

Note.
Shown as amended by the District Probate Registries (Amendment) Order 1994, SI 1994/1103 as from 23 May 1994, and the District Probate Registries (Amendment No 2) Order 1994, SI 1994/3079, as from 16 January 1995.

The Lord Chancellor, in exercise of the power conferred on him by section 104 of the Supreme Court Act 1981, hereby makes the following Order:

A2.28

1   This Order may be cited as the District Probate Registries Order 1982 and shall come into operation on 20 April 1982.

A2.29

2— (1) District probate registries shall be established at the places specified in column 1 of the Schedule to this Order.

(2) The name of every place so specified shall be the name of the district probate registry at that place except that the name of the district probate registry at Cardiff shall be the Probate Registry of Wales.

A2.30

3   District probate sub-registries shall be established at the places specified in column 2 of the Schedule to this Order, and each sub-registry shall be attached to and under the control of the registrar of the district probate registry appearing opposite it in column 1 of the Schedule to this Order.

A2.31 *Rules, Orders and Regulations*

A2.31

4 [(1)] Every district probate registrar shall arrange for an officer of a district probate registry or of a district probate sub-registry to attend, for the purpose of personal applications for a grant of probate or administration, at such places and such times as [the Lord Chancellor, after consulting the Lord Chief Justice, may specify], and any such place may be styled a probate office.

[(2) The Lord Chief Justice may nominate a judicial office holder (as defined in section 109(4) of the Constitutional Reform Act 2005) to exercise his functions referred to in rules 5A and 38.]

Para (1): numbered as such by SI 2006/680, art 2, Sch 1, para 46(1), (2) from 3 April 2006: see SI 2006/680, art 1.
Para (1): words 'the Lord Chancellor, after consulting the Lord Chief Justice, may specify' in square brackets substituted by SI 2006/680, art 2, Sch 1, para 46(1), (3) from 3 April 2006: see SI 2006/680, art 1.
Para (2): inserted by SI 2006/680, art 2, Sch 1, para 46(1), (4) from 3 April 2006: see SI 2006/680, art 1.

A2.32

5 The District Probate Registries Order 1968 and the District Probate Registries (Amendment) Order 1981 are hereby revoked.

A2.33

SCHEDULE

Column 1	Column 2
District Probate Registries	Sub-registries
Birmingham	Stoke-on-Trent
Brighton	Maidstone
Bristol	Bodmin, Exeter
[Cardiff]	Bangor, Carmarthen
Ipswich	Norwich, Peterborough
Leeds	Lincoln, Sheffield
Liverpool	Chester, Lancaster
...	...
Manchester	Nottingham
Newcastle-upon-Tyne	Carlisle, Middlesbrough, York
Oxford	[Gloucester,] Leicester
Winchester	

Entry relating to 'Cardiff' inserted and entry omitted revoked, by SI 1994/3079, art 4; word in square brackets in entry relating to 'Oxford' inserted by SI 1994/1103, art 3.

THE NON-CONTENTIOUS PROBATE RULES 1987

SI 1987/2024

Note.
Shown as amended by the Non-Contentious Probate (Amendment) Rules 1991, SI 1991/1876, Non-Contentious Probate (Amendment) Rules 1998, SI 1998/1903,Non-Contentious Probate (Amendment) Rules 1999, SI1999/1015 Non-Contentious Probate (Amendment) Rules 2003, SI 2003/185, Non-Contentious Probate (Amendment) Rules 2004, SI 2004/2985,Civil Partnership Act 2004 (Amendments to Subordinate Legislation) Order 2005, SI 2005/2114, Adoption and Children Act (Consequential Amendments) Order 2005, SI 2005/3504, Mental Capacity Act 2005 (Transitional and Consequential Provisions) Order 2007, SI 2007/1898, Non-Contentious Probate (Amendment) Rules 2009, SI 2009/1893. New/inserted text is inside square brackets.

ARRANGEMENT OF RULES

RULE
1. Citation and commencement
2. Interpretation
3. Application of other rules
4. Applications for grants through solicitors [or probate practitioners]
5. Personal applications
6. Duty of [district judge or] registrar on receiving application for grant
7. Grants by registrars
8. Oath in support of grant
9. Grant in additional name.
10. Marking of wills
11. Engrossments for purposes of record
12. Evidence as to due execution of will
13. Execution of will of blind or illiterate testator
14. Evidence as to terms, condition and date of execution of will
15. Attempted revocation of will
16. Affidavit as to due execution, terms, etc, of will
17. Wills proved otherwise than under section 9 of the Wills Act 1837
18. Wills of persons on military service and seamen
19. Evidence of foreign law
20. Order of priority for grant where deceased left a will
21. Grants to attesting witnesses, etc
22. Order of priority for grant in case of intestacy
23. Order of priority for grant in pre-1926 cases
24. Right of assignee to a grant
25. Joinder of administrator
26. Additional personal representatives
27. Grants where two or more persons entitled in same degree
28. Exceptions to rules as to priority
29. Grants in respect of settled land
30. Grants where deceased died domiciled outside England and Wales
31. Grants to attorneys
32. Grants on behalf of minors
33. Grants where a minor is a co-executor
34. Renunciation of the right of a minor to a grant
35. Grants in case of mental incapacity
36. Grants to trust corporations and other corporate bodies
37. Renunciation of probate and administration
38. Notice to Crown of intended application for grant
39. Resealing under Colonial Probates Acts 1892 and 1927
40. Application for leave to sue on guarantee
41. Amendment and revocation of grant

A2.40 Rules, Orders and Regulations

42. Certificate of delivery of Inland Revenue affidavit
43. Standing searches
44. Caveats
45. Probate actions
46. Citations
47. Citation to accept or refuse or to take a grant
48. Citation to propound a will
49. Address for service
50. Application for order to attend for examination or for subpoena to bring in a will
51. Grants to part of an estate under section 113 of the Act
52. Grants of administration under discretionary powers of court, and grants ad colligenda bona
53. Applications for leave to swear to death
54. Grants in respect of nuncupative wills and copies of wills
55. Application for rectification of a will
56. Notice of election by surviving spouse to redeem life interest
57. Index of grant applications
58. Inspection of copies of original wills and others documents
59. Issue of copies of original wills and other documents
60. Taxation of costs
61. Power to require application to be made by summons
62. Transfer of applications
62A. Exercise of a registrar's jurisdiction by another registrar
63. Power to make orders for costs
64. Exercise of powers of judge during Long Vacation
65. Appeals from district judges or registrars
66. Service of summons
67. Notices, etc
68. Application to pending proceedings
69. Revocation of previous rules

Schedules
        First Schedule—Forms
        Second Schedule—Revocations

The President of the Family Division, in exercise of the powers conferred upon him by section 127 of the Supreme Court Act 1981, and section 2(5) of the Colonial Probates Act 1892, and with the concurrence of the Lord Chancellor, hereby makes the following Rules:

A2.40

1   Citation and commencement.—

These Rules may be cited as the Non-Contentious Probate Rules 1987, and shall come into force on 1st January 1988.

A2.41

2   Interpretation

(1) In these Rules, unless the context otherwise requires—

    'the Act' means the [Senior Courts Act 1981];
    'authorised officer' means any officer of a registry who is for the time being authorised by the President to administer any oath or to take any affidavit required for any purpose connected with his duties;
    'the Crown' includes the Crown in right of the Duchy of Lancaster and the Duke of Cornwall for the time being;
    ['district judge' means a district judge of the Principal Registry;]

The Non-Contentious Probate Rules 1987 **A2.42**

'grant' means a grant of probate or administration and includes, where the context so admits, the resealing of such a grant under the Colonial Probates Acts 1892 and 1927;
'gross value' in relation to any estate means the value of the estate without deduction for debts, incumbrances, funeral expenses or inheritance tax (or other capital tax payable out of the estate);
['judge' means a judge of the High Court;]
'oath' means the oath required by rule 8 to be sworn by every applicant for a grant;
'personal applicant' means a person other than a trust corporation who seeks to obtain a grant without employing a solicitor [or probate practitioner], and 'personal application' has a corresponding meaning;
['probate practitioner' means a person to whom section 23(1) of the Solicitors Act 1974 does not apply by virtue of section 23(2) of that Act [or section 55 of the Courts and Legal Services Act 1990;]]
['registrar' means the district probate registrar of the district probate registry—
   (i) to which an application for a grant is made or is proposed to be made,
   (ii) in rules 26,40,41 and 61(2), from which the grant issued, and
   (iii) in rules 46,47 and 48, from which the citation has issued or is proposed to be issued;]
'registry' means the Principal Registry or a district probate registry;
['the senior district judge' means the Senior District Judge of the Family Division or, in his absence, the senior of the district judges in attendance at the Principal Registry;]
< ... >
< ... >
'the Treasury Solicitor' means the solicitor for the affairs of Her Majesty's Treasury and includes the solicitor for the affairs of the Duchy of Lancaster and the solicitor of the Duchy of Cornwall;
'trust corporation' means a corporation within the meaning of section 128 of the Act as extended by section 3 of the Law of Property (Amendment) Act 1926.

(2) A form referred to by number means the form so numbered in the First Schedule; and such forms shall be used wherever applicable, with such variation as a [district judge or] registrar may in any particular case direct or approve.

Para (1): in definition 'the Act' words 'Senior Courts Act 1981' in square brackets substituted by the Constitutional Reform Act 2005, s 59(5), Sch 11, Pt 1, para 1(2). Date in force: 1 October 2009: see SI 2009/1604, art 2(d).
Para (1): definition 'district judge' inserted by SI 1991/1876, r 6(a).
Para (1): definition 'judge' inserted by SI 1991/1876, r 6(b).
Para (1): in definition 'personal applicant' words 'or probate practitioner' in square brackets inserted by SI 1998/1903, r 3(a). Date in force: 14 September 1998: see SI 1998/1903, r 1(1).
Para (1): definition 'probate practitioner' inserted by SI 1998/1903, r 3(b). Date in force: 14 September 1998: see SI 1998/1903, r 1(1).
Para (1): in definition 'probate practitioner' words 'or section 55 of the Courts and Legal Services Act 1990;' in square brackets inserted by SI 2004/2985, r 2. Date in force: 7 December 2004: see SI 2004/2985, r 1.
Para (1): definition 'registrar' substituted by SI 1991/1876, r 6(c).
Para (1): definition 'the senior district judge' substituted, for definition 'the Senior Registrar' as originally enacted, by SI 1991/1876, r 6(d).
Para (1): definition 'statutory guardian' omitted revoked by SI 1991/1876, r 2.
Para (1): definition 'testamentary guardian' omitted revoked by SI 1991/1876, r 2.
Para (2): words in square brackets substituted by SI 1991/1876, r 7(1).

A2.42

[3 **Application of other rules—**

(1) Subject to the provisions of these rules and to any enactment, the rules of the Supreme Court 1965 as they were in force immediately before 26th April 1999 shall

A2.42 Rules, Orders and Regulations

apply, with any necessary modifications to non-contentious probate matters, and any reference in these rules to those rules shall be construed accordingly.

(2) Nothing in Order 3 of the Rules of the Supreme Court shall prevent time from running in the Long Vacation.]
Substituted by SI 1999/1015, r 2 from 26 April 1999: see SI 1999/1015, r 1.

A2.43

4 Applications for grants through solicitors [or probate practitioners].—

(1) A person applying for a grant through a solicitor [or probate practitioner] may apply at any registry or sub-registry.

(2) Every solicitor [or probate practitioner] through whom an application for a grant is made shall give the address of his place of business within England and Wales.
Provision heading: words 'or probate practitioners' in square brackets inserted by SI 1998/1903, r 4(a) from 14 September 1998: see SI 1998/1903, r 1(1).
Para (1): words 'or probate practitioner' in square brackets inserted by SI 1998/1903, r 4(b) from 14 September 1998: see SI 1998/1903, r 1(1).
Para (2): words 'or probate practitioner' in square brackets inserted by SI 1998/1903, r 4(b) from 14 September 1998: see SI 1998/1903, r 1(1).

A2.44

5 Personal applications.—

(1) A personal applicant may apply for a grant at any registry or sub-registry.

(2) Save as provided for by rule 39 a personal applicant may not apply through an agent, whether paid or unpaid, and may not be attended by any person acting or appearing to act as his adviser.

(3) No personal application shall be proceeded with if—
  (a) it becomes necessary to bring the matter before the court by action or summons, [unless a judge, district judge or registrar so permits];
  (b) an application has already been made by a solicitor [or probate practitioner] on behalf of the applicant and has not been withdrawn; or
  (c) the [district judge or] registrar so directs.

(4) After a will has been deposited in a registry by a personal applicant, it may not be delivered to the applicant or to any other person unless in special circumstances the [district judge or] registrar so directs.

(5) A personal applicant shall produce a certificate of the death of the deceased or such other evidence of the death as the [district judge or] registrar may approve.

(6) A personal applicant shall supply all information necessary to enable the papers leading to the grant to be prepared in the registry.

(7) Unless the [district judge or] registrar otherwise directs, every oath or affidavit required on a personal application shall be sworn or executed by all the deponents before an authorised officer.

(8) No legal advice shall be given to a personal applicant by any officer of a registry and every such officer shall be responsible only for embodying in proper form the applicant's instructions for the grant.
Para (3): in sub-para (a) words ', unless a judge, district judge or registrar so permits' in square brackets inserted by SI 1998/1903, r 5 from 14 September 1998: see SI 1998/1903, r 1(1).

Para (3): in sub-para (b) words 'or probate practitioner' in square brackets inserted by SI 1998/1903, r 6 from 14 September 1998: see SI 1998/1903, r 1(1).
Para (3): in sub-para (c) words 'district judge or' in square brackets inserted by SI 1991/1876, r 7(1).
Para (4): words 'district judge or' in square brackets inserted by SI 1991/1876, r 7(1).
Para (5): words 'district judge or' in square brackets inserted by SI 1991/1876, r 7(1).
Para (7): words 'district judge or' in square brackets inserted by SI 1991/1876, r 7(1).

A2.45

6 Duty of [district judge or] registrar on receiving application for grant.—

(1) A [district judge or] registrar shall not allow any grant to issue until all inquiries which he may see fit to make have been answered to his satisfaction.

(2) Except with the leave of a [district judge or] registrar, no grant of probate or of administration with the will annexed shall issue within seven days of the death of the deceased and no grant of administration shall issue within fourteen days thereof.
Provision heading: words in square brackets inserted by SI 1991/1876, r 7(1).
Paras (1), (2): words in square brackets inserted by SI 1991/1876, r 7(1).

A2.46

7 Grants by registrars.—

(1) No grant shall be made by a ... registrar—

(a) in any case in which there is contention, until the contention is disposed of; or
(b) in any case in which it appears to him that a grant ought not to be made without the directions of a judge or a [district judge].

(2) In any case in which paragraph (1)(b) applies, the ... registrar shall send a statement of the matter in question to the Principal Registry for directions.

(3) A [district judge] may either confirm that the matter be referred to a judge and give directions accordingly or may direct the ... registrar to proceed with the matter in accordance with such instructions as are deemed necessary, which may include a direction to take no further action in relation to the matter.
Paras (1), (3): words omitted revoked, and words in square brackets substituted, by SI 1991/1876, r 7(2), (3).
Para (2): words omitted revoked by SI 1991/1876, r 7(2).

A2.47

8 Oath in support of grant.—

(1) Every application for a grant other than one to which rule 39 applies shall be supported by an oath by the applicant in the form applicable to the circumstances of the case, and by such other papers as the [district judge or] registrar may require.

(2) Unless otherwise directed by a [district judge or] registrar, the oath shall state where the deceased died domiciled.

(3) Where the deceased died on or after 1st January 1926, the oath shall state whether or not, to the best of the applicant's knowledge, information and belief, there was land vested in the deceased which was settled previously to his death and not by his will and which remained settled land notwithstanding his death.

A2.47 Rules, Orders and Regulations

(4) On an application for a grant of administration the oath shall state in what manner all persons having a prior right to a grant have been cleared off and whether any minority or life interest arises under the will or intestacy.
Paras (1), (2): words in square brackets inserted by SI 1991/1876, r 7(1).

A2.48

9 Grant in additional name.—

Where it is sought to describe the deceased in a grant by some name in addition to his true name, the applicant shall depose to the true name of the deceased and shall specify some part of the estate which was held in the other name, or give any other reason for the inclusion of the other name in the grant.

A2.49

10 Marking of wills.—

Subject to paragraph (2) below, every will in respect of which an application for a grant is made—

(a) shall be marked by the signatures of the applicant and the person before whom the oath is sworn; and
(b) shall be exhibited to any affidavit which may be required under these Rules as to the validity, terms, condition or date of execution of the will.

(2) The [district judge or] registrar may allow a facsimile copy of a will to be marked or exhibited in lieu of the original document.
Para (2): words in square brackets inserted by SI 1991/1876, r 7(1).

A2.50

11 Engrossment for purposes of record.—

(1) Where the [district judge or] registrar considers that in any particular case a facsimile copy of the original will would not be satisfactory for purposes of record, he may require an engrossment suitable for facsimile reproduction to be lodged.

(2) Where a will—

(a) contains alterations which are not to be admitted to proof; or
(b) has been ordered to be rectified by virtue of section 20(1) of the Administration of Justice Act 1982,

there shall be lodged an engrossment of the will in the form in which it is to be proved.

(3) Any engrossment lodged under this rule shall reproduce the punctuation, spacing and division into paragraphs of the will and shall follow continuously from page to page on both sides of the paper.
Para (1): words in square brackets inserted by SI 1991/1876, r 7(1).

A2.51

12 Evidence as to due execution of will.—

(1) Subject to paragraphs (2) and (3) below, where a will contains no attestation clause or the attestation clause is insufficient, or where it appears to the [district judge or] registrar that there is doubt about the due execution of the will, he shall before

admitting it to proof require an affidavit as to due execution from one or more of the attesting witnesses or, if no attesting witness is conveniently available, from any other person who was present when the will was executed; and if the [district judge or] registrar, after considering the evidence, is satisfied that the will was not duly executed, he shall refuse probate and mark the will accordingly.

(2) If no affidavit can be obtained in accordance with paragraph (1) above, the [district judge or] registrar may accept evidence on affidavit from any person he may think fit to show that the signature on the will is in the handwriting of the deceased, or of any other matter which may raise a presumption in favour of due execution of the will, and may if he thinks fit require that notice of the application be given to any person who may be prejudiced by the will.

(3) A [district judge or] registrar may accept a will for proof without evidence as aforesaid if he is satisfied that the distribution of the estate is not thereby affected.
Para (3): words in square brackets inserted by SI 1991/1876, r 7(1).

A2.52

13   Execution of will of blind or illiterate testator.—

Before admitting to proof a will which appears to have been signed by a blind or illiterate testator or by another person by direction of the testator, or which for any other reason raises doubt as to the testator having had knowledge of the contents of the will at the time of its execution, the [district judge or] registrar shall satisfy himself that the testator had such knowledge.
Words in square brackets inserted by SI 1991/1876, r 7(1).

A2.53

14   Evidence as to terms, condition and date of execution of will.—

(1) Subject to paragraph (2) below, where there appears in a will any obliteration, interlineation, or other alteration which is not authenticated in the manner prescribed by section 21 of the Wills Act 1837, or by the re-execution of the will or by the execution of a codicil, the [district judge or] registrar shall require evidence to show whether the alteration was present at the time the will was executed and shall give directions as to the form in which the will is to be proved.

(2) The provisions of paragraph (1) above shall not apply to any alteration which appears to the [district judge or] registrar to be of no practical importance.

(3) If a will contains any reference to another document in such terms as to suggest that it ought to be incorporated in the will, the [district judge or] registrar shall require the document to be produced and may call for such evidence in regard to the incorporation of the document as he may think fit.

(4) Where there is a doubt as to the date on which a will was executed, the [district judge or] registrar may require such evidence as he thinks necessary to establish the date.
Paras (1), (4): words in square brackets inserted by SI 1991/1876, r 7(1).

A2.54

15   Attempted revocation of will.—

Any appearance of attempted revocation of a will by burning, tearing, or otherwise destroying and every other circumstance leading to a presumption of revocation by the testator, shall be accounted for to the [district judge's or] registrar's satisfaction.

A2.54 Rules, Orders and Regulations

Words in square brackets inserted by SI 1991/1876, r 7(5).

A2.55

16 Affidavit as to due execution, terms, etc, of will.—

A [district judge or] registrar may require an affidavit from any person he may think fit for the purpose of satisfying himself as to any of the matters referred to in rules 13, 14 and 15, and in any such affidavit sworn by an attesting witness or other person present at the time of the execution of a will the deponent shall depose to the manner in which the will was executed.
Words in square brackets inserted by SI 1991/1876, r 7(1).

A2.56

17 Wills proved otherwise than under section 9 of the Wills Act 1837.—

(1) Rules 12 to 15 shall apply only to a will that is to be established by reference to section 9 of the Wills Act 1837 (signing and attestation of wills).

(2) A will that is to be established otherwise than as described in paragraph (1) of this rule may be so established upon the [district judge or] registrar being satisfied as to its terms and validity, and includes (without prejudice to the generality of the foregoing)—

   (a) any will to which rule 18 applies; and
   (b) any will which, by virtue of the Wills Act 1963, is to be treated as properly executed if executed according to the internal law of the territory or state referred to in section 1 of that Act.

Para (2): words in square brackets inserted by SI 1991/1876, r 7(1).

A2.57

18 Wills of persons on military service and seamen.—

Where the deceased died domiciled in England and Wales and it appears to the [district judge or] registrar that there is prima facie evidence that a will is one to which section 11 of the Wills Act 1837 applies, the will may be admitted to proof if the registrar is satisfied that it was signed by the testator or, if unsigned, that it is in the testator's handwriting.
Words in square brackets inserted by SI 1991/1876, r 7(1).

A2.58

19 Evidence of foreign law.—

Where evidence as to the law of any country or territory outside England and Wales is required on any application for a grant, the [district judge or] registrar may accept—

   (a) an affidavit from any person whom, having regard to the particulars of his knowledge or experience given in the affidavit, he regards as suitably qualified to give expert evidence of the law in question; or
   (b) a certificate by, or an act before, a notary practising in the country or territory concerned.

Words in square brackets inserted by SI 1991/1876, r 7(1).

A2.59

20 Order of priority for grant where deceased left a will.—

Where the deceased died on or after 1 January 1926 the person or persons entitled to a grant in respect of a will shall be determined in accordance with the following order of priority, namely—

- (a) the executor (but subject to rule 36(4)(d) below);
- (b) any residuary legatee or devisee holding in trust for any other person;
- (c) any other residuary legatee or devisee (including one for life) or where the residue is not wholly disposed of by the will, any person entitled to share in the undisposed of residue (including the Treasury Solicitor when claiming bona vacantia on behalf of the Crown), provided that—
    - (i) unless a [district judge or] registrar otherwise directs, a residuary legatee or devisee whose legacy or devise is vested in interest shall be preferred to one entitled on the happening of a contingency, and
    - (ii) where the residue is not in terms wholly disposed of, the [district judge or] registrar may, if he is satisfied that the testator has nevertheless disposed of the whole or substantially the whole of the known estate, allow a grant to be made to any legatee or devisee entitled to, or to share in, the estate so disposed of, without regard to the persons entitled to share in any residue not disposed of by the will;
- (d) the personal representative of any residuary legatee or devisee (but not one for life, or one holding in trust for any other person), or of any person entitled to share in any residue not disposed of by the will;
- (e) any other legatee or devisee (including one for life or one holding in trust for any other person) or any creditor of the deceased, provided that, unless a [district judge or] registrar otherwise directs, a legatee or devisee whose legacy or devise is vested in interest shall be preferred to one entitled on the happening of a contingency;
- (f) the personal representative of any other legatee or devisee (but not one for life or one holding in trust for any other person) or of any creditor of the deceased.

Paras (c), (e): words in square brackets inserted by SI 1991/1876, r 7(1).

A2.60

21 Grants to attesting witnesses, etc.

Where a gift to any person fails by reason of section 15 of the Wills Act 1837, such person shall not have any right to a grant as a beneficiary named in the will, without prejudice to his right to a grant in any other capacity.

A2.61

22 Order of priority for grant in case of intestacy.—

(1) Where the deceased died on or after 1st January 1926, wholly intestate, the person or persons having a beneficial interest in the estate shall be entitled to a grant of administration in the following classes in order of priority, namely—

- (a) the surviving [spouse or civil partner];
- (b) the children of the deceased and the issue of any deceased child who died before the deceased;
- (c) the father and mother of the deceased;

A2.61 Rules, Orders and Regulations

(d) brothers and sisters of the whole blood and the issue of any deceased brother or sister of the whole blood who died before the deceased;
(e) brothers and sisters of the half blood and the issue of any deceased brother or sister of the half blood who died before the deceased;
(f) grandparents;
(g) uncles and aunts of the whole blood and the issue of any deceased uncle or aunt of the whole blood who died before the deceased;
(h) uncles and aunts of the half blood and the issue of any deceased uncle or aunt of the half blood who died before the deceased.

(2) In default of any person having a beneficial interest in the estate, the Treasury Solicitor shall be entitled to a grant if he claims bona vacantia on behalf of the Crown.

(3) If all persons entitled to a grant under the foregoing provisions of this rule have been cleared off, a grant may be made to a creditor of the deceased or to any person who, notwithstanding that he has no immediate beneficial interest in the estate, may have a beneficial interest in the event of an accretion thereto.

(4) Subject to paragraph (5) of rule 27, the personal representative of a person in any of the classes mentioned in paragraph (1) of this rule or the personal representative of a creditor of the deceased shall have the same right to a grant as the person whom he represents provided that the persons mentioned in sub-paragraphs (b) to (h) of paragraph (1) above shall be preferred to the personal representative of a spouse [or civil partner] who has died without taking a beneficial interest in the whole estate of the deceased as ascertained at the time of the application for the grant.

Para (1): in sub-para (a) words 'spouse or civil partner' in square brackets substituted by SI 2005/2114, art 2(6), Sch 6, para 2(1), (2) from 5 December 2005: see SI 2005/2114, art 1.
Para (4): words 'or a civil partner' in square brackets inserted by SI 2005/2114, art 2(6), Sch 6, para 2(1), (3) from 5 December 2005: see SI 2005/2114, art 1.

A2.62

23 Order of priority for grant in pre-1926 cases.—

Where the deceased died before 1 January 1926, the person or persons entitled to a grant shall, subject to the provisions of any enactment, be determined in accordance with the principles and rules under which the court would have acted at the date of death.

A2.63

24 Right of assignee to a grant.—

(1) Where all the persons entitled to the estate of the deceased (whether under a will or on intestacy) have assigned their whole interest in the estate to one or more persons, the assignee or assignees shall replace, in the order of priority for a grant of administration, the assignor or, if there are two or more assignors, the assignor with the highest priority.

(2) Where there are two or more assignees, administration may be granted with the consent of the others to any one or more (not exceeding four) of them.

(3) In any case where administration is applied for by an assignee the original instrument of assignment shall be produced and a copy of the same lodged in the registry.

A2.64

25 Joinder of administrator.—

(1) A person entitled in priority to a grant of administration may, without leave, apply for a grant with a person entitled in a lower degree, provided that there is no other person entitled in a higher degree to the person to be joined, unless every other such person has renounced.

(2) Subject to paragraph (3) below, an application for leave to join with a person entitled in priority to a grant of administration a person having no right or no immediate right thereto shall be made to a [district judge or] registrar, and shall be supported by an affidavit by the person entitled in priority, the consent of the person proposed to be joined as administrator and such other evidence as the [district judge or] registrar may direct.

(3) Unless a [district judge or] registrar otherwise directs, there may without any such application be joined with a person entitled in priority to administration—

(a) any person who is nominated under paragraph (3) of rule 32 or paragraph (3) of rule 35;
(b) a trust corporation.

Paras (2), (3): words in square brackets inserted by SI 1991/1876, r 7(1).

A2.65

26 Additional personal representatives.—

(1) An application under section 114(4) of the Act to add a personal representative shall be made to a [district judge or] registrar and shall be supported by an affidavit by the applicant, the consent of the person proposed to be added as personal representative and such other evidence as the [district judge or] registrar may require.

(2) On any such application the [district judge or] registrar may direct that a note shall be made on the original grant of the addition of a further personal representative, or he may impound or revoke the grant or make such other order as the circumstances of the case may require.

Words in square brackets inserted by SI 1991/1876, r 7(1).

A2.66

27 Grants where two or more persons entitled in same degree.—

(1) Subject to paragraphs (1A), (2) and (3) below, where, on an application for probate, power to apply for a like grant is to be reserved to such other of the executors as have not renounced probate, notice of the application shall be given to the executor or executors to whom power is to be reserved; and unless the [district judge or] registrar otherwise directs, the oath shall state that such notice has been given.

(1A) Where power is to be reserved to executors who are ... partners in a firm, ... notice need not be given to them under paragraph (1) above if probate is applied for by another partner in that firm.

(2) Where power is to be reserved to partners of a firm, notice for the purposes of paragraph (1) above may be given to the partners by sending it to the firm at its principal or last known place of business.

A2.66 Rules, Orders and Regulations

(3) A [district judge or] registrar may dispense with the giving of notice under paragraph (1) above if he is satisfied that the giving of such a notice is impracticable or would result in unreasonable delay or expense.

(4) A grant of administration may be made to any person entitled thereto without notice to other persons entitled in the same degree.

(5) Unless a [district judge or] registrar otherwise directs, administration shall be granted to a person of full age entitled thereto in preference to a guardian of a minor, and to a living person entitled thereto in preference to the personal representative of a deceased person.

(6) A dispute between persons entitled to a grant in the same degree shall be brought by summons before a [district judge or] registrar.

(7) The issue of a summons under this rule in a registry shall be noted forthwith in the index of pending grant applications.

(8) If the issue of a summons under this rule is known to the [district judge or] registrar, he shall not allow any grant to be sealed until such summons is finally disposed of.

Paras (1), (1A): substituted for original para (1) by SI 1991/1876, r 8(1).
Para (1A): words omitted revoked by SI 1998/1903, r 7(1) from 14 September 1998: see SI 1998/1903, r 1(1).
Paras (3), (5), (6), (8): words in square brackets inserted by SI 1991/1876, r 7(1).
Para (7): substituted by SI 1998/1903, r 7(2) from 14 September 1998: see SI 1998/1903, r 1(1).

A2.67

28 Exceptions to rules as to priority.—

(1) Any person to whom a grant may or is required to be made under any enactment shall not be prevented from obtaining such a grant notwithstanding the operation of rules 20, 22, 25 or 27.

(2) Where the deceased died domiciled outside England and Wales rules 20, 22, 25 or 27 shall not apply except in a case to which paragraph (3) of rule 30 applies.

A2.68

[29 Grants in respect of settled land.—

(1) In this rule 'settled land' means land vested in the deceased which was settled prior to his death and not by his will and which remained settled land notwithstanding his death.

(2) The person or persons entitled to a grant of administration limited to settled land shall be determined in accordance with the following order of priority:

    (i) the special executors in regard to settled land constituted by section 22 of the Administration of Estates Act 1925;
    (ii) the trustees of the settlement at the time of the application for the grant; and
    (iii) the personal representatives of the deceased.

(3) Where there is settled land and a grant is made in respect of the free estate only, the grant shall expressly exclude the settled land.]
Substituted by SI 1991/1876, r 9.

A2.69

30 Grants where deceased died domiciled outside England and Wales.—

(1) Subject to paragraph (3) below, where the deceased died domiciled outside England and Wales, [a district judge or registrar may order that a grant, limited in such way as the district judge or registrar may direct,] do issue to any of the following persons—

- (a) to the person entrusted with the administration of the estate by the court having jurisdiction at the place where the deceased died domiciled; or
- (b) where there is no person so entrusted, to the person beneficially entitled to the estate by the law of the place where the deceased died domiciled or, if there is more than one person so entitled, to such of them as the [district judge or] registrar may direct; or
- (c) if in the opinion of the [district judge or] registrar the circumstances so require, to such person as the [district judge or] registrar may direct.

(2) A grant made under paragraph (1)(a) or (b) above may be issued jointly with such person as the [district judge or] registrar may direct if the grant is required to be made to not less than two administrators.

(3) Without any order made under paragraph (1) above—

- (a) probate of any will which is admissible to proof may be granted—
  - (i) if the will is in the English or Welsh language, to the executor named therein; or
  - (ii) if the will describes the duties of a named person in terms sufficient to constitute him executor according to the tenor of the will, to that person; and
- (b) where the whole or substantially the whole of the estate in England and Wales consists of immovable property, a grant in respect of the whole estate may be made in accordance with the law which would have been applicable if the deceased had died domiciled in England and Wales.

Para (1): first words in square brackets substituted and other words in square brackets inserted by SI 1991/1876, rr 7(1), 10.
Para (2): words in square brackets inserted by SI 1991/1876, r 7(1).

A2.70

31 Grants to attorneys.—

(1) Subject to paragraphs (2) and (3) below, the lawfully constituted attorney of a person entitled to a grant may apply for administration for the use and benefit of the donor, and such grant shall be limited until further representation be granted, or in such other way as the [district judge or] registrar may direct.

(2) Where the donor referred to in paragraph (1) above is an executor, notice of the application shall be given to any other executor unless such notice is dispensed with by the [district judge or] registrar.

[(3) Where the donor referred to in paragraph (1) above lacks capacity within the meaning of the Mental Capacity Act 2005 (c 9) and the attorney is acting under an enduring power of attorney or lasting power of attorney, the application shall be made in accordance with rule 35.]

Paras (1), (2): words in square brackets inserted by SI 1991/1876, r 7(1).
Para (3): substituted by SI 2007/1898, art 6, Sch 1, para 13(1), (2) from 1 October 2007: see SI 2007/1898, art 1.

A2.71 Rules, Orders and Regulations

A2.71

32 Grants on behalf of minors

(1) Where a person to whom a grant would otherwise be made is a minor, administration for his use and benefit, limited until he attains the age of eighteen years, shall, unless otherwise directed, and subject to paragraph (2) of this rule, be granted to

- [(a) a parent of the minor who has, or is deemed to have, parental responsibility for him in accordance with—
  - [(i) section 2(1), 2(1A), 2(2), 2(2A), 4 or 4ZA of the Children Act 1989,]
  - (ii) paragraph 4 or 6 of Schedule 14 to that Act, or
  - (iii) an adoption order within the meaning of section 12(1) of the Adoption Act 1976 [or section 46(1) of the Adoption and Children Act 2002], or
- [(aa) a person who has, or is deemed to have, parental responsibility for the minor by virtue of section 12(2) of the Children Act 1989(a) where the court has made a residence order under section 8 of that Act in respect of the minor in favour of that person; or]
- [(ab) a step-parent of the minor who has parental responsibility for him in accordance with section 4A of the Children Act 1989; or]
- (b) a guardian of the minor who is appointed, or deemed to have been appointed, in accordance with section 5 of the Children Act 1989 or in accordance with paragraph 12, 13 or 14 of Schedule 14 to that Act]; [or]
- [(ba) a special guardian of the minor who is appointed in accordance with section 14A of the Children Act 1989; or
- (bb) an adoption agency which has parental responsibility for the minor by virtue of section 25(2) of the Adoption and Children Act 2002; or]
- [(c) a local authority which has, or is deemed to have, parental responsibility for the minor by virtue of section 33(3) of the Children Act 1989 where the court has made a care order under section 31(1)(a) of that Act in respect of the minor and that local authority is designated in that order;]

provided that where the minor is sole executor and has no interest in the residuary estate of the deceased, administration for the use and benefit of the minor limited as aforesaid, shall, unless a [district judge or] registrar otherwise directs, be granted to the person entitled to the residuary estate.

[(2) A district judge or registrar may by order appoint a person to obtain administration for the use and benefit of the minor, limited as aforesaid, in default of, or jointly with, or to the exclusion of, any person mentioned in paragraph (1) of this rule; and the person intended shall file an affidavit in support of his application to be appointed.]

(3) Where there is only one person competent and willing to take a grant under the foregoing provisions of this rule, such person may, unless a [district judge or] registrar otherwise directs, nominate any fit and proper person to act jointly with him in taking the grant.

Para (1): sub-paras (a), (b) substituted by SI 1991/1876, r 3.
Para (1): sub-para (a)(i) substituted by SI 2009/1893, rr 2, 3. Date in force: 1 September 2009: see SI 2009/1893, r 1.
Para (1): in sub-para (a)(iii) words 'or section 46(1) of the Adoption and Children Act 2002' in square brackets inserted by SI 2005/3504, art 4(a). Date in force: 30 December 2005: see SI 2005/3504, art 1.
Para (1): sub-para (aa) inserted by SI 1998/1903, r 8(1). Date in force: 14 September 1998: see SI 1998/1903, r 1(1).
Para (1): sub-para (ab) inserted by SI 2005/3504, art 4(b). Date in force: 30 December 2005: see SI 2005/3504, art 1.
Para (1): in sub-para (b) word 'or' in square brackets inserted by SI 1998/1903, r 8(2). Date in force: 14 September 1998: see SI 1998/1903, r 1(1).

Para (1): sub-paras (ba), (bb) inserted by SI 2005/3504, art 4(c). Date in force: 30 December 2005: see SI 2005/3504, art 1.
Para (1): sub-para (c) inserted by SI 1998/1903, r 8(3). Date in force: 14 September 1998: see SI 1998/1903, r 1(1).
Para (1): words 'district judge or' in square brackets inserted by SI 1991/1876, r 7(1).
Para (2): substituted by SI 1991/1876, r 4.
Para (3): words in square brackets inserted by SI 1991/1876, r 7(1).

A2.72

33   Grants where a minor is a co-executor.—

(1)   Where a minor is appointed executor jointly with one or more other executors, probate may be granted to the executor or executors not under disability with power reserved to the minor executor, and the minor executor shall be entitled to apply for probate on attaining the age of eighteen years.

(2)   Administration for the use and benefit of a minor executor until he attains the age of eighteen years may be granted under rule 32 if, and only if, the executors who are not under disability renounce or, on being cited to accept or refuse a grant, fail to make an effective application therefor.

A2.73

34   Renunciation of the right of a minor to a grant.—

(1)   The right of a minor executor to probate on attaining the age of eighteen years may not be renounced by any person on his behalf.

(2)   The right of a minor to administration may be renounced only by a person [appointed] under paragraph (2) of rule 32, and authorised by the [district judge or] registrar to renounce on behalf of the minor.

Para (2): first word in square brackets substituted and second words in square brackets inserted by SI 1991/1876, rr 5, 7(1).

A2.74

35   Grants in case of [lack of mental capacity].—

(1)   Unless a [district judge or] registrar otherwise directs, no grant shall be made under this rule unless all persons entitled in the same degree as the [person who lacks capacity within the meaning of the Mental Capacity Act 2005] referred to in paragraph (2) below have been cleared off.

(2)   Where a [district judge or] registrar is satisfied that a person entitled to a grant [lacks capacity within the meaning of the Mental Capacity Act 2005 to manage] his affairs, administration for his use and benefit, limited until further representation be granted or in such other way as the [district judge or] registrar may direct, may be granted in the following order of priority—

   (a)   to the person authorised by the Court of Protection to apply for a grant;
   (b)   where there is no person so authorised, to the lawful attorney of the [person who lacks capacity within the meaning of the Mental Capacity Act 2005] acting under a registered enduring power of attorney [or lasting power of attorney];
   (c)   where there is no such attorney entitled to act, or if the attorney shall renounce administration for the use and benefit of the [person who lacks

A2.74 Rules, Orders and Regulations

capacity within the meaning of the Mental Capacity Act 2005], to the person entitled to the residuary estate of the deceased.

(3) Where a grant is required to be made to not less than two administrators, and there is only one person competent and willing to take a grant under the foregoing provisions of this rule, administration may, unless a [district judge or] registrar otherwise directs, be granted to such person jointly with any other person nominated by him.

(4) Notwithstanding the foregoing provisions of this rule, administration for the use and benefit of the [person who lacks capacity within the meaning of the Mental Capacity Act 2005] may be granted to such [other person] as the [district judge or] registrar may by order direct.

(5) [Unless the applicant is the person authorised in paragraph (2)(a) above,] notice of an intended application under this rule shall be given to the Court of Protection.

Provision heading: words 'lack of mental capacity' in square brackets substituted by SI 2007/1898, art 6, Sch 1, para 13(1), (3) from 1 October 2007: see SI 2007/1898, art 1.
Para (1): words 'district judge or' in square brackets inserted by SI 1991/1876, r 7(1).
Para (1): words 'person who lacks capacity within the meaning of the Mental Capacity Act 2005' in square brackets substituted by SI 2007/1898, art 6, Sch 1, para 13(1), (4) from 1 October 2007: see SI 2007/1898, art 1.
Para (2): words 'district judge or' in square brackets in both places they occur inserted by SI 1991/1876, r 7(1).
Para (2): words 'lacks capacity within the meaning of the Mental Capacity Act 2005 to manage' in square brackets substituted by SI 2007/1898, art 6, Sch 1, para 13(1), (5)(a) from 1 October 2007: see SI 2007/1898, art 1.
Para (2): in sub-paras (b), (c) words 'person who lacks capacity within the meaning of the Mental Capacity Act 2005' in square brackets substituted by virtue of SI 2007/1898, art 6, Sch 1, para 13(1), (5)(b) from 1 October 2007: see SI 2007/1898, art 1.
Para (2): in sub-para (b) words 'or lasting power of attorney' in square brackets inserted by SI 2007/1898, art 6, Sch 1, para 13(1), (5)(c) from 1 October 2007: see SI 2007/1898, art 1.
Para (3): words 'district judge or' in square brackets inserted by SI 1991/1876, r 7(1).
Para (4): words 'person who lacks capacity within the meaning of the Mental Capacity Act 2005' in square brackets substituted by SI 2007/1898, art 6, Sch 1, para 13(1), (6) from 1 October 2007: see SI 2007/1898, art 1.
Para (4): words 'other person' in square brackets substituted by SI 1998/1903, r 9(1) from 14 September 1998: see SI 1998/1903, r 1(1).
Para (4): words 'district judge or' in square brackets inserted by SI 1991/1876, r 7(1).
Para (5): words from 'Unless' to 'paragraph (2)(a) above,' in square brackets inserted by SI 1998/1903, r 9(2) from 14 September 1998: see SI 1998/1903, r 1(1).

A2.75

36 Grants to trust corporations and other corporate bodies.—

(1) An application for a grant to a trust corporation shall be made through one of its officers, and such officer shall depose in the oath that the corporation is a trust corporation as defined by these Rules and that it has power to accept a grant.

(2)

    (a) Where the trust corporation is the holder of an official position, any officer whose name is included on a list filed with the [senior district judge] of persons authorised to make affidavits and sign documents on behalf of the office holder may act as the officer through whom the holder of that official position applies for the grant.

    (b) In all other cases a certified copy of the resolution of the trust corporation authorising the officer to make the application shall be lodged, or it shall be deposed in the oath that such certified copy has been filed with the [senior district judge], that the officer is therein identified by the position he holds, and that such resolution is still in force.

(3) A trust corporation may apply for administration otherwise than as a beneficiary or the attorney of some person, and on any such application there shall be lodged the consents of all persons entitled to a grant and of all persons interested in the residuary estate of the deceased save that the [district judge or] registrar may dispense with any such consents as aforesaid on such terms, if any, as he may think fit.

(4)

(a) Subject to sub-paragraph (d) below, where a corporate body would, if an individual, be entitled to a grant but is not a trust corporation as defined by these Rules, administration for its use and benefit, limited until further representation be granted, may be made to its nominee or to its lawfully constituted attorney.

(b) A copy of the resolution appointing the nominee or the power of attorney (whichever is appropriate) shall be lodged, and such resolution or power of attorney shall be sealed by the corporate body, or be otherwise authenticated to the district judge's or registrar's satisfaction.

(c) The nominee or attorney shall depose in the oath that the corporate body is not a trust corporation as defined by these Rules.

(d) The provisions of paragraph (4)(a) above shall not apply where a corporate body is appointed executor jointly with an individual unless the right of the individual has been cleared off.

Para (2): words in square brackets substituted by SI 1991/1876, r 7(4).
Paras (3), (4): words in square brackets inserted by SI 1991/1876, r 7(1), (5).

A2.76

37 Renunciation of probate and administration.—

(1) Renunciation of probate by an executor shall not operate as renunciation of any right which he may have to a grant of administration in some other capacity unless he expressly renounces such right.

(2) Unless a [district judge or] registrar otherwise directs, no person who has renounced administration in one capacity may obtain a grant thereof in some other capacity.

[(2A) Renunciation of probate or administration by members of a partnership—

(a) may be effected, or
(b) subject to paragraph (3) below, may be retracted by any two of them with the authority of the others and any such renunciation or retraction shall recite such authority.]

(3) A renunciation of probate or administration may be retracted at any time with the leave of a [district judge or] registrar; provided that only in exceptional circumstances may leave be given to an executor to retract a renunciation of probate after a grant has been made to some other person entitled in a lower degree.

(4) A direction or order giving leave under this rule may be made either by the registrar of a district probate registry where the renunciation is filed or by [a district judge].

Paras (2), (3): words in square brackets inserted by SI 1991/1876, r 7(1).
Para (2A): inserted by SI 1998/1903, r 10 from 14 September 1998: see SI 1998/1903, r 1(1).
Para (4): words in square brackets substituted by SI 1991/1876, r 7(3).

A2.77 Rules, Orders and Regulations

A2.77

38 Notice to Crown of intended application for grant.—

In any case in which it appears that the Crown is or may be beneficially interested in the estate of a deceased person, notice of intended application for a grant shall be given by the applicant to the Treasury Solicitor, and the [district judge or] registrar may direct that no grant shall issue within 28 days after the notice has been given.
Words in square brackets inserted by SI 1991/1876, r 7(1).

A2.78

39 Resealing under Colonial Probates Acts 1892 and 1927.—

(1) An application under the Colonial Probates Acts 1892 and 1927 for the resealing of probate or administration granted by the court of a country to which those Acts apply may be made by the person to whom the grant was made or by any person authorised in writing to apply on his behalf.

(2) On any such application an Inland Revenue affidavit or account shall be lodged.

(3) Except by leave of a [district judge or] registrar, no grant shall be resealed unless it was made to such a person as is mentioned in sub-paragraph (a) or (b) of paragraph (1) of rule 30 or to a person to whom a grant could be made under sub-paragraph (a) of paragraph (3) of that rule.

(4) No limited or temporary grant shall be resealed except by leave of a [district judge or] registrar.

(5) Every grant lodged for resealing shall include a copy of any will to which the grant relates or shall be accompanied by a copy thereof certified as correct by or under the authority of the court by which the grant was made, and where the copy of the grant required to be deposited under subsection (1) of section 2 of the Colonial Probates Act 1892 does not include a copy of the will, a copy thereof shall be deposited in the registry before the grant is resealed.

(6) The [district judge or] registrar shall send notice of the resealing to the court which made the grant.

(7) Where notice is received in the Principal Registry of the resealing of a grant issued in England and Wales, notice of any amendment or revocation of the grant shall be sent to the court by which it was resealed.
Paras (3), (4), (6): words in square brackets inserted by SI 1991/1876, r 7(1).

A2.79

40 Application for leave to sue on guarantee.—

An application for leave under section 120(3) of the Act or under section 11(5) of the Administration of Estates Act 1971 to sue a surety on a guarantee given for the purposes of either of those sections shall, unless the [district judge or] registrar otherwise directs under rule 61, be made by summons to a [district judge or] registrar and notice of the application shall be served on the administrator, the surety and any co-surety.
Words in square brackets inserted by SI 1991/1876, r 7(1).

A2.80

41 Amendment and revocation of grant.—

(1) Subject to paragraph (2) below, if a [district judge or] registrar is satisfied that a grant should be amended or revoked he may make an order accordingly.

(2) Except on the application or with the consent of the person to whom the grant was made, the power conferred in paragraph (1) above shall be exercised only in exceptional circumstances.
Para (1): words in square brackets inserted by SI 1991/1876, r 7(1).

A2.81

42 Certificate of delivery of Inland Revenue affidavit.—

Where the deceased died before 13th March 1975 the certificate of delivery of an Inland Revenue affidavit required by section 30 of the Customs and Inland Revenue Act 1881 to be borne by every grant shall be in Form 1.

A2.82

43 Standing searches.—

[(1) Any person who wishes to be notified of the issue of a grant may enter a standing search for the grant by lodging at, or sending by post to any registry or sub-registry, a notice in Form 2.]

(2) A person who has entered a standing search will be sent an office copy of any grant which corresponds with the particulars given on the completed Form 2 and which—

(a) issued not more than twelve months before the entry of the standing search; or
(b) issues within a period of six months after the entry of the standing search.

(3)

(a) Where an applicant wishes to extend the said period of six months, he or his solicitor [or probate practitioner] may lodge at, or send by post to, the registry or sub-registry at which the standing search was entered written application for extension.

(b) An application for extension as aforesaid must be lodged, or received by post, within the last month of the said period of six months, and the standing search shall thereupon be effective for an additional period of six months from the date on which it was due to expire.

(c) A standing search which has been extended as above may be further extended by the filing of a further application for extension subject to the same conditions as set out in sub-paragraph (b) above.
Para (1): substituted by SI 1991/1876, r 11(1).
Para (3): in sub-para (a) words 'or probate practitioner' in square brackets inserted by SI 1998/1903, r 6 from 14 September 1998: see SI 1998/1903, r 1(1).
Para (3): in sub-para (a) words from 'the registry' to 'search was entered' in square brackets substituted by SI 1991/1876, r 11(2).

A2.83   *Rules, Orders and Regulations*

A2.83

44   Caveats.—

(1)   Any person who wishes to show cause against the sealing of a grant may enter a caveat in any registry or sub-registry, and the [district judge or] registrar shall not allow any grant to be sealed (other than a grant ad colligenda bona or a grant under section 117 of the Act) if he has knowledge of an effective caveat; provided that no caveat shall prevent the sealing of a grant on the day on which the caveat is entered.

(2)   Any person wishing to enter a caveat (in these Rules called 'the caveator'), or a solicitor [or probate practitioner] on his behalf, may effect entry of a caveat—

- (a)   by completing Form 3 in the appropriate book at any registry or sub-registry; or
- (b)   by sending by post at his own risk a notice in Form 3 to any registry or sub-registry and the proper officer shall provide an acknowledgment of the entry of the caveat.

(3)

- (a)   Except as otherwise provided by this rule or by rules 45 or 46, a caveat shall be effective for a period of six months from the date of entry thereof, and where a caveator wishes to extend the said period of six months, he or his solicitor [or probate practitioner] may lodge at, or send by post to, the registry or sub-registry at which the caveat was entered a written application for extension.
- (b)   An application for extension as aforesaid must be lodged, or received by post, within the last month of the said period of six months, and the caveat shall thereupon (save as otherwise provided by this rule) be effective for an additional period of six months from the date on which it was due to expire.
- (c)   A caveat which has been extended as above may be further extended by the filing of a further application for extension subject to the same conditions as set out in sub-paragraph (b) above.

[(4)   An index of caveats entered in any registry or sub-registry shall be maintained and upon receipt of an application for a grant, the registry or sub-registry at which the application is made shall cause a search of the index to be made and the appropriate district judge or registrar shall be notified of the entry of a caveat against the sealing of a grant for which the application has been made.]

(5)   Any person claiming to have an interest in the estate may cause to be issued from the [nominated registry] a warning in Form 4 against the caveat, and the person warning shall state his interest in the estate of the deceased and shall require the caveator to give particulars of any contrary interest in the estate; and the warning or a copy thereof shall be served on the caveator forthwith.

(6)   A caveator who has no interest contrary to that of the person warning, but who wishes to show cause against the sealing of a grant to that person, may within eight days of service of the warning upon him (inclusive of the day of such service), or at any time thereafter if no affidavit has been filed under paragraph (12) below, issue and serve a summons for directions.

(7)   On the hearing of any summons for directions under paragraph (6) above the [district judge or] registrar may give a direction for the caveat to cease to have effect.

(8)   Any caveat in force when a summons for directions is issued shall remain in force until the summons has been disposed of unless a direction has been given under paragraph (7) above or until it is withdrawn under paragraph (11) below.

(9) The issue of a summons under this rule shall be notified forthwith to the [nominated registry].

(10) A caveator having an interest contrary to that of the person warning may within eight days of service of the warning upon him (inclusive of the day of such service) or at any time thereafter if no affidavit has been filed under paragraph (12) below, enter an appearance in the [nominated registry] by filing Form 5; and he shall serve forthwith on the person warning a copy of Form 5 sealed with the seal of the court.

(11) A caveator who has not entered an appearance to a warning may at any time withdraw his caveat by giving notice at the registry or sub-registry at which it was entered, and the caveat shall thereupon cease to have effect; and, where the caveat has been so withdrawn, the caveator shall forthwith give notice of withdrawal to the person warning.

(12) If no appearance has been entered by the caveator or no summons has been issued by him under paragraph (6) of this rule, the person warning may at any time after eight days after service of the warning upon the caveator (inclusive of the day of such service) file an affidavit in the [nominated registry] as to such service and the caveat shall thereupon cease to have effect provided that there is no pending summons under paragraph (6) of this rule.

(13) Unless a [district judge or, where application to discontinue a caveat is made by consent, a registrar] by order made on summons otherwise directs, any caveat in respect of which an appearance to a warning has been entered shall remain in force until the commencement of a probate action.

(14) Except with the leave of a [district judge] no further caveat may be entered by or on behalf of any caveator whose caveat is either in force or has ceased to have effect under paragraphs (7) or (12) of this rule or under rule 45(4) or rule 46(3).

[(15) In this rule, 'nominated registry' means the registry nominated for the purpose of this rule by the senior district judge or in the absence of any such nomination the Leeds District Probate Registry.]

Para (1): words 'district judge or' in square brackets inserted by SI 1991/1876, r 7(1).
Para (2): words 'or probate practitioner' in square brackets inserted by SI 1998/1903, r 6 from 14 September 1998: see SI 1998/1903, r 1(1).
Para (3): in sub-para (a) words 'or probate practitioner' in square brackets inserted by SI 1998/1903, r 6 from 14 September 1998: see SI 1998/1903, r 1(1).
Para (4): substituted by SI 1998/1903, r 11(1) from 14 September 1998: see SI 1998/1903, r 1(1).
Para (5): words 'nominated registry' in square brackets substituted by SI 1998/1903, r 11(2) from 14 September 1998: see SI 1998/1903, r 1(1).
Para (7): words 'district judge or' in square brackets inserted by SI 1991/1876, r 7(1).
Para (8): words in square brackets inserted by SI 1991/1876, r 12(1).
Para (9): words 'nominated registry' in square brackets substituted by SI 1998/1903, r 11(2) from 14 September 1998: see SI 1998/1903, r 1(1).
Para (10): words 'nominated registry' in square brackets substituted by SI 1998/1903, r 11(2) from 14 September 1998: see SI 1998/1903, r 1(1).
Para (10): words omitted revoked by SI 1991/1876, r 12(2).
Para (12): words 'nominated registry' in square brackets substituted by SI 1998/1903, r 11(2) from 14 September 1998: see SI 1998/1903, r 1(1).
Para (13): words in square brackets substituted by SI 1991/1876, rr 7(3), 12(3).
Para (14): words in square brackets substituted by SI 1991/1876, r 7(3).
Para (15): inserted by SI 1998/1903, r 11(3) from 14 September 1998: see SI 1998/1903, r 1(1).

A2.84

45 Probate actions.—

(1) Upon being advised by the court concerned of the commencement of a probate action the [senior district judge] shall give notice of the action to every caveator other than the plaintiff in the action in respect of each caveat that is in force.

A2.84 Rules, Orders and Regulations

(2) In respect of any caveat entered subsequent to the commencement of a probate action the [senior district judge] shall give notice to that caveator of the existence of the action.

(3) Unless a [district judge] by order made on summons otherwise directs, the commencement of a probate action shall operate to prevent the sealing of a grant (other than a grant under section 117 of the Act) until application for a grant is made by the person shown to be entitled thereto by the decision of the court in such action.

(4) Upon such application for a grant, any caveat entered by the plaintiff in the action, and any caveat in respect of which notice of the action has been given, shall cease to have effect.
Paras (1), (2): words in square brackets substituted by SI 1991/1876, r 7(4).
Para (3): words in square brackets substituted by SI 1991/1876, r 7(3).

A2.85

46   Citations.—

(1) Any citation may issue from the Principal Registry or a district probate registry and shall be settled by a [district judge or] registrar before being issued.

(2) Every averment in a citation, and such other information as the registrar may require, shall be verified by an affidavit sworn by the person issuing the citation (in these Rules called the 'citor'), provided that the [district judge or] registrar may in special circumstances accept an affidavit sworn by the citor's solicitor [or probate practitioner].

(3) The citor shall enter a caveat before issuing a citation and, unless a [district judge] by order made on summons otherwise directs, any caveat in force at the commencement of the citation proceedings shall, unless withdrawn pursuant to paragraph (11) of rule 44, remain in force until application for a grant is made by the person shown to be entitled thereto by the decision of the court in such proceedings, and upon such application any caveat entered by a party who had notice of the proceedings shall cease to have effect.

(4) Every citation shall be served personally on the person cited unless the [district judge or] registrar, on cause shown by affidavit, directs some other mode of service, which may include notice by advertisement.

(5) Every will referred to in a citation shall be lodged in a registry before the citation is issued, except where the will is not in the citor's possession and the [district judge or] registrar is satisfied that it is impracticable to require it to be lodged.

(6) A person who has been cited to appear may, within eight days of service of the citation upon him (inclusive of the day of such service), or at any time thereafter if no application has been made by the citor under paragraph (5) of rule 47 or paragraph (2) of rule 48, enter an appearance in the registry from which the citation issued by filing Form 5 and shall forthwith thereafter serve on the citor a copy of Form 5 sealed with the seal of the registry.
Para (1): words 'district judge or' in square brackets inserted by SI 1991/1876, r 7(1).
Para (2): words 'district judge or' in square brackets inserted by SI 1991/1876, r 7(1).
Para (2): words 'or probate practitioner' in square brackets inserted by SI 1998/1903, r 6 from 14 September 1998: see SI 1998/1903, r 1(1).
Para (3): words in square brackets substituted by SI 1991/1876, r 7(3).
Para (4): words 'district judge or' in square brackets inserted by SI 1991/1876, r 7(1).
Para (5): words 'district judge or' in square brackets inserted by SI 1991/1876, r 7(1).

47 Citation to accept or refuse or to take a grant.—

(1) A citation to accept or refuse a grant may be issued at the instance of any person who would himself be entitled to a grant in the event of the person cited renouncing his right thereto.

(2) Where power to make a grant to an executor has been reserved, a citation calling on him to accept or refuse a grant may be issued at the instance of the executors who have proved the will or the survivor of them or of the executors of the last survivor of deceased executors who have proved.

(3) A citation calling on an executor who has intermeddled in the estate of the deceased to show cause why he should not be ordered to take a grant may be issued at the instance of any person interested in the estate at any time after the expiration of six months from the death of the deceased, provided that no citation to take a grant shall issue while proceedings as to the validity of the will are pending.

(4) A person cited who is willing to accept or take a grant may, after entering an appearance, apply ex parte by affidavit to a [district judge or] registrar for an order for a grant to himself.

(5) If the time limited for appearance has expired and the person cited has not entered an appearance, the citor may—

- (a) in the case of a citation under paragraph (1) of this rule, apply to a [district judge or] registrar for an order for a grant to himself;
- (b) in the case of a citation under paragraph (2) of this rule, apply to a [district judge or] registrar for an order that a note be made on the grant that the executor in respect of whom power was reserved has been duly cited and has not appeared and that all his rights in respect of the executorship have wholly ceased; or
- (c) in the case of a citation under paragraph (3) of this rule, apply to a [district judge or] registrar by summons (which shall be served on the person cited) for an order requiring such person to take a grant within a specified time or for a grant to himself or to some other person specified in the summons.

(6) An application under the last foregoing paragraph shall be supported by an affidavit showing that the citation was duly served.

(7) If the person cited has entered an appearance but has not applied for a grant under paragraph (4) of this rule, or has failed to prosecute his application with reasonable diligence, the citor may—

- (a) in the case of a citation under paragraph (1) of this rule, apply by summons to a [district judge or] registrar for an order for a grant to himself;
- (b) in the case of a citation under paragraph (2) of this rule, apply by summons to a [district judge or] registrar for an order striking out the appearance and for the endorsement on the grant of such a note as is mentioned in sub-paragraph (b) of paragraph (5) of this rule; or
- (c) in the case of a citation under paragraph (3) of this rule, apply by summons to a [district judge or] registrar for an order requiring the person cited to take a grant within a specified time or for a grant to himself or to some other person specified in the summons;

and the summons shall be served on the person cited.

Paras (4), (5), (7): words in square brackets inserted by SI 1991/1876, r 7(1).

A2.87 Rules, Orders and Regulations

A2.87

48 Citation to propound a will.—

(1) A citation to propound a will shall be directed to the executors named in the will and to all persons interested thereunder, and may be issued at the instance of any citor having an interest contrary to that of the executors or such other persons.

(2) If the time limited for appearance has expired, the citor may—
- (a) in the case where no person has entered an appearance, apply to a [district judge or] registrar for an order for a grant as if the will were invalid and such application shall be supported by an affidavit showing that the citation was duly served; or
- (b) in the case where no person who has entered an appearance proceeds with reasonable diligence to propound the will, apply to a [district judge or] registrar by summons, which shall be served on every person cited who has entered an appearance, for such an order as is mentioned in paragraph (a) above.

Para (2): words in square brackets inserted by SI 1991/1876, r 7(1).

A2.88

49 Address for service.—

All caveats, citations, warnings and appearances shall contain an address for service in England and Wales.

A2.89

50 Application for order to attend for examination or for subpoena to bring in a will.—

(1) An application under section 122 of the Act for an order requiring a person to attend for examination may, unless a probate action has been commenced, be made to a [district judge or] registrar by summons which shall be served on every such person as aforesaid.

(2) An application under section 123 of the Act for the issue by a [district judge or] registrar of a subpoena to bring in a will shall be supported by an affidavit setting out the grounds of the application, and if any person served with the subpoena denies that the will is in his possession or control he may file an affidavit to that effect in the registry from which the subpoena issued.

Words in square brackets inserted by SI 1991/1876, r 7(1).

A2.90

51 Grants to part of an estate under section 113 of the Act.—

An application for an order for a grant under section 113 of the Act to part of an estate may be made to a [district judge or] registrar, and shall be supported by an affidavit setting out the grounds of the application, and—
- (a) stating whether the estate of the deceased is known to be insolvent; and
- (b) showing how any person entitled to a grant in respect of the whole estate in priority to the applicant has been cleared off.

Words in square brackets inserted by SI 1991/1876, r 7(1).

A2.91

52 Grants of administration under discretionary powers of court, and grants ad colligenda bona.—

An application for an order for—

(a) a grant of administration under section 116 of the Act; or
(b) a grant of administration ad colligenda bona,

may be made to a [district judge or] registrar and shall be supported by an affidavit setting out the grounds of the application.
Words in square brackets inserted by SI 1991/1876, r 7(1).

A2.92

53 Applications for leave to swear to death.—

An application for leave to swear to the death of a person in whose estate a grant is sought may be made to a [district judge or] registrar, and shall be supported by an affidavit setting out the grounds of the application and containing particulars of any policies of insurance effected on the life of the presumed deceased together with such further evidence as the [district judge or] registrar may require.
Words in square brackets inserted by SI 1991/1876, r 7(1).

A2.93

54 Grants in respect of nuncupative wills and copies of wills.—

(1) Subject to paragraph (2) below, an application for an order admitting to proof a nuncupative will, or a will contained in a copy or reconstruction thereof where the original is not available, shall be made to a [district judge or] registrar.

(2) In any case where a will is not available owing to its being retained in the custody of a foreign court or official, a duly authenticated copy of the will may be admitted to proof without the order referred to in paragraph (1) above.

(3) An application under paragraph (1) above shall be supported by an affidavit setting out the grounds of the application, and by such evidence on affidavit as the applicant can adduce as to—

(a) the will's existence after the death of the testator or, where there is no such evidence, the facts on which the applicant relies to rebut the presumption that the will has been revoked by destruction;
(b) in respect of a nuncupative will, the contents of that will; and
(c) in respect of a reconstruction of a will, the accuracy of that reconstruction.

(4) The [district judge or] registrar may require additional evidence in the circumstances of a particular case as to due execution of the will or as to the accuracy of the copy will, and may direct that notice be given to persons who would be prejudiced by the application.
Paras (1), (4): words in square brackets inserted by SI 1991/1876, r 7(1).

A2.94

55 Application for rectification of a will.—

(1) An application for an order that a will be rectified by virtue of section 20(1) of the Administration of Justice Act 1982 may be made to a [district judge or] registrar, unless a probate action has been commenced.

A2.94 Rules, Orders and Regulations

(2) The application shall be supported by an affidavit, setting out the grounds of the application, together with such evidence as can be adduced as to the testator's intentions and as to whichever of the following matters as are in issue:—

(a) in what respects the testator's intentions were not understood; or
(b) the nature of any alleged clerical error.

(3) Unless otherwise directed, notice of the application shall be given to every person having an interest under the will whose interest might be prejudiced[, or such other person who might be prejudiced], by the rectification applied for and any comments in writing by any such person shall be exhibited to the affidavit in support of the application.

(4) If the [district judge or] registrar is satisfied that, subject to any direction to the contrary, notice has been given to every person mentioned in paragraph (3) above, and that the application is unopposed, he may order that the will be rectified accordingly.
Paras (1), (4): words in square brackets inserted by SI 1991/1876, r 7(1).
Para (3): words ', or such other person who might be prejudiced,' in square brackets inserted by SI 1998/1903, r 12 from 14 September 1998: see SI 1998/1903, r 1(1).

A2.95

56 Notice of election by surviving spouse [or civil partner] to redeem life interest.—

(1) Where a surviving spouse [or civil partner] who is the sole or sole surviving personal representative of the deceased is entitled to a life interest in part of the residuary estate and elects under section 47A of the Administration of Estates Act 1925 to have the life interest redeemed, he may give written notice of the election to the [senior district judge] in pursuance of subsection (7) of that section by filing a notice in Form 6 in the Principal Registry or in the district probate registry from which the grant issued.

(2) Where the grant issued from a district probate registry, the notice shall be filed in duplicate.

(3) A notice filed under this rule shall be noted on the grant and the record and shall be open to inspection.
Provision heading: words 'or civil partner' in square brackets inserted by SI 2005/2114, art 2(6), Sch 6, para 2(1), (4) from 5 December 2005: see SI 2005/2114, art 1.
Para (1): words 'or civil partner' in square brackets inserted by SI 2005/2114, art 2(6), Sch 6, para 2(1), (4) from 5 December 2005: see SI 2005/2114, art 1.
Para (1): words 'senior district judge' in square brackets substituted by SI 1991/1876, r 7(4).

A2.96

[57 Index of grant applications—

(1) The senior district judge shall maintain an index of every pending application for a grant made in any registry or sub-registry.

(2) Every registry or sub-registry in which an application is made shall cause the index to be searched and shall record the result of the search.]
Substituted by SI 1998/1903, r 13 from 14 September 1998: see SI 1998/1903, r 1(1).

A2.97

58 Inspection of copies of original wills and other documents.—

An original will or other document referred to in section 124 of the Act shall not be open to inspection if, in the opinion of a [district judge or] registrar, such inspection would be undesirable or otherwise inappropriate.
Words in square brackets inserted by SI 1991/1876, r 7(1).

A2.98

59 Issue of copies of original wills and other documents.—

Where copies are required of original wills or other documents deposited under section 124 of the Act, such copies may be facsimile copies sealed with the seal of the court and issued either as office copies or certified under the hand of a [district judge or] registrar to be true copies.
Words in square brackets inserted by SI 1991/1876, r 7(1).

A2.99

[60 Taxation of costs.—

[(1) Order 62 of the Rules of the Supreme Court 1965 shall not apply to costs in non-contentious probate matters, and Parts 43, 44 (except rules 44.9 to 44.12), 47 and 48 of the Civil Procedure Rules 1998 ('the 1998 Rules') shall apply to costs in those matters, with the modifications contained in paragraphs (3) to (7) of this rule.

(2) Where detailed assessment of a bill of costs is ordered, it shall be referred—

(a) where the order was made by a district judge, to a district judge, a costs judge or an authorised court officer within rule 43.2(1)(d)(iii) or (iv) of the 1998 Rules;

(b) where the order was made by a registrar, to that registrar or, where this is not possible, in accordance with sub-paragraph (a) above.

(3) Every reference in Parts 43, 44, 47 and 48 of the 1998 Rules to a district judge shall be construed as referring only to a district judge of the Principal Registry.

(4) The definition of 'costs officer' in rule 43.2(1)(c) of the 1998 Rules shall have effect as if it included a paragraph reading–

'(iv) a district probate registrar.'

(5) The definition of 'authorised court officer' in rule 43.2(1)(d) of the 1998 Rules shall have effect as if paragraphs (i) and (ii) were omitted.

(6) Rule 44.3(2) of the 1998 Rules (costs follow the event) shall not apply.

(7) Rule 47.4(2) of the 1998 Rules shall apply as if after the words 'Supreme Court Costs Office' there were inserted ', the Principal Registry of the Family Division or such district probate registry as the court may specify'.

(8) Except in the case of an appeal against a decision of an authorised court officer (to which rules 47.20 to 47.23 of the 1998 Rules apply), an appeal against a decision in assessment proceedings relating to costs in non-contentious probate matters shall be dealt with in accordance with the following paragraphs of this rule.

(9) An appeal within paragraph (8) above against a decision made by a district judge, a costs judge (as defined by rule 43.2(1)(b) of the 1998 Rules) or a registrar, shall lie to a judge of the High Court.

A2.99   *Rules, Orders and Regulations*

(10) Part 52 of the 1998 Rules applies to every appeal within paragraph (8) above, and any reference in Part 52 to a judge or a district judge shall be taken to include a district judge of the Principal Registry of the Family Division.

(11) The 1998 Rules shall apply to an appeal to which Part 52 or rules 47.20 to 47.23 of those Rules apply in accordance with paragraph (8) above in the same way as they apply to any other appeal within Part 52 or rules 47.20 to 47.23 of those Rules as the case may be; accordingly the Rules of the Supreme Court 1965 and the County Court Rules 1981 shall not apply to any such appeal.]
Substituted by SI 1991/1876, r 13.
Substituted by SI 2003/185, rr 4, 5 from: 24 February 2003: see SI 2003/185, r 1; for transitional provisions see r 3 thereof.

A2.100

61   Power to require application to be made by summons.—

(1) Subject to rule 7(2), a [district judge or] a registrar may require any application to be made by summons to a [district judge or] registrar in chambers or a judge in chambers or open court.

(2) An application for an inventory and account shall be made by summons to a [district judge or] registrar.

(3) A summons for hearing by a [district judge or] registrar shall be issued out of the registry in which it is to be heard.

(4) A summons to be heard by a judge shall be issued out of the Principal Registry.
Paras (1)–(3): words in square brackets inserted by SI 1991/1876, rr 7(1), 14.

A2.101

62   Transfer of applications.—
A registrar to whom any application is made under these Rules may order the transfer of the application to another [district judge or] registrar having jurisdiction.
Words in square brackets inserted by SI 1991/1876, r 7(1).

A2.102

[62A   Exercise of a registrar's jurisdiction by another registrar.—
A registrar may hear and dispose of an application under these Rules on behalf of any other registrar by whom the application would otherwise have been heard, if that other registrar so requests or an application in that behalf is made by a party making an application under these Rules; and where the circumstances require it, the registrar shall, without the need for any such request or application, hear and dispose of the application.]
Inserted by SI 1998/1903, r 14 from 14 September 1998: see SI 1998/1903, r 1(1).

A2.103

63   Power to make orders for costs.—
On any application dealt with by him on summons, the … registrar shall have full power to determine by whom and to what extent the costs are to be paid.
Words omitted revoked by SI 1991/1876, r 7(2).

A2.104

64 Exercise of powers of judge during Long Vacation.—

All powers exercisable under these Rules by a judge in chambers may be exercised during the Long Vacation by a [district judge].
Words in square brackets substituted by SI 1991/1876, r 7(3).

A2.105

65 Appeals from [district judges or] registrars.—

(1) An appeal against a decision or requirement of a [district judge or] registrar shall be made by summons to a judge.

(2) If, in the case of an appeal under the last foregoing paragraph, any person besides the appellant appeared or was represented before the [district judge or] registrar from whose decision or requirement the appeal is brought, the summons shall be issued within seven days thereof for hearing on the first available day and shall be served on every such person as aforesaid.
Para (1): words 'district judge or' in square brackets inserted by SI 1991/1876, r 7(1), (6).
Para (2): words 'district judge or' in square brackets inserted by SI 1991/1876, r 7(1), (6).
Para (3): inserted by SI 2003/185, r 6 from 24 February 2003: see SI 2003/185, r 1; for transitional provisions see r 3 thereof.

A2.106

66 Service of summons.—

(1) A judge [or district judge] or, where the application is to be made to a district probate registrar, that registrar, may direct that a summons for the service of which no other provision is made by these Rules shall be served on such person or persons as the [judge, district judge or] registrar] [may direct].

(2) Where by these Rules or by any direction given under the last foregoing paragraph a summons is required to be served on any person, it shall be served not less than two clear days before the day appointed for the hearing, unless a judge or [district judge or] registrar at or before the hearing dispenses with service on such terms, if any, as he may think fit.
Para (1): words 'district judge' in square brackets substituted by SI 1991/1876, r 7(3).
Para (1): words 'judge, district judge or registrar' in square brackets substituted by SI 1998/1903, r 15 from 14 September 1998: see SI 1998/1903, r 1(1).
Para (1): words 'may direct' in square brackets substituted by SI 1991/1876, r 7(7).
Para (2): words 'district judge or' in square brackets inserted by SI 1991/1876, r 7(1).

A2.107

67 Notices, etc.—

Unless a [district judge or] registrar otherwise directs or these Rules otherwise provide, any notice or other document required to be given to or served on any person may be given or served in the manner prescribed by Order 65, rule 5 of the Rules of the Supreme Court 1965.
Words in square brackets inserted by SI 1991/1876, r 7(1).

A2.108   *Rules, Orders and Regulations*

A2.108

68   Application to pending proceedings.—

Subject in any particular case to any direction given by a judge or [district judge or] registrar, these Rules shall apply to any proceedings which are pending on the date on which they come into force as well as to any proceedings commenced on or after that date.
Words in square brackets inserted by SI 1991/1876, r 7(1).

A2.109

69   Revocation of previous rules.—

(1) Subject to paragraph (2) below, the rules set out in the Second Schedule are hereby revoked.

(2) The rules set out in the Second Schedule shall continue to apply to such extent as may be necessary for giving effect to a direction under rule 68.

A2.110

SCHEDULE 1
FORMS

Rule 2(2)

FORM 1   Certificate of Delivery of Inland Revenue Affidavit

Rule 42

And it is hereby certified that an Inland Revenue affidavit has been delivered wherein it is shown that the gross value of the said estate in the United Kingdom (exclusive of what the said deceased may have been possessed of or entitled to as a trustee and not beneficially) amounts to £......... and that the net value of the estate amounts to £.........

And it is further certified that it appears by a receipt signed by an Inland Revenue officer on the said affidavit that £......... on account of estate duty and interest on such duty has been paid.

FORM 2   Standing Search

Rule 43(1)

In the High Court of Justice Family Division

[The Principal or .... District Probate Registry]

I/We apply for the entry of a standing search so that there shall be sent to me/us an office copy of every grant of representation in England and Wales in the estate of—

Full name of deceased: ....

Full address: ....

Alternative or alias names: ....

Exact date of death: ....

which either has issued not more than 12 months before the entry of this application or issues within 6 months thereafter.

Signed ....

Name in block letters...

Full address ....

Reference/(if any) ....

Words in square brackets substituted by SI 1991/1876, r 11(3).

FORM 3   Caveat

Rule 44(2)

In the High Court of Justice Family Division

The Principal [or .... District Probate] Registry.

Let no grant be sealed in the estate of (*full name and address*) deceased, who died on the   day   of .... 19/20 ... ... without notice to (*name of party by whom or on whose behalf the caveat is entered*).

Dated this ... . day of ... . 20 ....

(*Signed*)   (*to be signed by the caveator's solicitor or probate practitioner or by the caveator if acting in person*)

whose address for service is: ....

Solicitor[/probate practitoner] for the said ... . (*If the caveator is acting in person, substitute 'In person'.*)

Words 'or probate practitioner' in square brackets inserted by SI 1998/1903, r 16(a) from 14 September 1998: see SI 1998/1903, r 1(1).
Words '/probate practitioner' in square brackets inserted by SI 1998/1903, r 16(b) from 14 September 1998: see SI 1998/1903, r 1(1).

FORM 4   Warning to Caveator

Rule 44(5)

In the High Court of Justice Family Division

[(The nominated registry as defined by rule 44(15))]

A2.110 Rules, Orders and Regulations

To .... of .... a party who has entered a caveat in the estate of .... deceased.

You have eight days (starting with the day on which this warning was served on you):

(i) to enter an appearance either in person or by your solicitor [or probate practitioner], at the [(name and address of the nominated registry)] setting out what interest you have in the estate of the above-named .... of .... deceased contrary to that of the party at whose instance this warning is issued; or

(ii) if you have no contrary interest but wish to show cause against the sealing of a grant to such party, to issue and serve a summons for [directions by a district judge of the Principal Registry or a registrar of] a district probate registry.

If you fail to do either of these, the court may proceed to issue a grant of probate or administration in the said estate notwithstanding your caveat.

Dated this .... day of .... 20 .....

Issued at the instance of ....

(Here set out the name and interest (including the date of the will, if any, under which the interest arises) of the party warning, the name of his solicitor [or probate practitioner] and the address for service. If the party warning is acting in person, this must be stated.) .... Registrar

Words '(The nominated registry as defined by rule 44(15))' in square brackets substituted by SI 1998/1903, r 17(b) from 14 September 1998: see SI 1998/1903, r 1(1).
Words 'or probate practitioner' in square brackets in both places they occur inserted by SI 1998/1903, r 17(a) from 14 September 1998: see SI 1998/1903, r 1(1).
Words '(name and address of the nominated registry)' in square brackets substituted by SI 1998/1903, r 17(c) from 14 September 1998: see SI 1998/1903, r 1(1).
Words from 'directions by' to 'a registrar of' in square brackets substituted by SI 1991/1876, r 7(8).

FORM 5   Appearance to Warning or Citation

Rules 44(10), 46(6)

In the High Court of Justice Family Division

The Principal (or   District Probate) Registry

Caveat No .... dated the ...... day of .... 20 ....

(Citation dated the ...... day of .... 20 .....

Full name and address of deceased: ....

Full name and address of person warning (or citor): ....

(Here set out the interest of the person warning, or citor, as shown in warning or citation.)

Full name and address of caveator (or person cited) ....

The Non-Contentious Probate Rules 1987 **A2.110**

(*Here set out the interest of the caveator or person cited, stating the date of the will (if any) under which such interest arises.*)

Enter an appearance for the above-named caveator [or person cited] in this matter.

Dated this .... .. day of .... 20 ... ...

(*Signed*) ....

whose address for service is: ....

Solicitor[/Probate practitioner] (*or* 'In person') ....

Words '/probate practitioner' in square brackets inserted by SI 1998/1903, r 18 from 14 September 1998: see SI 1998/1903, r 1(1).

FORM 6   Notice of Election to Redeem Life Interest

Rule 56

In the High Court of Justice Family Division

The Principal (*or* .... District Probate) Registry

In the estate of .... deceased.

Whereas .... of .... died on the .... day of .... 20 ..... .

wholly/partially intestate leaving his/her lawful wife/husband[/civil partner] and ... . lawful issue of the said deceased;

And whereas Probate/Letters of Administration of the estate of the said   were granted to me, the said .... [and to .... of ....] at the Probate Registry on the .... day of .... 20 ...... ;

And whereas (the said .... has ceased to be a personal representative because ....) and I am (now) the sole personal representative;

Now I, the said .... hereby give notice in accordance with section 47A of the Administration of Estates Act 1925 that I elect to redeem the life interest to which I am entitled in the estate of the late .... by retaining £ .... its capital value, and £ .... the costs of the transaction.

Dated this .... day of . . .. 20 ..... .

(Signed) ....

To the [senior district judge] of the Family Division.

Words '/civil partner' in square brackets inserted by SI 2005/2114, art 2(6), Sch 6, para 2(1), (5) from 5 December 2005: see SI 2005/2114, art 1.
Words 'senior district judge' in square brackets substituted by SI 1991/1876, r 7(4).

A2.111 *Rules, Orders and Regulations*

A2.111

SCHEDULE 2
REVOCATIONS

Rule 69

Rules revoked	References
The Non-Contentious Probate Rules 1954	SI 1954/796
The Non-Contentious Probate (Amendment) Rules 1961	SI 1961/72
The Non-Contentious Probate (Amendment) Rules 1962	SI 1962/2653
The Non-Contentious Probate (Amendment) Rules 1967	SI 1967/748
The Non-Contentious Probate (Amendment) Rules 1968	SI 1968/1675
The Non-Contentious Probate (Amendment) Rules 1969	SI 1969/1689
The Non-Contentious Probate (Amendment) Rules 1971	SI 1971/1977
The Non-Contentious Probate (Amendment) Rules 1974	SI 1974/597
The Non-Contentious Probate (Amendment) Rules 1976	SI 1976/1362
The Non-Contentious Probate (Amendment) Rules 1982	SI 1982/446
The Non-Contentious Probate (Amendment) Rules 1983	SI 1983/623
The Non-Contentious Probate (Amendment) Rules 1985	SI 1985/1232

THE PARENTAL RESPONSIBILITY AGREEMENT REGULATIONS 1991

SI 1991/1478

Note.
These regulations are amended and the Schedule substituted by the Parental Responsibility Agreement (Amendment) Regulations 2005, SI 2005/2808, with effect from 30 December 2005.

Citation, commencement and interpretation

A2.112

1— (1) These Regulations may be cited as the Parental Responsibility Agreement Regulations 1991 and shall come into force on 14 October 1991.

(2) In these Regulations, 'the Principal Registry' means the principal registry of the Family Division of the High Court.

Form of parental responsibility agreement

A2.113

[2 Form of parental responsibility agreement]
[A parental responsibility agreement—

(a) under section 4(1)(b) of the Children Act 1989 (c 41) (acquisition of parental responsibility by father), shall be made in form C(PRA1) set out in the Schedule to these Regulations; ...
(b) under section 4A(1)(a) of that Act (acquisition of parental responsibility by step-parent), shall be made in form C(PRA2) set out in that Schedule[; and]
[(c) under section 4ZA(1)(b) of that Act (acquisition of parental responsibility by second female parent) shall be made in Form C(PRA3) set out in that Schedule].]

Substituted by SI 2005/2808, regs 2, 3. Date in force: 30 December 2005: see SI 2005/2808, reg 1.

In para (a) word omitted revoked by SI 2009/2026, regs 2, 3(a). Date in force: 1 September 2009: see SI 2009/2026, reg 1.

In para (b) word '; and' in square brackets inserted by SI 2009/2026, regs 2, 3(b). Date in force: 1 September 2009: see SI 2009/2026, reg 1.

Para (c) inserted by SI 2009/2026, regs 2, 3(c). Date in force: 1 September 2009: see SI 2009/2026, reg 1.

Recording of parental responsibility agreement

A2.114

3— (1) A parental responsibility agreement shall be recorded by the filing of the agreement, together with [sufficient copies for each person with parental responsibility for the child], in the Principal Registry.

(2) Upon the filing of documents under paragraph (1), an officer of the Principal Registry shall seal the copies and send one to [each person with parental responsibility for the child].

(3) The record of an agreement under paragraph (1) shall be made available, during office hours, for inspection by any person upon—
(a) written request to an officer of the Principal Registry, and
(b) payment of such fee as may be prescribed in an Order under [section 92 of the Court Fees Act 2003 (Fees)].

Para (1): words 'sufficient copies for each person with parental responsibility for the child' in square brackets substituted by SI 2005/2808, regs 2, 4(a) from 30 December 2005: see SI 2005/2808, reg 1.

Para (2): words 'each person with parental responsibility for the child' in square brackets substituted by SI 2005/2808, regs 2, 4(b) from 30 December 2005: see SI 2005/2808, reg 1.

Para (3): in sub-para (b) words 'section 92 of the Courts Act 2003 (Fees)' in square brackets substituted by SI 2004/3123, art 4, Schedule, Pt 3 from 17 November 2004: (no specific commencement provision).

[SCHEDULE]
[FORM C(PRA1)]

[Regulation 2]

A2.115

Substituted by SI 2009/2026, regs 2, 4, Schedule. Date in force: 1 September 2009: see SI 2009/2026, reg 1.

A2.115 *Rules, Orders and Regulations*

C(PRA1) (09.09)

Parental Responsibility Agreement Keep this form in a safe place
Section 4(1)(b) Children Act 1989   *Date recorded at the Principal Registry of the Family Division:*

Read the notes on the other side before you make this agreement.
This is a Parental Responsibility Agreement regarding the Child   *Full Name*

	Gender	*Date of birth*	*Date of 18th birthday*
Between			
the Mother	*Name*		
	Address		
and the Father	*Name*		
	Address		

We declare that we are the mother and father of the above child and we agree that the child's father shall have parental responsibility for the child (in addition to the mother having parental responsibility).

Signed (Mother)	Signed (Father)
Date	Date

Certificate of Witness	The following evidence of identity was produced by the person signing above:	The following evidence of identity was produced by the person signing above:
	Signed in the presence of: *Name of Witness*	Signed in the presence of: *Name of Witness*
	Address	*Address*
	Signature of Witness	*Signature of Witness*
	[A Justice of the Peace] [Justices' Clerk] [An assistant to a justices' clerk] [An officer of the court authorised by the judge to administer oaths]	[A Justice of the Peace] [Justices' Clerk] [An assistant to a justices' clerk] [An Officer of the court authorised by the judge to administer oaths]

Notes about the Parental Responsibility Agreement

Read these notes before you make the agreement.

About the Parental Responsibility Agreement

The Parental Responsibility Agreement Regulations 1991 A2.115

The making of this agreement will affect the legal position of the mother and the father. You should both seek legal advice before you make the Agreement. You can obtain the name and address of a solicitor from the Children Panel (020 7242 1222)

or from

— your local family proceedings court, or county court
— a Citizens Advice Bureau
— a Law Centre
— a local library.

You may be eligible for public funding.

When you fill in the Agreement

Please use black ink (the Agreement will be copied). Put the name of one child only. If the father is to have parental responsibility for more than one child, fill in a separate form for each child. **Do not sign the Agreement.**

When you have filled in the Agreement

Take it to a local family proceedings court, or county court, or the Principal Registry of the Family Division (the address is below).

A justice of the peace, a justices' clerk, an assistant to a justices' clerk, or a court official who is authorised by the judge to administer oaths, will witness your signature and he or she will sign the certificate of the witness. **A solicitor cannot witness your signature.**

To the mother: When you make the declaration you will have to prove that you are the child's mother so take to the court the child's full birth certificate. You will also need evidence of your identity showing a photograph and signature (for example, a photocard, official pass or passport). **Please note that the child's birth certificate cannot be accepted as sufficient proof of your identity.**

To the father: You will need evidence of your identity showing a photograph and signature (for example, a photocard, official pass or passport).

When the Certificate has been signed and witnessed

Make 2 copies of the Agreement form. You do not need to copy these notes.

Take, or send, this form and the copies to **The Principal Registry of the Family Division, First Avenue House, 42–49 High Holborn, London, WC1V 6NP.**

The Registry will record the Agreement and keep this form. The copies will be stamped and sent back to each parent at the address on the Agreement. The Agreement will not take effect until it has been received and recorded at the Principal Registry of the Family Division.

Ending the Agreement

Once a parental responsibility agreement has been made it can only end

— by an order of the court made on the application of any person who has parental responsibility for the child

A2.115 Rules, Orders and Regulations

— by an order of the court made on the application of the child with permission of the court
— when the child reaches the age of 18.

C(PRA1) (**Notes**) (12.05)

Step-Parental Responsibility Agreement
Section 4A(1)(a) Children Act 1989

Keep this form in a safe place
Date recorded at the Principal Registry of the Family Division:

Read the notes on the other side before you make this agreement.
This is a Step-Parental Responsibility Agreement regarding
the Child   *Full Name*

	Gender	Date of birth	Date of 18th birthday
Between			
Parent A	Name		
	Address		
and *the other parent (with parental responsibility)	Name		
	Address		
and the step-parent	Name		
	Address		

We declare that	we are the parents and step-parent of the above child and we agree that the above mentioned step-parent shall have parental responsibility for the child (in addition to those already having parental responsibility).		
	Signed (Parent A)	*Signed (Other Parent)	Signed (Step-Parent)
	Date	Date	Date
Certificate of witness	The following evidence of identity was produced by the person signing above:	The following evidence of identity was produced by the person signing above:	The following evidence of identity was produced by the person signing above:
	Signed in the presence of: Name of Witness	Signed in the presence of: Name of Witness	Signed in the presence of: Name of Witness
	Address	Address	Address

430

The Parental Responsibility Agreement Regulations 1991

*If there is only one parent with parental responsibility, please delete this section	Signature of Witness	Signature of Witness	Signature of Witness
	[A Justice of the Peace] [Justices' Clerk] [An assistant to a justices' clerk] [An Officer of the Court authorised by the judge to administer oaths]	[A Justice of the Peace] [Justices' Clerk] [An assistant to a justices' clerk] [An Officer of the Court authorised by the judge to administer oaths]	[A Justice of the Peace] [Justices' Clerk] [An assistant to a justices' clerk] [An Officer of the Court authorised by the judge to administer oaths]

C(PRA2) (09.09)

Notes about the Step-Parent Parental Responsibility Form

Read these notes before you make the Agreement.

About the Step-Parental Responsibility Agreement

The making of this agreement will affect the legal position of the parent(s) and the step-parent. You should seek legal advice before you make the Agreement. You can obtain the name of a solicitor from the Children Panel (020 7242 1222) or from:

— your local family proceedings court, or county court,
— a Citizens Advice Bureau,
— a Law Centre,
— a local library.

You may be eligible for public funding

When you fill in the Agreement

Please use black ink (the Agreement will be copied). Put the name of one child only. If the step-parent is to have parental responsibility for more than one child, fill in a separate form for each child. **Do not sign the Agreement.**

When you have filled in the Agreement

Take it to a local family proceedings court, or county court, or the Principal Registry of the Family Division (the address is below).

A justice of the peace, a justices' clerk, an assistant to a justices' clerk, or a court official who is authorised by the judge to administer oaths, will witness your signature and he or she will sign the certificate of the witness. **A solicitor cannot witness your signature.**

To Parent A and the Other Parent with parental responsibility:

When you make the declaration you will have to prove that you have parental responsibility for the child. You should therefore take with you to the court one of the following documents:

A2.115 Rules, Orders and Regulations

— the child's full birth certificate and a marriage certificate or a civil partnership certificate to show that the parents were married to each other or were in a civil partnership with each other at the time of birth or subsequently,'
— a court order granting parental responsibility,
— a registered Parental Responsibility Agreement Form between the child's mother and father or other parent
— if the birth was registered after the 1 December 2003, the child's full birth certificate showing that the parents jointly registered the child's birth.

You will also require evidence of your (both parents') identity showing a photograph and signature (for example, a photocard, official pass or passport). (**Please note that the child's birth certificate cannot be accepted as sufficient proof of your identity.**)

To the step-parent: When you make the declaration you will have to prove that you are married to, or the civil partner of, a parent of the child so take to the court your marriage certificate or certificate of civil partnership.

You will also need evidence of your identity showing a photograph and signature (for example, a photocard, official pass or passport).

When the Certificate has been signed and witnessed

Make sufficient copies of the Agreement Form for each person who has signed the form. You do not need to copy these notes.

Take, or send, the original form and the copies to: **The Principal Registry of the Family Division, First Avenue House, 42–49 High Holborn, London, WC1V 6NP.**

The Registry will record the Agreement and retain the original form. The copies will be stamped with the seal of the court and sent back to every person with parental responsibility who has signed the Agreement Form and to the step-parent. The Agreement will not take effect until it has been received and recorded at the Principal Registry of the Family Division.

Ending the Agreement

Once a step-parent parental responsibility agreement has been made it can only end:

— by an order of the court made on the application of any person who has parental responsibility for the child,
— by an order of the court made on the application of the child with permission of the court,
— when the child reaches the age of 18.

Parental Responsibility Agreement
Section 4ZA Children Act 1989
(Acquisition of parental responsibility
by second female parent)
Read the notes on the other side before
you make this agreement

Keep this form in a safe place
Date recorded at the Principal Registry of the Family Division

This is a Parental Responsibility Agreement regarding
the Child   *Full Name*

    Gender   *Date of birth*   *Date of 18th birthday*

The Parental Responsibility Agreement Regulations 1991

Between the Mother	*Name* *Address*
and other parent (Second female parent)	*Name* *Address*
We declare that	we are the parents and step-parent of the above child and we agree that the above mentioned step-parent shall have parental responsibility for the child (in addition to the mother having parental responsibility for the child).

	Signed (Mother)	Signed (Other parent)
	Date	Date
Certificate of witness	The following evidence of identity was produced by the person signing above:	The following evidence of identity was produced by the person signing above:
	Signed in the presence of: *Name of Witness*	Signed in the presence of: *Name of Witness*
	Address	*Address*
	Signature of Witness	*Signature of Witness*
	[A Justice of the Peace] [Justices' Clerk] [An assistant to a justices' clerk] [An officer of the court authorised by the judge to administer oaths]	[A Justice of the Peace] [Justices' Clerk] [An assistant to a justices' clerk] [An officer of the court authorised by the judge to administer oaths]

C(PRA3) (09.09)

Notes about the Parental Responsibility Agreement

Read these notes before you make the agreement.

This form is for use by a mother and a woman who is a parent of the child by virtue of section 43 of the Human Fertilisation and Embryology Act 2008 (the 'other parent').

About the Parental Responsibility Agreement

The making of this agreement will affect the legal position of the mother and other parent. You should both seek legal advice before you make the Agreement. You can obtain the name and address of a solicitor from the Children Panel (020 7242 1222)

A2.115 *Rules, Orders and Regulations*

or from

— your local family proceedings court, or county court
— a Citizens Advice Bureau
— a Law Centre
— a local library

You may be eligible for public funding.

When you fill in the Agreement

Please use black ink (the Agreement will be copied). Put the name of one child only. If the other parent is to have parental responsibility for more than one child, fill in a separate form for each child. **Do not sign the Agreement.**

When you have filled in the Agreement

Take it to a local family proceedings court, or county court, or the Principal Registry of the Family Division (the address is below)

A justice of the peace, a justices' clerk, an assistant to a justices' clerk, or a court official who is authorised by the judge to administer oaths, will witness your signature and he or she will sign the certificate of the witness. **A solicitor cannot witness your signature.**

To the mother:	When you make the declaration you will have to prove that you are the child's mother so take to court the child's full birth certificate. You will also need evidence of your identity showing a photograph and signature (for example, a photocard, official pass or passport). **Please note that the child's birth certificate cannot be accepted as sufficient proof of your identity.**
To the other parent:	You will need evidence of your identity showing a photograph and signature (for example, a photocard, official pass or passport)

When the Certificate has been signed and witnessed

Make 2 copies of the Agreement form. You do not need to copy these notes, please send a copy of the child's full birth certificate with the two copies of the Agreement.

Take, or send, this form and the copies to **The Principal Registry of the Family Division, First Avenue House, 42–49 High Holborn, London, WC1V 6NP.**

The Registry will record the Agreement and keep this form. The copies will be stamped and sent back to each parent at the address on the Agreement. The Agreement will not take effect until it has been received and recorded at the Principal Registry of the Family Division.

Ending the Agreement

Once a parental responsibility agreement has been made it can only end

— by an order of the court made on the application of any person who has parental responsibility for the child
— by an order of the court made on the application of the child with permission of the court

— when the child reaches the age of 18

C(PRA3) (Notes) (09.09)]
Substituted by SI 2009/2026, regs 2, 4, Schedule. Date in force: 1 September 2009: see SI 2009/2026, reg 1.

INHERITANCE TAX (DELIVERY OF ACCOUNTS) (EXCEPTED ESTATES) REGULATIONS 2004

SI 2004/2543

Note.
In force from 1 November 2004 (with effect from 6 April 2004 in relation to deaths occurring on or after that date): see reg 1.

After consultation with the Lord Chancellor and the Scottish Ministers, the Commissioners of Inland Revenue, in exercise of the powers conferred on them by section 256(1) of the Inheritance Tax Act 1984, make the following Regulations:

A2.118

1 Citation, commencement and effect

These Regulations may be cited as the Inheritance Tax (Delivery of Accounts) (Excepted Estates) Regulations 2004, shall come into force on 1st November 2004 and shall have effect in relation to deaths occurring on or after 6th April 2004.

A2.119

2 Interpretation

In these Regulations—

'the Board' means the [Commissioners of Inland Revenue];
'the 1984 Act' means the Inheritance Tax Act 1984;
'an excepted estate' has the meaning given in regulation 4;
'IHT threshold' means the lower limit shown in the Table in Schedule 1 of the 1984 Act applicable to—
   (a) chargeable transfers made in the year before that in which a person's death occurred if—
      (i) that person died on or after 6th April and before 6th August, and
      (ii) an application for a grant of representation or, in Scotland, an application for confirmation, is made before 6th August in that year; or
   (b) chargeable transfers made in the year in which a person's death occurred in any other case,
and for this purpose 'year' means a period of twelve months ending with 5th April;
'the prescribed period' in relation to any person is the period beginning with that person's death and ending—

A2.119 *Rules, Orders and Regulations*

(a) in England, Wales and Northern Ireland, 35 days after the making of the first grant of representation in respect of that person (not being a grant limited in duration, in respect of property or to any special purpose); or

(b) in Scotland, 60 days after the date on which confirmation to that person's estate was first issued;

['section 131 rights' means the rights of issue under section 131(2) of the Civil Partnership Act 2004;]

'spouse[, civil partner] and charity transfer' has the meaning given in regulation 5;

'value' means value for the purpose of tax.

In definition 'the Board' words 'Commissioners for Her Majesty's Revenue and Customs' in square brackets substituted by SI 2006/2141, regs 2, 3 from 1 September 2006: see SI 2006/2141, reg 1(2).

Definition 'section 131 rights' inserted by SI 2005/3230, reg 15(1), (2)(b) from 5 December 2005: see SI 2005/3230, reg 1.

In definition 'spouse, civil partner and charity transfer' words ', civil partner' in square brackets inserted by SI 2005/3230, reg 15(1), (2)(a) from 5 December 2005: see SI 2005/3230, reg 1.

A2.120

3 Accounts

(1) No person is required to deliver an account under section 216 of the 1984 Act of the property comprised in an excepted estate.

(2) If in reliance on these Regulations a person has not delivered an account paragraphs (3) and (4) apply.

(3) If it is discovered at any time that the estate is not an excepted estate, the delivery to the Board within six months of that time of an account of the property comprised in that estate shall satisfy any requirement to deliver an account.

(4) If the estate is no longer an excepted estate following an alteration of the dispositions taking effect on death within section 142 of the 1984 Act, the delivery to the Board within six months of the date of the instrument of variation of an account of the property comprised in that estate shall satisfy any requirement to deliver an account.

A2.121

4 Excepted estates

(1) An excepted estate means the estate of a person immediately before his death in the circumstances prescribed by paragraphs (2), (3) or [(5)].

(2) The circumstances prescribed by this paragraph are that—

(a) the person died on or after 6th April 2004, domiciled in the United Kingdom;

(b) the value of that person's estate is attributable wholly to property passing—
 (i) under his will or intestacy,
 (ii) under a nomination of an asset taking effect on death,
 (iii) under a single settlement in which he was entitled to an interest in possession in settled property, or
 (iv) by survivorship in a beneficial joint tenancy or, in Scotland, by survivorship in a special destination;

(c) of that property—
 (i) not more than [£150,000] represented value attributable to property which, immediately before that person's death, was settled property; and

Inheritance Tax (Delivery of Accounts) etc Regulations 2004 **A2.121**

(ii) not more than [£100,000] represented value attributable to property which, immediately before that person's death, was situated outside the United Kingdom;
[(ca) that person was not a person by reason of whose death one of the alternatively secured pension fund provisions applies;]
(d) that person died without having made any chargeable transfers during the period of seven years ending with his death other than specified transfers where, subject to paragraph (7), the aggregate value transferred did not exceed [£150,000]; and
(e) the aggregate of—
   (i) the gross value of that person's estate,
   (ii) subject to paragraph (7), the value transferred by any specified transfers made by that person, and
   (iii) the value transferred by any specified exempt transfers made by that person,
did not exceed the IHT threshold.

(3) The circumstances prescribed by this paragraph are that—

(a) the person died on or after 6th April 2004, domiciled in the United Kingdom;
(b) the value of that person's estate is attributable wholly to property passing—
   (i) under his will or intestacy,
   (ii) under a nomination of an asset taking effect on death,
   (iii) under a single settlement in which he was entitled to an interest in possession in settled property, or
   (iv) by survivorship in a beneficial joint tenancy or, in Scotland, by survivorship in a special destination;
(c) of that property—
   (i) subject to paragraph (8), not more than [£150,000] represented value attributable to property which, immediately before that person's death, was settled property; and
   (ii) not more than [£100,000] represented value attributable to property which, immediately before that person's death, was situated outside the United Kingdom;
(d) that person died without having made any chargeable transfers during the period of seven years ending with his death other than specified transfers where, subject to paragraph (7), the aggregate value transferred did not exceed [£150,000];
(e) the aggregate of—
   (i) the gross value of that person's estate,
   (ii) subject to paragraph (7), the value transferred by any specified transfers made by that person, and
   (iii) the value transferred by any specified exempt transfers made by that person,
did not exceed £1,000,000; and
(f) the aggregate of—
$A - (B + C)$
does not exceed the IHT threshold, where—
A is the aggregate of the values in sub-paragraph (e),
B, subject to paragraph (4), is the total value transferred on that person's death by a spouse[, civil partner] or charity transfer, and
C is the total liabilities of the estate.

[(4) In Scotland, if legitim or section 131 rights could be claimed which would reduce the value of the spouse, civil partner or charity transfer, the value of B is reduced—

(a) to take account of any legitim or section 131 rights claimed, and

A2.121 *Rules, Orders and Regulations*

(b) on the basis that any part of the remaining legitim fund, which has been neither claimed nor renounced at the time of the application for confirmation, will be claimed in full, and
(c) on the basis that all section 131 rights, which have been neither claimed nor renounced at the time of the application for confirmation, will be claimed in full.]

(5) The circumstances prescribed by this paragraph are that—

(a) the person died on or after 6th April 2004;
[(b) that person was never domiciled in the United Kingdom or treated as domiciled in the United Kingdom by section 267 of the 1984 Act;
(ba) that person was not a person by reason of whose death one of the alternatively secured pension fund provisions applies; and]
(c) the value of that person's estate situated in the United Kingdom is wholly attributable to cash or quoted shares or securities passing under his will or intestacy or by survivorship in a beneficial joint tenancy or, in Scotland, by survivorship in a special destination, the gross value of which does not exceed [£150,000].

(6) For the purposes of paragraphs (2) and (3)—

'specified transfers' means chargeable transfers made by a person during the period of seven years ending with that person's death where the value transferred is attributable to—
(a) cash;
(b) personal chattels or corporeal moveable property;
(c) quoted shares or securities; or
(d) an interest in or over land, save to the extent that sections 102 and 102A(2) of the Finance Act 1986 apply to that transfer or the land became settled property on that transfer;
'specified exempt transfers' means transfers of value made by a person during the period of seven years ending with that person's death which are exempt transfers only by reason of—
(a) section 18 (transfers between spouses [or civil partners]),
(b) section 23 (gifts to charities),
(c) section 24 (gifts to political parties),
(d) section 24A (gifts to housing associations),
(e) section 27 (maintenance funds for historic buildings, etc), or
(f) section 28 (employee trusts)
of the 1984 Act.

(7) For the purpose of paragraphs (2)(d) and (e) and (3)(d) and (e), sections 104 (business property relief) and 116 (agricultural property relief) of the 1984 Act shall not apply in determining the value transferred by a chargeable transfer.

(8) Paragraph (3)(c)(i) does not apply to property which immediately before the person's death was settled property, to the extent that the property is transferred on that person's death by a spouse[, civil partner] or charity transfer.

[(9) In this regulation 'the alternatively secured pension fund provisions' means the following sections of the 1984 Act—

(a) section 151A (person dying with alternatively secured pension fund);
(b) section 151B (relevant dependant with pension fund inherited from member over 75); and
(c) section 151C (dependant dying with other pension fund).]

Para (1): reference to '(5)' in square brackets substituted by SI 2006/2141, regs 2, 4(1), (2) from 1 September 2006: see SI 2006/2141, reg 1(2).

Inheritance Tax (Delivery of Accounts) etc Regulations 2004 **A2.122**

Para (2): in sub-para (c)(i) sum '£150,000' in square brackets substituted by SI 2006/2141, regs 2, 4(1), (3)(a) from 1 September 2006: see SI 2006/2141, reg 1(2).
Para (2): in sub-para (c)(ii) sum '£100,000' in square brackets substituted by SI 2006/2141, regs 2, 4(1), (3)(b) from 1 September 2006: see SI 2006/2141, reg 1(2).
Para (2): sub-para (ca) inserted by SI 2006/2141, regs 2, 4(1), (3)(c) from 1 September 2006: see SI 2006/2141, reg 1(2).
Para (2): in sub-para (d) sum '£150,000' in square brackets substituted by SI 2006/2141, regs 2, 4(1), (2) from 1 September 2006: see SI 2006/2141, reg 1(2).
Para (3): in sub-para (c)(i) sum '£150,000' in square brackets substituted by SI 2006/2141, reg 4(1), (3)(a) from 1 September 2006: see SI 2006/2141, reg 1(2).
Para (3): in sub-para (c)(ii) sum '£100,000' in square brackets substituted by SI 2006/2141, regs 2, 4(1), (3)(b) from 1 September 2006: see SI 2006/2141, reg 1(2).
Para (3): sub-para (ca) inserted by SI 2006/2141, regs 2, 4(1), (3)(c) from 1 September 2006: see SI 2006/2141, reg 1(2).
Para (3): in sub-para (d) sum '£150,000' in square brackets substituted by SI 2006/2141, regs 2, 4(1), (3)(d) from 1 September 2006: see SI 2006/2141, reg 1(2).
Para (3): in sub-para (f) in definition of 'B' words ', civil partner' in square brackets inserted by SI 2005/3230, reg 15(1), (3)(a). Date in force: 5 December 2005: see SI 2005/3230, reg 1.
Para (4): substituted by SI 2005/3230, reg 15(1), (3)(b). Date in force: 5 December 2005: see SI 2005/3230, reg 1.
Para (5): sub-paras (b), (ba) substituted, for sub-para (b) as originally enacted, by SI 2006/2141, regs 2, 4(1), (4)(a) from 1 September 2006: see SI 2006/2141, reg 1(2).
Para (5): in sub-para (c) sum '£150,000' in square brackets substituted by SI 2006/2141, regs 2, 4(1), (4)(b) from 1 September 2006: see SI 2006/2141, reg 1(2).
Para (6): in definition 'specified exempt transfers' in para (a) words 'or civil partners' in square brackets inserted by SI 2005/3230, reg 15(1), (3)(c). Date in force: 5 December 2005: see SI 2005/3230, reg 1.
Para (8): words ', civil partner' in square brackets inserted by SI 2005/3230, reg 15(1), (3)(d). Date in force: 5 December 2005: see SI 2005/3230, reg 1.
Para (9) : inserted by SI 2006/2141, regs 2, 4(1), (5) from 1 September 2006: see SI 2006/2141, reg 1(2).

A2.122

5   Spouse[, civil partner] and charity transfers

(1)   For the purposes of these Regulations, a spouse[, civil partner] or charity transfer means any disposition (whether effected by will, under the law relating to intestacy or otherwise) of property comprised in a person's estate—

   (a)   subject to paragraph (2), to the person's spouse [or civil partner] within section 18(1) of the 1984 Act; and
   (b)   subject to paragraph (3), to a charity within section 23(1) of the 1984 Act or for national purposes within section 25(1) of the 1984 Act.

(2)   A transfer is not a spouse [or civil partner] transfer within paragraph (1)(a) if either spouse [or civil partner] was not domiciled in the United Kingdom at any time prior to the transfer.

(3)   A transfer is not a charity transfer within paragraph (1)(b) if the property becomes comprised in a settlement as a result of the disposition.

Provision heading: words ', civil partner' in square brackets inserted by SI 2005/3230, reg 15(1), (4)(c). Date in force: 5 December 2005: see SI 2005/3230, reg 1.
Para (1): words ', civil partner' in square brackets inserted by SI 2005/3230, reg 15(1), (4)(a)(i). Date in force: 5 December 2005: see SI 2005/3230, reg 1.
Para (1): in sub-para (a) words 'or civil partner' in square brackets inserted by SI 2005/3230, reg 15(1), (4)(a)(ii). Date in force: 5 December 2005: see SI 2005/3230, reg 1.
Para (2): words 'or civil partner' in square brackets in both places they occur inserted by SI 2005/3230, reg 15(1), (4)(b). Date in force: 5 December 2005: see SI 2005/3230, reg 1.

A2.123 Rules, Orders and Regulations

A2.123

6 Production of information

(1) Subject to paragraph (3), a person who by virtue of these Regulations is not required to deliver to the Board an account under section 216 of the 1984 Act of the property comprised in an excepted estate, must produce the information specified in paragraph (2) to the Board in such form as the Board may prescribe.

(2) The information specified for the purpose of paragraph (1) is—
- (a) the following details in relation to the deceased—
    - (i) full name;
    - (ii) date of death;
    - (iii) marital [or civil partnership] status;
    - (iv) occupation;
    - (v) any surviving spouse [or civil partner], parent, brother or sister;
    - (vi) the number of surviving children, step-children, adopted children or grandchildren;
    - (vii) national insurance number, tax district and tax reference;
    - (viii) if the deceased was not domiciled in the United Kingdom at his date of death, his domicile and address;
- (b) details of all property to which the deceased was beneficially entitled and the value of that property;
- (c) details of any specified transfers, specified exempt transfers and the value of those transfers;
- (d) the liabilities of the estate; and
- (e) any spouse[, civil partner] or charity transfers and the value of those transfers.

(3) Paragraph (1) does not apply if the information specified in paragraph (2) has been produced in an account under section 216 of the 1984 Act of the property comprised in the excepted estate that has been delivered to the Board.

Para (2): in sub-para (a)(iii) words 'or civil partnership' in square brackets inserted by SI 2005/3230, reg 15(1), (5)(a)(i). Date in force: 5 December 2005: see SI 2005/3230, reg 1.
Para (2): in sub-para (a)(v) words 'or civil partner' in square brackets inserted by SI 2005/3230, reg 15(1), (5)(a)(ii). Date in force: 5 December 2005: see SI 2005/3230, reg 1.
Para (2): in sub-para (e) words ', civil partner' in square brackets inserted by SI 2005/3230, reg 15(1), (5)(b). Date in force: 5 December 2005: see SI 2005/3230, reg 1.

A2.124

7 (1) The information specified in regulation 6(2) must be produced to the Board by producing it to—
- (a) a probate registry in England and Wales;
- (b) the sheriff in Scotland;
- (c) the Probate and Matrimonial Office in Northern Ireland.

(2) Information produced in accordance with paragraph (1) is to be treated for all purposes of the 1984 Act as produced to the Board.

(3) The person or body specified in paragraph (1) must transmit the information produced to them to the Board within one week of the issue of the grant of probate or confirmation.

A2.125

8 Discharge of persons and property from tax

(1) Subject to paragraph (2) and regulation 9, if the information specified in regulation 6 has been produced in accordance with these Regulations, all persons shall

on the expiration of the prescribed period be discharged from any claim for tax on the value transferred by the chargeable transfer made on the deceased's death and attributable to the value of the property comprised in an excepted estate and any Inland Revenue charge for that tax shall then be extinguished.

(2) Paragraph (1) shall not apply if within the prescribed period the Board issue a notice to—

(a) the person or persons who would apart from these Regulations be required to deliver an account under section 216 of the 1984 Act, or
(b) the solicitor or agent of that person or those persons who produced the specified information pursuant to regulation 6,

requiring additional information or documents to be produced in relation to the specified information produced pursuant to regulation 6.

A2.126

9 Regulation [8] shall not discharge any person from tax in the case of fraud or failure to disclose material facts and shall not affect any tax that may be payable if further property is later shown to form part of the estate and, in consequence of that property, the estate is not an excepted estate.
Reference to '8' in square brackets substituted by SI 2006/2141, regs 2, 5 from 1 September 2006: see SI 2006/2141, reg 1(2).

A2.127

10 Transfers reported late

An account of an excepted estate shall, for the purposes of section 264(8) of the 1984 Act (delivery of account to be treated as payment where tax rate nil), be treated as having been delivered on the last day of the prescribed period in relation to that person.

A2.128

11 Revocation

The Inheritance Tax (Delivery of Accounts) (Excepted Estates) Regulations 2002 and the Inheritance Tax (Delivery of Accounts) (Excepted Estates) (Amendment) Regulations 2003 are revoked in relation to deaths occurring on or after 6th April 2004.

A2.135A *Rules, Orders and Regulations*

LASTING POWERS OF ATTORNEY, ENDURING POWERS OF ATTORNEY AND PUBLIC GUARDIAN REGULATIONS 2007

SI 2007/1253

PART 1
PRELIMINARY

A2.135A

1   Citation and commencement

(1) These Regulations may be cited as the Lasting Powers of Attorney, Enduring Powers of Attorney and Public Guardian Regulations 2007.

(2) These Regulations shall come into force on 1 October 2007.

A2.135B

2   Interpretation

(1) In these Regulations—

'the Act' means the Mental Capacity Act 2005;
'court' means the Court of Protection;
'LPA certificate', in relation to an instrument made with a view to creating a lasting power of attorney, means the certificate which is required to be included in the instrument by virtue of paragraph 2(1)(e) of Schedule 1 to the Act;
'named person', in relation to an instrument made with a view to creating a lasting power of attorney, means a person who is named in the instrument as being a person to be notified of any application for the registration of the instrument;
'prescribed information', in relation to any instrument intended to create a lasting power of attorney, means the information contained in the form used for the instrument which appears under the heading 'prescribed information'.

A2.135C

3   Minimal differences from forms prescribed in these Regulations

(1) In these Regulations, any reference to a form—

(a) in the case of a form set out in Schedules 1 to 7 to these Regulations, is to be regarded as including a Welsh version of that form; and
(b) in the case of a form set out in Schedules 2 to 7 to these Regulations, is to be regarded as also including—
   (i) a form to the same effect but which differs in an immaterial respect in form or mode of expression;
   (ii) a form to the same effect but with such variations as the circumstances may require or the court or the Public Guardian may approve; or
   (iii) a Welsh version of a form within (i) or (ii).

A2.135D

4 Computation of time

(1) This regulation shows how to calculate any period of time which is specified in these Regulations.

(2) A period of time expressed as a number of days must be computed as clear days.

(3) Where the specified period is 7 days or less, and would include a day which is not a business day, that day does not count.

(4) When the specified period for doing any act at the office of the Public Guardian ends on a day on which the office is closed, that act will be done in time if done on the next day on which the office is open.

(5) In this regulation—

'business day' means a day other than—
    (a) a Saturday, Sunday, Christmas Day or Good Friday; or
    (b) a bank holiday under the Banking and Financial Dealings Act 1971, in England and Wales; and

'clear days' means that in computing the number of days—
    (a) the day on which the period begins, and
    (b) if the end of the period is defined by reference to an event, the day on which that event occurs,
are not included.

PART 2
LASTING POWERS OF ATTORNEY

Instruments intended to create a lasting power of attorney

A2.135E

6 Maximum number of named persons

The maximum number of named persons that the donor of a lasting power of attorney may specify in the instrument intended to create the power is 5.

A2.135F

7 Requirement for two LPA certificates where instrument has no named persons

Where an instrument intended to create a lasting power of attorney includes a statement by the donor that there are no persons whom he wishes to be notified of any application for the registration of the instrument—

    (a) the instrument must include two LPA certificates; and
    (b) each certificate must be completed and signed by a different person.

A2.135G

8 Persons who may provide an LPA certificate

(1) Subject to paragraph (3), the following persons may give an LPA certificate—

    (a) a person chosen by the donor as being someone who has known him personally for the period of at least two years which ends immediately before the date on which that person signs the LPA certificate;

A2.135H Rules, Orders and Regulations

   (b) a person chosen by the donor who, on account of his professional skills and expertise, reasonably considers that he is competent to make the judgments necessary to certify the matters set out in paragraph (2)(1)(e) of Schedule 1 to the Act.

(2) The following are examples of persons within paragraph (1)(b)—
   (a) a registered health care professional;
   (b) a barrister, solicitor or advocate called or admitted in any part of the United Kingdom;
   (c) a registered social worker; or
   (d) an independent mental capacity advocate.

(3) A person is disqualified from giving an LPA certificate in respect of any instrument intended to create a lasting power of attorney if that person is—
   (a) a family member of the donor;
   (b) a donee of that power;
   (c) a donee of—
      (i) any other lasting power of attorney, or
      (ii) an enduring power of attorney,
   which has been executed by the donor (whether or not it has been revoked);
   (d) a family member of a donee within sub-paragraph (b);
   (e) a director or employee of a trust corporation acting as a donee within sub-paragraph (b);
   (f) a business partner or employee of—
      (i) the donor, or
      (ii) a donee within sub-paragraph (b);
   (g) an owner, director, manager or employee of any care home in which the donor is living when the instrument is executed; or
   (h) a family member of a person within sub-paragraph (g).

(4) In this regulation—
   'care home' has the meaning given in section 3 of the Care Standards Act 2000;
   'registered health care professional' means a person who is a member of a profession regulated by a body mentioned in section 25(3) of the National Health Service Reform and Health Care Professions Act 2002; and
   'registered social worker' means a person registered as a social worker in a register maintained by—
      (a) the General Social Care Council;
      (b) the Care Council for Wales;
      (c) the Scottish Social Services Council; or
      (d) the Northern Ireland Social Care Council.

A2.135H

9 Execution of instrument

(1) An instrument intended to create a lasting power of attorney must be executed in accordance with this regulation.

(2) The donor must read (or have read to him) all the prescribed information.

(3) As soon as reasonably practicable after the steps required by paragraph (2) have been taken, the donor must—
   (a) complete the provisions of Part A of the instrument that apply to him (or direct another person to do so); and

(b) subject to paragraph (7), sign Part A of the instrument in the presence of a witness.

(4) As soon as reasonably practicable after the steps required by paragraph (3) have been taken—

(a) the person giving an LPA certificate, or
(b) if regulation 7 applies (two LPA certificates required), each of the persons giving a certificate,

must complete the LPA certificate at Part B of the instrument and sign it.

(5) As soon as reasonably practicable after the steps required by paragraph (4) have been taken—

(a) the donee, or
(b) if more than one, each of the donees,

must read (or have read to him) all the prescribed information.

(6) As soon as reasonably practicable after the steps required by paragraph (5) have been taken, the donee or, if more than one, each of them—

(a) must complete the provisions of Part C of the instrument that apply to him (or direct another person to do so); and
(b) subject to paragraph (7), must sign Part C of the instrument in the presence of a witness.

(7) If the instrument is to be signed by any person at the direction of the donor, or at the direction of any donee, the signature must be done in the presence of two witnesses.

(8) For the purposes of this regulation—

(a) the donor may not witness any signature required for the power;
(b) a donee may not witness any signature required for the power apart from that of another donee.

(9) A person witnessing a signature must—

(a) sign the instrument; and
(b) give his full name and address.

(10) Any reference in this regulation to a person signing an instrument (however expressed) includes his signing it by means of a mark made on the instrument at the appropriate place.

Registering the instrument

A2.135I

10 Notice to be given by a person about to apply for registration of lasting power of attorney

Schedule 2 to these Regulations sets out the form of notice ('LPA 001') which must be given by a donor or donee who is about to make an application for the registration of an instrument intended to create a lasting power of attorney.

A2.135J

11 Application for registration

(1) Schedule 3 to these Regulations sets out the form ('LPA 002') which must be used for making an application to the Public Guardian for the registration of an instrument intended to create a lasting power of attorney.

A2.135K *Rules, Orders and Regulations*

(2) Where the instrument to be registered which is sent with the application is neither—

(a) the original instrument intended to create the power, nor
(b) a certified copy of it,

the Public Guardian must not register the instrument unless the court directs him to do so.

(3) In paragraph (2) 'a certified copy' means a photographic or other facsimile copy which is certified as an accurate copy by—

(a) the donor; or
(b) a solicitor or notary.

PART 3
ENDURING POWERS OF ATTORNEY

A2.135K

23 Notice of intention to apply for registration of enduring power of attorney

(1) Schedule 7 to these Regulations sets out the form of notice ('EP1PG') which an attorney (or attorneys) under an enduring power of attorney must give of his intention to make an application for the registration of the instrument creating the power.

(2) In the case of the notice to be given to the donor, the attorney must also provide (or arrange for the provision of) an explanation to the donor of—

(a) the notice and what the effect of it is; and
(b) why it is being brought to his attention.

(3) The information provided under paragraph (2) must be provided—

(a) to the donor personally; and
(b) in a way that is appropriate to the donor's circumstances (for example using simple language, visual aids or other appropriate means).

A2.135L

24 Application for registration

(1) Schedule 8 to these Regulations sets out the form ('EP2PG') which must be used for making an application to the Public Guardian for the registration of an instrument creating an enduring power of attorney.

(2) Where the instrument to be registered which is sent with the application is neither—

(a) the original instrument creating the power, nor
(b) a certified copy of it,

the Public Guardian must not register the instrument unless the court directs him to do so.

(3) 'Certified copy', in relation to an enduring power of attorney, means a copy certified in accordance with section 3 of the Powers of Attorney Act 1971.

A2.135M

25 Notice of objection to registration

(1) This regulation deals with any objection to the registration of an instrument creating an enduring power of attorney which is to be made to the Public Guardian under paragraph 13(4) of Schedule 4 to the Act.

(2) A notice of objection must be given in writing, setting out—

(a) the name and address of the objector;
(b) if different, the name and address of the donor of the power;
(c) if known, the name and address of the attorney (or attorneys); and
(d) the ground for making the objection.

A2.135N

26 Notifying applicants of non-registration of enduring power of attorney

Where the Public Guardian is prevented from registering an instrument creating an enduring power of attorney by virtue of—

(a) paragraph 13(2) of Schedule 4 to the Act (deputy already appointed),
(b) paragraph 13(5) of that Schedule (receipt by Public Guardian of valid notice of objection from person entitled to notice of application to register),
(c) paragraph 13(7) of that Schedule (Public Guardian required to undertake appropriate enquiries in certain circumstances), or
(d) regulation 24(2) of these Regulations (application for registration not accompanied by original instrument or certified copy),

he must notify the person (or persons) who applied for registration of that fact.

A2.135O

27 Registration of instrument creating an enduring power of attorney

(1) Where the Public Guardian registers an instrument creating an enduring power of attorney, he must—

(a) retain a copy of the instrument; and
(b) return to the person (or persons) who applied for registration the original instrument, or the certified copy of it, which accompanied the application.

(2) 'Certified copy' has the same meaning as in regulation 24(3).

A2.135P

28 Objection or revocation not applying to all joint and several attorneys

In a case within paragraph 20(6) or (7) of Schedule 4 to the Act, the form of the entry to be made in the register in respect of an instrument creating the enduring power of attorney is a stamp bearing the following words (inserting the information indicated, as appropriate)—

'THE REGISTRATION OF THIS ENDURING POWER OF ATTORNEY IS QUALIFIED AND EXTENDS TO THE APPOINTMENT OF .... (insert name of attorney(s) not affected by ground(s) of objection or revocation) ONLY AS THE ATTORNEY(S) OF .... (insert name of donor)'.

A2.135Q Rules, Orders and Regulations

A2.135Q

29 Loss or destruction of instrument registered as enduring power of attorney

(1) This regulation applies where—

    (a) a person is required by or under the Act to deliver up to the Public Guardian any of the following documents—
        (i) an instrument registered as an enduring power of attorney;
        (ii) an office copy of that registered instrument; or
        (iii) a certified copy of that registered instrument; and
    (b) the document has been lost or destroyed.

(2) The person who is required to deliver up the document must provide to the Public Guardian in writing—

    (a) if known, the date of the loss or destruction and the circumstances in which it occurred;
    (b) otherwise, a statement of when he last had the document in his possession.

PART 4
FUNCTIONS OF THE PUBLIC GUARDIAN
The registers

A2.135R

30 Establishing and maintaining the registers

(1) In this Part 'the registers' means—

    (a) the register of lasting powers of attorney,
    (b) the register of enduring powers of attorney, and
    (c) the register of court orders appointing deputies,

which the Public Guardian must establish and maintain.

(2) On each register the Public Guardian may include—

    (a) such descriptions of information about a registered instrument or a registered order as the Public Guardian considers appropriate; and
    (b) entries which relate to an instrument or order for which registration has been cancelled.

A2.135S

31 Disclosure of information on a register: search by the Public Guardian

(1) Any person may, by an application made under paragraph (2), request the Public Guardian to carry out a search of one or more of the registers.

(2) An application must—

    (a) state—
        (i) the register or registers to be searched;
        (ii) the name of the person to whom the application relates; and
        (iii) such other details about that person as the Public Guardian may require for the purpose of carrying out the search; and
    (b) be accompanied by any fee provided for under section 58(4)(b) of the Act.

(3) The Public Guardian may require the applicant to provide such further information, or produce such documents, as the Public Guardian reasonably considers necessary to enable him to carry out the search.

(4) As soon as reasonably practicable after receiving the application—

(a) the Public Guardian must notify the applicant of the result of the search; and
(b) in the event that it reveals one or more entries on the register, the Public Guardian must disclose to the applicant all the information appearing on the register in respect of each entry.

A2.135T

32   Disclosure of additional information held by the Public Guardian

(1) This regulation applies in any case where, as a result of a search made under regulation 31, a person has obtained information relating to a registered instrument or a registered order which confers authority to make decisions about matters concerning a person ('P').

(2) On receipt of an application made in accordance with paragraph (4), the Public Guardian may, if he considers that there is good reason to do so, disclose to the applicant such additional information as he considers appropriate.

(3) 'Additional information' means any information relating to P—

(a) which the Public Guardian has obtained in exercising the functions conferred on him under the Act; but
(b) which does not appear on the register.

(4) An application must state—

(a) the name of P;
(b) the reasons for making the application; and
(c) what steps, if any, the applicant has taken to obtain the information from P.

(5) The Public Guardian may require the applicant to provide such further information, or produce such documents, as the Public Guardian reasonably considers necessary to enable him to determine the application.

(6) In determining whether to disclose any additional information [relating] to P, the Public Guardian must, in particular, have regard to—

(a) the connection between P and the applicant;
(b) the reasons for requesting the information (in particular, why the information cannot or should not be obtained directly from P);
(c) the benefit to P, or any detriment he may suffer, if a disclosure is made; and
(d) any detriment that another person may suffer if a disclosure is made.

Para (6): word 'relating' in square brackets inserted by SI 2009/1884, regs 2, 4. Date in force: 1 October 2009: see SI 2009/1884, reg 1(1).

A2.135T *Rules, Orders and Regulations*

FAMILY PROVISION (INTESTATE SUCCESSION) ORDER 2009

SI 2009/135

The Lord Chancellor makes the following Order in exercise of the powers conferred by section 1(1)(a) and (b) of the Family Provision Act 1966.

In accordance with section 1(4) of that Act, a draft of this Order was laid before Parliament for forty days during which period neither House resolved that the Order not be made.

A2.135U

1   Citation and commencement

This Order may be cited as the Family Provision (Intestate Succession) Order 2009 and shall come into force on 1st February 2009.

A2.135V

2   Statutory legacy

In the case of a person dying after this Order comes into force, section 46(1) of the Administration of Estates Act 1925 shall apply as if the net sums charged by paragraph (i) on the residuary estate were—

(a) under paragraph (2) of the Table, the sum of £250,000; and
(b) under paragraph (3) of the Table, the sum of £450,000.

PART II—CONTENTIOUS BUSINESS

CPR PART 57 – PROBATE CLAIMS, RECTIFICATION OF WILLS, SUBSTITUTION AND REMOVAL OF PERSONAL REPRESENTATIVES

A2.153

57.1   Scope of this Part and definitions

[(1)   This Part contains rules about—

(a) probate claims;
(b) claims for the rectification of wills; < ... >
(c) claims and applications to—
    (i) substitute another person for a personal representative; or

450

(ii) remove a personal representative[; and
(d) claims under the Inheritance (Provision for Family and Dependants) Act 1975].

(2) In this Part:

(a) 'probate claim' means a claim for—
  (i) the grant of probate of the will, or letters of administration of the estate, of a deceased person;
  (ii) the revocation of such a grant; or
  (iii) a decree pronouncing for or against the validity of an alleged will;
not being a claim which is non-contentious (or common form) probate business;

(Section 128 of the [Senior Courts Act 1981] defines non-contentious (or common form) probate business.)

(b) 'relevant office' means—
  (i) in the case of High Court proceedings in a Chancery district registry, that registry;
  (ii) in the case of any other High Court proceedings, Chancery Chambers at the Royal Courts of Justice, Strand, London, WC2A 2LL; and
  (iii) in the case of county court proceedings, the office of the county court in question;
(c) 'testamentary document' means a will, a draft of a will, written instructions for a will made by or at the request of, or under the instructions of, the testator, and any document purporting to be evidence of the contents, or to be a copy, of a will which is alleged to have been lost or destroyed;
(d) 'will' includes a codicil.]

I PROBATE CLAIMS

A2.154

57.2 General

(1) This Section contains rules about probate claims.

(2) Probate claims in the High Court are assigned to the Chancery Division.

(3) Probate claims in the county court must only be brought in—

(a) a county court where there is also a Chancery district registry; or
(b) the Central London County Court.

(4) All probate claims are allocated to the multi-track.

A2.155

57.3 How to start a probate claim

A probate claim must be commenced—

(a) in the relevant office; and
(b) using the procedure in Part 7.

A2.156 Rules, Orders and Regulations

A2.156

57.4 Acknowledgement of service and defence

(1) A defendant who is served with a claim form must file an acknowledgement of service.

(2) Subject to paragraph (3), the period for filing an acknowledgement of service is—

(a) if the defendant is served with a claim form which states that particulars of claim are to follow, 28 days after service of the particulars of claim; and
(b) in any other case, 28 days after service of the claim form.

(3) If the claim form is served out of the jurisdiction under rule [6.32 or 6.33], the period for filing an acknowledgement of service is 14 days longer than the relevant period specified in rule [6.35] or [*Practice Direction B supplementing Part 6*] [Practice Direction 6B].

(4) Rule 15(4) (which provides the period for filing a defence) applies as if the words 'under Part 10' were omitted from rule 15.4(1)(b).

A2.157

57.5 Lodging of testamentary documents and filing of evidence about testamentary documents

(1) Any testamentary document of the deceased person in the possession or control of any party must be lodged with the court.

(2) Unless the court directs otherwise, the testamentary documents must be lodged in the relevant office—

(a) by the claimant when the claim form is issued; and
(b) by a defendant when he acknowledges service.

(3) The claimant and every defendant who acknowledges service of the claim form must in written evidence—

(a) describe any testamentary document of the deceased of which he has any knowledge or, if he does not know of any such testamentary document, state that fact, and
(b) if any testamentary document of which he has knowledge is not in his possession or under his control, give the name and address of the person in whose possession or under whose control it is or, if he does not know the name or address of that person, state that fact.

(A specimen form for the written evidence about testamentary documents is annexed to *the practice direction* [Practice Direction 57].)

(4) Unless the court directs otherwise, the written evidence required by paragraph (3) must be filed in the relevant office—

(a) by the claimant, when the claim form is issued; and
(b) by a defendant when he acknowledges service.

(5) Except with the permission of the court, a party shall not be allowed to inspect the testamentary documents or written evidence lodged or filed by any other party until he himself has lodged his testamentary documents and filed his evidence.

(6) The provisions of paragraphs (2) and (4) may be modified by a practice direction under this Part.

A2.158

57.6 Revocation of existing grant

(1) In a probate claim which seeks the revocation of a grant of probate or letters of administration every person who is entitled, or claims to be entitled, to administer the estate under that grant must be made a party to the claim.

(2) If the claimant is the person to whom the grant was made, he must lodge the probate or letters of administration in the relevant office when the claim form is issued.

(3) If a defendant has the probate or letters of administration under his control, he must lodge it in the relevant office when he acknowledges service.

(4) Paragraphs (2) and (3) do not apply where the grant has already been lodged at the court, which in this paragraph includes the Principal Registry of the Family Division or a district probate registry.

A2.159

57.7 Contents of statements of case

(1) The claim form must contain a statement of the nature of the interest of the claimant and of each defendant in the estate.

(2) If a party disputes another party's interest in the estate he must state this in his statement of case and set out his reasons.

(3) Any party who contends that at the time when a will was executed the testator did not know of and approve its contents must give particulars of the facts and matters relied on.

(4) Any party who wishes to contend that—

    (a) a will was not duly executed;
    (b) at the time of the execution of a will the testator was not of sound mind, memory and understanding; or
    (c) the execution of a will was obtained by undue influence or fraud,

must set out the contention specifically and give particulars of the facts and matters relied on.

(5)

    (a) A defendant may give notice in his defence that he does not raise any positive case, but insists on the will being proved in solemn form and, for that purpose, will cross-examine the witnesses who attested the will.
    (b) If a defendant gives such a notice, the court will not make an order for costs against him unless it considers that there was no reasonable ground for opposing the will.

A2.160

57.8 Counterclaim

(1) A defendant who contends that he has any claim or is entitled to any remedy relating to the grant of probate of the will, or letters of administration of the estate, of the deceased person must serve a counterclaim making that contention.

A2.161 Rules, Orders and Regulations

(2) If the claimant fails to serve particulars of claim within the time allowed, the defendant may, with the permission of the court, serve a counterclaim and the probate claim shall then proceed as if the counterclaim were the particulars of claim.

A2.161

57.9 Probate counterclaim in other proceedings

(1) In this rule 'probate counterclaim' means a counterclaim in any claim other than a probate claim by which the defendant claims any such remedy as is mentioned in rule 57.1(2)(a).

(2) Subject to the following paragraphs of this rule, this Part shall apply with the necessary modifications to a probate counterclaim as it applies to a probate claim.

(3) A probate counterclaim must contain a statement of the nature of the interest of each of the parties in the estate of the deceased to which the probate counterclaim relates.

(4) Unless an application notice is issued within 7 days after the service of a probate counterclaim for an order under rule 3.1(2)(e) or 3.4 for the probate counterclaim to be dealt with in separate proceedings or to be struck out, and the application is granted, the court shall order the transfer of the proceedings to either—

(a) the Chancery Division (if it is not already assigned to that Division) and to either the Royal Courts of Justice or a Chancery district registry (if it is not already proceeding in one of those places); or
(b) if the county court has jurisdiction, to a county court where there is also a Chancery district registry or the Central London County Court.

(5) If an order is made that a probate counterclaim be dealt with in separate proceedings, the order shall order the transfer of the probate counterclaim as required under paragraph (4).

A2.162

57.10 Failure to acknowledge service or to file a defence

(1) A default judgment cannot be obtained in a probate claim and rule 10.2 and Part 12 do not apply.

(2) If any of several defendants fails to acknowledge service the claimant may—

(a) after the time for acknowledging service has expired; and
(b) upon filing written evidence of service of the claim form and (if no particulars of claim were contained in or served with the claim form) the particulars of claim on that defendant;

proceed with the probate claim as if that defendant had acknowledged service.

(3) If no defendant acknowledges service or files a defence then, unless on the application of the claimant the court orders the claim to be discontinued, the claimant may, after the time for acknowledging service or for filing a defence (as the case may be) has expired, apply to the court for an order that the claim is to proceed to trial.

(4) When making an application under paragraph (3) the claimant must file written evidence of service of the claim form and (if no particulars of claim were contained in or served with the claim form) the particulars of claim on each of the defendants.

(5) Where the court makes an order under paragraph (3), it may direct that the claim be tried on written evidence.

A2.163

57.11 Discontinuance and dismissal

(1) Part 38 does not apply to probate claims.

(2) At any stage of a probate claim the court, on the application of the claimant or of any defendant who has acknowledged service, may order that—
   (a) the claim be discontinued or dismissed on such terms as to costs or otherwise as it thinks just; and
   (b) a grant of probate of the will, or letters of administration of the estate, of the deceased person be made to the person entitled to the grant.

II RECTIFICATION OF WILLS

A2.164

57.12 Rectification of Wills

(1) This Section contains rules about claims for the rectification of a will.

(Section 20 of the Administration of Justice Act 1982 provides for rectification of a will. Additional provisions are contained in rule 55 of the Non-Contentious Probate Rules 1987.)

(2) Every personal representative of the estate shall be joined as a party.

(3) *The practice direction* [Practice Direction 57] makes provision for lodging the grant of probate or letters of administration with the will annexed in a claim under this Section.

III SUBSTITUTION AND REMOVAL OF PERSONAL REPRESENTATIVES

A2.165

57.13 Substitution and Removal of Personal Representatives

(1) This Section contains rules about claims and applications for substitution or removal of a personal representative.

(2) Claims under this Section must be brought in the High Court and are assigned to the Chancery Division.

(Section 50 of the Administration of Justice Act 1985 gives the High Court power to appoint a substitute for, or to remove, a personal representative.)

A2.166   *Rules, Orders and Regulations*

(3) Every personal representative of the estate shall be joined as a party.

(4) *The practice direction* [Practice Direction 57] makes provision for lodging the grant of probate or letters of administration in a claim under this Section.

(5) If substitution or removal of a personal representative is sought by application in existing proceedings, this rule shall apply with references to claims being read as if they referred to applications.

IV CLAIMS UNDER THE INHERITANCE (PROVISION FOR FAMILY AND DEPENDANTS) ACT 1975

A2.166

57.14   Scope of this Section

This Section contains rules about claims under the Inheritance (Provision for Family and Dependants) Act 1975 ('the Act').

A2.167

57.15   Proceedings in the High Court

(1) Proceedings in the High Court under the Act shall be issued in either—

    (a)   the Chancery Division; or
    (b)   the Family Division.

(2) The Civil Procedure Rules apply to proceedings under the Act which are brought in the Family Division, except that the provisions of the Family Proceedings Rules 1991 relating to the drawing up and service of orders apply instead of the provisions in Part 40 and *its practice direction* [Practice Direction 40B].

A2.168

57.16   Procedure for claims under section 1 of the Act

(1) A claim under section 1 of the Act must be made by issuing a claim form in accordance with Part 8.

(2) Rule 8.3 (acknowledgment of service) and rule 8.5 (filing and serving written evidence) apply as modified by paragraphs (3) to (5) of this rule.

(3) The written evidence filed and served by the claimant with the claim form must have exhibited to it an official copy of—

    (a)   the grant of probate or letters of administration in respect of the deceased's estate; and
    (b)   every testamentary document in respect of which probate or letters of administration were granted.

(4) Subject to paragraph (4A), the time within which a defendant must file and serve—

    (a)   an acknowledgment of service; and

(b) any written evidence,

is not more than 21 days after service of the claim form on him.

(4A) If the claim form is served out of the jurisdiction under rule 6.32 or 6.33, the period for filing an acknowledgment of service and any written evidence is 7 days longer than the relevant period specified in rule 6.35 or the *Practice Direction B supplementing Part 6* [Practice Direction 6B].

(5) A defendant who is a personal representative of the deceased must file and serve written evidence, which must include the information required by *the practice direction* [Practice Direction 57].

PRACTICE DIRECTION 57 – PROBATE
THIS PRACTICE DIRECTION SUPPLEMENTS CPR PART 57

I PROBATE CLAIMS

General

A2.169

1.1 This Section of this practice direction applies to contentious probate claims.

1.2 The rules and procedure relating to non-contentious probate proceedings (also known as 'common form') are the Non-Contentious Probate Rules 1987 as amended.

How to start a probate claim

A2.170

2.1 A claim form and all subsequent court documents relating to a probate claim must be marked at the top 'In the estate of [name] deceased (Probate)'.

2.2 The claim form must be issued out of—

(1) Chancery Chambers at the Royal Courts of Justice; or
(2) one of the Chancery district registries; or
(3) if the claim is suitable to be heard in the county court-
(a) a county court in a place where there is also a Chancery district registry; or
(b) the Central London County Court.

There are Chancery district registries at Birmingham, Bristol, Caernarfon, Cardiff, Leeds, Liverpool, Manchester, Mold, Newcastle upon Tyne and Preston.

(Section 32 of the County Courts Act 1984 identifies which probate claims may be heard in a county court.)

2.3 When the claim form is issued, the relevant office will send a notice to Leeds District Probate Registry, Coronet House, Queen Street, Leeds, LS1 2BA, DX 26451 Leeds (Park Square), telephone 0113 243 1505, requesting that all testamentary

A2.171 *Rules, Orders and Regulations*

documents, grants of representation and other relevant documents currently held at any probate registry are sent to the relevant office.

2.4 The commencement of a probate claim will, unless a court otherwise directs, prevent any grant of probate or letters of administration being made until the probate claim has been disposed of.

(Rule 45 of the Non-Contentious Probate Rules 1987 makes provision for notice of the probate claim to be given, and section 117 of the Senior Courts Act 1981 for the grant of letters of administration pending the determination of a probate claim. Paragraph 8 of this practice direction makes provision about an application for such a grant.)

Testamentary documents and evidence about testamentary documents

A2.171

3.1 Unless the court orders otherwise, if a testamentary document is held by the court (whether it was lodged by a party or it was previously held at a probate registry) when the claim has been disposed of the court will send it to the Leeds District Probate Registry.

3.2 The written evidence about testamentary documents required by this Part—

(1) should be in the form annexed to this practice direction; and
(2) must be signed by the party personally and not by his solicitor or other representative (except that if the party is a child or patient the written evidence must be signed by his litigation friend).

3.3 In a case in which there is urgent need to commence a probate claim (for example, in order to be able to apply immediately for the appointment of an administrator pending the determination of the claim) and it is not possible for the claimant to lodge the testamentary documents or to file the evidence about testamentary documents in the relevant office at the same time as the claim form is to be issued, the court may direct that the claimant shall be allowed to issue the claim form upon his giving an undertaking to the court to lodge the documents and file the evidence within such time as the court shall specify.

Case management

A2.172

4 In giving case management directions in a probate claim the court will give consideration to the questions—

(1) whether any person who may be affected by the claim and who is not joined as a party should be joined as a party or given notice of the claim, whether under rule 19.8A or otherwise; and
(2) whether to make a representation order under rule 19.6 or rule 19.7.

Summary judgment

A2.173

5.1 If an order pronouncing for a will in solemn form is sought on an application for summary judgment, the evidence in support of the application must include written evidence proving due execution of the will.

5.2 If a defendant has given notice in his defence under rule 57.7(5) that he raises no positive case but—

(1) he insists that the will be proved in solemn form; and
(2) for that purpose he will cross-examine the witnesses who attested the will;

any application by the claimant for summary judgment is subject to the right of that defendant to require those witnesses to attend court for cross-examination.

Settlement of a probate claim

A2.174

6.1 If at any time the parties agree to settle a probate claim, the court may—

(1) order the trial of the claim on written evidence, which will lead to a grant in solemn form;
(2) order that the claim be discontinued or dismissed under rule 57.11, which will lead to a grant in common form; or
(3) pronounce for or against the validity of one or more wills under section 49 of the Administration of Justice Act 1985.

(For a form of order which is also applicable to discontinuance and which may be adapted as appropriate, see Practice Form No. CH38)

(Section 49 of the Administration of Justice Act 1985 permits a probate claim to be compromised without a trial if every 'relevant beneficiary', as defined in that section, has consented to the proposed order. It is only available in the High Court.)

6.2 Applications under section 49 of the Administration of Justice Act 1985 may be heard by a master or district judge and must be supported by written evidence identifying the relevant beneficiaries and exhibiting the written consent of each of them. The written evidence of testamentary documents required by rule 57.5 will still be necessary.

Application for an order to bring in a will, etc.

A2.175

7.1 Any party applying for an order under section 122 of the Senior Courts Act 1981 ('the 1981 Act') must serve the application notice on the person against whom the order is sought.

(Section 122 of the 1981 Act empowers the court to order a person to attend court for examination, and to answer questions and bring in documents, if there are reasonable grounds for believing that such person has knowledge of a testamentary document. Rule 50(1) of the Non-Contentious Probate Rules 1987 makes similar provision where a probate claim has not been commenced.)

7.2 An application for the issue of a witness summons under section 123 of the 1981 Act–

(1) may be made without notice; and
(2) must be supported by written evidence setting out the grounds of the application.

(Section 123 of the 1981 Act empowers the court, where it appears that any person has in his possession, custody or power a testamentary document, to issue a witness summons ordering such person to bring in that document. Rule 50(2) of the Non-Contentious Probate Rules makes similar provision where a probate claim has not been commenced.)

7.3 An application under section 122 or 123 of the 1981 Act should be made to a master or district judge.

A2.176 *Rules, Orders and Regulations*

7.4 A person against whom a witness summons is issued under section 123 of the 1981 Act who denies that the testamentary document referred to in the witness summons is in his possession or under his control may file written evidence to that effect.

Administration pending the determination of a probate claim

A2.176

8.1 An application under section 117 of the Senior Courts Act 1981 for an order for the grant of administration pending the determination of a probate claim should be made by application notice in the probate claim.

8.2 If an order for a grant of administration is made under section 117 of the 1981 Act—

(1) Rules 69.4 to 69.7 shall apply as if the administrator were a receiver appointed by the court;
(2) if the court allows the administrator remuneration under rule 69.7, it may make an order under section 117(3) of the 1981 Act assigning the remuneration out of the estate of the deceased; and
(3) every application relating to the conduct of the administration shall be made by application notice in the probate claim.

8.3 An order under section 117 may be made by a master or district judge.

8.4 If an order is made under section 117 an application for the grant of letters of administration should be made to the Principal Registry of the Family Division, First Avenue House, 42–49 High Holborn, London WC1V 6NP.

8.5 The appointment of an administrator to whom letters of administration are granted following an order under section 117 will cease automatically when a final order in the probate claim is made but will continue pending any appeal.

II RECTIFICATION OF WILLS

Scope of this section

A2.177

9. This Section of this practice direction applies to claims for the rectification of a will.

Lodging the grant

A2.178

10.1 If the claimant is the person to whom the grant was made in respect of the will of which rectification is sought, he must, unless the court orders otherwise, lodge the probate or letters of administration with the will annexed with the court when the claim form is issued.

10.2 If a defendant has the probate or letters of administration in his possession or under his control, he must, unless the court orders otherwise, lodge it in the relevant office within 14 days after the service of the claim form on him.

Orders

A2.179

11. A copy of every order made for the rectification of a will shall be sent to the Principal Registry of the Family Division for filing, and a memorandum of the order shall be endorsed on, or permanently annexed to, the grant under which the estate is administered.

III SUBSTITUTION AND REMOVAL OF PERSONAL REPRESENTATIVES

Scope of this section

A2.180

12. This Section of this practice direction applies to claims and applications for substitution or removal of a personal representative. If substitution or removal of a personal representative is sought by application in existing proceedings, this Section shall apply with references to the claim, claim form and claimant being read as if they referred to the application, application notice and applicant respectively.

Starting the claim

A2.181

13.1 The claim form must be accompanied by –

(1) either—
(a) a sealed or certified copy of the grant of probate or letters of administration, or
(b) where the claim is to substitute or remove an executor and is made before a grant of probate has been issued, the original or, if the original is not available, a copy of the will; and
(2) written evidence containing the grounds of the claim and the following information so far as it is known to the claimant—
(a) brief details of the property comprised in the estate, with an approximate estimate of its capital value and any income that is received from it;
(b) brief details of the liabilities of the estate;
(c) the names and addresses of the persons who are in possession of the documents relating to the estate;
(d) the names of the beneficiaries and their respective interests in the estate; and
(e) the name, address and occupation of any proposed substituted personal representative.

13.2 If the claim is for the appointment of a substituted personal representative, the claim form must be accompanied by—

(1) a signed or (in the case of the Public Trustee or a corporation) sealed consent to act; and
(2) written evidence as to the fitness of the proposed substituted personal representative, if an individual, to act.

A2.182 *Rules, Orders and Regulations*

Production of the grant

A2.182

14.1 On the hearing of the claim the personal representative must produce to the Court the grant of representation to the deceased's estate.

14.2 If an order is made substituting or removing the personal representative, the grant (together with a sealed copy of the order) must be sent to and remain in the custody of the Principal Registry of the Family Division until a memorandum of the order has been endorsed on or permanently annexed to the grant.

14.3 Where the claim is to substitute or remove an executor and the claim is made before a grant of probate has been issued, paragraphs 14.1 and 14.2 do not apply. Where in such a case an order is made substituting or removing an executor a sealed copy of the order must be sent to the Principal Registry of the Family Division where it will be recorded and retained pending any application for a grant. An order sent to the Principal Registry in accordance with this paragraph must be accompanied by a note of the full name and date of death of the deceased, if it is not apparent on the face of the order.

IV CLAIMS UNDER THE INHERITANCE (PROVISION FOR FAMILY AND DEPENDANTS) ACT 1975

Acknowledgment of service by personal representative – Rule 57.16(4)

A2.183

15. Where a defendant who is a personal representative wishes to remain neutral in relation to the claim, and agrees to abide by any decision which the court may make, he should state this in Section A of the acknowledgment of service form.

Written evidence of personal representative – Rule 57.16(5)

A2.184

16. The written evidence filed by a defendant who is a personal representative must state to the best of that person's ability—
   (1) full details of the value of the deceased's net estate, as defined in section 25(1) of the Act;
   (2) the person or classes of persons beneficially interested in the estate, and—
   (a) the names and (unless they are parties to the claim) addresses of all living beneficiaries; and
   (b) the value of their interests in the estate so far as they are known.
   (3) whether any living beneficiary (and if so, naming him) is a child or patient within the meaning of rule 21.1(2); and
   (4) any facts which might affect the exercise of the court's powers under the Act.

Separate representation of claimants

A2.185

17. If a claim is made jointly by two or more claimants, and it later appears that any of the claimants have a conflict of interests—

(1) any claimant may choose to be represented at any hearing by separate solicitors or counsel, or may appear in person; and
(2) if the court considers that claimants who are represented by the same solicitors or counsel ought to be separately represented, it may adjourn the application until they are.

Production of the grant

A2.186

18.1 On the hearing of a claim the personal representative must produce to the court the original grant of representation to the deceased's estate.

18.2 If the court makes an order under the Act, the original grant (together with a sealed copy of the order) must be sent to the Principal Registry of the Family Division for a memorandum of the order to be endorsed on or permanently annexed to the grant in accordance with section 19(3) of the Act.

18.3 Every final order embodying terms of compromise made in proceedings under the Act, whether made with or without a hearing, must contain a direction that a memorandum of the order shall be endorsed on or permanently annexed to the probate or letters of administration and a copy of the order shall be sent to the Principal Registry of the Family Division with the relevant grant of probate or letters of administration for endorsement.

Annex
A Form of Witness Statement or Affidavit About Testamentary Documents
(CPR Rule 57.5)

A2.187

(Title of the claim)

I [name and address] the claimant/defendant in this claim state [on oath] that I have no knowledge of any document—

(i) being or purported to be or having the form or effect of a will or codicil of [name of deceased] whose estate is the subject of this claim;
(ii) being or purporting to be a draft or written instructions for any such will or codicil made by or at the request of or under the instructions of the deceased;
(iii) being or purporting to be evidence of the contents or a copy of any such will or codicil which is alleged to have been lost or destroyed,

except ... [*describe any testamentary document of the deceased, and if any such document is not in your control, give the name and address of the person who you believe has possession or control of it, or state that you do not know the name and address of that person*] ...

[I believe that the facts stated in this witness statement are true] [*or jurat for affidavit*]

(NOTE: '*testamentary document*' *is defined in CPR rule 57.1*)

Note.
The term 'testamentary document' is defined in CPR rule 57.1.

Appendix III
FEES
(NON-CONTENTIOUS BUSINESS)

Appendix III
FEES (NON-CONTENTIOUS BUSINESS)

THE NON-CONTENTIOUS PROBATE FEES ORDER 2004

SI 2004/3120

Note.
Shown as amended by the Non-Contentious Probate Fees (Amendment) Order 2007, SI 2007/2174 and Non-Contentious Probate Fees (Amendment) Order 2009, SI 2009/1497. New/inserted text is inside square brackets.

A3.01

1

(1) This Order may be cited as the Non-Contentious Probate Fees Order 2004 and shall come into force on the 4th January 2005.

(2) In this Order—
- (a) a fee referred to by number means the fee so numbered in Schedule 1 to this Order;
- (b) 'assessed value' means the value of the net real and personal estate (excluding settled land if any) passing under the grant as shown—
  - (i) in the Inland Revenue affidavit (for a death occurring before 13th March 1975), or
  - (ii) in the Inland Revenue account (for a death occurring on or after 13th March 1975), or
  - (iii) in the case in which, in accordance with arrangements made between the President of the Family Division and the Commissioners of the Inland Revenue, or regulations made under section 256(1)(a) of the Inheritance Tax Act 1984 and from time to time in force, no such affidavit or account is required to be delivered, in the oath which is sworn to lead to the grant,

  and in the case of an application to reseal means the value, as shown, passing under the grant upon its being resealed;
- (c) 'authorised place of deposit' means any place in which, by virtue of a direction given under section 124 of the [Senior Courts Act 1981] original wills and other documents under the control of the High Court (either in the principal registry or in any district registry) are deposited and preserved;
- (d) 'grant' means a grant of probate or letters of administration;
- (e) 'district registry' includes the probate registry of Wales, any district probate registry and any sub-registry attached to it;
- (f) 'the principal registry' means the Principal Registry of the Family Division and any sub-registry attached to it.

A3.01 Fees (Non-Contentious Business)

Para (2): in sub-para (c) words 'Senior Courts Act 1981' in square brackets substituted by the Constitutional Reform Act 2005, s 59(5), Sch 11, Pt 1, para 1(2). Date in force: 1 October 2009: see SI 2009/1604, art 2(d).

A3.02

2. Fees to be taken

The fees set out in column 2 of Schedule 1 to this Order shall be taken in the principal registry and in each district registry in respect of the items described in column 1 in accordance with and subject to any directions specified in column 1.

A3.03

3. Exclusion of certain death gratuities

In determining the value of any personal estate for the purposes of this Order there shall be excluded the value of a death gratuity payable under section 17(2) of the Judicial Pensions Act 1981 or section 4(3) of the Judicial Pensions and Retirement Act 1993, or payable to the personal representatives of a deceased civil servant by virtue of a scheme made under section 1 of the Superannuation Act 1972.

A3.04

[4. Remission of fees

Schedule 1A applies for the purpose of ascertaining whether a party is entitled to a remission or part remission of a fee prescribed by this Order.]

A3.05

[5.

The Lord Chancellor may, on the ground of financial hardship or for other reasonable cause, remit in whole or in part any fee prescribed by this Order.]

A3.06

6.

(1) Where by any convention entered into by Her Majesty with any foreign power it is provided that no fee shall be required to be paid in respect of any proceedings, the fees specified in this Order shall not be taken in respect of those proceedings.

(2) Where any application for a grant is withdrawn before the issue of a grant, a registrar may reduce or remit a fee.

(3) Fee 7 shall not be taken where a search is made for research or similar purposes by permission of the President of the Family Division for a document over 100 years old filed in the principal registry or a district registry or another authorised place of deposit.

A3.07

7. Special exemption – Armed Forces

Where a fee has been paid or fees have been paid for the application of a grant (other than fee 3.2) and at the time of payment of that fee or those fees –

(a) the application for the grant was in respect of an estate exempt from Inheritance Tax by virtue of section 154 of the Inheritance Tax Act 1984 (exemption for members of the armed forces etc); and

(b) was in respect of a death occurring before 20th March 2003;

the Lord Chancellor shall upon receiving a written application refund the difference between any fee or fees paid and fee 3.2.

A3.08

8. Revocation

The Order specified in Schedule 2 in so far as it was made under section 128 of the Finance Act 1990 shall be revoked.

A3.09

SCHEDULE 1
FEES TO BE TAKEN

Column 1 Number and description of fee	Column 2 Amount of fee
1. Application for a grant On an application for a grant (or for resealing a grant) other than on an application to which fee 3 applies, where the assessed value of the estate exceeds £5,000	£40
2. Personal application fee Where the application under fee 1 is made by a personal applicant (not being an application to which fee 3 applies) fee 2 is payable in addition to fee 1, where the assessed value of the estate exceeds £5,000	£50
3. Special applications 3.1 For a duplicate or second or subsequent grant (including one following a revoked grant) in respect of the same deceased person, other than a grant preceded only by a grant limited to settled land, to trust property, or to part of the estate	£15
3.2 On an application for a grant relating to a death occurring on or after 20th March 2003 and in respect of an estate exempt from inheritance tax by virtue of section 154 of the Inheritance Tax Act 1984 (exemption for members of the armed forces etc)	£8
4. Caveats For the entry or the extension of a caveat	£15

A3.09 Fees (Non-Contentious Business)

Column 1 Number and description of fee	Column 2 Amount of fee
5. Search On an application for a standing search to be carried out in an estate, for each period of six months including the issue of a copy grant and will, if any (irrespective of the number of pages)	£5
6. Deposit of wills On depositing a will for safe custody in the principal registry or a district registry	£15
7. Inspection On inspection of any will or other document retained by the registry (in the presence of an officer of the registry)	£15
8. Copy documents On a request for a copy of any document whether or not provided as a certified copy:	
(a) for the first copy	£5
(b) for every subsequent copy of the same document if supplied at the same time	£1
(c) where copies of any document are made available on a computer disk or in other electronic form, for each such copy	£3
(d) where a search of the index is required, in addition to fee 8(a), (b) or (c) as appropriate, for each period of 4 years searched after the first 4 years	£3
9. Oaths Except on a personal application for a grant, for administering an oath,	
9.1 for each deponent to each affidavit	£5
9.2 for marking each exhibit	£2
10. Determination of costs For determining costs	The same fees as are payable from time to time for determining costs under the Civil Proceedings Fees Order [2008], (the relevant fees are set out in fee 5 in Schedule 1 to that Order)
11. Settling documents For perusing and settling citations, advertisements, oaths, affidavits, or other documents, for each document settled	£10

In Fee 10 the figure '2008' in square brackets substituted by SI 2008/2854, arts 2, 3. Date in force: 26 November 2008: see SI 2008/2854, art 1.

A3.10

[SCHEDULE 1A
REMISSIONS AND PART-REMISSIONS]

[Article 4]

Inserted by SI 2007/2174, art 4, Schedule. Date in force: 1 October 2007: see SI 2007/2174, art 1.
Substituted by SI 2009/1497, arts 2, 3, Schedule. Date in force: 13 July 2009: see SI 2009/1497, art 1.

[Interpretation

1 (1) In this Schedule—

'child' means a child or young person in respect of whom a party is entitled to receive child benefit in accordance with section 141, and regulations made under section 142, of the Social Security Contributions and Benefits Act 1992;

'child care costs' has the meaning given in the Criminal Defence Service (Financial Eligibility) Regulations 2006;

'couple' has the meaning given in section 3(5A) of the Tax Credits Act 2002;

'disposable monthly income' has the meaning given in paragraph 5;

'excluded benefits' means—

  (a) any of the following benefits payable under the Social Security Contributions and Benefits Act 1992—
    (i) attendance allowance paid under section 64;
    (ii) severe disablement allowance;
    (iii) carer's allowance;
    (iv) disability living allowance;
    (v) constant attendance allowance paid under section 104 or paragraph 4 or 7(2) of Schedule 8 as an increase to a disablement pension;
    (vi) council tax benefit;
    (vii) any payment made out of the social fund;
    (viii) housing benefit;
  (b) any direct payment made under the Community Care, Services for Carers and Children's Services (Direct Payments) (England) Regulations 2003 or the Community Care, Services for Carers and Children's Services (Direct Payments) (Wales) Regulations 2004;
  (c) a back to work bonus payable under section 26 of the Jobseekers Act 1995;
  (d) any exceptionally severe disablement allowance paid under the Personal Injuries (Civilians) Scheme 1983;
  (e) any pension paid under the Naval, Military and Air Forces etc (Disablement and Death) Service Pensions Order 2006;
  (f) any payment made from the Independent Living Funds; and
  (g) any financial support paid under an agreement for the care of a foster child;

'the Funding Code' means the code approved under section 9 of the Access to Justice Act 1999;

'gross annual income' means total annual income, for the 12 months preceding the application for remission or part remission, from all sources other than receipt of any of the excluded benefits;

'gross monthly income' means total monthly income, for the month in which the application for remission or part remission is made, from all sources other than receipt of any of the excluded benefits;

'the Independent Living Funds' has the meaning given in the Criminal Defence Service (Financial Eligibility) Regulations 2006;

A3.10 Fees (Non-Contentious Business)

'LSC' means the Legal Services Commission established under section 1 of the Access to Justice Act 1999;

'partner' means a person with whom the party lives as a couple and includes a person with whom the party is not currently living but from whom the party is not living separate and apart;

'party' means the individual who would, but for this Schedule, be liable to pay the fee required under this Order;

(2) Paragraphs 2, 3 and 4 do not apply to a party who is in receipt of funding provided by the LSC for the purposes of the proceedings for which a certificate has been issued under the Funding Code.

Full remission of fees—qualifying benefits

2   (1) No fee is payable under this Order if, at the time when a fee would otherwise be payable, the party is in receipt of a qualifying benefit.

(2) The following are qualifying benefits for the purpose of sub-paragraph (1)—

(a) income support under the Social Security Contributions and Benefits Act 1992;
(b) working tax credit, provided that no child tax credit is being paid to the party;
(c) income-based jobseeker's allowance under the Jobseekers Act 1995;
(d) guarantee credit under the State Pension Credit Act 2002; and
(e) income-related employment and support allowance under the Welfare Reform Act 2007.

Full remission of fees—gross annual income

3   (1) No fee is payable under this Order if, at the time when the fee would otherwise be payable, the party has the number of children specified in column 1 of the following table and—

(a) if the party is single, the gross annual income of the party does not exceed the amount set out in the appropriate row of column 2; or
(b) if the party is one of a couple, the gross annual income of the couple does not exceed the amount set out in the appropriate row of column 3.

Column 1 Number of children of fee-paying party	Column 2 Single	Column 3 Couple
no children	£13,000	£18,000
1 child	£15,930	£20,930
2 children	£18,860	£23,860
3 children	£21,790	£26,790
4 children	£24,720	£29,720

(2) If the party paying the fee has more than 4 children then the relevant amount of gross annual income is the amount specified in the table for 4 children plus the sum of £2,930 for each additional child.

Full and part remission of fees—disposable monthly income

4   (1) No fee is payable under this Order if, at the time when the fee would otherwise be payable, the disposable monthly income of the party is £50 or less.

(2) The maximum amount of fee payable is—

(a) if the disposable monthly income of the party is more than £50 but does not exceed £210, an amount equal to one-quarter of every £10 of the party's disposable monthly income up to a maximum of £50; and

(b) if the disposable monthly income is more than £210, an amount equal to £50 plus one-half of every £10 over £200 of the party's disposable monthly income.

(3) Where the fee that would otherwise be payable under this Order is greater than the maximum fee which a party is required to pay as calculated in sub-paragraph (2), the fee will be remitted to the amount payable under that sub-paragraph.

Disposable monthly income

5 (1) A party's disposable monthly income is the gross monthly income of the party for the month in which the fee becomes payable ('the period') less the deductions referred to in sub-paragraphs (2) and (3).

(2) There is to be deducted from the gross monthly income—
  (a) income tax paid or payable in respect of the period;
  (b) any contributions estimated to have been paid under Part 1 of the Social Security Contributions and Benefits Act 1992 in respect of the period;
  (c) either—
    (i) monthly rent or monthly payment in respect of a mortgage debt or hereditable security, payable in respect of the only or main dwelling of the party, less any housing benefit paid under the Social Security Contributions and Benefits Act 1992; or
    (ii) the monthly cost of the living accommodation of the party;
  (d) any child care costs paid or payable in respect of the period;
  (e) if the party is making bona fide payments for the maintenance of a child who is not a member of the household of the party, the amount of such payments paid or payable in respect of the period; and
  (f) any amount paid or payable by the party, in respect of the period, in pursuance of a court order.

(3) There will be deducted from the gross monthly income an amount representing the cost of living expenses in respect of the period being—
  (a) £315; plus
  (b) £244 for each child of the party; plus
  (c) £159, if the party has a partner.

Resources of partners

6 (1) For the purpose of determining whether a party is entitled to the remission or part remission of a fee in accordance with this Schedule, the income of a partner, if any, is to be included as income of the party.

(2) The receipt by a partner of a qualifying benefit does not entitle a party to remission of a fee.

Application for remission or part remission of fees

7 (1) An application for remission or part remission of a fee must be made to the court officer at the time when the fee would otherwise be payable.

(2) Where a claim for full remission of fees is made, the party must provide documentary evidence of, as the case may be—
  (a) entitlement to a qualifying benefit; or
  (b) gross annual income and, if applicable, the children included for the purposes of paragraph 3.

(3) Where a claim for full or part remission of fees under paragraph 4 is made, the party must provide documentary evidence of—

A3.10 Fees (Non-Contentious Business)

  (a) such of the party's gross monthly income as is derived from—
   (i) employment;
   (ii) rental or other income received from persons living with the party by reason of their residence in the party's home;
   (iii) a pension; or
   (iv) a state benefit, not being an excluded benefit; and
  (b) any expenditure being deducted from the gross monthly income in accordance with paragraph 5(2).

Remission in exceptional circumstances

8   Where it appears to the Lord Chancellor that the payment of any fee prescribed by this Order would, owing to the exceptional circumstances of the particular case, involve undue financial hardship, the Lord Chancellor may reduce or remit the fee in that case.

Refunds

9   (1) Subject to sub-paragraph (3), where a party has not provided the documentary evidence required by paragraph 7 and a fee has been paid at a time when, under paragraphs 2, 3 or 4, it was not payable, the fee will be refunded if documentary evidence relating to the time when the fee became payable is provided at a later date.

(2) Subject to sub-paragraph (3), when a fee has been paid at a time where the Lord Chancellor, if all the circumstances had been known, would have reduced or remitted the fee under paragraph 8, the fee or the amount by which the fee would have been reduced, as the case may be, will be refunded.

(3) No refund will be made under this paragraph unless the party who paid the fee applies within 6 months of paying the fee.

(4) The Lord Chancellor may extend the period of 6 months mentioned in sub-paragraph (3) if the Lord Chancellor considers that there is a good reason for an application being made after the end of the period of 6 months.]
Inserted by SI 2007/2174, art 4, Schedule. Date in force: 1 October 2007: see SI 2007/2174, art 1.
Substituted by SI 2009/1497, arts 2, 3, Schedule. Date in force: 13 July 2009: see SI 2009/1497, art 1.

A3.11

SCHEDULE 2
ORDER REVOKED

Title	*Reference*
The Non-Contentious Probate Fees (Amendment) Order 2000	SI 2000/642

Appendix IV
RATES OF INHERITANCE TAX AND CAPITAL TRANSFER TAX

A4.01 Deaths on or after 13 March 1975 and prior to 27 October 1977. First Table of rates of Capital Transfer Tax (Finance Act 1975, s 37; s 49 and Sch 11, para 1).

Range of value		Cumulative tax to bottom of range	Rate of tax on value within range
Exceeding	Not exceeding		
£	£	£	%
15,000	20,000	Nil	10
20,000	25,000	500	15
25,000	30,000	1,250	20
30,000	40,000	2,250	25
40,000	50,000	4,750	30
50,000	60,000	7,750	35
60,000	80,000	11,250	40
80,000	100,000	19,250	45
100,000	120,000	28,250	50
120,000	150,000	38,250	55
150,000	500,000	54,750	60
500,000	1,000,000	264,750	65
1,000,000	2,000,000	589,750	70
2,000,000		1,289,750	75

A4.02 Rates of Inheritance Tax and Capital Transfer Tax

A4.02 Deaths on or after 27 October 1977 and prior to 26 March 1980. First Table of rates of Capital Transfer Tax (Finance Act 1978, s 62 and Sch 10).

Range of value		Cumulative tax to bottom of range	Rate of tax on value within range
Exceeding	Not exceeding		
£	£	£	%
25,000	30,000	Nil	10
30,000	35,000	500	15
35,000	40,000	1,250	20
40,000	50,000	2,250	25
50,000	60,000	4,750	30
60,000	70,000	7,750	35
70,000	90,000	11,250	40
90,000	110,000	19,250	45
110,000	130,000	28,250	50
130,000	160,000	38,250	55
160,000	510,000	54,750	60
510,000	1,010,000	264,750	65
1,010,000	2,010,000	589,750	70
2,010,000		1,289,750	75

A4.03 Deaths on or after 26 March 1980 and prior to 9 March 1982. First Table of rates of Capital Transfer Tax (Finance Act 1980, s 85 and Sch 14).

Range of value		Cumulative tax to bottom of range	Rate of tax on value within range
Exceeding	Not exceeding		
£	£	£	%
50,000	60,000	Nil	30
60,000	70,000	3,000	35
70,000	90,000	6,500	40
90,000	110,000	14,500	45
110,000	130,000	23,500	50
130,000	160,000	33,500	55
160,000	510,000	50,000	60
510,000	1,010,000	260,000	65
1,010,000	2,010,000	585,000	70
2,010,000		1,285,000	75

Rates of Inheritance Tax and Capital Transfer Tax   A4.05

A4.04 Deaths on or after 9 March 1982 and prior to 15 March 1983. First Table of rates of Capital Transfer Tax (Finance Act 1982, s 90 and Sch 14).

Range of value		Cumulative tax to bottom of range	Rate of tax on value within range
Exceeding	Not exceeding		
£	£	£	%
55,000	75,000	Nil	30
75,000	100,000	6,000	35
100,000	130,000	14,750	40
130,000	165,000	26,750	45
165,000	200,000	42,500	50
200,000	250,000	60,000	55
250,000	650,000	87,500	60
650,000	1,250,000	327,500	65
1,250,000	2,500,000	717,500	70
2,500,000		1,592,500	75

A4.05 Deaths on or after 15 March 1983 and prior to 13 March 1984. First Table of rates of Capital Transfer Tax (Finance (No 2) Act 1983, s 8).

Range of value		Cumulative tax to bottom of range	Rate of tax on value within range
Exceeding	Not exceeding		
£	£	£	%
60,000	80,000	Nil	30
80,000	110,000	6,000	35
110,000	140,000	16,500	40
140,000	175,000	28,500	45
175,000	220,000	44,250	50
220,000	270,000	66,750	55
270,000	700,000	94,250	60
700,000	1,325,000	352,250	65
1,325,000	2,650,000	758,500	70
2,650,000		1,686,000	75

A4.06 *Rates of Inheritance Tax and Capital Transfer Tax*

A4.06 Deaths on or after 13 March 1984 and before 6 April 1985. First Table of rates of Capital Transfer Tax (Finance Act 1984, s 101).

Range of value		Cumulative tax to bottom of range	Rate of tax on value within range
Exceeding	Not exceeding		
£	£	£	%
64,000	85,000	Nil	30
85,000	116,000	6,300	35
116,000	148,000	17,150	40
148,000	185,000	29,950	45
185,000	232,000	46,600	50
232,000	285,000	70,100	55
285,000		99,250	60

A4.07 Deaths on or after 6 April 1985 and prior to 18 March 1986. First Table of rates of Capital Transfer Tax (SI 1985/429).

Range of value		Cumulative tax to bottom of range	Rate of tax on value within range
Exceeding	Not exceeding		
£	£	£	%
67,000	89,000	Nil	30
89,000	122,000	6,600	35
122,000	155,000	18,150	40
155,000	194,000	31,350	45
194,000	243,000	48,900	50
243,000	299,000	73,400	55
299,000		104,200	60

Rates of Inheritance Tax and Capital Transfer Tax A4.10

A4.08 Deaths on or after 18 March 1986 and before 17 March 1987. Table of rates of tax (Finance Act 1986, s 101 and Sch 19, para 36).

Range of value		Cumulative tax to bottom of range	Rate of tax on value within range
Exceeding	Not exceeding		
£	£	£	%
71,000	95,000	Nil	30
95,000	129,000	7,200	35
129,000	164,000	19,100	40
164,000	206,000	33,100	45
206,000	257,000	52,000	50
257,000	317,000	77,500	55
317,000		110,500	60

A4.09 Deaths on or after 17 March 1987 and before 15 March 1988. Table of rates of tax (Finance Act 1987, s 57).

Range of value		Cumulative tax to bottom of range	Rate of tax on value within range
Exceeding	Not exceeding		
£	£	£	%
90,000	140,000	Nil	30
140,000	220,000	15,000	40
220,000	330,000	47,000	50
330,000		102,000	60

A4.10 For deaths on or after 15 March 1988.

Effective dates	Taxable threshold	Rate of tax	Legislation
15/3/88–5/4/89	£110,000	40%	FA 1988, s136
6/4/89–5/4/90	£118,000	40%	SI 1989/468
6/4/90–5/4/91	£128,000	40%	SI 1990/680
6/4/91–9/3/92	£140,000	40%	SI 1991/735
10/3/95–5/4/95	£150,000	40%	FA [No2] 1992, s 72
6/4/95–5/4/96	£154,000	40%	SI 1994/3011

A4.10 *Rates of Inheritance Tax and Capital Transfer Tax*

Effective dates	Taxable threshold	Rate of tax	Legislation
6/4/96–5/4/97	£200,000	40%	FA 1996, s 183
6/4/97–5/4/98	£215,000	40%	FA 1997, s 93
6/4/98–5/4/99	£223,000	40%	SI 1998/756
6/4/99–5/4/00	£231,000	40%	SI 1999/596
6/4/00–5/4/01	£234,000	40%	SI 2000/967
6/4/01–5/4/02	£242,000	40%	SI 2001/639
6/4/02–5/4/03	£250,000	40%	FA 2002, s 118
6/4/03–5/4/04	£255,000	40%	SI 2003/841
6/4/04–5/4/05	£263,000	40%	SI 2004/771
6/4/05–5/4/06	£275,000	40%	FA 2005, s 98
6/4/06–5/4/07	£285,000	40%	FA 2005, s 98
6/4/07–5/4/08	£300,000	40%	FA 2005, s 98
6/4/08–5/4/09	£312,000	40%	FA 2006, s 155
6/4/09–5/4/10	£325,000	40%	FA 2006, s 155, subject to the potential application of IHTA 1984, s 8
6/4/10–5/4/11	£350,000	40%	FA 2007, s 4. *The Chancellor's Pre-Budget report on 9 December 2009 deferred this change until 6/4/11, subject to enactment of the Finance Bill in 2010.*

Appendix V
COSTS
(NON-CONTENTIOUS BUSINESS)

Appendix V
COSTS (NON-CONTENTIOUS BUSINESS)

SOLICITORS' (NON-CONTENTIOUS BUSINESS) REMUNERATION ORDER 2009

2009 No 1931

A5.01

1. Citation, commencement and revocation

(1) This Order may be cited as the Solicitors' (Non-Contentious Business) Remuneration Order 2009.

(2) This Order comes into force on 11th August 2009 and applies to all non-contentious business for which bills are delivered on or after that date.

(3) The Solicitors' (Non-Contentious Business) Remuneration Order 1994 is revoked except in its application to non-contentious business for which bills are delivered before this Order comes into force.

A5.02

2. Interpretation

In this Order—

'client' means the client of a solicitor;
'costs' means the amount charged in a solicitor's bill, exclusive of disbursements and value added tax, in respect of non-contentious business;
'entitled person' means a client or an entitled third party;
'entitled third party' means a residuary beneficiary absolutely and immediately (and not contingently) entitled to an inheritance, where a solicitor has charged the estate for his professional costs for acting in the administration of the estate and the only personal representatives are—
   (a) solicitors (whether or not acting in a professional capacity);
   (b) solicitors acting jointly with partners, managers or employees in a professional capacity;
   (c) employees of a solicitor sole practitioner acting in that capacity; or
   (d) managers or employees of a recognised body acting in that capacity;
'manager' has the same meaning as in the Legal Services Act 2007 (see section 207 of that Act);
'paid disbursements' means disbursements already paid by the solicitor;
'recognised body' means a body recognised by the Law Society under section 9 of the Administration of Justice Act 1985;

A5.03 *Costs (Non-Contentious Business)*

'registered European lawyer' means a registered European lawyer within the meaning of the European Communities (Lawyer's Practice) Regulations 2000 who is registered with the Law Society;

'residuary beneficiary' includes a person entitled to all or part of the residue of an intestate estate; and

'solicitor' includes a registered European lawyer and a recognised body.

A5.03

3. Solicitors' costs

A solicitor's costs must be fair and reasonable having regard to all the circumstances of the case and in particular to—

(a) the complexity of the matter or the difficulty or novelty of the questions raised;
(b) the skill, labour, specialised knowledge and responsibility involved;
(c) the time spent on the business;
(d) the number and importance of the documents prepared or considered, without regard to length;
(e) the place where and the circumstances in which the business or any part of the business is transacted;
(f) the amount or value of any money or property involved;
(g) whether any land involved is registered land within the meaning of the Land Registration Act 2002;
(h) the importance of the matter to the client; and
(i) the approval (express or implied) of the entitled person or the express approval of the testator to—
   (i) the solicitor undertaking all or any part of the work giving rise to the costs; or
   (ii) the amount of the costs.

A5.04

4. Security for costs

A solicitor may take from his client security for the payment of any costs, including the amount of any interest to which the solicitor may become entitled under article 5.

A5.05

5. Interest

(1) A solicitor may charge interest on the unpaid amount of his costs plus any paid disbursements and value added tax, subject to the remainder of this article.

(2) Where an entitlement to interest arises under paragraph (1), and subject to any agreement made between a solicitor and client, the period for which interest may be charged runs from one month after the date of delivery of a bill.

(3) Subject to any agreement made between a solicitor and client, the rate of interest must not exceed the rate for the time being payable on judgment debts.

(4) Interest charged under this article must be calculated, where applicable, by reference to—

(a) the amount specified in a determination of costs by the Law Society under Schedule 1A to the Solicitors Act 1974;
(b) the amount ascertained on taxation if an application has been made for the bill to be taxed.

Appendix VI
FORMS

APPENDIX VI SUMMARY

		Para
Part I – Forms for use in Non-contentious Probate Matters		
Affidavits		
1	General heading of affidavit (and other forms)	A6.01
24	Affidavit in proof of lack of capacity	A6.29
County court form		
59	Notice to Leeds District Probate Registry to produce documents	A6.64
Nomination		
63	Nomination of a second administrator; lack of mental capacity within the meaning of the Mental Capacity Act 2005 and minority or life interest (NCPR 35(3))	A6.68
Notices		
64	Form 6: Notice of Election to Redeem Life Interest – Rule 56	A6.69
Oaths		
66	Oath for probate (general form)	A6.71
93	Oath for administrators– net estate exceeding £125,000 for death on or after 1 December 2005: civil partner and minor child survive: application by civil partner who has parental responsibility for minor and nominated co-administrator	A6.98
101	Oath for administration to child or other issue having a beneficial interest– no surviving spouse [civil partner*]	A6.106
120	Oath for administration to attorneys of intestate's husband or widow or civil partner	A6.125
121	Oath for administration to attorney of intestate's father or mother	A6.126
122	Oath for administration to attorneys of intestate's child– another child being a minor	A6.127
124	Oath for administrator (grantee having become mentally incapable) or (grantee subsequently lacks capacity within the meaning of the Mental Capacity Act 2005 to manage his affairs)	A6.129
125	Oath for administrator (a former grant having been revoked)	A6.130
126	Oath for administration to mother of minor and nominated co-administrator	A6.131
128	Oath for administration to step-parent of minor and nominated co-administrator	A6.133
129	Oath for administration to guardian of minor and nominated co-administrator	A6.134
134	Oath for person appointed by the Court of Protection for use of a person who lacks capacity to manage his affairs within the meaning of the Mental Capacity Act 2005	A6.139
135	Oath for administrator by attorney acting under a registered enduring power of attorney /registered lasting power of attorney	A6.140
136	Oath for administrators appointed by district judge or registrar for the use of a person who lacks capacity	A6.141
149	Oath for administration – judicially separated spouse (death on or after 1 August 1970)	A6.154

150	Oath for administration – judicially separated civil partner (death on or after 5 December 2005)	A6.155
167	Oath for administration (will) to person authorised by Court of Protection where executor is lacks capacity to manage his affairs	A6.172
168	Oath for administration (will) to attorney acting under a registered enduring power of attorney or registered lasting power of attorney; for the use executor who lacks capacity	A6.173
169	Oath for administration (will) to person entitled to the residuary estate; for the use of executor who lacks capacity within the meaning of the Mental Capacity Act 2005 is lacks capacity to manage his affairs	A6.174
170	Oath for administration (will) under s 116 of the Senior Courts Act 1981	A6.175
173A	Oath for administration (will) to legatee in accordance with NCPR 30(3)(b); whole or substantially whole estate in England and Wales consists of immoveable property	A6.178A
191	Renunciation by two members of a partnership	A6.196
198	Subpoena to bring in a testamentary document	A6.203

Part I

FORMS FOR USE IN NON-CONTENTIOUS PROBATE MATTERS

AFFIDAVITS

A6.01

1. General heading of affidavit (and other forms)

In the High Court of Justice

Family Division

The Principal [*or* District Probate] Registry [*or* The Probate Registry of Wales].

In the estate of A B deceased.

[Note.–

Every affidavit must be expressed in the first person and unless the court otherwise directs must state the place of residence of the deponent and his occupation or, if he has none, his description (Order 41, r 1(4)). The occupation (if any) of a female deponent should therefore be stated, but if she has none, her marital status should be given.]

A6.29

24. Affidavit in proof of lack of capacity

(*Heading as in Form 1*)

I, C D, of   make oath and say that:

1. I am [*state qualifications*] and I have for the last   years attended E F of   in my professional capacity.

2. The said E F now suffers from an impairment of, or a disturbance in the functioning of the mind or brain and as a result is unable to make a decision for himself in relation to an application for a grant of representation and administration of the estate of A B deceased and in my opinion lacks capacity to manage his property and affairs within the meaning of the Mental Capacity Act 2005.

Sworn etc

[Note.–

A certificate in the form given in para 11.254 of this supplement by the Responsible Medical Officer (where the person is a patient who is resident in an institution) or by the person's doctor (in other cases) is normally sufficient in lieu of an affidavit.]

COUNTY COURT FORM

A6.64

59. Notice to Leeds District Probate Registry to produce documents

In the   County Court.
No.
Between   A B   Claimant,
                                and
                                C D   Defendant

1. An application has been made to this court to revoke the grant of probate of the will [or letters of administration of the estate] of [here insert the name and address of the testator or intestate] granted out of the   Probate Registry on the   day of   20 .

2. Such application will be heard by this court at   on the   day of   at am [or   pm]:

3. I therefore request that you will cause to be produced before the court on that day [the will and*] all documents which are in the principal registry or any district probate registry relating to the matter.

Dated this   day of   20 .

(Proper Officer)

[See County Court Rules 1981, Order 41, rule 2.]

[*To be left out when administration without will annexed has been granted.]

NOMINATION

A6.68

63. Nomination of a second administrator; lack of mental capacity within the meaning of the Mental Capacity Act 2005 and minority or life interest (NCPR 35(3))

(*Heading as in Form 1*)

1. A B of   deceased, died on the   day of   20   domiciled in England and Wales having made and duly executed his last will and testament bearing date the   day of   20 ;

2. C D the sole executor and residuary legatee and devisee named in the said will lacks capacity within the meaning of the Mental Capacity Act 2005 to manage her property and affairs;

3. I, E F, am the person authorised by the Court of Protection to apply for a grant of representation of the estate of the said deceased for the use and benefit of the said C D [or No one has been authorised by the Court of Protection to apply for a grant of representation of the estate of the said deceased for the use and benefit of the said C D and I, E F, am her lawful attorney acting under a registered enduring power/registered lasting power of attorney];

4. A life [or a minority] interest arises under the said will;

5. I, the said E F, hereby nominate G H of   to be my co-administrator in the estate of the said deceased, he being a fit and proper person to act in that capacity.

Dated this   day of   20   .

Signed by the said E F

in the presence of

[Name and address of witness.]

[Note.–

This form can be adapted where the person nominating is the person entitled to the residuary estate or where the deceased died intestate.]

NOTICES

A6.69

64. Form 6
Notice of Election to Redeem Life Interest
Rule 56

In the High Court of Justice Family Division

The Principal (or   District Probate) Registry

In the estate of   deceased.

Whereas   of   died on the   day of   20   wholly/partially intestate leaving me his/her/lawful   wife/husband/civil   partner and   his/her issue;

And whereas Probate/Letters of Administration of the estate of the said   were granted to me, the said   (and to   of   ) at the Probate Registry on the   day of   20 ;

And whereas (the said   has ceased to be a personal representative because   ) and I am (now) the sole personal representative;

Now I, the said   hereby given notice in accordance with section 47A of the Administration of Estates Act 1925 that I elect to redeem the life interest to which I am entitled in the estate of the late   by retaining £   its capital value, and £   the costs of the transaction.

Dated the   day of   20   .

(Signed)

To [senior district judge] of the Family Division.

[Form 6 in the First Schedule to the Non-Contentious Probate Rules 1987.]

OATHS

General notes.–

1 Except where otherwise stated, the following forms are applicable in cases where the deceased died on or after 1 January 1926.

Every oath should state the address including, if known, the postcode of the deceased.

In every oath to lead a grant of administration (with or without will annexed), the deponent must state whether there is a life interest or a minority interest (NCPR 8(4)).

Where there is a life interest or a minority interest, the grant must be made to a trust corporation, with or without an individual, or to not less than two individuals, unless it appears to the court to be expedient in all the circumstances to appoint an individual as sole administrator.

Where the death occurred on or after 1 January 1926, in every oath to lead a grant of probate or administration (with or without will annexed), the deponent must swear to the best of his knowledge, information and belief whether there was land vested in the deceased which was settled previously to his death (and not by his will) and which remained settled land notwithstanding his death (NCPR 8(3)).

The name, address and occupation of the deponent or status (if a female with no occupation) and, in certain cases, his relationship to the deceased, if any, must be shown (see para 4.94).

Every oath must state the age and where the deceased died in the United Kingdom and the death was recorded in the Register of Deaths the name and dates of birth and death as recorded in the Register should be given. If the deceased was known by any different names those names should also be included in the oath. In those cases in which the exact age is not known, the applicant should give the best estimate he can (Practice Directions [1981] 2 All ER 832, [1981] 1 WLR 1185, [1999] 1 All ER 832).

2 Excepted Estates:
   (i)   Where the deceased died on and after 5 April 2004 and the gross value plus chargeable value of any transfers does not exceed the prevailing

IHT threshold the gross value of the estate should be recited as not exceeding the prevailing threshold and the net value should be rounded up to the next whole thousand and expressed as 'not exceeding £...' (President's Direction 23 March 2002);

(ii) where the deceased died on or after 5 April 2004 and the gross value plus chargeable value of transfers does not exceed £1,000,000 and the net chargeable estate after deduction of spouse and/or charity exemptions only is less than the prevailing IHT threshold the exact gross and net values of the estate should be included in the oath and

(iii) where the deceased died before 5 April 2004 the gross value of the estate should continue to be expressed as not exceeding the prevailing limit for the date of death and the net value should be rounded up to the next whole thousand as in (i) above

3. In order to reduce the volume of applications which are stopped or rejected the following checks are suggested before probate papers are submitted to the probate registry. The practitioner should check that:

(i) correct personal details are included in the oath: complete names and any aliases of the deceased are accounted for, identity of the applicant is verified if a different name is used in the will, addresses, dates of birth and death and correct gross and net values of the estate as on the IHT form are included and in appropriate cases the 'excepted estate' clause;

(ii) clearing and title is correct;

(iii) holes, tears or mark are accounted for—by affidavit evidence of plight and condition or if acceptable to the registrar by certifying that nothing of a testamentary nature was attached;

(iv) papers appropriate to the application are complete: the oath, original will and codicil(s) together with two A4 clear plain copies of each testamentary paper, original renunciation(s), power(s) of attorney, IHT205/421 and fee.

A6.71

66. Oath for probate (general form)

(Heading as in Form 1)

I, C D [or we C D and E F] of   make oath and say that:

1. I [we] believe the paper writing now produced to and marked by me [us] to contain the true and original last will and testament [with two codicils, *or as the case may be*] of A B of   formerly of   deceased, who was born on the   day of   19   and who died on the   day of   20   aged   years, domiciled in England and Wales;

2. To the best of my [our] knowledge, information and belief, there was [no] land vested in the said deceased which was settled previously to his death, and not by his will, and which remained settled land notwithstanding his death*;

3. I am [We are] the son[s] of the said deceased and the sole executor [or two of the executors] [or the surviving executors] named in the said will;

[4. Notice of this application has been given to the executor(s) to whom power is to be reserved, save   **;]

5. I [We] will:
   (i) collect, get in and administer according to law the real and personal estate of the said deceased;
   (ii) when required to do so by the Court exhibit in the Court a full inventory of the said estate and render an account thereof to the Court; and
   (iii) when required to do so by the High Court, deliver up to that Court the grant of probate;
6. To the best of my [our] knowledge, information and belief the gross estate passing under the grant [does not exceed/amounts to] £   and that the net estate [does not exceed/amounts to] £   [and that this is not a case in which an Inland Revenue account is required to be delivered].

Sworn by (both) the

above-named deponent(s)

at

this   day of   20

Before me,

A Commissioner for Oaths.

[*If there is settled land, a general executor may take a grant 'save and except settled land' on swearing simply that there was such settled land, but the value of the settled land must not be included in the oath. In such a case the word 'estate' should be followed by the words 'save and except settled land' in each place where it occurs. For form of oath for probate save and except settled land where there has been a previous grant limited to settled land, see No. 85.

**Where there are several executors and they do not all prove, power is reserved to the non-proving executors. See paras 4.53 ff as to the requirements for giving notice to the other executor(s) or dispensing with giving such notice and the relevant statement in the oath.

The alternatives so marked should be deleted as appropriate. In those cases in which an Inland Revenue account is not required to be delivered (see Ch 8, and the Capital Transfer Tax (Delivery of Accounts) (Excepted Estate) Regulations), it will be sufficient to state in the oath the threshold figures into which the estate falls (see paras 4.199 and 4.200).]

A6.98

93. Oath for administrators—net estate exceeding £125,000 for death on or after 1 December 2005: civil partner and minor child survive: application by civil partner who has parental responsibility for minor and nominated co-administrator

(*Heading as in Form 1*)

We, C D, of   and E F, of   make oath and say that:

1. A B of   deceased, was born on the   day of   19   and died on the   day of   20   aged   years domiciled in England and Wales intestate, leaving the said C D, his[her] lawful civil partner and G H, his [her] son, together the only persons entitled to share in his [her] estate;

2. The said G H is now a minor of the age of   years;

3. There is no parent, guardian, special guardian, adoption agency local authority or any other person with parental responsibility for the said minor;

4. The said C D is the step-parent of the minor and has acquired parental responsibility for him under s 4A of the Children Act 1989 under an order [*or* under a duly recorded parental responsibility agreement];

5. A minority and a life interest arise under the intestacy;

6. To the best of our knowledge, information and belief there was no land vested in the said deceased which was settled previously to his [her] death and which remained settled land notwithstanding his [her] death;

7. I, the said E F, am the person nominated by the said C D as co-administrator of the estate of the said deceased;

8. We will:

   (i) collect, get in and administer [etc– *complete as in Form 90*].

[When the father or step-parent is relying on s 4 or 4A of the Children Act 1989 a sealed copy of the order or of the recorded parental responsibility agreement, as the case may be, must be produced on the application.]

A6.106

101. Oath for administration to child or other issue having a beneficial interest—no surviving spouse [civil partner*]

(*Heading as in Form 1*)

I, C D, of   make oath and say that:

1. A B of   deceased, was born on the   day of   19   and died on the   day of   19   /20   aged   years, domiciled in England and Wales, intestate, a widow [*or* a widower] [*or* a surviving civil partner*] [*or* a single man] [*or* a single woman] [*or* a bachelor] [*or* a spinster];

2. No life or minority interest arises under the intestacy;

3. [*add statement as to settled land*];

4. I am the son [*or* daughter] and the only person entitled to the estate [*or* one of the persons entitled to share in the estate] of the said intestate;

[*Or* I am the grandson [*or* granddaughter] (being the son [*or* daughter] of E F, the son [*or* daughter] of the said intestate who died in the lifetime of the said intestate) [*or* the son [*or* daughter] of E F, the son [*or* daughter] of the said intestate who died in the lifetime of the said intestate] and the only person entitled to the estate [*or* one of the persons entitled to share in the estate] of the said intestate;]

5. I will:

(i) collect, get in and administer [etc– *complete as* Form 90].

* Death on or after 5 December 2005.

[For additional wording which must be included in the oath when the deceased was a divorced man or woman or person whose civil partnership was dissolved, see Form 66 and Form 108 respectively and para 6.127.]

A6.125

120. Oath for administration to attorneys of intestate's husband or widow or civil partner

(*Heading as in Form 1*)

We, C D of   and F G of   make oath and say that:

1. A B of   deceased, was born on the   day of   19   and died on the   day of   20   aged   years, domiciled in England and Wales, intestate, leaving E B her lawful husband [*or* his lawful widow][*or* his/her lawful civil partner];
2. No minority but a life interest arises under the intestacy;
3. [*add statement as to settled land*];
4. We are the lawful attorneys of the said E B [*and if acting under an enduring power of attorney/registered lasting power of attorney*] acting under an enduring power of attorney which has not been registered and E B remains mentally capable of managing his affairs *or* registered lasting power of attorney and E B does not lack capacity to manage his affairs;
5. We will:
    (i) collect, get in and administer according to law the real and personal estate of the said deceased for the use and benefit of the said E B until further representation be granted;
    (ii) when required to do so by the Court, exhibit in the Court a full inventory of the said estate and render an account thereof to the Court; and
    (iii) when required to do so by the High Court, deliver up to the Court the grant of letters of administration;

[*etc as in Form 66*].

A6.126

121. Oath for administration to attorney of intestate's father or mother

(*Heading as in Form 1*)

I, C D, of   make oath and say that:

1. A B of   deceased, was born on the   day of   19   and died on the   day of   20   aged   years, domiciled in England and Wales intestate, a bachelor [spinster] [widower] [widow] [surviving civil partner] [single person] without issue or any other person entitled in priority to share in the estate by virtue of any enactment, leaving E F, his [or her] father [or mother] and the only person entitled to his [or her] estate;
2. No minority or life interest arises under the intestacy;
3. [add statement as to settled land];
4. I am the lawful attorney of the said E F [and if acting under an enduring power of attorney or lasting power of attorney] acting under an enduring power of attorney or which has not been registered and E B remains mentally capable of managing his affairs or does not lack capacity to manage his affairs;
5. I will:
    (i) collect, get in and administer according to law the real and personal estate of the said deceased, for the use and benefit of the said E F until further representation be granted;
    (ii) when required to do so by the Court exhibit in the Court a full inventory of the said estate and render an account thereof to the Court; and
    (iii) when required to do so by the High Court, deliver up to that Court the grant of letters of administration;

[etc as in Form 66].

[For additional wording which must be included in the oath when the deceased was a divorced man or woman or person whose civil partnership was dissolved, see Form 107/8 and para 6.127.]

A6.127

122. Oath for administration to attorneys of intestate's child—another child being a minor

(Heading as in Form 1)

We, C D of   and G H of   make oath and say that:
1. A B of   deceased, was born on the   day of   19   and died on the   day of   20   aged   years, domiciled in England and Wales intestate, a widow [or a widower][or a surviving civil partner] leaving E F her [or his] son and one of the persons entitled to share in her [or his] estate;
2. A minority but no life interest arises under the intestacy;
3. [add statement as to settled land];
4. We are the lawful attorneys of the said E F [and if acting under an enduring power of attorney or registered lasting power of attorney] acting under an enduring power of attorney which has not been registered or registered lasting power of attorney and E F remains mentally capable of managing his affairs or does not lack capacity to manage his affairs within the meaning of the Mental Capacity Act 2005;

5. We will:

    (i)   collect, get in and administer according to law the real and personal estate of the said deceased, for the use and benefit of the said E F until further representation be granted;

    (ii)   when required to do so [etc– *complete as in* Form 90].

[*See note* to Form 91.]

A6.129

124. Oath for administrator (grantee having become mentally incapable) or (grantee subsequently lacks capacity within the meaning of the Mental Capacity Act 2005 to manage his affairs)

(*Heading as in Form 1*)

I, C D, of   make oath and say that:

1. A B of   deceased, was born on the   day of   19   and died on the   day of   20   aged   years, domiciled in England and Wales, intestate, a widower [*or as the case may be*];

2. On the   day of   20   letters of administration of the estate of the said deceased were granted at the Principal [*or*   District Probate] Registry to E B, the son and only person entitled to the estate of the said deceased;

3. The said E B is now by reason of mental incapacity incapable of managing his affairs *or* now lacks capacity within the meaning of the Mental Capacity Act 2005 to manage his affairs, no person has been authorised by the Court of Protection to apply for a grant in the estate of the said deceased, and part of the estate of the said deceased remains unadministered;

4. [*add statement as to minority and life interests*];

5. [*add statement as to settled land*];

6. I am the lawful attorney of the said E B acting under a registered enduring power of attorney *or* lasting power of attorney;

7. I will:

    (i)   collect, get in and administer according to law the unadministered estate of the said deceased, for the use and benefit of the said E B and during his incapacity *or* while he lacks capacity;

    (ii)   when required to do so by the Court, exhibit in the Court a full inventory of the said estate and render an account thereof to the Court; and

(iii) when required to do so by the High Court, deliver up to that Court the grant of letters of administration;

[*etc as in Form 90 , but with reference to the unadministered estate*].

[Note.–

This form may be adapted for use where the former grantee was one of the persons entitled to share in the estate, in which case the applicant should be one of the other persons entitled to share.]

A6.130

125. Oath for administrator (a former grant having been revoked)

(*Heading as in Form 1*)

I, C D, of   make oath and say that:

1. A B of   deceased, was born and died on the   day of   20   aged   years, domiciled in England and Wales intestate, a widower [surviving civil partner], without issue, parent, or brother or sister of the whole blood or any other person entitled in priority to share in his estate by virtue of any enactment [*or as the case may be*];

2. Letters of administration of the estate of the said deceased were, on the   day of   20   granted at the Principal [*or* District Probate] Registry to E F, the cousin german of the whole blood of the said deceased, on the basis that the said deceased died intestate, a widower, without issue, parent, brother or sister of the whole or half blood or their issue, grandparent or uncle or aunt of the whole blood or any other person entitled in priority to share in the estate by virtue of any enactment, and that the said E F was one of the persons entitled to share in the estate of the said deceased;

3. The said letters of administration have been since voluntarily brought in by or on behalf of the said E F, and have been duly revoked and declared null and void;

4. [*add statement as to minority and life interests*];

5. [*add statement as to settled land*];

6. I am the nephew of the whole blood and one of the persons entitled to share in the estate of the said deceased;

7. I will:

   (i) collect, get in and administer [*etc– complete as in* Form 90].

A6.131

126. Oath for administration to mother of minor and nominated co-administrator

(*Heading as in Form 1*)

We, E F of   and G H of   make oath and say that:

1. A B of   deceased, was born on the   day of   19   and died on the   day of   20   aged   years, domiciled in England and Wales intestate, a single man leaving C D his son and the only person entitled to his estate, who is now a minor aged   years;

2. The marriage of the said intestate with the deponent E F was dissolved by final decree of the High Court of Justice [*or* of the   County Court] in England and Wales dated the   day of   20   and that the said intestate did not thereafter remarry;

3. The said E F is the mother of the said minor and that there is no step-parent, guardian, special guardian of the said minor or adoption agency or local authority or any other person with parental responsibility for him;

4. That the said E F has by a nomination dated the   day of   20   nominated the deponent G H to be her co-administrator;

5. A minority but no life interest arises under the intestacy.

6. [*add statement as to settled land*];

7. We will:

    (i) collect, get in and administer according to law the real and personal estate of the said intestate, for the use and benefit of the said minor until he attains the age of eighteen years;

    (ii) when required to do so by the Court, exhibit in the Court a full inventory of the said estate and render an account thereof to the Court; and

    (iii) when required to do so by the High Court, deliver up to that Court the grant of letters of administration;

[*etc as in Form 90*].

[This form may be adapted where the mother has parental responsibility by virtue of an adoption order made within the meaning of s 12 of the Adoption Act 1976. The oath must state that she is the adopter or one of the adopters of the minor by such order and a copy of the order must be produced.]

A6.133

128. Oath for administration to step-parent of minor and nominated co-administrator

(*Heading as in Form 1*)

We E F of   and G H of   make oath and say that:

1. A B of   deceased, was born on the   day of   19   and died on the   day of   20   aged   years, domiciled in England and Wales intestate, a single woman leaving C D her son and the only person entitled to her estate who is now a minor aged   years;

2. The marriage of the said intestate with the deponent E F was dissolved by final decree of the High Court of Justice [*or* of the   County Court] in England and Wales dated the   day of   20   and the said intestate did not thereafter remarry;

3. The said E F is the step-mother of the said minor and has acquired parental responsibility for him under s 4A of the Children Act 1989 [by virtue of an order] [or parental responsibility agreement] which is subsisting;

4. There is no guardian or special guardian of the said minor or adoption agency or local authority or any other person with parental responsibility for him;

5. The said E F has by a nomination dated the   day of   19   /20   nominated the said G H to be her co-administrator;

6. A minority but no life interest arises under the intestacy;

7. [add statement as to settled land];

8. We will:

[as in *Form 126*]

A6.134

129. Oath for administration to guardian of minor and nominated co-administrator

(*Heading as in Form 1*)

We, C D of   and M N of   make oath and say that:

1. A B of   deceased, was born on the   day of   19   and died on the   day of   20   aged   years, domiciled in England and Wales intestate, a widow, leaving E B and G B, her children and the only persons entitled to share in her estate, who are both now minors, aged   years and   years respectively;

2. I B, deceased, the father of the said minors having parental responsibility for them, by his will dated the   day of   20   and proved on the   day of   20   at the Principal [or   District Probate] Registry, appointed the said C D to be guardian of his said children;

3. There is no other guardian or special guardian of the said minors or adoption agency or local authority or any other person with parental responsibility for them, or either of them;

4. The said C D has by an instrument in writing dated the   day of   19   /20   nominated the said M N to be his co-administrator;

5. A minority but no life interest arises under the intestacy;

6. [add statement as to settled land];

7. We will:

   (i) collect, get in and administer according to law the real and personal estate of the said intestate, for the use and benefit of the said minors, and until one of them attains the age of eighteen years;

   (ii) when required to do so [etc– *complete as in* Form 90].

[Note.–

This form may be adapted where the guardian has parental responsibility under one of the other parts of s 5 of the Children Act 1989 or in accordance with para 12, 13 or 14 of Sch 14 to that Act.]

A6.139

134. Oath for person appointed by the Court of Protection for use of a person who lacks capacity to manage his affairs within the meaning of the Mental Capacity Act 2005

(*Heading as in Form 1*)

I, C D, of   make oath and say that:

1. A B of   deceased, was born on the   day of   19   and died on the   day of   20   aged   years, domiciled in England and Wales intestate, a bachelor [spinster] [widower] [widow] [surviving civil partner][single person] without issue or any other person entitled in priority to share in the estate by virtue of any enactment leaving E B, his father and the only person entitled to his estate;
2. The said E B now lacks capacity to manage his affairs within the meaning of the Mental Capacity Act 2005;
3. I am the person authorised by an order of the Court of Protection dated the   day of   20   in the matter of the said E B, to apply for letters of administration of the estate of the said A B;
4. No minority or life interest arises under the intestacy;
5. [*add statement as to settled land*];
6. I will:
    (i) collect, get in and administer according to law the real and personal estate of the said deceased, for the use and benefit of the said E B until further representation be granted;
    (ii) when required to do so [etc– *complete as in* Form 90].

[Note.–

See also Form 124 for oath for further grant where original grantee becomes incapable.]

A6.140

135. Oath for administrator by attorney acting under a registered enduring power of attorney /registered lasting power of attorney

(*Heading as in Form 1*)

I, C D, of   make oath and say that:

1. A B of   deceased, was born on the   day of   19   and died on the   day of   20   aged   years, domiciled in England and Wales intestate, a widower [*or as the case may be*], leaving E F, his son and the only person entitled to his estate;

2. The said E F is now by reason of mental incapacity incapable of managing his affairs [*or* the said E F now lacks capacity to manage his affairs within the meaning of the Mental Capacity Act 2005];

3. No person has been authorised by the Court of Protection to apply for a grant in the estate of the said deceased;

4. No minority or life interest arises under the intestacy;

5. [*add statement as to settled land*];

6. I am the lawful attorney of the said E F, acting under a registered enduring power of attorney [*or* I am the lawful attorney of the said E F acting under a registered lasting power of attorney];

7. I will:

    (i) collect, get in and administer according to law the real and personal estate of the said deceased, for the use and benefit of the said E F until further representation be granted;

    (ii) when required to do so [etc– *complete as in* Form 90].

A6.141

136. Oath for administrators appointed by district judge or registrar for the use of a person who lacks capacity

(*Heading as in Form 1*)

We, C D of   and G H of   make oath and say that:

1. A B of   deceased, was born on the   day of   19   and died on the   day of   20   aged   years, domiciled in England and Wales intestate, a bachelor [spinster] [widower] [widow] [surviving civil partner][single person] without issue or parent or any other person entitled in priority to share in the estate by virtue of any enactment leaving E F, his brother of the whole blood and the only person entitled to his estate, who is now lacks capacity to manage his affairs within the meaning of the Mental Capacity Act 2005;

2. No minority or life interest arises under the intestacy;

3. [*add statement as to settled land*];

4. By order of Mr District Judge [*or* Registrar]   dated the   day of   20   it was ordered that letters of administration of the estate of the said deceased be granted to us under and by virtue of rule 35(4) of the Non-Contentious Probate Rules 1987, the grant to be for the use and benefit of the said E F limited until further representation be granted;

5. We will:

(i) collect, get in and administer according to law the real and personal estate of the said deceased, for the use and benefit of the said E F until further representation be granted;

(ii) when required to do so [etc– *complete as in* Form 90].

A6.154

149. Oath for administration—judicially separated spouse (death on or after 1 August 1970)

(*Heading as in Form 1*)

I, C D, of   make oath and say that:

1. A B of   deceased, was born on the   day of   19   and died on the   day of   20   aged   years, domiciled in England and Wales, intestate, leaving E F, his lawful widow [*or* her lawful husband];

2. By decree of the High Court of Justice [*or* of the   County Court] in England and Wales, dated the   day of   20   it was decreed that the said A B be judicially separated from the said E F;

3. At the date of death of the said deceased the said decree remained in force and the separation thereunder continued;

4. [*Insert clearings, e.g.* The said deceased died without issue or parent or any other person entitled in priority to share in the estate by virtue of any enactment;]

5. [*Add statement as to minority and life interests.*]

6. [*Add statement as to settled land.*]

7. I am the brother of the whole blood and only person entitled to [*or* one of the persons entitled to share in] the estate of the said deceased;

8. I will:

    (i) collect, get in and administer [etc– *complete as in* Form 90].

A6.155

150 Oath for administration—judicially separated civil partner (death on or after 5 December 2005)

(*Heading as in Form 1*)

I, C D, of   make oath and say that:

1. A B of   deceased, was born on the   day of   19   and died on the   day of   20   aged   years, domiciled in England and Wales, intestate, leaving E F, his lawful civil partner;

2. By a separation order of the High Court of Justice [*or* of the   County Court] in England and Wales, dated the   day of   20   it was ordered that the said A B be y separated from the said E F;

3. At the date of death of the said deceased the said separation order remained in force and the separation thereunder continued;

4. [*Insert clearings, e.g.* The said deceased died without issue or parent or any other person entitled in priority to share in the estate by virtue of any enactment;]

5. [*Add statement as to minority and life interests.*]

6. [*Add statement as to settled land.*]

7. I am the sister of the whole blood and only person entitled to [*or* one of the persons entitled to share in] the estate of the said deceased;

8. I will:

    (i) collect, get in and administer [etc– *complete as in* Form 90].

A6.172

167. Oath for administration (will) to person authorised by Court of Protection where executor is lacks capacity to manage his affairs

(*Heading as in Form 1*)

I, C D, of   make oath and say that:

1. A B of   deceased, was born on the   day of   19   and died on the   day of   20   aged   years, domiciled in England and Wales, having made and duly executed his last will and testament and thereof appointed E F sole executor;

2. The said E F is now lacks capacity to manage his affairs within the meaning of the Mental Capacity Act 2005;

3. By an order of the Court of Protection dated the   day of   20   I was duly authorised to apply for letters of administration (with will) of the estate of the said deceased for the use and benefit of the said E F;

4. [*add statement as to minority or life interest*];

5. [*add statement as to settled land*];

6. I believe the paper writing now produced to and marked by me to contain the true and original last will and testament of the said deceased;

7. I will:

    (i) collect, get in and administer according to law the real and personal estate of the said deceased for the use and benefit of the said E F until further representation be granted;

    (ii) when required to do so by the Court [etc– *complete as in* Form 151].

A6.173

168. Oath for administration (will) to attorney acting under a registered enduring power of attorney or registered lasting power of attorney; for the use executor who lacks capacity

(Heading as in Form 1)

I, C D, of   make oath and say that:

1. A B of   deceased, was born on the   day of   19   and died on the   day of   20   aged   years, domiciled in England and Wales, having made and duly executed his last will and testament;

2. E F, the sole executor named in the said will, is now by reason of mental incapacity incapable of managing his affairs [or now lacks capacity to manage his affairs within the meaning of the Mental Capacity Act 2005];

3. No one has been authorised by the Court of Protection to apply for a grant of representation of the estate of the said deceased for the use and benefit of the said E F;

4. I am the lawful attorney of the said E F acting under a registered enduring power of attorney [or I am the lawful attorney of the said E F acting under a registered lasting power of attorney];

5. [add statement as to minority or life interest];

6. [add statement as to settled land];

7. I believe the paper writing now produced to and marked by me to contain the true and original last will and testament of the said deceased;

8. I will:

   (i) collect, get in and administer according to law the real and personal estate of the said deceased for the use and benefit of the said E F until further representation be granted;

   (ii) when required to do so [etc– complete as in Form 151].

A6.174

169. Oath for administration (will) to person entitled to the residuary estate; for the use of executor who lacks capacity within the meaning of the Mental Capacity Act 2005

(Heading as in Form 1)

I, C D, of   make oath and say that:

1. A B of   deceased, was born on the   day of   19   and died on the   day of   20   aged   years, domiciled in England and Wales, having made and duly executed his last will and testament;

2. E F, the sole executor named in the said will, is now lacks incapacity to manage his affairs within the meaning of the Mental Capacity Act 2005;

3. No one has been authorised by the Court of Protection to apply for a grant of representation of the estate of the said deceased for the use and benefit of the said E F;

4. There is no lawful attorney of the said E F acting under a registered lasting power of attorney *or* registered enduring power of attorney [*or* G H, the lawful attorney of the said E F acting under a registered lasting power of attorney/ registered enduring power of attorney, has renounced administration for the use and benefit of the said E F];

5. I am the residuary legatee and devisee named in the said will;

6. [*add statement as to minority or life interest*];

7. [*add statement as to settled land*];

8. I believe the paper writing now produced to and marked by me to contain the true and original last will and testament of the said deceased;

9. I will:

   (i) collect, get in and administer according to law the real and personal estate of the said deceased for the use and benefit of the said E F until further representation be granted;

   (ii) when required to do so [etc– *complete as in* Form 151].

A6.175

170. Oath for administration (will) under s 116 of the Senior Courts Act 1981

(*Heading as in Form 1*)

I, C D, of   make oath and say that:

1. A B of   deceased, was born on the   day of   19   and died on the   day of   19   /20   aged   years, domiciled in England and Wales, having made and duly executed his last will and testament;

2. On the   day of   20   it was ordered by Mr District Judge [Registrar]   of this Division that letters of administration (with will annexed) of the estate of the said deceased be granted to me under and by virtue of s 116 of the Senior Courts Act 1981 [*recite any limitations given in order*];

3. [Add statement as to life and minority interests.]

4. [Add statement as to settled land.]

5. I believe the paper writing now produced to and marked by me to contain the true and original last will and testament of the said deceased;

6. I will:

   (i) collect, get in and administer according to law the real and personal estate of the said deceased [*add, if applicable*, limited as aforesaid];

   (ii) when required to do so by the Court [etc– *complete as in* Form 151].

511

A6.178A

173A.

Oath for administration (will) to legatee in accordance with NCPR 30(3)(b); whole or substantially whole estate in England and Wales consists of immoveable property

(*Heading as in Form 1*)

I, C D, of   make oath and say that:

1. I believe the paper writing now produced to and marked by me to contain the true and original last will and testament of A B of   deceased, who was born on the   day of   19   and who died on the   day of   /20   aged   years, domiciled in Spain;

2. E F, the sole executor named in the said will has renounced probate thereof [*and/or*, No executor, residuary legatee or devisee in trust or residuary legatee or devisee is named in the said will];

3. [*add statement as to minority and life interests*];

4. [*add statement as to settled land*];

5. The whole estate in England and Wales consists of immoveable estate;

6. I am the devisee named in the will entitled to the said estate;

. I will:

   (i) collect, get in and administer according to law the real and personal estate of the said deceased;

   (ii) when required to do so by the Court, exhibit in the Court a full inventory of the said estate and render an account thereof to the Court; and

   (iii) when required to do so by the High Court, deliver up to that Court the grant of letters of administration;

[*etc– complete as in Form 171.*]

[Note.–

*Where application is made by a legatee (or devisee) on the ground that substantially the whole estate is immoveable the case must be submitted to the district judge or registrar for his decision whether the facts bring the case within the terms of the rule, having regard to the size of the estate. The following statement should then be added at the end of the oath: '£   of the total value of the known estate of £   is immoveable estate'.

This form may be adapted where the deceased dies intestate]

A6.196

191. Renunciation by two members of a partnership

(*Heading as in Form 1*)

A B of   deceased, died on the   day of 20   having made and duly executed his last will and testament, bearing date the   day of 20 [and codicil bearing date the   day of 20] and thereof appointed as executors [and residuary legatees and devisees in trust]* the partners at the date of his death in the firm of C D and Co of   [*or* the firm which at that date had succeeded to and carried on its practice. At that date of death of the deceased the firm of E F & Co had succeeded to and was carrying on its practice.]**

The partners in the firm of C D and Co [E F & Co]** were

(*names of all partners who qualify as executors*)

We the said G H and J K of   with the authority of the other said partners do hereby declare that neither we nor any of the other said partners have intermeddled in the estate of the deceased and will not hereafter intermeddle therein with intent to defraud creditors, and we do hereby renounce all our and their right and title to probate and execution of the said will [and codicil][and to letters of administration (with the said will [and codicil]annexed) of the estate of the said deceased.]*

Signed by the said A B and C D as a deed this

day of   20   in the

presence of

(*Witnesses' names, addresses and occupations*)

[*These words must be included in the form where the executors are also entitled in the character (or any other lower character) under NCPR 20 and have to be cleared off in that character by the applicant for the grant (Registrar's Direction (1952) 27 November).]

[**Complete as appropriate if the renunciation is by the partners of a successor firm authorised by the will or if the firm has converted to an incorporated practice and members of the practice are the qualifying executors.]

SUBPOENAS

A6.203

198. Subpoena to bring in a testamentary document

(*Heading as in Form 1*)

Elizabeth the Second, by the grace of God, of the United Kingdom of Great Britain and Northern Ireland and of our other realms and territories Queen, Head of the Commonwealth, Defender of the Faith.

To   of

It appears by an affidavit of   Sworn on the   day of   and filed in the Principal Registry of the Family Division of our High Court of Justice [*or* in the   District Probate Registry], that a certain document, being or purporting to be testamentary, namely [*here describe the document*], bearing date the   day of   20   of A B, deceased, late of   who died on the   day of   20   is now in your possession, custody or power:

We command you that, within eight days after service hereof on you, inclusive of the day of such service, you do bring into and leave with the proper officer of the Principal Registry of the Family Division [*or* in the   District Probate Registry] aforesaid the said document now in the possession, custody or power of you the said   :

Witness, the Right Honourable [   ] Lord High Chancellor of Great Britain, the   day of   20   .

(Signed)

District Judge/Registrar.

Subpoena issued by   of   solicitor for

[*To be indorsed prominently on the front of the copy to be served:*] You the within-named   are warned that disobedience to this subpoena by the time therein limited would be a contempt of court punishable by imprisonment.

[*Also to be indorsed on the copy to be served:*]

1. N.B.– The Principal Registry of the Family Division of the High Court of Justice is at First Avenue House, High Holborn, London WC1V 6NP and the proper officer referred to is the Probate Manager [*or* The   District Probate Registry is at   and   the proper officer referred to is the Probate Manager].

2. If you the said   deny that the testamentary document(s) referred to is/are in your possession, custody or power, you may swear an affidavit to that effect and file it in the (issuing) registry. (*Registrar's Direction* (1989) 23 *June.*)

[For form of affidavit to lead subpoena, see Form 38.]

[For subpoena to bring in a testamentary document in a probate claim, see CP51: A6.259.]

Index

Access to Health Records Act 1990
    definitions,   A1.469–A1.470
Addition of parties
    Court of Probate,   28.04
Administration *ad colligenda bona*
    practice,   11.358
Administration *de bonis non*
    mentally incapable person, for,   13.48
Administration of Estates Act 1925
    definitions,   A1.127
Administration of Estates (Small Payment) (Increase of Limit) Orders
    1975,   A2.03–A2.05
    1984,   A2.34–A2.37
Administration pending determination of probate claim
    claim, grant limited to,   11.358
    practice,   11.356
Administration with will de bonis non
    legal proceedings, in respect of,   13.53
    legatee, to,   13.52
    mentally incapable person, for,   13.48
Administrator
    selection by court, dispute between executors,   14.13
    subsequent lack of capacity,   17.17–17.19
Adoption Act 1976
    general provisions
        status of adopted children,   A1.297
Adoption and Children Act 2002
    glossary,   A1.548
    minor and consequential amendments,   A1.547
    placement for adoption and adoption orders,   A1.517–A1.518
    registers,   A1.534
Affidavits
    forms, non-contentious business
        general heading,   A6.01
        proof of lack of capacity,   A6.29

Affidavits—*contd*
    rectification of will, supporting application for,   3.264
Agricultural property relief
    inheritance tax,   8.86–8.92
Alterations in valuation of estate
    administration before 1972
        affidavit of true value,   16.58
        further security,   16.57
        practice,   16.66
    grant marked by HMRC
        inheritance tax,   16.56
Amount of estate
    alterations in
        administration before 1972,   16.57–16.58, 16.66
        grant marked by HMRC inheritance tax,   16.56
    calculation
        assets,   8.59–8.63
        foreign property,   8.71
        liabilities,   8.69–8.70
        lifetime gifts,   8.57
    probates, and
        introduction,   4.202
        relevant estate,   4.218
        statement by applicant,   4.206
Applications
    ex parte, types of,   25.12
    mode of,   25.102–25.103
    notice, without,   25.12
Appointee of court, grants to
    use of persons under disability, for,   11.274–11.279
Assessment of costs
    non-contentious proceedings,   4.278
Association of Certified Chartered Accountants
    approved body, as,   1.32A, 2.03
Attorney
    limited grants to for use and benefit of person entitled,   11.31

Index

Attorneys, grants to
    form of oath, 11.80
    form of power, 11.40–11.42A
    substituted attorney, to, 11.65
    use and benefit of person entitled, for, 11.31

Births and Deaths Registration Act 1953
    general provisions, A1.148–A1.150

Blind testator
    evidence of execution, A2.52

Burden of proof
    want of knowledge and approval, as to, 34.50

Business property relief
    inheritance tax, 8.77

Calendars of grants
    searches, 21.01–21.02

Caveats
    warning A2.83

Cessate grants
    incapable executor, for, 13.92–13.93
    minors, and, 13.108
    persons under disability, 11.282
    recovery from incapacity, and, 13.111–13.115

Chain of executorship
    use and benefit of incapable executor, 4.81

Charity
    gift of residue to, 5.88A

Children
    parental responsibility agreements, A2.112–A2.115

Children Act 1989
    definitions, A1.463
    general provisions
        effect and duration of orders, A1.460
        parental responsibility, A1.448, A1.450A
        residence and contact, A1.455

Citations
    issue and service of, A2.85

Civil partnership
    contemplation of, will made in, 3.52
    jurisdiction, A2.130D–A2.130E
    recognition of judgments, A2.130F–A2.130L
    revocation of will by, 3.45

Civil Partnership Act 2004
    specified relationships, A1.567

Civil Procedure Rules 1995
    amendment, A2.190
    family provision claims,
        generally, A2.166–A2.168
        Practice Direction, A2.183–A2.187

Civil Procedure Rules 1995—*contd*
    probate claims,
        definitions, A2.153
        generally, A2.154–A2.163
        Practice Direction, A2.169–A2.176
        scope, A2.153
    rectification of wills,
        definitions, A2.153
        generally, A2.164
        Practice Direction, A2.177–A2.179
        scope, A2.153
    removal of personal representatives,
        definitions, A2.153
        generally, A2.165
        Practice Direction, A2.180–A2.182
        scope, A2.153
    substitution of personal representatives,
        definitions, A2.153
        generally, A2.165
        Practice Direction, A2.180–A2.182
        scope, A2.153

Clearance letters
    practice, 8.142

Colonial grants, resealing of
    application for, A2.78
    documents required, 18.71

Consular Conventions Act 1949
    application, A1.137

Contentious business
    addition of parties, Court of Probate, 28.04
    associated actions, removal of personal representative, 41.02
    Civil Procedure Rules
        definitions, A2.153
        generally, A2.154–A2.163
        Practice Direction, A2.169–A2.176
        prior to 15th October 2001, A2.136–A2.152
        scope, A2.153
    costs of propounding testamentary document, 40.10
    defences
        revocation of grants, 34.70
        want of knowledge and approval, 34.50
    denial of interest, 32.06
    hearings, place of, 39.01
    jurisdiction of county court, 26.12
    parties
        addition of, 28.04
        persons being, 28.01
    place of trial, 39.01
    removal of personal representative, 41.02
    statements of interest 32.06

Index

Copies of grant
    registration, for,   4.250
Copies of will for grant
    generally,   4.229–4.230
    need for,   4.231
Corrective accounts
    practice,   8.141
Costs of contentious business
    opposition to grant, unsuccessful
        parties,   40.13–40.14
    propounding a will, beneficiaries,   40.10
Costs of non-contentious business
    assessment,   4.278
    solicitor's charges,   4.272–4.277
    Orders,   A5.01–A5.20
Council of Licensed Conveyancers
    approved body, as,   2.03
    probate practice, rules for,   2.03
    statutory provisions,   A1.480A
County court
    jurisdiction,   26.12
County Courts Act 1984
    probate proceedings, effect of order
        of judge,   A1.394
Court of Protection
    authority of,   11.247–11.248
    person lacking capacity, notice
        of,   11.249–11.252
    replacement of,   11.237D, 11.246
    will for mentally disordered person
        exercise of powers,   3.440
        rules,   3.441
Courts and Legal Services Act 1990
    Council for Licensed
        Conveyancers,   A1.480A
Crown
    intended application for grant,
        notice of,   A2.78

De bonis non, grant
    papers required,   34.77
Death on active service
    inheritance tax relief,   8.109
Defences
    incapacity due to old age or
        illness,   34.31
    precedents
        incapacity,   34.31
        revocation,   34.70
    revocation of grants,   34.70
    want of knowledge and approval,
        burden of proof,   34.50
Deponent's details in grant
    change of name,   4.105A
Deposit of wills
    Regulations,
        citation,   A2.08
        definitions,   A2.09

Deposit of wills—*contd*
    Regulations—*contd*
        general provisions,   A2.10–A2.16
        schedules,   A2.17
District judge of Principal Registry
    applications without notice,   25.12
District probate registrars
    exercise of jurisdiction by another
        registrar,   A2.102
    applications without notice,   25.12
    jurisdiction
        administration pending suit,   2.65
    Order 1982,   A2.28–A2.33
District probate registries
    fees and tax, payment of,   2.79
    location,   2.59
Domicile and Matrimonial
    Proceedings Act 1973
    general provisions,   A1.240
Double taxation relief
    inheritance tax, on,   8.111, 8.116

Enduring power of attorney
    form of,   11.42, 11.42A, 11.259
    lawful attorney acting under,
        application for grant,   11.257–11.263
    lodging for inspection,   11.262
    loss or destruction of
        instrument,   A2.135Q
    non-registration, notification,   A2.135N
    objection or revocation not
        applying to all joint and
        several attorneys,   A2.135P
    registration,   11.260, A2.135K–A2.135O
    regulations,   11.41A, A2.135K–A2.135Q
    replacement of,   11.41, 11.23E
    statutory provision,   A1.591
Evidence of execution
    knowledge and approval,   3.133
Ex parte applications
    types of,   25.12
Execution of will (after 1963)
    evidence of knowledge and
        approval,   3.133
Execution of will in accord with
    law of place of execution
    definitions
        internal law,   3.408
Executors
    appointees
        incorporated practices,   4.48
        mental incapacity,   4.34
    appointment, form of,   4.49

Index

Executors—*contd*
  chain of executorship, and
    use and benefit of incapable
      executor, 4.81
  lack of capacity, 11.241, 11.242
  selection of administrator, disputes, 14.13
  subsequent lack of capacity, 17.16, 17.20

Executor's oath
  amount of estate
    death on and after 6 April
      2004, 4.204, 4.206–4.207
    introduction, 4.202
    relevant estate, 4.218
    statement by applicant, 4.206
  change of name
    deponent, 4.105A
  deponent's details
    change of name, 4.105A
  settling, 4.92

Family Division
  probate jurisdiction
    common form business, 1.32

Family Law Act 1986
  general provisions
    declaration of status, A1.416

Family Law Reform Act 1987
  general provisions
    general principle, A1.424
    parental rights and duties, A1.425
    property rights, A1.431

Family Provision (Intestate Succession) Orders
  1972, A2.01–A2.02
  1977, A2.06–A2.07
  1981, A2.18–A2.19
  1987, A2.38–A2.39
  1993, A2.116–A2.117
  2009, A2.135U–A2.135V

Fees
  grant of probate, for
    grant, on, 4.260
    remission, 4.261
  non-contentious probate, Order, A3.01–A3.11
  table of, 1.44, 1.45

Forms
  non-contentious probate
    affidavits
      general heading, A6.01
      proof of lack of capacity, A6.29
      county court form, A6.64
      nominations, A6.68
      notices, A6.69

Forms—*contd*
  non-contentious probate—*contd*
    oaths
      administrator appointed by
        district judge or registrar
        for use of person lacking
        capacity, A6.141
      attorney of intestate's child, A6.127
      attorney of intestate's father or
        mother, A6.126
      attorney of intestate's
        husband, widow or civil
        partner, A6.125
      child or other issue having
        beneficial interest, A6.106
      civil partner, A6.98
      executor lacking capacity, A6.174
      former grant having been
        revoked, A6.130
      general form, A6.71
      grantee having become
        mentally incapable or
        lacking capacity, A6.129
      guardian of minor and
        nominated
        co-administrator, A6.134
      judicially separated civil
        partner, A6.155
      judicially separated spouse, A6.154
      mother of minor and
        nominated
        co-administrator, A6.131
      person appointed by Court of
        Protection, A6.139, A6.172
      registered enduring/lasting
        power of attorney,
        attorney acting under, A6.140, A6.173
      step-parent of minor and
        nominated
        co-administrator, A6.133

Gender Recognition Act 2004
  appeals, A1.548I
  applications, A1.548A–A1.548H
  certificates, A1.548J–A1.548K
  definitions, A1.548Z
  general provisions, A1.548L–A1.548Y

Government debt
  small sums, and, 1.82

Grant in common form
  issue (district registries)
    applicants, 2.71
    lodging papers, 2.71
    postal applications, 2.71
  issue (Principal Registry)
    applicants, 2.03
    settling documents, 2.06

Index

Grant in common form—*contd*
payment without
    government debt, 1.82
    National Debt annuities, 1.82
    savings bank annuities, 1.82
procedure (district registries)
    applicants, 2.71
    fees and tax payment, 2.79
procedure (Principal Registry)
    applicants, 2.03
small sums
    government debt, 1.82
    National Debt annuities, 1.82
    savings bank annuities, 1.82
Guarantees
    application for leave to sue on, A2.79

Hearings
    contentious business, place of, 39.01
Her Majesty's Revenue and Customs
    regulations by, 8.02
Human Fertilisation and Embryology Act 2008
    application of provisions, A1.592B
    father, meaning, A1.592C– A1.592I
    general provisions, A1.592X–A1.592Z
    marriage or civil partnership,
        reference to, A1.592Q– A1.592R
    mother, meaning, A1.592A
    parental orders, A1.592V– A1.592W
    registration, A1.592S– A1.592T
    woman to be other parent, A1.592J–A1.592Q, A1.592U

IHT200
    reporting procedures, 8.3G
IHT205
    revised version of, 8.02
Impounding grant
    abandonment 17.67
Incapable executor
    cessate grants, 13.92–13.93
Incapable person
    impounding grant, abandonment 17.67
    executors, as, 4.34
    renunciation
        attorney, by, 15.46
        Court of Protection appointee,
            by, 15.43–15.45
        revocation, 17.64–17.66
Incapacity of grantee(s)
    defences, old age or illness, 34.31
    revocation of grant
        one of two or more grantees, 17.13–17.20
        sole grantee, 17.64–17.66

Inheritance provision, orders for
Civil Procedure Rules,
    generally, A2.166–A2.168
    Practice Direction, A2.183–A2.187
    Rules of the Supreme Court, A2.189
Inheritance tax (IHT)
    account summary, receipt, 2.79
    alteration in amount o estate, 4.212
    credit, grant on, 8.23
    current forms, 8.25
    delivery of accounts,
        1981 Regulations, A2.20–A2.27
        2004 Regulations, A2.118–A2.128
    estate for purposes of, 8.09
    exemptions, 8.25
    Finance Act 1986, A1.616
    gifts with reservation, 8.143
    indexation, A2.129–A2.130
    instalment-option property, 8.23
    interests including settled property, 8.74
    payment, 2.15A, 8.133
    payment before grant
        exceptions, 8.23
        postponement, 8.24
    payment from bank or building
        society account, 4.255
    personal applicant, completion and
        preparation of forms by, 2.97
    postal remittance, 2.15
    pre-owned assets, treatment of, 8.143
    property removed from scope, 8.10
    provisional, grants for, 8.18
    rates, 8.13, A1.597, A4.10
    Regulations
        delivery of accounts (1981), A2.20–A2.27
        delivery of accounts (2004), A2.118–A2.128
    reliefs
        agricultural property, 8.86–8.92
        business property, 8.77
        death on active service, 8.109
        double taxation, 8.111, 8.116
        introduction, 8.76
        quick succession, 8.118
    scope, 8.06–8.11
    variations in distribution of
        estate, 8.101
    reporting procedures, 8.34G
    settled property, treatment of
        interests in, 8.11, A1.598
    valuation of assets, 8.63
Inheritance Tax Act 1984
    general provisions, A1.595– A1.611

Index

Inland Revenue (IR) account
  administration
    assessment
      generally, 8.124–8.130
      introduction, 8.122–8.123
    Cap A5C
      generally, 8.34–8.34J
      not used, where, 8.34D
      obtaining, 8.34E
      revocation of grant, 8.34D
      subsequent grant, application
        for, 8.34–8.34C
    Cap A5N, 8.34E
    clearance letters, 8.142
    completion, 8.48
      valuation of estate, 8.63
    corrections, 8.141
    delivery of accounts,
      1981 Regulations, A2.20–A2.27
      2004 Regulations, A2.118–A2.128
    examination, 8.136–8.140
    excepted estate, 8.02–8.03, A2.131–A2.135
    forms
      Cap A5C, 8.34–8.34J
      Cap A5N, 8.34E
      Current, 8.25
    IHT200
      payment, 8.133
      scope, 8.06–8.11
      valuation of estate, 8.63
    IHT400, 8.26–8.31
    payment of tax, 8.133, 8.135
      bank or building society account,
        from, 4.255
    personal application, 2.97
    practice, completion of account, 8.48
    Regulations,
      delivery of accounts, A2.20–A2.27
    reporting procedures, 8.34G
Intestacy
  distribution of estate
    death on or after 1 January
      1926, 6.39–6.40, 6.44
    statutory trusts, failure of, 6.86
    equal rights to apply for grant, 8.34H
    issue of intestate, distribution to, 6.52
    order of priority for grant, A2.61
    person entitled on lacking
      capacity, 11.270–11.271
    spouse of civil partner of intestate
      lacking capacity, 11.272–11.273
    surviving, failure of kin within
      classes entitled to share, 6.85

Intestacy—*contd*
  succession
    family provision Rules. *See*
      Family Provision (Intestate
      Succession) Orders
    interest and capitalisation,
      Rules, A2.07A–A2.07D
Intestates' Estates Act 1952
  provisions of,, A1.147
IR account
  assessment, 2.14, 8.130
  Cap A5C
    generally, 8.34–8.34J
    not applicable, second or
      subsequent grant, 8.38
    not used, where, 8.34D
    obtaining, 8.34E
    revocation of grant, 8.34D, 8.36
    subsequent grant, application
      for, 8.34–8.34C
  clearance letters, 8.142
  completion, 8.45–8.52
    valuation of estate, 8.63
  corrections, 8.141
  delivery of accounts,
    1981 Regulations, A2.20–A2.27
    2004 Regulations, A2.117–A2.128
  excepted estate, 8.02–8.03, A2.131–A2.135
  forms
    Cap A5C, 8.34–8.34J
    Cap A5N, 8.34E
    IHT205, 8.02
    Obtaining, 8.44
  inheritance tax, and
    payment, 8.133
    scope, 8.06–8.11
    valuation of estate, 8.63
  intestacy, equal rights to apply on, 8.34H
  minority grant, 8.34I
  necessity for, 8.01
  no estate other than trust property, 8.33
  no known next of kin, grant for
    estate with, 8.34J
  PA1, submission of, 8.34F
  payment of tax
    before grant, 8.17–8.24
    generally, 8.133
  personal applications, 2.97, 8..01B
  practice
    completion of account, 8.48
  pre-owned assets, treatment of, 8.143
  reporting procedures, 8.34G
  reservation of benefit, 8.143
  settled land, 8.32

Index

IR account—*contd*
  solicitor applications, 8.01A

Joint wills
  revocation, 3.222

Jurisdiction of court
  county court, 26.12

Knowledge and approval
  evidence of execution, and, 3.133

Lasting power of attorney
  attorney, renunciation by, 15.46
  certificates, A2.135F, A2.135G
  enduring power, replacement of, 11.41, 11.237E
  execution of instrument, A2.135H
  form of, 11.42A, 11.237E
  lawful attorney acting under,
    application for grant, 11.263A–11.263E
    lodging for inspection, 11.263D, A2.135I, A2.135J
  regulations, A2.135E–A2.135J
  statutory provision, A1.583
Legitimacy Act 1976, A1.281–A1.282
Letters of administration, grant of
  additional administrator,
    subsequent appointment of, 6.23
  administrator's oath,
    death after 1925 but before 5 April 1988, description of applicant, 6.386
  adopted persons, to, 6.246
  applicant, description of, 6.384–6.385
  child en ventre sa mère, where, 6.122
  children or other issue, grants to, 6.170, 6172
  civil partner, to, 6.37, 6.45, 6.95
  husband or wife, to, 6.45, 6.95–6.96
  impounding, abandonment 17.67
  legitimated persons, to,
    children of void marriage, 6.221A
  number of administrators, 6.21
  persons entitled where intestacy since January 1926, 6.37
  revocation
    incapable person, 17.64–17.66
    to whom granted, 6.17–6.18
    children or other issue, 6.170A–6.175
    creditor, to, 6.369
Letters of administration (will annexed), grant of
  circumstances of grant, 5.01–5.02
  deeds of assignment executed before 1 December 2003, 5.249

Letters of administration (will annexed), grant of—*contd*
  grant to persons entitled to share in undisposed-of estate, 5.192–5.205
  impounding, abandonment 17.67
  minor or person lacking capacity, for, 5.258
  oath
    minority or life interest, 5.266
    order of property, 5.08
  persons entitled to share in undisposed-of estate
    deceased left surviving spouse or civil partner, 5.192–5.202
    failure of gift over, 5.204, 5.205
    no surveying spouse or civil partner, 5.203
  persons interested in residuary estate,
    adopted person, 5.60, 5.73, 5.78
    gift to charities, 5.88A
  revocation, incapable person, 17.64–17.66
  to whom granted
    death by murder or manslaughter, 5.187
Life interests
  attorney of spouse and person having interest joined, 7.35
  one of several children of full age, and, 7.29
  surviving spouse or civil partner, and, 7.25
Life interests, election for redemption of
  notice of election A2.95, A2.110
  surviving spouse or civil partner, right of, 16.36
Limited grants
  attorneys, to, 11.31–11.80
  minors, for use of, 11.159
  persons under disability, for use and benefit of, 11.237–11.282
Limited liability partnership
  appointment as executor, 4.47
Living persons, wills of
  deposit
    depositories, 20.01

Mariners, wills by
  'at sea', 3.376
Manslaughter
  administration with will annexed, and, 5.187
Mental Capacity Act 2005
  deprivation of liberty, A1.586A
  enduring powers of attorney, A1.591
  lasting powers of attorney,, A1.583

Index

Mental Health Act 1983
  repealed provisions,   A1.387–A1.391
Mentally disordered persons, wills for
  Court of Protection, exercise of
    powers of,   3.440
  Court of Protection rules,   3.441
  effect,   3.455
  execution,   3.442
  Mental Capacity Act 2005,   3.438–3.441
  power to make,   3.438–3.441
Minority interests
  attorney of spouse and person
    having interest joined,   7.35
  district judge's or registrar's order
    not required,   7.23
  one of several children of full age,   7.28–7.29
  surviving spouse or civil partner,
    and,   7.25
Minors
  cessate grant   13.108
  grant on behalf of,   A2.71
    co-executor, as   A2.72
    generally,   11.123–11.124
    renunciation,   A2.73
  renunciation
    attorney, by,   15.46
    Court of Protection appointee,
      by,   15.43–15.45
Minors, grants for use of
  adoptive parents, to,   11.159, 11.163
  generally,   11.123–11.124
  parents, to,   11.149, 11.152, 11.159–11.163
Murder
  administration with will annexed,
    and,   5.187
Mutual wills
  revocation,   3.222

National Debt annuities
  small sums, and,   1.82
National insurance benefits
  small sums, an,   1.91–1.92
Nominations
  forms,   A6.68
Non-contentious business
  administrator, joinder,   A2.64
  appeals,   A2.105
  application for grant,   A2.43–A2.45
  citations,   A2.85–A2.87
  costs
    orders for,   A2.102
    taxation,   A2.99
  fees
    Order,   A3.01–A3.11
    table of,   1.44–1.45
  foreign law, evidence of,   A2.58

Non-contentious business—*contd*
  forms
    affidavits
      general heading,   A6.01
      Inland Revenue, certificate of
        delivery,   A2.110
      proof of lack of capacity,   A6.29
    appearance to warning or
      citation,   A2.110
    caveat,   A2.110
    election to redeem life interest,   A2.110
    standing search,   A2.110
    warning to caveator,   A2.110
  Long Vacation, exercise of powers
    during,   A2.104
  method of application,   25.102–25.103
  order of priority of grant,   A2.59, A2.62–A2.67
  order to attend for examination,   A2.89
  pending proceedings,   A2.108
  personal representatives,
    additional,   A2.65
  probate action,   A2.84
  rules,   1.42–1.43, A2.40–A2.111
  service of summons,   A2.106
  settled land, and,   A2.68
  summons, application by,   A2.100
  transfer of applications,   A2.101
  trust corporation, grant to,   A2.75
Non-Contentious Probate Rules 1987
  citation and commencement,   A2.40
  current,   1.42
  forms,   A2.110
  general provisions,   A2.43–A2.108
  interpretation,   A2.41
  other rules, application of,   A2.42
  revocations,   A2.109, A2.111

Partnership
  appointment as executor, succeeded
    by limited liability partnership,   4.47
Personal representative
  removal of,
    action for,   41.02
    Civil Procedure Rules,
      definitions,   A2.153
      generally,   A2.165
      Practice Direction,   A2.180–A2.182
      scope,   A2.153
    Rules of the Supreme Court,   A2.188
  substitution,
    Civil Procedure Rules,
      definitions,   A2.153
      generally,   A2.165
      Practice Direction,   A2.180–A2.182
      scope,   A2.153
    Rules of the Supreme Court,   A2.188

Index

Persons under disability
  administration *de bonis non*, and, 13.48
  administration, grant of, 11.237F, 11.237G
    other persons having equal right, clearing off, 11.239–11.242
  cessate grants, 11.282
  lack of mental capacity
    grant in case of, A2.74
    guiding principles, 11.237A, 11.237B
    inability to make decision as, 11.237C
    statutory provisions, 11.237–11.238
  lasting powers of attorney, 11.41, 11.237E
  passing over, 11.264
  physical incapacity, 11.284
  sole grantee lacking capacity, 13.49

Persons under disability, grants for use of A2.74
  appointees of district judge or registrar, to, 11.274–11.279
  attorney under enduring power, to, 11.257–11.263
  attorney under lasting power, to, 11.263A–11.263E
  cessate, 11.282
  foreign domicile, 11.243
  notice to Court of Protection, 11.249–11.252
  oath, wording, 11.244–11.245
  one person entitled on intestacy, where, 11.270–11.271
  persons authorised by Court of Protection, to, 11.246–11.248
  persons with equal right, to, 11.239–11.242
  proof of incapacity, 11.253–11.256
  residuary legatee, to, 11.265–11.269
  spouse or civil partner of intestate lacking capacity, where, 11.272–11.273
  supervening incapacity after issue of grant, 11.281

Place of trial
  contentious business, 39.01

Presumed death
  leave to swear to death, A2.92

Principal Registry
  general procedure calendar, 2.81

Prior rights to grant, order to pass over
  method of application, 25.102–25.103

Probate
  chain of executorship
    use and benefit of incapable executor, 4.81

Probate—*contd*
  copies of will
    generally, 4.229–4.230
    need for, 4.231
  costs of non-contentious proceedings
    assessment, 4.278
    solicitor's charges, 4.272–4.277
    Orders, A5.01–A5.20
  deponent's details
    change of name, 4.105A
  double, 13.270
  executors
    incorporated practices, 4.48
    succession, 4.48
  executor's oath
    amount of estate, 4.202, 4.206
    settling, 4.92
  fees
    grant, on, 4.260
    remission, 4.261
  impounding, abandonment 17.67
  notice to Treasury Solicitor, 4.227
  practice, meaning, 2.03A
  proof
    copies for registration, 4.250
    members of Royal Family, 4.247–4.249
  revocation, incapable person, 17.64–17.66

Probate claims
  addition of parties, Court of Probate, 28.04
  associated actions, removal of personal representative, 41.02
  Civil Procedure Rules
    generally, A2.153–A2.163
    Practice Direction, A2.169–A2.176
  costs of propounding testamentary document, 40.10
  defences
    revocation of grants, 34.70
    want of knowledge and approval, 34.50
  denial of interest, 32.06
  hearings, place of, 39.01
  jurisdiction of county court, 26.12
  parties
    addition of, 28.04
    persons being, 28.01
  place of trial, 39.01
  removal of personal representative, 41.02
  statements of interest 32.06
  trial
    place of, 39.01

Probate jurisdiction
  common form business, 1.32

Index

Probate practitioner
  new classes of,   1.32
Proof of grant
  copies for registration,   4.250
  deponent's details
    change of name,   4.105A
  executor's oath
    amount of estate,   4.202, 4.206
    relationship of applicant,   4.190
    settling,   4.92
  fees
    grant, on,   4.260
    remission,   4.261
  HMRC account,   4.254
  members of Royal Family,   4.247–4.249
Pronouncing against solemn will,
  claims for
    costs of contentious business, and
      unsuccessful parties,   40.13–40.14
Propounding a will
  costs of contentious business, scale
    for beneficiaries,   40.10
Provision out of estate, orders for
  procedure
    Principal Registry, in,   16.48
Public Guardian
  additional information, disclosure
    of,   A2.135T
  Court of Protection, official of,   11.237D
  registers,   A2.135R–A2.135T

Quick succession relief
  inheritance tax, on,   8.118

Recovery from incapacity
  cessate grants,   13.111–13.115
Rectification of wills
  applications for
    affidavit in support,   3.264
    generally,   A2.94
  Civil Procedure Rules
    generally,   A2.164
    grant, lodging,   A2.178
    orders,   A2.179
Removal of representatives
  applications for,   41.02
  Civil Procedure Rules
    definitions,   A2.153
    scope,   A2.153
Renunciation
  executor, by   A2.76
    attorney, and,   11.71–11.72
  incapable person, on behalf of
    attorney, by,   15.46
    Court of Protection appointee,
      by,   15.43–15.45
  minors, on behalf of
    attorney, by,   15.46

Renunciation—*contd*
  minors, on behalf of—*contd*
    Court of Protection appointee,
      by,   15.43–15.45
Resealing
  colonial grants, of
    documents required,   18.71
Residuary legatees
  capacity to manage affairs,
    lacking,   11.268–11.269
  grants for use of persons under
    disability,   11.265–11.267
Revocation of grant
  defence, summary of cases,   34.70
  incapable person,   17.64–17.66
  incapacity of grantee(s)
    one of two or more grantees,   17.13–17.20
  sole grantee,   17.64–17.66
  supervening defect in grant
    ground of,   17.09
    incapacity of grantee(s),   17.13–17.20
Revocation of wills
  defence, summary of cases,   34.70
Rules of Supreme Court
  and see Civil Procedure Rules
  inheritance provision,   A2.189
  probate claims,   A2.136–A2.152
  removal of personal
    representatives,   A2.188
  substitution of personal
    representatives,   A2.188

Savings bank annuities
  small sums, and,   1.82
Searches
  calendars of grants, of,   21.01–21.02, 21.07
  grant of representation, for,   21.33–21.34
  standing,   A2.82, A2.110
  wills proved since 11 January
    1858   21.04
Second administrator
  surviving spouse or civil partner,
    and,   7.25
Settled land
  beneficial entitlement to,   8.11
  grants   A2.68
Settling documents
  executor's oath, and,   4.92
Small sums
  government debt,   1.82
  National Debt annuities,   1.82
  savings bank annuities,   1.82
Solicitors
  non-contentious remuneration
    generally,   4.272–4.277
    Orders,   A5.01–A5.20

Index

Statements of claim
  defence
    revocation of grants, 34.70
    want of knowledge and
      approval, burden of proof, 34.50
Sub-registries
  location, 2.59
Substituted attorney
  grants to, 11.65
Substitution of representatives
  applications for, 41.02
  Civil Procedure Rule application,
    definitions, A2.153
    generally, A2.165
    Practice Direction, A2.180–A2.182
    scope, A2.153
Supervening defect in grant
  incapacity of grantee(s), 17.13–17.20
  revocation, ground for, 17.09
Supreme Court Act 1981 [Senior
  Courts Act 1981]
  general provisions
    distribution of business, A1.363
    jurisdiction, A1.317
Surviving spouse or civil partner
  life interests, and, 7.25

Transmission of executorship
  use and benefit of incapable
    executor, 4.81
Trial of claim
  place of, 39.01
Trust
  age 18–25, 8.11
  bereaved minors, 8.11
Trust corporations
  grant to, A2.75
Trustee
  new or additional, power of
    appointing, A1.79
Two or more grantees
  subsequently lacking capacity,
    revocation, 17.13–17.20

Value of estate
  alterations in
    administration before 1972, 16.57–16.58, 16.66
    grant marked by HMRC
      inheritance tax, 16.53
  calculation
    assets, 8.59–8.63
    foreign property, 8.71
    liabilities, 8.69–8.70
    lifetime gifts, 8.57

Value of estate—*contd*
  probates, and
    introduction, 4.202
    relevant estate, 4.218
    statement by applicant, 4.206

Want of knowledge and approval
  burden of proof, 34.50
Warning to caveat
  form, A2.110
Wills
  blind or illiterate testator, will of, A2.52
  condition of
    pin or clip marks on, 3.156
  copy
    inspection of, A2.97
    issue of, A2.98
  deposit
    certificate, A1.17
    Regulations, A2.08–A2.17
  due execution, evidence of, A2.51–A2.57
  engrossment, A2.50
  envelope, endorsement on, A2.17
  execution
    signature, 3.70
  joint
    revocation, 3.222
  mentally disordered person, for
    Court of Protection, exercise of
      powers of, 3.440
    Court of Protection rules, 3.441
    effect, 3.455
    execution, 3.442
    Mental Capacity Act 2005, 3.438–3.441
    power to make, 3.438–3.441
  mutual
    revocation, 3.222
  nuncupative, A2.93
  privileged wills
    sailors at sea, 3.376
  signature
    form, 3.70
  republication
    effect confirming codicil, 3.188
  revocation
    contemplation of civil
      partnership, exception for
      will made in, 3.50
    contemplation of marriage,
      exception for will made in, 3.50
    formation of civil partnership,
      by, 3.45
Witnesses
  attesting, grant to, A2.60